Sports,
Jobs,
and Taxes

SPORTS, JOBS, AND TAXES

The Economic Impact of Sports Teams and Stadiums

Roger G. Noll and
Andrew Zimbalist, Editors

BROOKINGS INSTITUTION PRESS
Washington, D.C.

Library of Congress Cataloging-in-Publication data
Sports, jobs, and taxes : the economic impact of sports teams and
  stadiums / Roger G. Noll and Andrew Zimbalist, editors.
      p.   cm.
      ISBN 0-8157-6110-4 (alk. paper). — ISBN 0-8157-6111-2 (pbk. : alk
  paper)
      1. Sports franchises—Economic aspects—United States.   2. Sports
  teams—Economic aspects—United States.   3. Stadiums—Economic
  aspects—United States.   4. Urban economics—United States.
  I. Noll, Roger G.   II. Zimbalist, Andrew.
  GV716.S647   1997
  338.4'3796'0973—dc21   97-33764
                                                                      CIP

9 8 7 6 5 4 3 2 1

The paper used in this publication meets the minimum requirements of the American
National Standard for Information Sciences—Permanence of Paper for Printed Library
Materials, ANSI Z39.48–1984.

Typeset in Times Roman

Composition by Harlowe Typography Inc.
Cottage City, Maryland

Interior illustration by John Julius Maria

Printed by R. R. Donnelley and Sons Co.
Harrisonburg, Virginia

FOREWORD

America is in the midst of an unprecedented boom in construction of sports facilities. Nearly half of U.S. professional sports teams either are playing in a new facility or expect to have one within a few years. This book examines the economics, finance, and politics of the stadium boom.

With rare exceptions, facilities for professional sports are heavily subsidized. State and local governments frequently contribute to the capital cost of stadiums and forgive their owners some taxes. The federal government helps out by granting a tax exemption for interest on the debt of state and local governments that is used for financing stadiums. In many cases, the total subsidy for sports facilities exceeds $10 million a year for as long as thirty years. The total subsidy for all of these facilities runs into the billions of dollars. Advocates of stadium projects frequently justify subsidies by arguing that teams and facilities have a beneficial effect on the local economy. These claims are buttressed by numerous reports showing annual economic benefits from new stadiums in excess of $100 million.

One objective of this book is to examine the validity of these claims. The authors explain the appropriate methodology for calculating the costs and benefits of a sports facility and then examine several recent stadium projects and proposals. In every case, the authors find that the local economic impact of sports teams and facilities is far smaller than proponents allege; in some cases it is negative. These findings are valid regardless of whether the benefits are measured for the local neighborhood, for the city, or for the entire metropolitan area in which a facility is located.

The unattractive economics of stadiums raise a second issue: if stadiums are poor investments, why, in the era of limited government and skepticism about the value of public construction projects, are expensive stadiums still being subsidized? The studies in this book reach two conclusions: local politics, and the bargaining power that sports teams now enjoy because of their scarcity.

Stadium proponents typically comprise some very well organized interests that have much to gain from these projects. In cities where stadium measures are placed on the ballot, stadium proponents typically outspend the opposition by more than twenty to one. Because stadium referendums are usually held in special elections with low turnout, this spending differential gives stadium proponents considerable advantage.

In addition, stadium proposals usually are accompanied by a threat that a local team will move elsewhere or by a larger agreement to bring a new team to the community. Hence the stadium proposal is inextricably linked to the presence of a team. As a result sports fans must consider the value of having a local team as well as the cost of a new stadium. Because the annualized per capita cost of a new stadium typically is only a few dollars, fans may vote for a stadium that they believe is excessively lavish because they are given no reasonable alternative except not having a team.

In the introduction and conclusion, the editors offer their views about the cause of lavish public investments in sports facilities. The primal cause is the monopoly status of each professional sport, which keeps the number of teams lower than the market can support. The relative scarcity of teams forces cities that could be financially viable franchise locations into competitive bidding whenever a team becomes available through expansion or the termination of a lease. Monopoly leagues maximize their profits in part by creating this competition among cities for teams. Thus, the editors conclude, the most effective remedy for the escalating subsidies of sports facilities is competition: forcing each sport to form several separate leagues that make independent decisions about how many teams to include and where they should be located.

The original versions of the chapters in this book were presented at a conference at the Brookings Institution on October 7–8, 1996. The editors are especially grateful to Gemma Park for organizing the conference and shepherding the manuscript through the publication process. Among the sources of financial support for authors of the case studies were the Fisher Center for Real Estate and Urban Economics at the University of California, the Ohio Urban University Program, and the Lilly Endowment.

The authors gratefully acknowledge the following sources for providing extensive data: the Florida Sports Foundation, the Florida Department of Revenue, the Sporting News, the Baseball Hall of Fame, Edward Cline of the Maryland Stadium Authority, Joe Foss of the Baltimore Orioles, and Martin Greenberg of the Sports Law Institute of the University of Wisconsin-Milwaukee.

The project enjoyed capable research assistance from Chris Anderson, Julie Anzalone, Craig Cottrell, Ellen Cyran, Jocelyn Fagan, Betty Hosler, Richard Nelson, Sandra Sullivan, Craig Vandermause, Don and Helen Yoder, and Elaine Zimmerman. Special thanks go to Venka McIntyre for editing the manuscript; to Gary Gordon, Cynthia Iglesias, and Helen Kim for authenticating facts and references; to Carlotta Ribar for proofreading; and to Sherry Smith for preparing the index.

The views expressed in this book are those of the authors and should not be ascribed to the persons or organizations whose assistance is acknowledged or to the trustees, officers, or staff members of the Brookings Institution.

MICHAEL H. ARMACOST
President

September 1997
Washington, D.C.

CONTENTS

xi

SPORTS,
JOBS,
AND TAXES

1

"BUILD THE STADIUM— CREATE THE JOBS!"

ROGER G. NOLL AND ANDREW ZIMBALIST

 The title of this chapter captures the essence of the issues explored in this book. It was the campaign slogan for the proponents of a publicly subsidized football stadium in San Francisco to replace Candlestick (3-Com) Park.[1] On June 3, 1997, the citizens of San Francisco voted on two measures. The first proposed to dedicate the land now occupied by Candlestick Park for a new football stadium and a shopping center, to be owned in part by 49ers owner Eddie DeBartolo. The second authorized the city to float a $100 million bond issue to contribute to stadium construction. Both measures squeaked through with winning margins under 1 percent of the vote.[2]

As is apparent from the slogan, proponents argued that a new football stadium and shopping center would bring substantial economic benefits to the city through increased spending and jobs, especially in the economically depressed Hunters Point district just north of the project. Stadium advocates also predicted that new revenues from sales and other taxes would pay the interest and amortization on the bond and so ensure that these benefits would be costless to the city.

Although the details of campaigns for sports facilities differ from city to city, the basic case for subsidizing them is the same everywhere. First, as in San Francisco, a major facility is said to generate new jobs, primarily because people who attend sports events spend money at the facility and on other activities while traveling to and from it. Second, a team or an important sports event reputedly makes a community a "major league city," thereby garnering free publicity and attracting new businesses. Third, although a city might pay hundreds of millions of dollars in subsidies to attract or to retain a team or a regular national sporting championship, the additional tax revenues and lease payments are claimed to be sufficient to offset these subsidies and to make a publicly financed stadium a good investment. The purpose of this book is to examine the validity of these assertions.

Publicly subsidized facilities for professional sports are hardly a new phenomenon. The Los Angeles Memorial Coliseum, built to host the 1932 Olympic Games, has served as the home for a series of professional football teams, the collegiate USC Trojans and UCLA Bruins, and even the Los Angeles Dodgers baseball team.[3] Likewise, Municipal Stadium in Cleveland served the football Browns and the baseball Indians for four decades, beginning soon after World War II. Another Memorial Stadium, this one in Baltimore, has welcomed a baseball team (the Orioles) and three football teams (two in the National Football League [NFL], and one in the Canadian Football League). But, historically, publicly financed stadiums were exceptions to the rule. Until about 1960, the vast majority of new facilities were privately owned, usually by one of the teams that played in them.

Stadium ownership and financing began to change when major league professional sports became a national rather than a regional phenomenon with all teams snugly packed into the northeast quadrant of the country. Economic and population growth in the South and West, combined with improved and less expensive transportation, caused teams and leagues to look to the Sun Belt for places to relocate or to place an expansion franchise. Some teams apparently preferred being a monopolist in a western or southern city to being a competitor in a multiteam market and so departed Boston (Braves) for Milwaukee, Cleveland (Rams) for Los Angeles, Philadelphia (A's) for Kansas City, St. Louis (Browns) for Baltimore, Chicago (football Cardinals) for St. Louis, and New York (Dodgers and Giants) for Los Angeles and San Francisco. Other teams left smaller monopolies (Milwaukee Braves, Minneapolis Lakers, St. Louis Hawks) for larger Sun Belt markets (Atlanta, Los Angeles, Atlanta, respectively). At the same time, leagues began an expansion process that, over three decades, added more than fifty teams to the four major professional sports: baseball, basketball, football, and hockey.

The process of relocation and expansion enabled many cities to become prospective sites for a major league franchise and to compete to be the next lucky recipient of a team. Competition took the form of providing a subsidized playing facility. Only rarely did the team end up owning the stadium: the Dodgers are one such case, but even then the site was donated by the city. The more common arrangement was that the city owned the stadium, although sometimes, as in Cleveland and St. Louis, the city let the team or a corporate affiliate operate it.

Since the late 1950s, the sports industry has experienced a prolonged economic boom. Revenues from attendance, broadcasting, and concessions have shown rapid, steady growth. Meanwhile, the proportion of team revenues needed to cover stadium costs has declined because of the increasing eagerness of state and local governments to compete for teams by subsidizing them. In response to these attractive financial prospects, the industry has burgeoned. Established leagues have created new teams, and new leagues have emerged in all the major professional sports, with several surviving long enough to see many of their teams incorporated into existing leagues. Although the growth in revenues was the most important reason for this expansion, the willingness of cities to provide subsidized stadiums cannot be discounted as a significant additional incentive.

Since the beginning of the new stadium arrangements around 1960, most major league teams have been the beneficiaries of at least one new, subsidized facility. Almost all have had facilities built or substantially renovated. And many have had more than one new home.

Anaheim Stadium, to cite one example, was built for baseball's California (now Anaheim) Angels in the early 1960s and then was massively renovated to accommodate the NFL's Rams in the late 1970s. This renovation made the stadium a far better site for football, but less attractive for baseball. Then poor on-field performance caused Rams' attendance to fall, and less than twenty years after the renovation the Rams fled to a new stadium in St. Louis.

Atlanta and San Francisco have similar stories, but with happier endings. Fulton County, Georgia, built a new stadium in the 1960s that attracted baseball's Braves and football's Falcons, then gave the teams separate new homes in the 1990s. San Francisco's much maligned Candlestick Park was built for the National League Giants in the late 1950s, was renovated substantially for the NFL 49ers in the 1970s, and now is slated for replacement by separate facilities by the year 2000.

In Boston and New York, the ultimate outcome remains in doubt. The NFL New England Patriots built their own stadium in Foxboro in the early 1970s, but likewise now seek a publicly subsidized facility and have initiated a competition among Boston, Foxboro, and Providence to provide it. New York City built Shea Stadium in the 1960s for new teams in the National League (Mets) and American Football League (Titans/Jets) plus the established NFL team, the Giants. The Giants and Jets left in the 1980s to play in a new stadium in the New Jersey suburbs. New York also substantially renovated Yankee Stadium in the 1970s, but now the Yankees are threatening to leave the city, also for New Jersey, if a new stadium is not constructed within a few years.

In Salt Lake City, the Utah Jazz, a member of the National Basketball Association (NBA), is playing in its second Salt Palace (now named the Delta Center), which replaced the first after less than two decades. The NBA San Antonio Spurs, having played in the Hemisphere Arena and the Alamo Dome for the past twenty years, now seek a third new facility. And the Houston Oilers plan to move to Nashville in 1998, where a new stadium is being built for them. Less than a decade earlier, in 1987, Houston had made $67 million in improvements to the Astrodome, after the Oilers threatened to move to Jacksonville.[4]

The all-time winner in per capita frequency of facility construction is probably the Twin Cities, whose almost farcical experience with sports is recounted in detail in chapter 7. The Twin Cities' major league franchises in baseball and football began playing in renovated Metropolitan Stadium in 1960–61, then moved to the Humphrey Metrodome in 1982, whereupon the former facility was torn down. In 1996 the Twins grew unhappy again, and now another stadium is in the planning stages. The Met Center was built to welcome a National Hockey League (NHL) team in 1967. A few years later St. Paul built a similar facility, the Civic Center, which for a while housed a World Hockey Association team. In 1990 a third arena, the Target Center, opened for the NBA expansion Timberwolves. In 1993 the NHL team moved to Dallas. In 1995, in the wake of this departure and competition from the other arenas, Minneapolis razed the Met Center. At present St. Paul is trying to attract another NHL team by promising a major renovation of the Civic Center.

These are by no means isolated examples. In 1997 the number of franchises in the major professional sports, including the most recent expansions, total 113. Between 1989 and 1997, thirty-one new stadiums and arenas were built. At least thirty-nine additional teams are seeking new facilities, are in the process of finalizing the deal to build one, or are waiting to move into one.[5]

These new sports facilities are not cheap. One recent study estimated that the average cost of six new arenas for basketball and hockey that opened in 1995 and 1996 exceeded $150 million.[6] As reported in chapter 11, the new Gund Arena in Cleveland's Gateway Center cost approximately $150 million, not including the site. A new stadium for baseball or football, along with site acquisition and preparation, now runs at least $200 million, which, as reported in chapters 8 and 11, was roughly the cost of the new baseball parks in Baltimore and Cleveland. Frequently these costs are far more: the total cost of the new baseball stadium in Milwaukee is expected to hit $322 million, which is also roughly the expected cost of the new football stadium for the San Francisco 49ers.[7]

By contrast, Tampa's Houlihan Stadium, built in 1967, cost $14 million. The Civic Center in St. Paul, built in the 1970s, cost $19 million. The New England Patriots spent approximately $20 million to build Foxboro Stadium, and Rich Stadium in Buffalo was built for $23 million. (In current dollars, these costs would be in the neighborhood of $60 million.) Kansas City built a baseball stadium and a football stadium on the same site for $55 million (about $150 million in current dollars). In the 1980s the Dallas Cowboys and the Miami Dolphins spent about $75 million (about $100 million in 1997 dollars) on new stadiums.

The harbinger of things to come was the New Orleans Superdome, which was completed in 1975 at a cost of about $163 million, approximately $450 million in today's dollars. For a long while this project stood out as a wild anomaly. Today it would fit nicely in the upper range of standard experience.

The trends in the number and expense of stadiums and arenas raise several related questions. First, are these facilities worth it: to the teams, the leagues, and the cities that foot part of the bill? Second, what are the effects of teams and stadiums on a metropolitan area, a city, and its local neighborhood? Third, who actually pays for stadiums, and who benefits from them? Fourth, why do cities subsidize sports facilities, and what determines the amount of subsidy that a team receives?

Stadium Economics versus Stadium Financing

These questions cannot be addressed without a precise sense of the economic and financial issues surrounding sports facilities. The public debate typically conflates the issues. Most serious is its failure to distinguish between stadium economics and stadium financing. (For simplicity, we call these issues "stadium economics and financing," but when we use these terms, we mean to include all types of sports facilities.) Stadium financing refers to the narrow question of who pays for constructing and operating the stadium. Stadium economics refers to the wider question of how the stadium (and the events inside it) affect aggregate economic welfare.

Typically, the debate over stadium economics focuses on job and income creation in the community in which a facility is built, but the range of potential economic effects is far broader: it encompasses regional and national wealth, as well as the welfare of sports fans and the distribution of income. Indeed, the debate is so broad in scope that it cannot proceed satisfactorily without considering the total costs and benefits to society arising from the stadium.

To reiterate, stadium financing strictly refers to the expenditures and revenues directly associated with building and operating the stadium. Typically, the financial responsibility for these expenditures is shared by the team, other private sector entities, local government, and, occasionally, state government. To pay for its contribution to a new sports facility, the public sector relies on some combination of rents, taxes, and fees on activities related to the stadium; other taxes; and cuts in other public services. Stadium financing provides the link between the expenditures on the stadium and these sources of revenues. Clearly, stadium financing is both a narrower and a less important issue than stadium economics.

Most of this book is about stadium economics. Subsequent chapters explore the basic economic rationale for publicly subsidized sports facilities. The overriding conclusion of this discussion is that the economic case for publicly financed stadiums cannot credibly rest on the benefits to local business, as measured by jobs, income, and investment. Thus, as explained in some detail in chapter 2, the case for subsidies must rest on consumption benefits, which in this case is consumer satisfaction from the presence of a local team that is not reflected in traditional market transactions such as selling tickets, concessions, broadcast rights, and other goods and services.

The case studies that constitute the second half of the book deal with both economics and financing. The two subjects are certainly closely linked, but the relationship is incomplete and complicated. By way of introducing these complexities, in this chapter we lay out the basics of stadium financial arrangements and explain why stadium financial plans typically overstate the extent to which a stadium can be said to pay for itself.

Stadium Financing

The life of a stadium proceeds in three (sometimes four) stages. First, a site is acquired and existing facilities that are not usable for the stadium are destroyed. Second, the stadium and its supporting infrastructure—sewage linkups, utility connections, parking, transportation access—are built. Third, repair, maintenance, and operations activities are undertaken to support the events in the facility.

Occasionally, there is a fourth stage: the stadium may be razed for some other use. Of course, if the purpose of tearing down the stadium is to build another sports facility, this activity coincides with the first phase in building a new facility, so one should be careful not to double-count these expenditures; however, if the stadium site is to be used for something other than a sports facility, the phase four costs, to the extent that they exceed the costs of replacing the original alternative use for the stadium, represent the last payment for the life of the facility.

On the cost side, most (but not necessarily all) of these activities must be paid for by someone. Thus one aspect of stadium financing is to decide who will pay which bills. The standard practice is for local and sometimes state government to pay for most, if not all, site preparation. In some cases, governments will also pay for acquiring the land but as often as not will already own it. In that case, dedicating the land to a stadium does not require a cash payment and so does not figure into the financing arrangements. The proposed new stadiums in San Francisco and for the Yankees in New York City, for example, are all on publicly owned land. As a result the reported "cost" of these stadiums does not include any value for the site, even though in all cases the site could be sold for other valuable activities and so has a real economic cost to the community.

The team and the locality usually share responsibility for site preparation and the direct construction costs, although the nature of this arrangement varies greatly among stadiums. Once constructed, lease terms regarding the sharing of stadium revenues, defrayal of operating and maintenance costs, and responsibility for stadium management also differ substantially among the teams. (See the appendix to this chapter for a compilation of stadium lease agreements.)

Sources of Revenues

One of the most important recent trends in professional sports has been the growth in nontraditional sources of revenue. In the 1950s most of a team's revenues came from inside the stadium, and stadium-related revenues consisted almost entirely of ticket sales, with minor additional amounts collected from concessions, publications, and in-stadium advertising. In the 1960s, because of the growth in the popularity of sports and the unfortunate policy decision to grant antitrust immunity to leagues in selling their broadcast rights, revenues from broadcasting shot up and, in some cases, surpassed in-stadium revenues; nonetheless, ticket sales in the 1970s continued to dominate in-stadium revenues.[8] Reflecting this reality, league revenue-sharing rules (and, later, collective bargaining over the share of revenues that went to players) focused primarily on the two main sources of revenues: broadcasting and ticket sales.

Then came a new trend in the 1980s: a rapid growth in revenues from other sources. Concessions became a far more important part of revenues, as can be seen in the dramatic improvement in the quantity and quality of food, beverages, and sports memorabilia that are available for sale at sporting events. Because of the growing profitability of concessions, providers of concessions products have been willing to pay increasingly large amounts for the right to have access to the stadium. Financial plans typically include between $5 million and $15 million for the sale of rights related to concessions.

In some cases, concession rights are exclusive. A soft drink or beer manufacturer, for example, may purchase exclusive "pouring rights" at all concession stands. These rights have two sources of value: the profits from sales within the stadium, and the additional marketing value of association with the team or stadium as its "official soft drink." In other cases, vendors purchase nonexclusive rights simply to have a location inside the stadium. Several restaurant chains may acquire the right to place competing outlets in the stadium. Sometimes these rights are accompanied by an authorization to associate the team or stadium with the license holder in marketing.

The significance of the pure association with the stadium, unrelated to in-stadium sales, is apparent from the emergence of another significant source of revenues: stadium naming rights. The good old days of Fenway Park, Yankee Stadium, and the several Memorial stadiums are quickly waning as companies purchase the right to have the stadium named after them. Of course, some stadium names always have had a business connection, such as Wrigley Field and Busch Stadium, but these were limited to instances in which team ownership was linked to another product. (Recent commercial uses of stadium names are summarized in table 1-1.)

The practice of giving names to facilities that have no connection to ownership, history, or the city began when the New England Patriots financed the construction of their Foxboro facility by selling the name to the Schaefer Brewing Company. Although still relatively rare, selling a facility's name is growing in frequency. The San Francisco Giants plan to move from 3-Com Stadium (née Candlestick) to Pacific Bell Park, which in the original plans was named after its location in China Basin. Other examples are the Arco Arena, the home of the Sacramento Kings, the Great Western Forum, the home of the Lakers and Kings in Los Angeles, and the aforementioned Delta Center in Salt Lake City. The money involved in selling stadium names has become substantial, ranging from $20 million to $50 million for Pacific Bell Park. Because these prices are so high, selling names of facilities is likely to become common.

In addition, a variety of seating categories have been invented that, for a fee, provide fans with special perquisites. Examples are the luxury box and the personal seat license (PSL), both of which usually do no more than provide the holder with the option to buy a ticket in a particular stadium location. Usually this location has special amenities, although the PSL frequently provides nothing more than a better view of the game. Stadium financial plans vary with respect to the importance of these revenues. The financial plan for Pacific Bell Park

Table 1-1. *Sports Facility Naming Rights*

Facility	Location	Price[a] (millions of dollars)	Term (years)	Price per year (millions of dollars)	Team (league)
Stadiums					
Banc One Ball Park	Phoenix	66.00	30	1.00+	Diamondbacks (MLB)
Pacific Bell Park	San Francisco	50.00[a]	24	2.08	Giants (MLB)
Ericsson Stadium	Charlotte	20.00	10	2.00	Panthers (NFL)
Miller Park	Milwaukee	41.20	20	2.00	Brewers (MLB)
Trans World Dome	St. Louis	26.00	20	1.30	Rams (NFL)
Coors Field	Denver	15.00[a]	10	1.50	Rockies (MLB)
Cinergy Field	Cincinnati	6.00+	5	1.20	Reds (MLB), Bengals (NFL)
Turner Field	Atlanta				Braves (MLB)
Tropicana Field	St. Petersburg	30.00			Devil Rays (MLB)
Pro Player Park	Miami	20.00	10		Marlins (MLB), Dolphins (NFL)
Jacobs Field	Cleveland	13.90	20	0.70	Indians (MLB)
Houlihan's Stadium	Tampa Bay	10.00	5		Buccaneers (NFL)
Arenas					
MCI Center	Washington, D. C.	44.00[a]	10+	Undetermined	Bullets (NBA), Capitals (NHL)
Pepsi Center	Denver	68.00[a]	20	3.40	Nuggets (NBA)
Continental Airlines Arena	East Rutherford, N.J.	29.00	12	2.40	Nets (NBA)
Fleet Center	Boston	30.00	15	2.00	Bruins (NHL), Celtics (NBA)
Core States Spectrum	Philadelphia	40.00	29	1.37	Flyers (NHL) 76ers (NBA)
Molson Centre	Montreal	30.00	20	1.50	Canadians (NHL)
Target Center	Minneapolis	18.75	15	1.25	Timberwolves (NBA)
RCA Dome	Indianapolis	10.00	10	1.00	Colts (NFL)
USAir Arena	Landover, Md.	10.00	10	1.00	Bullets (NBA), Capitals (NHL)
Canadian Airlines Saddledome	Calgary	10.00	20	0.50	Flames (NHL)
GM Place	Vancouver	18.50	20	0.93	Grizzlies (NBA), Canucks (NHL)

Arena	City			Team
Key Arena	Seattle	15.10	15	1.00	Supersonics (NBA)
America West Arena	Phoenix	26.00	30	0.87	Suns (NBA)
United Center	Chicago	36.00	20	1.80	Bulls (NBA), Blackhawks (NHL)
Marine Midland Arena	Buffalo	15.00	20	0.75	Sabers (NHL)
Delta Center	Salt Lake City	25.00	20	1.25	Jazz (NBA)
Air Canada Center	Toronto	14.00	20	0.70	Raptors (NBA)
Gund Arena	Cleveland	14.00	20	0.70	Cavaliers (NBA)

Sources: Alan Friedman (Team Marketing Report) and Paul J. Much (Houlihan Lokey Howard and Zukin). *1997 Inside the Ownership of Professional Sports Teams: The Complete Directory of the Ownership and Financial Structure of Pro Sports* (Chicago: Team Marketing Report, 1997).

a. These deals involved more than naming rights. The Coors Field deal includes pouring rights and some equity in the team; the Pacific Bell deal includes rights to develop a theme park; the MCI Center deal includes signage rights inside; the Pepsi Center deal includes pouring rights in two buildings. The details of these deals are generally proprietary, and full information is not available. Auxiliary rights for other facilities are probable.

anticipates about $40 million from this source, whereas the plan for the Carolina Panthers' facility raised $150 million from various types of seating licenses.

All of these revenue sources typically are committed at least in part to financing a new stadium. The standard financial plan divides the expenditures on stadium construction into three components: those to be financed by the various forms of up-front payments such as pouring rights, naming rights, and special seat licenses; those to be paid by team owners out of their own pockets (perhaps financed by a loan); and those to be paid initially from either the budget of a local government or the sale of bonds. Of course, bond sales simply spread the city's payment over a number of years, rather than concentrate them during the period of construction.

Public or Private Financing?

What makes stadium financing particularly confusing is that the allocation of responsibility for expenditures and revenues varies greatly from one location to the next. Arrangements are generally regarded as "public" if the facility is paid for and managed by the local government authority and any deficit is covered by that government. Examples of this form of public financing are the renovations to the Oakland Coliseum for the relocation of the Raiders back to Oakland and the construction of the new stadium in St. Louis to attract the Rams. By contrast, when direct construction costs are paid by the team, the financing is considered "private." Examples in this category are the new football stadium for the NFL expansion team in Charlotte, the Carolina Panthers, and the new baseball stadium in San Francisco for the Giants.

Another difference between these two types of arrangements is who receives the revenues from the sale of the special rights. In Oakland and St. Louis, the stadium authority sold these rights (and allocated the revenues to various stadium costs), whereas in Charlotte and San Francisco the team performed this function. In both cases, the source of a significant portion of the revenues for paying for the facility was neither the team nor the city, but the people who purchase these rights. The nature of these arrangements depends primarily on who owns the facility, the team or a government authority. Ownership, in turn, determines whether the team or the city will absorb the risk that the revenues from these rights will be less than the amount that is assumed in the financial plan.

A government's financial commitment is more uncertain if it retains both ownership and control over the sale of these rights, which means that the cost to the local government is more open-ended and unlikely to be known in advance. Thus the extent to which a facility is publicly subsidized is not accurately measured by the formal allocation of responsibility for paying for the stadium. Transferring the responsibility to sell stadium naming rights, pouring rights, executive boxes, club seats, and PSLs from the team to the city does not increase the magnitude of the city's financial commitment by the amount of the transfer. Instead, the effect is far more subtle and difficult to predict in advance. The subsidy arising from this transfer is derived completely from the reallocation of the risk that the cost of the stadium and the revenues from these rights sales will differ from the original estimate. Whereas these risks can be substantial, they are always much less than the gross cost of the facility.

Another important aspect of the financing plan is the mechanism by which the local government compares its expenditures on and revenues from the stadium. On the cost side is the government's share of the direct expenditures in all phases of the life of the stadium, perhaps including interest if the government's cost is financed in part by borrowing. On the revenue side are the rents paid by the team, the incremental tax revenues arising from the stadium, and whatever additional revenues are derived from sources that are unrelated to the stadium, such as general tax increases or expenditure reductions.

Stadium financial plans differ substantially in the scope of stadium-related tax collections that are balanced against city expenditures. In almost all cases, the plan includes rents and taxes on in-stadium revenues. In some cases (though rarely), the stadium pays some form of property tax, and if so these also are counted as stadium-related tax revenues. Inside the stadium, concession revenues typically pay standard state and local sales taxes, and ticket sales pay special ticket taxes and sometimes special assessments that are earmarked for covering stadium construction costs. In addition, some financial plans attribute to the stadium certain tax revenues collected on the outside. If the stadium is said to generate new business in the surrounding community, for example, the financial plan may attribute some sales, income, and property taxes off-site to the existence of the facility. This type of revenue is called "tax increment financing" and was used in San Francisco to generate a financial plan for the new 49ers facility that shows no net expected cost to the city.

A stadium financing plan might also include an earmarked tax that is unrelated to the sports facility. Many stadium financial plans include new taxes that are specifically used for financing the stadium: the Maryland state lottery is used to help pay for the new facilities at Camden Yards (see chapter 8); a special sales tax will finance new stadiums in Cincinnati; and similar arrangements pay for the Alamo Dome in San Antonio, Coors Field in Denver, Arlington Park (Texas Rangers), and the new facilities for the Arizona Diamondbacks and Seattle Mariners. Alcohol and tobacco taxes are paying for Jacobs Field in Cleveland (see chapter 11); hotel taxes help to pay for New Comiskey Park in Chicago, the Trans World Dome in St. Louis, and new arenas in Miami and Orlando; and a special assessment on car rentals is dedicated to pay for America West Arena in Phoenix.

Frequently, stadium proponents claim that a facility is "self-financing." The meaning of this term is that rent plus tax collections directly attributable to and earmarked for the stadium are expected to be sufficient to cover the city's expenditures. It does not mean that the net increase in revenues due to the stadium is sufficient to pay for it.

Sources of Errors in Financial Plans

In view of all these sources of revenues, one potential pitfall in devising a stadium financing plan is that gross and net revenues may be confused. The gross revenues from rent and taxes are the total collections from activities attributed to the stadium. But this sum overstates the contribution of the facility to local government revenues, for three reasons.

First, unless the team that will play in the new stadium is certain not to play in the city if the new stadium is not built, the appropriate baseline is the revenues that would be collected if the team played in an existing facility. In the contemporary environment of professional sports, most teams credibly can threaten to leave their present home, or not to locate in a new one, if their demands are not met, although the threat that the city will lose a team forever may be far less credible. The departure of the Raiders and Rams from Los Angeles, for example, is likely to cause only a temporary loss of professional football there because the city remains attractive as a franchise site to many teams in lesser metropolitan areas and to the entire league. Furthermore, Cleveland, Baltimore, and St. Louis lost their NFL teams but eventually landed replacements. A similar deal is said to be in the works for Houston, which lost its Oilers after the 1996 season.

Second, as discussed in greater detail in several chapters of this book, the gross revenues spent at the stadium (and hence the tax collections derived from them) are in part substitutes for other entertainment and recreation expenditures by sports fans. To the extent that the departure of the Rams and Raiders has increased attendance at college football games, games in other professional sports, motion pictures, and restaurants, the lost tax revenues from the stadiums is offset to a significant degree by increased tax revenues from these sources. Thus all of the gross tax collections within a stadium cannot properly be attributed to it because some of that tax revenue would have been collected elsewhere had the stadium not been built or used.

Third, if a financial plan includes substantial "indirect" tax revenues arising from increased expenditures outside the stadium, coming first from an anticipated increase in tourism and then from the so-called multiplier effect of these expenditures in the local economy, the tax revenues are almost certainly overstated. Several chapters of this book contain detailed analyses of the overall economic growth effect of stadiums. The overwhelming consensus of opinion in these studies is that the local economic effect of a sports facility is between nonexistent and extremely modest. If stadiums do not contribute to an increase in local economic activity, they cannot cause a significant increase in revenues from local taxes.

To illustrate these pitfalls in stadium financing, consider the proposal for the new football stadium in San Francisco. This plan contemplates building a shopping mall adjacent to the stadium. The financial plan for the stadium dedicates rent, in-stadium taxes, and the tax revenues from the shopping mall to help pay for the interest and amortization on $100 million in bonds that will be used to pay for part of the stadium. As a result, according to San Francisco 49ers president Carmen Policy, the city "is almost not at risk for anything."[9]

The implicit assumptions behind the conclusion that this deal is self-financing are, first, that no development would occur at the site if the stadium were not constructed, and second, that not a penny of business in the stadium or at the new shopping center will substitute for sales at other retail outlets in San Francisco. As to the first assumption, the presence of the stadium actually makes the shopping center a little less financially attractive because the shared parking facilities will be clogged with fans attending the home games. Hence building the football stadium would be more costly to the city than a plan that contemplated a shopping center with no stadium (and hence no subsidy). As to the second assumption, the shopping center intends to feature the low-end shops of national chains (Nordstrom's Rack and the Gap's Old Navy), plus branches of several famous San Francisco restaurants. It is difficult to imagine that this would not compete with stores of the same and similar chains that are located elsewhere in the city. For these reasons, the assessment by state assembly member Don Perrata, who represents Oakland, is probably on target: "Getting the public to believe it's not going to cost any money . . . is a fool's errand."[10]

Another problem that can plague a stadium financial plan arises from the uncertainty surrounding revenue forecasts, particularly those relating to the future popularity of the team. Sales taxes, ticket taxes, and usually rental payments depend on attendance at games. If a financial plan assumes that the stadium will cause a permanent, substantial increase in rent and tax collections, it is implicitly expecting the stadium to generate a nontransitory increase in attendance. This is a dangerous assumption.

Historical experience indicates that a team's attendance usually does increase sharply when a new or renovated facility is opened. The novelty of the new facility attracts fans, and an additional boost to attendance occurs because the quality of a team usually improves when a new facility is opened. This is indeed what happened after the opening of Oriole Park in Baltimore, Jacobs Field in Cleveland, and Coors Field in Denver. The typical explanation for this effect is that the improved financial position of the team enables it to hire better players; however, this explanation reverses the cause-effect relationship. Teams in new facilities hire better players because the effect of doing so on revenues is greater in a new facility. Thus a team can prolong the attendance effect of stadium novelty by fielding a stronger team. This effect is weakest in football, which has far greater sharing of in-stadium revenues and so a weaker incentive for a team to increase attendance.

At the level of an entire league, revenue enhancements that depend on improved team quality cannot be sustained if all teams are in the process of acquiring new facilities. If all teams build a new stadium, each one cannot possibly expect to win more games and thereby hold onto the attendance increase arising from the effect of a new stadium on team quality. In the end, all teams, on average, will be as good as they were before the stadium boom took place; therefore, average revenue will be permanently enhanced only insofar as better facilities induce additional attendance and more and better concessions stands generate extra sales. Because the construction of new stadiums in a league is sequential, the fortunes of the team generally are such that, for a few years, it will experience a large revenue enhancement arising from both having a new stadium and an improved team, but as other new stadiums open and other teams improve, attendance and revenue will gradually decline until, two or three decades later, the team is given another new facility.

A realistic financial plan must take into account this long-term effect of new stadiums: that is, it should exhibit an initial increase but then a general decline in the revenues associated with a new stadium. A plan based on the assumption that the initial revenue increase will be sustained over the life of the stadium is likely to be too optimistic. And, if the plan indicates that on an annual basis tax revenues and expenditures are roughly balanced, then the reality is that in the back half of the plan, tax revenues are unlikely to cover these costs.

The Economics of Stadium Financing

Because the sale of various rights within a stadium plays a prominent role in stadium financing, it is essential to know exactly how these markets operate. An extremely important source of the incessant and seemingly endless demand for new playing facilities lies in these nontraditional sources of revenue. The growing popularity of sports has caused attendance to increase, but there are very real limits to pure attendance growth as a source of revenue.

To begin, in responding to demand a team usually can do almost as well by increasing ticket prices as by increasing the number of tickets sold. Studies of the market for sporting events typically find that the demand elasticity is close to 1, so that revenues from the sale of tickets—ticket price times attendance—do not exhibit a great deal of variance with respect to changes in ticket prices. In addition, the nature of each sport creates a physical limit to the number of good seats that can be created. As a result, the "ideal" stadium size and seating configuration for each sport has not changed a great deal for several decades.

For these reasons, concessions, special seating arrangements, and marketing connections have accounted for a growing fraction of revenues in sports. As with traditional in-stadium sources, each team is either a local monopolist or duopolist in marketing these rights locally within its sport. Hence the team can extract more than competitive profits from these sources.

Commercial Licensing Arrangements

The first two types of rights sales—concessions and marketing connections—are similar to each other, but distinct from the various seating rights. A team or stadium authority has basically two approaches to generating revenues from commercial licensing. One is to charge a royalty that is based on sales, and the other is to charge a fixed fee that is not based on sales. This distinction signifies, of course, that there is a trade-off between these two sources of revenues.

The profitability of a commercial license has an upper bound, and no matter how the rights are sold the team cannot collect more than these profits. Hence, if the up-front payment is increased, the team's maximum royalty payment must decline. Thus, in negotiating a stadium financing plan, the initial fee for gaining the commercial license is paired with a subsequent royalty rate. In this sense, to use commercial up-front rights fees as a means to finance a stadium entails an agreement to reduce future royalties from these same sources.

At the same time, the trade-off between up-front rights fees and continuing royalty rates gives rise to a puzzling question: what difference does it make how these arrangements are patterned, and whether the team or the commercial licensees pay for the stadium? Presumably the team or the stadium authority is free to charge nothing for, say, pouring rights and other concessions rights, to borrow money to pay for the stadium, and then to pay off the loan with the higher royalty rates that concessionaires would be willing to pay, given that they paid no up-front rights fees. Why, then, is so much emphasis placed on these sources of revenue?

One answer is an artifact of the 1986 Tax Reform Act, which, as discussed below, accords a more favorable tax status to up-front license fees than to royalties. Another answer is purely economic. A team or stadium authority wants to give commercial licensees the maximum incentive to sell concessions and products with a marketing connection to the team. A royalty is a form of sales tax, which creates a disincentive to expand sales. Moreover, the royalty can create inefficiencies in that the person holding the license rationally will not sell products to a customer who is not willing to pay the cost of the product plus the royalty, but who is willing to pay some intermediate amount between cost and cost plus a royalty. By discouraging such sales, a royalty system reduces the profits that can be extracted from the licensed product.

The preceding argument seems to suggest that a team should never structure a rights agreement that includes any royalties at all. The entire deal should be based on an up-front payment, with the commercial licensee collecting all of the revenues from product sales. Unfortunately, this arrangement creates another problem. The value of the license depends on the quality of the team. Better teams will have higher attendance and so will sell more concessions and confer greater value on firms that hold the right to market a connection with the team. Hence, in order to create an incentive for the teams to be strong, the holder of a commercial license will want the amount it pays for the license to depend on sales of licensed products, whether cola and beer in the stadium, sports clothing in and out of the stadium, or unrelated products outside.

The upshot of this argument is that the optimal method for the team to market its rights is to combine up-front fees and royalties. The former sharpens the incentive of the licensee to sell licensed products, and the latter sharpens the incentive of the team to field a team that will have higher value to the commercial licensee.

With respect to stadium financing, the connection between up-front fees and a new stadium is subtle and indirect. Most apparently, if a team or stadium authority sets the up-front fees too high, the consequences will be, first, lower royalty rates, and second, a reduced incentive by the team to maintain its quality. In an earlier era, when concession revenues and other commercial licenses were not very important, this effect would not be particularly important; however, as the significance of these revenue sources grows, this disincentive has ever greater relevance. Hence an overemphasis on commercial rights fees to finance a stadium can undermine the likely future quality of the team, the revenues derived from the stadium, and, to the extent that the financing of the stadium depends on these revenues, the financial viability of the stadium financing package. This argument, then, constitutes one more source of concern about the out-years in stadium financing plans.

Special Seating and the Strange Case of PSLs

The second type of license fee is for access to certain types of seats: luxury boxes, premium seating, and the like. Typically, financing plans use revenues from these sources to pay for the stadium. An especially interesting source of revenue is the personal seat license, whereby a customer pays a fixed fee to obtain the right to buy season tickets. PSLs can be perpetual, as they are for the new San Francisco Giants ballpark, but more commonly they cover a fixed period, such as the ten-year life of a PSL for tickets to the Oakland Raiders games.[11] Likewise, the rights inhering in a PSL usually can be sold, but sometimes a change in ownership requires a payment to the team.

PSLs were first used by the Dallas Cowboys in 1968 to help finance Texas Stadium.[12] Called "seat options," they were priced at $300 to $1,000 and had a life of forty years. The next use did not occur until 1986, when a variant of the PSL, called "charter seat rights," was used to collect advance ticket revenues of sufficient magnitude to persuade the NBA to expand to Charlotte, which it did by creating the Hornets. These revenues were converted to a down payment on the first year's season tickets.

The contemporary model for PSLs was implemented in 1993 by the owners of the NFL expansion team in Charlotte, the Carolina Panthers. The team raised $150 million through the sale of PSLs, of which $50 million went for taxes and $100 million was used to help pay for a new stadium. PSL prices ranged from $600 to $5,400. In 1995 St. Louis followed suit to attract an NFL team by selling PSLs for between $250 and $4,500. The sale raised $70 million, which eventually paid for, among other things, the relocation fees to the Rams and the NFL. Later that year, the Oakland Coliseum launched a PSL plan, charging $250 to $4,000 for ten-year PSLs, with a target revenue of nearly $100 million. PSLs subsequently have been adopted as part of the financing plan of new baseball parks in Cincinnati, Milwaukee, and San Francisco, and new football stadiums in Baltimore, Boston, Cincinnati, Nashville, and the Maryland suburbs of Washington, D.C.

PSLs and similar seating licenses have obvious attractions as a means of financing a stadium. First, they reduce the financial exposure of teams and governments for a new stadium. Second, in comparison with taxes, they place the financing burden on sports fans, who derive the benefits of a new stadium. Moreover, whereas sales and property taxes tend to be regressive, seat licenses tend to be progressive. Thus the movement toward financing stadiums partly by selling seat licenses has many desirable effects.

The economics of PSLs is deceptively complicated. At one level, they should have the same basic relationship with ticket prices that up-front commercial rights fees have with subsequent royalties. From the demand side, a fan has a maximum willingness to pay for season tickets to a sports team for each of the next ten years. Ignoring possible variability in team quality, the fan is willing to pay either a sequence of payments each year, the discounted present value of that sequence of payments today, or any combination of fixed payments and annual ticket purchases that has the same discounted present value. Thus the immediate effect of a PSL system should be to reduce the price of season tickets by a corresponding amount.

The main problem with the preceding analysis is that one cannot assume the sale of PSLs will have no impact on team quality. As with commercial rights, PSLs affect the incentives of both teams and fans. If PSLs lower long-term season ticket prices, they reduce the incentive of the team to field good teams. Moreover, this effect is amplified by the incentive that the system gives fans to continue to buy season tickets. First, a PSL expires if the ticket is not purchased, so a fan must either buy tickets or sell the license to avoid losing all of its value. Second, if PSLs lower season ticket prices to PSL holders, the minimum quality of team that must be fielded in order to keep the fan buying tickets will be lower. Of course, if fans recognize that a PSL system has poor incentive properties for the team, they will not pay as much for a PSL, and the introduction of a PSL system will lower the sum of the revenues a team will receive from PSLs and subsequent ticket sales.

Whether teams somehow do charge lower season ticket prices over the duration of the license is not at all clear. Most agreements do not specify future pricing rules. The one that does, the Oakland Raiders' PSL, states that ticket prices will remain below $50 through 1997 and will increase by no more than 5 percent a year thereafter; however, $50 is already at the top of NFL ticket prices, the team is not selling out its games, and in any case the 1997 prices average $51, so it is not clear that this price cap has any effect or value.[13]

The actual nature of the rights conferred by a PSL are obscure. If good season tickets are in excess demand, as is the case in some cities, a PSL might be interpreted as guaranteeing the holders that they will not be excluded. In reality, teams typically allow season ticket holders automatically to renew their tickets each year, and one's position in the season ticket queue is lost only if season tickets are not renewed. Hence ensuring access under excess demand does not seem to be the motivation for buying PSLs.

If a PSL can be sold, this might appear to ensure a certain value to one's season tickets; as a practical matter, however, season ticket renewal rights can be sold in any case simply by not changing the name associated with the tickets. A sports team has no way of knowing whether a ticket is used by the person who bought it, and whether a change of address entails a change of residence or the identity of the purchaser. Hence it is simply not obvious that a PSL confers any rights beyond those held by a normal season ticket holder.

The implication of the preceding discussion is that as a purely economic matter PSLs appear to be a very bad idea for everyone concerned—teams, fans, and stadium authorities—because they confer no extra benefits, generate no extra sources of revenues, and tend to reduce team quality and thereby team revenues. Why, then, do they exist?

The first possible reason is that PSLs are induced by a perversity in the institutional arrangements of baseball and football. In these sports, ticket revenues are shared between the home and visiting team. In baseball, ticket license revenues and premium seating fees are not shared, and in football these revenues are not necessarily shared if they are used to pay for a stadium.[14] The baseball and football rules create a strong financial incentive to pay for stadiums through PSLs rather than through stadium rents on ticket sales. If a team sells a PSL and in return credibly commits to charge lower ticket prices, the effect is to cause other teams in the league to pay part of the cost of its stadium. (By contrast, concession revenues are not shared, whether they are collected as up-front fees or royalties.)

Suppose that the relevant discount rate is 10 percent. In the NFL, if a ten-year PSL costs $700, the equivalent reduction in season ticket prices is $100 a year for ten years. If this reduction occurs, visiting teams lose 40 percent of the cut in ticket sales ($40 a year), which has a present value of $280. If the present value of the team's share of stadium costs is really $700, the visiting teams are actually paying $280 of this cost by forgoing the share of revenues that they would have received had ticket prices been higher but no PSL had been sold.

The second explanation for the existence of PSLs is that they also are encouraged by a perversity in the federal tax system.[15] The Tax Reform

Act of 1986 withdrew the right to use tax-exempt bonds to finance sports facilities if more than 10 percent of interest and amortization was accounted for by revenues from the stadium. Tax exemption is important, because it reduces the city's interest cost of indebtedness by as much as 30 percent, as explained in chapter 4.

The rule about tax exemption was written in such a way that PSL sales did not count in the 10 percent limitation, but rental payments do. If a city is collecting money from ticket sales to pay for the stadium, it can do so in two ways. It can charge rent and tax ticket sales, or it can sell PSLs. The former count toward the 10 percent limit, but the latter do not; hence the city prefers to use PSLs in order to preserve its tax exemption. Likewise, the city would rather have the team sell PSLs and pay lower rent and taxes than finance the stadium itself from higher rents and taxes.

The same incentive is present for using up-front commercial licensing fees to pay for a stadium. If the trade-off is between, say, higher rents and taxes on concessions versus an up-front rights fee, federal tax rules count the former toward the 10 percent limit but not the latter. Hence the team and stadium authority will prefer up-front fees if doing so enables them to retain the tax exemption for the bonds that finance part of the stadium.

The preceding analysis leads to a rather sobering conclusion that one often encounters in analyzing federal tax policy. The recent boom in seat licenses, stadium naming rights, and other up-front licensing fees may have been artificially induced by yet another loophole in the tax code. Cities, teams, and their tax consultants may have done nothing more than invent a legal evasion of the 1986 tax reform. And the 1986 attempt to reduce the use of state and local debt to subsidize private businesses may have succeeded only in creating yet another distortion, in this case leading to practices that reduce the incentive to field high-quality teams.

A third possible reason for the existence of PSLs is that they may increase total revenues from the stadium. The argument that PSLs increase revenues is that the act of purchasing a PSL confers a special benefit: a sense of participation in bringing in a new team or keeping an old one, and a sense of personal ownership in the new stadium. In essence, a PSL is a kind of private good for achieving a public purpose, something akin to voluntary contributions to a charity.

Charitable contributions generally are subject to the problem of free riding. Because a single person has little effect on whether the charitable goal is achieved, each potential donor has little instrumental incentive to make a contribution. Hence one would expect total donations to be substantially less than the value of the civic purpose to which the funds are put. Nevertheless, this argument alone does not support the conclusion that PSLs must have no charitable component. The key point is that even if people are prone to contribute less to a civic purpose than the value of that purpose to them, they still might contribute a significant amount. If so, some nontrivial portion of PSL revenue may be a net increment to the revenue stream of teams and stadiums.

If this motivation explains part of the revenue from PSL sales, PSLs make a real contribution to stadium financing, and the various distortions discussed above are less important than they otherwise would be. Moreover, the argument would apply with equal force to long-term sales of other premium seats, such as luxury boxes, if these revenues also are used to help finance a stadium. One implication of this account, of course, is that part of PSL charges for stadium construction should not lead to a comparable reduction in season ticket sales over the life of the PSL. Likewise, higher premium seating charges for stadium finance should be feasible if they are used to pay for a stadium. And, finally, if the thrill of participating in attracting a new team to a city is part of the motive, this component of the value of a PSL should evaporate when the team begins to play, so that the price of subsequent resale of PSLs should fall more rapidly than the remaining life in the first few years after they are issued.

Unfortunately, too few teams and stadium authorities have used PSLs and other premium seating revenues to finance stadiums to permit an empirical test of these propositions. Nevertheless, one interesting fact has emerged: the success of PSLs has been quite variable. The most successful PSL can be found in Charlotte, where sales achieved expectations, but others have fallen short. The worst experience is in Oakland.[16]

Oakland sold PSLs through a local government entity, the Oakland Football Marketing Association, whose proceeds net of selling costs went to the city and county to offset their investment in renovating the Coliseum to accommodate the Raiders. In the original financial plan, PSL revenues (including fees from special clubs for PSL holders) were expected to produce $99.1 million. After one year, the actual revenues were $58.9 million, a shortfall in excess of $40 million.

Also, the Oakland financial plan expected renovation to cost $100 million, but the actual cost was $130 million because the plan failed to include several important items: notably, a scoreboard, improved seat covers, and field drainage to accommodate rain (which occurs only in the football season). Instead of breaking more or less even (with an expected loss of less than $1 million), the stadium renovation was $70 million in the red after the first year. Although some of this loss may be recovered through PSL sales in subsequent years, it would be optimistic to believe that most of the cost of the stadium renovation will not be paid out of increased taxes and reduced public services.

The extent to which PSLs distort the decisions of teams and stadium authorities, and reflect additional distortions created by federal taxes and league revenue-sharing arrangements, remains quantitatively uncertain. Nevertheless, the distortions arising from revenue sharing and taxation are likely to be an important part of the attractiveness of PSLs to both teams and stadium authorities. Regardless of altruistic motives behind the sale of PSLs and other seating rights, an extremely attractive feature of these revenue sources is that they are not paid by the team, the fans, or local government. Instead, these financing arrangements pass part of the cost of stadium construction on to teams in other cities and to federal taxpayers through the tax-exempt status of local bonds.

Why Cities Subsidize Sports Facilities

The upshot of the discussion of stadium financing to this point is that the government pays a significant fraction of the cost of sports facilities. Most financing plans actually do conclude that the facilities are subsidized, but the actual magnitude of the subsidy is typically greater than the estimate in the plan owing to numerous systematic errors in estimating the costs and revenues of a stadium.

The obvious question that arises is why such subsidies exist. Part of the answer probably lies in the fact that the social and psychological significance of sports substantially exceeds its economic value, so that in the absence of economic and political distortions in the relationship between teams and cities, some subsidies are bound to emerge (see chapter 2). Part of the answer may lie in a widespread belief that sports facilities are an engine of local economic development. Most of this book is devoted to demonstrating that this belief is mistaken. Still another part of the answer is that public ownership enables teams and cities to capture federal tax benefits for constructing stadiums, thereby causing people who live elsewhere to pay part of the cost of a facility for the hometown team (see chapter 4). And, part of the answer also may lie in the peculiar politics of sports, in which teams, other interests that benefit from sports facilities, and their political representatives control the agenda of public decisionmaking about sports facilities and make use of that power to give the public a choice among bad alternatives (see chapter 5).

The preceding are only some of the economic and political reasons for public subsidies. The fact that teams want subsidies and that governments are willing to provide them does not necessarily mean subsidies will emerge. In virtually all lines of business, providers would love to charge more, and most consumers would be willing to pay more rather than do without. Nevertheless, firms and consumers continue to transact at prices below the level that would extract the maximal feasible amount from consumers and maximize industry profits. Two additional factors explain why subsidies actually are paid: the relatively weak bargaining position of cities, and the fundamental economic irrationality of most new stadiums as purely private investments.

Monopoly Leagues

Although professional sports has expanded considerably since the 1950s, the number of teams in each sport remains substantially lower than the number of cities that can support a major league team. Moreover, because of the rising popularity of professional sports, the minimum size of a metropolitan area that can support a team is shrinking. Consider what happens when expansion is contemplated or an established team plans to relocate. In either case, many more cities bid for franchises than the number of teams that are available. Until the 1980s, cities such as Charlotte, Jacksonville, Nashville, Phoenix, and St. Petersburg would have been unlikely candidates to bid for a franchise, let alone win one. The success of these small-city franchises indicates that many comparable cities are also good candidates for new teams. Likewise, multiple teams seem to be viable in the largest markets.

The reason for the excess demand for teams among cities is the structure of the sports industry. All major sports are controlled by monopoly leagues. Like monopolists anywhere, these leagues profit from a scarcity of teams. By creating a situation in which several cities that are viable franchise sites do not have teams, the leagues set up competitive bidding for any team that becomes available, whether through expansion or relocation. Cities that lack a team then become credible threats to induce an existing team to move, as well as provide a hungry pack of suitors when a league decides to expand. This situation bids up the price for franchises and the subsidy that a city must expect to pay in order to capture or to retain a team. The underlying economics of this process are discussed in chapter 2.

Normally, monopolistic behavior such as this would attract entry in the form of new leagues. Indeed, several leagues have tried to enter professional sports throughout the postwar era, but none has succeeded since the World Hockey League and the American Basketball Association merged some of their teams into the established NHL and NBA in the 1970s. The lack of successful entry since the 1970s also is based on the structural features of sports. The success of a professional sports team depends greatly on the success of its league. The problem is not just that one team needs other teams to play, but that a league must include some major cities. The presence of at least some teams from large cities has two major benefits, both of which are related to the media.

First, national television has become a very important source of revenue for all sports and is essential to the success of a major league. A league must include big cities to offer an attractive package of television rights, partly because so much of the TV audience is in large cities and partly because fans in smaller communities are more likely to watch a team from a large city than from a smaller one.

Second, the free publicity that arises from coverage of a league by national media is far more extensive if the league includes teams in national media centers such as Chicago, Los Angeles, and New York. The relationship between the media and sports is synergistic: sports coverage sells newspapers and increases audience ratings, but it also enhances interest in sports.

For these reasons, a presence in at least some of the largest metropolitan areas is essential to the success of a major professional sports league. The great problem for new leagues entering large cities is to find the necessary sports facilities. Because existing teams have exclusive rights to nearly all facilities of major league caliber, a new team usually must gain access to a new facility soon after it is created. Of course, established teams also play in facilities that are subsidized, so that to compete on equal footing, the new league must be able to obtain comparable subsidies. But cities are less likely to subsidize a new team in a new league if the city already has a team or two in the established league. Hence a new league faces enormous problems, not just in locating in big cities but also in getting the league off the ground, even though there are many other cities that would welcome the new league, subsidize its teams, and support its games. For these reasons, competitive entry is no longer a serious threat to existing monopoly sports leagues.

Stadiums as Poor Investments

Stadium subsidies exist also because stadiums are seldom financially attractive as private investments. As already explained, stadiums are not financially viable if they must both improve the profitability of a team and pay for themselves. That is why local governments have difficulty finding a combination of rents, fees, and taxes to pay for a stadium.

If a team were not subsidized directly by payments from state and local governments and indirectly by the federal interest subsidy on government debt, interest and amortization for a stadium would be roughly 10 percent of its construction costs, including site acquisition and clearance. In no sport would the incremental revenue that is kept by a team be sufficient to pay for the stadium, except in two cases.

First, a dual-purpose basketball and hockey facility could plausibly pay for itself. In these sports, game revenues are not shared, so all of the revenue enhancement from a new facility is kept by the home team. In addition, arenas can be used for other events, such as circuses and trade shows. Second, the baseline revenues for an expansion team are zero, which means that the revenues from a new facility are entirely a gain to the team. At the same time, all of the team's costs are incremental to building the stadium. Thus a privately financed facility is worth building if the excess of revenues over costs exceeds the interest and amortization on the stadium, in other words, if the annual profit is $20 million to $30 million, depending on the sport. Whereas such profits are conceivable, they would be exceptional in all sports.

For established teams, stadiums are extremely unlikely to pay for themselves. The gross incremental revenue from a stadium frequently does exceed its annualized cost, but these greater revenues also cause increases in other costs, especially player salaries. Professional athletes receive salaries that are roughly proportional to the revenues that they generate, so that much of the revenue enhancement from a new stadium inevitably goes to players. As shown in chapter 5, most of the incremental revenues from Oriole Park at Camden Yards were spent on player salaries. This increase would have been less if baseball had an effective salary cap, but because Camden Yards would have caused the salary cap to increase, and because no salary cap is completely free of loopholes, even with a cap players can be expected to capture a substantial part of the revenue increase.

The bottom line is that for the most part facilities are not financially viable when assessed on the basis of the incremental profit that a team can expect over the life of the facility. If teams had to pay for their own facilities, stadiums would have to be much smaller and much less elaborate.

Why Build a Stadium?

The foregoing analysis suggests the possibility of a cheaper way to subsidize teams: simply pay them the incremental profits that a stadium would provide, rather than pay for a stadium. To return to the case of Camden Yards, the owners of the Baltimore Orioles seem to benefit from the presence of the new ballpark by only a few million dollars a year. Hence, if Baltimore and the state of Maryland had simply paid the Orioles $5 million a year, these governments could have saved a substantial amount of money, the Orioles' bottom line would be improved, and the federal government would avoid several million dollars in annual interest subsidies.

Why, then, do cities and teams fail to follow that course? The answer to this question most likely lies in the politics of stadiums. One possibility, of course, is that the new stadium provides the city with sufficient spillover benefits to make the facility worthwhile. However, as the remaining chapters of the book indicate, this is unlikely to be the case. We suspect that, as a political matter, the explanation lies in two areas. First, some of the interests behind a stadium, such as local contractors and construction unions, cannot benefit unless the stadium is actually built. Second, people in general are more willing to subsidize a team indirectly by providing a stadium, even if it costs more. Perhaps they prefer to have a better team, in which case the benefit to fans of the extra expenditures on players more than offsets the cost to the team. Of course, this benefit is likely to be temporary if, as time progresses, other teams also acquire new stadiums.

Conclusions

Stadium financing is a complicated business. The effect of stadiums on the cash flow of teams and cities suggests that new facilities rarely, if ever, are worthwhile. Sometimes they can be financially catastrophic.

Subsidized sports facilities do not exist because they are financially valuable assets in their own right. They exist, instead, because most cities have decided that a subsidized team is better than no team at all, and because scarcity in the number of teams gives owners the advantage in bargaining with cities.

Appendix
Summaries of Lease Agreements in Professional Sports

Major League Baseball

ANAHEIM (CALIFORNIA) ANGELS (name changed for 1997 season). Anaheim Stadium built in 1996/97 (till construction complete). Capacity in 1996: 64,593. Luxury suites in 1996: 104 @ $22,000–$32,000, but none in 1997 season owing to renovation construction.

Lease began in 1996 for thirty-three years (until 2029). Team can escape lease after twenty years. Lease can be extended for three-year period. Team controls *all* stadium revenue. Team pays city $2 ticket surcharge for every admission over 2.6 million. Team pays city 25 percent of revenues exceeding $2 million from non–baseball events. The team is controlled by the Walt Disney Co. (general partner). Disney also helped finance stadium renovations (Disney, 70 percent; city, 30 percent).

ATLANTA BRAVES. Atlanta-Fulton County Stadium, opened 1964. Capacity: 60,700. Luxury suites: 60 @ $125,000–$200,000 per year. Lease expired December 31, 1996.

Rent: equal to 5 percent of gate on first 1.2 million paid admissions plus 10–16.5 percent of gross concessions receipts plus game-day expenses of stadium authority minus $193,368. Team also pays $20,000 for stadium club rental and $192,000 for stadium cleaning yearly. Authority keeps all parking and signage (except at concessions spaces) revenues. Braves retain 39 percent of net concessions revenue.

TURNER FIELD. Built 1996. Capacity: 49,831. Private suites: 59. Party suites: 3. Lease expires in 2017.

Annual operator's fee: $500,000 per year, plus any annual revenues from naming rights above $1.5 million up to a maximum of $250,000 per year. Braves retain 91.5 percent of parking revenues, 100 percent of concessions revenues, 100 percent of advertising revenues, 100 percent of suite revenues, and 50 percent of revenues from non–baseball events. Braves are responsible for operations and maintenance. Opened for baseball in 1997.

BALTIMORE ORIOLES. Oriole Park at Camden Yards, built in 1992 for $210 million. Capacity: 48,262. Luxury suites: 72 @ $55,000–$110,000 per year. Club seats: 3,800 @ $30 per game plus $500 annual fee, or $2,075 per season. Lease is for thirty years.

Rent: 7 percent of net admissions receipts. Team pays Maryland Stadium Authority (owner) between 1.7 percent and 7.5 percent of gross concessions revenues. Authority operates parking but team receives 50 percent of net receipts. Team retains 90 percent of luxury suite rentals, signage, and club seat revenues. Authority is responsible for all maintenance except field conditions.

BOSTON RED SOX. Team owner, John L. Harrington, owns park.

CHICAGO CUBS. Team owner, Tribune Co., owns park.

CHICAGO WHITE SOX. Comiskey Park, built in 1991. Capacity: 44,321. Luxury suites: 102 @ $60,000–$90,000 a year. Club seats: 1,800 @ $1,620 a season. Lease is through 2009.

Rent: $1 per year. Illinois Sports Facility Authority receives 35 percent of sum of local broadcast revenues and signage exceeding $10 million. Team retains all signage except that stipulated above and retains all parking revenue. Team retains all income from stadium club and concessions. City pays for stadium insurance and all capital repairs above $500,000.

CINCINNATI REDS. Cinergy Field. Formerly Riverfront Stadium, built in 1970. Capacity: 52,952 (baseball), 59,754 (football). Luxury suites: 20 @ $77,220 a year, including tickets for all Reds and Bengals games. Lease is through 2017.

Rent: $175,000 plus 7.5 percent of ticket revenue above $2.3 million. Team retains 90 percent of gross concessions revenue and 30 percent of suite rental fee (Bengals receive 62.5 percent and city 7.5 percent). City retains all parking revenue.

CLEVELAND INDIANS. Jacobs Field, built in 1994. Capacity: 42,865. Luxury suites: 122 @ $36,000–$96,000 a year plus tickets ($23 each). Club seats: 2,064 @ $1,600 club fee plus $23 a game. Lease is through 2014.

Rent: $.75 per ticket sold after 1.85 million paid admissions up to 2.25 million, $1 per ticket between 2.25 and 2.5 million attendance, and $1.25 per ticket for attendance above 2.5 million. Team retains all parking, signage, concessions, and luxury and club seat revenues.

COLORADO ROCKIES. Coors Field, built in 1995. Capacity: 50,200. Luxury suites: 52 @ $73,000–$110,000 a year. Club seats: 4,400 @ $28 per game. Lease expires 2012.

Rent: Team retains all revenues generated at the stadium, including all suite, club seat, signage, and concessions revenues. Team also receives all revenue from the sale of naming rights. Team is responsible for park maintenance and operations. There is also a provision for the team to pay the authority 2.5 percent of the team's net taxable income if the partners take a 5 percent cash return in any given year on their paid-in capital (and this return shall be deducted from the taxable basis).

DETROIT TIGERS. Tiger Stadium, built in 1912. Capacity: 52,416. Luxury suites: 4, 2 of which are sold to the public at $2,500 per game. Club seats: 3,773 @ $1,620 a year. Lease expires 2008.

Rent: $1.00 a year plus $.90 per ticket sold, not to be less than $150,000 or more than $400,000. Team retains signage, concessions, and parking income. Team covers operations and maintenance.

FLORIDA MARLINS. Team owns park.

HOUSTON ASTROS. The Astrodome, built in 1965. Capacity: 54,350. Luxury suites: 65 @ $21,000–$68,000 a year. Skyboxes: 72 @ $288 per game. Club seats: 100 @ $60 per game. Lease expires on August 16, 2005.

Rent: $735,020 for 1997 season plus a $100,000 special-purpose additional rent; plus 2 percent of parking or $125,000, whichever is greater.

All revenue from baseball events and non–baseball events goes to the team. Team covers operations and most maintenance expenses.

KANSAS CITY ROYALS. Ewing Kauffman Stadium, built in 1973. Capacity: 40,625. Luxury suites: 19 @ $32,000–$42,000. Lease expires 2015.

Rent: $450,000, plus 5 percent of gross gate receipts between $7.5 and $12.5 million, 4 percent of gross receipts between $12.5 and $17.5 million and 2 percent of gross receipts above $17.5 million. The team retains all revenues from signage, suite rentals, and concessions. Authority covers operations and maintenance.

LOS ANGELES DODGERS. Team owns park.

MILWAUKEE BREWERS. County Stadium, built in 1953. Capacity: 53,192. No luxury suites or club seats.

Rent: $1 per ticket sold up to 1 million tickets; 5 percent of gross receipts from 1 to 1.5 million tickets; 7 percent of gross receipts from 1.5 to 2 million tickets and 10 percent of gross above 2 million tickets. County retains 100 percent of parking revenues. Signage is shared on roughly a 50/50 basis. Team retains all net concessions revenue up to 1 million attendance and above 1 million pays the county 10 percent of gross concessions revenues. County covers maintenance and shares operations expenses with the team.

MINNESOTA TWINS. Hubert H. Humphrey Metrodome, built in 1982. Capacity: 48,678. Luxury suites: 113 owned by the Vikings and 2 owned by the Twins @ $39,000–$78,000. For Vikings-owned suites, Twins tickets must be purchased at $17 a seat. Lease expires in 2009.

Rent: 10 percent ticket tax. Team retains between 75 percent and 100 percent of signage, but cannot use scoreboard for commercial advertising. Team receives 35 percent of gross concessions receipts until 1 million tickets sold and 45 percent thereafter. Team retains no parking revenue. Team pays utility and insurance costs. Authority covers other operations and all maintenance costs.

MONTREAL EXPOS. Olympic Stadium (Le Stade Olympique), built in 1976. Capacity: 46,418. Luxury suites: 36 @ C$44,000–C$62,144. Club seats: 151 @ C$3,483.

Rent: 6.5 percent on gross receipts up to 1 million tickets sold; 7.5 percent on next 800,000 tickets and 9.5 percent on ticket sales above 1.8 million. Expos receive no income from luxury suite sales.

NEW YORK METS. Shea Stadium, built in 1964. Capacity: 55,601. Luxury suites: 46 @ $95,000–$205,000. Club seats: 3,885 @ $25 per game. Lease expires 2004.

Rent: The greater of $300,000 or a percent of gross receipts. Team receives 15 percent commission on luxury suites revenue. City receives 8 percent of development cost of suites. Team retains remaining 50 percent of luxury suite rentals. Team controls and retains 100 percent of signage and concessions revenues. City retains all parking revenues. City is responsible for all maintenance and shares in operations expenses.

NEW YORK YANKEES. Yankee Stadium, built in 1923. Capacity: 57,545. Luxury suites: 19 @ $102,000. Club seats: 5,000 @ $2,187 per season. Lease expires 2002, with two five-year renewal options.

Rent: minimum rent is $200,000. Five percent of gross gate and gross concessions for attendance up to 750,000; 7.5 percent of gross gate and concessions for attendance between 750,000 and 1.5 million; 10 percent of gross gate and concessions for attendance above 1.5 million. Team receives 100 percent of signage revenues, except signage on stadium exterior. Team retains 100 percent of all luxury suite income and 50 percent of parking. Team pays operations and normal maintenance costs, but may deduct many of these costs from its rental obligations. In practice, the Yankees, claiming various deductions, have paid less than $1 million in rent since the late 1980s.

OAKLAND ATHLETICS. Oakland-Alameda County Stadium, built in 1966. Capacity: 47,313. Luxury suites: 53 skyboxes and 10 plaza suites @ $35,000–$65,000. Club seats: 2,700 @ $1,620–$2,025 per season. Lease expires 2004.

Rent: $250,000 a year, plus $100,000 for parking rights, $100 for each club seat membership and 10 percent of net club seat revenue, and $10,000 a year for use of DiamondVision. Team retains all luxury suite income up to $750,000 and 50 percent thereafter, 100 percent of signage, and 50 percent of concessions. Beginning in 1997, city will collect a $.25 surcharge per ticket.

PHILADELPHIA PHILLIES. Veterans Stadium, built in 1971. Capacity: 62,530. Luxury suites: 89 @ $90,000–$180,000, and 59 super boxes @ $22,000–$80,000. Club seats: 1,296 @ $1,539 a year. Lease expires 2011, with two five-year renewal options.

Rent: greater of $160,000 or 10 percent of ticket sales in excess of $1.6 million, with provision that city credits team against rental obligation equal to 50 percent of the city's gross concession receipts. City retains all parking revenue. Phillies retain 100 percent of luxury suite income, but must reimburse Eagles for value of football tickets. Phillies must also pay the city 10 percent of gross receipts from pay television. Phillies cover the bulk of operations expenses.

PITTSBURGH PIRATES. Three Rivers Stadium, built in 1970. Capacity: 47,972. Loge boxes: 110 @ $18,000 per season plus $25 per game. Lease expires in 2010. Rent: 10 percent of net receipts plus a 10 percent amusement tax on every ticket. Team retains no revenue from parking, 70 percent of net concessions revenue, 33 percent of signage from concourse, and no revenues from loge box rentals. Team covers operations and maintenance expenses.

SAN DIEGO PADRES. Qualcomm Stadium at Jack Murphy Field (renamed in 1997), built in 1968. Capacity: 47,750. Luxury suites: 78 @ $34,000–$70,000 a year. Club seats: 582 at $27 a game. Lease expires 2000.

Rent: 10 percent of first $15 million in ticket sales and 8 percent thereafter. Team retains 29 percent of luxury suite rentals, 50 percent of parking revenues above $1.5 million, and 100 percent of gross concessions revenues.

SAN FRANCISCO GIANTS. 3-Com Park, built in 1960. Capacity: 63,000. Luxury suites: 85 @ $29,880–$74,700 a year. Club seats: 6,900 lower seats @ $1,660 a year, and 2,000 upper seats @ $1,286 a year. Lease is through 2008.

Rent: Team pays greater of $125,000 minimum rental, or 5 percent of paid admissions. Team pays $.25 per ticket to city-sponsored after-school sports program. City controls all parking and retains revenues.

SEATTLE MARINERS. Kingdome, built in 1976. Capacity: 59,158. Luxury suites: 19 @ $35,000–$190,000 a year. Lease expired March 14, 1997. Team has two five-year renewal options.

Rent: greater of 7 percent of gate receipts for first 1 million tickets sold or $160,000 plus 5 percent of gate from first 1 million. Team retains approximately 45 percent of gross concessions and parking revenues, 100 percent of baseball novelty revenues, and 40 percent of net revenues from suite rentals for 48 suites, and 100 percent of net revenues from remaining 29 suites. Mariners pay $318,000 for signage rights and keep 75 percent of signage revenue, except DiamondVision, in which case the team keeps 50 percent. Team pays county $9,750 for game-day expenses for 1996 season and 5 percent of any reported net operating profits for the franchise. County covers operations and maintenance.

ST. LOUIS CARDINALS. Team owns park. Busch Stadium, built in 1966. Capacity: 57,078. Luxury suites: 64 @ $30,000–$33,000. Club seats: 592 @ $8,505 per season.

TAMPA BAY DEVIL RAYS. Tropicana Field (formerly ThunderDome, 1990), completed for baseball in 1997. Capacity: 46,000. Luxury suites: 65 @ $40,000–$140,000. Lease expires 2027.

Rent: $.50 for each ticket sold up to 3.3 million tickets and $.75 above 3.3 million, with the first $250,000 of these funds paid into a maintenance account. Team operates and maintains stadium and receives a $4.2 million management fee from the city. Team retains all revenues generated for baseball and non–baseball events. Team also retains between 80 and 85 percent of naming rights to stadium.

TEXAS RANGERS. The Ballpark at Arlington, built in 1994. Capacity: 49,178. Luxury suites: 121 @ $40,000–$200,000. Club seats: 5,386 @ $1,215–$1,328 per season. Lease expires in 2024.

Rent: base rent of $2 million a year, and until bond obligations retired an additional $1.5 million a year, along with a $1 surcharge per ticket sold. Team retains 100 percent of parking and signage, and 95 percent of luxury club suite rentals through 1999 and 100 percent thereafter. Team receives all revenues from non-baseball events. Team pays operations and maintenance costs above sum collected by the ticket surcharge.

TORONTO BLUE JAYS. SkyDome, built in 1989. Capacity: 50,516. Skyboxes: 161 @ $100,000–$225,000. Club seats: 5,700 @ C$4,000.

Rent: A consortium of thirty businesses owns the facility.

National Basketball Association

ATLANTA HAWKS. The Omni, built in 1972. Capacity: 16,378. Luxury suites: 16 @ $175,000–$180,000. New facility planned for 1999.

Rent: 10 percent of gross ticket sales. Atlanta-Fulton County Recreation Authority controls 100 percent of parking revenue. All suite revenue goes to the Authority, but team is paid for the tickets.

BOSTON CELTICS. FleetCenter, built in 1995. Capacity: 18,600. Luxury suites: 104 @ $125,000–$200,000. Club seats: 2,350 @ $10,650–$12,250 a year.

Rent: no payment made. Suite revenue divided among Celtics, Bruins, and loan debt. Celtics receive suite ticket money.

CHARLOTTE HORNETS. Charlotte Coliseum, built in 1988. Capacity: 24,042. Luxury suites: 12 @ $73,500–$126,000. Lease expires in 2000.

Rent: the greater of 12 percent of net ticket sales or $3,500 per home game up to a maximum of $9,000 per home game. Team and city split luxury suite net revenue. City retains all parking revenues (approximately $100,000 per game) and all concessions revenues, except game-day sales of basketball novelties. Team retains all signage revenues. Operating and maintenance expenses are the responsibility of the Authority, but the team reimburses the Authority for game-day personnel.

CHICAGO BULLS. United Center, built in 1994. Capacity: 21,711. Luxury suites: 216 @ $85,000–$175,000. Club seats: 3,300 at $40 per ticket plus $1,000 annual fee.

Rent: United Center Bulls and Blackhawks Joint Venture own the arena. They are assessed a reduced rate property tax of between $600,000 and a maximum of $1 million per year.

CLEVELAND CAVALIERS. The Gund Arena at Gateway, built in 1994. Capacity: 20,562. Luxury suites: 92 @ $85,000–$150,000. Club seats: 2,000 @ $6,955, $7,955, and $8,587 per season a year. Lease expires in 2024.

Rent: 27.5 percent of suite revenue, 48 percent of club seat revenue and $.75 per ticket in excess of 1.85 million tickets up to 2.5 million tickets, and $1.00 per ticket in excess of 2.5 million. These ticket thresholds apply to all basketball and non–basketball events held at Gund Arena. Team retains all parking, signage, and concessions revenues from all events at the arena. Provisions are made for additional rental payments if an NHL hockey team plays at the arena or if parking revenues exceed $1.5 million annually. Team retains any proceeds from arena naming rights. Cavs are responsible for operations and routine maintenance expenses.

DALLAS MAVERICKS. Reunion Arena, built in 1980. Capacity: 18,042. No suites or club seats. Lease expires 2008, with two five-year renewal options.

Rent: If per game receipts are less than or equal to $324,000, team pays $10,000 or 7 percent of receipts, whichever is less. If per game receipts exceed $324,000, team pays $10,000 plus 5 percent of receipts in excess of $324,000. Team retains 50 percent of signage revenues from static advertising and 100 percent from nonstatic advertising. Team receives 10.8 percent of gross concessions up to $4,320 per game when sales exceed $40,000. Team receives 25 percent of parking revenue from season parking passes. The city is responsible for most operations and all maintenance expenses.

DENVER NUGGETS. McNichols Sports Arena, built in 1975. Capacity: 17,171. Luxury suites: 27 @ $90,000. Lease expires 2008.

Rent: greater of 5 percent of net ticket income or $250,000, with maximum of $350,000. Nuggets receive a fixed payment of $140,000 for concessions. Nuggets retain no parking revenue, all luxury suite revenue, and 70 percent of signage revenue until city share reaches $200,000, and 100 percent thereafter. Except for game-day expenses, city covers operations and maintenance costs.

DETROIT PISTONS. Palace of Auburn Hills, built in 1988. Capacity: 21,454. Luxury suites: 180 @ $40,000–$200,000. Club seats: 1,000 @ $6,500. Team owner owns facility.

GOLDEN STATE WARRIORS. Oakland Coliseum, built in 1966; opening night, November 8, 1997. Capacity: 19,200. Luxury suites: 72 @ $95,000–$125,000 a year. Club seats: 3,000 @ $75–$200 per ticket; $8,200, $6,150, $3,690, $3,075 per season.

Rent: Team pays $1.5 million a year and $500,000 management fee. Team pays Coliseum $7.4 million per year for rental of suites, club seats, courtside seats. Team pays ticket surcharge not to exceed 5 percent. Net income will be split between team and Coliseum up to $7.5 million. After that figure is reached, team receives 75 percent and Coliseum 25 percent.

HOUSTON ROCKETS. Summit Arena, built in 1975. Capacity: 15,997. Luxury suites: 20 @ $65,000–$70,000. Lease expires 2003.
   Rent: minimum payment of $22,500 per game. Team retains 50 percent of signage income. Arena is subleased from IHL Houston Aeros.

INDIANA PACERS. Market Square Arena, built in 1974. Capacity: 16,530. Patio boxes: 36 @ $10,650. Lease expires in 2023.
   Rent: $150,000. If team makes a profit, team reimburses city for maintenance and utilities. Team retains 100 percent of signage, 50 percent of parking, and gross concessions revenues. Under terms of the lease, city has right of first refusal on sale of the team. Except for fire insurance, Authority pays for operations and maintenance.

LOS ANGELES CLIPPERS. Memorial Sports Arena, built in 1959. Capacity: 16,021. Luxury suites: 2 @ $7,500 per seat. Lease expires June 30, 1998, with a five-year renewal option.
   Rent: $15,000 per game. For playoff games, 6 percent of gross ticket sales. Team retains 50 percent of luxury suite income, 100 percent of signage for basketball events and 50 percent for other events. Team receives 22.5 percent of concessions sales from all events. Team retains 67 percent of income from Clipper Club and 42.5 percent of parking.

LOS ANGELES LAKERS. Team owns arena. Great Western Forum, built in 1967. Capacity: 17,505. No suites. Club seats: 2,400 @ $9,200 per season.

MIAMI HEAT. Miami Arena, built in 1988. Capacity: 15,200. Luxury suites: 16 @ $70,000–$120,000. Lease expires in 1998.
   Rent: $600,000. Team receives between 47.5 percent and 100 percent of net concessions from basketball games. Team retains 100 percent of suite revenues minus $225,000, 100 percent of signage minus $275,000, and 50 percent of parking revenues. The Authority covers operations and maintenance costs. Team covers liability insurance.

MILWAUKEE BUCKS. Bradley Center Arena, built in 1988. Capacity: 18,633. Skyboxes: 68 @ $50,000–$70,000.

Rent: no rental payment. The team receives between 13.75 percent and 30 percent of gross concessions revenue, 100 percent of courtside signage, and approximately 50 percent of skybox revenues. Other than insurance for the Bradley Center, the Authority covers operations and maintenance expense.

MINNESOTA TIMBERWOLVES. Target Center Arena, built in 1990. Capacity: 19,006. Luxury suites: 68 @ $50,900–$100,000. Club seats: 702 @ $64, $84, or $175 per game. Lease expires 2024.

Rent: $2.9 million in 1995, rising at a maximum of 2 percent per year over the next thirty years. Team and Ogden Entertainment Services share all revenues from suites at games.

NEW JERSEY NETS. Continental Airlines Arena, built in 1981. Capacity: 20,039. Luxury suites: 29 @ $145,000–$200,000. Club seats: 66 @ $205 per game. Lease expires after 1999–2000 season.

Rent: 5 percent of gross ticket sales of sales between $5 and $6 million, 12.5 percent for sales between $6 and $7 million, 10 percent for sales between $7 and $8 million, 15 percent for sales between $8 and $11 million, 5 percent for sales between $11 and $15 million, and 15 percent for sales above $15 million. In addition, a 10 percent admission tax is levied on all tickets. Team receives 25 percent of net suite revenues, 50 percent of parking for first 4,000 vehicles and 25 percent thereafter, 50 percent on concessions.

NEW YORK KNICKS. Team owns arena. Madison Square Garden, built in 1968. Capacity: 19,763. Luxury suites: 89 @ $250,000–$300,000 a year. Club seats: 2,600 @ $110–$115 per game.

ORLANDO MAGIC. Orlando Arena, built in 1989. Capacity: 16,010. Luxury suites: 26 @ $80,000. Lease expires in 1998, with two five-year renewal options.

Rent: $9,000 per game and 25 percent of revenue from luxury suite rental. Team retains 100 percent of signage except in concourse areas, where city retains 100 percent. Team receives 50 percent of net concessions income from team events. Team receives no parking revenue. City is responsible for operations and maintenance costs.

PHILADELPHIA 76ERS. Team owners own facility. CoreStates Center, built in 1996. Capacity: 18,168. Luxury suites: 126 @ $75,000–$135,000. Club seats: 1,880 @ $6,000, $9,000, or $12,500 per season.

PHOENIX SUNS. America West Arena, built in 1992. Capacity: 19,023. Luxury suites: 88 @ $60,000–$70,000. Club seats: 2,270 @ $3,300 per season. Lease expires in 2032.

Rent: team pays zero rent. Team retains 90 percent of hard concessions revenue and 60 percent of gross suite revenue. Team receives no parking revenue and 60 percent of signage. Team pays for insurance and utilities. City covers other operations and all maintenance expense.

PORTLAND TRAIL BLAZERS. Team and arena owned by team owner. Rose Garden, built in 1995. Capacity: 21,538. Luxury suites: 70 @ $65,000–$135,000. Club seats: 2,505 @ $4,000–$13,000 per season.

SACRAMENTO KINGS. Arena owned by team. ARCO Arena, built in 1988. Capacity: 17,317. Luxury suites: 30 @ $110,000–$130,000. Club seats: 412 @ $2,500.

SAN ANTONIO SPURS. Alamodome, built in 1993. Capacity: 20,662. Luxury suites: 64 available for basketball @ $61,000–$100,000. Club seats: 6,000 available for basketball @ $22–$46 per game. Lease expires May 25, 1999.

Rent: $5,000 per game. Team retains 80 percent of suite and club seat revenue. Team receives 100 percent of signage from arena and concourse; for other signage team receives 40 percent. Team retains 100 percent of parking revenue on 3,200 spaces after paying a $50,000 yearly rental on these spaces for Spurs games. Team pays operations and city pays maintenance expenses.

SEATTLE SUPERSONICS. Key Arena, built in 1994. Capacity: 17,072. Luxury suites: 58 @ $50,00–$135,000. Club seats: 1,702 @ $4,100–$5,125 a year. Lease expires 2009.

Rent: $800,000, adjusted yearly by the consumer price index and 8.5 percent of ticket sales for pre- and post-season games. Team receives 100 percent of signage income after $750,000 payment to city over fifteen years of lease. Team receives 20 percent of suite revenue with share increasing to 40 percent by 2004. Team receives 40 percent of club seat revenue with share rising to 60 percent by 2004. Team invests in equipment for concessions and receives 100 percent of game-day net revenues and 60 percent of gross concessions revenues for other events, with share declining to 30 percent by 2004. City receives 100 percent of parking, and the first $750,000 of naming rights, and 50 percent thereafter. The city covers maintenance and most operations and game-day expenses.

TORONTO RAPTORS. Arena owned by consortium of thirty businesses. Air Canada Arena, built in 1996. Capacity: 25,356 skydome. Luxury suites: 55 @ C$150,000. Club seats: 1,400 @ C$2,960 per season and C$4,000 subscription fee.

UTAH JAZZ. Arena owned by team owner. Delta Center, built in 1991. Capacity: 19,911. Luxury suites: 56 @ $40,000–$90,000. Skyboxes: 18 @ $40,000–$90,000 a year. Club seats: 668 @ $90–$160 per game.

VANCOUVER GRIZZLIES. Arena owned by Orca Bay Sports and Entertainment. General Motors Place, built in 1995. Capacity: 19,193. Luxury suites: 88 @ $C65,000–130,000. Club seats: 2,200 @ C$89 per game.

WASHINGTON BULLETS. Arena owned by team owners. USAir Arena, built in 1973. Capacity: 18,756. Luxury suites: 40 @ $31,000–$75,000. MCI Center opening 1997/98 season. Luxury suites: 110 @ $100,000–175,000. Club seats: 3,000 @ $7,500 per season.

National Football League

ARIZONA CARDINALS. Stadium owned by Arizona State University. Sun Devil Stadium, built in 1958. Capacity: 73,273. Skyboxes: 67 @ $42,500–$46,500. Club seats: 4,928 @ $675–$1,800 per season. Lease expires in 1998 with four five-year renewal options.

Rent: greater of 10 percent of ticket receipts or $50,000 per game. Team receives 100 percent of suite revenues and revenues from advertising on message board and video display. Team receives 50 percent of net parking revenues and 50 percent of net concessions income. The university is responsible for all operations and maintenance expense.

ATLANTA FALCONS. Georgia Dome, built in 1992. Capacity: 71,228. Luxury suites: 203 @ $20,000–$120,000. Club seats: 5,600 @ $1,800 a year. Lease expires 2022.

Rent: 10 percent of net ticket proceeds, but Authority pays Falcons $4 million each year of lease. Team receives 70 percent of net stadium revenues up to $2,857,144 and 50 percent of revenues thereafter. Otherwise, Authority retains all concessions, parking suite, and signage income.

BALTIMORE RAVENS. Memorial Stadium, built in 1954. Capacity: 68,400. No luxury suites. Club seats: 1,850 @ $35,000–$75,000 for boxes of 15–31 seats.

Rent: All stadium revenues to team until new park at Camden Yards is built. Zero rent. Stadium Authority pays all operations and maintenance expenses. Team pays day-of-game expenses.

Camden Yards, projected completion for 1998 season. Capacity: 70,000. Luxury suites: 108. Club seats: 7,500. Lease is for thirty years.

Rent: zero rent. Team (actually the stadium operator corporation, owned by Art Modell) receives 100 percent of stadium revenues. The team pays no rent but is responsible for day-of-game expenses and maintenance.

BUFFALO BILLS. Rich Stadium, built in 1973. Capacity: 80,024. Luxury suites: 88 @ $25,000–$50,000. Club seats: 1,002 @ $1,669 per season. Lease expires in 1997.

Rent: 9 percent of gross ticket sales up to $5 million, 4 percent between $5 and $7.5 million, and 2 percent thereafter. Team receives 50 percent of net concessions and parking revenue, and 100 percent of signage and suite revenues. Team pays for stadium maintenance.

CAROLINA PANTHERS. Stadium owned by team owners. Ericsson Stadium, built in 1996. Capacity: 72,500. Luxury suites: 160 @ $40,000–$296,000 a year. Club seats: 10,998 @ $975–$2,975 per season plus $600–$5,400 PSL fee.

CHICAGO BEARS. Soldier Field, built in 1924. Capacity: 66,944. Luxury suites: 116 @ $65,000–$80,000. Lease expires January 31, 2000.

Rent: 12 percent of gross ticket receipts plus $1 surcharge per ticket. Team retains 80 percent of suite revenue, and no parking, concessions, or signage revenue. Team covers operations and city covers maintenance expenses.

CINCINNATI BENGALS. Cinergy Field, built in 1970. Capacity: 60,389. Luxury suites: 20 @ $47,220 plus $30,000 for tickets (or $77,200 total), for Bengals and Reds.

Rent: 10 percent of gross ticket receipts. Bengals retain 62.5 percent of suite rental fee and 10 percent of gross food and beverage concessions revenues at football games and 100 percent of football novelty sales. Team does not earn revenue from parking or signage. Team maintains the football field during season. Other maintenance is done by the city. This lease was renegotiated in 1993, when the city agreed to pay the Bengals a $2.75 million annual subsidy and to add luxury boxes as well as a club section to the facility. New lease terms negotiated in 1996 hold until new stadium is ready; see chapter 9.

DALLAS COWBOYS. Texas Stadium, built in 1971. Capacity: 65,675. Luxury suites: 379 @ $250,000–$1.5 million per term of lease. Lease expires 2009 with an option to renew for twenty-five years.

Rent: greater of $950,000 or sum of 8 percent of stadium revenue. Team controls all stadium operations and retains all revenues, except parking.

DENVER BRONCOS. Mile High Stadium, built in 1948. Capacity: 76,273. Luxury suites: 60 @ $38,000–$80,000. Lease expires in 2018.

Rent: 6.5 percent of gross gate receipts plus 8 percent of gross luxury suite revenues. City and county levy a 10 percent seat tax and retain all concessions, parking, and signage revenues. City covers operations and maintenance.

DETROIT LIONS. Pontiac Silverdome, built in 1975. Capacity: 80,368. Luxury suites: 102 @ $24,000–$27,500. Club seats: 7,384 @ $45 per game. Lease expires 2004.

Rent: $12,000 per month or 7 percent of gross ticket receipts, whichever is greater. City collects a $1.50 surcharge per ticket, and retains all signage, concessions (except football novelties), luxury suite, and parking income. The city pays most operations and all maintenance expense.

GREEN BAY PACKERS. Lambeau Field, built in 1957. Capacity: 60,789. Boxes: 198 @ $24,000–$30,000. Club seats: 1,920 @ $85 per game. Team has the option of a series of one-year leases through 2024.

Rent: $25,000 per game plus $15,000 of city services and $2 per ticket, and 10 percent of gross revenues for all non–football events. Team controls parking, concessions, and advertising and retains all income from these sources and luxury suites. Except utilities, city covers operations and maintenance expense.

HOUSTON OILERS. Astrodome, built in 1965. Capacity: 59,969. Luxury suites: 65 @ $37,500–$52,500. Lease expires in 1997. Team moving to Nashville.

Rent: approximately $3 million. Team retains suite revenue and 25 percent of parking for Oilers games.

INDIANAPOLIS COLTS. RCA Dome, built in 1983. Capacity: 60,272. Luxury suites: 96 @ $22,500–$45,000. Lease expires in 2014.

Rent: $250,000 per year plus $25,000 for playoff games. Team receives greater of $500,000 or 50 percent of luxury suite rental revenues. Team receives no parking, concessions, or signage income and is not responsible for maintenance, operation, or game-day expenses, except ticket takers and security. City collects a 5 percent tax on tickets.

JACKSONVILLE JAGUARS. Jacksonville Municipal Stadium, built in 1946 and renovated in 1995. Capacity: 73,000. Luxury suites: 75 @ $50,000–$80,000. Club seats: 11,000 @ $1,537. Lease expires in 2020.

Rent: $250,000 per year through 2000, $500,000 next five years, $1 million next ten years, and $1.25 million last ten years. There is also a $2.50 ticket surcharge. Team receives all suite, concessions, signage, and parking revenues but pays a $2 per car surcharge to the city. Any naming rights revenue will be split 50/50 between the city and the team.

KANSAS CITY CHIEFS. Arrowhead Stadium, built in 1972. Capacity: 79,239. Luxury suites: 80 @ $27,500–$82,250. Club seats: 10,199 @ $700 annual fee plus $41 per game. Lease expires 2015.

Rent: $450,000 a year, plus 5 percent on ticket sales for sales between $7.5 and $12.5 million, 4 percent on sales for sales between $12.5 and $17.5 million, and 2 percent for sales above $17.5 million. Team retains all signage and luxury suite revenues, and a percentage of parking revenues. The team is responsible for operations and normal maintenance. City covers all game-day, operations, and maintenance expenses, except liability insurance, which is provided by the team.

MIAMI DOLPHINS. Stadium owned by team owner. Pro Player Stadium, built in 1987. Capacity: 74,916. Luxury suites: 215 @ $55,000–$150,000. Club seats: 10,209 @ $600–$1,500 a year.

MINNESOTA VIKINGS. Hubert H. Humphrey Metrodome, built in 1982. Capacity: 64,035. Luxury suites: 113 @ $24,000–$61,000 for all events, or $24,000–$26,000 for Vikings games only. Lease expires 2009.

Rent: 10 percent of ticket receipts. Team receives 10 percent of gross concessions sales at football games plus 100 percent of football novelty sales. Team pays $1 million annual fee for right to retain luxury suite revenue up to 1997, then $1.3 million a year after 1997; Twins receive base ticket revenue only. Authority retains signage revenue, except in a few spaces designated for the Vikings. Vikings cover game-day expenses and associated utility charges. Authority covers other operations and maintenance costs.

NEW ENGLAND PATRIOTS. Stadium owned by team owner. Foxboro Stadium, built in 1971. Capacity: 60,292. Luxury suites: 42 @ $33,000–$125,000.

NEW ORLEANS SAINTS. Louisiana Superdome, built in 1975. Capacity: 70,852. Luxury suites: 137 @ $26,000–$57,000 a year. Club seats: 14,077 @ $50 per game. Lease expires 2018 with two five-year extension options.

Rent: greater of $25,000 per game or 5 percent of gross ticket receipts, with a yearly cap of $800,000. Team receives 100 percent of signage, suite, and parking revenues. Team also receives 42 percent of gross concessions receipts. The Authority pays all operations and maintenance expenses, and all game-day personnel expenses up to 650 employees.

NEW YORK GIANTS. Giants Stadium, built in 1976. Capacity: 78,024. Luxury suites: 72 @ $115,000. Lease expires in 2026.

Rent: 13 percent of gross ticket sales in 1996, 11 percent in 1997, and 10 percent in 1998 and after. Team receives 50 percent of net signage income (except for scoreboard), 50 percent of net concessions revenue, and 20 percent of gross parking receipts.

NEW YORK JETS. Giants Stadium, built in 1976. Capacity: 78,024. Luxury suites: 72 @ $115,000. Lease expires in 2008.

Rent: 15 percent of gross ticket sales. Team receives 50 percent of net signage income (except for scoreboard), 50 percent of net concessions revenue and 25 percent of net parking revenues. Authority covers all operations and maintenance expenses.

OAKLAND RAIDERS. Oakland Alameda Coliseum, built in 1966, renovated in 1996. Capacity: 62,500. Luxury suites: 143 @ $30,000–$150,000. Club seats: 9,000 @ $1,610 per season. Lease expires in 2010.

Rent: $500,000 plus $1 surcharge per ticket. Team retains 100 percent of suite rentals; 50 percent of club seat rentals for 10 years, and 100 percent thereafter; and 50 percent of revenues from parking, signage, concessions, and naming rights.

PHILADELPHIA EAGLES. Veterans Stadium, built in 1971. Capacity: 65,352. Luxury suites: 89 @ $78,000–$180,000. Lease expires 2012.

Rent: team retains 100 percent of suite revenue (percentage falls to 30 percent in 2001), 15 percent of gross concessions revenue, and no parking revenue. Team maintains skyboxes and pays utilities. City is responsible for other operations and all maintenance expenses.

PITTSBURGH STEELERS. Three Rivers Stadium, built in 1970. Capacity: 59,600. Loge boxes: 110 @ $18,000 per season plus tickets. Lease expires April 30, 2009.

Rent: minimum is $450,000, capped at $852,000. Team receives 10 percent of loge box revenue, 30 percent of net concessions revenue, and no parking and 33 percent of net concourse signage revenue. A 5 percent amusement tax is levied per ticket.

SAN DIEGO CHARGERS. Qualcomm Stadium, built in 1967. Capacity: 60,794. After renovation, luxury suites: 110 @ $34,000–$70,000. Club seats: 7,800. Lease expires in 2020.

Rent: 10 percent on first $6 million ticket sales and 8 percent thereafter. Team retains 71 percent of suite revenue, 33 percent of net parking revenue, 33 percent of gross concessions revenues up to $705,207 and 100 percent thereafter, and 25 percent of signage. City ticket surcharge of $.75.

SAN FRANCISCO 49ERS. 3-Com Park at Candlestick Point, built in 1960. Capacity: 70,140. Luxury suites: 94 @ $35,000–$88,000. Lease expires in 2008 with three five-year renewal options.

Rent: 10 percent of gross ticket sales, plus the greater of $7,500 per luxury box or 15 percent of gross suite revenues. Team retains 58 percent of gross parking revenues, 100 percent of concessions up to gross revenues of $4.5 million and 85 percent thereafter, 100 percent of scoreboard, and no signage revenue. The rent is reduced by 50 percent of payments to the city for concessions and parking from football games, as well as by the sum spent by the team on repairs and improvements to the facility. City is responsible for maintenance.

SEATTLE SEAHAWKS. Kingdome, built in 1976. Capacity: 66,400. Luxury suites: 48 @ $55,000–$80,000. Lease expires in 2005.

Rent: 7 percent of gross ticket sales, plus 7 percent of gross rental proceeds from fifteen press-level loges. Team receives 30 percent of gross concessions revenue and 100 percent of concessions rights payments, no parking or signage revenue, and a proportion varying from 10 percent to 50 percent of suite and loge income.

ST. LOUIS RAMS. TransWorld Dome, built in 1995. Capacity: 65,321. Luxury suites: 124 @ $55,000–$110,000. Club seats: 6,500 @ $700–$2,200. Lease expires in 2025.

Rent: $250,000 plus 50 percent of game-day expenses (estimated at $250,000). Team retains 75 percent of signage income up to $6 million and 90 percent thereafter, 100 percent of concessions, 100 percent of suite and club income, 75 percent of naming rights income, and $1.50 per parking space sold for the season. Authority covers the rest of game-day and operations expenses, as well as all maintenance.

TAMPA BAY BUCCANEERS. Houlihan's Stadium, built in 1967. Capacity: 74,301. Luxury suites: 59 @ $32,000–$90,000.

Rent: $63,000 per game. The team retains all revenue from ticket sales, signage, suite, concessions, naming rights, and parking. Team also receives 27.5 percent of concessions and parking revenue from non–football events. Houlihan's restaurant chain is 70 percent owned by Malcom Glazer, the owner of Bucs, and pays $10 million for naming rights, but this money reverts to Glazer. Authority pays operations and maintenance, as well as day-of-game expenses.

WASHINGTON REDSKINS. RFK Memorial Stadium, built in 1961. As of opening of Redskins Stadium 1997, capacity: 78,000. Luxury suites: 280 @ $59,950–$159,950. Club seats: 15,044 @ $995–$1,995 per season.

Rent: estimated at $2 million. Team receives 50 percent of concessions revenue.

National Hockey League

ANAHEIM MIGHTY DUCKS. Arrowhead Pond of Anaheim, built in 1993. Capacity: 17,174. Luxury suites: 84 @ $69,000–$99,0000. Club seats: 2,731 @ $4,000–$6,900 per season. Lease expires in 2023.

Rent: 7.5 percent of gross gate receipts. Team retains between 45 and 55 percent of all suite and club seat revenues, 50 percent of net parking receipts, 22.5 percent of gross concessions revenues plus 15 percent of food and beverage sales to club seats, and 5 percent of food and beverage sales to suites, 100 percent of hockey-related advertising, and 50 percent of non-hockey advertising, 50 percent of naming rights up to $1 million annually, and 100 percent above this. Facility manager, Ogden, on behalf of the city, is responsible for all operations and maintenance expenses.

BOSTON BRUINS. Arena and team owned by New Boston Garden Corp. FleetCenter, built in 1995. Fleet Bank paid $30 million for fifteen-year naming rights. Capacity: 17,565. Luxury suites: 104 @ $175,000–$258,000. Club seats: 2,350 @ $10,650–$12,250, includes all Bruins and Celtics games. Suite revenue divided among Bruins, Celtics, and loan debt.

BUFFALO SABRES. Marine Midland Arena, opened September 21, 1996. Capacity: 18,595. Luxury suites: 80 @ $55,000–$100,000. Club seats: 5,000 @ $2,537 per season. Team controls all arena revenue.

Rent: $1.75 million. Team gets 85 percent of concessions, 70 percent of net signage, and 100 percent of luxury suite revenues. City is responsible for maintenance.

CALGARY FLAMES. Canadian Airlines Saddledome, built in 1983. Capacity: 18,700. Luxury suites: 72 @ C$36,000–$85,000. Club seats, 1,400 @ C$3,100 per season. Lease expires in 2015.

Rent: 12 percent of first $5 million in ticket revenue; 11 percent of next $5 million; 10 percent of revenue above $10 million. Team receives 40 percent of luxury suite revenue, 70 percent of dasherboard advertising, and no revenue from parking. Team manages arena.

CHICAGO BLACKHAWKS. Arena jointly owned with owner of Chicago Bulls. United Center, built in 1994. Capacity: 20,500. Luxury suites: 216 @ $53,000–$175,000. Club suites: 3,300 @ $1,000 annual fee plus $50 per game.

COLORADO AVALANCHE. McNichols Sports Arena, built in 1975. Capacity: 16,061. Luxury suites: 27 @ $90,000. New arena planned.

Rent: Team pays 5 percent of gross ticket receipts or an amount based on per game attendance. Team receives 100 percent of net concession revenue received by city and 68 percent of parking receipts.

DALLAS STARS. Reunion Arena, built in 1980. Capacity: 16,924. No suites. Club seats: 5,154 @ $52.50–$82.50 per game. Lease expires in 2003 with three five-year options to renew.

Rent: For gate receipts up to $324,000 per game, the lesser of 7 percent of gate or $10,000; above $324,000, $10,000 plus 5 percent of receipts above this level. Team receives 50 percent of net advertising profits, 10.8 percent of gross concessions revenues of first $40,000 in sales, and 100 percent of net revenues above this level, 25 percent of parking revenues from season's passes and 30 percent of gross parking revenues after city receives $20,000 annually. The city is responsible for most operations and all maintenance expenses.

DETROIT RED WINGS. Joe Louis Sports Arena, built in 1979. Capacity: 19,275. Luxury suites: 83 @ $55,000–$175,000.

Rent: 10 percent of ticket receipts plus 10 percent of gross concessions revenues, 5 percent of merchandise sales, and approximately 7 percent of suite revenues. The team retains the balance of net arena revenues.

EDMONTON OILERS. Edmonton Coliseum, built in 1974. Capacity: 16,437. Luxury suites: 39 @ C$32,000–$125,000. Club seats: 3,000 @ C$55–$60 per game. Lease expires in 2004, with six five-year renewal options.

Rent: team receives 50 percent of luxury suite revenue and no parking revenue.

FLORIDA PANTHERS. Miami Arena, built in 1988. Capacity: 14,703. Luxury suites: 16 @ $70,000–$120,000, includes Miami Heat and Panthers games. Yearly lease.

Rent: $9,000 minimum per game or 7.5 percent of gross ticket sales above $200,000, plus a $.75 per ticket surcharge. Team receives 45 percent of all concessions revenues paid to the city, and 100 percent of net revenues from NHL or team-related merchandise sales. Suite revenue and advertising controlled by Heat.

HARTFORD WHALERS. Hartford Civic Center, built in 1975. Capacity: 15,635. Luxury suites: 45 @ $60,000–$72,000. Club seats: 300 @ $5,000 per season. Team bought out lease in 1997.

Rent: No rent paid. Team receives 85 percent of suite revenue above a guaranteed amount and 100 percent of hockey-related advertising but receives no concessions revenues. City is responsible for operations and maintenance expenses.

LOS ANGELES KINGS. The Great Western Forum, built in 1967. Capacity: 16,005. No suites. Club seats: 2,400 @ $9,200 per season. Lease expires 2018.

Rent: 12.5 percent of gross ticket receipts.

MONTREAL CANADIANS. Arena owned by team owner. Molson Centre, built in 1996. Capacity: 21,273. Luxury suites: 135 @ C$64,000–C$140,000. Club seats: 2,676 @ C$1,600 annual fee plus C$70 per game.

NEW JERSEY DEVILS. Continental Airlines Arena, built in 1981. Capacity: 19,040. Luxury suites: 29 @ $145,000–$200,000. Lease expires in 2007.

Rent: 10 percent of gross ticket sales up to $20 million, 9 percent from $20 million to $30 million, and 8 percent above $30 million. Team receives 40 percent of gross suite revenues and 88 percent of gross club seat revenues (club seats to be added). Team receives 34.2 percent of all concession revenue and 50 percent of gross revenue paid to the Authority from existing and new restaurants, 35 percent of parking for hockey games, and 30 percent of arena naming rights (twelve-year deal valued at $29 million). Team retains 100 percent from all on-ice advertising. Authority covers operations and maintenance.

NEW YORK ISLANDERS. Nassau Veterans Memorial Coliseum, built in 1972. Capacity: 16,297. Luxury suites: 33 @ $84,000–$260,000. Club seats: 292 @ $80–90 per game. Promenade seats: 139 @ $90 per game. Lease through 2015.

Rent: Islanders give a share of suite revenue to the Coliseum.

NEW YORK RANGERS. Arena owned by Madison Square Garden Ltd. Partnership. Madison Square Garden, built in 1968. Capacity: 18,200. Luxury suites: 89 @ $250,000–$300,000, includes tickets to all Rangers and Knicks games. Club seats: 3,775 @ $95, $110, and $125 per game.

OTTAWA SENATORS. Corel Centre, built in 1996. Capacity: 18,500. Luxury suites: 148 @ C$39,000–C$150,000. Club seats: 2,500 @ C$3,177.72–C$3,769.75 per season. Lease year to year.

Rent: C$3.9 million. Ogden bought concessionaire rights for thirty years for an initial investment toward arena construction of C$50 million.

PHILADELPHIA FLYERS. CoreStates Center, built in 1996. Capacity: 17,380. Luxury suites: 126 @ $75,000–$155,000 for all 76ers and Flyers games. Club seats: 1,880 @ $6,000–$12,500 per season.

Rent: 25 percent of luxury suite revenues will go each to the Flyers and 76ers; the remaining 50 percent will go to Spectator (facility manager), which will use the funds to pay off the construction debt.

PHOENIX COYOTES. AmericaWest Arena, built 1992. Capacity: 16,210. Luxury suites: 88 @ $60,000–$70,000. Club seats: 2,270 @ $3,300 per season.

PITTSBURGH PENGUINS . Civic Arena, built in 1961. Capacity: 17,180. Luxury suites: 55 @ $67,500–$135,000; and 88 club seats @ $3,600 per season. Lease expires in 2011.

Rent: $325,000. Team sells arena advertising. Teams pays insurance and utilities; Authority covers other operations and all maintenance costs.

SAN JOSE SHARKS. San Jose Arena, built in 1993. Capacity: 17,190. Luxury suites: 68 @ $62,000–$125,000. Club seats: 3,000 @ $63–$73 per game. Lease expires in 2008 with three five-year renewal options.

Rent: $500,000 a year, and beginning in 1997 team will pay city 20 percent of net luxury suite revenue. City receives first $250,000 of naming rights revenues annually, plus 50 percent of excess above $500,000. Team receives 100 percent of concession revenue, 100 percent of hockey-related advertising, and 50 percent of fixed signage. Team receives 100 percent of parking minus $100,000 payment to city.

ST. LOUIS BLUES. Kiel Center Arena, built in 1994. Capacity: 19,260. Luxury suites: 90 @ $37,500–$120,000. Club seats: 1,684 @ $3,990 per season.
    Rent: team receives 50 percent of arena's cash flow. There is overlap of several individuals who are in the syndicate owning the team and in the syndicate owning the private arena.

TAMPA BAY LIGHTNING. Ice Palace, built in 1996. Capacity: 19,500. Luxury suites: 72 @ $55,000–$100,000. Club seats: 3,300 @ $2,100–$2,500 per season. Lease expires 2026. Team retains all arena revenues.

TORONTO MAPLE LEAFS. Arena owned by team owners. Maple Leaf Garden, built in 1931. Capacity: 15,847. Luxury suites: 85 @ $32,500–$185,000.

VANCOUVER CANUCKS. Arena owned by Orca Bay Sports and Entertainment. General Motors Place, built in 1995. Capacity: 18,422. Luxury suites: 74 @ C$65,000–C$130,000. Club seats: 2,195 @ C$3,915 per season.

WASHINGTON CAPITALS. Arena owned by team owners. MCI Center, opening 1997–98 season. Luxury suites: 110 @ $100,000–$175,000. Club seats: 3,000 @ $7,500 per season.

SOURCES. Alan Friedman (Team Marketing Report) and Paul J. Much (Houlihan Lokey Howard and Zukin), *1997 Inside the Ownership of Professional Sports Teams: The Complete Directory of the Ownership and Financial Structure of Pro Sports* (Chicago: Team Marketing Report, 1997). The publisher does not guarantee that this work is absolutely accurate or without errors in some cases. Readers should therefore not rely on any of the information presented in this appendix where such reliance might cause loss or damage. The publisher disclaims all warranties, including the implied warranties of merchantability and fitness for a specific purpose.

Notes

1. Edward Epstein, "Key Questions on Stadium Deal: Here Are Some Answers, but 49ers Scramble for Specifics," *San Francisco Chronicle,* April 10, 1997, p. A1.
2. *San Jose Mercury News,* June 5, 1997, p. 1A.
3. The Dons of the All-American Football Conference, the Rams of the National Football League, the Chargers of the American Football League, the Sun of the World Football League, the Express of the U.S. Football League, and the Raiders of the National Football League all played in the Coliseum. For an excellent compendium of the history of sports franchises, see James Quirk and Rodney D. Fort, *Pay Dirt: The Business of Professional Team Sports,* 3d ed. (Princeton University Press, 1997).
4. Martin J. Greenberg, "Current Trends in Facility Leases," October 14, 1995, processed, p. 4.
5. Ibid., p. 3.
6. Kenneth Shropshire, *The Sports Franchise Game: Cities in Pursuit of Sports Franchises, Events, Stadiums, and Arenas* (University of Pennsylvania Press, 1995), p. 2.
7. *Inside the Ownership of Professional Team Sports* (Chicago: Team Marketing Report, 1997), p. 60; Epstein, "Key Questions on Stadium Deal," p. A1.
8. For data on the revenues of professional sports in the period 1950 to 1970, see Roger G. Noll, ed., *Government and the Sports Business* (Brookings, 1974), especially chap. 1. For data in more recent periods, see Quirk and Fort, *Pay Dirt;* the annual sports issue of the business magazine *Financial World;* and *Inside the Ownership.*
9. Dennis J. Opatrny and Eric Brazil, "49ers Kick Off Stadium Plans," *San Francisco Examiner,* February 2, 1997, p. A14.
10. Ibid.
11. Edward Epstein and John King, "Handshake in Ballpark Lease: Giants to Pay $1.2 Million Annual Rent," *San Francisco Chronicle,* December 17, 1996, p. A17; Renee Koury, "How Raiders Deal Went Sour," *San Jose Mercury News,* February 21, 1997, pp. 1A, 28A. The unsold Raiders PSLs are being reduced in duration by one year each year they are not sold, with a concomitant 10 percent price cut after the first year.
12. The following is taken from *Inside the Ownership,* pp. 29–36.
13. Ibid., p. 189.
14. The NFL system evolved from its internal revenue-sharing agreements and its collective bargaining agreement with the players. The former requires that all ticket revenues be shared (except the premium on luxury boxes), including PSL revenue, after an allowance for taxes and stadium costs. The latter places a cap on player salaries that is based on a concept called "defined gross revenues." Over the years, the types of revenues that are included in calculating the cap have been negotiated and have been subject to change; in the last collective bargaining agreement the revenues used to calculate the salary cap were linked to those shared among teams. The new agreement states that PSL revenues are included in defined gross revenues unless the PSL revenues are used to finance a stadium and the NFL exempts the PSL sales from its interteam revenue-sharing arrangements. Conflicting interpretations of these new arrangements have given rise to conflict and litigation within the NFL, including lawsuits over the relocation of the Rams and the Raiders.
15. The distortions and costs of federal tax treatments of sports facilities are discussed in greater detail in chapter 4.
16. The details about the Oakland Coliseum plan are taken from Renee Koury, "Raiders Seat Licenses Cut 10%," *San Jose Mercury News,* February 21, 1997, pp. 1B, 2B; and Koury, "How Raiders Deal Went Sour," pp. 1A, 28A.

2

THE ECONOMIC IMPACT OF SPORTS TEAMS AND FACILITIES

ROGER G. NOLL AND ANDREW ZIMBALIST

 A major league sports franchise places local government in an awkward position: the city must either provide subsidized playing facilities or lose its teams to other communities that are more willing to subsidize them. Proponents of such subsidies contend that a sports facility is a good investment, because it generates positive net economic benefits for the community. Opponents counter that publicly financed sports facilities absorb scarce government funds, which ought to be used for either tax reductions or programs having a higher social or economic payoff. To make an informed judgment about a stadium proposal, how can citizens and city officials determine the true economic impact of these facilities?

This chapter sets forth the conceptual foundation for a valid economic impact study of a new sports facility. In doing so it explains why independent economic analysis arrives at conclusions far different from those of studies sponsored by stadium proponents. A valid economic impact study also sheds light on how cities compete for teams; how this competition affects the magnitude of stadium subsidies; and how it distorts the location of teams, the design of stadiums, and the operation of sports leagues.

Public Investment Economics and Sports Facilities

All levels of government commonly undertake public investments. Ultimately, these investments are based on political considerations, for they are financed through budget allocations made by elected politicians, in response to electoral incentives created by constituents, contributors, and lobbyists. Nevertheless, policy debates about public investments typically focus on two issues: whether the project provides amenities and other direct consumption benefits that justify the expenditure, and whether the project will make a net positive contribution to economic development.

Stadiums as Public Consumption

A classic example of an investment that can provide valuable public consumption benefits is a park. According to federal officials, the primary benefits of the National Park System are recreation for visitors and conservation of places of outstanding historical importance or natural beauty. Likewise, local governments invest in parks primarily to provide amenities and recreational benefits for their constituents.

The parallel argument for sports facilities is that attracting and retaining a major league sports team is a valid end in itself because the team is valuable to local residents, above and beyond any contribution of the sports facility and the team to the local economy. Thus if a subsidy is needed to retain or to attract a team, the city should provide it. Although this is rarely the primary argument of stadium proponents, the notion that a sports team provides significant public consumption benefits is not frivolous.

The cultural importance of major league team sports in American society most assuredly exceeds its economic significance as a business. A sports team derives revenue from fans who attend games and who follow team broadcasts. These revenues are actually remarkably small. In 1996 a reasonable estimate of the average gross revenue from all sources for a major league sports team is about $75 million in football, $65 million in baseball, $55 million in basketball, and $30 million in hockey.[1] These revenues are trivial compared with the economic activity in even the smallest major league city, and substantially smaller than many businesses. In Jacksonville, Florida, for example, the gross revenues of its National Football League team account for about 0.4 percent of metropolitan area effective buying income (EBI), or total disposable income;

in St. Louis the figure is 0.2 percent of EBI; and in New York 0.02 percent.[2]

By measures such as revenue, a sports team is a considerably smaller business than many less visible enterprises. To take but one example, a major university is not only larger than any sports team, but many exceed the size of an entire league. Stanford University expects to generate revenues of approximately $1.5 billion in fiscal 1997.[3] In 1994 fifty universities each received more than $75 million in research grants from the federal government. The top ten universities together received approximately $2.8 billion in federal grants in 1994, which was more than the combined revenues of the NFL and the National Hockey League, or the combined revenues of Major League Baseball and the National Basketball Association.[4] Similarly, total undergraduate tuition payments at a good private university with six thousand or more undergraduates (including payments from funds that endow scholarship aid) exceeded the revenues of any professional sports team.[5]

The number of people who actually attend games is remarkably small. Over the course of an entire season, an average baseball team sells about two million tickets, and in other sports the total number of tickets sold is in the hundreds of thousands. In all cases, the majority of tickets are sold in blocks, for the season or for several games. Consequently, the number of individuals who attend at least one game per season is much smaller than the number of tickets sold and constitutes a small fraction of the total population of a metropolitan area. Far more people watch or listen to broadcasts of the games of local teams, although even the audience is only a small percentage of the households in a given metropolitan area.

Nevertheless, it would be inaccurate to conclude from these figures that major league team sports are unimportant. The reason is that one does not need to attend a game or tune in to a broadcast to derive consumer benefits from a local sports team. A major league game is a newsworthy event that is covered extensively by the press, and sports coverage takes up a large share of local newspapers and news broadcasts. The fact that local media devote so much attention to sports and place much greater emphasis on local teams than on teams from other areas implies that their customers are intensely interested in local teams. These sports fans consume coverage of local sports events, and the media report such events, without providing compensation to the team.

For these reasons, a major league sports event creates a classic "externality," a benefit accruing to people who are neither buyers nor sellers of the production of the game. The presence of this externality causes the direct demand for games that is experienced by sports teams to understate the total value of sports to local consumers. Hence some consumers who never attend a game or buy a product associated with the local team nevertheless may have a considerable willingness to pay to prevent the team from relocating to another community.

The practical significance of the preceding argument is, of course, extremely difficult to quantify. Whether the value of the external benefits of a major league team to consumers really does exceed stadium subsidies is uncertain, but by no means implausible. For example, for a stadium that receives a subsidy of $250 million in a metropolitan area with a population of five million, per capita capital costs are $50, and the per capita annualized cost of servicing the debt (interest plus amortization) to finance the stadium is about $5. It does not vastly stretch credulity to suppose that, say, a quarter of the population of a metropolitan area derives $20 per person in consumption benefits annually from following a local sports team. If so, the consumption benefits of acquiring and keeping a team exceed the costs, and one would expect a local government's decision to subsidize a stadium in order to achieve this objective to be politically popular.

Stadiums and Economic Growth

Despite the plausibility of the argument that subsidies for sports facilities generate more than compensating consumption benefits, proponents of subsidized stadiums are far more likely to emphasize the effect of a stadium on the local economy. All levels of government commonly make investments for the purpose of facilitating economic growth. Obvious examples are investments in streets and highways, airports, and public education. Indeed, in the mid–nineteenth century, the construction of the U.S. railroad system was facilitated by federal land grants and local subsidies of terminals.[6] Given that public investment can be economically beneficial, how should one evaluate the contribution of a public investment such as a stadium to economic growth?

The answer to that question comes from a well-developed subfield of economics, which is devoted to ascertaining whether public investments contribute enough to economic growth to offset their costs. The central objective of such analysis is to determine whether the stream of new economic activity that is created by an investment produces an adequate return. Thus the evaluation of a public investment is conceptually similar, although very different in detail, to the analysis that a private company undertakes to determine whether to build a new production facility.

The benefits and costs of a public investment fall into four general categories: direct benefits, indirect benefits, initial costs, and the costs of operation. Direct benefits can be described as the value consumers attach to the output from the public investment. In the case of a stadium, the net direct benefits include (a) any incremental consumer surplus from all of the consumption activities produced at the stadium for inhabitants of the city (games, broadcasts, and concession products such as food, beverages, parking, programs, clothing, and souvenirs) above the consumer surplus engendered by goods and services that were previously consumed (but substituted for by the stadium); (b) incremental consumer surplus from any additional expenditures on stadium-related activities over and above pre-stadium consumer expenditures (after netting out the welfare loss from the reduction in savings); and (c) any externalities accruing to residents because of the existence of the team. Indirect benefits include all of the additional consumption that takes place in response to the generation of any new income in the production of these consumer products. Indirect benefits arise only if the public investment and its use cause a net increase in income, rather than a reallocation of income among products and businesses.

If an investment does not generate a net increase in income, the public investment can be worthwhile only if the direct consumption benefits exceed the costs. Under normal circumstances, if all the benefits of an investment are direct consumption benefits, the private sector will have adequate incentives to make the investment because consumers will pay enough for the products of the investment to enable private investors to recover their costs.[7] Of course, for reasons given in the previous section, a local sports team is not "normal" if it produces significant externalities. Nevertheless, proponents of sports facilities contend that local teams generate economic growth as well as consumption benefits and so are like investments in infrastructure and education.[8] According to this argument, sports teams attract tourism and new business to a community. To evaluate this argument, it is necessary to ascertain the magnitude of the net increase in income that a stadium generates.

Costs, as already discussed, consist of the initial cost of the investment and the stream of costs associated with producing the stream of consumer benefits from the facility. Whereas the evaluation of consumer benefits comports conceptually with common sense, the proper evaluation of costs is much misunderstood and is a frequent source of error in evaluating public investments. The relevant cost concept in this case is not the actual financial costs to a local government, but what economists call the opportunity cost of the investment, which is defined as the sacrifice in other outputs that is necessary to undertake the investment. In other words, the economic cost of an investment is the sacrifice in other activities that was required to undertake the investment, which is not necessarily the amount spent on the project.

For two reasons, opportunity costs can depart substantially from financial costs. First, a public investment is costly to society only if the resources used to build and operate it are transferred from other valuable economic activities. If the relevant sectors of the economy are operating at full employment, the financial cost of acquiring these resources (the wages of labor, the prices paid for equipment, materials, and land) is usually a reasonably accurate indicator of the sacrifice in other products that is required for the public investment. But if the economy is not at full employment, or if some resources are devoted to activities in which these resources have low productivity, the opportunity cost of the public investment can be less than the amount actually paid for these resources. In times of recession, a government usually pays more for resources than their current earnings (which may be zero if they are unemployed), in which case the direct financial cost of the investment exceeds its opportunity cost.

Second, the financial costs of public investments ultimately are paid from taxation, either immediately or eventually to pay off public debt. In general, taxation imposes an additional opportunity cost because it reduces the consumption of taxed goods. The real economic cost to society of the tax system is not the taxes that are paid, for tax collections are simply transferred to those who build and operate the public investment. Whereas taxpayers naturally regard these taxes as a cost to themselves, from the perspective of society as a whole taxes are simply transferred from one pocket to another and so are not themselves a net social cost. Rather, the social cost of taxation is the reduction in net consumption benefits that is caused by imposing a tax. These costs consist of the costs of tax compliance (of collecting taxes and enforcing the tax code) plus the "dead-weight loss" of driving a wedge between the cost of products, as measured by their market price, and the total amount paid by consumers, which includes the tax.

Economics research indicates that the opportunity cost of taxes is significant. Although different methods produce different estimates, a common conclusion is that the social cost of taxation exceeds tax collections by about 25 percent.[9] The implication is that if an economy is operating at full employment, the opportunity cost of a subsidy can be substantially greater than its financial cost. Suppose that the economic cost of the tax system is 25 percent of tax collections. Then, with full employment the true cost of a $200 million subsidy for a sports facility would be $250 million.

Another common misconception about public investments is that the income they generate ought to be counted as part of their benefits. By way of example, the wages to be paid to construction workers are frequently assumed to be a benefit of a publicly financed sports facility. This perception is incorrect on several counts.

If project workers would otherwise be employed at the same wage if the project were not undertaken, there is no net income arising from the public investment. Instead, the public investment is crowding out other activities of equal cost, and the workers are affected only insofar as the source of their income has changed. The key point is that under conditions of full employment, expenditures on the project, including the wages of construction workers, are a cost, not a benefit, because these expenditures approximately measure the sacrifice in the production and consumption of other goods that must be made in order to build the facility.

If the workers would otherwise be unemployed, the financial costs of hiring them to build the stadium are ignored in the economic impact analysis, so that nothing is subtracted from the consumption benefits of the stadium to cover the wages of the workers. Of course, citizens pay taxes, which are then paid to the workers, but it would constitute double-counting to ignore the tax payments as part of costs (because the opportunity cost of the workers is zero) and then to add in the wages of the workers as a benefit.

Moreover, the societal benefits of employing unemployed workers can be obtained without undertaking the public investment. The local government instead could simply give the money to the workers as unemployment insurance, or employ half the workers to dig a hole and the other half to fill it up, thereby generating the same amount of income and number of jobs. Thus the benefits of a stadium investment compared with unemployment insurance or make-work public employment arise from its contribution to consumption, not the transfer of income to the construction workers.

Because of the significance of opportunity costs, a public investment should be evaluated in terms of the best alternative way to use the same resources. The presence of unemployment may be a legitimate rationale for a public investment program, but it is not a rationale for building a stadium, rather than making some other public investment. In order for the stadium to be the best choice, it must generate net benefits that exceed the alternative uses. That is, the stadium not only must be more attractive than unemployment insurance and digging and filling holes, but more attractive than an equal investment in schools, streets, parks, and subsidies for other private businesses. The opportunity forgone in building a stadium is not the cost of the stadium, but the benefits from the other ways this money could be spent (including tax reductions).

The preceding discussion leads to an extremely important general conclusion about the evaluation of public investments for society as a whole: a public investment can be worthwhile in only three circumstances. First, society may have unemployed resources that can be used most productively by subsidizing investment. Second, if society is fully employed, it may be spending too little on investment in relation to current consumption (that is, more investment, although sacrificing some current consumption, would cause a more than compensating increase in consumption in the future). Systematic underinvestment is likely only if an investment produces significant externalities (such as the externalities that arguably arise from the presence of a local sports team) or if capital markets do a poor job of financing some forms of viable private investments.[10] Third, the productivity of the subsidized investment, as measured by the value of the consumption that it creates, exceeds the productivity of all other feasible investments. In all cases, in order for a public investment to contribute to economic welfare, it must increase future consumption. And, in the first two cases, this objective is accomplished because the public investment causes a net increase in total investment.

If a public subsidy does cause a net increase in investment or investment productivity, its benefits are not limited to the direct consumption benefits of the investment. Additional benefits will be derived from increased consumption that arises from the additional income created by producing the net addition to direct consumption. In short, the public investment has a "multiplier effect" because producing the direct benefits causes an increase in real income, which in turn is spent on further consumption. Hence a proper evaluation of a public investment differs significantly from the purely profit-oriented evaluation of a normal private investment. The latter requires only that direct consumer benefits exceed costs so that the firm can charge prices in excess of average costs and thereby earn a profit. By contrast, in evaluating a public investment one must take into account the additional net benefits that accrue in other industries due to the multiplier effect.

Local versus Societal Effects

Thus far the main concern of this discussion has been the global effects of an investment: whether it causes a net increase in total economic activity. The underlying assumption here is that the political unit responsible for the investment will take into account all of its economic consequences. But public expenditures may have worldwide consequences, as illustrated by the decision of France, Germany, Spain, and the United Kingdom to subsidize investments in Airbus to facilitate its effective competition with U.S. aircraft manufacturers. These countries are unlikely to take into account either the benefits or the costs that arise from the Airbus program in other nations (and in particular, any loss in aircraft production efficiency that arises from transferring aircraft sales from Boeing to Airbus).

A fundamental tension exists between global economic analysis of the type described above and the principle of democratic responsiveness. An investment can have two kinds of global net benefits: internal net benefits (which accrue to people who live within the political jurisdiction undertaking the investment) and external net benefits (which accrue to people outside the same jurisdiction). If the primary concern of voters is the effects of an investment on their own welfare, and if external effects are significant, public officials will be unresponsive to the demands of their constituents should they base decisions on global effects, yet will pursue inefficient investment policies when they consider only internal net benefits. Put another way, to pass a global benefit-cost test (which includes both internal and external effects), an investment must generate a net increase in total worldwide wealth and consumer welfare, whereas to pass a local (purely internal) benefit-cost test, an investment need only reallocate wealth and consumer benefits in favor of the political jurisdiction that is undertaking the investment.

Investments in sports facilities can have international implications and so create this dilemma, as they do when Canadian and American cities compete for the same sports franchise. From the perspective, say, of all signatories to the North American Free Trade Agreement (NAFTA), no aggregate economic welfare may be at stake in deciding whether a sports team locates in Canada or the United States; however, in neither nation is the decision to invest in a sports facility likely to incorporate the lost benefits to the other nation from losing (or not attracting) a team. Consequently, in each country the economic benefits of building a facility to attract a team are likely to include the gross consumer benefits, not the net benefits in comparison with other locations.

In practice, of course, the international implications of subsidies to sports facilities are not likely to be very important, so that a purely national analysis of stadium investments is not likely to misstate appreciably its global economic consequences. Nevertheless, the example is instructive, because subsidies for sports facilities usually are provided by state and local governments, in competition with other state and local governments within the same nation.

The major difference between international competition and competition among localities in the same country is that in the latter case productive resources are highly mobile, more so than in even reasonably fully integrated free-trade areas such as NAFTA and the European Union. More than is the case internationally, competition among localities within the same nation induces businesses and workers to relocate from other communities. By contrast, international competition primarily affects the market share that a domestic firm can capture from foreign competitors.

To be deemed worthwhile, a local public investment, such as a sports stadium, must create a net economic benefit to the locality that pays for the facility. To generate a net increase in local economic activity under conditions of full employment, the investment must attract sales from outside the local area. This net increase in local economic activity can be, but need not be, a global net increase. In particular, if a local public investment simply causes a reallocation of economic activity among localities, a city that gains from the reallocation can perceive its investment to be worthwhile even if its gain is exactly offset by reduced economic activity elsewhere.

In the case of professional sports, luring an existing team from another locality usually is more attractive than participating in the net economic growth of major league sports by obtaining an expansion franchise. Established teams are usually better than expansion franchises and, in any case, have a history and traditions that add to their value in the eyes of sports fans. Moreover, the monopoly structure of all major league professional sports enables leagues to create scarcity in teams in order to maximize the value of established franchises. Scarcity in teams is achieved by pursuing a strategy of very slow expansion that leaves many viable franchise locations without a team. These cities then compete for established franchises by offering subsidized playing facilities.

The Dependence of Estimated Net Benefits on Arbitrary Line Drawing

An important consequence of the propensity of governments to consider only internal benefits and costs is that the magnitude of net benefits depends precisely on how the lines are drawn to differentiate internal and external effects. At one extreme, consider the effects of a sports facility on the neighborhood in which it is constructed. Most likely, residents of the neighborhood account for a very small fraction of the taxes used to pay for the facility; hence the loss of consumption benefits through taxation probably will be very small. Likewise, almost no event inside the stadium will matter economically to the neighborhood. Nearby residents are likely to account for a tiny fraction of attendance inside the stadium, so that the staging of contests will generate virtually no direct benefits to the neighborhood.

Indirect neighborhood benefits, arising from the additional consumption generated by employment within the stadium, are also likely to be unimportant. Nearly all of the income generated by a sports team goes to players, managers, executives, and owners. Only if they choose to move near the new stadium will the neighborhood experience an indirect benefit, arising from their neighborhood consumption expenditures. Because this circumstance is highly unlikely, nearly all of the income earned by the team is irrelevant as far as the neighborhood is concerned. A more plausible neighborhood benefit is that some local residents will find part-time jobs at the stadium, such as taking tickets, parking cars, or selling concessions. Of course, these jobs would arise regardless of where the stadium is located, but the extent to which neighborhood residents hold these jobs plausibly depends on where the stadium is located. The neighborhood benefits to the extent that these jobs increase the income of neighborhood residents.

Some neighborhood businesses may receive indirect benefits in the form of an increase in sales during both the construction and operation of a sports facility. First construction workers, and then fans attending games, are likely to live outside the neighborhood and to increase their patronage of restaurants, bars, parking lots, and gas stations near the stadium. The neighborhood effect from fans, of course, is greatly diminished by the modern tendency to enclose all these commercial activities within the ballpark or arena. Whereas under conditions of full employment these effects are likely to be reallocations of business from other localities, the additional income of nearby businesses, net of their production costs, will cause an increase in wealth and consumption by neighborhood residents. Indeed, the increase in neighborhood net income is a rough approximation of the increased value of consumption.

To the extent that the stadium does cause some increase in neighborhood income and consumption, the additional indirect benefits that are generated by the multiplier effect are likely to be quite small. In general, as the size of the area that is regarded as internal grows smaller, so, too, does the proportion of a resident's income that is spent within the area. The area near the stadium is likely to have a less diverse array of retail stores than an entire city or metropolitan area, so that neighborhood residents are likely to spend a considerable fraction of their income outside the neighborhood. As a result, the multiplier that is appropriate for measuring the total amount of economic activity that the stadium creates in its neighborhood is likely to be small in comparison with the multiplier for a larger area, such as an entire city. Finally, the new facility might cause increased local congestion and pollution, and even a change in the local crime rate. In calculating the neighborhood's net benefits, these spillover effects must also be taken into account. In some cases, neighborhood residents believe that these undesirable spillover effects are so large that they vociferously oppose a stadium proposal. For example, residents of South Boston created "Sack the Stadium," an organization that intensely opposed a plan to build a stadium for the New England Patriots in their community.[11]

By contrast, consider the internal net benefits from the perspective of the entire metropolitan area. Now the direct consumption benefits from the major league sports team and the costs of constructing the stadium, including the cost of taxation, are far more important, for most of these benefits and costs will accrue to residents of the metropolitan area. At the same time, the choice of lunch spots, watering holes, and gas stations by construction workers and fans who live in the metropolitan area, and the identity of the employees who work in the stadium, are a substitution of economic activity in one neighborhood for business in another and so make no net contribution to metropolitan economic activity. Likewise, the negative spillovers in the neighborhood of the stadium will not affect most citizens in a metropolitan area.

Recall that under conditions of full employment, local economic growth and the multiplier effects are not achieved unless the public investment increases "exports" to other areas, which then generate additional income and consumption benefits locally. Likewise, as increases in local income are spent and generate more consumption, the subsequent rounds of the multiplier effect will be higher for the metropolitan area because more of the increased consumption will occur somewhere in the metropolitan area than in any given neighborhood.

These examples illustrate some general principles about the relationship between the size of the political unit that is contemplating a public investment and the investment's "internal" effects. Most obviously, the fraction of global benefits and costs that are regarded as internal increases as the size of the relevant political jurisdiction increases. Following from this observation, the global effects of a sports facility are likely to be almost completely internalized at the national level.

At the level of a metropolitan area, the primary distortion in an internal benefit-cost analysis will be that the transfer of direct consumption benefits and indirect economic growth effects from other metropolitan areas will be counted as a net benefit. From a national standpoint, this transfer is generally a matter of indifference. At the level of a political jurisdiction within a metropolitan area, a reallocation of entertainment expenditures by metropolitan area residents from other local jurisdictions will be counted as an internal effect, even though at the level of the metropolitan area this reallocation is generally a matter of indifference. Consequently, as one moves to ever smaller jurisdictions, defined in terms of the fraction of the metropolitan area that they include, the difference between a politically relevant and a comprehensive benefit-cost analysis grows larger, and jurisdictions are increasingly likely to base their decisions on the effects of the investment on the allocation of activity in contrast to its global net benefits.

Identifying a Team's Net Exports

An important distinction between metropolitan and submetropolitan effects lies in the nature of the "exports" that generate local economic growth. The external sources of income are in-stadium revenues accounted for by fans who reside outside the relevant political jurisdiction, plus other team revenues, such as those connected with broadcasting or licensing, that are paid by businesses outside the jurisdiction. If a team locates within a metropolitan area, gross regional exports increase to the extent that the team attracts tourists and sells broadcasting and licensing rights to national firms.

From the team's gross exports must be subtracted the team's "imports." For example, if out-of-town fans buy concessions, but these goods are produced elsewhere, the external payments must be subtracted from concession sales to determine net concession exports. Likewise, to the extent that players, managers, executives, and owners live outside the metropolitan area, the net export value of the team consists only of the portion of income that is spent locally, and not the part that is transferred to the residence location of these personnel.

The details about the true net exports of a team are important because they determine the first-order amount of economic growth created by a team, which is then used in a multiplier formula to calculate the net benefits of a team to local residents. Typically, economic impact studies of stadiums are susceptible to two errors related to net exports that cause the benefits of the facility to be overestimated: the first is to overstate the extent to which a stadium attracts tourists; the second is to overstate the extent to which the income generated by the team is retained in the local community.

To estimate the exports attributable to a team, local economic impact studies frequently conduct surveys of those in attendance at games to ascertain where fans live and then count as tourists attracted by the team all fans who reside outside the area. Additional survey instruments are used to ascertain how much the average tourist spends on hotels, restaurants, shopping, and other consumer activities. The sports facility is then credited with creating new tourism expenditures equal to the number of nonresident fans times average tourist spending. These expenditures are then multiplied by a number derived from studying the effects of new industrial facilities to ascertain the overall increase in local economic activity that is accounted for by the imports. Typical values of this multiplier range from 1.5 to 2.0. Thus the estimated net exports said to be caused by a sports team are the product of three numbers: the number of nonresidents attending the game, the average amount spent by tourists who visit the city, and the regional multiplier. Of course, the expenditures of a fan on tickets and concessions may be a tiny fraction of this total, if the total includes several days of expenditures on hotels, restaurants, other tourist attractions, and other consumer goods, all then multiplied by some number nearer 2 than 1.

Trouble with Tourism and Multipliers

The procedure just described overstates the net exports arising from a professional team in that it credits the sports facility with drawing to the community all nonresidents in attendance at a game. Obviously, if tourists who attend sporting events visited the city for another purpose, or have their visits paid by local residents, these calculations are in error. The following examples illustrate the point.

—Executives from a nonresident client corporation of a law firm visit the city to discuss pending litigation against their company. The law firm owns a luxury box at the local baseball stadium, and during the visit some of the firm's lawyers take the visiting executives to a baseball game.

—A professor of Japanese art at a local university receives a grant from the National Endowment for the Humanities to hold a conference about some recently discovered nineteenth-century wood prints and invites several colleagues from Japanese universities. While in town, the Dodgers are playing the local baseball team, and Hideo Nomo is scheduled to pitch, so the Japanese visitors attend the game.

—As a result of a divorce, one parent is separated geographically from two children but makes a point each weekend to visit the children, and occasionally takes them to the ball game.

—A family decides to spend a vacation at Disneyland. One evening during the visit, the family attends a baseball game at Anaheim Stadium, only a few blocks away.

In all of these cases, the standard practice for evaluating the economic effect of a sports team would attribute all the visitors' expenditures to the baseball team, not just the expenditures at the ball park. In other words, the baseball team would be given the credit for the law firm getting its nonresident client, for the professor getting a federal grant to pay for the Japanese visitors, for the parent deciding to exercise visitation rights for the children, and for all Disneyland visitors who also attend either a Dodgers or an Angels game.

How important are these errors? We do not know, but they are likely to be substantial. The survey instruments used in these calculations do not attempt to ascertain causality in any form, including who actually paid for the ticket or why the nonresident is visiting the city. Teams do sell tickets, even season tickets, to nonresidents, but rarely are data about ticket sales made public.

Despite the lack of systematic information with which to evaluate the magnitude of these errors, several observations can be made that shed some qualitative light on them. First, the importance of sports teams in attracting tourism is almost certainly declining as the number of teams grows. Until the 1950s, major league professional sports were confined almost entirely to a few cities in the northeast quadrant of the nation. The only exceptions were the NFL teams in California. Consequently, the vast majority of Americans could attend a game only by traveling a great distance to one of these cities. Subsequently, expansion and relocation brought multiple teams in each sport to every region of the country. The result is not only that a much higher fraction of the population now has a local team, but that tourists have less reason to plan vacation trips around the opportunity to attend a major league game. A visit to any large city brings a tourist to the home of a major league sports franchise.

In addition, with the growth in demand for sports, a much larger fraction of attendance is now accounted for by season ticket sales. Most teams in football and basketball, many teams in hockey, and even some teams in baseball sell all of their good seats on a season-ticket basis. Hence planning a vacation on the expectation of seeing a game at Fenway Park, Giants Stadium, Madison Square Garden, or even lesser-known venues such as the Duck Pond[12] and the Shark Tank[13] would be difficult at best because a family would have a strong chance of being unable either to buy good tickets or to purchase any tickets at all.

Most likely, these factors are increasing the proportion of inadvertent attendance by nonresidents that has nothing to do with their visit and is actually arranged by local residents. Hence, as the number of teams grows and more teams sell all or most good seats as season tickets, the magnitude of the error in the traditional economic impact analysis of a sports facility will probably grow as well.

Just as gross exports are overstated, so, too, is there a tendency to overstate the extent to which the income generated by a team remains in the local economy. In reality, the main source of external revenue for a sports team is not attendance by nonresidents, but broadcasting and licensing income. National broadcast revenue is important in all sports, but in football it amounts to more than half of all revenue, and in baseball it is more than $10 million per team. Local broadcasting, which is significant in all sports other than football, is usually sponsored by national firms: breweries, oil companies, automobile manufacturers, manufacturers of shaving materials, and so on. Likewise, product licensing agreements, whether sold primarily by the league (as is the case in the NFL) or by individual teams (which is more common in other sports), are usually with national manufacturers of consumer products such as clothing, athletic equipment, soft drinks, and beer. Hence, with some exceptions, these revenues are gross exports for a local sports team. (Net exports would subtract the magnitude of licensing fees that are derived from local sales and the increase in non–locally produced goods as a result of national advertising.) If these revenues were retained in the local community, they would be a substantial source of new income to which the multiplier effect might apply. But to calculate net exports (and hence the net income subject to a multiplier effect), one must subtract from the gross income of the team all income that accrues outside the local community.

In all professional sports, more than half of the gross revenue of a team goes to athletes. A significant portion of the rest goes to owners, executives, on-field managers and coaches, and scouts. To the extent that these personnel do not reside locally, almost all of their income is immediately transferred out of the area in which it is earned. The amounts transferred make no contribution to local economic growth. In addition, teams spend additional funds outside the area: for equipment, travel, and minor league players, coaches, and managers, among other things.[14] In baseball, and to a lesser extent football, additional expenditures are incurred in pre-season training at facilities outside the local metropolitan area.

The magnitude of these external transfers and expenditures is substantial and varies enormously among sports and teams. The career of an athlete, a manager, or a coach is short, and even those with long careers are likely to change teams several times during their tenure. Consequently, athletes and managers are notoriously unlikely to have much attachment to the cities in which they work; rather, they tend to select a permanent residence on the basis of the attractions of the city. In particular, many are drawn to locations where they were raised or where they attended college. In some cases, these considerations cause athletes and managers to reside in the area where they play, but in many cases they do not. In any event, to the extent that a team's roster includes players, coaches, and a manager who live elsewhere, their salaries should be excluded from calculating the local economic impact of their team. Likewise, the earnings of an absentee owner or executive also should be subtracted.

Yet another concern is whether standard multiplier analysis is a valid way of dealing with the local income of a sports team. The premise of multiplier analysis is that a certain portion of the income generated by an investment is spent on consumption, and that some significant fraction thereof is spent locally and itself is devoted primarily to consumption. The extent to which this income is spent on consumption depends, first, on how much is paid in taxes, and, second, on the decision by the income recipient in allocating disposable (after-tax) income between consumption and savings. In both cases, even after taking into account the income that is earned by nonresident employees of a team, standard regional multipliers are likely to overstate the extent to which the income of a sports team contributes to local economic growth through a multiplier effect.[15]

One source of this overestimate is the unusually high incomes of the people who earn almost all of the income generated by a sports team. Multiplier analysis is based on observing the consequences of investments that employ ordinary people earning ordinary incomes. Athletes, coaches, managers, executives, and owners account for nearly all of the income generated by a sports team, and the incomes they enjoy are far larger than the average wage. Team personnel therefore pay a higher share of their income in income-related taxes, and so have proportionately less disposable income. Also, whereas most Americans save a tiny fraction of disposable income, high-income individuals have higher savings rates. Moreover, because athletes have very short careers in comparison with other high-income occupations, they have an even stronger motive to save, in order to smooth annual consumption over their lives.

For these reasons, a lower proportion of the income of athletes and other high-salaried team employees is spent on consumption than would be the case for the income generated by other businesses. Consequently, the income generated by a sports team should have a much smaller multiplier effect than the income generated by other new businesses.

The magnitude of the overstatement of net exports and the regional multiplier effect is not known. To calculate these effects would require detailed expenditure studies of athletes and other employees of sports teams, and such studies have never been undertaken. Moreover, these studies would have to be done separately for each team, because teams differ in the residences and expenditure patterns of their athletes. What is known is that the typical economic impact study of a team and stadium does not assess the validity of the standard assumptions, in spite of the powerful reasons to believe that these standard assumptions introduce significant errors that systematically overstate the economic benefits of a sports facility.

Another economic benefit of sports teams, proponents claim, is that industry is more likely to locate in cities with major league sports franchises. This tendency is said to have been one reason that Jacksonville vigorously pursued an NFL expansion team. According to this argument, corporate executives prefer cities with major league sports teams, and so in a close decision about where to locate a new business facility they will favor these cities. In fact, several business leaders have openly stated that they consider the status of major league sports when making such decisions.

There is no systematic evidence that this assertion is true, and some even indicates otherwise. Chapter 14, for example, shows that sports teams have no long-run employment effect, and other research on corporate location decisions finds that, statistically, costs (including taxes net of subsidies), the quality of the local labor force, and city amenities (such as the quality of education and health care) are the factors that affect corporate location decisions. In any event, the relevant question is not whether a sports team makes a city more attractive for corporate executives, but whether the most effective way to spend $200 million to $300 million with a view to attracting new business is to build a stadium to attract a team. By contrast, the same amount could be spent on industrial parks, local tax exemptions for new business facilities, computers for local schools, or an endowment for a high-quality electrical engineering and computer science program at a local university. Furthermore, to the extent that the facility has a lease that is unfavorable to the city, the stadium may experience net operating losses, which would have an adverse effect on the city's fiscal situation. This, in turn, would put pressure on both services and taxes and tend to discourage corporate relocations.

Summary of Economic Impact Analysis

A valid economic impact analysis consists of a comprehensive statement of the net benefits to a relevant population arising from a public expenditure. Economic impact analysis constitutes a test of whether the benefits exceed the costs and can be summarized as a simple algebraic expression:

Net benefits = (consumption value of a team to fans)

− (annual cost of stadium + team operating cost)

− (environmental, congestion, and public safety costs)

+ (increase in local income x multiplier).[16]

The consumption value of a stadium has three components: attendance, broadcasting, and the externality value of simply having a local team. Stadium costs are net of rent, if any, and any increase in local tax revenues that is due to the stadium but they include local government costs of stadium operations, even public services such as police. The consumption benefits include the value of broadcasts of local teams (rather than distant ones) to consumers, and team operating cost includes all costs associated with broadcasting as well as playing games. And, just as the positive externality of having a team must be included in the equation, so, too, must the negative externalities associated with travel to games, such as additional air pollution, traffic congestion, and security problems.

Local income can increase in two ways: through increased sales to people outside the community (net exports), and through higher-productivity jobs for local residents. Both effects can arise from either the use to which the investment is put (the direct effects) or the spillover effect on other local businesses (the indirect effect). The indirect effect includes incidental expenditures by fans and nonresident team employees in the local community. The direct and indirect increases in local income include only additional income earned by residents of the political unit that is paying the subsidy and so exclude any income retained by owners and employees who do not live in the community.

The multiplier, m, is calculated as:

$$m = 1/(1 - s),$$

where $s = c * f$; c = fraction of the increment to pre-tax income that is spent on consumption; and f = fraction of local consumption expenditures that generate an increase in local net income. Typically, taxes and savings account for more than 30 percent of income, and among the highly paid employees who earn most of the income that is generated by a sports team, this fraction is likely to be even higher. Even if consumption occurs locally, the businesses that experience added sales will also have additional costs of goods sold that are paid to residents outside the local community (such as the food sold at restaurants and grocery stores, the clothing sold at department stores, and the rights fees for the films shown at the local movie theater). For ordinary public investments in a relatively large metropolitan statistical area (MSA), a reasonable value for c is ⅔ and for f is ½, so $s = $ ⅓ and $m = 1.5$. Most likely, for sports facilities, the multiplier is lower for several reasons. First, most of the income of sports teams goes to high-income individuals, who allocate more income to taxes and savings than the typical wage earner. Second, athletes are likely to live outside the city in which they play, and even those who live in the city are more likely, along with the team's executives, to spend larger shares of their income outside the area than is true for employees of typical businesses. Third, prices for food items at a ballpark or arena are considerably higher than at average retail establishments, and a large part of this price differential is siphoned off by the concessionaire, which more often than not is based in another city. Thus a sports multiplier might be conservatively estimated with the following parameter values: c is 0.5 (assuming state and federal taxes equal to one-third of income and savings equal to 25 percent of disposable income), f is 0.3 (assuming one-fourth of consumption expenditures are outside the area), so $s = 0.15$ and the multiplier for sports teams is 1.2. Finally, it is important to stress that the proper multiplier is applied not to gross spending, but to that portion of spending that constitutes a net increase in the income of local residents (or local value added).

The Economics of Competition for Teams

The next important question to consider is whether interjurisdictional competition for teams distorts decisions about subsidies, the design of stadiums, and the location and operation of teams. To address this question, we take as given two conditions that are discussed in chapter 1. First, as a political matter, local governments channel subsidies primarily through stadiums rather than direct cash payments. Second, the number of teams is smaller than the number of financially viable franchise locations, so that cities compete for either existing teams or a very limited number of expansion teams. The latter assumption enables us to simplify the analysis by contemplating the outcome of a process in which many cities compete for a single team. The outcome of this simplified process does not differ substantially from what happens when there are many cities bidding for a much smaller number of teams, as in the recent spectacles of ten or more cities bidding for two expansion franchises in each sport.

We also assume that teams seek to maximize long-run profits, including the resale value of the team. This assumption is compatible with the view that teams will evaluate competing bids by giving an advantage to their existing home, but it does assume that if a team is offered a substantially better deal to relocate, it will do so. Somewhat surprisingly, this assumption does not produce dramatically different results from the theory publicly espoused by some sports executives, namely, that owners seek to maximize the quality of their team, rather than profits.[17] These two views produce similar results because team quality is improved by increasing expenditures on players, training, and coaching, and a team with higher revenues is able to spend more on team quality. The results differ primarily in the way teams dispose of their profits.

The practical consequence of the assumption that teams maximize profits is that this assumption makes the bidding among cities consequential: these bids determine the distribution of teams among cities. Of course, frequent moves and threats to move by teams in all sports provide evidence that this assumption is not wildly incorrect. Thus in the following analysis teams are relatively passive players, calculating the long-run effect of location (including subsidies but also including all other sources of revenues) on the value of the team to the owner, and locating where this value is maximized.

An important point to bear in mind is that the issue at hand is the subsidy to the team, not the total amount spent by a city on a stadium. To the extent that the stadium generates additional tax revenues for the city, the stadium is not subsidized but is a form of business investment by the city. Typically, stadiums will have a direct effect on local tax revenues through sales taxes on tickets and concessions, and another effect through increases in indirect income and the multiplier process in increments to taxes on retail sales and perhaps property (if the stadium increases property values). Thus the analysis in this section refers to the excess of stadium expenditures over the amount that would be justified as an investment by its effects on future tax revenues.

In the case of stadiums that cost a state or local government hundreds of millions of dollars, it is obvious that most of the cost of the facility is a subsidy. For twenty-five stadiums constructed between 1978 and 1992, the average subsidy was nearly $7 million a year.[18] Because stadiums have since become so much more expensive than the average during this period, the annualized subsidy of recent facilities is most likely even greater. Counting all forms of taxes to all levels of government, the direct gross tax revenues from a team are likely to be in the range of 10 to 15 percent of gross revenues, consisting of rent (if any), sales taxes on tickets, concessions, parking, and the increment to other retail sales through indirect effects and the multiplier, and perhaps income tax on the earnings of players and other employees.

For example, if a football team sells 600,000 tickets at a price of $35, collects another $20 in gross concession and amenities sales from each customer, and sells $4 million of signage, total stadium revenues are $37 million. (These assumptions are within the range experienced by existing teams.) Even a 10 percent sales tax would generate only $3.7 million in taxes. If the indirect effects create an equal amount of new spending outside the stadium, which is quite optimistic, gross sales tax revenues are, at most, double this amount. Of course, most of this revenue is a substitution for other taxes (because stadium revenues from residents are a substitute for other consumption). If the team's payroll is $50 million and state and local income and payroll taxes average 10 percent (a very high number), at most another $5 million is added to all government coffers; however, to the extent that this income is earned by residents of other states, tax collections by subsidizing governments will be less than this amount. Consequently, the increase in local and state tax revenues from the stadium would be at most $12.4 million under favorable assumptions, and probably much less.

By contrast, the annualized cost of a $250 million stadium with a thirty-year life will be about $25 million in interest and depreciation, plus several million more in stadium maintenance and local public services. Moreover, to qualify for tax-exempt debt, the rents and taxes from the operation of the facility must not exceed 10 percent of the financing costs.[19] Hence, for both economic and legal reasons, it is reasonable to conclude that most of the cost of a stadium to a city is, in fact, a subsidy.

Under the assumption that the team locates where it is most valuable, competition among cities will proceed until the last bid prevents all other cities from matching the offer. Of course, this does not imply that the winning bid contains the highest subsidy, for the team will also take into account other sources of revenue. A metropolitan area with a large population, high per capita income, and a large surrounding broadcast region with no competition in the same sport will produce higher revenues from attendance and broadcasting, so a large area need not bid as much as a less attractive location to attract a team. On the other hand, to the extent that a sport engages in extensive revenue sharing, the attraction of a local market is relatively less important in differentiating among cities. For example, the NFL engages in far more revenue sharing than any other sport and so has the smallest variance among teams in total annual revenues. Hence NFL teams are likely to make location decisions primarily on the basis of competing bids for subsidies. The movement of the Los Angeles teams to Oakland and St. Louis, the Houston Oilers to Nashville, and Cleveland to Baltimore, would be far more difficult to understand in the other sports, where local market demand is far more important to the overall profitability of a team.

If the benefit to the team of the attributes of the local market are important, the best markets do not need to bid their maximum willingness to pay to obtain a team. If an average market makes a bid that equals the net economic benefit of a team (including consumption value plus the net gain in economic activity), a strong market can win the team by bidding the same amount, or even less. Hence better markets can succeed with lower subsidies, and to the extent that the strength of the local market to a team is correlated with the net economic benefits of the team to the community, better markets are more likely to derive a net economic benefit from a team. However, with extensive revenue sharing, as in the NFL, this effect is attenuated. Thus one consequence of more equal revenue sharing is that better markets must bid more for teams, and a greater proportion of the total economic benefits of the sport is transferred to teams. In short, the NFL is able to extract larger subsidies from local governments than the other sports, relative to the value of its teams, because it engages in extensive revenue sharing.

The cornerstone of the economics of subsidy competition among cities is the calculation by a local government of the amount that it is willing to spend to attract or to retain a team beyond its tax benefits. Two factors affect the amount that a local government is willing to bid. The first is the estimated magnitude of the internal net benefits, and the second is the degree to which the local political process translates these expected net benefits into effective political representation and action.

The maximum amount that a local government can pay to subsidize a team without doing economic harm to its constituents is the internal net benefit of having a team that would arise if the team received no subsidy. This internal net benefit includes the consumption benefits to constituents, the net transfers of economic activity to the local juris-diction if the team locates there, and the multiplier effects of these transfers. If many cities are bidding for a team, the city that, in prin-ciple, can bid the most is the one for which all of these internal net benefits are greatest.

From the preceding discussion, three factors appear to account for one city having an economic advantage over another in competing for a sports franchise. First, one city can derive a greater net consumption benefit from a team. All else equal, this puts larger cities at an advantage over smaller ones, because larger cities have more people who can derive a personal benefit from a local team. Of course, all else may not be equal. A smaller city may have a greater proportion of diehard sports fans, a higher per capita income (so the intensity of its interest in sports is backed up by greater purchasing power), or fewer cultural and enter-tainment attractions that deflect attention from a sports team. Likewise, a local government that includes a larger proportion of the sports fans in a metropolitan area is at an advantage. Because only residents "count" in internal benefit-cost analysis, a government containing a higher pro-portion of the intense sports fans will have a higher maximum bid. Finally, if a city has fewer teams, it is will also have an advantage in bidding, because the presence of some teams is likely to reduce the consumer benefits of attracting still another team. This effect is likely to be stronger if a city already has a team in the same sport.

Second, cities that expect to experience a larger reallocation of economic activity from other communities are at an advantage. In general, this effect works in the opposite way from the first. Within a metropolitan area, each locality will benefit from the relocation of a team from outside the metropolitan area to within its jurisdiction. But a smaller jurisdiction will derive a greater benefit because it has more to gain from reallocations within the metropolitan area. Most of the expenditures of fans attending a game are by residents of the metropolitan area who decide to spend discretionary dollars on professional sports, rather than on movies, restaurants, the theater, or other things. These expenditures amount to a substitution of sporting events for other local consumption activities. Notwithstanding differences in whether the income from these expenditures is retained inside the metropolitan area, the net effect of this reallocation of local consumption activity is zero and so is irrelevant from the standpoint of net economic activity within the metropolitan area. However, if a local government contains a small proportion of these other businesses and expects to retain a significant proportion of the expenditures associated with attendance at games, it will perceive a net internal benefit from the purely redistributive effects of the stadium. A metropolitan-wide government perceives no internal benefit from these reallocations of local expenditures.

Third, a city will experience a larger multiplier effect from the location of a team if the community captures a larger proportion of the consumption expenditures that are generated from the net local income (if any) that the team generates. This effect again works in favor of communities that are larger and more diverse, including communities that contain extensive retail sales outlets. Thus a wealthy bedroom suburb may attract the star athletes but experience a small multiplier effect because its residents spend all of their income elsewhere. A central city that contains extensive retail shopping may attract no star athletes, but if they spend money at its retail shops, the city may experience a significant multiplier effect.

Similarly, a metropolitan area is more likely to experience a net gain from a team if the surrounding hinterland is heavily populated and contains no other teams. For example, because Camden Yards is only forty-five minutes from downtown Washington, D.C. (and half that from some D.C. suburbs), the Baltimore Orioles attract a significant number of fans from outside the Baltimore metropolitan area and so generate unusually large "net export" sales. Were a baseball team to locate in the District of Columbia, neither the Orioles nor the new team would be likely to generate much in the way of sales in the other community. Thus, if neither Baltimore nor Washington has a team in a sport, each city's willingness to bid will be enhanced by the possibility of generating revenue from residents of the other city. The maximum feasible bid for either city is lower if the other has a team.

Briefly, the advantage of a metropolitan government is that it incorporates all of the consumer benefits from attracting a sports team, plus all of the net export benefits a team creates. The advantage of a community that is smaller than a metropolitan area is that it takes into account transfers of consumption expenditures within the metropolitan area. Whether a metropolitan consortium of governments has the greater advantage depends on the relative importance of these effects. From the preceding arguments, one might expect metropolitan area governments to be more likely to have the advantage when an area has an especially intense unsatisfied demand for sports, as would be the case when it is acquiring its first team and when its surrounding region is populous and lacks competing teams. In larger metropolitan areas (both absolutely and relative to the surrounding regional population), a subgovernment is at an advantage because the transfer effects within the metropolitan area are likely to loom larger. Moreover, because a strong retail sales base is a necessary condition for capturing indirect benefits, the governments having the greatest advantage with respect to the redistributive effects of a stadium are likely to be either central cities or large suburbs with extensive retail shopping, as compared with small bedroom suburbs.

From the standpoint of economic efficiency, aggregate economic welfare is maximized if teams locate in areas where they generate the greatest global net economic benefit. Competition among metropolitan areas (or among states) is broadly consistent with this outcome. The primary factor entering into the maximum bid of metropolitan areas is the magnitude of net consumer benefits, that is, the intensity of fan demand for a sports team. A possibly important second factor is the extent to which employees of the team (primarily the players) relocate to the area in which the team plays. Cities that retain more players will retain more of the net income generated by a team and so enjoy greater net exports and a larger multiplier effect. These benefits are not economically valueless from a global perspective, since presumably, all else equal, players would rather live where they play and so derive value if their team locates in a city that is a desirable place to live.

If bidding takes place among metropolitan areas, the ranking of the maximum amounts that competing areas can bid and still benefit from having the team is likely to be roughly the same as the actual global net benefits of the team. Thus, assuming an efficient political process (wherein the welfare of citizens is accurately represented by elected officials) or equal distortions in the political process across cities, competitive bidding would tend to cause teams to be located in areas where they contribute the most to economic welfare. The primary problem from this competition is that, holding aggregate economic benefits constant, a smaller metro area with a compensatingly larger nearby regional population center can have the advantage because it counts the transfer of economic activity from its hinterland as a net internal benefit.

If submetropolitan governments also bid for teams, the conclusion that the bidding process is reasonably efficient is no longer sustainable. Submetropolitan governments are primarily the result of historical accident and state rules about forming and merging local governments. Metropolitan areas vary enormously in the extent to which local government is fragmented, from areas in which one city accounts for a large proportion of the metropolitan area (examples are Houston and Jacksonville) to areas that contain many medium-size cities and no city that accounts for even as much as a fourth of the metropolitan area population (examples are Boston, San Francisco Bay, and Los Angeles). One would expect governments that cover nearly all of the metropolitan area to succeed in a bidding war only when they are very large or have an especially intense demand for professional sports, such as when they have no teams.

For these reasons, areas with more than one large population center, such as the Baltimore-Washington and San Francisco Bay areas, are likely to express a willingness to pay for teams (owing to the reallocation effect inside the metropolitan area) that is more than the global economic value of locating a team in the metro area. If so, bidding by medium-size submetropolitan governments (such as Oakland, San Jose, and the New Jersey suburbs of New York) may cause them to outbid areas in which the global economic value of the team is greater. If so, bidding among cities leads to a misallocation of teams. If the location that maximizes consumer welfare (that is, the location that fans would most prefer for a team) is not in a jurisdiction that would benefit from the local reallocation of retail expenditures that follows the team, the team will not locate optimally. Consequently, the winner in a competition among metropolitan areas will not necessarily be the area in which the team generates the greatest amount of fan satisfaction.

Notwithstanding the efficiency of subsidy competition in allocating teams among cities, for most cities the bidding process strips most of the benefit of a team from the local government and its constituents. Except for a few very large, lucrative markets, competing cities are likely to be reasonably similar in their attractiveness as a sports market and the net economic benefit (including externalities) that the city would derive from a team. Because the winning bid must be high enough so that no other city would derive a net benefit from the team at that price, the city that acquires the team will derive little net benefit from winning.

The Effect of Monopoly Leagues

The magnitude of sports subsidies is certainly due primarily to the fact that leagues monopolize franchises, but not entirely so. Imagine that the number of professional teams in a sport is determined solely by competitive market conditions (as in other industries), rather than by a monopoly league. In this circumstance, if a city lost a team but was a financially viable location, another would quickly replace the departing team. And, when a city grew large enough to become a viable franchise site, a team would be created to serve the market. Hence no city that is a viable franchise location would have to pay anything in subsidies to acquire a team.

Nevertheless, a completely competitive market for teams would not put an end to subsidies. The externality value of a local team would still exist. Hence a city that has no team and is not quite large enough to make a team financially viable can derive a net benefit by providing a subsidized facility. Thus if leagues freely expand in response to the presence of sites where teams are financially viable, teams in better markets receive no subsidies, but additional, subsidized teams emerge in smaller markets.

The question arising from this argument is how many teams would there be, and how many of the existing teams would be subsidized, if leagues were not monopolies? Indeed, if monopoly sports leagues are altruistic, rather than profit maximizing, they would expand in precisely the way described above. How do we know that the new expansion franchises, with their large stadium subsidies, are not the kinds of teams that need a subsidy to make them financially viable?

The simple answer to the preceding question is that recent expansion franchises have paid extremely high fees to join their league. For example, the price of the NFL expansion teams in Charlotte and Jacksonville, taking into account the fact that the teams did not receive equal shares of broadcasting revenue, was in the range of $175 million to $200 million.[20] Thus most of the subsidy received was not a benefit to the teams, but a payment to the monopoly league to create an expansion franchise. In a normal business, new firms do not need to pay established businesses for the right to enter an industry. The expansion fee was roughly the amount necessary to compensate the NFL for the fact that, eventually, the new team would receive a full share of national television and licensing revenues. The value of the NFL's national broadcasting and licensing rights increases after an expansion because audience ratings, hence advertising revenues, and licensing income rise in the area that obtains a team. However, because some residents of the expansion city watched NFL games and bought NFL products before the expansion, and because expansion cities are usually from areas with a below-average market, the increased revenues from these rights are likely to be substantially smaller than the share of rights income that is paid to the expansion team. Hence existing teams are likely to experience a decline in their revenues following expansion. Of course, an increase in the number of competitors is likely to have the same effect in any industry. Only because sports leagues are monopolies can they extract compensation from entrants. The expansion fee represents compensation to existing teams for more extensive sharing of the monopoly profits from broadcasting.

The Reason for Bogus Impact Analysis

The main thrust of the preceding analysis is that stadiums are subsidized because sports teams create local consumption value that owners can extract from state and local government because leagues are monopolies. An interesting puzzle in this story is why cities claim that stadiums are good investments and use bogus economic impact studies to buttress this pretense. The most plausible explanation for bogus studies is political. They create the illusion of a greater public benefit than, in fact, a team creates. We are skeptical of any explanation that rests on permanent, massive mistakes on the part of citizens, but in this case such an explanation does not require a completely pessimistic view of voters. For instance, in a community in which 54 percent of the voters expect no personal consumer benefit from a team and so are inclined against a stadium subsidy and 46 percent are diehard sports fans who favor it, a bogus economic impact study that misleads only 5 percent of the voters can switch the outcome. Thus, if bogus studies can sway only a relatively few people, the interests that benefit from facility construction (the sports team, local contractors, construction unions, real estate operators, bankers) are motivated to produce them. Regardless of whether a new sports facility pays off as an economic investment for the city, an influential study, even if bogus, can cause political officials to be more responsive to this powerful coalition of local interest groups.

The effectiveness of bogus economic studies can only be enhanced by the one-sided political environment in which stadium proposals are debated. Local media, owing to their symbiotic relationship with sports, are likely to favor a stadium initiative. Moreover, the well-organized interests favoring the stadium are likely to outspend opponents by awesome amounts. For example, in June 1997 San Francisco and the state of Washington held referenda on whether to subsidize a new NFL football stadium. Both referenda won by tiny margins. In San Francisco, proponents outspent opponents by 25 to 1, while in Washington the spending ratio was an amazing 80 to 1![21] If as few as 2 percent of voters were misled by the incorrect claims about the economic effects of the stadium proposals in these campaigns, the bogus studies determined the outcome in these elections. With campaign spending so unequal, such an outcome surely is not implausible.

Conclusion

The system of bidding for teams by promising subsidized stadiums arises in part because Americans are intensely interested in sports. Subsidies also arise because localities that lure a sports team usually experience a modest increase in net economic activity. The amount of the increased activity depends, among other things, on the extent to which people from outside the city attend sporting events and spend money at the stadium and in the surrounding neighborhood, and the extent to which high-salaried employees of the team choose to live in the same community.

Whether a team can increase global economic welfare by relocating depends completely on the consumption value of sports itself. Teams are likely to experience higher fan interest in some cities than in others. If relocation increases attendance, broadcast audiences, and overall fan interest, it improves economic welfare. Consequently, with a few important qualifications, teams should be free to relocate where demand is most intense once they have fulfilled their contractual obligations to their host city.

If stadium subsidies were motivated solely by consumer welfare and there were no distortions in the incentives facing cities, bidding among cities for teams would not cause a misallocation of teams among cities. The primary effect of these subsidies would be to transfer income from citizens in general to those who are engaged in sports, owners as well as players. Misallocation occurs because cities differ in the extent to which they perceive economic benefits from the transfer of business that accompanies a sports team. A city's willingness to bid depends on the perceived value of the team to consumers, the extent to which the political unit subsidizing the facility is the beneficiary of transfers of business from other jurisdictions, and the political influence of the private economic interests that benefit from a stadium project. In general, large cities that constitute a small fraction of the population of a market area are at an advantage in competing for teams. A large market area is beneficial because it enables the city to capture substantial consumption benefits from having a team and a larger share of the indirect effects of the team. Yet a subgovernment that does not contain the entire market area is at an advantage because it increases the fraction of the economic activity associated with a team that is transferred from nearby jurisdictions.

Economic impact studies of a sports facility raise many complex questions and are difficult to evaluate. One source of these difficulties is the uniqueness of the sports industry. A sports team is very different from most businesses that cities try to attract, such as shopping centers, corporate headquarters, or manufacturing facilities. These operations are more likely to attract sales from other communities—that is, to have high net exports—and so are likely to induce a net increase in local economic activity. In addition, standard formulas for calculating indirect and multiplier effects, because they are based on ordinary businesses paying ordinary wages, are less accurate when applied to a sports team in which almost all of the income is earned by a relatively small number of people who are very highly paid.

Unfortunately, the standard method of assessing economic impact overstates the extent to which a team generates a net increase in business (its net exports) and then overstates again the multiplier effects arising from this business. However, it also ignores the consumer benefits of having a team. These benefits may be large enough to offset the subsidy, even if the team has no net effect on local economic activity, although quantifying them is extremely difficult. Most likely, these consumer benefits presumably are the real reason that cities are willing to spend so much on attracting and keeping a team.

If the real reason for extensive subsidization of major league team sports is public consumption, the validity of the economic impact studies is not very important. But if the purpose of sports subsidies is consumption, not economic development, the effect of luring a major league sports franchise to the local economy is to substitute sports events for other forms of discretionary spending, such as movies, restaurants, recreational activities, and media. One consequence of this substitution is a highly regressive redistribution of income. Far more than half of the gross revenue of sports teams is paid as salaries to players, managers, coaches, and executives. These salaries are substantially above median income. Moreover, if stadiums are financed by sales and property taxes or lottery revenues, the financing is also regressive. In other words, redirecting consumer expenditures from almost all other consumer goods to sports stadiums redistributes income from people with lower incomes to people who are very wealthy. The exceptions are when sports substitutes for some other forms of popular entertainment, such as rock concerts and movies, which also remunerate performers handsomely.

The magnitude of stadium subsidies is greatly increased by the monopoly structure and behavior of professional sports leagues. The scarcity of teams is caused by a very slow expansion process that leaves many viable franchise sites without a team. Then, league processes for governing relocation, which involve prior discussions with league officials and ultimately supermajority approval by other teams, have the effect of allowing a city to negotiate with only one team at a time. In 1991–92, Victor Kiam sought to move the New England Patriots out of the Boston area. He attempted to negotiate with representatives from several cities, including Baltimore and Jacksonville, but the NFL central office prohibited these discussions in order to preserve these cities as competitors for the 1995 expansion.[22] As a result of those league policies, when a team becomes available, it can enjoy many potential suitors and no competition for their attention.[23]

An important part of the subsidy is simply the extraction of monopoly prices from cities; however, the profits to owners of sports teams are a relatively small part of the total amount of the subsidy. By far the biggest effect of subsidized stadiums is that perfectly good facilities are forced to retire prematurely and new facilities are far more elaborate and costly than is justified by the business that they generate. The next largest effect is that player salaries capture more than half of the value of the subsidy, as explained in chapter 1.

One way to reduce such subsidies would be simply to cap them. In the mid–nineteenth century, local governments frequently overextended themselves in offering subsidies to railroads so as to influence decisions about routes and terminals. States responded to these problems by regulating both railroads and local government subsidies. Of course, the problem with this approach is that sometimes a subsidy is a perfectly valid action for a community. If subsidies were banned, communities that cannot support a team from direct revenues but that are willing to pay a subsidy would not be able to have a team. If one sets an upper bound on subsidies and does nothing else, monopoly sports leagues will still expand too slowly, and all cities will have to pay the maximum amount, not just those in which the team needs the subsidy to be viable.

If the primary cause of massive stadium subsidies is monopoly sports leagues, the most effective policy is not to regulate stadiums and leagues, but to make leagues competitive. Monopoly sports leagues fail to expand into cities that are viable franchise sites, and fail to add extra teams in areas that could support them, because existing owners benefit from a scarcity of teams. This scarcity bids up both stadium subsidies and the franchise value of teams. But leagues can succeed in making franchises scarce only because the threat of competitive entry by another league is minimal. If there were multiple leagues, a league would derive no benefit and would suffer a cost from a failure to expand into an area that could support a team, or to add a team to an area that could support multiple teams.

For the most part, an industry as localized as a sports team is not likely to generate much local economic development, especially in an entire metropolitan area rather than a city within that area. Stadium subsidies facilitate building expensive monuments to sports that benefit no one and transfer income from ordinary people to highly paid players, owners, and executives. Moreover, they arise because sports leagues are monopolies that by and large have been created and protected by public policy.

Notes

1. *Financial World*, June 17, 1997, pp. 47–49.
2. EBI data are from the *1996 Commercial Atlas and Marketing Guide* (New York: Rand McNally, 1996), pp. 40–43.
3. Stanford University, *Stanford University Budget Plan 1997/98*, 1997.
4. U.S. National Science Foundation, *Federal Support to Universities, Colleges and Nonprofit Institutions*, Document NSF 95-331 (Washington, D.C.: Government Printing Office), 1995.
5. If undergraduate tuition is $18,000, total payments from 6,000 undergraduates amount to $108 million. Including graduate students and undergraduates, Stanford collected $258 million in tuition in 1995–96.
6. Local government decisions in the nineteenth century to subsidize railroads have many parallels to contemporary decisions to subsidize stadiums. The former are examined in Mark T. Kanazawa and Roger G. Noll, "The Origins of State Railroad Regulation: The Illinois Constitution of 1870," in Claudia Goldin and Gary D. Libecap, eds., *The Regulated Economy: An Historical Approach to Political Economy* (University of Chicago Press, 1994), pp. 13–54.
7. A subsidy for an investment that produces only direct consumption benefits can enhance efficiency in two circumstances. First, if some direct benefits are externalities, private investors may underinvest in the activity. Second, if the activity that makes use of the investment exhibits economies of scale, output prices that fully recover investment costs exceed the incremental cost of production, and so exclude some consumers who value the product more highly than the incremental cost of providing it to them. Public subsidies can improve efficiency in this case if they permit lower output prices. In the case of sports facilities, however, teams charge profit-maximizing prices regardless of the source of funds for the stadium.
8. For example, one justification for public subsidies of education and student loans is that students who lack sufficient funds to pursue income-enhancing education have inadequate access to capital markets because they lack collateral for educational loans. An argument of this form is not likely to apply to sports stadiums because both stadiums and franchises are frequently used as collateral for loans by sports teams.
9. John B. Shoven and John Whalley, "Applied General-Equilibrium Models of Taxation and International Trade: An Introduction and Survey," *Journal of Economic Literature*, vol. 22 (September 1984), p. 1032; and A. Lans Bovenberg and Lawrence H. Goulder, "Optimal Environmental Taxation in the Presence of Other Taxes: General Equilibrium Analysis," *American Economic Review*, vol. 86 (September 1996), pp. 994.
10. The literature on firm locations emphasizes the importance of linkages with suppliers and customers; taxation and regulation are generally important, but less so than the structure of the local or regional economy. The classic paper on firm location decisions is Dennis W. Carlton, "The Location and Employment Choices of New Firms: An Econometric Model with Discrete and Continuous Endogenous Variables," *Review*

of Economics and Statistics, vol. 65 (August 1983), pp. 440–49. See also James E. Rauch, "Does History Matter Only When It Matters Little? The Case of City-Industry Location," *Quarterly Journal of Economics,* vol. 58 (August 1993), pp. 843–67.

11. Tina Cassady, "South Boston Stadium Foes to Hold Fundraisers," *Boston Globe,* February 21, 1997.

12. The home of Disney's Anaheim Mighty Ducks of the National Hockey League.

13. The unofficial name of the San Jose Arena, home of the Sharks of the NHL.

14. Travel expenses refer to transportation of team personnel and equipment. Because each team plays half of its games on the road, hotel and food expenditures out of town by the local team and media are roughly equal to local spending by visiting teams and media.

15. In addition to the problems associated with the application of multiplier analysis to sports projects, more general questions apply to all attempts to calculate a multiplier effect for any small, specialized activity. Multiplier analysis is based on broad assumptions about average conditions, including constant returns to scale in production and constant income elasticities of demand across all consumer goods. Tiny projects with initial income effects on an atypical segment of the population are not likely to satisfy these conditions.

16. The formula can be expressed as either the annual net economic benefit from the facility, in which case capital expenditures are converted to annual interest plus amortization for a loan to finance the cost of the facility, or as the total increase in wealth that is created by the facility, in which case the benefits and costs that appear as annual streams are expressed as their discounted present value.

17. An owner who seeks to maximize team quality is not necessarily performing an altruistic public service for the community. Some owners may be motivated by the personal satisfaction of fielding a winning team, in which case team quality is personal consumption, rather like a hobby. Or, owners may own a team as part of a larger business enterprise for which total profits are maximized if the team is of a higher quality than would maximize profits just from the team. For example, the ownership connection between the Atlanta Braves and the Turner Broadcasting System probably raises the optimal team quality of the Braves.

18. James P. Quirk and Rodney Fort, *Pay Dirt: The Business of Professional Team Sports* (Princeton University Press, 1992), pp. 170–71.

19. Dennis Zimmerman, *Tax Exempt Bonds and the Economics of Professional Sports Stadiums,* CRS Report 96-460E (Washington, D.C.: Congressional Research Service, 1996), pp. 5–6. See also chapter 4.

20. The expansion fee for these teams was $140 million. Allan Friedman and Paul J. Much, *Inside the Ownership of Professional Sports Teams: The Complete Directory of the Ownership and Financial Structure of Pro Sports* (Chicago: Team Marketing Report, Inc., 1996). In addition, they must have experienced some start-up costs. Public estimates of broadcasting revenues in 1996 show a gap of more than $20 million between established NFL teams and the expansion clubs in Charlotte and Jacksonville. *Financial World,* June 17, 1997, p. 49. The discounted present value of $20 million for three years, using a 10 percent discount rate, is $54 million.

21. San Francisco data are from Philip J. Trounstine and Brandon Bailey, "Strategy: Funds, Fees, Foot Soldiers Combined to Give 49ers Win in Overtime," *San Jose Mercury News,* June 5, 1997, p. 20A.

22. Jon Morgan, *Glory for Sale: Fans, Dollars and the New NFL* (Baltimore: Bancroft Press, 1997), p. 162; and Frank Cooney, "NFL Could Find Itself in Court Again If It Snubs Jacksonville," *San Francisco Examiner,* November 7, 1993, p. L8.

23. Bud Adams, the owner of the Houston Oilers, in commenting about the Rams deal in St. Louis, remarked: "If you had asked NFL teams if they would be interested in the same deal in St. Louis, seven or eight would have raised their hands and there would be a stampede . . . like the running of the bulls at Pamplona," *Sporting News,* March 27, 1997.

3

THE EMPLOYMENT EFFECT OF TEAMS AND SPORTS FACILITIES

ROBERT A. BAADE AND ALLEN R. SANDERSON

 As the preceding chapters have indicated, a growing concern of state and local governments in the United States is whether to subsidize professional sports teams and their playing facilities. Those who support such subsidies believe that teams and stadiums spur economic development and thus should be considered investments.[1] A useful exercise, then, would be to determine whether building a new stadium, or otherwise subsidizing professional sports, actually does stimulate job growth beyond what could be expected from an alternative use of public and private funds.

A number of recent studies concerned with the economic impact of professional sports show a clear trend toward a moderation of projected benefits. The growing tendency to exercise restraint in projecting such benefits may reflect, in part, the view that budget constraints impose limits on leisure spending. This more conservative approach is particularly evident in the distinction some now make between "gross" and "net" economic impact, as can be seen in a report commissioned by King County to determine the impact of the Seattle Mariners on the economies of King County, the city of Seattle, and the state of Washington.[2] The distinction has more than trivial implications. The authors of the King

County report, Conway and Associates, estimated that in a gross sense the Mariners created 2,249 jobs, while at the state level the "new money" attributable to professional sports was responsible for about 427 jobs, or approximately one-fifth of the gross estimate.

Although less dramatic, the implications of the distinction at the county and city levels remain substantial. The figures for 1993, Conway reported, were 1,805 gross jobs for King County and 1,535 for Seattle, 685 net jobs for the county and 577 for the city. Clearly, new spending dissipates as the area of analysis expands. In the case of Mariner fans, what those residing in Olympia spend at games in Seattle represents new spending in Seattle but little in the way of a change in net spending in the state.

From a practical and policymaking perspective, the debate about job creation could be resolved in large part if impact assessments consistently used net as opposed to gross figures. The experience of a cross section of cities in the United States during the past quarter century shows scant evidence that professional sports create a significant number of new jobs.[3] The primary reason for the excessive optimism of many appraisals of this job creation potential is their assumption that an increase in sport-generated revenues necessarily corresponds to an expansion of the local economy. The fact is that the demand for labor derives from the demand for goods and services. If professional sports do not correlate with an increase in net new spending, jobs will not be created. Our empirical analysis indicates that spending on spectator sports is largely offset by reductions in other forms of leisure spending by consumers and other fiscal commitments by governmental entities. As a consequence, sports account for negligible increases in net new spending and new jobs. This assertion and the evidence presented here reflect elementary budgetary constraints, which in turn affect the spending of individuals, families, and state and local governments.

However, the number of jobs created is not the sole factor to indicate the employment effect of professional sports. Two others also merit attention: the types of jobs sports subsidies generate, and the costs involved in creating jobs through such subsidies. These three factors are the central concern of this chapter.

Issues Related to Estimating Job Creation

Estimates of the impact of professional sports teams and stadiums on local and regional employment vary widely. In rationalizing public subsidies for a National Football League franchise, team owners in Jacksonville, Florida, asserted that their team would pump $130 million a year into the Jacksonville economy and create 3,000 jobs.[4] Those advocating a subsidy for a new NFL franchise in Baltimore (the former Cleveland Browns) estimated 1,394 new jobs.[5] Others have been far less optimistic. If sports creates jobs at all, states a recent report, the impact is likely to be one-tenth as large as that estimated by boosters in Jacksonville.[6] In part, these radically divergent views on economic impact and job creation may reflect important structural differences in the cities analyzed. They may also reflect some differences in objective economic reality. But it is not only economic conditions or contexts that differ: perceptions about the workings of the economies analyzed differ as well.

In an analysis of economic contexts for sports subsidies, several conditions assume critical importance. First, the extent to which such subsidies create jobs varies with the degree to which the metropolitan or regional economy is operating near its productive capacity. In the same vein, the level of unemployment in those labor markets most affected by an expanding professional sports industry will determine the number of jobs created. Expansionary pressures in a fully employed economy realign economic activity unless resources expand to meet the increased demand for them (see chapter 2).

Second, potential economic benefits and stimuli for a local labor market will be dampened considerably if expenditures migrate beyond the immediate area. In professional sports, money that goes to owners, players, coaches, team executives and broadcasts is overwhelmingly spent beyond the geographic area in which the teams play and the fans reside. In other words, most of the money in sports is earned by people in national rather than local or regional labor markets.

Third, many of the new stadiums and arenas being built are replacement facilities. Replacing infrastructure for sports does not lead to an expansion of the local economy but rather maintains economic activity at or near its former level once the construction phase of the new facility project ends. Employment estimates provided as a rationale for replacing an "obsolete" structure with a new facility should not be interpreted as jobs gained but rather as jobs not lost. To a large extent, a new stadium or arena simply relocates the workplace while leaving the work force largely unaltered. In addition, one should distinguish between the total current employment at an existing facility and the net incremental effect due to a new stadium. Furthermore, both depend on whether a city expects a team to leave an area if an owner's demand for new construction or renovation is unmet.

Fourth, a stadium that hosts games for a regionally isolated franchise—for example, Major League Baseball's Colorado Rockies in Denver—will likely attract fans from greater distances than a franchise in a saturated sports market, such as the northeastern United States. All else being equal, the isolated sports franchise will boost the local economy more than the franchise competing for fans in a regional market with an abundance of teams, since the sports product is more likely to be exported beyond the borders of the metropolis.

A related point here is that job creation will depend on the extent to which net increases in expenditures originate from outside the immediate geographic or political area. If movies and restaurants are good substitutes for each other within a city, increased consumer spending on one may come at the expense of the other. If significant numbers of consumers of either activity are drawn from outside the city, a net increase in spending is possible for a narrowly defined area. Hence net job creation resulting from professional sports could hinge on the fan base that resides in the central city versus the suburbs (or beyond) or may even occasionally cross a state boundary, as in the case of the St. Louis Cardinals and Rams, the Washington Redskins, and the several New York-area franchises.

Fifth, stadiums integrated into a commercial, residential development improve the prospects for stadium-inspired economic growth. Many sports facilities constructed in the post–World War II era, beginning with County Stadium in Milwaukee and Memorial Stadium in Baltimore, accommodated the preference for automobile transportation and population shifts within an urban area from the central city to the suburbs. Surrounding a stadium with a sea of asphalt or concrete eases entry and egress of automotive traffic, but mitigates the spillover of stadium pedestrian traffic into other commercial sites in the city, particularly in the stadium's environs. New sports facilities in downtown Cleveland, Baltimore, and Denver have departed from automobile-inspired designs and locations. The early evidence indicates that these more synergistic urban stadium plans may promote neighborhood economic development beyond that experienced by facilities shaped by automotive imperatives. (An alternative explanation for a rediscovery of central cities is that suburban political entities have weighed the costs and benefits and then rejected the advances of teams: the Chicago White Sox and Chicago Bears are two recent examples in which owners explicitly sought suburban locations but could not obtain the necessary financial commitments and then turned back to the city of Chicago and the state of Illinois.)

A few other factors may affect employment: the "occupancy rate" or hours of operation (a football stadium is only used 10 days, or maybe 50 hours a year, whereas a baseball park may be used 80 days or 300 hours a year, and a mall perhaps 360 days or about 3,000 hours);[7] differences between utilization for repetitive events (such as regular season games) versus less frequent occurrences (such as playoff games, an All-Star game or Super Bowl, or even a periodic political convention); the distinction between a burst of activity during, say, the construction and postconstruction phases versus steady-state operations; and short-term versus long-term effects, such as increased attendance that may accompany a new team or new facility (or a team that is performing better on the field or court than usual) for a few years until the "novelty effect" wears off and interest returns to more normal levels.

Contextual differences suggest that stadium and team economic contributions are best measured individually, but some general principles do apply and can help account for the differences in the estimated and real economic contributions of professional sports to local and regional economies. The first point to note is that the methodology used to assess economic impact will in part be task-oriented, and that is why approaches vary in past assessments. In the most general sense, the methodology will depend on whether one's objective is to provide economic estimates (prospective analysis) or evidence on past experience (retrospective analysis). Those who advocate the use of public funds for sports infrastructure conduct prospective analysis. They justify such public financing through promises of substantial increases in area output, income, jobs, and tax revenues. The most sophisticated of these prospective models have a general equilibrium character and are supply-based, input-output structures.[8]

Given the number of stadiums being built, their cost, and the equity issues involved, a growing number of public finance scholars are turning their attention to the economic impact of these projects. Some have begun questioning the accuracy of the projections.[9] In general, independent scholarship has concluded that studies claiming substantial contributions to the local and regional economies from professional sports systematically exaggerate the real contribution.[10]

Problems exist on both the demand and supply sides. On the supply side, even when subsidy advocates employ the methods of Regional Economic Models Incorporated (REMI) in their analysis, they often ignore certain constraints that clearly impair the growth potential of any large, public project. The balanced-budget constraint confronted by local and state government, for example, compels trade-offs that mitigate the economic impact of facilities for professional sports.[11] This and other resource constraints—especially in private capital and labor markets—must be taken into account if the impact of professional sports is to be measured more precisely.[12] In other words, a gross measure of the economic growth induced by sports is not appropriate justification for a subsidy: the proper standard for gauging its economic contribution is a net measure of growth.

The distinction between net and gross measures assumes critical importance on the demand side as well. Individuals and families have limited leisure budgets, defined in both terms of time and money. Money spent on watching professional sports events is money not spent on other leisure activities. In practice, many subsidy supporters have neglected, in some instances ignored, this substitution effect, with the result that estimates of the benefits to having a team or the costs of losing one are in many cases biased. To estimate how much Major League Baseball's host cities lost during the players' 1994 strike, for example, it is not enough simply to count lost ticket and concession revenues at the ballpark and reduced sales at sports bars and other firms in the immediate area. The fact is, fans may have changed the locus of their recreational spending without measurably reducing the total. Indeed, reports that Hollywood enjoyed its best September ever during the players' strike indicates that leisure spending was not reduced but rather reallocated. Recent research confirms this expected result: "The strike had little, if any, economic impact on host cities. Retail trade appeared to be almost completely unaffected by the strike. . . . The relationship between a city's economic performance before and during the strike essentially was no different for cities that hosted teams and those that did not."[13] The strike may well have determined to some extent where people drank beer in Chicago and Boston during August and September of 1994, but it almost certainly had little or no impact on the total amount of beer consumed in those cities.

Measures of the contribution of professional sports to local and regional economies may be biased in yet another respect. Because the benefits of professional sports are dispersed across much of the population, it is difficult to measure the benefits to an individual spectator.

More amenable to measurement, since it was more concentrated, is the cost to those who lost a job or considerable income during the 1994 strike. In reality, it is easier to estimate the economic effects for the small number of people who experience a large gain or loss than it is to calculate the effects of the far larger group of people who experience only a very small effect, either as spectators or as owners and employees of the myriad of businesses that are substitutes or complements for sporting events. Many analysts are unable to resist the temptation to measure that which is easiest to measure and to ignore the rest, even though the latter may be far more important in the aggregate. (This is akin to calculating the losers versus winners with the removal of tariff protection: it is easier to find those whose jobs have been eliminated—and their sizable losses make their case more compelling for the media—than it is to add up the marginal gains for thousands of consumers who benefit from lower prices and a wider selection.)

From the perspective of the metropolitan area as a whole, economic activity increases if the professional sports services are exported or provide a substitute for services that would otherwise be imported. Furthermore, if the professional sports industry expands at the expense of other industries as a consequence of resource constraints, there is no reason to expect contracting industries to be any less prone to export than professional sports.

The demand for goods and services produced within a metropolis or a region can also be affected by changes in the distribution of income. This certainly applies to an expansion of professional sports, an industry characterized by a highly skewed distribution of income. The major part of the revenues from professional sports go to players, coaches, and top administrators (diehard fans are the other principal beneficiary), whereas only a small part goes to vendors, ticket takers, parking lot attendants, and other service workers. Also, as already mentioned, to the extent that owners and players do not live in the host city and repatriate their earnings to their primary residences or invest their returns beyond the area in which the team is located, the expansion of the professional sports industry may actually precipitate a net outflow of funds from the metropolitan or regional economy.

In sum, current research has thus far failed to construct a model adequate to the task of accurately predicting the economic contribution of professional sports. (Alternatively, it may be that the modelers have not yet found the motivation to apply themselves adequately to the task of projecting the contribution of sports to the local or regional economy.) The purpose of this discussion is not to compensate for the deficiencies of prospective analysis and to offer an all-encompassing model, but rather to use retrospective analysis to provide a mechanism through which the economic promises of subsidy advocates can be filtered. The first step to that end is to consider the promises that have been made to date.

Profiling Jobs Created by Professional Sports

According to all the available evidence, the jobs generated by professional sports activities are concentrated in the nonmanufacturing sector: both gross and net estimates suggest the concentration may be as high as 98 percent.[14] More specifically, almost all such jobs can be placed under "trade" and "services," in accordance with Standard Industrial Classification (SIC) conventions. Furthermore, professional sports activities are seasonal, and each event is completed during what constitutes a portion of a workday; most jobs in professional sports therefore qualify as part-time and seasonal work. Their concentration in the nonmanufacturing sectors would apply to the largest, most diverse metropolitan economies. Needless to say, this concentration should not be used to indict professional sports or to imply that cities should not provide jobs of this nature, but it does help explain why professional sports do not induce the same magnitude of economic activity as some alternative uses of the public funds earmarked for stadium construction (such as subsidizing an industrial park).

It seems that the only mechanism through which sports would contribute to job creation in the manufacturing sector would be if they served as a magnet for enterprises engaged in manufacturing. Although this claim is sometimes made by subsidy advocates, no evidence has yet been found to support it.[15]

The nonmanufacturing sectors of the U.S. economy certainly include many highly skilled, highly paid workers. However, most service and trade employment within the professional sports industry is in the part-time, low-wage end of those sectors. This situation has important implications for net new spending and overall job creation that occurs indirectly as a consequence of professional sports activities. If most of the

Table 3-1. *Compensation for Major League Baseball Players and Stadium Workers, Milwaukee, 1994*

Compensation	Players	Grounds crew	Ushers
Pay	$1.2 million on average per year for all Major League baseball players	$4.85 to $6.56 per hour	$5.40 to $6.38 per hour
Pension	Yes	No	No
Health insurance	Yes	No	No
Uniforms	Supplied	Supplied[a]	Charged to worker
Food	Free postgame buffet	Discounts on brats and hot dogs	Discounts on brats and hot dogs

Source: Robert L. Rose, "Stadium Workers Say Union Solidarity Doesn't Extend to Millionaire Players," *Wall Street Journal*, March 9, 1995, p. B11.

a. Grounds crew members each pay a $25 deposit for uniforms.

proceeds from sports spending are concentrated in the hands of owners, players, and the top administrators of professional sports organizations, it is conceivable that the sports industry has a negative impact on job creation. This could occur if the leisure industry in a city developed a greater professional sports orientation, and if the highly compensated individuals in the sports industry resided in the host city only part of the time and invested their earnings and profits elsewhere. In such cases, leisure spending does not remain in the city, but is deflected to those places in which players and owners reside. It is possible that locally owned leisure establishments could be replaced by professional sports enterprises whose income is distributed toward absentee owners and players. If professional sports induces a net decrease in spending that occurs through a growing current account deficit with the world beyond the metropolis, jobs could in theory be lost. The point, of course, is that there is no assurance that an expansion of the professional sports sector creates jobs. Anything is possible. The compensation of major league baseball players and selected stadium workers for 1994 illustrates this and some of the other points just discussed (table 3-1). Note that most of the part-time, stadium-related jobs are held by people who are moonlighting; thus this work is not their primary source of income.

The Cost of Job Creation through Professional Sports

Few issues are more controversial in state and local government politics than subsidies for private enterprise. Alabama, for one, was widely
criticized inside and outside the state for bidding $300 million in 1993 to
secure the first Mercedes-Benz AG auto plant in the United States. The
plant was expected to accommodate 1,500 workers, and therefore the
subsidy averaged out to $200,000 per job created.[16] A recent review of
this case and other states' incentives to lure corporations noted that, on
a per job basis, Alabama paid far more than neighboring states paid for
other automobile plants. In addition, the Mercedes deal is now expected
to generate only a fraction of the statewide jobs projected originally, and
Alabama's commitment is about 20 percent higher than originally estimated.[17] According to Governor James Edgar of Illinois, reckless state
competition for private enterprise has encouraged states to adopt voluntary guidelines to "de-escalate the bidding wars that have too often pen-
alized existing business and squandered precious resources."[18] In July
1990 the Arizona state legislature authorized the use of more than $240
million to finance the construction of a retractable dome stadium for use
by the Arizona Diamondbacks, a Major League Baseball expansion franchise. The Arizona Office of Sports Development commissioned a study
by Deloitte & Touche to estimate the economic impact of the franchise.
In the stadium's operational phase, the state was expected to gain 340
full-time equivalent jobs.[19] On a base of $240 million, taxpayers in the
state of Arizona are paying approximately $705,800 for each job
created.[20]

From a purely economic perspective, as an investment the much criticized Alabama subsidy would be rated better than the one in Arizona.
This would be true not only because the initial outlay per job was substantially less, but also because most of the jobs created through Alabama's investment would be qualitatively better.

To turn to a national example, it has been estimated that the Local
Public Works Capital Development and Investment Act of 1976 (LPW I)
and the Local Public Works Capital Employment Act of 1977 (LPW II)
created direct and indirect jobs at an average cost of $37,000 for a person-
year.[21] If the nominal cost of creating those jobs doubled between 1980
and 1996 (that is, adjusting for inflation), the average cost per person-
year would be $74,000. By any economic standard, the cost of creating

jobs through professional sports is substantial, defined both in terms of current outlay and the present value of the returns through job creation.

A Model for Estimating Professional Sports Job Creation

Ideally, to estimate the capacity of professional sports to create jobs, a model should include the myriad of independent variables that influence city growth. In theory, a well-conceived and crafted construct would isolate the stadium and team variables, to allow one to estimate their separate impacts. Arguably, no urban growth models have yet been conceived with all the necessary data that would allow for an unbiased, consistent estimate of a stadium's or team's impact on a city's economy. No existing model, and probably no model that is practicable, can isolate stadium and team effects for all the cities that have built a new stadium and attracted, kept, or lost a major league team during the past four decades.[22]

Data limitations and the relative insignificance of professional sports in a large, diverse metropolitan economy argues for a model-building strategy that compensates for, or somehow circumvents, these deficiencies. For the purposes of this study, equation (3-1) is used to estimate jobs created by professional sports teams to include the construction of their facilities.

$$CE_{i,t}/SE_{j,t} = \beta_0 + \beta_1 CRPCY_{i,t}/SRPCPY_{j,t}$$
$$(3\text{-}1) \qquad + \beta_2 CAWW_{i,t}/SAWW_{j,t} + \beta_3 CPOP_{i,t}/SPOP_{j,t}$$
$$+ \beta_4 NT_i + \beta_5 NS_i + \beta_6 TREND + e_i,$$

where $CE_{i,t}/SE_{j,t}$ = city i's share of state employment in the amusement and recreation industry (SIC 79) or the commercial sports industry (SIC 794) at time t; $CRPCY_{i,t}/SRPCPY_{j,t}$ = ratio of city i's real per capita personal income to the state j's at time t; $CPOP_{i,t}/SPOP_{j,t}$ = city i's share of state population at time t; $CAWW_{i,t}/SAWW_{j,t}$ = ratio of average hours worked per week in the durable goods sector in the city relative to the state at time t; NT_i = number of professional sports teams in city i at time t; NS_i = number of new stadiums in city i at time t; $TREND$ = a variable assigned a value of one for the first observation and numbered consecutively for each observation thereafter; and e_i = stochastic error.

This model addresses the economic insignificance of professional sports to a large, diverse metropolitan economy by focusing attention on the sector of the economy most likely to be affected by changes in the professional sports industry: amusement and recreation (SIC 79).[23] In particular, if a city's teams manage their facilities, a change in the number of teams hosted by the city is far more likely to surface in statistics for key economic indicators recorded in SIC 79.[24] Employment is one statistic generally reported by the SIC category at the two-digit level.

How does this model account for the net financial flows that result from professional sports activities that, in turn, determine job creation? As alluded to earlier, many economic impact studies tacitly assume that spending in conjunction with sports spectating represents spending that would not otherwise occur. This notion underlies the use of gross as opposed to net measures of spending changes induced by professional sports. Such an assumption is not entirely realistic. Spectating is but one option with regard to the use of leisure time and money. If aggregate spending does not increase with a city's acquisition of a new stadium or professional sports franchise, it may well be because sports expenditures supplant spending on other leisure pursuits. If leisure spending substitutions by citizens of a municipality are complete, professional sports will induce economic growth only if they attract money from outside the city (exportation of sports services) or keep money inside the city previously spent outside the city's walls (import substitution).

Equation (3-1) is designed to provide evidence on the extent to which professional sports increase the spending and income in the metropolitan statistical area (MSA; the term "city" and MSA are used synonymously throughout this analysis; see note 22) by improving its balance of trade position with the outside world. It was also designed to dispense with the need to specify each variable that may be important in determining city economic growth. More specifically, it factors out rather than making explicit those elements that shape the business cycle or define economic trends for a city and the state in which it is located. Since professional sports affect the host MSA's economy relatively more intensively than is true for the state's economy (the leisure substitution effect is more complete the larger the area analyzed), it is one element that distinguishes the city's economic performance from that of the state. This design ensures that the contribution of professional sports is not netted out of the financial flows for a metropolitan area.

Several other conventions relating to the model's specification should be mentioned. First, the length of time a stadium or arena could be considered new was drawn from earlier research about the duration of a stadium's "novelty effect." In baseball, the novelty of a new stadium was assumed to last somewhere between seven and eleven years.[25] For the purposes of this analysis, a stadium was considered new if it was less than eleven years old, that is, if the "number of new stadiums" variable (NT) increased by one for each addition to an MSA's stock of sports facilities, and decreased by one when a stadium reached eleven years of age.[26]

The novelty effect cannot be expected to be the same for each MSA, and the procedure used in this analysis was to run regressions characterizing the stadium as new for a period not longer than ten years and not shorter than five years for each city. Such a procedure served two purposes: it allowed us to determine if a statistically significant novelty effect did exist, that is, to determine whether statistical significance was related to the length of time a stadium was construed as new or novel; and it provided a range of values for the new stadium coefficients. In no instance did the specification of the duration of the novelty effect alter our findings with regard to statistical significance; that is, if the new stadium coefficient was statistically insignificant for five years, it remained insignificant for a new stadium specification of six through ten years. This finding suggests that it is not the novelty of a new stadium that is decisive in determining whether the facility induces increases in metropolitan employment measurably different from zero, but other factors, such as the city's proximity to other teams in the same league. The size of the stadium coefficient did on occasion vary by small amounts for different specifications of the length of the novelty effect; the stadium impact that is reported in tables 3-2 and 3-3 records the largest stadium coefficients. In other words, our approach was conservative; we made the strongest possible case for the stadium's contribution. The particular specification for how long a stadium was considered new, the novelty specification that yielded the largest coefficient, is identified in appendix table 3A-2.

Second, since individual cities are examined over time, the Cochrane-Orcutt iterative procedure was used to address the potential serial correlation problem.

Third, the number of teams and new stadiums are not highly correlated. In the overwhelming majority of cases, new stadiums have been or are being constructed for teams currently residing in those MSAs, or teams are taking up residence in a city that already has an appropriate

Table 3-2. Estimated Impact of Stadiums and Teams on Employment in the Amusement and Recreation Industry (SIC 79), Selected U.S. Cities[a]

City	Constant β_0	Real income ratio β_1	Leisure time ratio β_2	Population ratio β_3	Number of teams β_4	Number of new stadiums β_5	Trend β_6	R^2
Cincinnati	.38* (2.42)	−.29 (−1.83)	n.a.	.011 (.04)	.01 (1.50)	.014 (2.02)	.003** (3.36)	.71
Denver	−1.51 (−1.22)	.78 (1.32)	n.a.	2.05 (1.52)	.0347* (2.30)	−.033 (1.44)	−.01* (2.11)	.75
Detroit	1.08** (5.48)	−.37* (−2.27)	n.a.	−.10 (−.36)	n.a.	−.30 (−.44)	−.35** (−5.91)	.85
Kansas City	.31 (.27)	−.89 (−1.76)	1.01 (1.41)	−.51 (−.32)	.04* (2.50)	.01 (.72)	.00 (.24)	.33
Minneapolis	−1.72** (−3.34)	1.01** (4.89)	n.a.	2.32 (3.64)	.06 (1.86)	−.07* (−4.11)	−.003 (−1.44)	.66
New Orleans	1.91** (3.57)	−.36 (−1.32)	n.a.	−2.73** (−2.33)	−.01 (−.42)	−.02 (−1.20)	−.01** (−5.61)	.90
Pittsburgh	−.57 (−1.52)	.15 (.82)	n.a.	3.36 (1.89)	−.01 (−.72)	−.03* (−3.19)	.002 (1.0)	.40
San Diego	.023 (.80)	.05* (2.18)	n.a.	−.59** (.28)	.003* (2.08)	−.001 (.36)	−.001** (6.63)	.85
Seattle	.31 (1.03)	.16 (1.07)	n.a.	.17 (.27)	−.036** (−2.66)	.03 (1.95)	.004 (1.00)	.51
Tampa Bay	.05 (.28)	.02 (.11)	n.a.	.42 (.60)	.01 (.95)	−.01 (1.35)	−.00 (−.53)	.44

Source: Authors' calculations.
a. See the appendix to this chapter for conventions.
*Significant at the 5 percent level.
**Significant at the 1 percent level.

Table 3-3. Estimated Impact of Stadiums and Teams on Employment in the Commercial Sports Industry (SIC 794), Selected U.S. Cities[a]

City	Constant β_0	Real income ratio β_1	Leisure time ratio β_2	Population ratio β_3	Number of teams β_4	Number of new stadiums β_5	Trend β_6	R^2
Cincinnati	.31 (.97)	−.22 (−.68)	n.a.	.23 (.31)	−.01 (−.37)	.017 (1.36)	.04* (3.07)	.56
Denver	.04 (.02)	−.20 (−.17)	n.a.	.66 (.26)	.04 (1.4)	−.00 (−.00)	.004 (.74)	.47
Detroit	−.21 (−.27)	.45 (.78)	na.a	.18 (.19)	n.a.	.024 (1.11)	.01 (1.18)	.78
Kansas City	−.46 (−.63)	−.96* (−2.90)	1.77* (3.54)	−.56 (−.45)	.037* (4.01)	.029 (2.10)	.01 (2.99)	.74
Minneapolis	−1.35 (−1.73)	.95* (3.05)	n.a.	2.09** (2.13)	.01 (.23)	−.05 (1.85)	−.005 (1.57)	.23
New Orleans	2.66* (3.10)	−.79 (−1.85)	n.a.	−3.44 (−1.86)	−.03 (−1.65)	−.01 (−.59)	−.01* (−4.63)	.72
Pittsburgh	−8.07* (−5.98)	−.75 (−1.69)	n.a.	39.66* (6.55)	.07 (1.96)	−.05* (−2.57)	.06* (7.20)	.69
San Diego	.06 (.90)	−.01 (−.11)	n.a.	−.56 (1.41)	.003 (.75)	.004 (.60)	.002* (4.36)	.78
Seattle	.42 (.57)	.17 (.47)	n.a.	−.20 (−.12)	−.04 (−1.31)	.03 (.65)	.01 (.90)	.46
Tampa Bay	.68 (3.58)	−.32** (−2.15)	n.a.	−2.10* (−2.89)	.01 (.41)	−.02** (2.12)	.003* (2.88)	.45

Source: Authors' calculations.
a. See the appendix to this chapter for conventions.
*Significant at the 1 percent level.
**Significant at the 5 percent level.

Table 3-4. *Job Creation Estimates for Cities Exhibiting Statistically Significant, Positive Coefficients, Selected Years*[a]

City	Number of jobs in SIC 79 for year of event[b]	Job creation coefficient[c]	Jobs created[d]
Denver			
1960 (Broncos)[e]	3,838	.0347	133
1967 (Nuggets)	4,645	.0347	161
Kansas City[f]			
1960 (Chiefs)[e]	6,636	.04	265
1969 (Royals)	8,903	.04	356
San Diego			
1960 (Chargers)[f]	42,801	.003	128
1969 (Padres)	52,072	.003	158

Source: Authors' calculations.
a. Coefficients as represented in table 3-2.
b. Jobs created can be calculated on the basis of the year the team actually began to play in the city since the coefficient that we have estimated is based on historical data.
c. Coefficients from table 3-2.
d. *County Business Patterns* identifies "paid employees for pay period," and it is this statistic that we use for calculating our jobs created estimates. "Paid employees" does not distinguish between full- and part-time employment. The figures recorded in this table, therefore, are not to be construed as full-time equivalents.
e. Since information for employment in SIC 79 is not available for 1960, 1962 figures were used.
f. The Chiefs and the Royals operate the stadiums in which they play. See James P. Quirk, "The Quirk Study: A Close Look at the Two Proposals," *St. Louis Post Dispatch*, January 18, 1987, pp. 5i–8i. This is significant in light of 1987 SIC conventions. See note 24 for an explanation.

facility. Of the 155 changes in the professional sports industry among the thirty-five major-league cities during the thirty-year period from 1958 through 1987, only 11 of the changes combined a new team with a new stadium. In considering the number of changes for metropolitan areas individually, cities typically experienced three or four changes during the sample period for this study, 1958 through 1993.

Fourth, statistics were constructed from Bureau of Labor Statistics, *County Business Patterns* (various years). In constructing the data set, we took care to ensure consistency. Any scholar who has used metropolitan statistics over time is aware that the Department of Commerce changes its definition of a metropolis fairly frequently, as well as its SIC classification of various goods. All changes in SIC classifications were considered to ensure a uniform data set.

Fifth, although the model specifies a "leisure-time" variable $(CAWW_{i,t}/SAWW_{j,t})$, in the empirical analysis, the coefficient for the variable was reported only in the case of Kansas City, since the leisure variable improved the explanatory power of the equation only for that MSA.[27] The empirical record represented by tables 3-3 and 3-4 reflects the fact that a better fit was most often achieved when the leisure variable was excluded. This does not suggest that the leisure variable does not add anything to the analysis, but rather indicates that there are fewer observations on leisure availability by city, and the inclusion of the variable usually does not compensate for the observations lost when it was included. Kansas City was the sole exception in this regard. It should also be noted that consistent data for average hours worked per week were available for the durable goods industry only. Thus data for this industry were used as a proxy for leisure time for the city and state economies.

Empirical Results and Analysis

Tables 3-2 and 3-3 record the results for the regressions run using equation (3-1) for the ten MSAs that constitute our sample for the period 1958 through 1993 (see appendix table 3A-1).[28] Because some data are unavailable, there are 27 degrees of freedom for all cities except Kansas City. In the case of Kansas City, there were 10 degrees of freedom. This data set and empirical results are what we used to estimate the role professional sports play in determining employment in the "amusement and recreation" industry (SIC 79) and "commercial sports industry" (SIC 794).

Recall that the dependent variable for equation (3-1) was defined as the MSA's share of the state value for employment in either the amusement and recreation (SIC 79) or commercial sports industry (SIC 794). The dependent variable was specified in this way on the expectation that those same factors that account for trends in the leisure industry in both cities and states (such as demographic changes or the business cycle) separately from the independent variables specified would in part be "factored out." For example, a general downward trend in economic activity for the state imitated exactly by the city would leave the city-state ratio of overall economic activity unaltered. If leisure spending traced general economic activity for both the state and city, the ratio of city-state leisure spending would be unaffected by changes in general business conditions. That is, the effect of the business cycle would be accounted for, and there would be no need to specify those variables that determine changes in business conditions.

We had some initial expectations with regard to the signs of the coefficients for the independent variables specified in the equation. We expected a city's share of state amusement and recreation or leisure spending to vary directly with the ratio of city to state real per capita income (an income effect). Our a priori expectations were confirmed only 50 percent of the time.

With respect to the leisure variable, we had no expectations since this variable implicitly incorporates an income and substitution effect. If residents of a particular city work longer hours than the residents of the state in which the city is located, there is presumably less leisure time to consume but more money available for leisure consumption. At least in the case of Kansas City, the income effect apparently dominates the substitution effect. We expected to find that the more the state's population is concentrated in an MSA, the greater will be the concentration of state amusement and recreation (commercial sports) jobs in that city, all else equal. In a majority of cases, the population coefficient was positive.

If professional sports induces job growth, we expected a city's share of state jobs in the amusement and recreation industry (commercial sports industry) to increase with the addition of a professional sports team or the operation of a new facility. This expectation echoes the theory alluded to earlier. Professional sports must export its services to the rest of the state (region), create an import-substitution industry, or in some other way increase aggregate spending to induce an economically significant addition to the city's economy. Of the twenty sports variable coefficients in tables 3-2 and 3-3 (β_4 and β_5), nine emerged as statistically significant. Of those nine, only five exhibited a positive sign.

The relative infrequency of positive coefficients for either the team or stadium variables prompts two general observations. First, adding a professional sports team or stadium to a city's economy appears to realign leisure spending rather than adding to it and is therefore neutral with regard to job creation. Second, the fan base supporting professional sports appears to be insufficiently "foreign" to the city to contribute significantly to metropolitan economic activity. The exportation of the services of the teams or stadiums or the import substitution created is generally insufficient to induce job growth that is measurably different from zero.[29]

The presence of only one positive, statistically significant coefficient for the team variable in table 3-3 requires further explanation, given the portion of the commercial sports sector constituted by professional sports. One interpretation of these results is that in some cases the substitutions in leisure spending induced by changing a city's professional sports landscape may in large measure occur in the commercial sports sector. Research indicates that individuals and families budget a certain amount of time and money for commercial sports activities and therefore substitute spending across teams and seasons within a city.[30]

The presence of statistically insignificant or negative coefficients in table 3-2 should not be surprising. It is plausible that the realignment of leisure spending is such that no net jobs are created or that jobs are lost. To cite but one possible argument, the β_4 (number of teams) or β_5 (number of new stadiums) coefficients could be positive or negative depending on how labor-intensive and export-prone the expanding professional sports industry in a particular MSA is in relation to the contracting enterprises that constitute the leisure industry. Therefore, the negative coefficient for the stadium variable for Pittsburgh (table 3-2) or the negative team variable for Seattle (table 3-2) may imply that the stadium or team uses labor less intensively per dollar spent on its activities than the leisure activities for which it substitutes. Or, it could imply that the contracting leisure industries exported more of their product than does the expanding professional sports industry. An alternative explanation for the negative stadium coefficient in Pittsburgh is that leisure time spent at Three Rivers Stadium translated into fewer dollars (and fewer jobs) than the leisure activities for which the stadium substitutes, including those at the stadium replaced by Three Rivers Stadium.[31]

Furthermore, the health of the MSA's economy may well determine the sign and size of the stadium coefficient. For example, a fully employed MSA may well compel a more complete substitution of employment within the amusement and recreation industry than an economy characterized by slack demand for labor. Indeed, there is not even a guarantee that the construction of the sports facility will enhance the MSA's economy. During the construction phase of the project, it may be that in-migration of construction labor is necessary to build the facility if the MSA is at or near full employment. In such instances, funds that MSA residents provide for stadium construction may well be repatriated by the migrating labor to their residences, some of which may be outside the MSA. In this scenario the balanced-budget multiplier may well be significantly less than one (see note 12).

The information recorded in tables 3-2 and 3-3 indicates that of the four positive, statistically significant coefficients for the number of teams and new stadiums, three were significant at the 5 percent level, while only one was significant at the 1 percent level. Of the five negative, statistically significant coefficients for the number of teams and new stadiums, four were significant at the 1 percent level, while only one was significant at the 5 percent level. In all, only 10 percent of the coefficients (2.5 percent at the 1 percent level of significance) indicated a positive correlation between number of teams or new stadiums and employment in either the amusement and recreation industry (SIC 79) or the commercial sports industry (SIC 794). By contrast, 12.5 percent of the coefficients (10 percent at the 1 percent level of significance) indicated a negative correlation between number of teams or new stadiums and employment in SIC 79 or SIC 794.

Table 3-4 summarizes our estimates of job creation for those cities in which there was a statistically significant, positive coefficient for either the team or stadium variable. The largest positive, statistically significant β_4 coefficient (number of teams) for the amusement and recreation industry was for Kansas City. Indeed, it is noteworthy that statistically significant, positive team coefficients were found only in cities west of the Mississippi. It may be that western cities in the United States are more geographically isolated in a sports sense (no other team is present within several hundred miles) and are therefore more likely to have a regional following. In other words, these cities are more likely to export their sports services and thus add to aggregate spending in the city. If we multiply the Kansas City β_4 coefficient by the number of amusement and recreation jobs in the state of Missouri, the Kansas City Chiefs added 265 jobs to the Kansas City economy when the Chiefs began play in that city in 1962 (the Chiefs played in Dallas in 1960 and 1961). The Royals, on the other hand, contributed 356 jobs to the Kansas City economy when they initiated play in 1969. Using an analogous procedure, we estimated that sports teams in San Diego and Denver accounted for less than 200 jobs each when they started out. These results conform to the projections for job creation based on net as opposed to gross spending changes initiated by sports. (We attempted to locate economic impact studies for the Chiefs and Royals that projected job creation from the adoption of the teams; unfortunately, we were unable to secure or even determine if formal economic impact studies were performed.) Recall, however, that these estimates are calculated for only the statistically significant cases in which sports exert a positive impact. Such cases are atypical. It is also important to note that we are measuring metropolitan job creation, which may well come at the expense of jobs elsewhere in the state or adjacent areas in neighboring states.

To help put a stadium's job creation potential in sharper profile, consider how many jobs a $250 million investment (the public sector's contribution for the new stadium for the Arizona Diamondbacks) in the stock market could support assuming a real return of 8 percent, or $20 million, a year. If we assume that average annual wages plus benefits equal $40,000 ($25,000), the stock market investment would support 500 (800) people. These job creation figures exceed by a substantial amount those estimated in conjunction with investments in stadiums.

Conclusions and Policy Implications

The usual justification for public subsidies for professional sports is that teams and stadiums induce economic expansion, increase spending, create jobs and provide other positive externalities. This view can be challenged on both quantitative and qualitative grounds. For jobs to be created within a metropolis, professional sports would have to either induce an increase in aggregate spending on city goods and services or induce spending shifts toward industries with a more labor-intensive character. In general, the results of this study do not support a positive correlation between professional sports and job creation. This finding suggests that professional sports realign economic activity within a city's leisure industry rather than adding to it.

Furthermore, there is evidence to indicate that creating jobs through subsidies for sports is inefficient and costly. In addition, the jobs created can be characterized as low-paying, and the present value of the return on a city's investment is likely to be quite low in comparison with investment alternatives such as a subvention for the location of an industrial park or department store. An important distinction between a city vying for one of these enterprises and one negotiating to attract or retain a sports franchise, perhaps through a commitment to construct a new playing facility for it, is that professional sports leagues are cartels, and as such they have the power to limit the supply of teams. This tilts the financial leverage to the team or league and is yet another reason why the benefits of a team or stadium are so low for the metropolitan areas involved. In other words, the expected returns have been captured by the cartel in the form of the concessions they demand. (An automobile assembly plant, such as the Mercedes plant cited earlier in the chapter, falls in the middle of the competition-to-cartel spectrum, and thus a city's financial exposure will be greater for an auto plant than a department store but less than for a professional sports franchise.) Only a change in the fundamental structure of our professional sports industries can level the economic playing field for cities.

Not only can a sports cartel extract most of the potential benefits from a city in the form of subvention concessions, with the end result being a low rate of return on the city's investment and few net jobs, as we have demonstrated, but also the interaction of these cartels across leagues may reduce potential gains even further or turn them into losses. For example, the fact that the NFL and MLB support team demands for separate instead of shared playing facilities—or even require this as a condition for awarding an expansion franchise—means that cities with both football and baseball teams now must have two stadiums, each used a small fraction of the potential "commercial year." This also reduces the effective "half-life" of any stadium by employing additional interleague pressures for the latest technological or revenue-generating features. (The cartel also dangles the prospect of a future All-Star game or Super Bowl, complete with an impact study showing the millions of dollars to be gained by the host community, as a further enticement to cooperate.) In addition, unlike a service station that can be converted into a dry cleaning establishment or convenience store if demand conditions change, a football or baseball stadium has few alternative commercial uses, which makes a team's threat to leave town more credible. Cost overruns that have to be absorbed by the city instead of the franchise, or financial exposure if ticket sales or attendance goals are not met, or other such problems are all too common features of most sports facility contractual arrangements. All of these factors combine to put cities at a tremendous disadvantage in their quest for economic development when they have to square off against a professional sports team and the parent cartel, and against the "parents" in a related league as well. Only a change in the fundamental structure of our professional sports industries can level the economic playing field for cities.

Our results suggest that professional sports have been oversold by professional sports boosters as a catalyst for economic development. Regional economic models, even the sophisticated models constructed by Regional Economic Models Incorporated, are potentially misleading if those estimating the impact of professional sports do not conduct their analysis through general rather than partial equilibrium systems. Cities should be aware that the professional sports industry is relatively small and that the associated substitutions in leisure spending can mute an impact identified in a partial equilibrium framework. As a consequence, cities should be wary of committing substantial portions of their capital budgets to building stadiums and otherwise subsidizing professional sports in the expectation of strong income and job growth. Professional sports are not a major catalyst for economic development.

Appendix

Table 3A-1. *Ten Sample Cities with Their Counties*

City	Counties
Cincinnati	Clermont, Ohio; Hamilton, Ohio; Warren, Ohio; Boone, Kentucky; Campbell, Kentucky; Kenton, Kentucky; Dearborn, Indiana.
Denver	Adams, Colorado; Arapahoe, Colorado; Denver, Colorado; Douglas, Colorado; Jefferson, Colorado; Boulder, Colorado; Clear Creek, Colorado; Gilpin, Colorado.
Detroit	Lapeer, Michigan; Livingston, Michigan; Macomb, Michigan; Oakland, Michigan; St. Clair, Michigan; Wayne, Michigan.
Kansas City	Cass, Missouri; Clay, Missouri; Jackson, Missouri; Platte, Missouri; Ray, Missouri; Johnson, Kansas; Wyandotte, Kansas.
Minneapolis	Anoka, Minnesota; Carver, Minnesota; Chisago, Minnesota; Dakota, Minnesota; Hennepin, Minnesota; Isanti, Minnesota; Ramsey, Minnesota; Scott, Minnesota; Washington, Minnesota; Wright, Minnesota.
New Orleans	Jefferson, Louisiana; Orleans, Louisiana; St. Bernard, Louisiana; St. Tammany, Louisiana.
Pittsburgh	Allegheny, Pennsylvania; Washington, Pennsylvania; Westmoreland, Pennsylvania; Beaver, Pennsylvania.
San Diego	San Diego, California.
Seattle	King, Washington; Snohomish, Washington; Pierce, Washington.
Tampa Bay	Hillsborough, Florida; Pasco, Florida; Pinellas, Florida.

Table 3A-2. *Length of Novelty Effect for Ten Sample Cities*

City	Length of novelty (years)[a]
Cincinnati	8
Denver	7
Detroit	7
Kansas City	8
Minneapolis	7
New Orleans	7
Pittsburgh	10
San Diego	10
Seattle	7
Tampa Bay	7

Source: Authors' calculations.
a. Regressions were run for each city using different specifications for the length of the novelty effect. The results recorded in tables 3-2 and 3-3 in the text were consistent with the maximum value for the job creation attributable to the team or the stadium.

Notes

1. Other arguments may include the production of positive externalities, such as reductions in crime or increases in civic pride or unity, or increased tax revenues derived from a higher sales volume. The externality argument is beyond the scope of this chapter, though it should be noted that it is virtually never mentioned by proponents of sports subsidies as a principal reason for their position, but almost as a "yes, but . . ." response to criticisms that such subsidies are poor financial investments. With regard to the claim for increased retail sales and tax revenue, it is implicitly discussed here in the remarks on employment that would theoretically generate sales and taxes.

2. Richard S. Conway and William B. Beyers, "Seattle Mariners Baseball Club Economic Impact," Conway and Associates, August 1994, processed.

3. Robert A. Baade, "Professional Sports as Catalysts for Metropolitan Economic Development." *Journal of Urban Affairs,* vol. 18, no. 1 (1996), pp. 1–17.

4. Erle Norton, "Football at Any Cost: One City's Mad Chase for an NFL Franchise," *Wall Street Journal,* October 13, 1993, p. A1.

5. Dennis Zimmerman, "Tax-Exempt Bonds and the Economics of Professional Sports Stadiums," *CRS Report for Congress,* May 29, 1996.

6. Baade, "Professional Sports as Catalysts."

7. In this regard, a sports stadium, especially a football-only facility, could actually retard economic development in the immediate area because it is closed so much of the time. Complementary commercial activity would be unlikely to gravitate to an "anchor" with such limited hours of operation.

8. The state-of-the-art models used by subsidy advocates have been provided by Regional Economic Models Incorporated (REMI). REMI is located in Amherst, Massachusetts.

9. More than half of the cities that have professional sports stadiums are planning, or have started to build, new facilities or have plans for renovating current stadiums and arenas. See Kerry Johnson and Mark Belko, "Super Stadiums: Bait of Burden," *Pittsburgh Post-Gazette,* October 29, 1995, p. A1. The cost to taxpayers of facilities constructed so far

in the 1990s has been well in excess of $4 billion. Robert A. Baade and Allen R. Sanderson, "Cities under Seige: How the Changing Financial Structure of Professional Sports Is Putting Cities at Risk and What to Do about It," in Wallace Hendricks, ed., *Advances in the Economics of Sports,* vol. 2 (Greenwich, Conn.: JAI Press, 1997), pp. 77–114.

10. See, for example, Benjamin A. Okner, "Subsidies of Stadiums and Arenas," in Roger G. Noll, *Government and the Sports Business* (Brookings, 1974), pp. 325–47; Robert A. Baade and Richard F. Dye, "The Impact of Stadiums and Professional Sports on Metropolitan Area Development," *Growth and Change,* Spring, 1990; Dean Baim, *The Sports Stadium and a Municipal Investment* (Westport, Conn.: Greenwood Press, 1992); James P. Quirk, "The Quirk Study: A Close Look at the Two Proposals," *St. Louis Post Dispatch,* January 18, 1987, pp. 5i–8i; Mark S. Rosentraub and others, "Sport and Downtown Development Strategy: If You Build It, Will Jobs Come?" *Journal of Urban Affairs,* vol. 16, no. 3 (1994), pp. 228–39.

11. Edwin S. Mills, "The Misuse of Regional Economic Models," *Cato Journal,* vol. 13 (Spring/Summer 1993), pp. 29–39.

12. Many economic impact studies use what amounts to a "government expenditure" multiplier to estimate the economic impact. When taxes are used in estimating the economic impact during the construction phase of the project, a "balanced-budget" multiplier, or something close to it, should be used since the stadium-inspired tax increase reduces consumer spending. Theoretically, the size of the multiplier during both the construction and operational phase of the stadium will be determined by the sum of the spending increases (injections) and decreases (leakages) triggered by the facility.

13. John F. Zipp, "The Economic Impact of the Baseball Strike of 1994," *Urban Affairs Review,* vol. 32 (November 1996), pp. 157–85.

14. Conway and Beyers, "Seattle Mariners."

15. Robert A. Baade and Richard F. Dye, "An Analysis of the Economic Rationale for Public Subsidization of Sports Stadiums," *Annals of Regional Science* vol. 22 (July 1988), pp. 37–47.

16. E. S. Browning and Helena Cooper, "Ante Up: States' Bidding War over Mercedes Plant Made for Costly Chase; Alabama Won the Business, but Some Wonder If It Also Gave Away the Farm, Will Image Now Improve?" *Wall Street Journal,* November 23, 1993, p. A1.

17. Allen R. Myerson, "O Governor, Won't You Buy Me a Mercedes Plant?" *New York Times,* September 1, 1996, sec. 3, p. 1.

18. Browning and Cooper, "Ante Up," p. A1.

19. Deloitte & Touche, Arizona Office of Sports Development, "Economic Impact Study of a Major League Baseball Stadium and Franchise," December 1993, processed.

20. Since a sales tax is being used to subsidize the sports infrastructure for the MLB Arizona Diamondbacks, some of the expense will be borne by people outside Arizona. That does not change the fact that Arizona citizens are paying an extraordinary amount of money for each job created through this investment in professional sports.

21. Robert L. Hall, *Public Works as a Countercyclical Tool,* Hearings before the Joint Economic Committee, 96 Cong. 1 sess. (GPO, June 17, 1980), p. 9.

22. "City" as used here refers to the metropolitan statistical area (MSA). Detroit, for example, is the Detroit MSA and not the city of Detroit; the city of Detroit represents a part of the Detroit MSA.

23. A principal reason for concentrating on this one sector instead of the aggregate metropolitan economy is that a sports franchise is, in terms of employment or retail sales revenues, a relatively small business, on a par with a medium-size department store in the central city. Full-time employment for all twenty-eight MLB teams is less than 2,000,

including 700 players. And baseball spending is about 30 cents for every $1,000 of GDP. See Allen R. Sanderson, "Bottom-Line Drive," *University of Chicago Magazine,* June 1995. In addition, professional sports franchises, with few exceptions (such as the Green Bay Packers), are located in multibillion-dollar economies; thus it would be virtually impossible to detect any overall impact of job creation attributable to a team or facility. By limiting our study to the most appropriate employment subcategory, we are looking for an impact in the area in which it is most likely to occur.

24. The *Standard Industrial Classification Manual, 1987* (p. 381), specifies that "stadiums and athletic fields are included only if the operator is actually engaged in the promotion of athletic events. Establishments primarily engaged in operating stadiums and athletic fields are classified in Real Estate, Industry Group 651." However, the trend at present and in the relatively recent past has been toward teams managing the facility in which they play because it is profitable for them to do so. Furthermore, the Tax Reform Act of 1986 creates an incentive for cities to offer more favorable leases for teams to qualify for tax-exempt bonds for financing stadium construction (the 10 percent rules). See Zimmerman, "Tax-Exempt Bonds." One aspect of a more favorable lease is to allow the team to function as the stadium operator.

25. Roger G. Noll, "Attendance and Price Setting," in Roger G. Noll, ed., *Government and the Sports Business* (Brookings, 1974), pp. 115–57.

26. Accepting a novelty effect of this duration means that it is impossible to include several of the newest arenas in our analysis, and some critics might argue that Camden Yards, Jacobs Field, Coors Field, and the TWA Dome for the St. Louis Rams constitute a new generation of stadiums that, unlike others noted in this study, will have sizable impacts on those metropolitan areas. Two points are worth noting. First, inasmuch as a large body of literature, now including our analysis, points overwhelmingly to the insignificance of sports franchises and stadiums in terms of being catalysts for economic development, the burden of proof that there is another set of experiences for which this is not the case clearly lies with those who make that claim. Second, there is some evidence that the novelty effect may be shortening, not lengthening: 1996 baseball attendance at Skydome, the Ballpark at Arlington, and the New Comiskey Park (three of the newer stadiums) is off in relation to MLB as a whole. When New Comiskey Park opened in 1991, attendance that year averaged 36,677 (capacity is 44,700). Despite a strong team on the field, including a pennant-winning team in 1993 and one that was leading its division on August 11, 1994, when the players' strike ended the season, White Sox attendance has fallen every year since the new park opened. Per-game attendance in 1996 was 42 percent lower than in 1991.

Failure to control for other factors, such as team quality, may also lead to erroneous notions about the drawing capacity of a new facility. In Cleveland, for example, the Indians play to packed houses in Jacobs Field, but right next door in Gund Arena, which opened at the same time as Jacobs Field, the Cavaliers showed the largest percentage drop in the NBA between the 1994–95 and 1995–96 seasons. See Noll, "Attendance and Price Setting."

27. The leisure variable identified in this analysis was one of many possible specifications that could have been used. Unemployment in the MSA might have been another, but such a statistic does not provide as good a proxy, in our opinion, for the work/leisure choices or disposable income that we surmise correlates with the demand for professional sports entertainment. Since the variable added to the explanatory power of the equation only in the case of Kansas City, it may well be that there are better ways of representing leisure, or that leisure availability varies across MSAs and states insufficiently to influence the value of the dependent variables. It is our sense that the latter interpretation applies.

28. In selecting cities for the sample, we sought to meet certain criteria. First the city had to host a team in one of the four major professional sports: baseball, basketball,

football, or hockey. Second, the timing of the stadium construction or the adoption of a team had to allow for a sufficient number of observations before and after the change in the professional sports industry in the metropolis to permit an evaluation of how the economic landscape changed as a consequence. Third, a sufficient amount of data by county and SIC 79 and 794 had to exist to permit valid statistical analysis. Fourth, it was hoped that the metropolises that met the first three criteria would constitute a reasonable geographic cross section of major urban centers in the United States. It should also be noted that since our aim was to determine how professional sports contributed to job growth in various cities, we saw no need to pool the observations for all metropolises represented in the sample and run a pooled regression.

29. We made no attempt to distinguish the job creation induced by the various professional sports or to differentiate the economic impact of the first stadium/arena built by an MSA from that of the second, third, fourth, and beyond. A greater incidence of statistically significant results would have compelled a more systematic analysis in this regard. Further research did not appear to be promising in light of the substantial substitution effect that appeared to underlie our empirical results. We have no reason to suspect that the substitution effect will not mitigate the economic impact of new arenas or stadiums for any of the sports, no matter how many facilities exist in the MSA. However, we would not discourage others from extending our research in the ways implied here.

30. Noll, "Attendance and Price Setting"; Baade and Dye, "The Impact of Stadiums and Professional Sports." Although beyond the scope of this paper, a complementary area for analysis would be to look for a similar impact within an urban area if patrons of the arts, when faced with a new subscription series or museum option, make similar trade-offs between theater, ballet, symphony, and opera tickets and an exciting exhibition at one museum. This could even occur across entertainment/recreation boundaries: recent evidence shows that January 1996 was the lowest attendance month ever recorded by Phoenix area art and cultural museums, a period in which Phoenix was the host city for Super Bowl XXX. In January 1994 attendance at the Phoenix Art Museum was 13,415; in January 1995 it increased to 15,842; but during January 1996, the month in which Super Bowl XXX and related activities to that game took place, attendance was only 7,551. In January 1997 attendance was 20,031. For the Heard Museum, renowned for its historical and cultural exhibits on the Southwest, attendance for January 1994, 1995, 1996, and 1997 was 14,297, 17,249, 14,044, and 16,109, respectively. (Data furnished to the authors by these museums.)

31. A word of caution is advisable at this point. Data on commercial sports are inconsistently provided. In some years for some counties, data are not disclosed, and the Department of Commerce notes on occasion that the sensitive nature of the data precludes disclosure. We can only speculate as to what that means, but for the scholar attempting to develop a uniform data set, it makes the data, and results derived therefrom, suspect.

4

SUBSIDIZING STADIUMS

Who Benefits, Who Pays?

DENNIS ZIMMERMAN

 By now, the message of this volume should be apparent: the additional labor and capital income a community obtains from a sports-related facility—whether a stadium, arena, or training center—generally is inadequate to justify public subsidy of that facility. This financial performance is not necessarily an indication of an incorrect economic decision. As explained in chapter 2, to ascertain whether a stadium is worthwhile, one must add public and private consumption benefits to these income-based benefits, and must weigh who receives the total benefits against who pays for the stadium subsidy. It may well be that the dominant political coalition's (or the median voter's) share of these total benefits exceeds its share of the local costs of financing.

Who benefits from the facility and who pays for it depend upon how people use their income and leisure (patterns of private consumption and public consumption) and the sources of people's incomes (wages, dividends, capital gains, and so on). Rarely does the decisionmaking behind the construction of a stadium or other facility include much serious discussion of its true financial impact and distributional patterns between sports fans and nonfans, high income and low income, capital income and wages, races, city and suburbs. Much of the information provided to citizens about the financial impact and distributional patterns often is incorrect or misleading. Stadium proponents usually overstate the magnitude of the income-based benefits and frequently assert that the facility will cost taxpayers nothing.

Under the benefit principle of taxation, each taxpayer's financial contribution to the provision of a publicly provided service should be a function of the benefits received from that service. This principle implies a system of tax prices that is equitable and that promotes economic efficiency by discouraging over- or underprovision of public services. The benefit principle is a particularly appropriate guideline to follow when most of the benefits accruing to the dominant political coalition are consumed privately rather than collectively, as is likely to be the case for professional sports.

This chapter examines the public financing of professional sports facilities—referred to as stadiums here—in the context of the benefit principle of taxation. The analysis is based on the experience of twenty-one stadiums. The central concerns are which groups of taxpayers benefit from the stadium, what size of local public subsidy and of federal subsidy is provided by the exemption of the interest income on stadium debt from federal income tax, and which groups of local and federal taxpayers pay for the subsidies.

Current evidence suggests that the dominant local political coalition probably manages to obtain substantially greater benefits than costs from publicly financed stadiums. Yet sufficient options for raising local taxes and reducing local spending are available so that policymakers could structure the incidence of stadium finances to approximate more closely the incidence of stadium benefits than generally is the case. Obviously, local governments have chosen not to do this. Because local governments have little leverage against the market power of the professional sports leagues, subsidies are likely to continue. Nevertheless, the federal government could restructure tax-exempt bond law to reduce the federal subsidy and encourage local governments to rely more on the benefit principle of taxation.

The Incidence of Economic Benefits and Costs

To implement the benefit principle of taxation, revenue must be raised or spending on other programs decreased in such a manner that the distribution of stadium costs matches the distribution of stadium benefits. The distribution of most stadium benefits is beyond the control of local officials. It is logical, therefore, to begin with the distribution of stadium benefits, which can serve to guide local officials in their choice among alternative revenue sources for financing the stadium.

Benefits

Each taxpayer's benefits depend upon the uses of income and leisure (consumption) and the sources of income (wages, dividends, capital gains, and so on). I begin with the uses of income and leisure. Consumption of professional sports is essentially a private good. A stadium is an exclusionary device, one that denies private consumption benefits to those who are unwilling to pay for the privilege of viewing the game. (Those watching television or listening to radio must "pay" by being subjected to commercials, and some also must pay cable fees.) Thus it seems reasonable to conclude that viewers enjoy substantial private consumption benefits (including consumer surplus) not available to those who ignore the games.[1] Furthermore, the majority of these beneficiaries are likely to live in the surrounding metropolitan area and region and therefore outside the local jurisdiction in which the stadium is located.

The design of new stadiums tends to focus on added luxury and prime seating at premium prices, and on marketing these seats to those with the means to purchase season tickets for individual use or business entertainment. Even viewing games on television may require cable or satellite payments. At the same time, teams decry their inability to attract minorities and families to the stadium. All this suggests that the incidence of private consumption benefits is becoming more and more concentrated among the middle- and upper-income segments of the local population and business community. If minorities and low-income households are concentrated in the central cities, then a substantial portion of central city residents receive relatively few private consumption benefits.

The public consumption benefits provided by stadiums arise from the satisfaction people get from living in a "big league" town, from having another topic of conversation that is common to most citizens, from reading about its successes and failures in the newspaper, and the like.[2] These benefits have the potential to be large in the aggregate because no citizen can be excluded from their consumption, and one citizen's consumption does not reduce the consumption available to other citizens.

However, these benefits probably are relatively small for each individual, particularly when they are compared with the magnitude of the private consumption benefits accruing to a devoted fan who buys season tickets or a luxury box. One might argue that these benefits are valued equally by all individuals, although a better case can be made that fans, and particularly those who view games, are likely to value them more.

Some citizens also benefit from the sources side of their income in that their employment or business sales are directly related to sports. The profusion of luxury suites for business entertainment serves to increase the share of these types of benefits: that is, a main (if not the only) purpose of buying these seats is to increase sales or worker productivity in the business that pays for the tickets. These benefits arise from taxpayers' sources of income rather than from their uses of income. These economic benefits are also emphasized in the studies that stadium proponents use to lobby for public subsidy of stadiums. Indeed, the only benefits for which they estimate dollar values are those pertaining to increased income. As discussed elsewhere in this book, these studies tend to overstate local economic benefits because they draw on optimistic assumptions about the increase in additional spending generated by a stadium. Invariably, these studies fail to compare the stadium's benefits with the sources-of-income benefits available from alternative local investments.

A case in point is the benefits assessment prepared by the Maryland Department of Business and Economic Development (part of the state's executive branch) for the stadium Maryland is constructing for the National Football League's Baltimore Ravens. Optimistic assumptions about increased spending led the department to estimate economic benefits of $111 million and 1,394 additional jobs (table 4-1). Because the stadium proved to be politically controversial, these estimates were reviewed by the Maryland Department of Fiscal Services (part of the state's legislative branch). More realistic assumptions produced the much lower figures of $33 million and 534 additional jobs. Thus Maryland taxpayers had the unusual advantage of more realistic, publicly available information about the magnitude of the economic benefits available to taxpayers.

The last row of table 4-1 makes a rough attempt to compare the economic benefits of the stadium with the economic benefits from the best alternative public investment or tax reduction. The Economic Development Department estimates returns to the state will be 1,394 full-time "jobs created," which amounts to a cost of $127,000 per job created by the stadium. In contrast, the 5,200 full-time jobs created or retained

Table 4-1. *Assumptions and Opportunity Cost in Assessing Economic Impact of Baltimore's Football Stadium*

Source of estimate	Economic benefits (millions of dollars)	Jobs created	Cost of investment (millions of dollars)	Cost per job (thousands of dollars)
Department of Business and Economic Development	110.6	1,394	177	127
Department of Fiscal Services	33.0	534	177	331
Sunny Day Fund Development Activities	n.a.	5,200	32.5	6.25

Sources: Maryland Department of Business and Economic Development, *The Impact of a Baltimore Pro Football Team on the Economy of Maryland* (1995); Maryland Department of Fiscal Services, *Estimated Impact of a Football Stadium at Camden Yards* (1996); and Office of the Governor, *Summary of Legislation Proposed by Parris N. Glendening, Governor, Kathleen Kennedy Townsend, Lt. Governor,* 1996 Session of the Maryland General Assembly, n.d.

n.a. Not available.

by the state's Sunny Day Fund for economic development have cost Maryland's taxpayers $32.5 million, or $6,250 per job. As an income generator or a job creator, the stadium appears to be a poor investment compared with Maryland's Sunny Day Fund. The stadium will impose losses on Maryland taxpayers in comparison with alternative investments.

Although in the aggregate these sources-of-income benefits are small and perhaps even negative, they are positive and might be large for some individuals and businesses. The history of state and local debt finance in the nineteenth and early twentieth centuries is replete with examples of bond issuance for canals, railroads, and land development schemes at least partly motivated by a desire to spur real estate development and values.[3] For many cities, stadium building seems to be the modern-day counterpart to railroads. Chambers of commerce, downtown business associations, and real estate boards are frequent proponents. Bringing more activity into downtown has a positive impact on downtown real estate values. The early bird gets the worm, and the capital gains. Chapter 8 presents the theoretical argument that the economic benefits from stadiums are likely to be capitalized into property values. Most of these sources-of-income benefits probably accrue to the better-off segment of the population.

Costs

As with benefits, each taxpayer's share of costs depends on the uses of income and leisure and the sources of income. The benefits discussion provides some guidance for choosing financing options. First, because both private and public consumption benefits are enjoyed by taxpayers in all jurisdictions within the metropolitan area, the tax base should cover the entire geographic attendance area. This principle is particularly important if the stadium is located in a central city, because attendance patterns suggest that minorities and the poor, who constitute a substantial share of central city residents, receive relatively few consumption benefits. Second, the largest share of subsidy costs probably should be paid for by those who receive private benefits (and substantial consumer surplus) from viewing the games, which argues for a substantial ticket tax or a tax on other stadium-related revenue.

Third, most citizens probably attach some value to the public consumption benefits from the stadium, which might seem to argue for a broadly based tax that touches all citizens, such as a property tax. If these benefits are valued much more by those who view the games, however, one might wish to consider additional stadium-related user charges, such as a higher ticket tax and a tax on cable TV fees.[4]

Fourth, gains from the sources side of income are probably fairly concentrated among real estate interests, those who receive the few jobs created, and businesses using their luxury boxes for business entertainment. This might argue for a special taxing district if substantial appreciation in property values is expected, and for an additional tax on tickets associated with luxury boxes to account for their source-of-income benefits (as distinct from their use-of-income benefits).

How consistent is stadium financing with the benefit principle of taxation? Although an evaluation of all stadium financing deals is beyond the scope of this discussion, the dimensions of the issue can be illustrated with reference to several. In the case of the Metrodome, Minneapolis used four revenue sources to finance the local subsidy for this project: a 10 percent ticket tax, a 2.5–3.0 percent tax on hotels/motels located in Minneapolis, a 2.0 percent tax on liquor sales in Minneapolis, and the parking revenue from existing city parking garages (see chapter 7). Did this financing package comport with the benefit principle?

—The ticket tax seems consistent with the benefit principle. It is collected from citizens who are the primary beneficiaries of the stadium, and it is not geographically restricted.

—The hotel/motel tax probably is not consistent with the benefit principle. To the extent the tax applies to rooms occupied by those attending Metrodome events, it is consistent because the tax is shared by hotel/

motel owners who benefit through measured sales and hotel/motel users who derive consumption benefits. But this desirable attribute is probably more than offset by three distortionary factors introduced by the tax. First, the tax is restricted geographically: it applies only in Minneapolis. No tax is paid by renters and owners of rooms located outside Minneapolis that receive stadium-related patronage. Second, renters and owners of rooms located in Minneapolis pay tax for patronage that is not stadium related. Third, the tax exports some of the financing burden beyond the political decisionmaking unit.

—The liquor tax fails the benefit principle. Neither the private nor the public consumption benefits seem to be related to liquor consumption. And if liquor consumption was so related, it would fail because it applies only in Minneapolis. Perhaps inappropriate "sin" taxes are adopted because they tend to rouse little organized opposition.

—Ceding revenue from city-owned parking garages is more difficult to judge. A great deal depends on how the city responds to this revenue loss. If the city simply reduces spending, the incidence of the tax depends on who benefited from the spending that was eliminated. If the revenue is replaced, it depends on the incidence of the source of replacement revenue. In any case, ceding a revenue source makes it much more difficult for the citizens to estimate the distribution of the subsidy unless the city's response to the reduced revenue is made explicit.

In summary, only one element of the Metrodome financing package is clearly consistent with the benefit principle: the ticket tax. Two omissions from the financing package are noteworthy. None of these revenue sources are related to the public consumption benefits that stadium proponents claim are enjoyed by all citizens. If previous arguments about the existence and relative size of public consumption are correct, such a revenue source should be part of the financing package, albeit not the major part. In a prior unsuccessful effort to build a stadium, downtown Minneapolis business interests, perhaps recognizing that they would benefit disproportionately, offered to create a special downtown taxing district to assume some liability for losses that might be incurred by the stadium. Had this idea been implemented when the stadium finally received approval, the financing package would have been more consistent with the benefit principle.

A few financing options used in other stadium projects deserve some mention. The Baltimore Ravens football stadium and the proposed Northern Virginia baseball stadium are to be financed in part by state lottery revenue. The claim has been made by proponents that the lottery revenue costs Maryland and Virginia taxpayers nothing. This is, of course, misinformation designed to obscure the incidence of stadium finance. The incidence depends upon several factors. Those who play the lottery are spread across the entire state and pay an implicit tax. This implicit tax is regressive in that lower-income people tend to spend a higher proportion of their income on the lottery than do higher-income people.[5] Thus the distribution of the tax is not consistent with either the geographic or income distribution of private and public consumption benefits. And if the lottery is already in existence and the money is being spent on other public services, some citizens suffer a loss of benefits from these forgone services. This means lottery financing entirely ignores any attempt to tax those who benefit from the sources side of income.

The primary financing source for the proposed Milwaukee Brewers stadium is a five-county sales tax. This tax does have the advantage of trying to target the primary geographic attendance area. But it is also regressive, is not focused on the private or public consumption beneficiaries, and makes no effort to tax those who benefit from the sources side of income.

For most stadium deals, the distribution of the financial costs among citizens does not seem to be consistent with the distribution of the benefits. Recently, two additional sources of revenue seem more promising: personal seat licenses (PSLs) and licensing arrangements such as naming and pouring rights. PSLs ask consumers and businesses that derive the most benefits from a sports team (as indicated by the fact that they buy the most expensive tickets) to finance the stadium. License fees ask businesses to pay for the right to profit from an association with the stadium. Thus both sources of revenue are consistent with the benefits principle. Indeed, because they are voluntary payments, not mandatory taxes, these revenues are assured of being paid by beneficiaries.

The Federal Subsidy of Stadiums

An important factor in the local decision to subsidize a stadium is that a substantial share of the public subsidy is paid by federal, not local, taxpayers. This federal subsidy arises because some portion of the local government's debt financing for the stadium is in the form of bonds whose interest income is exempt from federal income taxes. This exemption causes the interest rate on these tax-exempt bonds to be lower than the interest rate on taxable bonds of equivalent risk. Thus stadiums financed with tax-exempt bonds have lower interest costs than if they were financed with taxable private debt. These lower interest payments are paid for by federal taxpayers in the form of forgone federal tax receipts from the interest income that would have been taxed had taxable debt been used to finance the stadium.[6] How important is this federal subsidy?

The Size and Share of the Federal Subsidy

Private ownership of a stadium would require a rental payment at least equal to the sum of fixed costs (depreciation of buildings and equipment, a market rate of return on invested capital, and property taxes) plus operating expenses. This market-based approach was used in an earlier study to estimate the annual subsidies received in 1989 by users of twenty-one publicly financed stadiums with forty-year useful lives.[7] The results are presented in the first five columns of table 4-2. Of these stadiums, Lambeau Field opened first, in 1957 (column 1), and the Orlando and Miami Arenas opened last, in 1988. The original cost of each stadium is presented in column 2. Column 3 contains estimates of the fixed cost that would have been incurred in 1989 had the stadiums been privately financed (depreciation and property taxes both based on replacement cost, plus a pre-tax real return on equity). Column 4 contains estimates of the public authority's operating income or loss (revenue minus variable cost) in 1989.[8] This operating income (loss) is deducted from (added to) fixed costs to obtain the total public subsidy in column 5.

These one-year subsidies totaled $171.6 million in 1989 and are quite substantial for some stadiums. That year users of the Superdome received a subsidy of approximately $40.0 million;[9] the Orlando Arena, $14.7 million; the Cincinnati Riverfront Stadium, $11.6 million; and the Kansas City Arrowhead Stadium, the Hoosier Dome, and the Seattle Kingdome, each about $10.7 million. At the other end of the scale, users of Green Bay's Lambeau Field and the L.A. Sports Arena received subsidies of $174 thousand and $451 thousand, respectively.

In order to calculate the federal share of this *annual* total subsidy, it is first necessary to calculate the interest savings for local taxpayers (the value of the federal subsidy) over the *lifetime* of each stadium. I illustrate this lifetime subsidy with a hypothetical $225 million stadium financed 100 percent with thirty-year tax-exempt bonds rather than with the av-

Table 4-2. *Federal and Local Subsidies to Users of Selected Publicly Owned Stadiums, 1989*
Thousands of dollars

Stadium	(1) Year opened	(2) Original cost	(3) Fixed cost[a]	(4) Net operating income	(5) Total public subsidy	(6) Interest rate spread (percentage points)[b]	(7) Maximum federal subsidy[c] Dollars	(8) Percentage of total
Green Bay Lambeau Field	1957	969	324	150	174	0.76	5	2.9
L.A. Sports Arena	1959	5,000	1,385	934	451	1.03	41	9.2
Atlanta-Fulton County Coliseum	1964	18,000	5,728	(1,478)	7,206	1.29	237	3.3
Anaheim Stadium	1966	24,000	7,290	5,605	1,685	1.37	346	20.5
San Diego Jack Murphy Stadium	1967	26,000	7,835	(64)	7,899	1.33	365	4.6
Salt Lake City Salt Palace	1969	17,000	4,800	(639)	5,439	2.05	363	6.7
Cincinnati Riverfront Stadium	1970	45,000	11,676	118	11,558	2.09	968	8.4
Kansas City Arrowhead Stadium	1972	53,000	13,286	2,599	10,687	2.80	1,469	13.7
Atlanta Omni	1972	17,000	3,848	1,130	2,718	2.80	471	17.3

Stadium	Year							
Buffalo Rich Stadium	1973	22,000	4,680	0	4,680	2.45	517	11.1
Denver McNichols Arena	1975	13,000	2,483	(799)	3,282	2.92	341	10.4
Louisiana Superdome	1975	168,000	32,112	(7,922)	40,034	2.92	4,406	11.0
Pontiac Silverdome	1975	56,000	10,716	205	10,511	2.92	1,469	14.0
Seattle Kingdome	1976	67,000	12,082	1,535	10,547	2.39	1,398	13.3
New Jersey Giants Stadium	1976	68,000	12,612	5,150	7,462	2.39	1,419	19.0
New Jersey Byrne Meadowlands Arena	1981	85,000	11,917	2,541	9,376	4.46	2,875	30.7
Minnesota Metrodome	1982	62,000	7,775	5,554	2,221	4.14	1,932	87.0
Hoosier Dome/ Market Square Arena	1984	77,000	9,683	(1,100)	10,783	2.59	1,484	13.8
Charlotte Coliseum	1985	55,000	7,167	3,632	3,535	3.18	1,294	36.6
Orlando Arena	1988	110,000	14,812	128	14,684	2.54	2,014	13.7
Miami Arena	1988	50,000	6,693	(11)	6,704	2.54	915	13.7

Sources: James P. Quirk and Rodney D. Fort. *Pay Dirt: The Business of Professional Team Sports* (Princeton University Press, 1992); Moody's Investors Service. *Moody's Municipal and Government Manual, 1990* (1990); and Board of Governors, Federal Reserve System. *Annual Statistical Digest and Banking and Monetary Statistics* (various issues).

a. Assumes a 9 percent pre-tax real rate of return on invested capital (Quirk and Fort assumed a 10 percent rate), a forty-year stadium life with straight-line depreciation based on replacement cost, and property taxes equal to 2 percent of replacement cost.

b. Moody's corporate and state and local long-term Aa bond yields. Bonds used to finance a stadium in year X are assumed to be issued in December of year X-2 (for example. the yields for the Miami arena are those that prevailed in December 1986).

c. Present value of thirty-year interest savings allocated across forty-year life of stadium such that the subsidy remains a constant fraction of the remaining real value of the stadium.

Table 4-3. *Interest Savings and Federal Revenue Loss on Hypothetical $225 Million Stadium Financed with Thirty-Year Tax-Exempt Bonds*
Millions of dollars

	Interest rate differential	
Savings/loss	2%	4%
Value of interest savings		
Undiscounted	69.8	139.5
Discounted at 7 percent	37.7	75.4
Savings (present value) as percentage of construction cost	16.8	33.6
Present value of federal revenue loss	47.1	94.2

Source: Calculated by the author.

erage $50 million stadium in table 4-1. The $225 million is comparable to the cost of stadiums being built today—it cost $233 million for Chicago's Comiskey Park in 1991, $225 million for Denver's Coors Field in 1995, $244 million for Cleveland's Jacobs Field in 1994, and $250 million for the proposed stadiums in Milwaukee and Northern Virginia—and provides a better idea of the magnitude of the typical maximum federal subsidy for new stadiums.

The interest rate spread (differential) between long-term taxable corporate bonds and long-term tax-exempt state and local bonds, each rated Aa by Moody's Investors Service, has ranged from 2 percent to 4.5 percent over the past quarter century. The interest expense savings, assuming $\frac{1}{30}$ of the bond principal is retired at the end of each year, are presented in table 4-3 for interest rate differentials of 2 percent and 4 percent, both undiscounted and discounted at a rate of 7 percent.

The present discounted value of the interest savings, if the interest rate spread is 2 percent, is $37.7 million. This interest saving is equal to almost 17 percent of the $225 million construction cost. Should the interest rate differential be twice as high, the present value of the savings doubles to $75.4 million, about 34 percent of construction cost. The cost to local taxpayers and tenants of professional sports stadiums clearly is reduced by the substantial decrease in interest expense made possible by tax-exempt bonds.

The federal taxpayers' revenue loss usually exceeds the value of the interest savings to state and local taxpayers. The present value of the federal revenue loss on these $225 million of bonds is between $47.1 million and $94.2 million, depending on the interest rate differential.[10]

With this background, consider now the twenty-one stadiums in table 4-2 for which the 1989 total subsidy was calculated. The first step in estimating the annual (1989) value of the tax-exempt bond subsidy is to make a calculation similar to that in table 4-3 for each of these twenty-one stadiums, assuming that 100 percent of each stadium's original cost was financed with tax-exempt thirty-year noncallable serial bonds. The present value of the thirty-year interest savings is based on the interest rate differential in column 6 of table 4-2, and is allocated across the forty-year life of the stadium such that the annual subsidy is a constant fraction of the undepreciated real value of the stadium.[11] The dollar value of the maximum federal subsidy and the federal share of the total subsidy for each stadium is presented in columns 7 and 8.[12] The one-year federal subsidies total $24.3 million and represent 9.8 percent of the total public subsidy.

Several factors determine these federal subsidies and subsidy shares. Other things equal, more recently built stadiums tend to have higher federal subsidies and subsidy shares because they are more costly (require larger bond issues) and because more of the original investment is undepreciated (this implies a larger dollar payment for rate of return). Lambeau Field and the L.A. Sports Arena were built in the 1950s and, in 1989, had but eight and ten years of useful life remaining, respectively. Their federal subsidies were $5,000 and $41,000.

The difference in interest rates between taxable and tax-exempt bonds is also important. As illustrated in column 6 of table 4-2, bonds for the Byrne Meadowlands Arena were issued in 1979 when this spread was very high (4.46 percent); its federal subsidy and share are substantially higher than those for the Hoosier Dome's comparably sized bond issue in 1982, which experienced a smaller interest rate difference (2.59 percent).

The most important factor explaining the federal subsidy share is the rental contract with stadium tenants and whether it requires a large subsidy from local taxpayers. Anaheim Stadium was built in 1966. In absolute terms, its federal subsidy was small ($346,000), because the value of the original bond issue was small in 1989 dollars and only seventeen years of useful life remained. But its federal subsidy share is 20.5 percent of the total subsidy, which is much higher than for stadiums of comparable vintage. Jack Murphy Stadium was built one year later for almost the same cost, yet its federal subsidy share is only 4.6 percent of a much larger total subsidy. Column 4 shows that Anaheim Stadium's rental contract produced a $5.6 million operating profit for the public stadium authority to offset its facility subsidy; Jack Murphy Stadium's rental contract produced a $64,000 operating loss for San Diego. In effect, Anaheim Stadium uses its operating profit to pay a substantial share of its fixed cost, thereby reducing the annual subsidy required of state and local taxpayers.

The federal share of the Metrodome's total subsidy is 87.0 percent, which implies that most of this stadium's subsidy is being provided by federal, not local, taxpayers. The size of the bond issue, share of useful life remaining, and interest rate differential contribute to this high federal share. But the Hoosier Dome (built two years later) has a greater original cost and more remaining useful life than the Metrodome, yet has a federal share of only 13.8 percent. And the Byrne Meadowlands Arena (one year older) has an even higher interest rate differential than the Metrodome, yet has a federal share of only 30.7 percent. The Metrodome's rental agreement, which generates an operating profit of $5.5 million for the public authority, is primarily responsible for reducing the state and local share of the subsidy and boosting the federal share almost to 90 percent. In contrast, the Hoosier Dome has an operating loss of $1.1 million.

To summarize, the public sector provides large subsidies to professional sports stadiums, and the federal share of these subsidies is significant. As has been shown by the Metrodome, in a given year it is possible for federal taxpayers to be providing almost all of a stadium's subsidy. But even for the Metrodome, local taxpayers also provide a substantial subsidy over the life of the stadium. The annual subsidy for the Metrodome through 1994 (including additional investment made between 1982 and 1994 that is not included in the subsidy calculations shown in table 4-2) averaged $15 million in 1994 dollars (see chapter 7). According to my calculations, the federal share of this annual subsidy was 30 percent, or $4.5 million (1994 dollars), and the local subsidy $10.5 million a year.

The Incidence of the Federal Subsidy

It is not difficult to determine whether the federal subsidy satisfies the benefit principle of taxation. The effect of fiscal policy on the size of the nation's employment pie is determined by the spending, revenue, and deficit totals in the federal budget. These totals determine the effect of the budget on national output, which in turn determines the number of jobs in the economy. Once these budget totals have been established in the congressional budget resolution, the congressional budget process mandates that any proposal to expand a specific program or cut a tax must be offset by a change elsewhere in the budget. Thus a change in any individual program or tax has a zero effect on job creation and economic activity unless it is able to alter the structural elements of the economy affecting the natural rate of unemployment. To reduce the natural rate of unemployment it is necessary to decrease the levels of structural and frictional unemployment through such programs as job training, relocation assistance, and better information about job availability, or increasing productivity through net increases in investment in physical capital and research.[13]

Tax-exempt bonds do not accomplish this objective. The discussion in chapter 2 makes clear that the net economic benefits from a stadium diminish as the geographic span of the subsidizing unit of government increases. Unless the fans attending the games come from foreign countries, all spending is made by residents of the political jurisdiction providing the tax-exempt bond subsidy: the United States of America. Except for those few U.S. residents who will reduce their savings to attend games, all of this spending is offset by reductions in spending on alternative entertainment or other activities.

Thus to the federal taxpayer, very few economic benefits are created to offset the cost of the subsidy. The subsidy is only worthwhile to federal taxpayers if they value spending and associated jobs and public consumption in one location more than they value them in another location. If that is the case, it is only this differential valuation that should be included in taxpayer benefits. But it is unlikely that federal taxpayers value stadiums differently according to their location: the subsidy is not approved for some locations and disapproved for others. It is, in effect, an entitlement program without regard to the location of the spending and associated jobs.

Of course, none of this holds true for the local taxpayer. From the perspective of the dominant political coalition at the local level, the benefits from the federal subsidy are concentrated among the relatively few, and the costs of the increased federal taxes or reduced federal spending necessary to pay for the lost federal revenue are diffused among 250 million people.[14] In the case of the Metrodome, if one assumes that the aggregate value of the benefits at least equals the value of the public subsidy, the federal subsidy reduced the cost of the local subsidy to Minnesota taxpayers by 30 percent and benefits exceeded costs by $4.5

million a year. This also helps explain the seemingly uneconomic decision of local governments to subsidize professional sports stadiums.

Federal Tax-Exempt Bond Policy and Local Finance Options

Options for making stadium finances more consistent with the benefit principle of taxation are limited. More information might help local taxpayers form a dominant political coalition that demands a better financing package. But such information probably is not a central part of most stadium debates precisely because it is not in the interests of the dominant political coalition.

Improvement in stadium financing may be most likely to arise from federal policy changes. The current structure of the tax-exempt bond law provides a costless federal subsidy to local taxpayers, establishes incentives for local governments *not* to utilize the benefit principle of taxation to finance the local subsidy, and fails to apply to stadium bonds some tax-exempt bond rules that increase the cost of construction projects for most other private users of tax-exempt bonds. Altering the treatment of stadium bonds would serve two purposes: the federal revenue loss would be reduced with no loss of benefits to federal taxpayers; and local taxpayers would be confronted with prices more nearly reflecting the full cost of the stadium subsidy. To understand the bond law changes that could effect these changes, it is first necessary to understand the economics and history of the tax-exempt bond law.

Private Use of Tax-Exempt Bonds: History and Economic Rationale

Adam Smith might ask why the federal government of a nation usually devoted to markets free of government interference would subsidize the capital facilities of selected private businesses (such as professional sports teams) by allowing them to use tax-exempt bonds. It is a complicated story, but one whose telling is essential to the understanding both of current tax law that enables such subsidies and legislative options that would change them.[15]

The first modern income tax law in the United States, in 1913, excluded from taxable income the interest income earned by holders of the debt obligations (bonds) of states and their political subdivisions. This treatment was believed to be consistent with the Tenth Amendment to the

Constitution and the doctrine of intergovernmental tax immunity: one level of government could not impose taxes on income received by individuals or businesses pursuant to contracts with another level of government (the bond is a contract between a state or local government and the bondholder) because such a tax would be equivalent to a tax on the government.[16]

This provision of the Internal Revenue Code did not limit the purposes for which state and local governments issue bonds, though some states may have been constrained by their own laws. Eventually state and local officials began to issue bonds and use the proceeds to make loans to private businesses and private individuals for such things as manufacturing and commercial facilities, owner-occupied housing, and student loans. State and local taxpayers generally did not object to the issuance of bonds for these private purposes because the bond issues were structured to pay the debt service with revenue from the private capital facility being built or loan made, thereby avoiding any need to tax residents.

This situation prevailed until 1968 when Congress attempted to make bond issuance conform more closely to the economic, as opposed to the legal, rationale for the interest exemption. The economic rationale for this federal taxpayer-financed subsidy is that state and local public capital facilities tend to be underprovided because their benefits spill over political boundaries. The sheer number of state and local jurisdictions implies that any one jurisdiction's political boundaries likely fail to encompass all individuals and businesses who benefit from its public services. Thus some of the collective consumption benefits spill over the border of a taxing jurisdiction, as in the case of some educational services or environmental projects. Collective consumption benefits from providing such goods exceed the benefits to taxpayers in the providing jurisdiction. Because taxpayers tend to be unwilling to pay for services received by nonresidents, it may be desirable for a higher level of government (which does receive payments from the nonresident spillover beneficiaries) to subsidize residents' consumption in order to induce state and local governments to provide the proper, that is, a larger, number of facilities.

This economic perspective suggests that the subsidy be restricted to capital facilities that generate benefits to the general public. The Revenue and Expenditure Control Act of 1968 (P.L. 90-364) began partial application of this restriction. It declared state and local bonds to be taxable if more than 25 percent of the bond proceeds were used by a nongovernmental entity *and* if more than 25 percent of the debt service (interest and principal repayment) was secured by property used directly or indirectly in a private business.

Congress made an exception to this requirement for a limited list of "exempt facilities" and types of loans, specifically including sports facilities. This exception enabled continued tax-exempt bond financing of sports stadiums when a professional sports team used more than 25 percent of the stadium's useful service and when more than 25 percent of the debt service was paid for with revenue generated by the stadium through rents, ticket taxes, shares of concession and parking facilities, and the like. These user-type financing fees met little resistance from state and local taxpayers, probably because nonusers of the stadium perceived it to be a free good: that is, general taxes were not being levied to pay for the stadium.

This situation prevailed essentially unchanged until the Tax Reform Act of 1986 (P.L. 99-514), which adopted several provisions affecting private-use bonds. First, a bond issue was deemed to be a "private-activity" bond and taxable if more than 10 percent of the bond proceeds were used by a nongovernmental entity *and* more than 10 percent of the debt service was secured by property used directly or indirectly in a private business. A bond issue that did not exceed one of these tests was deemed to be a "governmental" bond and tax-exempt. Second, sports facilities were removed from the list of "exempt facilities" that retain eligibility for financing with tax-exempt private-activity bonds even though the bonds exceed the two 10 percent tests. Third, the total volume of most tax-exempt private-activity bonds for exempt facilities that could be issued by all the political jurisdictions in a state was limited to the *greater* of $50 per resident or $150 million (sections 141, 142, and 146 of the Code).

Current Practice in Stadium Bond Financing

Promoters of stadiums did not immediately react to this change in the law because $2.7 billion of bond financing for virtually every stadium in the planning or gleam-in-the-eye stages was allowed to remain eligible for tax-exempt financing by both general and stadium-specific transition rules included in the 1986 act. Under these transition rules the bonds had to be issued before the end of 1990. But nongrandfathered stadiums built after 1986 have been forced to alter their financial arrangements, and it is these stadiums that have been receiving considerable attention for their apparently generous public subsidies.

Eligibility for tax-exempt bonds now requires that stadium bonds be issued as governmental bonds; they can exceed one but not both of the 10 percent bond tests. Since professional sports teams almost always will consume more than 10 percent of a stadium's useful services, stadium bond issues generally exceed the use test. In order to avoid exceeding the security interest test, a stadium bond issue must be structured so that no more than 10 percent of the debt service for the bonds is secured, *directly or indirectly,* by property used in a trade or business. This precludes paying for debt service directly with stadium-related revenue, or indirectly with general revenue (for example, taxes or lottery receipts) that is replaced with infusions of revenue earned from the stadium. Thus stadiums now being financed with tax-exempt bonds cannot generate stadium-based payments that exceed 10 percent of the debt service on the bond issue. In practical terms, this means state and local taxpayers must be willing to pay at least 90 percent of the debt service from some revenue source other than stadium-generated revenue.[17]

The effect of these changes in bond law can be seen in the terms negotiated for new stadiums. For instance, the proposed $250 million stadium for the Milwaukee Brewers baseball team envisions a $160 million tax-exempt bond issue, a $40 million capital contribution from the team, and a $50 million loan from the state to be financed with taxable debt. The tax-exempt bond issue is to be paid with a five-county regional sales tax of 0.1 percent. Public revenue generated from the stadium will not exceed 10 percent of the debt service on $160 million.

The $200 million Baltimore football stadium is being financed with $99 million in cash and $86 million in tax-exempt bonds. Both the cash and the debt service on the bonds are to be paid from state lottery funds. Public receipt of stadium-generated revenue is not to exceed 10 percent of the debt service on $86 million. In both these deals, the tax-exempt bonds are being serviced with revenue generated from public sources other than the stadium.

The 1986 act has had two noteworthy effects. It virtually requires that, if a stadium is financed in part by a state or local government bond, it must provide a highly favorable lease to its professional tenants.[18] And the act redistributes the burden for debt service among local taxpayers, as general revenue sources must be substituted for stadium-related revenues. This makes it more difficult to finance the local public subsidy in a manner consistent with the benefit principle of taxation.

It may be possible for these effects to be circumvented by careful structuring of governmental units. A tax is not considered to be stadium related if it is "generally applicable." For example, sports is entertainment. If a local government were to apply a 5 percent tax to all types of entertainment (movie theaters, concerts, theater), this "generally applicable" entertainment tax would not violate the 10 percent rule even if stadium-related revenue exceeded 10 percent of debt service on the tax-exempt bonds. Of course, such an action would elicit considerable resistance from other forms of entertainment, making circumvention difficult.

A stadium authority can itself be established as a separate unit of government. It appears that the current private-activity bond law can be interpreted in such a way that, were the authority to manage several stadiums (as does Maryland's stadium authority), a ticket tax would be generally applicable provided all stadiums under the authority's control were subject to the tax. Or the stadium authority could erect a small movie theater on the grounds of the stadium, charge a generally applicable admissions tax for movie and stadium tickets whose revenue exceeds 10 percent of stadium debt service, and not violate the 10 percent of debt-service rule. Such circumventions of the 10 percent rule are being discussed during the long-running comment period for the proposed regulations the U.S. Department of Treasury issued in 1994 to provide guidance for applying the private-activity bond rules.

Federal Policy Options

The discussion now turns to three options for reducing the financial incentives that would otherwise lead team owners and the dominant local political coalition to decide that taxpayers should subsidize stadiums: eliminate the use of tax-exempt bonds; require the bonds to be issued as private-activity bonds, which means they will not be tax-exempt unless they receive an allocation from the state private-activity volume cap; and require the value of the tax-exempt bond subsidy to be included in the revenues to be shared by league teams.

ELIMINATION. Local governments cannot issue tax-exempt private-activity bonds to finance stadiums for professional sports teams, but they can issue governmental bonds for this purpose. The authority to issue federal tax-exempt governmental bonds for stadiums could be withdrawn, as has been proposed by Senator Daniel Moynihan (Democrat of New York) in the Stop Tax-Exempt Arena Debt Issuance Act (STADIA) of 1996 (S. 1880). STADIA is consistent with the notion that these stadium projects provide no economic benefits for the federal taxpayer and would force local officials and team owners to share more of the costs, and thereby would reduce the incentive for stadium construction. The Moynihan bill would make it easier for local officials to use the benefit principle of taxation since they would no longer be constrained by a 10 percent of debt service rule for stadium-related revenue.

Some believe elimination would also be consistent with the intent of Congress in 1986. The general explanation of the 1986 act states: "The Act repeals the prior-law exceptions permitting tax-exemption for interest on bonds to finance sports facilities."[19] This seemingly unambiguous statement of intent is supported by H.R. 3838, the House bill that led ultimately to the Tax Reform Act of 1986. This bill proposed repeal of the security interest test.[20] Had repeal been adopted, stadium bonds would have been eliminated because they would always exceed the one remaining test, the 10 percent use test.

The House and Senate conferees decided to retain the security interest test, apparently to avoid prohibiting tax-exempt bond use for public facilities managed by private entities that do not generate any substantial revenue, such as New York City's zoos and libraries. Some might argue that retention of the security interest test need not indicate waning congressional intent to eliminate bonds for stadiums. Rather, it might be viewed as a reasonable response to the problem of maintaining bond issuance authority for such privately managed public entities, particularly if legislators generally believed that stadium proponents would be unable to induce state and local taxpayers to switch to governmental bond financing.

The 1986 act could have included an outright prohibition of governmental bonds for stadiums. At that time, Congress had never imposed an outright prohibition on tax-exempt bond use for any activity financed with governmental bonds. Two such prohibitions were enacted, however, in the Omnibus Budget Reconciliation Act of 1987 (P.L. 100-203). This act generally eliminated the ability of municipalities to use tax-exempt governmental bonds to finance the takeover of investor-owned electric and gas utilities in order to convert them into municipal utilities (section 141(d) of the Code). The act also denied the use of governmental bonds to finance residential rental property that is not located within the jurisdiction of the issuer [section 148(b)(2)(E)]. Thus precedent does exist for such a prohibition directed to a specific activity.

With these two exceptions, the tax-exempt bond law currently allows state and local governments to issue tax-exempt bonds whose proceeds will be used by governmental or private entities for virtually any activity, provided taxpayers agree to pay 90 percent or more of the debt service on the bonds from other revenue sources. For example, nothing in the federal tax law would prevent a local government from issuing bonds to finance a privately owned car dealership, provided at least 90 percent of the debt service on the bonds was paid from general revenue (meaning the dealership's revenue contributions to the local government did not exceed 10 percent of the debt service). Constraints on such projects would have to come from the state's constitution, state and local statutes, or citizen resistance encountered in the political process required to implement such a policy.

In fact, U.S. tax-exempt bond law currently allows for federal subsidy of certain private businesses that requires less fiscal responsibility of local taxpayers than they have for stadium bonds. For example, tax-exempt small-issue industrial development bonds can be issued for up to $10 million of private investment in manufacturing facilities and the debt service on those bonds can be paid by revenue generated from the manufacturing facility, not from local taxes. In other words, these are exempt private-activity bonds issued for facilities that exceed both the use and security interest tests but retain the tax-exempt bond issuance privilege, albeit subject to state volume caps. This contrasting federal tax treatment raises the question of what rationale would justify total denial of bond subsidy for stadium projects that are alleged to stimulate economic development but allow subsidy for privately owned manufacturing facilities that are also alleged to stimulate economic development, particularly when the evidence suggests that manufacturing facilities are no more successful at generating benefits for federal taxpayers than are stadium projects.[21]

LIMITATION. An alternative option would reverse the policy decision made in 1986 that eliminated the use of tax-exempt private-activity bonds to finance stadiums and ushered in the use of tax-exempt governmental bonds. The reverse policy would deny governmental bond financing and permit tax-exempt private-activity bond financing that is subject to the state volume cap.

Implementation would entail repeal of the security interest test for stadium bonds, in effect adopting a more targeted variant of the repeal originally proposed by H.R. 3838, as passed by the House in 1985. The use of governmental bonds to finance stadiums housing professional teams would be precluded because such bonds would always fail the 10 percent use test. Stadium bonds for which private use exceeds 10 percent of bond proceeds would be classified as private-activity bonds, and stadiums would be added to the list of private activities for which tax-exempt private-activity bonds can be issued. These bonds would be subject to the state volume cap.

This scheme would have several beneficial effects. Use of the volume cap for a stadium would force most states and local governments to forgo taxpayers' benefits from other bonds: small-issue industrial development bonds, mortgage revenue bonds for first-time home buyers, student loans, and so on. State and local governments would be forced to weigh their taxpayers' benefits from a bond-financed stadium investment against their taxpayers' benefits from other bond-financed private activities, all of which provide few net benefits to the federal taxpayer. In addition, local governments would not be subject to the 10 percent of debt service rule and could use the benefit principle if they chose.

If states in which stadiums are built already use most of their private-activity bond allotment, stadium bonds would replace tax-exempt private-activity bonds issued for other purposes. Tax-exempt bond financing of stadiums would entail no additional cost to federal taxpayers.

Requiring private-activity bond financing would also subject stadium bonds to a series of restrictions that do not apply when issued as governmental bonds. These restrictions taken together would reduce the public subsidy, raise the cost of stadium projects, and perhaps reduce the volume of stadium bonds.

—No portion of the proceeds of a tax-exempt private-activity bond issue may be used to finance a "skybox or other private luxury box" (Section 147(e) of the Code). Tenants are pressuring cities to replace or upgrade stadiums that are quite new, such as the Charlotte and Miami facilities built in 1988, owing to inadequate luxury seating. The exclusion of luxury seating revenue from sports leagues' pool of shared revenue increases the return on luxury seating investments relative to alternative investments (such as developing better players or more appealing give-aways and promotional efforts).

—Issuance costs financed with the proceeds of a tax-exempt private-activity bond issue are limited to 2 percent of bond proceeds. Costs in excess of 2 percent must be financed with more expensive revenue sources (Section 147(g) of the Code).

—Tax-exempt private-activity bonds issued for construction of facilities must rebate arbitrage profits earned on unspent bond proceeds even if the requirement for spending an increasing share of bond proceeds over a two-year period is met (Section 148(f)(C) of the Code).

—Advance refunding to take advantage of favorable interest rate changes that precede call dates on the original stadium bond issue is prohibited for private-activity bonds (Section 149(d) of the Code).

—Private-activity bonds issued to finance purchase of an existing stadium must make rehabilitation expenditures that equal or exceed the dollar value of the bond issue (Section 147(d) of the Code).

INCLUDE VALUE OF BOND SUBSIDY IN REVENUE-SHARING BASE. Owners desire luxury seating because it allows them to price-discriminate and capture considerable consumer surplus. But owners are also attracted because the revenue is not included in the revenues shared among the teams, thereby increasing the return per dollar of revenue for the team. The return from local subsidy of a stadium could be reduced by following the same logic. Alter the tax-exempt bond law to require that the annual interest savings on the tax-exempt debt used to finance a stadium be included in the pool of revenue shared among all league teams. This would reduce the owner's return from the federal subsidy, and hence the pressure an owner would apply to local governments to subsidize these investments.

Conclusions

The benefit principle of taxation requires that those who benefit from a public expenditure should pay for it. The studies by proponents of publicly financed stadiums emphasize the income that a stadium generates. These benefits are vastly overstated as net benefits to the community, but they do represent rough approximations of the gross benefits to businesses associated with sports: the team, the concession suppliers, some nearby local businesses, and businesses that buy season tickets as a means of increasing their own sales. According to the benefits principle, these businesses, plus citizens who derive the consumption benefits, should pay for the stadium. Thus the benefits principle implies stadium financing by such things as ticket taxes, PSLs, stadium license fees, and a tax on broadcasting fees.

In practice, most stadiums are not financed in this manner. Instead, most stadiums are financed by local broadly based (general) taxes and higher federal income taxes that make up for the federal revenue lost through tax-exempt bonds. The tax reforms of 1986 have actually made matters worse by insisting that stadium revenues cannot be used to pay for more than 10 percent of the debt service on tax-exempt bonds. Thus a necessary condition to improve stadium financing is to revise this portion of the tax code, either by eliminating tax exemptions for sports facilities or by removing the 10 percent cap on the use of stadium revenues to pay for these bonds.

Notes

1. The consumer surplus for major league baseball fans in 1985 was estimated to average $18.4 million per franchise, and to range from $54.1 million (Los Angeles Dodgers) to $5.4 million (Cleveland Indians). Daraius Irani, "Public Subsidies to Stadiums: Do the Costs Outweigh the Benefits?" *Public Finance Review*, vol. 25 (March 1997), pp. 238–53.

2. See chapter 2 in this volume; and Thomas V. Chema, "When Professional Sports Justify the Subsidy: A Reply to Robert A. Baade," *Journal of Urban Affairs*, vol. 18 (March 1996), pp. 19–22.

3. Dennis Zimmerman, *The Private Use of Tax-Exempt Bonds: Controlling Public Subsidy of Private Activities* (Urban Institute Press, 1991), chap. 2.

4. It is possible that the aggregate value of public consumption benefits is greater for those who do not view games than for those who do, since there are many more of the former than the latter, but the issue here is the size of the tax for each individual in the two groups, not the size of the group.

5. Charles T. Clotfelter and Philip J. Cook, *Selling Hope: State Lotteries in America* (Harvard University Press, 1989).

6. Relatively little has been written about the tax-exempt bond subsidy of publicly financed sports stadiums. See Benjamin A. Okner, "Subsidies of Stadiums and Arenas," in Roger G. Noll, ed., *Government and the Sports Business* (Brookings, 1974), pp. 325–48; and James Quirk and Rodney D. Fort, *Pay Dirt: The Business of Professional Team Sports* (Princeton University Press, 1992). Both studies forgo explicit discussion of tax-exempt bonds, leaving this federal subsidy subsumed within estimates of the total public subsidy. Were the policy at issue here an evaluation of the federal subsidy to state and local government business enterprises, one would want to estimate the federal tax revenue forgone by not taxing the pre-tax return on a privately financed and owned stadium.

7. Quirk and Fort, *Pay Dirt,* tables 4.14–4.16.

8. Rental contracts usually include payments based on shares of revenue from admissions (sometimes termed an admissions tax), concessions, parking, and luxury boxes. These revenues are offset by operating expenses for such things as labor, management, and supplies.

9. Were the Superdome privately financed, its cost presumably would have been better controlled. Private owners would have realized that use of the facility could not generate a revenue stream adequate to provide a market rate of return on a facility costing $168 million.

10. If the marginal tax rate of the bond purchaser who clears the market is lower than the average marginal tax rate of all purchasers of the bonds (meaning some of the bonds are purchased by those with marginal tax rates above the market-clearing rate), the revenue loss exceeds the value of the interest savings. Zimmerman estimated the interest savings on tax-exempt bonds to be about 60 percent of revenue loss before the 1986 tax act, and about 80 percent after 1986, owing to the decrease in progressivity of the marginal rate structure. Zimmerman, *Private Use of Tax-Exempt Bonds.*

Some might argue that this revenue loss should be reduced by the revenue loss that would result from interest deductions on the debt-financed portion of the alternative privately financed stadium. This is not done here. The creditors of a 100 percent debt-financed private stadium would pay taxes on their interest income. If some portion were equity financed, even higher taxes would be paid, and this revenue-loss estimate would be understated.

11. Although the bonds issued to finance these stadiums all are retired after thirty years, one cannot assume state and local taxpayers receive zero subsidy for the last ten years of the forty-year stadium life. Had taxpayers been forced to pay the higher interest cost for thirty years, those higher expenses would show up over the next ten years as some combination of higher taxes, lower services, and higher debt burden.

12. If some portion of a stadium was financed with current revenue, calculating the federal subsidy on the basis of 100 percent tax-exempt financing still is reasonable. The stadium probably was each government's marginal investment; any current funding simply shifted the extra tax-exempt bonds to other planned investments. The estimate does overstate the actual subsidy if some portion of the original cost was financed with taxable debt or if call provisions were exercised.

13. For a more complete discussion of these issues, see Jane G. Gravelle, Donald W. Kiefer, and Dennis Zimmerman, *Is Job Creation a Meaningful Policy Justification?* Library of Congress, Congressional Research Service Report 92-697 E (September 8, 1992); and Paul N. Courant, "How Would You Know a Good Economic Policy If You Tripped over One? Hint: Don't Just Count Jobs," *National Tax Journal,* vol. 47 (December 1994), pp. 863–81.

14. Interestingly, this implies a belief on the part of local taxpayers that their jurisdiction is more successful than the average jurisdiction in obtaining a federal subsidy for a purely local program. If they believed otherwise, they would see that their stadium benefits are more than offset by the increased federal taxes and reduced federal spending necessary to pay for federal subsidies captured by other local governments.

15. For a more complete discussion, see Zimmerman, *Private Use of Tax-Exempt Bonds.*

16. The U.S. Supreme Court in 1988 rejected this constitutional protection for the tax exemption, maintaining that the exemption is based in U.S. statutes. See *South Carolina v. Baker,* 485 U.S. 505 (1988).

17. Unresolved at this point is the tax treatment of bonds issued to finance facilities "related to" a stadium. For example, the new Washington Redskins stadium in Maryland

is privately financed with public financing for road improvements and parking. The Treasury Department has issued proposed regulations on such facilities for public comment. See Department of the Treasury, Internal Revenue Service, 59 Fed. Reg. 67658–90 (December 30, 1994). The federal subsidies calculated in this chapter do not account for related-facility financings that were not counted as part of the stadium bond issue.

18. This does not preclude negotiating a lease agreement requiring the team to assume the operating cost of the stadium. These payments would not be counted in the 10 percent rule.

19. Joint Committee on Taxation, *General Explanation of the Tax Reform Act of 1986 (H.R. 3838, 99th Congress: Public Law 99-514)* (GPO, May 4, 1987), p. 1175.

20. *Tax Reform Act of 1985, H.R. 3838,* H. Rept. 99-426, 99 Cong. 1 sess. (GPO, December 7, 1985), p. 520.

21. Dennis Zimmerman, *Small-Issue Industrial Development Bonds*, Library of Congress, Congressional Research Service Report 94-771 E (October 4, 1994).

5

DIRECT DEMOCRACY
AND THE STADIUM MESS

RODNEY FORT

*I believe the citizens should have a say in this issue. If the voters pass this,
we'll move forward. If the voters don't pass this, we'll still move forward.*
— Mayor Jay Tibshraeny, Chandler, Arizona[1]

 One way for the public to participate in decisions about
sports stadiums is through the process of direct democracy,
that is, through referenda and initiatives.[2] Voting on ballot
measures provides the public with a means of expression.
However, such votes can fall prey to the participation problems plaguing
all democratic activity. In conventional wisdom, ballot initiatives ensure
that the majority will prevails, but in reality the outcome of a democratic
process depends on which voters turn out to vote and what amount and
quality of information is available on which to base a decision. Because
both turnout and information can be biased, it is not clear that direct
democracy does drive the outcome closer to the "will of the people."

Votes on stadium issues have now occurred often enough to provide
some insight into the preferences of state and local residents on these
issues, as well as into the relationship between citizens and their government. Typically, when a stadium issue appears on the ballot, it is a
referendum that is the culmination of a complex political process. In
some cases, usually when taxes are changed or bonds are issued, a referendum may be required, whereas in other cases public officials place a
stadium measure on the ballot even though it is not required. Now and
then, citizens use the initiative process to force a public vote, as occurred

when Cincinnati approved a sales tax increase to finance new stadiums for the Bengals and the Reds. Four cases in which ballot measures played a role in the decision about whether to build a publicly subsidized stadium are discussed in chapters 7, 9, 11, and 12.

As this book makes clear, the decision to provide a substantial subsidy to professional sports through a publicly financed facility is highly controversial; hence the efficiency and legitimacy of such a decision is a matter of considerable concern.[3] Owners want the new revenue sources that accompany new or improved stadiums, especially the luxury boxes and other facilities that generate revenues that are not shared. Some local interests want the direct, indirect, and psychic values that go along with teams that are stadium tenants. For Nashville Mayor Phil Bredesen, the local benefits are substantial:

> First, the economic impact, which does not totally justify the investment but justifies a piece of it. Second, the intangible benefits of having a high-profile NFL team in the community at a time when cities are competing for attention is positive. Third, it is an amenity that a lot of people want. We build a golf course and parks and libraries and lots of things because people in the community want them, and certainly there are substantial numbers of people who want this. Fourth, the location of the stadium represents the redevelopment of an industrial area close to downtown, certainly a positive in its own right and a significant factor in the public's mind. Taken together, it makes a very compelling argument for going ahead with this.[4]

The pursuit of these benefits occurs in a setting in which professional sports leagues artificially restrict the number of teams below the competitive level. By constantly keeping a supply of possible host cities on line, current host cities are in the inevitable position of accepting or denying deals often described as "blackmail" or "extortion." Recently, team owners used Jacksonville and Tampa Bay/St. Petersburg as leverage against local governments in Chicago, Cleveland, San Francisco, and Seattle, as well as against state governments in Illinois and Washington.

Elsewhere I have referred to this situation as "the stadium mess," whereby local governments cave in to the ever-increasing demands of team owners.[5] Cities without teams eagerly undertake expensive investments in hopes of attracting teams, and cities with teams are forced to counter by offering improvements in their stadiums and leases that match the offers from other communities.

It is difficult to find fault with cities that already have teams and that respond to a threat to move by cutting rents and giving a larger share of concession revenues to keep a team. Losing money on an existing facility in the short run may be the best one can do (and the short run can be pretty long for a stadium) because the maintenance and financing costs of the stadium are mostly fixed and independent of whether the team remains. Likewise, from a political perspective, losing more money but keeping the major league tenant may be more attractive than the alternative simply because economic losses are likely to be incurred whether the team stays or goes.

The incentives facing cities without teams can be just as relentless. As the other chapters in this volume show, stadiums are sold as panaceas for depressed and declining downtown areas, using estimations of economic impact that would make Rosy Scenario blush. They also are widely trumpeted as being crucial to the image of a metropolitan area and a key to attracting other businesses. Politicians certainly appear to find electoral profit in the pursuit of teams through the construction of fancy stadiums.

On one occasion the public did arise to exact political punishment for a stadium giveaway. Shortly after the state representative from Racine, Wisconsin, changed his vote in favor of financing a new stadium for the Brewers, he was recalled by popular vote. But the rarity of such events leads one to doubt that direct democracy, through recalls or ballot measures, can ameliorate the stadium mess. A series of votes in the San Francisco area have made clear to the Giants and their supporters that voters prefer a new baseball stadium that is downtown and, except for the use of public land and transportation infrastructure, want the project to be strictly privately financed, but it remains to be seen whether these preferences will be honored. Likewise, the advisory vote in Seattle (King County) on a new Mariners ballpark put pressure on local officials to make the public financial obligation much more specific and the expected payback more direct, but did not prevent a large subsidy. Politicians may not take the advice of the voters to heart, but at least preference was revealed.

If the preceding examples eventually end up being "the good," others represent "the bad and the ugly." The passage of the Denver sales tax referendum, instrumental in obtaining for that city the Rockies expansion franchise, actually served the interests of the few over the many.[6] Other examples, detailed later in the discussion, reveal that some problems with the process may bring stadium votes to the people. "The intangible benefits," Benjamin Okner has noted, "cannot be disregarded just because it is not possible to put a price tag on most of them. Their perceived value to various communities is illustrated by the large number of cities that now provide publicly supported sports facilities."[7] Despite the possibility of intangible benefits from stadiums, the data from ballot measures indicate that even though a large number of cities provide publicly financed facilities, these subsidies may not reflect voter preferences. The old Progressive battle cry, "The only cure for democracy is more democracy," rings hollow in this context.

This chapter describes direct democracy and examines whether voter preferences are served by it. The chapter includes a detailed, descriptive look at some recent votes spanning the possible direct democracy outcomes. The primary conclusion is that the median voter's preferences regarding the amount of public spending on stadiums probably are not being met. Essentially, direct democracy gets mixed reviews. The stadium mess can be expected to continue as long as professional sports leagues are able to restrict the number of teams, thereby using the cities that lack teams as bargaining leverage over existing franchise hosts.

Direct Democracy and Voter Preferences

The basic idea behind direct democracy is that direct citizen participation in governance enhances political legitimacy. According to this view, a more "hands-on" decisionmaking process produces policies that are more legitimate in the eyes of participants.[8] A related argument is that, under direct democracy, the outcome more closely reflects the actual preferences of voters. Under representative democracy, legislators might be corrupt or inept, or might face intense pressures from well-organized special interests, and so make decisions that serve the interests of only a minority of their constituents. For the case at hand, direct democracy would be expected to legitimize stadium funding choices and reveal the will of voters on these issues.

Perhaps the most appealing example of just how direct democracy might help concerns the prisoner's dilemma that state and local representatives might perceive themselves to be facing. Former Washington, D.C., mayor Sharon Pratt Kelly stated quite succinctly how and why cities chase sports franchises:

The mayors of American cities are confronted with a prisoner's dilemma of sorts. If no mayor succumbs to the demands of a franchise shopping for a new home then the teams will stay where they are. This, however, is unlikely to happen because if Mayor A is not willing to pay the price, Mayor B may think it is advantageous to open up the city's wallet. Then to protect his or her interest, Mayor A often ends up paying the demanded price.[9]

Intense competition among as many as ten prospective franchise sites, including most notably the Sun Coast Dome in St. Petersburg, Florida, before the expansion of Major League Baseball to Denver, Miami, Phoenix, and St. Petersburg, testifies to the veracity of Mayor Kelly's explanation. Once St. Petersburg had committed to the philosophy of "If you build it, they will come," other cities seeking to attract or to retain a team felt more pressure to build an elaborate new baseball stadium because St. Petersburg became a credible threat to win the competition for an available franchise. That this sort of prisoner's dilemma might be avoided under direct democracy has been a point of contention among referendum theorists for years.

An implication of Mayor Kelly's observation is that in order to understand why politicians might choose the referendum path, one must understand the most important differences between representative and direct democracy as devices for making policy. The key question she raises is whether resorting to a referendum can help elected officials either escape the prisoner's dilemma or at least avoid being held accountable by disappointed voters for the ultimate choice that is made. A related question is whether easy access to the initiative process also is a useful check on stadium decisions by politicians that depart from the interests of most citizens.

Unfortunately, for several reasons direct democracy frequently is no better, and can be worse, than representative democracy in deciding policy issues. What, precisely, are the general properties of direct democracy and how do they apply to the case of votes on stadiums?

In representative democracy, a candidate for office offers voters a long list of positions on policy issues, enunciates general political values, and reveals personal characteristics that voters can use to infer the candidate's likely positions on issues that are not explicitly mentioned in the campaign. By contrast, a referendum usually deals with a single issue, in this case a proposal for building and paying for a stadium. This fundamental difference between representative and direct democracy has several important consequences.

In campaigning for office, candidates need considerable resources to bring their messages to the voters. They obtain these resources from people and groups with intense preferences about certain public policy issues. These citizens give money and time to candidates who advocate positions that they find especially desirable. The pathology that this process can create is that only an extreme position on an issue may attract contributions, so that candidates who depart from the preferences of most voters on that issue are more successful at the polls because they have more resources to use during the campaign. In theory, direct democracy could correct this problem by giving voters the opportunity to block or to reverse a "sell-out" by their elected representatives on an issue that generates a large amount of special-interest support.

Chapter 2, concerning the benefits and costs of teams and stadiums, provides the information necessary to apply this idea to the case of sports stadiums. If stadiums have a net economic benefit, the source is a relatively small individual willingness to pay on the part of a large number of sports fans. Otherwise, the economic beneficiaries of a team and a stadium are concentrated in a very small proportion of the population: the team, the press that generates income by reporting about sports, the industries that will build the stadium or sell concessions in it, and perhaps a few businesses near the stadium that stand to gain by its presence. These interests have a very large individual stake in getting a stadium improved. On the other side, the per capita cost of a stadium subsidy is small, and the decline in other businesses through the substitution of sports for other entertainment is spread across a large number of firms throughout the metropolitan area, none of which is likely to experience a large loss. Thus a stadium issue is ripe for control by special interest politics. Most citizens have little at stake in the matter one way or the other, so that even though the net economic benefits of the stadium may be negative, the losers are unlikely to cast votes for local offices on the basis of this loss. By contrast, the extremely high per capita stakes of the industries that stand to benefit are likely to lead them to base their decisions about whom to support (through publicity and contributions) on whether a candidate supports the stadium.

For several reasons, direct democracy is not likely to solve the problem of representation bias in representative democracy and may produce results that depart even further from the preferences of most citizens. Most obviously, the campaign for a ballot measure, whether a referendum or an initiative, suffers from precisely the same bias as a campaign for office. The higher personal stakes of the proponents of a stadium are likely to induce them to take a far more active role than the opponents in the campaign for a ballot measure. Proponents are far more likely than opponents to be willing to pay the cost of putting an initiative on the ballot, and in the case of both an initiative and a referendum, they are likely to make larger contributions than opponents to finance the campaign. As reported elsewhere in this book, proponents of stadiums typically outspend opponents by an overwhelming margin. But even if this bias does not arise, so that Mayor Kelly's prisoner's dilemma places politicians between two well-organized interests, direct democracy has several characteristics that can prevent it from producing results that truly reflect majority preferences.

One problem is that direct democracy creates substantial barriers to political compromise. Direct democracy asks citizens to vote on each issue separately, so that it provides fewer opportunities for logrolling and consensus building than arise in a legislative setting. If the vote covers only one issue—such as a stadium subsidy—there is nothing to trade in a logrolling context, and consensus can be difficult to achieve if proponents have nothing to offer in exchange for other politicians' support.

Although logrolling is widely regarded as suspicious, if not downright undesirable, in reality most citizens usually prefer compromises across issues to the result of a sequence of single-issue votes. The reason for this preference is illustrated by a simple example, depicted in figure 5-1, which shows the choice of spending for two activities, sports facilities and new schools, in a three-person, majority-rule democracy. Points A, B, and C represent the "ideal point," or the most preferred combination of these two activities, for each of the three voters. For each person, as policy moves away from the ideal bundle of expenditures, that voter's welfare diminishes. The circles drawn around each ideal point in figure 5-1 represent combinations of spending on stadiums and schools that each voter finds equally desirable in relation to other combinations, and equally undesirable in comparison with the ideal point. For example, for the circle surrounding point A, voter A is indifferent to all the bundles on that circle, would prefer any bundle inside the circle to any combination on the circle, and would prefer any point on the circle to any bundle outside the circle.

Figure 5-1. *School Spending*

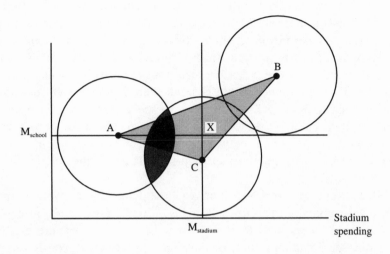

M_school

M_stadium

Stadium spending

In the example in figure 5-1, if voters are asked to decide each issue separately and are allowed to consider all possible levels of spending for each purpose, theory predicts that the resulting policy will be the median position on each issue. In the example, this outcome is C's ideal point on stadiums and A's ideal point on schools, which is shown as X in figure 5-1. The logic behind this prediction is as follows. Any stadium spending proposal that is less than C's ideal ($M_{stadium}$) can be beaten by $M_{stadium}$ (B and C will vote for $M_{stadium}$), and any spending proposal that exceeds $M_{stadium}$ will be beaten by $M_{stadium}$ (A and B will vote for $M_{stadium}$). Thus $M_{stadium}$ is the only proposal for stadium spending that can beat all other proposals, and it will be the outcome of the election if voters are allowed to consider it. By the same logic, M_{school} (the ideal level of school spending for voter A) will be the winner for spending on schools.

In almost all cases, the outcome of a series of single-issue votes can be defeated by many other proposals. In figure 5-1, for example, the shaded lens between A and C contains bundles that both voter A and voter C would prefer to X, even though both of these voters would obtain one of their "most preferred" outcomes on a series of single-issue votes. Thus if both A and C compromise on the issue that they can win on a single-issue vote—logroll, if you will, their positions—both can be made better off.

Of course, the example in figure 5-1 does not prove that logrolled results are necessarily better, but it does demonstrate two important points. First, a majority of voters is very likely to prefer policymaking processes that permit direct trade-offs across issues to the result of an issue-by-issue voting process that prohibits such trade-offs. Second, majority-rule votes are not a powerful tool for deciding which policies are best for society because, in general, there is no clear-cut majority-rule winner. In figure 5-1, any point in the shaded lens between A and C can defeat X, but all of these bundles can be defeated by other proposals that appeal to a coalition between A and B, and all of these outcomes can be defeated by another set of proposals appealing to a coalition between B and C.

One natural way to choose among all the points that can win majority approval is unanimous approval—that is, a combination that is preferred by all three voters to at least some other outcomes. In figure 5-1, the spending combinations that are unanimously preferred consist of the bundles within the triangle ABC. This triangle includes point X, but it also includes innumerable other bundles. Thus the criterion of unanimous consent is not very powerful in deciding which bundle to select.

Another natural way to identify the socially most desirable combination of policies is to take into account the intensities of preferences of voters. Voting enables citizens to express a simple preference among candidates or policy proposals, but it does not enable them to express the intensity of their preferences. By contrast, in a market, consumers express the intensity of their preferences by demonstrating their willingness to pay, such as by making a higher bid at an auction or buying a larger quantity of a much-desired product. One reason that economists advocate the use of benefit-cost analysis for selecting among policy alternatives is that benefits and costs are measures of the intensities of preferences. Benefits resemble the maximum bid at an auction, whereas costs measure the sacrifice of resources that is necessary to obtain these benefits and so resemble the reservation price of the person who has offered the item for sale at auction.

The analysis in figure 5-1 takes no account of intensities of preferences. For example, voter B may care little about how much is spent on schools or stadiums. Nevertheless, B will vote to spend more than X if given the chance. In a representative democracy, B (or B's representative) might be perfectly willing to let A and C decide how much to spend on schools and stadiums in return for a small reward: say, an outcome on some third issue (not shown in the picture) about which B cares more deeply. In this case, an outcome near the edge of the triangle ABC along the line between A and B plausibly could be the best outcome for all three voters.

Representative democracy facilitates logrolled compromises of this type. Unlike the single-issue feature of the referendum, legislators easily can make compromises across issues by trading their votes. If, in the example, each voter is represented faithfully by a legislator who seeks to bring policy as close as possible to the voter's ideal position, legislators will seek logrolled compromises that reflect the intensities of voter preferences, and on balance citizens will be more satisfied with the bundle of policies that emerge from this process.

Of course, elected representatives are unlikely to be completely faithful representatives of their constituents for two main reasons. First, citizens are not likely to observe completely and accurately the activities of their representatives in the legislative process as compromises are negotiated. Consequently, citizens are not likely to know whether their representatives obtained the best possible deal for them. Second, legislators are not likely to know with much precision the preferences of their constituents on all issues. Legislators observe only votes on the entire package of positions and attributes that they offered during the election, and they receive contributions and volunteer effort only from a few citizens who have atypically strong feelings about the election or a particular issue at stake in the election. Consequently, even the best intentions by legislators still are likely to lead to mistakes in representing the interests of constituents.

Direct democracy offers a solution to both of these problems. Citizen preferences can be made clearer, and faithless or erroneous decisions by representatives can be corrected; however, these advantages of direct democracy can be obtained only by sacrificing opportunities for compromise across issues.

Thus far the discussion has focused on circumstances in which voters have a full range of choice among either candidates for office (and the associated bundles of policies that are represented on the ballot) or the details of single-issue ballot measures. This form of analysis implicitly assumes that both representative and direct democracy are highly competitive in that both candidates and ballot measures are numerous. If elections are intensely competitive in this way, the centralizing tendencies of policy choice through legislative compromises and the power of the median voter have a chance to work. In practice, representative democracy is likely to be more competitive than direct democracy. Because running for office is relatively easy, elected officials—especially those who make decisions that are widely at variance with citizen preferences—typically face several competitors for office, whereas rarely are citizens given the opportunity to vote for several ballot propositions that propose different details for the same policy issue. The reason is straightforward: putting a measure on the ballot and informing voters about its consequences is expensive.

Even if voters were given multiple options on a ballot measure, it is far from obvious that they would carefully study them all to pick the very best, since doing so would be difficult and time-consuming. Research on direct democracy finds that citizens exhibit considerable ignorance about ballot measures, and, as a result, are susceptible to being unduly influenced by advertising, especially if one side of the issue is substantially better financed than the other.[10] These problems would be more severe if voters were called upon to select among numerous alternatives. Plausibly, voters facing a referendum with numerous alternatives on the same issue would simply rebel, concluding that elected officials were not doing their jobs because they failed to place a single reasonable proposal before the voters. Consequently, in a referendum voters almost always face only two choices: retain the status quo, or adopt a proposed alternative.

This feature of direct democracy has profound consequences for policy outcomes that have been made clear and concrete in the so-called setter model.[11] Instead of assuming that access to the ballot is competitive, the setter model examines the polar extreme: the case in which one person (for example, the mayor) or group (for example, the city council) controls access to the ballot. In this circumstance, the setter proposes the amount of spending for a particular purpose, and voters either accept or reject the proposal. For the purposes of this chapter, the setter typically wants to spend more on a stadium than the median voter would prefer. For example, the setter might be a political leader like the one Mayor Kelly describes who faces a demand from a local team and reluctantly decides to try to keep the team by supporting a new publicly financed stadium that is more expensive than most voters would prefer.

The requirement that the approval of the median voter be obtained constrains the setter's pursuit of spending. But a setter who controls the reversion point—the outcome that will occur if the proposal is rejected—can obtain more spending than the median voter prefers by making the reversion outcome highly undesirable. For example, the reversion threat

Figure 5-2. *The Power of the Setter*

A	B	C + D	E
No team	Obsolete stadium	No frills	Taj Mahal

can be that owners will move the team. Thus the reversion threat is used to induce the pivotal voter to favor too much spending because the only alternative, no spending at all, is worse.

The power of the setter is illustrated in figure 5-2, which depicts four possible outcomes of a debate about a stadium. The outcome on the extreme left is no team, and is the preferred position of citizen A. To the right of this position is having a team that plays in an unattractive, obsolete facility. Citizen B prefers this outcome. Next to the right is a new no-frills facility that would be an improvement over the existing obsolete stadium, but that would have no extras, such as luxury boxes, a fancy restaurant, elaborate offices for team executives, and an internal shopping mall for extensive concessions. Citizens C and D prefer this option. Finally, the possibility on the extreme right is a Taj Mahal, an elaborate facility with all the trimmings. Citizen E prefers this outcome.

In this example, the winning proposal, if all alternatives were considered, would be the no-frills stadium, which beats all other proposals by a vote of either 3 to 2 or 4 to 1. But suppose that the setter (the team acting through the mayor) prefers the Taj Mahal, keeps all other options off the ballot, and credibly threatens that "no team" will be the result if a new stadium is not built. In this case, voters C and D, and maybe even voter B, might prefer the Taj Mahal to no team, even though all voters but E would prefer the no-frills facility to the Taj Mahal. If voters believe either that the no-frills facility will never make the ballot or that the team will leave unless it obtains the Taj Mahal of stadiums, the Taj Mahal will win majority approval. Hence, in this case direct democracy offers no solution to the prisoner's dilemma that was described by Mayor Kelly.

Even if the pivotal voter does not believe entirely in the reversion threat, the result of voting no may be an aged, substandard facility. In general, median voters will support any spending level that is preferred to their beliefs about the reversion. The more dire their beliefs about the reversion, such as loss of the team, the higher the spending level that pivotal voter will support. Given this, the setter can push the median voter to favor a proposal to spend far more than the preferred amount. If the setter has complete control over access to the ballot, the prediction is that the number and cost of stadiums will exceed the amounts preferred by a large majority of voters.

Some anecdotal evidence from minor league baseball and the Denver sales tax vote is consistent with the setter model.[12] The modus operandi is for the city and the team to agree on all the details (financing shares, leases with tenants, and infrastructure payment) before going to the voters.

In addition to restricting the alternatives that voters are allowed to consider, the setter frequently has another source of power: deciding when the referendum will take place. In general, citizens are more likely to vote if the election includes something that they care deeply about. Hence turnout tends to be higher in general elections, when numerous offices and ballot measures are at stake, than in special elections for a single office or ballot measure. Suppose that most of the citizens depicted in figure 5-2 simply do not care very much about whether the team stays or a stadium is built. In particular, suppose that only citizen E, a fanatical sports fan, cares deeply about the issue and strongly prefers the Taj Mahal to any other outcome. In this case, all voters might turn out for a general election, and if the threat that the team will move is not credible, the Taj Mahal proposal might lose. But if the setter calls a special election on the stadium issue and only E bothers to vote, the Taj Mahal will win.

The setter model also has been applied to understand the effect of the initiative process.[13] Initiatives have a direct effect and an indirect effect on policy. The direct effect is almost identical to the setter model, whereas the indirect effect refers to the response of elected officials to the presence of an initiative threat.

An implication of the problem of representation bias is that no one is likely to sponsor an initiative—to gather the necessary signatures and to raise the funds to campaign for it—unless the sponsor is very dissatisfied with current policy and so wants to make a profound change in the status quo. Because the initiative requires majority approval, a large change is likely to be possible only under one of two circumstances: the status quo is quite different from the preferred policy of the median voter, or the sponsor can expect to outspend the opposition by an enormous amount and so to succeed in misleading the median voter about the consequences of the proposed measure. The latter is most likely when only the sponsor cares deeply about the policy issue at stake.

In either of these cases, the sponsor of an initiative is likely to propose a new policy that deviates substantially from the preferences of the median voter. If policy already departs from median preferences in the opposite direction preferred by the sponsor, the process is precisely the same as the setter model. The sponsor places an initiative on the ballot that is a little better for the median voter than the status quo, but still far from the median ideal. If the sponsor anticipates misleading the median voter, the proposal will be as close to the sponsor's preference (and as far from the median preference) as misleading advertising will allow.[14]

Of course, a legislature can avoid initiatives that have the same characteristic as setter-dominated referenda simply by passing bills that are near the preferences of the median voter. Thus one indirect effect of the possibility of initiatives is that it might force a legislature to take actions that prevent policy from deviating too far from median preferences in order to forestall initiatives that reflect the setter bias. Unfortunately, Mayor Kelly gives us a reason to believe that elected officials will not always take such preemptive action. If an issue is divisive among citizens, elected officials may respond to the possibility of an initiative by simply not taking a public position on the divisive issue and letting initiatives deal with the problem.

In short, if elected officials face Mayor Kelly's prisoner's dilemma, the possibility of an initiative may cause them not to take action, thereby letting policy remain a long way from the preferred position of the median voter. The sponsor of an initiative who fills this void is likely to be someone with an atypical and intense policy preference, proposing a policy that also departs from the preferences of the median voter. In fact, there is considerable evidence that when the initiative process is available, legislative bodies are more prone to avoid confronting controversial issues.[15]

To the extent that the stadium issue is affected by the possibility of an initiative, the nature of its influence is likely to resemble the setter model. The vast majority of citizens have relatively little at stake in stadium subsidies, for the annualized cost of even the most heavily subsidized and expensive facilities is only tens of dollars per household. The people with unusually intense interests include team owners, construction interests, diehard sports fans, and sports journalists, all of whom are likely to have atypically favorable views about a new stadium and to advocate a more elaborate facility than most citizens would find ideal. Hence, to the extent that there is an initiative threat, it is for a measure that proposes the Taj Mahal, not a no-frills facility.

For the setter model of referenda and initiatives to be an accurate predictor of the outcome of direct democracy, ballot access must be restricted. The restrictions can be legal ones, such as rules that limit access to the ballot, or financial ones, such as the high cost of qualifying a measure for the ballot and campaigning for its passage. In addition, most voters must prefer moderate spending to either none at all or the level advocated by the most ardent proponents (that is, preferences must be "single-peaked" at moderate levels of spending). Finally, the ballot issue must be reasonably straightforward. Voting must be on a single dimension (such as spending on a stadium) rather than on a bundle of issues. If voters are confronted with a bundle of issues in the referendum, have weak estimates of the net result of the referendum (the costs, financing details, the potential for cost overruns, the lease agreement), or anticipate that a sequence of votes may be in the offing, then the median voter and the setter models are less insightful than other, more complex descriptions.

The upshot of this analysis is that direct democracy has certain pitfalls that can lead to excessive spending on stadiums compared with either the preferences of most citizens on that particular issue or the likely outcome of a legislative process. Whether this outcome will occur depends on the factual circumstances surrounding the ballot measure: the power and preferences of the setter/sponsor, the configuration and intensities of the preferences of voters, and the credibility of a draconian reversion should the measure fail. The history of stadium votes will indicate whether outcomes reflect median preferences.

Stadium Votes: A Brief History and Observations

Brief descriptions of the direct democracy votes used in this discussion appear in the appendix to this chapter. Table 5-1 is a condensed version. The votes varied widely in purpose: increasing the sales tax, repealing previous legislation that hindered public funding, issuing bonds, increasing property taxes, specifying expenditures without identifying financing

Table 5-1. *Sports Facility Votes and Their Outcomes*

Location	Date	Purpose	Yes	No	Percentage yes
Passed					
Arlington	1/19/91	Sales tax	21,924	11,936	64.7
Baltimore	1974	Enabling	91,981	45,175	67.1
Charlotte	5/3/86	Property tax	17,825	17,396	50.6
Cincinnati	3/19/96	Sales tax	—	—	61.4
Cleveland	5/8/90	Excise tax	—	—	51.7
Cleveland	11/95	Excise tax	—	—	—
Denver	8/14/90	Sales tax	—	—	54.0
Detroit	3/19/96	Bonds	—	—	—
Detroit	3/19/96	Bonds	—	—	—
Nashville	1996	Bonds	—	—	59.0
San Antonio	1989	Unknown	—	—	—
San Francisco	3/26/96	Approval	101,343	85,313	54.3
Failed					
Chicago	1986	Enabling	3,744	3,787	49.7
Cleveland	1984	Property tax	—	—	—
Colorado Springs	8/85	Bonds	13,364	21,837	38.0
Colorado Springs	4/89	Bonds	14,965	34,597	30.2
Durham	3/90	Bonds	9.051	12,984	41.1
Miami	11/2/82	Sales tax	108,963	223,774	32.7
Miami	1988	Unknown	—	—	—
Milwaukee	4/4/95	Lottery	348,818	618,377	36.1
New Jersey	1987	Bonds	473,904	972,783	32.8
Oklahoma City	—	Unknown	—	—	—
San Francisco	11/3/87	Approval	85,005	96,445	46.8
San Francisco	11/7/89	Approval	85,796	87,850	49.4
San Francisco	11/7/89	Approval	83,599	98,875	45.8
San Jose	11/6/90	Approval	85,313	89,269	48.9
San Jose	6/2/92	Utility tax	78,809	94,466	45.5
Santa Clara	11/6/90	Utility tax	126,906	129,652	49.5
Seattle	9/19/95	Sales tax	245,418	248,500	49.9

Source: See the appendix to this chapter.
—Unknown.

methods, raising excise taxes, enabling a sports lottery, eliciting public sentiment through "approval" votes, and increasing utility and hotel taxes. For the sample of votes listed in table 5-1, all were binding except for those listed as "approval" and the straw votes concerning Charlotte and Chicago.

Of the referenda in the sample, 41 percent passed (twelve of twenty-nine). Although there are not many observations of each funding type and one must be cautious in taking these observations very far, table 5-1 provides some evidence about the financing arrangements preferred by voters. Excise taxes were always approved, whereas utility taxes and a sports lottery were never approved. In addition, only one so-called approval vote passed out of five times that they were tried. The outcome for the rest of the issues is too mixed to support further general conclusions.

Table 5-1 also reveals that referenda occur predominantly in locations aiming to keep their current teams. The exceptions are Denver, Charlotte, Nashville, New Jersey, San Jose, and Santa Clara County. Denver's sales tax vote and New Jersey's bond issue were both in pursuit of an expansion team. Charlotte's sales tax straw vote reflected an attempt to attract a nearby minor league baseball team. Nashville's bond issue fulfilled its promise to the owners of the Houston Oilers in return for their move to Tennessee in 1997. The San Jose/Santa Clara votes concerned the possibility of a move by the baseball Giants. The remaining twenty-two elections all occurred in cities currently hosting professional sports teams at either the minor or major level.

Voting margins are known for twenty-two of the elections in table 5-1. The average yes vote for the eight that passed was 58 percent, and that for the losing propositions was 43 percent. Most of the elections were quite close. Fully 55 percent of the issues with known voting outcomes had yes votes between 45 and 55 percent. The closeness of so many of these elections provides some insight into whether the setter model or the median voter model better explains the outcome. If the reversion is much below the median ideal and vote margins are small, the inference from the setter model is that proposed spending exceeds the amount preferred by a majority of voters.[16] The setter tries to push spending to the highest level that the pivotal voter will approve, while everyone whose preferred spending level is less than what the pivotal voter prefers casts a no vote. In the setter model, referenda vary primarily in the amount of spending that is proposed. A draconian reversion outcome produces high spending, whereas a reasonably good status quo (in this case a stadium that a team would not plausibly abandon if the Taj Mahal is not approved) produces modest spending. By contrast, if the median voter's preferences are powerful, because ballot access is easy or because the setter has median preferences, the reversion point will be irrelevant to outcomes, and a moderate, centralizing outcome always will occur. In this case, variation in referenda will be manifest primarily in vote margins. A very bad status quo would lead to overwhelming support for the proposal that is favored by the median voter, whereas a reasonably good but slightly

Table 5-2. *The Distribution of Yes-Vote Percentages in Sports Facility Elections*

Yes vote (%)	Number of outcomes	Percentage of all outcomes
1–10	0	0
10–20	0	0
20–30	0	0
30–40	5	23
40–50	7	32
50–60	7	32
60–70	3	14
70–80	0	0
80–90	0	0
90–100	0	0
Total known	22	

Source: Author's calculation.
a. Note clustering around the 50 percent margin, which suggests that setters have been in operation.

inferior status quo would lead to a vote in which the median voter's preferred outcome just barely wins.

Table 5-2 shows the distribution of yes-vote percentages. If the setter logic is compelling, clustering close to the bare 50 percent margin supports the idea that setters have been in operation. A wide distribution would support the idea that the median preferences were being served. Compared with votes on hospitals and nuclear power, these outcomes are very concentrated around 50 percent.[17] This outcome indicates that the preferences of the pivotal median voter are violated frequently. Most likely, more often than not most citizens are voting in favor of stadiums but would prefer to see less spent on them. Again, such an observation probably is more warranted for nonrepeated elections; the San Francisco case may not fall under such an explanation.

Recent Direct Democracy Episodes

Additional detailed statistical analysis can lend more insight into the outcomes described in the preceding section. But that analysis must wait for another occasion. Here, case studies are presented detailing the (possibly) good, the bad, and the ugly of the voting process for stadiums. All in all, it is not clear that direct democracy has proven an aid to better public policy toward stadiums.

The first case concerns the Giants' quest for a new stadium. In the late 1980s, there were three elections in San Francisco, plus three votes aimed at keeping the Giants in the area but not in San Francisco, before a referendum was finally passed in 1996. In the Bay Area, the people had the opportunity to speak repeatedly. Eventually, with some of their options reduced because of expansion into Denver, Miami, Phoenix, and St. Petersburg, the Giants and their supporters were forced to realize that the people of San Francisco wanted a privately owned and financed downtown stadium.

On November 3, 1987, San Francisco voted on Proposition W, which proposed that a ballpark be built on land close to the Oakland Bay Bridge. San Francisco allows the mayor simply to put such an issue on the ballot, and that is what happened in this case; a few supervisors added their supporting signatures. Although the ballot specified that the park would be provided at no cost to the city, devoting valuable city land to the proposal carried a high opportunity cost. The referendum did specify that taxes would not increase and that all debt incurred would be repaid with nontax money. But the true economics behind the issue included a reduction in revenue from some taxes not paid on the ballpark land (see chapter 12).

While the ballot statement seems innocuous enough, debate was heated. In the public ballot statement of the San Francisco registrar of voters, proponents argued that passage would keep the Giants (and all the spending they represent) in town, help invigorate parts of the downtown area, and squelch the growing opinion that San Francisco was dying. Notable supporting statements were submitted by the mayor, most of the city supervisors, the chamber of commerce, and organized labor.

Although the setter logic arguably is less operational in a repeated-vote setting, elements of that strategy do appear here. In expressing the hopes of an expenditure-maximizing setter—namely, that the voters should believe that the reversion level is zero—Bob Lurie (chairman of the Giants) wrote: "The issue is not whether or not we should build a ballpark for Bob Lurie or for the Giants. This franchise will be around a lot longer than I, and they will always have a place to play. I just think it would be tragic if it is not in San Francisco."[18] The zero-level reversion threat could not be put more forcefully.

Opponents, a much more diverse mix of smaller groups (the Sierra Club, the Coalition for San Francisco Neighborhoods, and a booster club in favor of an alternative downtown site), countered mostly with quality-

Table 5-3. *The Early San Francisco Experience, Voting by Aggregate Area, 1987 and 1989*[a]

| Area | Proposition | | |
	W, 1987	P, 1989	V, 1989
Richmond		x	
Inner Richmond		x	
Pacific Heights/Marina	x	x	
Nob Hill/Russian Hill		x	
China Town/North Beach	x	x	
Downtown	x	x	
Fillmore		x	x
Haight Ashbury		x	x
Upper Market/Eureka Valley		x	x
Noe Valley/Diamond Heights		x	
Mission			x
Bernal Heights		x	x
Potero Hill			x
Bayview/Hunters Point	x		x
Visitacion Valley			x
Excelsior (Outer Mission)		x	
West of Twin Peaks		x	
Igleside	x		x
Lake Merced			
Inner Sunset		x	x
Citywide absentees			x

Source: Author's calculation.
a. x = majority of votes achieved.

of-life issues near the stadium location. But the most insightful among them argued that nothing in the referendum prohibited the diversion of existing taxes. Others did not believe the no-cost claims, especially with respect to support infrastructure, but also voiced fears of financial bailouts. The proposition failed 96,445 to 85,005, receiving a majority in five of twenty-one voting aggregates reported by the registrar of voters (see table 5-3).

The other two early San Francisco issues were on the November 7, 1989, ballot. Proposition P sought voter approval of a joint stadium venture agreement between the city and Spectacor Management Group (covering development, financing, land, amended zoning, revenue sharing, and ownership). Again, this proposition was put on the ballot by the mayor. Although it failed by the narrow margin of 87,850 to 85,796, it actually received a majority in fourteen of twenty-one voting aggregates reported by the registrar of voters (table 5-3). As table 5-2 shows, the margin of yes votes increased dramatically for this issue over the earlier one. Perhaps an explicitly stated mix of public and private financing and the new location were more favorable in voters' eyes.

The second issue on the same ballot was much less successful. Proposition V, on the ballot by initiative petition, asked voters if the Board of Supervisors should explore proposals to improve Candlestick Park at private expense instead of a proposal to construct a downtown baseball stadium. The referendum received a majority in only ten of twenty-one voting aggregates reported by the registrar of voters and failed by a much wider margin, 98,875 to 83,599. Taken as a whole, the early voting results in San Francisco indicated that a downtown ballpark was preferred to Candlestick and that, at most, there should be a mix of public and private funds.

Before the last vote in which San Francisco voters approved a ballpark, three other votes were taken in nearby localities. Basically, the Giants wanted help in paying for the park, and if San Francisco was reluctant, then maybe other communities would be less so. San Jose held city votes in 1990 and 1992 and voted with the rest of Santa Clara County in 1990.

On November 6, 1990, San Jose voted on Measure H. As in the first San Francisco election, the Giants wanted the city to participate in building a "sports facility for major league baseball" with tax dollars. Measure H failed by a vote of 89,269 to 85,313. On the same ballot, Santa Clara County voted on Measure G, which requested a 1 percent utility tax and a parking tax at any new stadium totaling $15 million per year, to pay the county's share of a projected $153 million construction cost. The expected finish date was 1994. The vote went 129,652 against to 126,906 in favor, with the following interesting observation. San Jose voted in favor, with Milpitas, Santa Clara, Sunnyvale, Stanford, the unincorporated areas, and absentees voting against. The results of Measures H and G are consistent with the observation that, while voters in San Jose were not interested in financing a stadium by themselves, they were willing to share the cost with the rest of the county. This view seems reasonable, given that the Giants probably would draw from the larger geographical area.

The final San Jose election came two years later, on June 2, 1992. The question was whether the city should finance most of a $265 million stadium project. The mechanism was a 2 percent increase in the city's utility tax, about $35 per year per household. Despite the fact the proponents raised $1 million for their campaign, the question went down to defeat with a 55 percent vote against.

An overview of the elections outside San Francisco shows a purposeful strategy that is too complex to be explained completely on the basis of the median voter model. First, the issue was structured to seek a generic commitment from San Jose or Santa Clara County. Second, efforts were aimed at playing the city off against the county, but still for a generic commitment. Failing these, the final try was to get specific about the funding relationship. This strategy is consistent with self-interested behavior on the part of the Giants, coupled with an ability to structure the contents of the ballot issue in a self-vying way. While having some setter model characteristics, no subsidy level acceptable to the voters and to the Giants was found.

After failing to generate public funding all over the Bay Area, the Giants did receive voter approval for a stadium. Proposition B passed on March 26, 1996, 101,343 yes to 51,222 no. The referendum was simple: whether to approve the China Basin site for the construction of a ballpark. The measure as written did not discuss financial arrangements. According to a popular source, the proponents of the referendum promised no use of public funds for construction, no new taxes, no use of general fund money, and no taxpayer liability.[19] Given the history of this nearly ten-year pursuit, a final synopsis would be that voters felt the Giants belonged downtown, rejected the many ways that public funding was requested to subsidize the Giants, but expressed a willingness to provide a valuable public site for the stadium. Direct democracy eventually made preferences clearer.

Nevertheless, voters' preferences regarding a new stadium still may not be fully reflected in the approved arrangement. This referendum, being only the most recent in a series, may not be perceived by anyone—voters, political leaders, and the Giants—as necessarily the last word. How any of these actors might behave if they thought that future votes were likely is unknown and far too complicated to deduce. Furthermore, although the Giants have faced opposition to proposed moves to San Jose, other areas in northern California—notably, Sacramento—are still a threat, so that the median voter in San Francisco may still perceive a draconian reversion.

Perhaps the most uncertain aspect of the San Francisco vote is that the measure did not specifically ask whether the Giants should pay for anything. Although public statements by proponents disavowed public subsidies for stadium construction, proponents did not make similar statements about whether the Giants should pay for the site and the other public expenditures on police and transportation access that go with a stadium. As a result, we do not know if the most recent result reflects the most preferred outcome for a majority of voters. Furthermore, since the ballot measure contained nothing specific about the type of financial arrangement that will eventually be chosen, and in light of the results discussed in the rest of the chapters in this volume, the promises by proponents for no public financing may have been cheap talk. It would be naive to ignore the history of other cities in which low information content in a referendum and manipulation of the final outcome have gone hand in hand (as in Cleveland and Cincinnati).

Even if the San Francisco case eventually becomes an example of "the good," other cases provide "the bad and the ugly." Seattle's recent referendum on a new stadium for the Mariners gave a clear directive: no public spending for a stadium. But this statement of the will of voters has been overridden by state politicians. On September 19, 1995, the stadium vote in King County failed by a narrow margin (246,500 to 245,418), but fail it did. Voters were unwilling to raise the sales tax by half a percent toward the projected $240 million cost of a retractable roof plus repairs for the Kingdome. Talk of relocating the team to the Washington, D.C.– Northern Virginia area surfaced immediately. Then, the governor stepped in, found some state funds and a way to ease a spending limitation for King County, and sent the issue back to the King County Council. After short deliberations, the subsequent council vote in early October, 1995, was in favor. As noted earlier, one use of a referendum is to see if sentiment is evenly split in order to begin logrolling and consensus building at the legislative level. There are many paths to stadium financing.

In the case of Seattle, the ultimate legislative logroll may be better or worse for most citizens, but the referendum did provide the information that opinion was closely divided on whether the community should build an elaborate, highly subsidized stadium. In this case, because the reversion point—"no team"—was highly credible, the median voter's most preferred outcome probably was for a less elaborate facility and a lower subsidy. But this option was not placed before the voters, and it is plausible that enough deals were made in the final stadium arrangement so that some of those who opposed a Seattle Taj Mahal were mollified by logrolls involving other policies.

Chicago and Milwaukee provide really ugly cases. The White Sox strategy in gaining support for their new Comiskey Park was interesting.[20] After shopping all over the Chicago area in search of a new stadium, the Sox settled on Addison, Illinois (DuPage County). The Sox mounted a $100,000 campaign on a nonbinding, advisory vote to the opponents' $3,000, only to lose by the barest of margins, 3,787 to 3,744 in 1986. But the action in Addison may have been part of a larger strategy. If the Sox had desired, they were not kept from further pursuits in DuPage County. In fact, a corresponding countywide referendum to create an open space, precluding any other chance for the Sox somewhere else in the county, was defeated 12,306 to 5,888. But rather than carry it further, the Sox employed the Tampa Bay–St. Petersburg ploy, threatening to move to Florida, and ended up back in their old neighborhood in a new Comiskey Park. The Illinois state legislature passed by one vote a $150 million package resting on a 2 percent tax on hotel and motel rooms in Chicago.

In the Milwaukee Brewers episode, a statewide referendum to create a special sports lottery, with proceeds going for stadium construction, was defeated resoundingly (64 percent against) in the spring of 1994. A county-by-county examination of the vote result reveals that the four Milwaukee metro area counties (Milwaukee, Ozaukee, Washington, and Waukesha) all voted in favor, typically by wide margins. But apparently the perceived benefits stopped there. All the remaining counties in the state voted no, including the three southeastern counties: Kenosha, Racine, and Walworth.

The rest of the Milwaukee story is similar to that of Seattle and Chicago. After two misfires, a financing plan was adopted by the state legislature on October 4, 1995, in the wee hours of the morning. The state plan increased the sales tax by 0.1 percent for the five counties surrounding the proposed new Milwaukee County Stadium. As always, rumored alternative locations for the Brewers made the vote interesting. Some of the debate centered on whether the alternative was Charlotte or Mexico City. Apparently, the stadium mess has the potential to take on international dimensions.

If the history of stadium referenda is any indication, direct democracy for stadium decisions must receive a mixed review. The San Francisco episode has produced the most favorable result in that the people spoke repeatedly and with purpose, although whether the eventual outcome will match the revealed preferences of voters remains to be seen. Other episodes (in Seattle, Chicago, and Milwaukee) reveal that direct democracy can reflect the Hobson's choice of a strong setter regime or can be ignored.

Conclusions

The virtue of direct democracy is that it "enables" voters. Their preferences can be expressed on each issue, rather than on a package of issues as represented by a candidate for office. But does it offer a way out of the stadium mess? The verdict from the first look undertaken here is mixed. The San Francisco case is cause for guarded optimism. But the data on the closeness of outcomes and the other examples (Seattle, Chicago, and Milwaukee) represent evidence to the contrary. The weight of all the empirical evidence seems to indicate that median voters are not getting their way. The pattern of vote splits is highly concentrated around the bare 50 percent majority. Furthermore, some of the measures policymakers use—such as creating a stadium authority and insulating it from public review—coupled with mayors who confront a prisoner's dilemma, do not favor the median voter. Cities are likely to spend more on stadiums than the median preference holder would desire. Where referenda fail, rather than having made some sort of compromise, teams will be left confronting dilapidated facilities. As long as there are more cities that are viable team locations than there are teams, the outcome is likely to be that the team will move.

That a careful judgment of the issue is required is clear. As long as professional sports leagues maintain an artificial shortage of teams, so that some cities can be used by team owners as leverage against current franchise hosts in their pursuit of better stadiums and leases, the stadium mess will continue. Direct democracy can have an ameliorative impact, as in the San Francisco case, but cannot be counted on to stem the tide. The typical result of direct democracy is consistent with the quotation at the beginning of this chapter: the people speak and stadium construction continues apace.

Yet opportunities abound for further useful work on the relationship between direct democracy and the stadium mess. First, a detailed model of voting dictates that the benefits and costs to different voters be closely examined. For example, it would be important to know the geographic dispersion of preferences. In Milwaukee and Santa Clara, the results show a clear pattern of support close to the proposed facility location. It should be expected that those closest to the proposed locations would have stronger preferences one way or the other.

Second, it would be interesting to see if the fortunes of the team at the time that the vote is taken influence the outcome of the vote. For example, in 1987 the Giants lost in the National League championship series and the referendum failed. In 1989 they won the National League pennant (but lost the World Series 4 to 0), and the vote that year was very close. The Giants did poorly in 1990 and the Santa Clara issue failed. On a related note, backers of the Mariners may have done better because they scheduled the election just before the team won a close race for the division championship, but before it lost the American League pennant to Cleveland. In any event, it should prove enlightening to pursue this fascinating topic further, especially since new data are being generated all the time (referenda were held on November 5, 1996, in Miami, Detroit, and Houston).

Appendix: Referenda by City

Not all referenda were held at the city level. Some were county issues, and some were statewide issues. Not all were for one team, either. Some were for a facility for two teams. As a result, this appendix lists the votes by the city that one would normally think that the referendum would affect.

Arlington, Texas. Proposition 1, January 19, 1991. New stadium for the Rangers. Sales tax increase of 0.5 cent to cover $135 million. Referendum passed 21,924 to 11,936.

Baltimore, Maryland. Question Q, 1974.[21] Repealed legislation dictating that Memorial Stadium is a memorial to veterans and no other stadium can be constructed with public funds. Referendum passed 91,981 to 56,175.

Chandler, Arizona. Unknown title. January 23, 1996. For Chandler Stadium for spring training for the Milwaukee Brewers. Sought $5 million in bonds ($6 per year in residential property taxes per $100,000 assessed value, $23 per year for businesses) to meet $9.2 million from Maricopa County Stadium District. Overall, estimates of the renovation costs are between $9 million and $12 million. Outcome unknown.

Charlotte, North Carolina. Nonbinding referendum, May 3, 1986. Straw vote in Mecklenberg County (lost the Charlotte Knights to Fort Mill, South Carolina) on a one-time increase in property tax, 1.7 cents per $100 assessed value to raise $2.7 million, for a new 5,000 seat stadium: 17,825 yes to 17,396 no. Commissioners went ahead.[22]

Chicago, Illinois. Addison, Illinois (DuPage County). Unknown title. 1986. White Sox request the hospitality of the citizens of Addison. Rejected, 3,787 to 3,744. A corresponding countywide referendum to create an open space, precluding any other chance for the Sox somewhere else in the county, was defeated 12,306 to 5,888.[23]

Cincinnati, Ohio. Hamilton County. Unknown title. March 19, 1996. Raise the county sales tax by 0.5 percent to raise more than $400 million to subsidize new, separate stadiums for the Reds and Bengals. Total cost is about $544.[24] Seventy percent of the tax revenue would go to paying for the stadiums while 30 percent would be used to offset a property tax rollback. Passed with 61.4 percent in favor.

Cleveland, Ohio. Cuyahoga County. Unknown title. 1984. Proposal for domed stadium for the Cleveland Indians financed with property taxes. Sources simply note that it happened and failed to pass.[25]

Cleveland, Ohio. State of Ohio. Unknown title. 1990. A small excise tax on the purchase of alcoholic beverages and cigarettes to share 50/50 in the stadium costs of $344 million for a new stadium for the Cleveland Indians and a new arena for the Cavaliers (known as the Gateway Project): 51.7 percent yes.

Cleveland, Ohio. Cuyahoga County. Unknown title. November 1995. To extend a sin tax on alcohol and cigarettes for ten years to help fund 15 percent of the $170 million to Cleveland Stadium (Browns). The referendum passed.

Colorado Springs, Colorado. Unknown title. August 1985. A $6 million bond issue to renovate Spurgeon Field to replace lower division minor league baseball with Joe Buzas's AAA Portland team: 13,364 yes, 21,837 no.[26]

Colorado Springs, Colorado. Unknown title. April 1989. A $37.5 million bond issue to finance $50 million arena. 14,965 yes, 34,597 no.[27]

Denver, Colorado. Baseball Stadium Question: "Shall, in support of efforts to gain a Major League Baseball team for Colorado, the Denver Metropolitan Major League Baseball Stadium District be authorized to levy and collect a uniform sales tax throughout the district at a rate not to exceed one-tenth of one percent for a period not to exceed twenty years, with the proceeds to be used, along with funds from other sources including the private sector, for the costs relating to a Major League Baseball stadium to be located within the district, provided that the tax will be levied and collected only upon the granting of a Major League Baseball franchise by Major League Baseball to be located within the district?" August 14, 1990. Passed 54 to 46.

Detroit, Michigan. Proposition A. March 19, 1996. Detroit votes for a new baseball stadium; $40 million in stadium bonds. Passed.

Detroit, Michigan. Proposition B. March 19, 1996. Detroit votes for a new baseball stadium. Along with Proposition A, the issue concerns $40 million in stadium bonds. Passed.

Durham, North Carolina. Unknown title. March 1990. Countywide vote for $11.28 million in general obligation bonds to build a new stadium and keep the Bulls. Failed: 9,051 yes, 12,984 no.[28]

Miami, Florida. Dade County Question: "Subject to this referendum, the Dade County Commission has enacted an ordinance authorizing a 1 percent increase in the sales tax during 1983 for use with private contributions to finance Sports stadium, Miami arena/exposition center, Performing arts and recreation centers, Other sports, arts and convention centers as are affordable. Remaining proceeds shall be used solely for property tax relief. Do you favor financing Sports, Arts and Recreation Centers with a 1-cent sales tax for 12 months only?" November 2, 1982. Failed: 108,963 yes, 223,774 no.[29]

Miami, Florida. Unknown jurisdiction. Unknown title. One failed in 1988.[30]

Milwaukee, Wisconsin. State of Wisconsin. Wisconsin Sports Lottery: "Shall section 24(6) of article IV of the constitution be amended to permit the state to operate lottery games that have their proceeds dedicated to athletic facilities?" Basically, creates a special funding source to pay for stadiums. April 4, 1995. Failed: 348,818 yes, 618,377 no.

Nashville, Tennessee. Unknown title. 1996. City vote for an $80 million bond issue toward $292 million total for 65,000 seat open-air stadium to open in 1998. Called for $144 million in local financing, $77 million state, and $71 million private (seat licenses). Approved by 59 percent.[31]

New Jersey. Public Question 3: "Shall the 'New Jersey Baseball Stadium Bond Act of 1987,' which authorizes the State to issue bonds in the amount of $185,000,000 for the purpose of providing funds for the acquisition and construction by the New Jersey Sports and Exposition Authority of a Major League Baseball stadium located in the State, the ownership thereof to be conveyed to the State upon completion, and to be operated by the Authority pursuant to a lease or other agreement with the State, including the land necessary for the stadium and land necessary for other projects of the authority which may be constructed on the site of the stadium; and in a principal amount sufficient to refinance any of the bonds if the same will result in present value savings, and providing the ways and means to pay the interest on the debt and also to pay and discharge the principal thereof, and which prohibits the issuance of these bonds until a commitment is obtained from a Major League Baseball team to locate in the State, to use the words 'New Jersey' as part of the team name, and use the baseball stadium for its home games, be approved?" 1987. Basically, a general obligation bond issue. Failed: 972,783 no, 473,904 yes.

Oklahoma City, Oklahoma. Unknown jurisdiction. Unknown title. The measure failed.[32]

San Antonio, Texas. Unknown jurisdiction. Unknown title. A referendum was passed in 1989.[33]

San Francisco, California. Proposition W: "Shall it be the policy of the people of San Francisco to build a baseball park at 7th and Townsend Streets at no cost to the City?" November 3, 1987. City/County vote with the idea that the park would be built on land provided at no cost to the city, there would be no increases in taxes, and all debt would be repaid with nontax money. San Francisco allows the mayor to simply put such an issue on the ballot. This one also was signed by a few supervisors. Failed: 96,445 to 85,005.

San Francisco, California. Proposition P: "Shall the City enter into an agreement with Spectacor Management Group, consistent with specified principles regarding the land acquisition, financing and construction of a new ballpark in the China Basin area, and shall certain zoning laws be amended to facilitate the construction of a ballpark in that area?" November 7, 1989. This issue really was whether the city and Spectacor should sign an agreement to pursue a joint stadium venture (encompassing development, financing, land, revenue sharing, and ownership) with amended zoning (forty-foot height limit in an industrial area would have to be waived). Spectacor would be paid $20 million out of hotel taxes and the city would assume liability for up to $10 million in overruns. Further, under the agreement with Spectacor the city would buy the land, prepare the site, and maintain title but forfeit property tax assessments. Failed: 87,850 to 85,796.

San Francisco, California. Proposition V: "Shall it be the policy of the people of the City and County of San Francisco for the board of Supervisors to explore proposals to improve Candlestick Park at private expense instead of any proposal to construct a downtown baseball stadium?" November 7, 1989. This proposition made the ballot by initiative petition (5 percent of the vote for mayor in 1987, 9,399 votes, were needed and 10,560 were collected). Failed: 98,875 to 83,599.

San Francisco, California. Proposition B. March 26, 1996. A referendum that promised no public funds would be used for construction, but the zoning exemptions requested in the earlier vote were included. Advertisements promised no new taxes, no general fund money, and no taxpayer liability.[34] Passed 101,343 yes, 51,222 no.

San Jose, California. Measure H: "Shall the City of San Jose participate in the building of a sports facility for Major League Baseball with the use of tax dollars?" November 6, 1990. Failed: 89,269 no, 85,313 yes.

San Jose, California. Unknown title. City to finance bulk of $265 million stadium project. Proponents raised $1 million for their campaign! One percent increase in city's utility tax, about $35 per year for average resident. June 2, 1992. Result: 55 percent no.

Santa Clara County, California. Measure G. One percent utility tax and parking tax at any new stadium worth $15 million per year to reach $153 million. Expected finish date was 1994. November 6, 1990. Failed: 129,652 to 126,906.

Seattle, Washington. Unknown title. It was a 0.5 percent sales tax increase to raise $240 million for Mariners retractable-roof stadium plus some repairs to the Kingdome. September 19, 1995. Failed: 246,500 no, 245,418 yes.

Notes

1. The mayor's comment referred to a referendum for renovations to Chandler Field, spring home of the Milwaukee Brewers. *Phoenix Gazette,* October 13, 1995, p. A1.

2. The distinction between an initiative and a referendum is not a simple one. An initiative is direct legislation by the voters, whereas a referendum is a vote on legislation that has already been approved through the normal legislative process. Usually an initiative is associated with a citizen petition, and a referendum with either a constitutional requirement or a decision by elected officials to place legislation on the ballot; however, this association is not completely accurate. The distinction between the two is confused by the fact that in some jurisdictions public officials, including legislative bodies, have the authority to place an initiative on the ballot, and in some cases citizens can petition to force a statute

to be ratified by the voters. One source of confusion is the constitutional necessity in some states that initiatives can only be amended by another initiative, so that new legislation followed by a referendum is not a pathway that is available to elected officials. For a discussion of the complexities of the instruments of direct democracy, see Bruce E. Cain and Roger G. Noll, "Principles of State Constitutional Design," in Bruce E. Cain and Roger G. Noll, eds., *Constitutional Reform in California: Making State Government More Effective and Responsive* (University of California Institute for Governmental Studies Press, 1995).

3. On the general issue of subsidized stadiums, see Benjamin A. Okner, "Subsidies of Stadiums and Arenas," in Roger G. Noll, ed., *Government and the Sports Business* (Brookings, 1974); James Quirk and Rodney Fort, *Pay Dirt: The Business of Professional Team Sports* (Princeton University Press, 1992), chap. 4; Andrew Zimbalist, *Baseball and Billions: A Probing Look inside the Big Business of Our National Pastime* (New York: Basic Books, 1992), chap. 6; and Rodney Fort, "The Stadium Mess," in Daniel R. Marburger, ed., *Stee-rike Four! What's Wrong with the Business of Baseball?* (Westport, Conn.: Greenwood, 1996).

4. National Football League, "National Voters Say 'Yes' to NFL," *NFL Report*, vol. 45 (Summer 1996), p. 4.

5. Fort, "The Stadium Mess."

6. George Sage, "Stealing Home: Political, Economic, and Media Power and a Publicly Funded Baseball Stadium in Denver," *Journal of Sport and Social Issues*, vol. 17 (1993), pp. 110–24.

7. Okner, "Subsidies of Stadiums and Arenas," p. 329.

8. For excellent histories and analyses of direct democracy, see David Butler and Austin Ranney, eds., *Referendums: A Comparative Study of Practice and Theory* (Washington, D.C.: American Enterprise Institute, 1978); and Thomas E. Cronin, *Direct Democracy: The Politics of Initiative, Referendum, and Recall* (Harvard University Press, 1989).

9. Quoted in Kenneth L. Shropshire, *The Sports Franchise Game: Cities in Pursuit of Sports Franchises, Events, Stadiums, and Arenas* (University of Pennsylvania Press, 1995), Foreword.

10. On information, advertising, and campaign finance in direct democracy, see E. Lee, "Representative Government and the Initiative Process," in John J. Kirlin and Donald R. Winkler, eds., *California Policy Choices*, vol. 6 (University of Southern California, School of Public Administration, 1990); Arthur Lupia, "Busy Voters, Agenda Control, and the Power of Information," *American Political Science Review*, vol. 86 (1992), pp. 390–413; and David B. Magleby, *Direct Legislation: Voting on Ballot Propositions in the United States* (Johns Hopkins University Press, 1984).

11. See Thomas Romer and Howard Rosenthal, "Median Voters or Budget Maximizers: Evidence from School Expenditure Referenda," *Economic Inquiry*, vol. 20 (1982), pp. 556–78; and Rodney Fort, "The Median Voter, Setters, and Non-Repeated Construction Bond Issues," *Public Choice*, vol. 56 (1988), pp. 213–31.

12. Arthur T. Johnson, *Minor League Baseball and Local Economic Development* (University of Illinois Press, 1993); and Sage, "Stealing Home."

13. See John A. Ferejohn, "Reforming the Initiative Process," In Cain and Noll, eds., *Constitutional Reform in California*; and Elisabeth R. Gerber, "Legislative Response to the Threat of Initiatives," *American Journal of Political Science*, vol. 40 (February 1996), pp. 99–128.

14. In light of these features of an initiative, Ferejohn has a novel proposal: make access to the ballot very easy (that is, require very few signatures) so that outlier proposals and unanticipated consequences are easy to correct. Ferejohn, "Reforming the Initiative

Process." Gerber makes other proposals that are similar in spirit: allow the legislature to amend qualified initiatives, and require that initiatives be reauthorized periodically (the "sunset" proposal). Elisabeth R. Gerber, "Reforming the California Initiative Process: A Proposal to Increase Flexibility and Legislative Accountability," in Cain and Noll, eds., *Constitutional Reform in California*.

15. See, generally, Gerber, "Reforming the California Initiative Process." For a detailed illustration of these ideas with respect to the history of taxation legislation and initiatives in California during the 1970s, see David O. Sears and Jack Citrin, *Tax Revolt: Something for Nothing in California* (Harvard University Press, 1982).

16. Fort, "The Median Voter."

17. Ibid. See also Rodney Fort, "A Recursive Treatment of the Hurdles to Voting," *Public Choice* vol. 85 (1995), pp. 45–69.

18. "Argument in Favor of Proposition W," Baseball Stadium.

19. *San Francisco Bay Guardian*, March 20, 1996, p. 22. See also chapter 12 in this volume.

20. Charles C. Euchner, *Playing the Field: Why Sports Teams Move and Cities Fight to Keep Them* (Johns Hopkins University Press, 1993), pp. 145–46.

21. Personal conversation with Betty Clark, Legislative Reference for Board of Supervisors of Elections, Baltimore City, 1991.

22. Johnson, *Minor League Baseball*, pp. 123–24.

23. Euchner, *Playing the Field*, pp. 145–46.

24. David Swindell, "Public Financing of Sports Stadiums: How Cincinnati Compares," Policy Insight, Buckeye Institute for Public Policy Solutions, Dayton, Ohio, February 1996.

25. Johnson, *Minor League Baseball*; Euchner, *Playing the Field*.

26. Johnson, *Minor League Baseball*, pp. 233–34.

27. Ibid.

28. Ibid., p. 210.

29. Euchner, *Playing the Field*, says there were three that failed.

30. Johnson, *Minor League Baseball*.

31. National Football League, "National Voters Say 'Yes'," p. 4.

32. See Euchner, *Playing the Field*.

33. Johnson, *Minor League Baseball*.

34. *San Francisco Bay Guardian*, March 20, 1996, p. 22.

6

STADIUMS AND
URBAN SPACE

MARK S. ROSENTRAUB

 For four decades the leaders of most central cities have watched with frustration the pace and extent of the growth of suburban areas and the dispersion away from downtown areas of many essential aspects of American life. Where once bedroom communities were little more than homes to commuters who journeyed "downtown" for work and shopping, some suburban cities have now grown to be center cities in their own right. The movement of production, manufacturing, and service industries to the suburbs, accompanied by the building of extensive recreational and retail centers miles from aging core areas, has created different commuting patterns and multinucleated urban centers. Downtown centers in Cleveland, Detroit, Indianapolis, and Dallas were once destinations for work, recreation, and retail activities. Today, virtually all needs of American life can be found in suburban and exurban communities. Few central cities have avoided a decline in retail and recreational activity coinciding with the growth of office complexes and production and manufacturing facilities that complement the substantial levels of residential development found in suburban areas. While a handful of primary cities' downtown areas remain dominant centers of employment, retail activity, and recreation within their regions (for example, New York City, Chicago, San Francisco), virtually every other core city in the nation must make major efforts to underscore its centrality in the economy and social life of its region. Indeed, in many areas, core cities have simply become less relevant or central to the economic and social life of many people.

In trying to keep some central business districts (CBDs) integral to their region's economic and social life, many public officials have latched onto sports strategies through the building of downtown sports facilities to reverse or retard certain elements of suburbanization. Many cities have developed policies and programs based on both the emotions generated by the nostalgic architecture of newer sports facilities and the excitement created when large numbers of people attend sporting events. In some ways, these new facilities and the development policies linked to sports and recreation have become the latest hope for emphasizing urban life, bringing jobs back to downtown areas, and invigorating people's interest in both visiting and living in downtown areas.

This is not the first effort to use recreation-based activities to revive center cities. In the 1980s the festival marketplace and shopping mall were seen as the most promising means of interesting people in downtown areas.[1] Today, justifications for the public's investment in the building of sports facilities incorporate a discussion of both the redevelopment efforts that can be led or jump-started by ballparks and arenas and the micro-level impacts of sports facilities and events on downtown areas. For many of the reasons discussed in chapter 2, even consultants whose reports are used to attract support for the building of sports facilities have conceded that the aggregate economic impact of teams and facilities may be far smaller than once believed. In a report for the city of Indianapolis regarding the economic impact of the Indianapolis Colts, Coopers & Lybrand noted:

> Adjustments must also be made to direct spending to reflect the fact that *much* of the economic activity associated with the Colts would likely impact the area economy in another form had the NFL game not taken place . . . an individual attending an NFL game at the RCA Dome may instead go to a movie had the Colt's franchise not hosted a game.[2]

These realizations have contributed to the need to justify public sector investments in sports facilities in terms of their expected impact on reviving or maintaining CBDs.

Are the justifications for the public's investment in sports facilities based on the contributions of these edifices to the centrality of cities any more valid than the previous claims of economic development? Can sports facilities reverse or slow the suburbanization trends so apparent in numerous urban areas? Or, are urban leaders again grasping at the latest elixir that will likely fail to change the decentralized and suburbanized life-style seemingly desired by most Americans? Because some sport and entertainment complexes such as Jacobs Field and Gund Arena in Cleveland are able to attract more than four million visitors to downtown areas that were essentially avoided for years, more and more mayors justify their investments in sports facilities as an effort to enhance the vitality of urban life. As the focus for justifying the public's investment in sports facilities has shifted from a reliance on regional development to one that stresses the enhancement of downtown, it seems important to determine if nostalgic ballparks, futuristic domed stadiums, or luxurious high-technology arenas (computerized food service, digital sound systems, state-of-the art video), located in a downtown area, can enhance the centrality of core cities and influence the patterns of suburbanization so ingrained in American life.

Sports Strategies, Culture, and Urban Policy

Sports policies implemented for downtown development can be divided into two broad groups: those based on team and local concerns to revitalize a small area of a city and those based on the creation of an export industry for a region.

Building Facilities for Teams and Revitalization

The objective of the most common program is to build a new facility or two for selected teams and to use these buildings to jump-start development or revitalize a downtown area. Policies of this nature assume that by attracting large crowds a downtown area will underscore its vitality, centrality, and potential for additional economic activity and development. The hope is that large crowds will encourage investments in related entertainment facilities such as restaurants, bars, and retail outlets (especially if a new mall is located near the sports facilities, as is frequently the case). If recreational and retail opportunities increase, it is then argued or hoped that corporations will be attracted back to the center, to expand downtown office complexes. If that occurs, new residential development will surely follow as higher-income families will be attracted to a lively downtown where they can both work and reside while enjoying a city's amenities. Principally, cities that focus on building one or two facilities are attempting to alter development and consumption (recreation) patterns within their region.

A secondary, and smaller, consumer group that is targeted by these facilities consists of individuals who might be conducting business or visiting friends and relatives in the area, and some tourists who might visit an area as a result of the presence of a team and a new facility. This latter group provides an export function in that a portion of the spending by these people brings new dollars to the region and city. To the extent that transferred recreational activity crosses municipal boundary lines within a metropolitan region, the central city may experience an intraregional export gain as well.

This kind of sports policy has been attempted by both more mature cities and newer central cities. Baltimore, Cincinnati, Cleveland, and Detroit are typical Rust Belt cities that have justified or planned facilities in an effort to emphasize the centrality of a downtown area. Dallas, Phoenix, Houston, and Sacramento represent younger, Sun Belt cities that have also planned, discussed, or built downtown sports facilities in an effort to change development and recreational patterns within their regions.

Sports and Facility Development as a Regional Export Industry

The second type of sports development policy is more directly export based for an entire region. Within this perspective the focus is on the development of facilities that can be used to host events that attract people from outside a region. There are far fewer examples of the second type of sports development programs or policies. Indianapolis is without doubt the best example of city whose sports development strategy for its downtown area emphasized hosting a large number of national and international events in addition to big league sports teams.[3] Over a period of three decades, Indianapolis built several facilities in an effort to become a capital city for amateur sports and conventions. Although regional residents attend some of the events associated with this strategy, the "target" audience is participants and fans from across the nation and world. In addition to being the home of the Colts, Indianapolis's domed stadium provides exhibition space for a successful convention center and a site for national and international sporting events, including the National Collegiate Athletic Association (NCAA) men's basketball championship and several track and field events. The National Basketball Association's Pacers play their home games in Market Square Arena, which also has been used for numerous amateur sports events. Recently, intrigued by Indianapolis's perceived success, St. Louis developed a domed stadium to attract the Rams from Anaheim. This facility is part of a new convention center and will be used in an attempt to make St. Louis a favored location for national and international sporting events.

The focus of this sports development policy is not a specific team but sports as a component of a larger recreational business that includes not only the games played by big league teams but also national and international competitions, concerts, meetings, and conventions. The professional team becomes a part of, or maybe even an anchor in, this constellation of activities, but the goal is to attract a large number of events, which in turn bring a large number of out-of-town visitors to a city. The anchor team may well impart name recognition and create publicity for the community, but the strategy is based on the hope that hosting events, competitions, and conventions will generate substantial export gains for the community as people from across the nation or from all parts of the world visit the city.

Regardless of the primary purpose of a sports development initiative, the hope intertwined with belief is that the presence of downtown sports facilities will change the view of the centrality of a CBD. This hope emanates from observations of the importance of sports in American culture.[4] If sports are important to people and American life, and this importance can be made synonymous with the CBD, then the downtown area, it is believed, will be invigorated. In view of the importance society places on sports, it may not be far-fetched to hope that bringing sports teams back to downtown areas and building architecturally splendid facilities could change land-use or recreational patterns in an urban area.

Beyond the cultural importance of sports, there are other examples of the use of architecturally exciting buildings to reinforce the centrality of core cities. Early in this century, the building of architecturally pleasing office buildings buttressed the centrality of the downtown areas as a place for commerce, shopping, fine dining, entertainment, and even residential life. New York's Empire State Building, Chrysler Building, and Rockefeller Center are certainly landmarks that reinforce the centrality of Manhattan for the region. Likewise in Chicago, Cleveland, Pittsburgh,

Philadelphia, and Boston, downtown office buildings, through their architecture, helped define the centrality of their CBDs. Could the construction of new ballparks and arenas that evoke memories of the grand buildings of the early parts of the twentieth century lead to a change in the use of urban space? Although it is unlikely that people will move back to the cities if a few new buildings and sports facilities are developed, would the presence of teams or the hosting of national and international sporting events in a downtown area change some land-use patterns or slow the pace of the decentralization of commerce and residential activities? Many sports advocates believe it would, and a mania of sorts has encased the furor of activity surrounding the construction of downtown sports facilities.

A First Look at Sports and the Use of Urban Space

Little is yet known about the impact of sports franchises and their facilities on the use of urban space. This is an important gap in the sports research field, for facilities that are well-integrated into an urban framework have substantial potential for both influencing development patterns and coupling attendance at a game or event with other activities. Facilities surrounded by acres of parking lots produce a very different set of interactions than a facility within walking distance of restaurants, office complexes, and other recreational facilities. Facilities that are architecturally distinguished or constitute an event in themselves evoke far different emotions than a facility fans see as an inconvenience. The most distinguished facilities can and do become tourist attractions regardless of the playing of a game or the hosting of an event. Both Oriole Park at Camden Yards and the Skydome in Toronto attract thousands of visitors who simply want to tour the facility. Since it is by now obvious that teams and facilities have a very small economic impact, and since new proposals for facilities stress the role of sports venues in maintaining the centrality of CBDs, the appropriate question to consider is whether teams and the facilities they use influence the use of urban space.

Assessing the Influence of Facilities and Teams on Spatial Patterns

The very small scale of economic activity produced by sports suggests that the presence or absence of a team or facility cannot reverse the

decentralization of residential and business activity.[5] Those patterns are
the result of the perception of costs and benefits by households and
businesses from alternative locations. Congestion, aesthetics, access to
labor, jobs, transportation systems, and the cost and quality of urban
services—all contribute to the prices offered by households and businesses for alternative sites.[6] Each of these factors would seem to dwarf
the value of any single amenity regardless of its attractiveness or integration with a neighborhood. As such, it would be foolish to expect the
preferences for a suburban life-style and the more horizontal organization
of space in any region to change because a new stadium was built in a
CBD or because a sports-export industry or set of events was able to find
a home in a downtown area. Any preliminary investigation into the
impact of facilities or export events on spatial patterns would find, at the
maximum, a slight slowing of the decentralization or suburbanization
process, if sports facilities had any impact at all. Furthermore, these
impacts, if they exist, must be studied in cities that have already developed one or two sports facilities and that have made a concerted effort
to develop an entire new export industry through the attraction of national and international events. For both sets of activities, the appropriate
null hypothesis is: "The presence of either sports facilities in a downtown
area or a set of facilities designed to attract numerous events with participants and fans from across the nation or around the world does not
influence the rate of suburbanization or the decentralization of urban life
in a region." In other words, research should focus on the rate of suburbanization and not on a reversal of existing trends. Thus the issue
explored here is the effect of sporting facilities on the relative concentration of both population and employment in downtown areas.

Studies of this nature generally rely on regression models to illustrate
the importance of a particular factor, such as a downtown sports facility
or a sports policy, controlling for the effects of several other variables
that are known to influence development. In such a model the presence
of downtown facilities for professional sports teams could be specified
with a dummy variable; one could even attempt to scale this variable for
the presence of more than one facility or the concentrated location of
several facilities. However, the operationalization of an independent variable for sports facilities presents some critical methodological problems.
For example, both Cleveland and Indianapolis built two new facilities,
but in Indianapolis's case one was attached to a thriving convention
center and was part of an amateur sports policy that directly increased

the number of days it was used. In Cleveland, neither facility was part of a convention center. Cleveland's new facilities are located adjacent to each other; Indianapolis's two sports facilities are separated by more than half a mile. Using a single variable to reflect the fact that both of these cities built two facilities that are used by professional sports teams would not precisely represent the differences between these developments and might make the results unreliable.

St. Louis is another city with two new downtown facilities, an arena for hockey and a domed stadium for football, but they are separated by a greater distance than the Indianapolis facilities. While this city's downtown developments also included several hundred million dollars in other investments, its domed stadium is part of a convention center. St. Louis, then, is attempting to implement an export policy based on sports and other events, but this relatively new policy and its facilities have yet to be established on a scale similar to the achievements in Indianapolis. Minneapolis has two relatively new sports facilities, but this city did not fully develop or articulate a sports and downtown development plan as did Indianapolis.[7] Cincinnati has one downtown facility, Riverfront Stadium, that is used by two teams. Pittsburgh's Three Rivers Stadium is "downtown" but is separated by a river from the CBD. These subtle but important differences make each city's sports investments unique.

The Cities Studied

This initial investigation into the relationship between sports facilities and patterns of the use of urban space was limited to an assessment of changing residential population and job locations in each of twelve metropolitan regions regarded by economic development specialists as reasonably similar.[8] Ten of these regions or cities are in the Midwest, and two cities, one with a downtown sports facility and one without, were drawn from the Southeast. In limiting this preliminary investigation to the Midwest and two southeastern cities that compete with these midwestern communities for development, the study ensured that the areas of concern were similarly affected by cost factors and national and regional development trends.

All of the cities selected for this study could also be classified as "sports cities" in that they host major sports programs or teams. The cities with downtown sports facilities each host at least two major professional sports teams. Two of the cities that do not have downtown sports facilities also have two professional sports teams using facilities located outside their CBDs. The three cities that did not have major professional sports teams had other important sports assets in that each hosts major collegiate sports programs. One was home to a professional sports team in the past and hosts an annual sporting event of national significance. Another city has hosted a soccer team since 1995. The last of these three cities has sought major sports teams for several years and, in 1995, secured the move of a National Football League team to its CBD.

The cities studied with downtown sports facilities were Indianapolis, Charlotte, Cincinnati, Cleveland, Pittsburgh, St. Louis, and Minneapolis. Charlotte was included in this group because of a new football stadium in its downtown area, its strategy of emphasizing downtown development in a fashion similar to that of the other communities, and its repeated competition with the other midwestern cities for economic development opportunities. Both Charlotte and Nashville are frequently identified as communities competing with Indianapolis, Columbus, Cincinnati, Louisville, and St. Louis for economic development opportunities. Although Charlotte's stadium opened only recently, it has been planned for the downtown area since the city was awarded an NFL franchise. As a result, a potential impact on development patterns has existed for several years, especially in view of the city's emphasis on enhancing its downtown region. The cities in the second group, those not having a downtown sports emphasis, were Columbus (Ohio), Kansas City, Louisville, Milwaukee, and Nashville.

Each of the twelve cities is part of a metropolitan area that experienced growth in private sector jobs from 1985 to 1995. The number of jobs in the five cities without downtown sports facilities increased by 19.9 percent; in the regions with downtown sports facilities, it increased 19.3 percent. The growth rates in the regions without downtown sports facilities ranged from 12.7 percent to 25.0 percent. In the regions with downtown sports facilities, the ranges were more extreme, 5.7 percent to 43.0 percent. All twelve regions also have enjoyed an expanding population base since 1990, and only the Pittsburgh region had fewer residents in 1995 than it had in 1980. From 1980 to 1995 the population in the seven regions with downtown sports facilities grew by 5.9 percent; the other regions grew by an average of 5.2 percent.

In the decade between 1970 and 1980, nine of the twelve counties studied also had at least a 16 percent increase in the number of private sector jobs. Two of the counties that enjoyed less growth decided to build downtown sports facilities (in Cleveland and Pittsburgh). One area with twice as much growth as the average for all twelve areas also decided to build downtown sports facilities. Both fast-growth and slow-growth areas were attracted to sports programs as a tool for development and economic expansion.

This study places primary emphasis on outcomes in Indianapolis. As already noted, Indianapolis, more than any city in America, has been implementing a downtown development program with national and international objectives for more than twenty years. Under the administration of three mayors, Indianapolis has completely rebuilt its downtown area while hosting the Pan American Games, the NCAA men's basketball finals several times, numerous national track and field competitions, the World Gymnastics Championships, and several national and international swimming events. The physical aspects of this policy included the building of office space for numerous amateur sporting organizations that moved their headquarters to downtown Indianapolis. To complement all of this development, a new convention center, several museums and theaters, and a new downtown mall were opened. The state of Indiana made substantial contributions to development in the CBD by building a new government center and expanding the Indiana University–Purdue University campus in Indianapolis. The private sector, responding to the downtown strategy, built several new office centers. The "glue" or guiding force behind these efforts, however, was the "sports strategy," with its export function. The concentrated set of activities in Indianapolis provides an excellent opportunity to determine if such a focused effort and the attraction of millions of fans from across the nation and world could affect the use of space in this region. Likewise, this case can shed light on whether Indianapolis can sustain this effort and remain a favored venue for events and the offices of amateur sporting organizations.

Data from Market Statistics, Inc., were used to tabulate private sector employment levels for 1985, 1990, and 1995 in four geographical areas for each of the twelve cities studied. This made it possible to calculate percentages to reflect the "size" of the CBD in relationship to total employment in the city, the center city's county, and the metropolitan region. The same calculations were then made for these four geographical areas. The downtown area is referred to as the CBD, as defined by the planning departments in each city. Population and employment within the city were also determined, as were the population and number of jobs within the county and metropolitan area in which the central city was located. Market Statistics, Inc., produces data by zip codes; maps were used to place zip codes into the appropriate geographical boundaries. A longer time frame would have been an asset for these analyses; however, reliable data at the zip code level for private sector employment do not exist prior to the early 1980s. Population data from the Bureau of the Census and the various cities and states were used to analyze demographic changes.

Population and employment statistics are but two measures of concentration and dispersion; another that could be used is population density. However, the centrality desired by many center city leaders for their communities can be reflected in the proportion of private sector jobs that exist in CBDs and the people who choose to live downtown. Civic leaders have long identified jobs and residential development as key factors in retaining the vitality of CBDs. Furthermore, if a CBD is an increasingly important business center bringing workers downtown, overall job levels or concentrations would certainly reflect the increasing use of space in the CBD for economic activities. If people decide to live downtown, other businesses will also locate there to provide the services needed by an expanding or stable population base. In addition, if the building of sports facilities changes recreational patterns, the concentration of service sector jobs in the CBD can be expected to increase. And if facilities with luxury seating become an attraction for certain businesses, a changing concentration of firms in the finance, insurance, and real estate fields (FIRE) might also reflect a different spatial pattern for the location of these firms.

Downtown Sports Facilities and Centrality

The analysis presented here reviews Indianapolis's export-based sports and downtown development policy and its outcomes for residential and employment patterns. These outcomes are then compared with those in the other cities that developed downtown sports facilities for particular teams. The outcomes for all cities with downtown facilities are then tabulated and compared to those cities without downtown facilities. Finally, the outcomes in the retail, service, and FIRE sectors of the economy for each region (by CBD, city, county, and region) and by city type (presence of downtown sports facilities or not) are discussed.

"Indiana-No-Place" and the Sports and Downtown Development Strategy

The city of Indianapolis found itself considering economic development policies and programs at the same time that many cities in North America were dealing with the Rust Belt's decline and recession. In the 1970s Indianapolis was a city with a declining job base, a deteriorating downtown core, and a small place in the national and international economic landscape. Comically, people in the region and elsewhere sometimes referred to the city as "Indiana-No-Place."[9] The city seemed to suffer from the absence of a national identity and distinction; it was simply one of several smaller midwestern cities that dotted the landscape from New York to Chicago. Some long-time residents of Indianapolis believe its image problems were best summarized on a late-night talk show when favorite son Kurt Vonnegut described the city as a "cemetery with lights" that came to life one day a year for the Indianapolis 500. A survey commissioned by the Greater Indianapolis Progress Committee in the mid-1970s found the city to have a "nonimage"—neither positive nor negative—in the national media and among convention planners. A finding of no image was actually a substantial improvement over earlier assessments of Indiana's capital city. Indianapolis had been called "Naptown" by some. John Gunther, in 1947, almost ended the city's future when he described Indianapolis as "an unkempt city, unswept, raw, a terrific place for basketball and auto racing, a former pivot (*sic*) of the Ku-Kluxers."[10] No image, or a nonimage, was probably a substantial improvement on Vonnegut's characterization and the view that Gunther portrayed. Yet, for a city with aspirations for regional and national leadership, a "nonimage" was as unsettling as the older negative view. Indianapolis's business and political leadership, as well as its citizenry, wanted a different image.[11]

Indianapolis's problems were not limited to its identity. Indianapolis was also shrinking in size. Between 1970 and 1980 the consolidated city of Indianapolis lost population while the metropolitan area grew by 4.5 percent. Indeed, in 1970 Indianapolis's population accounted for 59.0 percent of the metropolitan region. By 1980 the consolidated city contained only 54.5 percent of the region's population. When Indianapolis and its county consolidated in the early 1970s to form "UniGov" (unified government), a considerable amount of suburban land was joined with Indianapolis's older neighborhoods and downtown area. Four small cities

Table 6-1. *Population Growth in Indianapolis, 1970–95*

Area	1970	1980	1990	1995	Percentage change 1980–95
Consolidated Indianapolis	736,856	711,540	741,936	762,844	7.2
Percentage change		−3.4	4.3	2.8	
As a percentage of the region	59.0	54.5	53.7	51.5	
Metropolitan Indianapolis	1,249,870	1,305,911	1,380,491	1,482,298	13.5
Percentage change		4.5	5.7	7.4	

Source: Author's information provided by U.S. Bureau of the Census; Department of Metropolitan Development, City of Indianapolis and Marion County, Indiana; Indiana Business Research Center, School of Business, Indiana University.

within the county decided not to merge with Indianapolis and remained independent. When this annexation did not herald a period of substantial growth, Indianapolis's leadership realized that drastic policies were required to improve the image and attractiveness of the city and to reverse the deterioration and decline of the downtown core. Ironically, even with the intensive downtown development program, Indianapolis's share of the region's population continued to decline, falling to 51.5 percent in 1995 (table 6-1).

In the 1970s, economic growth, as measured by private sector jobs, was slightly lower in the Indianapolis area than in the other midwestern cities (16.7 percent growth versus 19.7 percent). The cause in large part was Indianapolis's dependency on automotive jobs and the decline in that industry. Fearing a continuing loss of economic importance, the city's community leaders in the 1970s turned their policy attention toward redeveloping downtown as a tool for enhancing the city's role in the region. A coalition of leaders from the public, private, and nonprofit sectors responded to Indianapolis's malaise by developing a program that would serve two objectives: establish a market niche for Indianapolis in amateur sports, and use this sports strategy to redevelop the downtown core as the cultural and economic center of the city and region.

As a first step in this direction, Indianapolis formed several organizations or partnerships to rebuild the city's image and downtown center. It created an economic development corporation to assist companies considering a move to Indianapolis and to help local corporations that might want to expand their operations within the city. The overriding mission for this organization was to encourage businesses to locate in downtown Indianapolis. Another group was created to market the city as a venue for sports events and as the headquarters location for amateur sports organizations. A third organization concentrated on the city's image in the national media, seeking to increase the positive exposure of the city in national and international publications.

A central component of Indianapolis's strategy was to build several facilities that would become the new anchors for the revitalized downtown and the core of the Indianapolis region. The downtown area targeted for the redevelopment effort is bounded by interconnections of two interstate highways on the east, north, and south (I-65 and I-70). The campus of Indiana University–Purdue University Indianapolis (IUPUI) and the White River form the western boundary of the redevelopment area. Redevelopment began with the construction of Market Square Arena in 1974, a 16,950-seat home for the Indiana Pacers. The city assumed complete responsibility for building the facility through its Department of Public Works. Later, when a food and beverage tax was implemented to help pay for the Hoosier Dome (renamed the RCA Dome after RCA purchased the naming rights in 1994), a new public entity, the Capital Improvements Board, assumed responsibility for Market Square Arena. The arena has no suites, but in the late 1980s a small club section of 144 seats was created behind one of the baskets. In 1995 these seats were converted to expensive individual seats. In 1983 a new lease was developed between the team and the city containing the following provisions:

—The Pacers are charged $150,000 and, if a profit is earned, the team reimburses the city for arena maintenance and utilities.

—The Pacers receive 100 percent of all advertising revenue inside the facility.

—The team and the parking facility operator (a public agency) share equally in all parking revenues.

—The team receives one half of the gross concession revenue for all events at the arena.

—If the team is sold and moves from Indianapolis, the city receives 50 percent of the amount paid for the franchise.

The Pacers have never earned a profit as defined by both the city and the team. As a result, the city has never received any payments to offset its utility, maintenance, and management expenses for Market Square Arena. The city's annual expenses exceed $1 million.[12] The team's lack of profits, the absence of luxury seating, and the low income from the sale of food and beverages, combined with escalating player salaries, have been cited to justify the Pacers' request for a new arena.

From 1974 through 1995 more than thirty major development projects were initiated downtown (table 6-2). The state of Indiana developed the new Government Center at a cost of $264 million and Indiana University's investment in its Indianapolis campus totaled more than $231 million. Seven of these projects were completely related to the sports identity Indianapolis tried to establish. In 1984 Indianapolis opened the 60,272-seat Hoosier, now RCA Dome, which became the home for the Indianapolis Colts and has hosted the NCAA Men's Basketball Final Four twice (this event will return to Indianapolis for the fourth time in 2000). Other new facilities include the Sports Center, a tennis stadium for the annual hard-court championships, the Indiana University Natatorium, the Indiana University Track and Field Stadium, the Velodrome (bicycle racing), and the National Institute for Fitness and Sports. By 1989 a total of seven national organizations (Athletics Congress of the USA, U.S. Canoe and Kayak Team, U.S. Diving, Inc., U.S. Gymnastics Federation, U.S. Rowing, U.S. Synchronized Swimming, and U.S. Water Polo) and two international organizations (International Baseball Association, International Hockey League) had moved their governing offices to Indianapolis.

The Dome was built at a cost of $78 million, and although its size greatly expanded the exhibition space for the city's convention center, there was considerable hope that the Dome's existence would bring an NFL franchise to Indianapolis. The public sector's investment was $48 million; the bonds sold to finance the facility are repaid through a countywide 1 percent tax on food and beverages consumed at restaurants, bars, and clubs. A local foundation provided the balance through a $30 million grant. In 1984 the Colts moved from Baltimore to Indianapolis and signed a twenty-year lease that expires in 2014 for the use of the 60,272-seat facility. The facility has no club seats, but there are ninety-six suites, one of the largest of which seats thirty people and is reserved for the city of Indianapolis. The Colts' lease for the RCA Dome contains the following provisions:

—The annual rental charge is $250,000 (or $25,000 per game). The team also pays this per game rate for any playoff games it hosts.

—The Colts receive the greater of $500,000 or 50 percent of the luxury suite license fees.

—The team does not share in the revenue earned from parking, stadium advertising, and from the sale of food and beverages.

—The team has no fiscal responsibility for any game-day expenses, or for the maintenance of the facility.

The Colts repeatedly have asked to renegotiate their lease to increase their income from the sale of luxury seating and the food and beverages on game day. To pressure Indianapolis to change the lease, the Colts have promoted an image that they would be willing to move to Cleveland or Los Angeles.

The projects identified in table 6-2 do not include all development that took place in the downtown area during this time period. Some developments (the city's monuments, a large park area, the state's refurbishing of the Capitol building, new fire stations, and the like) were not appropriate for consideration here because they would have taken place even if a sports strategy had not been specified. To be sure, there is a subjective element to this classification process; however, through interviews, it was ascertained which projects were specifically intended to be part of the strategy.[13]

Several important points emerge from table 6-2. First, $2.76 billion for capital development was invested in downtown Indianapolis. To place this figure in the context of more current economic development projects, this investment amounts to $4.52 billion in 1995 dollars. This clearly represents a substantial commitment of funds targeted to a specific area and in support of a tightly designed policy. Second, the commitment of private funds to the strategy was extensive. Indeed, more than half of the funds invested, 55.7 percent, were from the private sector. Third, the nonprofit sector also was an active participant, being responsible for 8.5 percent of the cost. Taken together, the private and nonprofit sectors were responsible for approximately two-thirds of the funds invested in the amateur sports and downtown redevelopment strategies. Fourth, the city of Indianapolis's investment amounted to less than one-sixth of the total, 15.8 percent. Fifth, the investment by the state of Indiana and Indiana University actually exceeded the expenditure made by the city of Indianapolis. Sixth, sports and recreation facilities accounted for approximately 10 percent of the total investment.

The city of Indianapolis was quite successful in leveraging funds for its sports strategy. Basically, a $2.76 billion investment for an economic development program required $436.1 million from the city of Indianapolis. For every dollar invested by the city, it was able to leverage $6.33. If the investment by the state in its office center and Indiana University on its Indianapolis campus is removed—on the grounds that these in-

Table 6-2. *Sources of Funds for Economic Development Projects*

Millions of dollars

Project	Year	Source of funds					Total
		Federal	State	City	Private	Philanthropic	
Sports related							140.8
Market Square Arena	1974	0	0	16	0	0	16
Sports Center	1979	0	0	4	1.5	1.5	7
Indiana University Track and Field Stadium	1982	0	1.9	0	0	4	5.9
Indiana University Natatorium	1982	1.5	7	0	0	13	21.5
Velodrome	1982	0.48	0	1.1	0	1.1	2.68
Hoosier Dome	1984	0	0	48	0	30	78
National Institute of Sports	1988	0	3	3	0	3	9
Recreation							131.9
Children's Museum	1976	0	0	0	0	25	25
Indiana Theater	1980	1.5	0	0	4.5	0	6
Walker Building	1985	2	0	0	0	1.4	3.4
Zoo	1988	0	0	0	0	37.5	37.5
Eiteljorg Museum	1989	0	0	0	0	60	60
Hotels							152
Hyatt Hotel/Bank	1977	0	0	0	55	0	55
Embassy Suites Hotel	1985	6.45	0	0	25.05	0	31.5
Westin Hotel	1989	0.5	0	0	65	0	65.5

Project	Year						Total
Retail							373.81
City Market	1986	0	0	0	0	4.7	4.7
Lockerbie Market	1986	1.8	0	0	14	0	15.8
Union Station	1986	16.3	0	1	36.01	0	53.31
Circle Centre Mall	1995	0	0	290	0	10	300
Offices and infrastructure							610.79
Capitol Tunnel	1982	1.4	0	0	0	0	1.4
Heliport	1985	2.5	0.12	0.6	2.36	0	5.58
Pan Am Plaza	1987	0	0	5.7	25	4.5	35.2
2 W. Washington offices	1982	1.2	0	0	11.8	0	13
1 N. Capitol offices	1982	3.2	0	0	10.41	0	13.61
Farm Bureau offices	1992	0	0	0	0	36	36
State Office Center	1992	0	264	0	0	0	264
Lilly Corporate expansion	1992	0	0	0	242	0	242
Residential							56.22
Lower Canal Apartments	1985	7.9	0	10.3	0	2	20.2
Lockfield Apartments	1987	0	0	0.62	24.6	0	25.22
Canal Overlook Apartments	1988	0	0	0	11	0	11
Other							1295.33
Indiana University	1990	0	231	0	0	0	231
Other projects	74–92	0	0	0	1008.53	0	1008.53
Property tax abatements	74–92	0	55.8	55.8	0	0	55.8
Total		46.7	507.0	436.1	1536.8	233.7	2760.33
Percent		1.7	18.4	15.8	55.7	8.5	100

Source: Author's information provided by Department of Metropolitan Development. City of Indianapolis and Marion County, Indiana.

vestments would have been made without an economic development plan—for each dollar spent by the city, it was able to leverage $4.20. However, it should be noted that the state of Indiana and Indiana University's components of the redevelopment of downtown were something city officials and leaders worked to secure through a variety of political avenues. Put another way, had the city not focused on a downtown economic development plan, the state and university might not have invested as much as they did. The state and Indiana University could have selected different sites for their expansions, or decided that a declining downtown was not where additional resources should be invested. With no possible way to know for certain whether these developments would have taken place, the leverage ratios with and without the involvement of the state and the university are reported.

How Did Downtown Indianapolis Change?

Three factors were examined to judge whether downtown Indianapolis was revitalized: size of the residential population living downtown, concentration of jobs in the CBD, and type of firms attracted to downtown Indianapolis. The very clear intent of Indianapolis's downtown development efforts, of which the sports strategy was the centerpiece, was to stabilize if not increase the number of jobs in the downtown or core area, and to reestablish the area as a competitive residential location.

POPULATION CHANGES. Table 6-3 summarizes the changes in population in the downtown area, the balance of the city, the entire county, and the metropolitan region from 1970 to 1995. The precipitous decline in the number of people willing to live downtown between 1970 and 1980, and then between 1980 and 1990, identifies the magnitude of the problem Indianapolis's leadership perceived. From 1970 to 1980, more than one quarter of the residents in downtown Indianapolis moved away. The city's population declined by 3.4 percent while the county's population dropped by 3.6 percent. At the same time, the region was growing, and by 1980 it had 4.5 percent more residents than it had in 1970. Suburbanization was firmly entrenched in the region and the declining years for the Rust Belt took its toll on Indianapolis.

The decade of the 1980s brought a rebound for the city (a 6.4 percent population increase), but not for downtown Indianapolis, which lost 12.5 percent of its population. Even in the years when the sports and down-

Table 6-3. *Population Changes in Downtown Indianapolis, the City of Indianapolis, Marion County, and Metropolitan Region, 1970–95*[a]

Area	1970 Number	1980 Number	1980 Percentage change	1990 Number	1990 Percentage change	1995 Number	1995 Percentage change
Downtown	108,880	80,274	−26.3	70,202	−12.5	70,449	0.4
Balance, city	627,976	631,266	0.6	671,734	6.4	692,395	3.1
Balance, county	56,913	53,693	−5.6	55,223	2.8	54,760	−0.8
Balance, metropolitan area	456,101	540,678	18.5	583,332	7.9	664,694	13.9
Share of regional population (percent)							
Downtown	8.7	6.1		5.1		4.8	
Balance, city	50.2	48.3		48.7		46.7	
Balance, county	4.6	4.1		4.0		3.7	
Balance, metropolitan area	36.5	41.5		42.2		44.8	

Sources: Author's information provided by Indiana Business Research Center, Indiana University; Department of Metropolitan Development, City of Indianapolis and Marion County, Indiana.

town strategy was clearly evident in the development of several new facilities, people continued to move away from the city center. Metropolitan Indianapolis continued to grow, adding an additional 7.9 percent to its population. The centrality of downtown as a place to live declined from 1970 through 1995, but the rate of decline was slower from 1990 to 1995. The centrality of the city also declined, and by 1995, 44.8 percent of the region's population lived outside of Marion County and the city of Indianapolis, an increase of 8.3 percentage points from 1970.

The most important population change took place between 1990 and 1995 when the population in downtown Indianapolis stabilized. Indeed, there was even a slight increase as several new apartment complexes opened. Several historic neighborhoods in the downtown areas also began enjoying a renaissance as houses were restored and others were built. The opening of Circle Centre Mall in 1995 represented the virtual completion of the entire sports and downtown development program. The city's decision in 1992 to complete the retail center that it had been discussing for more than a decade made a substantial contribution to the viability of living in the downtown area as the mall's presence ensured convenient access to services and products for those living in the city's center. Before the opening of the mall, retail trade had declined substantially in the downtown area. The stabilization of the residential population in downtown Indianapolis represents the attainment of one of the city's goals for the sport and downtown development process. However, the 2000 census must be performed before the city will know if the combined efforts to build sports and other facilities have created a durably attractive residential setting in downtown Indianapolis.

EMPLOYMENT CHANGES. The CBD's share of jobs in the region has steadily decreased since 1985 (table 6-4). Although the early success of the amateur sports policy did increase the number of jobs located in the downtown area, this increase was not sufficient to offset substantially higher growth rates in other sections of the region. Some of the early success from the amateur sports program began to wane in the early 1990s. More than 9,000 jobs were lost, and the CBD's share of private sector jobs in 1995 was below the 1985 level. In contrast, other areas within the city have attracted more jobs, and its share of private sector jobs in 1995 was virtually identical to the 1985 level. The proportion of jobs beyond the city–county borders of Indianapolis grew steadily from 1985 to 1995.

Table 6-4. *Number and Concentration of Private Sector Jobs in the Indianapolis Region, 1985–95*

Area	1985	1990	1995
Number of jobs/year			
Central business district	91,151	103,875	94,490
Balance of city	268,020	308,140	334,117
Balance of county	21,227	55,656	32,364
Balance of region	125,866	162,481	175,596
Share of jobs in region (percent)			
Central business district	18.0	16.5	14.8
Balance of city	52.9	48.9	52.5
Balance of county	4.2	8.8	5.1
Balance of region	24.9	25.8	27.6

Source: Author's information provided by Market Statistics, Inc.

Table 6-5. *Concentration of Retail, Service, and FIRE Sector Jobs in Indianapolis's Central Business District, 1985–95*

	1985		1990		1995	
Job	Number	Percentage of city	Number	Percentage of city	Number	Percentage of city
Retail	11,179	14.1	10,311	12.0	7,992	9.3
Other services	26,354	27.9	37,920	28.8	37,219	26.2
FIRE[a]	19,212	49.6	18,840	49.1	15,563	42.0

Source: Author's information provided by Market Statistics, Inc.
a. Finance, insurance, and real estate fields.

TYPES OF JOBS CREATED. Despite the loss of centrality in overall employment, the CBD might still have made gains in certain key sectors. For example, with the growing concentration of sporting and entertainment events in downtown Indianapolis, one might have anticipated a growth in service jobs. If more banking or finance firms chose to locate downtown, the number of jobs classified in the FIRE category could have grown; as table 6-5 shows, however, there has been a decline in the concentration of jobs in the retail, service, and FIRE sectors. The loss in centrality, compared with the city as a whole, was smallest for the service sector; the loss of centrality was largest for the FIRE sector with its higher-paying jobs. The concentration of retail jobs within the CBD, as a proportion of all retail jobs in the city of Indianapolis, also declined.

Indianapolis versus Other Cities with Downtown Sports Facilities

Outcomes in Indianapolis, with its pronounced export-oriented sports strategy, can be compared with changes in other cities that focused on building downtown facilities for teams.

POPULATION CHANGES. The residential population in the CBDs declined in all cities that had downtown sports facilities (table 6-6). Indianapolis had a slightly smaller percentage decline than the other cities, but in terms of the centrality of the CBD within each region, Indianapolis's decline was actually larger. In the 1990–95 period, however, whereas the other cities continued to lose downtown residents, the residential population in Indianapolis's CBD grew by 0.4 percent. During these same years the CBD's regional share of the population declined by 5.9 percent in Indianapolis, compared with more than 10 percent in the other cities. Although the Indianapolis region also has been growing at a faster rate than the other cities with downtown facilities, the city's share of the regional population has not fallen as fast as in the other cities. The cities with downtown facilities built for a specific team lost more centrality with regard to overall population levels in their region than did Indianapolis, but this may be a result of Indianapolis's consolidated status. For example, the other areas had greater increases in centrality for areas outside the city, whereas in the Indianapolis region the small cities outside the consolidated city–county had a loss of centrality.

EMPLOYMENT CHANGES. The export-based sports development program implemented by Indianapolis was more successful in slowing the suburbanization process than the facility-oriented efforts in other cities. From 1985 to 1995, while Indianapolis's CBD lost 17.8 percent of its jobs, CBDs in the other cities with downtown sports facilities lost 27.7 percent of their jobs (table 6-7). In terms of the growth of jobs in suburban areas, the rate of diffusion out of the center city's county was also greater in the other cities. Indianapolis's more export-based sports policy had a greater impact on slowing suburbanization trends than the sports facility orientations of the other cities (table 6-7).

Outcomes for Cities with and without Downtown Sports Facilities

The data and discussion that follow join outcomes in the Indianapolis area with those of other cities with sports policies and downtown facilities

Table 6-6. Absolute and Percentage Changes in Population in Cities with Downtown Sporting Facilities, 1970–95

Area	Population				Percentage change			
	1970	1980	1990	1995	1970–80	1980–90	1990–95	1980–95
Absolute changes								
Indianapolis								
Central business district	108,880	80,274	70,202	70,449	–26.3	–12.5	0.4	–12.2
Balance, city	627,976	631,266	671,734	692,395	–0.5	6.4	3.1	9.7
Balance, county	56,913	53,693	55,223	54,760	–5.6	2.8	–0.8	2.0
Balance, region	456,101	540,678	585,332	664,694	18.5	7.9	13.9	22.9
Other cities with downtown facilities								
Central business district	60,968	43,790	40,213	37,815	–28.2	–8.2	–6.0	–13.6
Balance, city	443,825	376,613	359,883	361,685	–15.1	–4.4	0.5	–4.0
Balance, county	581,594	603,207	625,272	646,617	3.7	3.7	3.4	7.2
Balance, region	1,000,521	1,069,864	1,136,964	1,154,936	6.9	6.3	1.6	8.0

	As percentage of the region's population				Percentage change			
	1970	1980	1990	1995	1970–80	1980–90	1990–95	1980–95
Changes in regional shares								
Indianapolis								
Central business district	8.7	6.1	5.1	4.8	–29.9	–16.4	–5.9	–21.3
Balance, city	50.2	48.3	48.7	46.7	–3.8	–0.8	–4.1	–3.3
Balance, county	4.6	4.1	4.0	3.7	–10.9	–2.4	–7.5	–9.8
Balance, region	40.6	41.5	42.2	44.8	2.2	1.7	6.2	8.0
Other cities with downtown facilities								
Central business district	2.9	2.1	1.9	1.7	–27.6	–9.5	–10.5	–19.0
Balance, city	21.3	18.0	16.6	16.4	–15.5	–7.8	–1.2	–8.9
Balance, county	27.9	28.8	28.9	29.4	3.2	0.3	1.7	2.1
Balance, region	47.9	51.1	52.6	52.5	6.7	2.9	–0.2	0.3

Source: Author's information provided by U.S. Bureau of the Census.

Table 6-7. *Concentration of Private Sector Jobs: Indianapolis and Other Cities with Downtown Facilities, 1985–90*

Percentage change

Area	1985	1990	1995	1985–90	1990–95	1985–95
Indianapolis region						
Central business district	18.0	16.5	14.8	−8.3	−10.3	−17.3
Balance of city	52.9	48.9	52.5	−7.6	7.4	−0.8
Balance of county	4.2	8.8	5.1	109.5	−42.0	21.4
Balance of region	24.9	25.8	27.6	3.6	7.0	10.8
Regions with downtown sports facilities						
Central business district	13.7	10.2	9.9	−25.5	−2.9	−27.7
Balance of city	20.6	17.8	17.8	−13.6	0.0	−13.6
Balance of county	29.5	35.3	28.9	19.7	−18.1	−2.0
Balance of region	36.1	36.8	43.4	1.9	17.9	20.2

Source: Author's information provided by Market Statistics, Inc.

to determine the differences between cities with and without downtown facilities.

POPULATION CHANGES. When all the cities with downtown sports facilities are examined alongside those without these structures in their CBDs, population loss in the downtown areas was slightly greater in the cities with downtown sports facilities (13.3 percent to 11.0 percent). The regional share of the population that lived in downtown areas, however, was consistently larger in cities without downtown sports facilities than in the other communities (table 6-8). At the regional level, both sets of communities had similar population increases; 5.9 percent in those with downtown sports facilities and 5.2 percent in the other communities.

EMPLOYMENT CHANGES. Across the ten years from 1985 to 1995, there was virtually no difference in the decline of employment opportunities in CBDs for cities with and without downtown sports facilities. Both groups of cities experienced a decline, with those cities without sports facilities in their downtown areas suffering a 0.6 percent greater loss than the other communities. From 1990 to 1995, cities with facilities in their downtown areas did better, suffering a decline of only 4.7 percent as compared with the 7.4 percent decline in jobs in the CBDs in the other cities (table 6-9).

Table 6-8. *Population Distribution by Area in Cities with and without Downtown Sporting Facilities: Population Levels and Regional Shares, 1970–95*

Area	Population				Percentage change			
	1970	1980	1990	1995	1970–80	1980–90	1990–95	1980–95
Absolute changes								
With downtown facilities								
Central business district	67,813	49,002	44,497	42,477	-27.7	-9.2	-4.5	-13.3
Balance, city	470,132	412,992	404,433	408,929	-12.2	-2.1	1.1	-1.0
Balance, county	506,639	524,705	543,837	562,066	3.6	3.6	3.4	7.1
Balance, region	922,747	994,266	1,057,873	1,084,902	7.8	6.4	2.6	9.1
Without downtown facilities								
Central business district	53,369	43,509	40,457	38,708	-18.5	-7.0	-4.3	-11.0
Balance, city	474,093	437,229	450,259	452,892	-7.8	3.0	0.6	3.6
Balance, county	209,460	244,428	255,217	273,273	16.7	4.4	7.1	11.8
Balance, region	401,107	532,402	547,879	558,005	32.7	2.9	1.8	4.8
Regional shares (percent)								
With downtown facilities								
Central business district	3.4	2.5	2.2	2.0	-26.5	-12.0	-9.1	-20.0
Balance, city	23.9	20.8	19.7	19.5	-13.0	-5.3	-1.0	-6.2
Balance, county	25.8	26.5	26.5	26.8	2.7	0.0	1.1	1.1
Balance, region	46.9	50.2	51.6	51.7	7.0	2.8	0.2	3.0
Without downtown facilities								
Central business district	4.7	3.5	3.1	2.9	-25.5	-11.4	-6.5	-17.1
Balance, city	41.7	34.8	34.8	34.2	-16.5	0.0	-1.7	-1.7
Balance, county	18.4	19.4	19.7	20.7	5.4	1.5	5.1	6.7
Balance, region	35.2	42.3	42.3	42.2	20.2	0.0	-0.2	-0.2

Source: Author's information provided by U.S. Bureau of the Census.

Table 6-9. *Changing Employment Concentrations in Regions with and without Downtown Sports Facilities, 1985–95*

Percentage change

Area	1985	1990	1995	1985–90	1990–95	1985–95
With downtown facilities						
Central business district	14.3	11.1	10.6	−22.4	−4.7	−26.0
Balance of city	25.0	22.3	22.8	−11.0	2.5	−8.8
Balance of county	26.1	31.4	25.4	20.6	−19.1	−2.4
Balance of region	34.4	35.2	41.1	1.7	17.0	19.0
Without downtown faciities						
Central business district	15.1	11.9	11.1	−20.7	−7.4	−26.6
Balance of city	30.4	25.8	25.7	−15.2	−0.3	−15.4
Balance of county	23.9	30.0	29.0	25.5	−3.3	21.4
Balance of region	30.6	32.3	34.2	5.4	6.0	11.7

Source: Author's information provided by Market Statistics, Inc.

Table 6-10. *Changing Proportion of Jobs in Central Business Districts, 1985–95*

	City CBD		County CBD		Region CBD	
Sector	Points[a]	Percent[b]	Points[a]	Percent[b]	Points[a]	Percent[b]
Cities with downtown facilities						
Retail	−4.5	−13.8	−4.0	−29.9	−4.5	−36.6
FIRE[c]	−1.9	−2.8	−11.3	−22.5	−1.0	−25.7
Other services	−2.9	−7.0	−2.9	−11.9	−3.6	−20.3
Cities without downtown facilities						
Retail	−3.9	−16.4	−3.7	−29.2	−2.9	−34.0
FIRE	−5.6	−12.4	−6.4	−19.3	−6.7	−26.2
Other services	−5.0	−14.6	−5.5	−22.3	−6.5	−35.3

Source: Author's information provided by Market Statistics, Inc.
a. Points = absolute change in percentages, 1985–95.
b. Percent = percentage change, 1985–95.
c. Finance, insurance, and real estate fields.

Changes in Employment in the Service, Retail, and FIRE Sectors

Evidence from the three sectors of the economy related to sports activities reveals declining job concentrations in the CBD of all cities (table 6-10). Moreover, the rates of decline do not differ dramatically between cities with and without downtown sports facilities. Looking first at concentrations of retail jobs, the CBD in cities without downtown sports facilities experienced slightly smaller losses of job concentration within the region. The pattern is reversed when jobs in the service and FIRE sectors are analyzed. The decline in job concentration was virtually the same in FIRE, but for other services the decline was substantially greater in the cities without downtown sports facilities.

The concentration of these jobs in the CBD in relation to the rest of the city was uniformly better for cities with a downtown sports facility. As a portion of city employment, the CBD did much better in the FIRE sector than the rest of the city and central county of the region in cities with sports facilities, although even here the CBD centrality suffered a decline.

Conclusions

The factors contributing to the decentralization of economic activity and the suburbanization of urban life are well known.[14] In many cities, efforts to retard, if not to reverse, this trend have included an emphasis on building sports facilities in downtown areas. Indianapolis initiated an aggressive downtown development program that focused on building an export-based sports program that included hosting numerous national and international events, as well as two big league franchises. In several other cities the policy focus has been limited to building facilities for specific teams in the hope that expanded economic development would occur to restore the centrality of the area for commerce, recreation, and residential life.

In contrast to cities that did not build downtown sports facilities, the experience of cities with these assets is not encouraging. For example, from 1980 to 1995, the population levels in downtown areas in cities with downtown sports facilities declined more than in the other communities. Job levels in the CBD areas declined in both sets of communities at relatively the same rate. CBDs with downtown sports facilities did lose fewer service sector jobs, but the presence of sports facilities did not substantially affect the loss of jobs in the FIRE or retail sectors.

Outcomes in Indianapolis were somewhat different.[15] For example, from 1985 to 1995, while other cities with downtown sports facilities had a decline of 27.7 percent in the number of jobs in their CBDs, and cities without downtown sports facilities exhibited losses of 26.6 percent, the decline in Indianapolis's CBD was 17.8 percent. Of course, Indianapolis differed in two ways from other cities. For one thing, it focused on export-oriented amateur sports rather than strictly on facilities' professional teams. But another difference was a large, balanced urban redevelopment plan that included many projects other than sports facilities. Nevertheless, even Indianapolis could only modestly retard suburbanization in its region when compared with other cities.

Other changes in Indianapolis suggest the initial gains from the sports strategy may have been short term in nature. First, some organizations that moved to Indianapolis in the 1970s and 1980s have now accepted incentive packages to relocate in other areas. The Amateur Athletic Union, for example, has moved to Florida. In June 1997, however, the National Collegiate Athletic Association accepted a $50 million incentive package to move to Indianapolis. Second, as the competition to host national and international sporting events has increased, those events are beginning to be rotated among cities. Indianapolis was one of the first cities with a sports corporation that actively recruited events for the city. Today, many other cities have a sports-oriented development focus, so that Indianapolis, which initially was successful in this market niche, must now share the benefits of these events with other communities. It is likely that some of the gains secured by Indianapolis in the 1980s and early 1990s will be lost in the future.

Sports is clearly important to a substantial number of people. This importance, however, does not make it an economic engine for development nor an elixir able to reverse or slow suburbanization and the decentralization of activities from downtown areas. Only Indianapolis, with its emphasis on export-based amateur sports, seemed able to retard suburbanization rates for certain jobs for a short period of time. With some amateur sporting organizations now moving to other areas and large-scale events being rotated among cities, Indianapolis's gains in employment opportunities for its CBD may be short lived. Although other analyses of other cities and the use of more precise statistical models will be needed before it can be concluded that downtown sports facilities do not reverse suburbanization trends, this first view of the potential of downtown facilities to invigorate CBDs suggests that great caution should be used before spending substantial amounts of the public's resources on this tool for redesigning urban space. The factors that attract businesses and people to suburban locations are more powerful than the roar of the crowds or the crack of a bat at nostalgic facilities, despite all their architectural splendor.

Notes

1. Philip Kotler, Donald H. Haider, and Irving Rein, *Marketing Places: Attracting Investment, Industry, and Tourism to Cities, States, and Nations* (New York: The Free Press, 1993).

2. Coopers & Lybrand, "Economic and Fiscal Impact Analysis of the Indianapolis Colts," A Report Prepared for the Capital Improvement Board, County of Marion (Indiana), May 30, 1996, draft, p. 3.

3. William A. Schaffer and others, *Beyond the Games: The Economic Impact of Amateur Sports in Indianapolis, 1977–91* (Indianapolis Chamber of Commerce, 1993).

4. John Wilson, *Playing by the Rules: Sport, Society, and the State* (Wayne State University Press, 1994).

5. Robert A. Baade, "Professional Sports as Catalysts for Metropolitan Economic Development," *Journal of Urban Affairs*, vol. 18, no. 1 (1996), pp. 1–17; Mark S. Rosentraub, "Does the Emperor Have New Clothes? A Reply to Robert Baade," *Journal of Urban Affairs*, vol. 18, no. 1 (1996), pp. 23–31.

6. Konrad Stahl, "Theories of Urban Business Location," in Edwin S. Mills, ed., *Handbook of Regional and Urban Economics*, vol. 2 (New York: North-Holland, 1987), pp. 759–820; Mahlon Straszheim, "The Theory of Urban Residential Location," in Mills, ed., *Handbook*, pp. 717–58.

7. Robert A. Baade, "Stadium Subsidies Make Little Economic Sense for Cities, A Rejoinder," *Journal of Urban Affairs*, vol. 18, no. 1 (1996), pp. 33–37.

8. See Baade, "Professional Sports as Catalysts for Metropolitan Economic Development."

9. William H. Hudnut, *The Hudnut Years in Indianapolis, 1976–1991* (Indiana University Press, 1995).

10. Ibid., p. 7.

11. Rosentraub, "Does the Emperor Have New Clothes?"

12. Jim Snyder, Special Assistant to the Mayor of Indianapolis, interview with the author, 1996.

13. Interviews were conducted with representatives of economic development organizations based in Indianapolis. In these discussions, the development specialists were asked to identify the cities or regions that they viewed as Indianapolis's competitors when firms evaluated Indianapolis as a "home" for a new facility.

14. Stahl, "Theories of Urban Business Location"; Straszheim, "The Theory of Urban Residential Location."

15. Schaffer and others, *Beyond the Games*.

7

STADIUMS AND
MAJOR LEAGUE SPORTS

The Twin Cities

JAMES QUIRK

 This chapter presents a historical study of the financial aspects of the construction and operation of facilities used by major league professional sports teams in the Twin Cities. It covers Met Stadium, Met Center, the Metrodome, and the Target Center and deals in part with the St. Paul Civic Arena. It also gives estimates of the subsidies provided to tenants of the facilities.

Early History

In general, major league sports were latecomers to the Twin Cities. However, there were a couple of flirtations in that direction before the arrival of the Vikings and Twins in 1961. The first major league team calling the Twin Cities home, however briefly, was a member of the Union Baseball League in 1884, the only season the league was in operation. For the last two weeks of that season, the team, formerly based in Chicago and then in Pittsburgh, played its games, all on the road, under the

I would like to thank Roger Simonson and Bill Lester of the MSFC, Phil Handy and John Moir of the city of Minneapolis, Maggie Sloss of the Minneapolis collection at the Minneapolis Public Library, and Pat Pahl of the Metropolitan Council, for their help.

name of the St. Paul Saints.[1] Thirty-seven years later, in 1921, a local professional football team named the Minneapolis Marines joined the American Professional Football League (renamed the National Football League one year later). The Marines had been one of the outstanding professional football teams in the country in the pre–World War I era, but the team was past its peak by 1921. The Marines disbanded in 1924, after four disastrous NFL seasons, returning in 1929 under a different name (the Minneapolis Red Jackets), but with the same optimistic owners, Johnny Dunn and Val Ness, who finally gave up for good in 1930, after two more losing NFL seasons.[2]

In 1947 major league sports returned to the Twin Cities, in the form of two professional basketball teams, one in St. Paul as a member of the newly organized Professional Basketball League (PBL), and one in Minneapolis, a team that had played the 1946–47 season as the Detroit Gems in the established National Basketball League (NBL). One other major pro basketball league was also in operation at the time, the Basketball Association of America (BAA), which had opened for business in the 1946–47 season.

Unfortunately, the St. Paul franchise, booked into the St. Paul Auditorium, was as short-lived as the Union League franchise in 1884: the PBL went under two weeks into the 1947–48 season. The Minneapolis NBL team, owned by Ben Berger and Morris Chalfan and renamed the Minneapolis Lakers, had a more interesting history.[3] When the PBL went out of business, there was an NBL reverse-order-of-finish draft of PBL players. Since Detroit had come in last in the 1946–47 NBL season, Minneapolis had the first pick in the draft, and hit the jackpot by choosing George Mikan, the dominant player of the early years of professional basketball. Under coach Johnny Kundla and with Mikan at center, the Lakers became the best team in basketball, winning the 1947–48 NBL title. Along with three other NBL teams, the Lakers moved to the BAA in 1948 and won that league's 1948–49 title. In 1949 the BAA absorbed the rest of the NBL and changed the name of the combined league to the National Basketball Association (NBA). The Lakers then won NBA titles in 1949–50, 1951–52, 1952–53, and 1953–54.

The Lakers played in a publicly owned facility, the Minneapolis Auditorium, but they were given no apparent special treatment because of this.[4] In fact, while the Lakers played their regular season games at the auditorium, they were obliged to find other quarters for playoff and championship games. The auditorium gave priority in scheduling during

March to the Sportsman's Show, a popular event that had been held at the auditorium for seventeen years before the Lakers arrived.

The Lakers were forced to move their playoff games to the Minneapolis Armory.[5] The armory, still standing today but boarded up and deserted, is located a few blocks from the Metrodome. In its heyday, during the 1940s and 1950s, it had a seating capacity of only 4,300. One year (1949–50) the armory was booked as well as the Minneapolis Auditorium, and the Lakers ended up playing their playoff games at the St. Paul Auditorium, not an ideal home court for a Minneapolis team.

By 1957 the bloom was definitely off the rose as far as the Lakers were concerned. The great teams were a thing of the past, and the team was drawing poorly in Minneapolis. There was a threat to move the team, and in response a local group of businessmen and supporters put together $200,000 to buy the team from Ben Berger and to furnish it with some working capital. The scheduling and attendance problems continued; in 1958–59, only twenty-two of the team's thirty-six home games were played in the Twin Cities. Before the 1959–60 season, the team decided to move its home base to the armory, investing $60,000 in new seats and other amenities. Despite the appeal of the refurbished armory and of Elgin Baylor, who had joined the Lakers in 1958, the team did not draw. The next year, Bob Short, who had acquired control of the team as a member of the 1957 buyout group, moved it to Los Angeles as the Los Angeles Lakers.

One of the striking things about the departure of the Lakers from Minneapolis is that there was an almost complete lack of effort by local or state officials to save the team for the city. As the story of Met Stadium makes clear, this was not because officials were opposed at the time to the use of public money to subsidize sports teams. Instead, it seems to have been the low level of esteem enjoyed by NBA basketball in the 1950s and early 1960s, even in the city whose team had dominated the sport just a few years earlier.

The Met

In 1953 Minneapolis businessmen, headed by Jerry Moore, president of the Minneapolis Chamber of Commerce, moved to bring a Major League Baseball team to the Twin Cities.[6] The first team that they courted was the St. Louis Browns, then owned by Bill Veeck. At the September 1953 meetings of the American League, for the second year in a row Veeck was trying to move the Browns. A Twin Cities delegation made a presentation to league owners asking for a vote in favor of a move of the Browns to either Minneapolis or St. Paul. The proposal was that the team would play in Parade Stadium in downtown Minneapolis while a new stadium was being built.

Unfortunately, Parade Stadium was woefully inadequate for major league baseball.[7] The American League turned down the bid of the Twin Cities group, and the group then was told that, before an American League team would be allowed to locate in the Twin Cities, there would have to be a stadium in place in the Twin Cities metropolitan area meeting the standards for major league play.

After the meeting, discussions were held between representatives from St. Paul and Minneapolis about a site for a new stadium. Following a long-established pattern in intercity negotiations between the two, talks broke down almost immediately, and in November 1953 St. Paul voters approved a $2 million bond issue to build a 12,500-capacity stadium, Midway Stadium, to house the American Association St. Paul Saints, awaiting the arrival of a major league team. Midway was located near the State Fair Grounds, about five miles from the downtowns of both cities. It replaced Lexington Park, located at Lexington and University avenues in St. Paul and owned by the Saints from the time it opened, in 1896.

The Minneapolis major league committee decided on a stadium to be located in Bloomington, roughly nine miles south of downtown Minneapolis and about twelve miles southwest of downtown St. Paul. A major attraction of Bloomington was cheap land, to be acquired through condemnation by the city of Bloomington. The stadium—Metropolitan Stadium, Met Stadium, or the Met—was designed to seat 23,500 for baseball but was expandable to 40,000. The cost of the proposed stadium was $4.5 million, with $0.5 million for site acquisition, $3.5 million for construction, and $0.5 million for working capital and financial costs. The stadium was financed through the issuance of city of Minneapolis revenue bonds, marketed primarily to local businesses and wealthy local citizens. There was virtually no controversy at all about funding the stadium, which was heavily backed by the *Minneapolis Star* and *Tribune* and by the leading local businesses, including Dayton's, General Mills, Pillsbury, Northwest National Bank, and First National Bank.

Met Stadium opened on April 22, 1956, and was the home park of the American Association Minneapolis Millers for the next five seasons.[8] The facility was operated by the Metropolitan Sports Area Commission, a public entity established in 1954 and consisting of four members from Minneapolis, one from Bloomington, and one from Richfield, another southern suburb of Minneapolis.

Negotiations were held with a number of teams—including the Philadelphia Athletics, the New York Giants, the Cincinnati Reds, and the Cleveland Indians—concerning a possible move to the Twin Cities. In the event, the Washington Senators, owned by Calvin Griffith, was the team that decided to make the move. Already by 1958 Griffith had promised to move the team to the Twin Cities, as soon as the American League approved a new expansion team to replace the Senators in Washington.

While most of the effort of Twin Cities leaders was directed toward acquiring a major league baseball team, it was actually major league football that committed to the Twin Cities first. There were conversations with Viola Wolfner, owner of the Chicago Cardinals, about moving that team to the Met, and two regular season Cardinals games were played at the Met in 1959. The Cardinals ended up in St. Louis instead, but an expansion franchise for the Twin Cities was approved by NFL owners in 1960, with play to begin in the 1961 season.[9]

On the baseball front, in 1960 Branch Rickey and William Shea organized the Continental League as a rival to Major League Baseball, with its primary objective to bring a National League team back to New York. One member of the proposed league was the Twin Cities. The Continental League disbanded before playing a game, after reaching an agreement with Major League Baseball under which National League teams were to be added in New York and Houston, with American League expansion to occur as well. At the 1960 American League meetings, Calvin Griffith proposed a move of the Senators to the Twin Cities (to Met Stadium) coupled with an expansion franchise for Washington. This was accepted by American League owners, and the Senators moved to the Twin Cities as the Minnesota Twins.

The Minnesota Twins and the Minnesota Vikings both began play at the Met in the 1961 season. For the individuals holding the revenue bonds issued to finance the Met, it could not have come at a better time. Between 1956 and 1961, the Met did not earn enough to cover required interest payments on the bonds, and the facility would have been in default except that certain large bondholders, civic-minded firms and individuals, agreed to wait for their money until major league sports made it to the stadium.[10]

On January 18, 1961, the Metropolitan Sports Area Commission (MSAC) signed an agreement (Baseball Playing Agreement) with the Washington American League Baseball Club, Inc., to the following effect:

—The agreement was for fifteen years.

—Baseball was given priority over football and other prospective tenants in scheduling and other matters.

—Stadium rental for regular season games was 7 percent of ticket sales after deducting the visitor and league shares (at the time, the visiting team got 30 cents per ticket, and the American League 6 cents per ticket); for post-season and All-Star games, the rental was $2,000 per game.

—If total attendance over the period 1961–65 was less than 3.75 million (an average of 750,000 a year), then the club did not have to pay any rent it owed until attendance reached 3.75 million.

—The club was to control the concessions operation, with the MSAC to receive 10 percent of gross concession revenues at baseball games, and 15 percent of gross concession revenues at football games. (Note that the Twins controlled the concessions at Vikings games as well as at Twins games.)

—The MSAC agreed to provide a seating capacity of 30,000 for the 1961 season and 40,000 for the 1962 and succeeding seasons.

—All parking revenues at Met Stadium, a major source of revenue for the facility, were assigned to the MSAC.[11]

The Vikings were definitely the "second" team in the Met, as indicated by the terms of the Twins' contract. The Vikings agreement was also for 15 years, with the MSAC collecting 10 percent of gross gate revenue, after deducting the visitor share (40 percent) and the league share. The Vikings received no concession income under the original agreement. The cost of the expansion was approximately $4.0 million. The city of Minneapolis issued $8.5 million of revenue bonds to pay for the expansion and to retire the outstanding bonds from the original 1955 financing of the Met.

The Metrodome

Sports writers, fans, and players all agree that the Met was a great baseball park. It had the intimacy of older stadiums and of the best new ones, and great sight lines. But the Met had major problems as a football stadium, not the least of which were weather related. During the first ten years the Twins played at the Met, the team outdrew the average American League team in every year. These were the years of Harmon Killebrew, Tony Oliva, Bob Allison, Rich Rollins, Zoilla Versalles, Jim Kaat, Earl Battey, and the rest, outstanding baseball teams playing in an almost ideal baseball setting. The early years of the Vikings were shaky ones on the field, but once Bud Grant arrived, the Vikings vied with the Cowboys for the title of the dominant team in the National Football Conference for the next ten years. On the other hand, while the Vikings essentially sold out the Met almost from the time they arrived, the Met capacity for football (47,000) was so small that the Vikings drew under the NFL per team average every year of their stay at the Met (1961–81).

By 1969 the Vikings and the NFL commissioner's office were beginning to apply pressure to do something about the stadium situation.[12] Over the next ten years, state and local politics and politicians were plagued with unresolved questions concerning the construction of a new stadium or renovation of the Met, threats of the Vikings and the Twins to move, and infighting among Minneapolis, St. Paul, and Bloomington concerning the siting of a new stadium.

Ultimately, in 1977, agreement was reached on funding a new stadium by the state of Minnesota, with the difficult siting issue being finessed by passing a law providing that an independent commission, appointed by the governor, should be charged with determining the kind of stadium to be built (domed versus open air, football versus multisport), and where it was to be located. The basic constraint on the commission was that no more than $55 million was to be raised by the sale of revenue bonds by the state to be spent on the stadium. Backup funding for "start-up" money and to cover possible future operating deficits took the form of a 2 percent metropolitan area liquor tax, beginning in August 1977.

The commission held hearings and did background research for eighteen months, from June 1, 1977, to December 1, 1978. A poll taken by Channel 5 in the Twin Cities, just before the commission's announcement on December 1, 1978, got the following responses: 38 percent of those polled wanted a new domed stadium, while 42 percent wanted the old stadium remodeled or left as is. Eighty-two percent of those polled opposed the use of taxpayer money to finance the remodeling of the Met or building a new stadium. When asked where it should be built, if a new stadium were approved, 65 percent voted for Bloomington versus 14 percent for Minneapolis, the rest undecided or voting for other sites.[13] On December 1, 1978, despite the poll results, the commission, by a vote of 4 to 3, recommended building a domed stadium at the Industry Square site in downtown Minneapolis.[14]

There was some tidying up to do. Members of the state legislature from St. Paul led a fight to change the backup funding to a 2 percent liquor tax applying only to Minneapolis, plus a 2.5 to 3 percent tax on hotels and motels, again collected only in Minneapolis. This was coupled with an arrangement with the city of Minneapolis, under which the city agreed to turn over to the stadium all net receipts from three city-owned parking ramps for a ten-year period, along with $75,000 a year in perpetuity from parking meters. The resulting bill passed, and a $55 million domed stadium in downtown Minneapolis, the Hubert H. Humphrey Metrodome, financed by state revenue bonds, was now alive and well.

The legislation authorizing the Metrodome also created a new public entity, the Metropolitan Sports Facilities Commission (MSFC), to replace the MSAC. Finally, in early August 1979, agreements were signed between the Twins and the Vikings and the MSFC.[15] The Twins' agreement contained the following provisions:

—The agreement is for thirty years, except that if the team is unable to sell the lesser of (a) 1.4 million tickets, or (b) the average number of tickets sold by all American League teams, for three successive seasons; or, if for three consecutive fiscal years, the team has a cumulative net operating loss, then the team can terminate the agreement at the end of the first baseball season following such occurrence.

—The Twins get 30 percent of gross revenue from concessions at Twins games until 1.4 million tickets are sold, after which the Twins get 20 percent.

—The rent is 7.5 percent up to 1 million admissions; no rent from 1.0 to 1.4 million; and then back to 7.5 percent on all tickets over 1.4 million a year.

—If lack of air-conditioning affects attendance in any of the first three years, MSFC must install air-conditioning.

—If the team breaks its lease, it must pay the average it has paid in the past, for the number of years remaining on the lease.

—The Twins were given $1 million to construct a new office complex in the Metrodome, to replace the office complex they had at Met Stadium.

The Vikings agreement included the following terms:

—The agreement is for thirty years, with no escape clause.

—Rent is 9.5 percent of net gate receipts.

—The Vikings get 10 percent of gross revenue from concessions at Vikings games.

—The penalty for breaking the lease is on the same basis as with the Twins, the penalty (over the remaining years under the contract) being the average the Vikings have paid to the stadium authority in the past.

In addition to these provisions, the law authorizing the Dome provided for the imposition of a 10 percent tax on admissions to the Dome, so that the effective rental rate for the Twins became 17.5 percent, and for the Vikings 19.5 percent, both among the highest rental rates in major league sports.[16]

One other contract was signed in early August between the Vikings and the MSFC, one relating to luxury boxes in the Dome.[17] Under this agreement, the Vikings were allowed to construct, maintain, and operate 112 boxes, for a period of twenty years. The Vikings agreed to pay $440,000 a year for the first five years, $700,000 a year for the second five years, $1 million a year for the third five years, and $1.3 million a year for every year after that, with the MSFC to get 30 percent of concession proceeds in the boxes. The agreement was renewable in twenty years.

Later, one other controversial agreement was signed, with the Minnesota Golden Gophers, who agreed to abandon Memorial Stadium on their Minneapolis campus for the Metrodome, under a twenty-seven-year no-rent agreement, with the university getting 30 percent of gross concession income at Gopher games. The usual 10 percent tax on admissions applies to Gopher tickets.

With the team agreements in place, construction began on the Dome, which ended up costing approximately $75 million to build.[18] This exceeded the $55 million of state funding under the authorizing legislation, but $7 million was provided by the Twins and the Vikings ($5 million of which represents the cost of the luxury boxes to the Vikings), and the remaining $13 million came from interest earnings during the construction period.[19] On a comparative basis, the Metrodome cost about the same (in real terms) as the 1984 Indianapolis Hoosierdome, while both were almost one-third less expensive (in real terms) than Seattle's 1976 Kingdome.[20] In part the relatively low construction cost of the Metrodome came about because certain capital costs were converted into current costs. For example, the Metrodome does not have its own heating system; instead, it buys heat supplied by the Metropolitan Hospital located a few blocks away. And, when air-conditioning was installed, Minnegasco, the natural gas public utility, invested in the ductwork and air-conditioning equipment and is recovering its investment through its monthly billings.[21]

The Metrodome, located between Fourth and Fifth Streets South, and between Eleventh Avenue and Chicago Avenue, opened in March 1982. A year later, after a typical baseball season with the usual humidity and heat in the Twin Cities, Calvin Griffith exercised his option under the baseball agreement, and air-conditioning was installed in the Dome, adding to operating cost an amount that has a capitalized value of about $10 million.

In 1984 Carl Pohlad purchased the Twins from Calvin Griffith, paying a price of about $35 million for the team and taking over the stadium contract from Griffith. Three years later, the team having drawn less than the American League average for five years running, Pohlad filed a notice to move it at the end of the 1987 season, and the Twins' stadium contract was renegotiated. Beginning with the 1988 season, the rent of 7½ percent of gate revenue was eliminated, and the Twins agreed to a ten-year contract. Under the new contract, the team can leave without penalty if the team loses money in three successive years beginning in 1995, or if the team draws less than the American League average in three successive years beginning in 1995. The Vikings have not renegotiated their stadium contract.[22]

Metrodome Finances

This brings up the general question: How did the Metrodome do, from a financial point of view, up to 1996? Table 7-1 reports Metrodome operating revenue, operating expenses, and operating income (before depreciation), from 1982 through 1995, net of direct subsidies. Average operating income net of direct subsidies over this period was $4.12 million a year, almost exactly equal to debt interest and amortization costs of about $4.03 million a year.[23]

One way to interpret the data is that stadium rentals coupled with the admission tax have provided the MSFC with (just) sufficient operating income to cover its indebtedness requirements, without the need for (further) direct public subsidies. Looking at things this way, the Metro-

Table 7-1. *Metrodome Operating Income, Net of Direct Subsidies, 1982–95*
Thousands of current dollars

Year	Parking[a]	Rent[b]	Concessions[c]	Admission tax	Other	Total	Operating expenses	Operating income[d]
1982	103	1,474	1,143	1,411	163	4,294	2,813	1,481
1983	142	1,692	1,839	1,789	87	5,549	2,901	2,648
1984	153	1,882	2,600	2,232	119	6,986	3,383	3,603
1985	147	1,447	2,411	2,369	250	6,624	4,162	2,462
1986	129	1,380	2,264	2,270	378	6,421	4,176	2,245
1987	211	1,995	3,651	3,410	460	9,727	5,682	4,045
1988	275	4,188	2,937	3,771	523	11,694	4,918	6,776
1989	311	3,259	2,376	4,207	650	10,803	6,398	4,405
1990	234	1,786	3,230	3,847	740	9,837	6,146	3,691
1991	190	2,012	3,587	4,669	938	11,396	6,247	5,149
1992	167	2,318	3,840	4,031	1,490	11,846	6,114	5,732
1993	243	2,905	2,759	4,056	1,843	11,806	6,457	5,349
1994	171	4,246	2,989	3,704	839	11,949	6,695	5,254
1995	137	4,622	2,898	3,562	856	12,075	7,290	4,785
Average	187	2,515	2,752	3,237	667	9,358	5,242	4,116

Source: Metropolitan Sports Facilities Commission, Financial Audit, annually, 1982–95.
a. Does not include the amount paid to the Metropolitan Sports Facilities Commission by the city of Minneapolis under the parking agreement.
b. Includes stadium rent and advertising fees. Rent totals exclude rents paid by Minnesota North Stars at Met Center, 1985–92.
c. Net of concession operating costs and tenants' share of concession receipts. expenses reimbursed by tenants are excluded both from revenue and cost, as are interest earnings and expenses.
d. Operating income (= total operating revenue less total operating expense).

Table 7-2. *Direct Subsidies to the Metrodome, 1977–95*

Thousands of current dollars

Year	Metropolitan liquor tax	Minneapolis liquor tax	Minneapolis parking	Total direct subsidies
1977	634	. . .	. . .	634
1978	4,022	. . .	. . .	4,022
1979	3,376	931	. . .	4,307
1980	. . .	2,905	. . .	2,905
1981	. . .	2,977	. . .	2,977
1982	. . .	3,264	105	3,369
1983	. . .	3,229	316	3,545
1984	. . .	2,519	409	2,928
1985	. . .	. . .	421	421
1986	. . .	. . .	434	434
1987	. . .	. . .	437	437
1988	. . .	. . .	458	458
1989	. . .	. . .	476	476
1990	. . .	. . .	493	493
1991	. . .	. . .	509	509
1992	. . .	. . .	373	373
1993	. . .	. . .	75[a]	75[a]
1994	. . .	. . .	75[a]	75[a]
1995	. . .	. . .	75[a]	75[a]
Total	8,033	15,825	4,429	28,287

Source: Metropolitan Sports Facilities Commission: Schedule of Outside Revenue Sources, 1993.
a. Estimated.

dome has fulfilled the basic financial objectives the legislature had in mind back in 1979, when the Metrodome was finally approved.

Table 7-2 identifies the sources and amounts of direct subsidies that were received by the MSFC between 1977 and 1995. Such direct subsidies became a relatively minor part of Metrodome financing after 1984 and have practically ceased in recent years. However, over the history of the Metrodome, from the preconstruction period through 1995, direct subsidies from Twin Cities taxpayers ($28 million) were fully half as large as operating income net of direct subsidies ($57 million).

Table 7-3 presents a more complete picture of Metrodome finances, including operating and nonoperating income. If the objective of Metrodome financial operations is to generate sufficient net income to cover depreciation and out-of-pocket costs, then table 7-3 shows that, netting out average direct subsidies of $2.01 million a year, annual depreciation of $3.35 million a year has been more than covered by operating and nonoperating revenue sources (net of direct subsidies). Beyond the direct subsidies provided by the liquor and hotel-motel taxes and parking rev-

Table 7-3. *Metrodome Net Income, 1977–95*
Thousands of current dollars

Year	Operating income	Depreciation	Direct subsidies	Net interest	Other nonoperating income[a]	Net income
1977	...	...	634	...	...	634
1978	...	...	4,022	...	...	4,022
1979	...	...	3,376	...	...	3,376
1980	...	...	2,905	2,774	...	5,679
1981	...	...	2,977	5,016	...	7,993
1982	1,481	(1,969)	3,368	(862)	...	2,018
1983	2,648	(2,605)	3,545	(2,946)	...	642
1984	3,603	(2,625)	2,928	(2,353)	...	1,553
1985	2,462	(2,655)	421	(1,118)	...	(890)
1986	2,245	(3,586)	434	(1,595)	...	(2,502)
1987	4,046	(3,103)	437	(1,731)	...	(351)
1988	6,776	(3,510)	458	(1,092)	3,819	6,451
1989	4,405	(2,398)	476	(366)	...	2,117
1990	3,691	(3,318)	493	(899)	2,870	2,837
1991	5,149	(3,714)	509	(1,364)	1,000	1,580
1992	5,732	(3,852)	373	(1,372)	...	881
1993	5,349	(4,304)	75[a]	(231)	...	889
1994	5,254	(4,313)	75[b]	(644)	(2,712)	(2,340)
1995	4,785	(4,933)	75[b]	(531)	...	(604)
Average[c]	4,116	(3,349)	2,021	(1,062)	356	2,428

Source: Metropolitan Sports Facilities Commission, *Financial Audit*, annually, 1982–95.

a. Figures in parentheses are negative values.

b. Other nonoperating income for 1988, condemnation award of $3,919; 1990, roof lawsuit settlement, $2,870; 1991, Viking real estate tax refund, $1,000; 1994, investments revalued or sold. $2,712.

c. Average is total divided by fourteen years, 1982–95.

enues, the state and local governments have provided ongoing indirect subsidies to the Metrodome and its tenants in the form of property tax relief, with the federal government providing subsidies through tax exemption of interest on state revenue bonds.[24]

This leads to the question of the overall size of the subsidies all government units provide to Metrodome tenants. The idea is to calculate the rental ("market rent") that would be charged for use of the Metrodome if it were operated on a for-profit basis. The difference between this and the operating income actually received by the Metrodome is then the amount of the overall subsidy provided to Metrodome tenants.

Note that in order for a privately financed stadium to operate profitably, it would have to charge a rent high enough to cover depreciation plus property taxes plus a market rate of return on investment. Furthermore, the relevant measure of investment is replacement cost and not the standard accounting measure of the lesser of historical cost or market value.

Table 7-4 presents a calculation of "market rent" over the period 1982–95, measured in 1994 dollars.[25] The (net) rent actually received by the Metrodome is the operating income (net of direct subsidies) by year, in 1994 dollars. The difference is the subsidy provided to tenants by the Metrodome, which averages out at $14.9 million a year, in 1994 dollars. Pro-rating this subsidy on the basis of the net revenues received by the Metrodome from various tenants, the Twins would receive a subsidy of about $5.2 million a year, the Vikings $6.7 million a year, the Gophers $0.9 million a year, and other tenants $2.1 million a year.

The subsidy arises in part from the fact that the Metrodome does not pay property taxes and it is financed using tax-exempt bonds at a cost of capital of less than 10 percent a year. Also, the facility has been directly subsidized by taxpayers, through the liquor and hotel-motel taxes levied in the early years, and through the transfer of parking revenues from the city of Minneapolis.

In addition, table 7-4 shows sizable net investments in the Metrodome after completion of initial construction in 1982. Between 1982 and 1995 approximately $32 million in 1994 dollars was spent on upgrading the Metrodome. Given that the Twins are talking about moving from the Metrodome to a new stadium in the near future, this raises questions about the future return on these upgrading investments. If the actual working life of the Metrodome as a multisport facility is only, say, eigh-

Table 7-4. *Calculation of Subsidies Provided by Metrodome to Tenants*

Millions of 1994 dollars

Year	Net investment[a]	Cumulative net investment[b]	Depreciation[c]	Property tax[d]	10 percent return[e]	Market rent[f]	Operating Income[g]	Estimated subsidy[h]
1979	15.7	...	...	...	...	...	...	...
1980	29.7	45.4	...	...	...	...	...	...
1981	55.0	100.4	...	...	...	...	...	...
1982	10.5	110.9	3.7	2.6	11.1	17.4	2.1	15.3
1983	3.3	114.2	3.8	2.7	11.4	17.9	3.4	14.5
1984	0.4	114.6	3.8	2.7	11.5	18.0	4.7	13.3
1985	0.5	115.1	3.8	2.8	11.5	18.1	3.2	14.9
1986	1.3	116.4	3.9	2.9	11.6	18.4	2.8	15.6
1987	1.6	118.0	3.9	3.0	11.8	18.7	4.9	13.8
1988	1.9	119.9	4.0	3.0	12.0	19.0	8.1	10.9
1989	2.0	121.9	4.0	3.0	12.2	19.2	5.2	14.0
1990	3.9	125.8	4.2	3.1	12.6	19.9	4.2	15.7
1991	3.3	129.1	4.3	3.2	12.9	20.4	5.6	14.8
1992	3.7	132.8	4.4	3.3	13.3	21.0	6.1	14.9
1993	4.6	137.4	4.6	3.4	13.7	21.7	5.5	16.2
1994	.7	138.1	4.6	3.4	13.8	21.8	5.3	16.5
1995	4.8	142.9	4.8	3.6	14.3	22.7	4.5	18.2
Average								14.9

Source: Net investment and operation income from Metropolitan Sports Facilities Commission Financial Audit, annually, 1982–95, adjusted for inflation.
a. The 1979 net investment represents the value of the site ($8.7 in current (1979) dollars), while other net investments are changes in the book value of the Metrodome, converted into 1994 dollars.
b. Replacement value of the facility at each point in time, measured in 1994 dollars.
c. Calculated on the basis of a thirty-year life, and is based on the replacement value figure shown.
d. Assumed to be 2.5 percent of replacement value.
e. Amount required to earn 10 percent on the replacement value.
f. Sum of depreciation plus property tax plus 10 percent return. Operating income is net of subsidy, and is stated in 1994 dollars.
g. Operating income is from table 7-1, adjusted for inflation.
h. Difference between market rent and operating income each year, in 1994 dollars.

teen years, rather than thirty years, the investments certainly will not pay off.

Met Finances

This brings the story of the Metrodome up to date. Now, to return to 1982 and the disposal of Met Stadium, an operation that was almost as messy and controversial as getting approval for the Metrodome. The Met was closed after the 1981 season. By law, the property had to be disposed of by mid-July 1982.

After the smoke generated by the bidding process had cleared, the MSFC announced that it had awarded the property to William Cooley and his syndicate, for a bid of $25.8 million. Some lawsuits surrounding the award had finally been resolved, and Cooley was scheduled to pay for the property in mid-1984. But then he announced that he was unable to make the required payment, and the property reverted back to the MSFC.

At this point, the eager bidders of 1982 were no longer around. The city of Bloomington stepped in and bought the property for $14.5 million and had the much dilapidated Met stadium torn down and removed. In 1985 Bloomington found a client for the 100-acre Met site in the Ghermezian brothers of Edmonton, Alberta, who put together an impressive financing package to convert the old Met property into what has become Minnesota's biggest tourist attraction, the Mall of America.

This ends the story of Met Stadium, except that the $14.5 million received for the Met site went into the coffers of the MSFC. This provided the commission with the working capital and reserves sufficient to satisfy levels specified in the bond indenture, and the Minneapolis liquor and hotel-motel taxes were eliminated. As of 1996, there had been no need to reimpose the taxes since that time.

With the sale of the Met site, it was now possible to assess the financial and economic success of the stadium over its lifetime. Table 7-5 presents the breakdown of revenue and expense items making up the operating income of Met Stadium from 1956 until 1981. During the five minor league years, the Met had an average operating income of only $53,000 a year, while the interest and amortization requirements ran roughly $225,000 a year. With the Twins and Vikings on board, the average operating income was $418,000 a year, which was roughly equal to the

Table 7-5. *Metropolitan Stadium Operating Income, Net of Direct Subsidies, 1956–81*

Thousands of current dollars

Year	Parking	Rent	Concessions	Other	Total	Operating expenses[a]	Operating income
Minor league operation							
1956	81	59	58		198	92	107
1957	57	72	71	30	230	147	84
1958	47	54	52	1	155	143	12
1959	43	54	11	72	180	110	69
1960	36	46	8		90	98	(8)
Average	53	57	40	21	171	118	53
Major league operation							
1961	235	267	101	2	605	296	309
1962	383	300	121	2	806	323	483
1963	377	311	124	2	814	332	482
1964	341	277	120	1	739	315	424
1965	467	298	157	2	925	453	473
1966	451	292	118	1	863	434	428
1967	515	329	147	1	993	508	485
1968	415	303	128	3	849	436	413
1969	489	405	162	5	1,060	485	575
1970	513	432	175	4	1,124	563	562
1971	391	356	141	6	893	545	348
1972	331	300	119	4	755	505	250
1973	377	405	156	4	942	519	424
1974	326	455	139	2	922	589	332
1975	396	446	175	4	1,021	666	355
1976	633	651	245	15	1,544	1,025	519
1977	784	685	280	80	1,829	1,157	672
1978	724	699	287	570[b]	2,280	2,068	212
1979	1,079	790	326	481[b]	2,675	2,250	425
1980	560	734	325	376[b]	1,995	1,514	481
1981	677	596	265	366[b]	1,904	1,769	135
Average	498	444	182	92	1,216	798	418

Sources: Metropolitan Sports Area Commission, Financial Audit, annually, 1956–77; and Metropolitan Sports Facilities Commission, Financial Audit, annually, 1977–81.

a. Some of the expenses incurred from 1978 on are related to planning for the Metrodome, but it has not been possible to segregate the costs specifically allocable to the Met Stadium.

b. Includes admission tax receipts: 1978, $454; 1979, $421; 1980, $345; 1981, $280.

interest and amortization requirements of about $425,000 a year. In brief, even with major league baseball and football teams in the stadium, the Met operated on a short leash, with not much in the way of surplus over and above the required payments on the $8.5 million in debt issued in 1961.[26]

Table 7-6 estimates the subsidies provided to the Twins and Vikings by the Met. Total subsidies to the two tenants averaged $5 million a year, 1961–81, in 1994 dollars. Thus the Metrodome roughly tripled the subsidies received by the Twins and the Vikings.

With the sale of the Met stadium site for $14.5 million in 1985, a natural question to ask is whether investment in the Met turned out to be a good decision from a purely financial point of view. In particular, taking into account all subsequent investments and the income derived from the Met as well as the final purchase of the Met site, was the present value of revenues greater than the present value of investments? The discount rate used in this calculation is 6 percent, roughly the average rate over the period on high-grade municipal bonds.

Table 7-7 presents the underlying data, as well as the present value of investments and revenues. Even with the $14.5 million payment for the Met site in 1985, the present value of revenues received by the Met is less than the present value of investments in the facility over its lifetime. In effect, what this comparison shows is that the city of Minneapolis's investment in the Met did not earn a 6 percent rate of return, even when the large ($14.5 million) liquidation value of the facility is taken into account, so that, on net balance and ignoring external and consumption effects, the Met turned out to be a losing investment for the city of Minneapolis.

The Met Center

The Twin Cities' experience with sports facilities does not end there, however. On March 11, 1965, the National Hockey League announced that it was expanding for the first time since the end of World War II. On February 2, 1966, the NHL awarded a franchise to a group of Twin Cities businessmen for a $2 million fee, subject to the proviso that they have an arena seating 12,500 available for the 1967–68 season. The Minnesota North Stars were now in business.

The group obtained approval from the MSAC to use land at the Met Stadium site and obtained financing from First National Bank. Except for the use of publicly owned land, only private money was used to finance the Metropolitan Sports Center (the Met Center), which was finished in one year at a cost of $5.8 million. The arena opened on October 21, 1967, with a seating capacity of 14,400. Tenants at the Met Center were the

Table 7-6. *Subsidies Provided by Metropolitan Stadium to Tenants, 1961–81*
Millions of 1994 dollars[a]

Year	Net investment	Cumulative net investment	Depreciation	Property tax	10 percent return	Market rent	Operating income[b]	Estimated subsidy
Minor league operation								
1956	34.0	34.0	1.1	.9	3.4	5.4	.8	4.6
1957	(1.1)	32.9	1.1	.8	3.3	5.2	.6	4.6
1958	(1.0)	31.9	1.1	.8	3.2	5.1	.1	5.0
1959	(1.0)	30.9	1.0	.8	3.1	4.9	.5	4.4
1960	(1.0)	29.9	1.0	.8	3.0	4.8	(.1)	4.9
Average								4.7
Major league operation								
1961	20.7	50.6	1.7	1.3	5.1	8.1	2.0	6.1
1962	(1.6)	49.0	1.6	1.2	4.9	7.7	3.0	4.7
1963	0.0	49.0	1.6	1.2	4.9	7.7	3.0	4.7
1964	(1.5)	47.5	1.6	1.2	4.8	7.6	2.9	4.7
1965	(1.5)	46.0	1.5	1.2	4.6	7.3	2.5	4.8

Year								
1966	(0.9)	45.1	1.5	1.1	4.5	7.1	2.3	4.8
1967	(0.9)	44.2	1.5	1.1	4.4	7.0	2.4	4.6
1968	(1.3)	42.9	1.4	1.1	4.3	6.8	1.9	4.9
1969	(1.2)	41.7	1.4	1.0	4.2	6.6	2.4	4.2
1970	(0.7)	41.0	1.4	1.0	4.1	6.5	2.2	4.3
1971	(0.3)	40.7	1.4	1.0	4.1	6.5	1.2	5.3
1972	(0.6)	40.1	1.3	1.0	4.0	6.3	.8	5.5
1973	(0.3)	39.8	1.3	1.0	4.0	6.3	1.2	5.1
1974	(0.3)	39.5	1.3	1.0	4.0	6.3	.9	5.4
1975	(0.5)	39.0	1.3	1.0	3.9	6.2	.9	5.3
1976	(0.5)	38.5	1.3	1.0	3.8	6.1	1.2	4.9
1977	(0.2)	38.3	1.3	1.0	3.8	6.1	1.4	4.7
1978	(0.6)	37.7	1.3	.9	3.8	6.0	.4	5.6
1979	(0.6)	37.1	1.2	.9	3.7	5.8	1.4	4.4
1980	(0.4)	36.7	1.2	.9	3.7	5.8	.8	5.0
1981	(0.3)	36.4	1.2	.9	3.6	5.7	.2	5.5
Average								5.0

Source: *Engineering News-Record* construction price index.
a. Figures in parentheses are negative values.
b. Operating income from table 7-5, adjusted for inflation.

Table 7-7. *Present Value of Investments and of Net Income,*
Metropolitan Stadium
Millions of current dollars

Year	Investment	Net income[a]
1956	4.2	0.1
1957	. . .	.1
1958	. . .	.0
1959	. . .	.1
1960	. . .	.0
1961	3.4	.3
1962	. . .	.5
1963	.2	.5
1964	. . .	.4
1965	. . .	.5
1966	.1	.4
1967	.2	.5
1968	. . .	.4
1969	.1	.6
1970	.1	.6
1971	.2	.3
1972	.1	.2
1973	.2	.4
1974	.2	.3
1975	.1	.4
1976	.1	.5
1977	.2	.7
1978	. . .	.2
1979	. . .	.4
1980	.1	.5
1981	.1	.1
1985	. . .	14.5
Present value	7.55	6.69

Source: Author's calculations.
a. Operating income from table 7-5, adjusted for inflation.

NHL North Stars, and a second team, the Minnesota Muskies of the just organized American Basketball Association (ABA). The Muskies stayed in town for only one year, to be replaced by the ABA Minnesota Pipers, who also played just one season before returning to Pittsburgh.[27]

The leasing arrangement relating to the stadium, the North Stars, and the MSAC was a unique one.[28] Under the contract, the North Stars agreed to turn over the title to the Met Center to the MSAC immediately. They also agreed to pay 10 percent of the gross receipts from most events and 10 percent of concessions and other income, with the MSAC retaining all parking income. Operating expenses were allocated between the two parties. However, these rental arrangements would only come into force at a future "payout date." Before the payout date, the North Stars agreed to pay the MSAC a flat fee of $400 a month. The payout date was to be that time at which, given the actual operating history of the Met Center, the cumulative amounts that would have been due to the MSAC under the rental arrangements would equal the amount invested by the North Stars in the facility, with interest calculated at the maximum of the market rate of interest, or 5+ percent. The team was to submit monthly statements to the MSAC as to the status of the progress toward the payout date. Additional investments in the Met Center required agreement by both parties, with the North Stars bearing the cost, and with the cost of such investments being incorporated into the calculation of the payout date. The agreement was for the expected lifetime of the facility, that is, thirty years.

From the North Stars' point of view, the arrangement saved them from paying land rent for the use of the Met Center site and also avoided property taxes on the Met Center, a total savings of perhaps $300,000 a year. The MSAC had obtained a major league sports tenant with a minimal investment, so that both parties found the arrangement attractive.

During the early years of the franchise, North Stars attendance was exceptional, but by the mid-1970s it was down, and the original owners were ready to get out. On June 14, 1978, the Gund brothers (George III and Gordon) took over the North Stars and their Met Center contract, merging their even more troubled Cleveland Barons into the North Star franchise. Details of the agreement between the local group and the Gunds are not known, but a guess is that the North Stars were sold for roughly the price of an expansion team, that is, $6 million.[29]

The North Stars recovered both on the ice and at the box office almost immediately. For seven consecutive years, the team made the playoffs, and they reached the Stanley Cup finals in 1980–81. Back in the board room, things were not so pleasant. The complicated provisions relating to the calculation of the payout date on the Met Center contract led to suits and countersuits by the MSFC and the North Stars, and the problems relating to the sale of the Met Stadium site, which also involved the Gunds, did not help matters. Ultimately, the problems were resolved, and a new contract was hammered out, one that in effect recognized the payout date had in fact finally arrived, but that reduced the rent of the

North Stars considerably below that envisaged in the original agreement. On January 17, 1985, the Gunds signed a new Met Center lease with the MSFC.

The new lease was for twenty years, with an option to extend for ten more. The North Stars were to retain operating control over the Met Center, to receive all revenues, and to pay all operating costs. They agreed to spend $3 million within a year for improvements to the Met and accepted a rental arrangement under which the MSFC received 1 percent of gross revenues for the first five years, 2 percent the next five, and 3 percent for all following years. There was no penalty clause in the contract, in case the team left town.[30]

By the late 1980s, the North Stars franchise was once again in trouble. In part this was because of team performance, but there were other factors at work as well. The entrance of the NBA Timberwolves into the Twin Cities market had a negative effect on North Stars' attendance, and non-hockey-related income at the Met Center was going to be hit hard when the Target Center opened for business.[31]

In April 1990 the North Stars were sold to Howard Baldwin and Morris Belzberg, under an arrangement enabling the Gunds to acquire an expansion franchise in San Jose for the 1991–92 season. The price paid for the team was $31.5 million.[32]

Two months later, the team was sold to Norman Green, who had been part owner of the Calgary NHL team. An indication of impending trouble for the franchise came in early July, with the firing of half the staff at the Met Center, because of a loss of non–hockey events bid away by the Target Center, which was scheduled to open in October 1990.

Attendance and related problems persisted, and Green began negotiations with both the St. Paul Civic Arena and the Target Center, and began investigating an alternative site for the team. At about this time, Green also was sued for sexual harassment on the job.[33] In March 1993 the NHL approved Green's request to move the North Stars to Dallas.[34]

With the North Stars gone, the Met Center, owned by the MSFC, was now empty. The MSFC organized a nineteen-member task force to determine what to do with the Met Center. A second commission was set up by Governor Arnie Carlson to recruit an NHL team to the Twin Cities. The complicating factor in both of these tasks was the Target Center, the Timberwolves' new arena in downtown Minneapolis, which was in financial trouble.

Table 7-8. *Annual Rental Income of the Twin Cities Met Center,*
1985–95

Thousands of dollars

Year	Income	Year	Income
1985	121,782	1989	126,881
1986	121,905	1990	220,217
1987	118,946	1991	309,106
1988	119,645	1992	244,065

Source: Roger Simonson, personal communication, June 1996.

Thus at the very time that the MSFC was trying to decide how to find a new occupant for the Met Center, the owners of the newly opened Target Center were trying to get the city, the state, the Metropolitan Council, anybody, to buy their arena. Under pressure from Gary Bettman, commissioner of the NHL, and with the support of members of the governor's commission, the MSFC voted in December 1993, to demolish the Met Center. This step was taken on Bettman's recommendation, to improve the Twin Cities' chances of obtaining a new NHL team, to be housed in the spanking new Target Center. The $1.2 million demolition was completed early in 1994.

As of mid-1996, the Met Center site had not been sold. However, the property had been appraised at $28 million, and negotiations were under way with representatives from the Mall of America and from the Airport Commission concerning disposal of the property.[35]

Because the Met Center was operated by the North Stars over its history, data are not available to determine the operating revenues of the facility. What can be calculated is the present value of the investments by the MSAC and MSFC in the facility versus the present value of rental income plus the prospective sales price of the site. Investments are simply the $140,000 purchase price of the site in 1956 (one-third of the original purchase price of the land acquired for Met stadium, since the Met Center occupied 50 of the 150 acres at that site) plus the $1.2 million demolition cost in 1994. Rental income was $4,800 a year from 1966 through 1984, with rentals under the 1985 agreement as shown in table 7-8.[36]

At a 6 percent rate of discount, the present value of income of the Met Center from 1956 up through 1992 is $245,000 versus a present value of investments of $140,000, excluding the demolition cost. Hence, even ignoring the huge increase in site value that took place between 1956 and

1996, the rents that the Met Center earned generated more than a 6 percent rate of return on the site investment back in 1956. If the land sells for something in the $25 million range within the next few years, then the rate of return on original investment will be far in excess of 6 percent, of course.

This long story of arenas, stadiums, and professional sports teams in the Twin Cities has not quite reach its end. There is one more controversial episode: the story of "Harv and Marv," the Timberwolves, and the Target Center.

The Target Center

Harvey Ratner and Marvin Wolfenson first came to public prominence in the Twin Cities in early 1987. The two were successful developers of residential property in the Twin Cities and were also the owners and operators of the Northwest Racquet, Swim and Health Clubs, with facilities throughout the Twin Cities. They had decided to make a bid for an NBA expansion team, to be housed in a new arena and health club complex, located in a depressed area of downtown Minneapolis north of 7th and Hennepin Avenues. The state of-the-art complex was to include a 19,000-capacity arena, along with 120,000 square feet of health facilities. On February 20, 1987, the Minneapolis city council voted, 11 to 1, to pitch in to help, by agreeing to issue $20 million in city bonds to provide the $15.4 million needed to pay for the land on which the complex would be built, plus reserves.

By the terms of the agreement, Ratner and Wolfenson would repay the city $380,000/year for twenty years. The city would also receive 5 percent of any profits of the combined operation—team, arena, and health club. In addition, if the team or arena were to be sold, the city would get between 10 and 20 percent of any profits made on the sale. In effect, the two owners were guaranteeing 50 percent of the cost of the land through direct repayments, and were providing the other 50 percent through their profit-sharing arrangement with the city. The announced estimated cost of the facility was $35 million.[37]

While there was metropolitan-wide support for acquiring an NBA team, building the new arena was another kettle of fish entirely. As of 1987, there were in operation in the Twin Cities the twenty-year-old Met

Center, with a capacity of 15,000; the fifteen-year-old St. Paul Civic Center Arena, a 16,000-capacity facility; and sixty-year-old Williams Arena on the campus of the university, with a seating capacity at the time of 16,549 for basketball, and another 7,775 for hockey.

The Civic Center Arena was built in the early 1970s by the city of St. Paul, for $19 million. In 1983, in a mirror-image reversal of the Met Center story, the Civic Center Arena was sold to a group of private investors and leased back by the city. It is located just east of the Seven Corners area of downtown St. Paul. The Civic Center contains a parking complex as well as the arena, with parking providing much of the Civic Center's income. The Civic Center Arena hosts conventions and shows, as well as various state high school tournaments (basketball, hockey), and has become a regular if not quite permanent site for the annual Western Collegiate Hockey Association tournament. The arena also has hosted the National Collegiate Athletic Association hockey tournament. Between 1973 and 1976, the Minnesota Fighting Saints of the World Hockey Association made their home at the arena, before going bankrupt and leaving the center with unpaid rent bills.

With the Met Center, the Civic Center, and Williams Arena on the premises, the need for yet another Twin Cities arena was not at all clear. Concerns expressed by civic leaders, especially from St. Paul, were vocal enough that, on April 10, 1987, the Minneapolis City Council asked the Metropolitan Council to study the "metropolitan significance" of the proposed arena.[38] The Met Council had been given the legal authority to delay proposed major metropolitan projects for up to a year, if necessary to assess negative environmental or economic effects, but had never exercised this authority in connection with any construction project. The particular problem that the Metropolitan Council was most concerned about was the impact of the Target Center on the two existing publicly owned arenas, Met Center and the Civic Center, both offering facilities and services directly competitive with those of the proposed Target Center.

In mid-June the council released the report of a consulting firm that it had hired, Economics Research Associates (ERA). In ERA's judgment, the Twin City arena market was in a state of excess capacity, but "the arena (system) is not necessarily overbuilt."[39] In particular, "It is our feeling . . . that . . . no events will be lost at existing facilities due to the presence of a new arena in the market."[40] A new arena in the Twin

Cities market, the report concluded, would result in a loss of less than 2 percent of total revenue at the Met Center, with even less severe effects on the Civic Center Arena.[41]

ERA also estimated the impact of the arena on income in the Twin Cities metropolitan area: the arena would spend $3.6 million a year on operating expenses, athletes would spend $0.9 million a year on hotel rooms and restaurant meals, spectators would spend $3.7 million on nonarena goods and services, and with other direct impact spending of $2.3 million the total spending in this category would amount to $10.3 million. Using a multiplier of between 1.3 and 1.5 to estimate indirect spending, ERA estimated a total direct and indirect economic impact of between $24 and $26 million a year. The overall multiplier of 2.3 to 2.5, it stated, was "standard for impact analysis in metropolitan areas."[42]

Interestingly, the ERA report did not consider the possibility that a new NBA team might be accommodated at one of the existing arenas, either the Met Center or the Civic Center Arena. In arriving at its conclusion that no existing events would be transferred from the Met Center or Civic Center Arena to the new arena, the report identified events not currently offered at these arenas, including "arena football, professional volleyball, women's basketball, and the martial arts."[43] It noted that "these are not now presented in the Twin Cities for two reasons: either they have not been available up to now (such as arena football or professional volleyball) or scheduling problems have precluded their showing."[44] The possibility of a third reason economists would find more convincing, namely that these events were not profitable, is not mentioned. Finally, there is a pro forma statement concerning the fact that expenditures at the new arena might simply be diversions from other spending within the metropolitan area, but no adjustment was made to the expenditure impact estimates to reflect such diversions.[45]

On the basis of the consultant's findings, the council concluded in its Metropolitan Significance Review Report that "there will be no substantial effects on any of the metropolitan systems and, therefore, that the proposed NBA arena project is not of metropolitan significance (with respect to existing legal standards)."[46] Thus the council took no action to interfere with the financing and development of the Target Center, but it did urge the Timberwolves to seek an alternative to a new arena, to play at the Met Center or the Civic Center Arena, or to participate with the University of Minnesota on a jointly financed campus-based arena.[47]

Ratner and Wolfenson decided instead to proceed with their plans for a privately financed arena at the downtown site in Minneapolis.

Between the summer of 1987 and the start of construction on the Target Center in 1988, the city of Minneapolis kicked in an additional $5.7 million to pay for road work and other ancillary costs relating to the new facility and also agreed to reduce the annual repayment by Harv and Marv from $380,000 to $225,000. It is not clear how this affected the implicit responsibility of the Timberwolves for the $20 million in city bonds issued to buy the land for the Target Center.

The Timberwolves played in the Metrodome during the 1988–89 and 1989–90 seasons, setting an NBA attendance record in their first season, 1.07 million, or 26,160 per game, and far exceeding the NBA average attendance in their second season: 779,470 as against 625,042.

Meanwhile, elaborations of the original design, inflation, and, most important, bedrock problems at the site, caused the cost of the arena to escalate rapidly. By the time that the Target Center opened, in October 1990, the construction cost was up to $104 million, triple the original $35 million estimate, and Ratner and Wolfenson were facing an interest bill of about $9 million a year on almost $100 million of loans covering the Target Center and the NBA franchise fee of $32.5 million.

Once in operation, the Target Center was quite successful in booking events, many of which had formerly played at the Met Center and at the Civic Center Arena: in its first year, the Target Center hosted 155 non-Timberwolves events, 30 more than the Met Center in the previous year. And the Timberwolves continued to draw crowds at levels above the NBA per team average. However, Ratner and Wolfenson were experiencing financial difficulties owing to debt-servicing costs associated with construction cost overruns at the Target Center. But one other important problem was that competition among the three arenas had bid the cost of events up to the point where, according to their own statements, the Target Center could not break even on its non–basketball operations.

It was not only the Target Center that was having financial problems. Table 7-9 shows that, except for a brief period in the 1980s, the St. Paul Civic Center has used parking revenues to subsidize its other activities. But the deficits incurred in the nonparking activities of the Civic Center increased markedly when the Target Center came into the picture. Between 1987 and 1989, before the Target Center, the average nonparking deficit was (−) $362,000 a year. Between 1990 and 1992, when all three

Table 7-9. *St. Paul Civic Center Authority Operating Income, 1970–95*
Thousands of current dollars[a]

Year	Events	Concessions	Total (A)	Parking (B)	Operating Income (A) + (B)
1970	(156)	36	(120)	2	(118)
1971	(146)	29	(117)	23	(94)
1972	(208)	43	(165)	47	(118)
1973	(229)	180	(49)	203	154
1974	(168)	285	117	188	305
1975	(453)	285	(168)	180	12
1976	(436)	308	(128)	210	82
1977	(378)	273	(105)	244	138
1978	(426)	380	(46)	291	244
1979	(495)	276	(219)	235	16
1980	(937)	521	(416)	388	(28)
1981	(830)	601	(229)	535	306
1982	(911)	789	(122)	681	560
1983	(718)	764	46	764	809
1984	(627)	992	365	812	1,178
1985	(750)	857	107	1,005	1,112
1986	(839)	978	139	1,010	1,149
1987	(736)	1,044	309	1,052	1,362
1988	(1,497)	919	(578)	1,272	694
1989	(1,801)	983	(818)	1,083	264
1990	(1,819)	1,028	(791)	601	(189)
1991	(1,845)	916	(929)	694	(235)
1992	(2,232)	1,125	(1,107)	1,096	(11)
1993	(1,637)	1,190	(447)	1,080	632
1994	(2,501)	1,788	(713)	1,161	448
1995	n.a.				
Average	(911)	662	(248)	595	347

Source: Civic Center Authority of St. Paul, Annual Financial Report, 1970–94.
a. Figures in parentheses are negative values.

facilities—the Civic Center Arena, Met Center, and Target Center—were operating, the average nonparking deficit rose to (−) $943,000 a year. And in 1993 and 1994, with the Met Center off the market, the average nonparking deficit was back down to $581,00 a year. Comparable data are not available for the Met Center, but what is known is that the Target Center made an attempt to recruit the North Stars from the Met Center (and failed), the North Stars left the Twin Cities just two and a half years after the Target Center opened, and the Met Center was demolished, only three years after the Target Center opened. So much for the forecast of Economics Research Associates that the Target Center would have only marginal impact on the other arenas in the area.

In any case, by 1992 the two venture capitalists of 1987 who had objected to government interfering with their decision to build an arena— after all, it was their money, wasn't it?—now were knocking on the government's door and asking to have the Target Center taken over as a public facility. It took two years to accomplish this task. Along the way, public takeover of the Target Center became linked to the effort to lure an NHL team to the Twin Cities to replace the departed North Stars. As noted earlier, once the North Stars had left, most of the movers and shakers in downtown Minneapolis mounted a campaign to demolish the Met Center. This meant that NHL hockey could be played in Minneapolis only at the downtown Target Center. What then surfaced was an argument as to why a return of NHL hockey required public ownership of the Target Center. Why? Because with private ownership of the arena structured as it was in 1994, the $9 million interest cost made it impossible to offer an NHL team the dollar incentives needed to make a move attractive, while allowing the Target Center to break even. Under public ownership financed by tax-free bonds, interest costs would be cut by $4 million or so a year, which would make it possible for the city or state to offer much more attractive terms to an incoming NHL team. Or at least that is the way the argument was stated.

But there was a widespread lack of public support for a buyout of the Target Center by any government body. Ratner and Wolfenson thus decided to try to sell their marketable commodity, namely, the Timberwolves. On May 23, 1994, came the stunning announcement that the Timberwolves had been sold to the Top Rank of Louisiana organization for $152.5 million, and that the team would be moved to New Orleans.[48] The announced price was at least $50 million above the highest value that had been assigned to the franchise in other negotiations.

On June 15 the NBA turned down the sale of the team. NBA documents filed in court stated that the Top Rank offer depended on $40 million of private equity (from individuals Top Rank could not identify), $76 million in bank loans that had not yet been committed by any specific bank, and $50 million in other undisclosed sources.[49]

There was legal maneuvering involving the NBA, the Timberwolves, and Top Rank, but finally, in August 1994, a southern Minnesota businessman, Glen Taylor, was announced as the purchaser of the Timberwolves under a deal negotiated as well with the state and with the city of

Minneapolis. Taylor began operating the team at that time, although it took until March 1995, before a formal contract was agreed to among all parties.[50]

Under the agreement, Taylor and a group of twelve limited partners (including Ratner and Wolfenson with a 10 percent interest) bought the T-Wolves for $88.5 million, while the Minneapolis Community Development Agency (MCDA) purchased the Target Center for $54.6 million. Taylor signed a thirty-year rental agreement with the Target Center containing an escape clause: he can move the team if the team loses money two years in a row. If he tries to move the team, however, a novel and creative part of the agreement provides that he must give the MCDA the option to buy the team at a price equal to $88.5 million plus an escalation factor of 3 percent a year.

Taylor agreed to pay a rental to the city of Minneapolis equal to the property tax on the arena, beginning at $2.8 million per year in 1994, but limited to a rise of no more than 2 percent a year. The city of Minneapolis provided the proceeds of a 3 percent tax on Target Center events, plus $90,000 a year in parking ramp revenues, and also assigned its share of property tax levied on the health club. The state of Minnesota, through the Minnesota Amateur Sports Commission, agreed to pay $750,000 a year through the year 2009 for up to fifty days' use of the Target Center for amateur sports events. Federal taxpayers were involved in the operation as well, providing subsidies through the tax-exempt character of the bonds issued to finance the purchase of the facility.

The Ogden Corporation, which had operated the arena for Ratner and Wolfenson, leased it from the MCDA for thirty years for $1 a year. Ogden receives all operating revenues, pays all operating and maintenance expenses, and guarantees the city of Minneapolis against operating deficits. Ogden is required to spend $300,000 a year on maintenance and repairs. The MCDA is responsible for capital improvements, which are expected to run to approximately $20 million over the thirty-year life of the agreement.

Finally, the health club at the Target Center was leased to Ratner and Wolfenson for thirty years, for $1 a year. The two are responsible for maintenance and repairs and for property taxes. The implicit value of the facility, as stated in the agreement, is $10 million; hence the lease is in effect a $10 million payment to Ratner and Wolfenson.

Financing of the deal went as follows. The Taylor syndicate borrowed $58.5 million from the banks to go along with $30 million of partnership equity capital. The city of Minneapolis issued $70.8 million in general obligation bonds, and the Minneapolis Community Development Agency issued $12.7 million in revenue bonds, to cover the purchase of the Target Center, to pay off the $20 million in bonds issued back in 1988 and 1989 to purchase the land, and to cover financing and reserve requirements.

In 1995 the city of Minneapolis issued general obligation bonds as variable rate bonds, converted six months later to staggered maturity (up to thirty years) fixed rate bonds, at an average interest rate of about 5.2 percent.[51]

To summarize, the interest and amortization payments plus capital improvements were funded through "tax-increment" property tax payments by the T-Wolves of $2.9 million a year, rising at most by 2 percent per year; the proceeds of a 3 percent tax on Target Center events; city of Minneapolis's contribution of $90,000 per year in parking revenues; $750,000 in MASC payments until 2009; and the city of Minneapolis's share of property taxes on the health club, roughly $90,000 in 1995.

Under the financing plan, as already mentioned, bond maturities are staggered to reflect rising revenues over time. But a simplified check can be run on the adequacy of the proposed financing, as follows. The level payment over thirty years required to amortize the $83.5 million of bonds is roughly $5.55 million a year. With the tax increment rising at 2 percent a year, the Timberwolves' payments will average $4.09 million a year over the thirty years. Estimated first-year payments under the entertainment tax are $.9 million (estimated Target Center revenue of $30 million); with an inflation rate of 3 percent a year, the average yield from the entertainment tax will run $1.5 million a year over the thirty years. Parking and property tax revenues should average $0.3 million a year, and average capital improvements are $0.67 million a year. MSAC payments of $750,000 for the first thirteen years of the agreement average out to $325,000 a year over the thirty years.

In sum, average revenues are ($4.09 + $1.5 + $0.3 − $0.67 + $.325) million = $5.55 million, or just equal to the amount needed to cover average interest and amortization payments. Needless to say, all uncertainties as to the sources of income are being borne by the city of Minneapolis, so that if revenues do not rise as expected, outside sources of money will have to be tapped.

The subsidies provided to the facility are masked, but it appears that the $750,000 payment by the MASC is in effect a direct subsidy from the state, and the same is true of the Minneapolis share of property taxes and the parking revenues that are being provided by the city, so that, in total, subsidies to the facility by the city and the state average $625,000 a year, with the federal tax-exemption subsidy in the neighborhood of $1.0 million a year. However, the main subsidy the city is providing is the assumption of risks relating to future repayments of debt obligations on the facility, and these might turn out to be large, indeed.

The outcome of the Timberwolves-Target Center deal appears to be as follows. The Glenn Taylor syndicate obtained an NBA team for $88.5 million at a time when NBA expansion franchises were selling for $125 million. The agreement providing for sale to the MCDA at a price reflecting franchise value escalating at the rate of only 3 percent (as compared with a historical rate of 25 to 30 percent during the 1980s and 1990s) could be an important factor limiting the value of the franchise to Taylor or any subsequent purchaser.[52] On the other hand, *Financial World* estimated the average net operating income of NBA teams in 1995 at almost $15 million a year, which suggests that Taylor and his group did quite well under the agreement.[53]

The city of Minneapolis will have invested $15.4 million to buy the land, $5.7 million to do the road work, $54.6 million to buy the arena— a total of $75.7 million—for an arena (including land and roads) that cost $125.1 million to build ($104 million construction + $21.1 million for land and roads). The problem is that, including the $15.4 million in land value and $5.7 million in roads, the appraised value of the arena was only $63.1 million.[54] Thus the city provided a subsidy of roughly $12.6 million to Ratner and Wolfenson in purchasing the Target Center.

By mid-1995, with the Target Center buyout an accomplished fact and with the Met Center safely demolished, it was now time to move on to the job of acquiring an NHL team to replace the North Stars. So the downtown Minneapolis establishment, the "usual suspects" in the professional sports game, started looking at likely NHL teams to bring to the Twin Cities. There was a team not all that far away that was ripe for the picking, namely, the Winnipeg Jets. The preferred landing place for the Jets was the Twin Cities, and in fact it was a syndicate headed by a Minnesotan that ended up buying and moving the team: to Phoenix, not to Minneapolis and the Target Center. What in the world went wrong?

The answer is that the Target Center–Timberwolves deal was only possible under terms that, in effect, signed away all the revenue sources of the Target Center to the Taylor syndicate or to the Ogden Corporation. There was nothing left to offer a prospective NHL team, beyond the kind of terms that the North Stars had rejected two years earlier as being inferior to the deal they already had at the Met Center. And, with the Met Center torn down, the option of offering a prospective team a refurbished Met Center went by the boards, too, although that arena might have been simply too outmoded to be worth the cost of a refurbishment.

One way to think of what happened is this. Proponents of the Target Center buyout and demolition of the Met Center had talked about the interest savings that would occur when the city took over the Target Center and municipal bonds replaced private bonds. According to their scenario, the money saved would then be available to entice a hockey team into town. What actually happened was that when the Taylor syndicate bought the Timberwolves for $88.5 million, the syndicate took on an interest and equity cost burden not much different from what Ratner and Wolfenson had when they owned the team and arena. Because of this, there was no saving on interest costs, just a shift of interest costs from the owners of the arena to the owners of the team.

Conclusion

This more or less concludes the history of arenas and stadiums and associated major league sports teams in the Twin Cities, as of mid-1997. However, the story is certainly ongoing. In June 1997 the NHL announced that it was locating an expansion team in St. Paul, beginning with the 2000 season. The expansion announcement was contingent on action by the city of St. Paul to demolish the existing Civic Center Arena and to build a state-of-the-art replacement facility. There are possible problems with this arrangement because of the existing indebtedness of the city, and the state of Minnesota might be called on to provide a major share of the funding.

On the baseball front, low attendance in recent years has activated that provision of the Twins' Metrodome contract that permits a move of the team from that facility. Following the 1996 season, Carl Pohlad, owner of the Twins, began serious lobbying for the construction of a new publicly financed, open air, baseball-only stadium. The city of Minneapolis has indicated a willingness to donate riverfront land for such a structure, and a special session of the Minnesota state legislature is tentatively scheduled to consider proposals in September 1997 for state financing of a Twins' stadium. With the Timberwolves, the new NHL team, and the

Twins all receiving sweetheart stadium or arena deals, can the Vikings be far behind?

Notes

1. See James Quirk and Rodney D. Fort, *Pay Dirt: The Business of Professional Team Sports* (Princeton University Press, 1992), p. 305.

2. For a history of the Minneapolis Marines, see James Quirk, "Johnny Dunn and the Minneapolis Marines: Minnesota's First NFL Team," manuscript, 1997.

3. Among the small stockholders in the Berger-Chalfan syndicate were two individuals, Harvey Ratner and Martin Wolfenson, who would later become well-known figures in Twin Cities sports history as "Harv and Marv" of Target Center fame.

4. See Stew Thornley, *Basketball's Original Dynasty: The History of the Lakers* (Minneapolis: Nordin Press, 1988); Thomas Zahn, *The Minneapolis Auditorium and Convention Center: A History* (City of Minneapolis, 1988).

5. The armory was built in 1934 for the Minnesota National Guard, at a cost of $793,000, but was also used as an arena for various sports and family events over its history.

6. Charles Johnson, *The History of the Metropolitan Stadium and Sports Center* (Midwest Federal, 1971), gives the details underlying the building and financing of Met Stadium and the acquisition of the Twins and the Vikings.

7. Parade Stadium was located on the northwest side of downtown Minneapolis, next to the Catholic Procathedral. The grounds had been acquired by the Park Board in 1904, but the stadium was not built until 1951, when $600,000 was invested in building the stadium, with bench-type seats and bleachers-only construction. The stadium seated 17,000 and was configured for football. In 1990, the stadium was torn down to make room for a statuary park. See C. Ben Wright, *Minneapolis Parks and Recreation* (privately printed, 1981).

8. The Millers left one of the most interesting ballparks in baseball, Nicollet Park, built in 1896 for $4,000 on a tiny plot of land at 31st Street and Nicollet Avenue. The right-field power alley in Nicollet was only 328 feet, so that routine flyballs could go for extra bases and even for home runs. The first year that Nicollet was open, Perry Werden hit 49 home runs, a record for all of baseball that held until Babe Ruth hit 54 in 1920. Joe Hauser, a long-time fixture at first base for the Millers, stroked out 69 homers in his banner year, 1933, a record for all of baseball that held for over fifty years. See Stew Thornley, *On to Nicollet: The Glory and Fame of the Minneapolis Millers* (Minneapolis: Nordin Press, 1988); and Dave Mona, "Nicollet Park," *Southside Pride*, May 1995, p. 17.

9. Originally, the football ownership group had been involved in the organization of the American Football League (AFL), but they left the AFL when offered an NFL franchise. The Minnesota AFL franchise was then assigned to Oakland. Three years later, this incident was a central part of the evidence submitted by the AFL in its (unsuccessful) antitrust suit against the NFL. *American Football League v. National Football League*, 205 F. Supp. (C.D. Md. 1962), 323 F. 2d 124 (4th Cir. 1963).

10. With the Met in as the major league park in the Twin Cities, Midway Stadium in St. Paul was out, and it was demolished in the mid-1970s, to be replaced by a smaller (6,500-capacity) stadium of the same name. The new Midway came into fashion, featuring outdoor minor league baseball. Mike Veeck's St. Paul Saints of the independent Northern League, starring a pig as mascot and ball boy (girl?), played to enthusiastic and season-long sellout crowds up to the time of Veeck's departure in 1997.

11. Metropolitan Sports Area Commission, Baseball Playing Agreement between the Metropolitan Sports Area Commission and the Washington American League Baseball Club, Inc., January 18, 1961.

12. See Amy Klobuchar, *Uncovering the Dome: Was the Public Interest Served in Minnesota's 10-Year Brawl Over the Metrodome?* (Minneapolis: Bolger Publications, 1982), for a detailed history of the political infighting in Minnesota concerning the financing of the Metrodome in the period from 1969 to 1981.

13. *Minneapolis Tribune*, November 26, 1978, p. 1A.

14. Several years earlier, a group of downtown Minneapolis businessmen, headed by John Cowles, publisher of the *Star Tribune*, had agreed to buy and clear the thirty-two-acre Industry Square site and to donate it to the state, if the state would build a stadium there. The cost involved to the business group was roughly $16 million.

15. Metropolitan Sports Facilities Commission, Metrodome Baseball Agreement, Minnesota Twins Baseball Club, and the Metropolitan Sports Facilities Commission, August 10, 1979; and Metropolitan Sports Facilities Commission, Football Use Agreement between the Minnesota Vikings and the MSFC, August 9, 1979.

16. For a summary of stadium contracts for Major League Baseball and the NFL, see Quirk and Fort, *Pay Dirt*, table 4.9, p. 146, and table 4.11, pp. 150–51.

17. Metropolitan Sports Facilities Commission, Private Spectator Box Option Agreement between the Minnesota Vikings and the MSFC, August 8, 1979.

18. Communication from Roger Simonson, financial officer of the MSFC, June 1996.

19. The funds available to the MSFC for investment during the construction period included the $55 million received from the sale of state revenue bonds, along with the proceeds of the Metropolitan (later Minneapolis) liquor and motel-restaurant taxes. The large interest earnings of the MSFC reflect the historically high short-term interest rates of the 1980–82 period.

20. See Quirk and Fort, *Pay Dirt*, chap. 4.

21. Communication from Roger Simonson, financial officer of MSFC, June 1996.

22. Communication from Bill Lester, managing director of the Metrodome, June 1996.

23. Direct subsidies excluded from the data shown in table 7-1 are MSFC receipts from the metropolitan-wide liquor tax (1977–79), and from the Minneapolis liquor and hotel-motel tax (1979–84), as well as subsidies from the city of Minneapolis in the form of parking receipts.

24. For a discussion of federal tax subsidies in connection with stadium finances, see Dennis Zimmerman, *Tax Exempt Bonds and the Economics of Professional Sports Stadiums*, CRS Report to the Congress 96-460E, May 29, 1996.

25. The net investment column includes the Metrodome site, shown as a net investment in 1977 of $15.7 million in 1994 dollars ($8.7 million in 1977 dollars). Excluded from the net investment figures are the investments by the Vikings and the Twins combined in 1981 ($10.7 million in 1994 dollars, $7 million in 1981 dollars).

26. The fact that, in the cases of both Met Stadium and the Metrodome, operating income almost exactly matches interest and amortization requirements is intriguing, especially given the large uncertainties present in stadium economics. One possibility is that discretionary operating costs rise to eliminate any surplus over interest and amortization requirements, in effect transferring such surpluses indirectly to facility tenants.

27. See Stew Thornley, "The Minneapolis Muskies," note, and "The Minnesota Pipers," note, both in the Minneapolis collection, Minneapolis Public Library.

28. Metropolitan Sports Facilities Commission, "North Star Payout Date," Dispute Background, July 27, 1984.

29. See Quirk and Fort, *Pay Dirt*, p. 468.

30. Communication from Roger Simonson, financial officer of the MSFC, June 1996.

31. In 1989, when the Timberwolves began play in Minneapolis, the Twin Cities market was the only one in its population class to have four major league sports teams. See Rodney D. Fort and James Quirk, "Cross-Subsidization, Incentives, and Outcomes in Professional Team Sports Leagues," *Journal of Economic Literature*, vol. 33 (September 1995), pp. 31–54.

32. Quirk and Fort, *Pay Dirt*, p. 468.

33. "Sports People: Hockey; Stars' Green Is Sued," *New York Times*, March 26, 1993, sec. B, p. 13.

34. "Hockey; Big D: Dollars Draw North Stars to Dallas," *New York Times*, March 11, 1993, sec. B, p. 16.

35. Communication from Roger Simonson, June 1992.

36. Ibid.

37. *Minneapolis Star Tribune*, February 21, 1987, p. 1.

38. A summary of the history of the Metropolitan Council's involvement in the Target Center issue is provided in Gene Knaff, Bill Byers, Pat Pahl, and Jane Davis, "Metropolitan Significance Review Report: Proposed Arena of the NBA Franchise for Minneapolis," Metropolitan Council, June 12, 1987.

39. *Ramifications of the Development of a New Arena in Downtown Minneapolis*, ERA Report, June, 1987, p. 5.

40. Ibid., p. 8.

41. Ibid., p. 74.

42. Ibid., p. 80

43. Ibid., p. 52.

44. Ibid., p. 57–58

45. "In calculating such impacts, however, it must be recognized that at least some of these expenditures will be divested from other goods and services, and will not represent additional economic impacts." Ibid., p. 86

46. Knaff and others, "Metropolitan Significance Review Report," p. 38.

47. Ibid.

48. "ProBasketball; New Orleans Getting Wolves," *New York Times*, May 24, 1994, sec. B, p. 11.

49. *Minneapolis Star Tribune*, June 16, 1995, p. 16A.

50. Minneapolis Community Development Agency, Terms of Arena Acquisition documents, March 8, 1995.

51. Target Center Finance Plan, City of Minneapolis Finance Department, March 23, 1995.

52. For a discussion of rates of inflation of NBA franchise prices in the 1980s, see Quirk and Fort, *Pay Dirt*, chap. 2,

53. "Values of Sports Teams," *Financial World*, May 20, 1996.

54. Minneapolis Community Development Agency, Terms of Arena Acquisition documents.

8

BALTIMORE'S CAMDEN YARDS BALLPARKS

BRUCE W. HAMILTON AND PETER KAHN

 The accepted wisdom is that municipal professional sports stadiums are a bad economic deal for cities, except for Oriole Park at Camden Yards.[1] Those who have studied the work of Robert Baade and the other contributors to this volume (particularly that of Roger Noll and Andrew Zimbalist) understand the basis for the first clause in the opening sentence. But there is also a widely held perception that the Baltimore experience breaks the mold, and that holds out the possibility that if only other cities can replicate Camden Yards magic, they too can get rich from professional sports.

There is, indeed, something behind the feeling that Camden Yards is different. In the decade before the 1992 opening of Camden Yards, Orioles attendance averaged 26,823 per game; average annual attendance reached an all-time high of 29,458 in the last four years before the move. In the five years since the move, average attendance has been 45,034.[2] The move to Camden Yards appears to have propelled the Orioles from a team with a weak financial base to one of the most financially successful

We thank Joseph Foss of the Orioles and Edward Cline of Maryland Stadium Authority for providing us with data and for their patient explanations of the workings of their respective organizations. We thank Roger Noll, Andrew Zimbalist, and Kenneth Shropshire for many helpful comments on earlier drafts.

teams in baseball.[3] If a new stadium is economically justified anywhere, that place must be Baltimore.

Our main task in this chapter is to ask whether Oriole Park at Camden Yards is, or at least might possibly be, an exception to the conventional wisdom that publicly financed sports stadiums are bad deals for cities. Is the ballpark good for Baltimore and Maryland, or just for the Orioles? Following that discussion, we present an abbreviated analysis of the Ravens' (National Football League) stadium at Camden Yards.

Taking account of all of the measurable benefits of the Camden Yards investment (that is, job creation and tax imports), we estimate that baseball at Camden Yards generates approximately $3 million in annual economic benefits to the Maryland economy, at an annual cost to the taxpayers of Maryland of approximately $14 million. The net annual cost is approximately $11 million, or about $14.70 a year per Baltimore metro household.[4] All of these identifiable benefits to the Maryland economy are in the form of tax and job imports; thus these benefits occur at the expense of neighboring economies. In addition, Maryland taxpayers bear only a portion of the true social costs of the stadium. It is likely that non-Marylanders may incur as much as approximately another $12 million per year because investment funds were diverted from the private sector to the stadium and distortions created by the taxation required to finance the stadium deficit.

Even at Camden Yards, public expenditure on the baseball stadium cannot be justified on the grounds of local economic development. If the public subsidy is justified at all, such justification must rest on public consumption externalities that accrue to Baltimoreans as a result of the presence of the Orioles. First, however, it is useful to briefly review the history of the Orioles in Baltimore and at Memorial Stadium, and the events leading up to the move to Camden Yards.

Prehistory

Beginning shortly after World War II, Baltimore's political leaders sought to attract major league baseball and football teams to the city. Since this was before the days of league expansion, the only route open to them was to attract an existing franchise from another city. That idea itself must also have seemed daunting; in the case of baseball, no major league franchise had changed cities since 1903, when the minor league

Baltimore Orioles became the New York Yankees. The only route open was to find a team that was in financial difficulty.

In 1947 the city of Baltimore began construction of Memorial Stadium, at a site on 33rd Street that had housed a prior sports stadium, Municipal Stadium, originally constructed in the 1920s. The stadium was home to a minor league baseball team and seated approximately 30,000 fans. Minor league Memorial Stadium had apparently been a financial boon to the city government; by 1950 it had turned a profit of $329,659 ($2.2 million in 1996 dollars) through rent and control of concessions.[5] But in its effort to attract major league franchises, the city invested heavily in the stadium (most important, it added an upper deck to bring seating capacity up to approximately 50,000).[6] The city invested approximately $7.5 million ($46.2 in 1996 dollars) in the early 1950s, when three separate $2.5 million bond issues were approved by voters.[7]

In 1953 the Dallas (Football) Texans/Colts, a bankrupt NFL team, moved to Baltimore and Memorial Stadium, becoming the Baltimore Colts.[8] The St. Louis (Baseball) Browns, also in poor financial and athletic condition, moved in the 1954 season and became the Baltimore Orioles.[9] The Browns had for years been underdog to the Cardinals in St. Louis, a town that was not big enough to support two franchises.

After World War II, it was clear that major league baseball was out of line with the national market, and that westward movement and expansion were both appropriate. Indeed, there was real concern within the American and National leagues that one of the minor leagues would become "major" and erode the majors' monopoly position then.[10] An obvious partial solution was to move teams (such as the Browns) out of two-team cities into western cities.[11] But movement west required coordination; one west coast team would be uneconomical. The American league was unable to put forth a coordinated plan to move two teams west, and Browns owner Bill Veeck was left to shop for a city on his own. Since Baltimore was one of only two cities with a municipal stadium (Milwaukee being the other),[12] it was a leading candidate to receive the Browns.[13] After vetoing the move before the 1953 season, the American League approved it after the 1953 season on the condition that Veeck relinquish control of the team. The team was bought by a group of Baltimore businessmen for $2.4 million ($14.1 million in 1996 dollars) and entered the 1954 season as the Baltimore Orioles.[14] Thus began the era in which cities constructed stadiums and leased them, generally at a loss, in order to attract or retain sports teams.

The Orioles gradually rose from the cellar of the league to become the dominant team in baseball in the late 1960s and early 1970s. It remained a major power in the American League through 1983 and then collapsed. The Orioles fielded consistently second-division teams for the next decade, and not until 1996 did they return to the American League playoffs.

The team's playing-field success was not reflected in the box office. Through 1978 the franchise was at best marginally profitable, drawing only a modest number of fans and television revenue. In the late 1960s and early to mid-1970s, post-season revenue was the difference between profit and loss.[15] With a few gaps, table 8-1 gives data on Orioles' profit, attendance, win/loss record, and rent, along with the city's subsidy. As a result of new owner Edward Bennett Williams's aggressive marketing, the Orioles became more profitable after 1979. The city's rent, which at the time was solely a percentage of profit, also rose substantially.[16]

With two teams in Philadelphia until the Athletics moved in 1955 and one thereafter, and one in Washington until the second Senators moved in 1972, the Orioles' market was quite limited; this limit was apparently exacerbated by three forces:

—The Colts, who came to Baltimore at essentially the same time as the Orioles, moved to playing-field respectability much more quickly than the Orioles.[17] Thus the Colts were the darlings of Baltimore in a way that the Orioles never were (even after the O's began winning consistently) until the Colts left Baltimore in 1985.[18]

—Again in contrast to the Colts, the Orioles did a poor job of attracting black fans. In part this was calculated, out of fear that large numbers of black fans would deter whites. In part, the Orioles lost any chance of black loyalty because the team itself was highly segregated. The Orioles' first black impact player was Frank Robinson, who joined the team in December 1965, but before his arrival they had had a very small number of black players, and most stayed only a season or two.[19] This was in marked contrast to the Colts, who had several black stars as early as the late 1950s.[20]

—Memorial Stadium was not well suited to accommodating a large fan base. Memorial Stadium is approximately five miles north of Baltimore's downtown district, occupying a plot of land in a largely residential neighborhood of two-story rowhouses. Within several blocks of the stadium is a small commercial district, consisting of a few restaurants and carry-out establishments.[21] The stadium is bounded on the south and east

Table 8-1. *Orioles Attendance, Performance, Rent*

Year	Calculated average[a]	Winning percentage	Profit (in dollars)	Rent[b] (in dollars)
1954	15,834	0.351		
1955	13,743	0.370		
1956	13,451	0.448		
1957	15,367	0.500		
1958	12,388	0.484		
1959	13,936	0.481	54,000	
1960	16,726	0.578	315,000	
1961	13,587	0.586 small		
1962	10,976	0.475 >0		
1963	10,755	0.531	99,262	
1964	16,177	0.599	301,092	
1965	11,495	0.580		
1966	17,961	0.606	500,000	
1967	14,923	0.472	−57,412	
1968	13,295	0.562	551,305	
1969	14,495	0.673		
1970	14,094	0.667		
1971	15,985	0.639		
1972	13,043	0.519	−214,582	
1973	13,315	0.599		
1974	13,008	0.562	82,700	
1975	14,738	0.566	−3,192	
1976	14,306	0.543	−102,531	
1977	15,529	0.602		838,417
1978	14,407	0.559	−234,141	308,851
1979	23,347	0.642	1,500,000	1,808,312
1980	22,468	0.617	1.5–2.0 million	1,190,594
1981	19,325	0.562		1,275,485
1982	21,798	0.580		244,684
1983	26,520	0.605		1,311.676
1984	26,918	0.525		
1985	26,655	0.512		
1986	24,977	0.451		
1987	23,535	0.414		
1988	22,442	0.335		
1989	32,503	0.537		
1990	30,572	0.472		
1991	32,313	0.414		
1992	44,598	0.549		
1993	45,562	0.525		
1994	46,951	0.563		
1995	43,034	0.493		
1996	45,024			
Totals	20,883	0.532		

Sources: On attendance and Winning PCT, see *Orioles 1996 Media Guide*, pp. 368, 346; on profit, see Miller; *The Baseball Business*, pp. 75, 76, 89, 101, 127, 129, 137, 189, 207, 214, 227, 232, 249, 272. On rent, see Johnson, "Economic and Policy. . . . ," p. 418.

a. Average calculated by using total attendance divided by the number of games played.

b. Rent figures are in 1996 dollars and are combined payment from the Orioles and the Colts to the city of Baltimore.

by four-lane (but not limited-access) residential streets, and on the north and west by two-lane streets. There are no expressways within twenty blocks of the stadium. Stadium property has parking for 2,800 cars, and an additional 2,200 spaces are available in the vicinity for a total of 5,000 spaces.[22] Access from Washington is fairly difficult, because there are no thoroughfares from outside Baltimore to the neighborhood of Memorial Stadium, and Baltimore's rail station is approximately twenty blocks away.[23]

According to team officials, the Memorial Stadium site could not accommodate more than about 30,000 fans because of limited parking.[24] If attendance rose above that figure, fans would still be cruising the streets during the third inning looking for parking.

In terms of city finances, the arrival of major league sports at Memorial Stadium meant two things: the city's annual profits on the stadium turned to losses, and the city entered a forty-year period in which the team owners almost continuously requested either improvements at Memorial Stadium or replacement of the stadium.[25] The pressure increased over the Memorial Stadium era largely because of three forces: the mobility of franchises,[26] free agency and the attendant increase in the cost of operating a major league team,[27] and the increasing obsolescence of Memorial Stadium.

Through most of the Memorial Stadium era, the city (which continued to own the facility) lost money, but city officials chose to believe that the teams brought enough economic benefit and image to the city to justify the expense. Despite warnings from team owners, city officials did not believe that either the Colts or the Orioles would leave Baltimore. In the case of the Colts, Baltimore's league-enforced protection ended in the winter of 1983–84, when a federal judge ruled that the NFL did not have the power to prevent the Oakland Raiders from moving to Los Angeles.[28] In the spring of 1984 the Colts left Baltimore for Indianapolis.

As for the Orioles, the team was locally owned from its arrival in 1953 until after the 1979 season, at which time it was sold to Edward Bennett Williams of Washington, D.C.[29] Williams repeatedly disavowed any intention of seeking Major League Baseball's permission to move the team to Washington; however, the disavowals were rather muted and the threat hung in the air. There seems to be little doubt that the league would have approved a move. Against this backdrop, the city, the state, and the Orioles agreed to the construction of Oriole Park at Camden Yards, and the state, through the Maryland Stadium Authority, ultimately lured the

Cleveland Browns (now the Baltimore Ravens) football team to Baltimore with the promise of a football-only stadium, also located at Camden Yards. The Orioles opened the 1992 season at Oriole Park at Camden Yards.[30]

The Orioles at Camden Yards

The Orioles' spectacular athletic collapse in 1984 was due in substantial measure to the team's precarious financial health over the previous two decades. The team's original rise to dominance had been based heavily on a strong farm system, and paradoxically the weakness of the farm system would also prove its downfall.[31] In the 1950s, before the days of free agency, established players could be obtained only through purchase or trade; the Orioles could afford neither so they resigned themselves to the slow process of developing their own talent. But playing-field success, when it came in the latter half of the 1960s, did not bring profits, and in the 1970s the team could not afford to maintain quality on both its flagship team and its farm system. The problem was exacerbated by the rising cost of major league players and expansion drafts that took rising players from the farm teams.[32] The Orioles' difficult decision between the major league team and the farm system would not have been necessary had the Orioles generated the kind of profit that other top-quality teams were generating. To the extent that the Orioles' poor attendance was due to the deficiencies of Memorial Stadium, the future success of the franchise required a new stadium. Thus the Orioles argued throughout the 1970s and 1980s that they needed a new stadium to attract more fans in order to generate enough revenue to compete with the more lucrative teams.

Of course, it is not necessary to invoke "need" to explain the Orioles' continued push for a new stadium; it is sufficient to note (or assume) that the owners wished to maximize profit from whatever source. During the latter years of the Memorial Stadium era, the Orioles were in a position to extract a larger subsidy, if not from Baltimore, then from another city. On the other hand, it is true that one consequence of the Orioles' failure to extract the "market" subsidy from the city is that they became increasingly unable to bid top dollar for talent.

Thus the Orioles had two objectives: first, to build a stadium that would attract more fans, and, second, to ensure that the new stadium had a substantial number of premium seats and luxury box seats. The latter was important because revenue from luxury boxes (over and above the "base" ticket price) is not shared with the league. After some political maneuvering, the Camden Yards area just west of Baltimore's Inner Harbor was chosen as the site for the new baseball stadium (and, when the time arrived, for the football stadium as well).

In the early 1970s, the Inner Harbor was a badly blighted section of the city made up largely of abandoned warehouses that were relics of an earlier era when ships had docked there.[33] Beginning in the late 1970s the Inner Harbor was the site of massive redevelopment; it now houses a substantial number of high-class hotels and restaurants, upscale retail shopping, legal and financial offices, and such tourist attractions as the National Aquarium, the Maryland Science Center, and Harborplace.[34] Most of these attractions are an easy walk from the stadium; others such as Little Italy and Fells Point are a short drive or water-taxi ride away.

In sharp contrast to Memorial Stadium, the Inner Harbor/Camden Yards area is readily accessible from all directions. In particular, Interstate 95 from Washington passes within easy access to stadium parking. In addition, there is rail access, with game-day trains stopping directly in front of the stadium. Under the terms of the Orioles' lease with Maryland Stadium Authority, the Camden Yards facility is to have 5,000 parking spaces. Before construction of the football stadium at Camden Yards, there were approximately 5,400 spaces, but the football stadium will reduce this to approximately 2,800.[35] In addition, since virtually no baseball games are played during normal business hours, a substantial part of the parking infrastructure in Baltimore's central business district is available for game parking. Within a one-mile walk of the stadium there are approximately 30,000 private off-street parking spaces.[36]

The ballpark, dedicated to baseball, has more than 48,000 seats and 72 luxury boxes.[37] The backdrop for the stadium (beyond the right-field wall) is a renovated B&O Railroad warehouse. This building, along with a view of the Baltimore skyline beyond center field, gives the stadium a downtown-Baltimore feel.

Effect of Move to Camden Yards: Attendance

As noted, the Orioles felt a financial need to increase attendance (and presumably an opportunity to extract more surplus from Baltimore). The thinking among planners was that the Camden Yards site would attract fans from throughout the Baltimore/Washington area both because of easy access and because of the other attractions at the Inner Harbor. The basic rationale for selecting the site was that the presence of multiple attractions would induce more attendance both at Orioles games and other downtown attractions than either could generate in the absence of the other.

As shown in figure 8-1, the Orioles enjoyed a massive increase in attendance when they moved to Camden Yards. It is hard to attribute the Orioles' jump in attendance to anything other than the move; there is no apparent positive effect of on-the-field performance upon attendance. Average attendance was 45,034 in the five years after the move, and 29,458 in the four years before.[38] Whereas average attendance rose throughout Major League Baseball during the late 1980s, this effect appears to be fully accounted for in the final Memorial Stadium years. The 29,457 figure is already approximately 6,000 above average attendance during the previous decade (during which the Orioles had two World Series appearances).[39]

Approximately 70 percent of the incremental Camden Yards fans come from outside the state of Maryland, whereas only about 10 percent of Memorial Stadium fans did so. By contrast, a city of Baltimore fan survey estimates that 31 percent of 1992 Camden Yards fans came from out of state; and Joseph Foss, vice chairman of business operations and finance for the Orioles estimates that in 1996 approximately 35 percent of fans came from out of state. If we accept the 10 percent figure for Memorial Stadium and the 31 percent Camden Yards figures for out-of-state fans, simple arithmetic tells us that 71 percent of the incremental fans came from out of state.[40]

The Honeymoon Effect

Several authors have suggested that a sports team has a "honeymoon" period with its fans after moving to a new stadium. If this is true in the case of the Orioles (that is, if average attendance in the neighborhood of 45,000 is not the steady state), then both the Orioles and the Maryland Stadium Authority will do less well than indicated by our projections. Furthermore, of course, the import-driven job-creation effect will be smaller than our calculations suggest.

The accepted wisdom is that the honeymoon begins to fade after three years and that the steady state is achieved in approximately eight years.[41]

FIGURE 8-1. *Historical Data on Orioles' Performance*

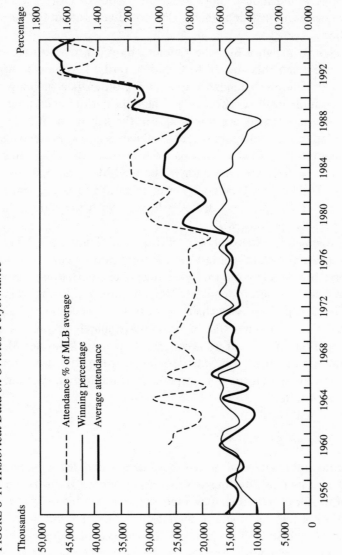

Source: Calculated by authors from data in *Baltimore Orioles Media Guide 1996*.

As of this writing, the Orioles have just completed their fifth year (1996) at Camden Yards; average attendance in 1996 was 45,024, virtually in- distinguishable from the average of prior years at Camden Yards.[42] At first blush, anyway, there is no fading honeymoon. On the other hand, 1995 could be influenced by the "Cal Ripken effect," and 1996 is the first Camden Yards year in which the Orioles made the playoffs, so one can speculate that there is a fading-honeymoon effect offset by a team-quality effect.[43]

In private conversation, Joseph Foss of the Orioles indicated that he believes there is indeed a very modest honeymoon effect. In 1992 the Orioles did virtually no "hustling" to sell groups of tickets. By 1996 they found it necessary to engage in modest marketing in order to maintain attendance in the 45,000 range. All told, though average attendance of about 45,000 may not be the steady state, *to date* it is difficult to discern any evidence of a significant honeymoon effect.

Economic Impact: The Geographic Perspective

As pointed out in chapter 2, the magnitude of economic benefits of a stadium depends heavily on the geographic boundary of analysis. The reason is that at the national level essentially all baseball spending is diverted from other venues; that is, it crowds out spending elsewhere. At the local level this need not be true; some of the economic activity and tax revenue may be crowded out not from the local economy but from a neighboring economy. Baltimore's gain is Washington's loss, but it is a genuine gain for Baltimore nonetheless.

For a different set of reasons, measurement of cost is also influenced by line drawing. For the nation as a whole, the true cost of a $200 million stadium is the return to the investment that was crowded out by the financing of the stadium, probably around 7 percent.[44] Thus the annual loss of national output resulting from a $200 million stadium is approxi- mately $14 million.

From the perspective of Maryland taxpayers, however, investment funds can be had for much less than a 7 percent real rate. The real (ex- post) yield on tax-exempt bonds is approximately 2 percent, and federal thirty-year Treasury bonds that benefit from state exemption generally yield approximately 1 percent above tax-exempts.[45] Thus from the per- spective of Maryland, the cost of funds is approximately 2 percent, and another 1 percent is borne by the federal treasury in the form of the federal tax exemption. Perhaps as much as another 5 percent is borne by the American public at large in the form of forgone output from the private alternative use of the funds.

A portion of the spread between the 7 percent opportunity cost of capital and the 2 percent real borrowing rate faced by the state of Maryland represents costs borne not by outsiders but by Marylanders themselves. First, Maryland is a part of the national economy (the Maryland population is 0.0201 percent of the national population). Second, it is reasonable to assume that a disproportionate share of the crowded-out investment would have occurred in Maryland, as construction of the stadium likely discouraged other entertainment-related investment in Baltimore. However, Marylanders' share of the burden of the opportunity cost depends not on where the alternative investment would have occurred, but where the returns would have been realized. If the returns would have been reaped by national capital owners, then only a relatively small portion of the spread between the borrowing and opportunity-cost rates would be borne by Marylanders. In the following discussion, we assume that Marylanders succeed in exporting the entire spread to the rest of the nation.

It is likely that Marylanders also export a large fraction of the deadweight loss generated by the tax financing of the state deficit. Taxation generates a deadweight loss by distorting the price system and thereby compromising its ability to direct resources to their most efficient use. Since most prices are determined in (at least) the national economy, the burden of much of this distortion is exported to the national economy.

There is a great deal of uncertainty as to the magnitude of the deadweight loss from taxes; one respected estimate places it at between 13 and 24 percent of the tax revenue.[46] If this estimate is approximately correct for the taxes that finance Camden Yards, then citizens (likely non-Marylanders, for the most part) incur approximately $2 million in annual deadweight-loss cost.

At the national level, there seems little debate over the proposition that new stadiums cost a lot and yield little. The more contentious question is whether some stadiums are justified at the local level. Accordingly, we conduct our economic impact analysis from the perspective of the state of Maryland (since it is the state that owns the stadium and incurs the financial obligations). But one should bear in mind that all of the benefits we identify are beggar-thy-neighbor benefits, and that substantial costs are borne by non-Marylanders.

It is also worth noting that there is considerable redistribution within the state. The costs take the form of incremental state taxes and lottery revenues and are presumably borne evenly geographically throughout the state. Benefits take two forms. The first significant benefit is imports of state sales taxes, also accruing on a statewide basis. The second, through the employment effect, is a rise in Baltimore property values. The latter effect is localized, of course, and therefore subsidized by non-Baltimore state taxpayers.

Effect of the Move to Camden Yards: Internal Rate of Return

We begin our economic analysis of the Camden Yards stadium with the following counterfactual: suppose that the Orioles had owned Memorial Stadium, and had constructed and owned the Camden Yards stadium and had received no subsidy from the state of Maryland. Suppose, in other words, that the pattern of ownership and rights to returns were like those of an ordinary business. Under this counterfactual, we calculate the internal rate of return to the move to Camden Yards as it would have appeared to the Orioles had they been a typical business.

According to a report published by *Financial World* magazine (which is published annually from 1991 to 1996 and includes data from 1990 through 1995), the Orioles' basic gate receipts rose $11.6 million (from $19.0 million to $30.6 million) between 1991 and 1992.[47] If we average their last two seasons at Memorial Stadium and their first four seasons at Camden Yards, respectively, their gate receipts have increased by $13.2 million.[48] More important, their stadium revenues increased by $16.5 million in 1992, and on average by $12.3 million.[49] Thus the Orioles' revenue (after remittance to visiting teams but before rent) rose by approximately $25.5 million as an apparent result of the move to Camden Yards. In addition, admission tax receipts (Maryland Stadium Authority's share of gate receipts) rose by approximately $1.8 million (approximately one-third of the $5 million admission tax receipts at Camden Yards).[50] Total stadium revenue therefore rose by approximately $27.3 million, of which $25.5 million is private return.[51]

The cost of site acquisition and construction at Camden Yards was approximately $200 million. We have no data on which to estimate the rate of depreciation of the new stadium, and there is wide variation in the ex-post lifetimes of prior stadiums. Memorial Stadium served as the home of the Orioles for thirty-nine years; other older stadiums such as

Yankee Stadium and Fenway Park continue to operate, whereas some newer stadiums have already been retired. Lacking firm guidance, we assume that the rate of economic depreciation is 5 percent.

Maintenance costs approximately $6 million a year.[52] For purposes of the current calculation, this should be netted against the maintenance cost at Memorial Stadium; unfortunately, we have been unable to determine the level of maintenance expenditure at Memorial. Here we assume that maintenance cost is the same at Camden Yards as at Memorial Stadium.

In keeping with our counterfactual, we should credit the Orioles with any salvage value of Memorial Stadium. As a stadium, the economic value of Memorial Stadium is surely very small or nil; though we are aware of no studies in this regard, it seems very likely that the best use of the site is to demolish the stadium and sell the land. And it is highly unlikely that land value in the Memorial Stadium neighborhood will more than cover demolition cost. Thus we provisionally assume no salvage value for Memorial Stadium.[53]

Under the above assumptions, the real internal rate of return on Camden Yards is equal to the net revenue increase ($25.5 million) less annual economic depreciation ($10 million) divided by the cost of the stadium ($200 million). The real internal rate of return is estimated to be 7.75 percent.

If the Orioles were in the business of manufacturing automobiles, this would be the end of the economic analysis; if the Orioles were to face a real borrowing rate of less than 7.75 percent, then the corporation would have to build a new facility that generated sufficient revenue to cover depreciation, incremental maintenance, and real interest. There would simply be no debate over the economic viability of the new stadium, any more than there would be over the economic viability of private investments in general.

Orioles' Actual Balance Sheet

Camden Yards is not owned by the Orioles; it is owned by the Maryland Stadium Authority. If the authority leased the stadium to the Orioles at a price that covered the capital and maintenance cost of the facility, ownership would make no difference. But the terms of the lease are much more favorable to the Orioles than that. Whereas the authority bears annual operating and capital cost of approximately $20 million ($14 million in real interest and depreciation and $6 million in maintenance), the Orioles pay only approximately $6 million in rent; a modest increase from the $3.6 million that they were paying in their last years at Memorial Stadium.[54] Thus, as an apparent result of the move to Camden Yards, the Orioles' net revenue rose by approximately $23 million per year ($25.5 revenue less $2.4 million incremental rent).

The move to Camden Yards enables the Orioles to do what they could not do at Memorial Stadium: spend competitively on the major league team. And, indeed, the payroll for the Orioles' roster rose by approximately the net revenue increase, $22 million.[55]

As an interesting aside, at the time of the move to Camden Yards, the Orioles' reported operating expenses fell by approximately $6 million (by 23 percent).[56] This coincides with replacement of the Orioles' prior lease, in which rent was based on profits to the current formula, which in turn was based solely on revenues. This suggests that costs were artificially inflated to avoid rental payments.[57]

There is, of course, nothing to ensure that the newfound $23 million will enable the Orioles to bid competitively for talent in the future. If the Orioles spend their money wisely and return to dominance in the American League, other cities might increase their subsidies to their teams. This will create greater rents for ballplayers and will leave some teams in financial peril.

Fiscal Balance Sheet at Camden Yards

The move to Camden Yards generated $27.3 million in incremental revenue ($25.5 million to the Orioles and $1.8 million to the Maryland Stadium Authority in the form of incremental admission tax receipts). Economic depreciation was estimated to be $10 million. If we assume a real (tax-free) interest rate of 2 percent, real interest cost of the stadium is $4 million; thus the net absolute return is $13.3 million a year (less any increase in operating cost).

Recall that the Orioles realized a net absolute return of approximately $23 million, indicating that they receive a subsidy of approximately $9.7 million from the state. Not surprisingly, essentially the same subsidy appears in the finances of the Maryland Stadium Authority. As already noted, real interest faced by Maryland citizens and depreciation are approximately $14 million a year, and operating cost is approximately

$6 million a year. The total cost to the state of carrying and operating the stadium is approximately $20 million.

The Maryland Stadium Authority recovers approximately $6 million in rent[58] and another $5 million in admissions tax revenue;[59] it incurs a deficit of approximately $9 million ($20 million in costs less $11 million in revenue). The federal treasury incurs another $2 million in interest subsidy. The private economy bears another $8 million in forgone return to crowded out investment and $2 million in deadweight loss resulting from the incremental taxes.[60]

The authority's deficit of $9 million must be financed by taxes.[61] Assuming a deadweight loss of 20 percent, then the dollar deadweight loss is approximately $1.8 million. As just mentioned, we did not estimate the distribution of this loss between Maryland and the rest of the nation.

Social Return on the Stadium

If our original counterfactuals were correct (that is, if the Orioles had built and financed the stadium), few would have bothered to address the question of the social return on the stadium.[62] Most economists would conclude that if the stadium passed the market test, then it likely passed the cost-benefit test as well. Any debate over social returns arises because the public subsidy is justified only if the stadium's social benefits exceed the private returns captured by the Orioles.

There seems little doubt that at the national level there are no such benefits, and thus that there is no justification for the federal tax subsidy previously identified. Indeed, the 1986 amendment to the Federal Tax Code was designed to eliminate the use of tax-exempt bonds to finance stadiums, and legislation currently under consideration is designed to tighten these restrictions.

Economic benefits to the state of Maryland might differ from those captured in the counterfactual private return in three kinds of circumstances.

CROWDING OUT. Our estimated 7.75 percent internal rate of return on Camden Yards rests on a $23.5 million increase in revenue. But to the extent that this $23.5 million represents expenditure that would have occurred elsewhere in the Maryland economy even without Camden

Yards, then the net effect on the local economy is correspondingly reduced. We can illustrate this by extending our counterfactual.

Assume now that before Camden Yards there were two stadiums in Baltimore: Memorial Stadium and Stadium X. Memorial attracted 29,000 patrons a year and Stadium X attracted 16,000. In 1992 all 45,000 were diverted to Camden Yards; both Memorial and Stadium X became worthless. Now suppose that the Orioles owned both Memorial Stadium and Stadium X (and that the maintenance on the two stadiums combined was equal to the $6 million maintenance cost at Camden Yards). Under this scenario, the move to Camden Yards is a $200 million investment that yields no revenue whatsoever: all of the "incremental" revenue generated at Camden Yards is crowded out from Stadium X; it is simply a $200 million white elephant.

In fact, from the perspective of Maryland citizens, it appears that the crowding out from "Stadium X," that is, from incremental fans to Camden Yards, is of only modest importance. As mentioned earlier, approximately 70 percent of incremental fans come from out of state, which suggests in turn that approximately 70 percent of the incremental revenue is generated by out-of-state fans. Thus approximately $7 million of the incremental revenue is crowded out from other venues in the state of Maryland, and $16 million is new spending in Maryland. We will discuss how to measure the benefit from importing expenditure shortly.

But we cannot lay crowding out to rest even for that 70 percent of the incremental revenue that is due to out-of-staters' expenditure. Some out-of-staters' Camden Yards expenditure may replace other expenditure they would have made in Baltimore (Stadium X expenditure). The crucial question is not the increment to out-of-staters' baseball expenditure, but the increment to out-of-staters' expenditure anywhere in the state. We have no specific evidence on this question, unfortunately. In the remainder of our analysis we assume that all incremental baseball expenditure by incremental out-of-staters represents expenditure diverted to Maryland; to the extent that this is not correct, we understate the degree of crowding out reflected in the Camden Yards revenue figures. Figure 8-2 shows the history of downtown Baltimore's hotel-tax receipts, in constant (1997) dollars, since 1984. After approximately 10 percent annual growth from 1984 through 1990, there has been virtually no trend subsequently. This graph, at any rate, offers no support for the conjecture that large numbers of incremental fans are coming to Baltimore to see the Orioles;

FIGURE 8-2. *Baltimore City Hotel Tax Revenue*

Millions of 1997 dollars

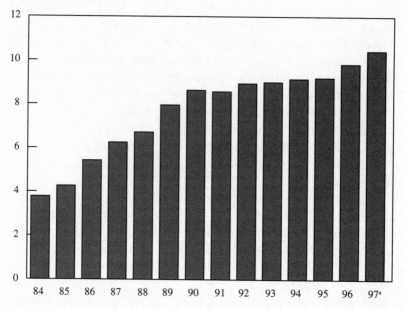

SOURCE: Data provided to the authors by Mrs. Helen J. Westfall, Baltimore City Department of Finance Accounting Assistant.
a. Data for fiscal 1997 (July 1996–June 1997) not available for May or June. The 1997 figure calculated by authors assuming May and June identical to previous year.

or if they are coming, they appear not to be staying in downtown Baltimore.

IMPORTING JOBS AND TAXES. If out-of-state residents pay more taxes in Maryland as a result of Camden Yards (and if these taxes are not offset by incremental expenses), then Marylanders' taxes are correspondingly reduced. Similarly, if out-of-staters spend money in Maryland and generate an increase in Maryland (mostly Baltimore) employment, the Maryland economy benefits in a manner we will describe shortly. We have already confronted the expenditure-importing question in another guise: to the extent that baseball expenditure is not an import, it merely reflects crowding out of other local expenditure.

In addition to sales-tax imports, holders of imported jobs pay income and property taxes. As a first approximation, however, it is not appropriate to count the income and property taxes generated by the job import as benefits to Maryland. These imported jobs are held by imported people, who require incremental expenditure on education, police protection, and the like; the incremental taxes approximately cover these expenses.

PUBLIC CONSUMPTION BENEFITS. If the citizens of Maryland obtain pleasure from the presence of the Orioles even when they neither attend the stadium nor listen to broadcasts, then this external benefit to the presence of the Orioles is not reflected in any of our financial figures. Note that it is most plausibly the presence of the Orioles in Baltimore that generates such public consumption benefits. It is far from clear that such public consumption benefits increase as a result of the team's move to Camden Yards. Thus at first glance it is doubtful that any such benefits should be counted as benefits of the move to Camden Yards.

There are, however, two reasons to believe that at least some such benefits should be attributed to the move.

—Had the Orioles remained at Memorial Stadium, it seems clear that they would not have been financially able to field competitive teams; if public consumption benefits depend at least partly on team quality, then at least a part of such benefits should be attributed to Camden Yards.

—Had the Orioles not been given a new stadium (or some other way to generate an additional $23 million in revenue), it is likely that the team would eventually have left Baltimore. Under this scenario, of course, the entire public consumption benefit to Marylanders is attributable to the stadium at Camden Yards.

The Benefit of Importing Expenditure and Jobs

We rely on a Baltimore City 1992 fan expenditure survey to estimate the magnitude of non-ballpark expenditure imports generated by the Orioles at Camden Yards. According to results of this survey, non-SMSA residents spent $46 million before and after games, mostly in Baltimore.[63] The same survey reports that 46 percent of fans were from out of the SMSA, and that 31 percent of fans were from out of state.[64] Assuming the $46 million is proportionally allocated between in-state and out-of-state non-Baltimoreans, total before-and-after-game expenditure by out-of-state residents was $31 million ($46 million × (0.31/0.46)).[65] Inasmuch as out-of-state attendance increased approximately fivefold as a result of the move to Camden Yards, we attribute 80 percent of the out-of-staters' expenditure, or $25 million, to Camden Yards.[66] Total incremental out-of-staters' expenditure is thus $41 million ($25 million in incremental nonstadium expenditure by out-of-staters, plus $16 million of the Orioles' revenue increase): the share of the Orioles' revenue increase that is attributable to incremental out-of-staters. In this section we discuss our method of converting this incremental expenditure figure to economic benefit for Maryland.

We begin by assuming that Baltimore is open to migration to and from the rest of the nation. This assumption carries the implication that in equilibrium nobody can increase utility by migrating, which in turn implies that any intercity wage differences must be offset by (indeed caused by) intercity differences in cost of living and amenities.[67] The (assumed) openness of migration between Baltimore and the rest of the nation means that, in equilibrium, real wage and unemployment rates (within individual occupations) will be equalized across the country, and it does not make sense to think of a sports team as enriching the citizens of Baltimore by reducing unemployment or raising real wages.[68] An influx of jobs (say, attendant to a rise in exports) does raise wages in a city, but only because it raises the cost of living. Without the wage increase new workers would be unwilling to migrate to the city to take the new jobs. Baltimore residents gain from an influx of jobs not because steady-state unemployment declines (any decline will be short-lived) nor because real wages rise, but because the present value of property values increase.

When the demand for a city's exports rises, the first consequence is an outward shift in the city's demand curve for labor, which causes wages to be bid up because the supply curve of urban labor is rising. As more workers are attracted to the city, the cost of living is driven up, primarily through a rise in the price of housing (the price of housing rises with city size, for reasons that are discussed in all major urban economics texts).[69] The interurban equalization of utility requires that house value rise by the present value of the wage increase. The entire present value of the economic benefit of an increase in exports (an increase in city size) is captured by local property owners; the present value of the wage increase is capitalized into house values. Workers who do not own houses see their entire wage increase disappear into rent increases. Thus the proper (present value) measure of the economic benefit realized by an increase in export demand is the aggregate increase in property values generated by the export surge, which equals the present value of the increase in the wages of the inframarginal workers. Consequently we can measure the benefit per household as either the annual induced wage increase per household (annual measure) or the average induced increase in house value (present value). The incidence of the benefit is the same regardless; the entire present value of the benefit is captured by those people (whether they are residents or whether they are employed) who own property at the time of the capitalization.

Baltimoreans receive economic benefit from incremental direct Orioles expenditures by precisely the same mechanism: if the presence of the Orioles creates incremental jobs, the equilibrium wage for inframarginal workers rises and the present value of this increase is capitalized into property values. The winners are the holders of property at the time of the job infusion. Thus the steps required to estimate the economic benefit from incremental out-of-staters' expenditure both inside and outside the ballpark are as follows: (1) determine the magnitude of incremental expenditure; (2) determine the number of jobs created directly by the incremental expenditure; (3) determine the appropriate multiplier via which to calculate the total employment effect; and (4) determine the effect of this induced employment on metro property values. The aggregate of this effect is the present value (measured by property value change) or the annual value (measured by the change in the annual wage bill of inframarginal workers) of the economic benefit (to Baltimoreans) of the Orioles' and out-of-staters' expenditures. Since we have already discussed step (1), we move directly to step 2.

DIRECT CREATION OF JOBS. Now we must determine the number of jobs directly created by the $41 million in out-of-staters' expenditures. We are aware of no estimates of this magnitude, so we proceed by making what we hope are reasonable assumptions. First, we assume that half of the $41 million is spent on labor in Baltimore.[70] Under this assumption the local wage bill generated by the $41 million is $20.5 million. The average salary of full-time employees in the United States in 1993 was $35,803 (inclusive of fringe benefits); applying this arithmetic, we estimate that out-of-staters' expenditure creates 575 new jobs ($20.5 million/$35,803).

Whereas this calculation method may be reasonable for most expenditure imports, it surely overstates job creation in this case. The Orioles spent virtually all of their incremental revenue on the major league roster payroll, and of course the number of players on the roster did not increase at all. However, the Oriole ballplayers surely spent a portion of their incremental income in Maryland, so assuming a zero employment effect from the Orioles' portion of the incremental revenue would understate the job-creation impact. In this calculation we assume that all of the non-ballpark spending creates jobs in the manner we have suggested, and that half of the ballpark spending does. On the basis of this calculation, we estimate that the incremental out-of-state expenditure is directly responsible for 460 new jobs in the Baltimore metro area.

SIZE OF MULTIPLIER. Several authors have argued that the expenditure multiplier for professional sports is likely to be quite small, even if the expenditure base is value added rather than gross expenditure. But we have argued that the calculation should be based on jobs. Hence we have calculated the number of local jobs directly due to the Orioles; and therefore we need to use an employment multiplier. The most important reason for assuming a small multiplier when the base is a professional sports payroll is that highly paid athletes save a high fraction of their income and spend much of the rest outside the local economy. But when using a jobs multiplier, this concern is negated and, if anything, reversed.[71] In our calculations we use an employment multiplier of 1.2, though for reasons noted above that may be a bit conservative. If the incremental out-of-staters' spending is directly responsible for 460 jobs in Baltimore, total job creation due to the Orioles' presence is approximately 460 × 1.2 or 550 new jobs.

EFFECT ON WAGES AND PROPERTY VALUES. The best evidence on this question comes from the Rosen regression:

$$\ln w_i = X_i\beta + \mu_i,$$

where w_i is the annual earnings in city i for a specified well-defined type of worker (such as a secretary), and X_i is a vector of metro area characteristics, including city size and amenities. Under the assumption of location equilibrium, the β's can be interpreted as the antilog of the workers' compensation for the X's. Rosen finds, for example, that the annual wage rises by $15 ($32 in 1996 dollars) with each additional rainy day per year, suggesting that the marginal worker is willing to pay $32 a year (in forgone wages) to live in a city with one more sunny day a year; or that the shadow price of a sunny day is $32. The natural interpretation of the coefficient on city size in this regression is the cost of an increment to city size. Mobility ensures that workers are able to receive compensation for enduring this cost. The regressions tell us that a 10 percent increase in the population of an urban area raises the average annual wage by $48 ($100 in 1996 dollars). Total employment in the Baltimore metro area is approximately 1.2 million;[72] applying the Rosen coefficient to Baltimore, an increment of 1,000 jobs raises the average annual wage by $0.80.

If the move to Camden Yards generated 500 new jobs, the average annual wage in Baltimore rose by about 40 cents as a result. This is the effect that is capitalized into the value of Baltimore houses. Assuming 1.6 workers per household (1.2 million workers/750,000 households) and a rent-to-value ratio of .1, the presence of the Orioles raises house values by approximately $6.50 each.[73]

We can also calculate the aggregate annual benefit induced by the job creation; at $0.40 per worker times 1.2 million workers, this benefit is approximately $480,000. Note that the method we have worked out is applicable to any job-creation activity in an urban area. Given the size of Baltimore and the parameter values we have assumed, creation of 1,000 incremental jobs generates approximately $0.80 in annual surplus per worker, for an aggregate annual benefit of just under $1 million. If an entrepreneur comes to Baltimore with an offer to bring 1,000 new jobs to town, then (on an aggregate costs-and-benefits basis) the city should be willing to pay up to $1 million to cement the deal.[74]

Importing Tax Revenue

If the move to Camden Yards generated few jobs and little multiplier benefit to Maryland citizens, did it still cause some direct importation of tax revenue? If out-of-state fans pay taxes to Maryland or its subdivisions, and if these taxes are not offset by incremental governmental expenditures, then the net drain on the state (plus municipalities) treasury is reduced by this amount. Each dollar of taxes paid by out-of-staters reduces, one for one, the tax liabilities of Marylanders. Here we examine such sources of additional revenue.

Recall that incremental spending by out-of-staters before and after games is $25 million. Revenue from 5 percent sales tax on this expenditure is $1.25 million. Approximately 24 percent of fans are incremental out-of-staters.[75] Thus 24 percent of admission tax revenue is attributable to new out-of-state spending; this comes to $1.2 million. In addition, approximately 70 percent of incremental stadium revenues are attributable to the same new out-of-staters; this expenditure is generally taxed at 5 percent, for another $0.43 million.

Table 8-2. *Benefits and Net Cost to Marylanders*

Millions of dollars

Benefit/Cost	Amount
Benefits of job creation	0.48
Out-of-stadium incremental taxes	1.25
Incremental admission tax	1.20
Sales tax on incremental stadium spending	0.43
Total	2.96
Capital cost	14
Net cost to Marylanders	11.04

Source: Authors' calculations.

Table 8-2 shows the components of incremental revenue to the citizens of Maryland. It appears that the state of Maryland spends approximately $14 million a year to attract approximately $3 million a year in job-creation and tax-import benefits. In addition, the federal treasury absorbs a subsidy of approximately $2 million; there is a deadweight loss of $2 million, and the excess of the opportunity cost of investment over the interest rate might be as high as another $8 million.

On some criteria, as seen earlier, Camden Yards is indeed a success. The stadium routinely sells out, and it generates enough incremental revenue to make the Orioles a competitive ball club. But it is most definitely not a success as a vehicle for job creation and economic development. In addition to their spending at the ballpark, Marylanders pay approximately $11 million, or approximately $14.70 per Baltimore household, a year to keep the Orioles in town.

This $11 million figure represents our best estimate of the annual subsidy borne by Marylanders. For an idea of the worst-case value of the subsidy, suppose that there is no tax or expenditure importing due to the Orioles' move; that all of the identified incremental expenditure would otherwise have been spent in the Maryland economy. Or equivalently, assume that despite their new stadium the Orioles leave Baltimore and that the stadium remains vacant. In that case the state's financial loss from Camden Yards is simply the carrying cost of the stadium, $14 million per year, or $18.70 per household per year.

Intangible Benefits

The citizens benefit from the presence of the Orioles in two additional ways, over and above any import of taxes and jobs.

—The amenity value of the O's and the business climate. If the presence of the O's is an amenity that attracts footloose businesses to Baltimore, then by the same reasoning as applied above, every 1,000-person
increase in employment yields aggregate annual benefits of approximately
$1 million.

—Economic fan surplus. The identification of a sports team like the
Orioles with a city surely generates some pleasure for its citizens beyond
that reflected in ticket sales. In this respect the economics of sports is
much different from the economics of, say, apples. A fan can derive
substantial pleasure from the Orioles and identify with them as "his"
team without ever attending a game, but he gets no such pleasure from
knowing that somebody is eating apples in Baltimore. This is a standard
externality; the Orioles produce a service for which some beneficiaries
pay nothing.

In fact, the two intangible benefits are simply different manifestations
of the same benefit. If the presence of the Orioles is a valuable amenity
for Baltimore residents, they will accept lower wages than they otherwise
would to work there, and as a result employers will find that labor is
cheap in Baltimore, and the city will expand. In other words, these public
consumption benefits, like job- and tax-import benefits, are capitalized
into local property values.

In principle, it is possible to measure the magnitude of this amenity
benefit, using the technique that Rosen employed to measure the effect
of city size and rainy days. Attempts to estimate the amenity value of
professional sports teams have not been successful, however, because the
number of sports teams is so highly correlated with city size. Inclusion
of some index of sports team presence as a regressor generally either
produces statistically insignificant coefficients or renders other coefficients, such as city size, insignificant.[76] Of course, these findings do not
mean that no sports-amenity effect exists, but rather that any such effect
as does exist cannot be statistically disentangled from other regressors
such as city size.[77] In the absence of statistical evidence, there is little to
do but to state what is by now obvious: before considering the present
value of the amenities generated by the Orioles, the cost of the subsidy
is approximately $14.70 per Baltimore SMSA household per year,[78] as-
suming that the above calculations are valid. It seems plausible (but not
verifiable) that the externalities generated by the Orioles are substantially
larger than this figure.

Suppose that the citizens of Baltimore were faced with a choice of climate change in the form of one additional rainy day per year or loss of the intangible benefits of the Orioles. It seems plausible that most would prefer the extra rainy day; according to Rosen, the disutility of this rainy day is approximately $45 per worker, or about $72 per household, per year. As citizens are actually paying about $15 per household per year to keep the Orioles in town, it seems likely that they are getting a substantial net surplus.

Declining Cities

Earlier we calculated that the Orioles at Camden Yards are directly and indirectly responsible for at most approximately 550 jobs in the Baltimore metro area and that these jobs, along with tax imports, generate economic benefit for Baltimore residents of approximately $3 million a year. Recall, too, that the job-creation portion of this benefit is achieved through city expansion, which raises property values. In this section we note that the effect of incremental jobs on city welfare is likely to depend critically on whether the city is expanding or shrinking, in other words, on whether the incremental jobs cause growth or diminish decline. This consideration is potentially very important in Baltimore. Between 1950 and 1990 the central city's population declined by 23 percent, from 950,000 to 736,000.[79]

Much of a city's infrastructure is irreversible (putty-clay) past investment. When a city's population declines, a portion of this capital becomes redundant. In the case of public infrastructure such as water mains and schools, a city's shrunken population frequently has little choice but to pay for upkeep on this excess capital. In the case of housing, the value of the stock declines as the demand curve shifts inward. A population decline of the magnitude suffered by Baltimore leaves the city with substantially more houses than households, and therefore a need to retire some houses from the stock. Frequently the cheapest way to retire houses is to abandon them.[80] In short, shrinkage imposes significant costs on the residents of a city. It is not harmful to be small; in equilibrium the same utility is available in small as in large cities, but becoming small can be very harmful, indeed. We are aware of no studies detailing the costs of shrinkage, nor of the incidence of these costs. However, it seems clear that the costs are substantial. This in turn suggests that capturing 540 jobs might be much more important for a shrinking than for an expanding city.

If this line of reasoning is correct, it does not necessarily imply that the public investment in Camden Yards was better than our prior calculations suggest. If the state has limited funds for job attraction, then getting the biggest possible job-creation bang for the dollar is more important for a shrinking than an expanding city.

The Political Economy of Camden Yards

Few in Baltimore were seriously concerned about the possibility of the Orioles leaving town until after the team was sold to Washington attorney Edward Bennett Williams and the Colts left town. During the 1970s, before either of these events, the teams' efforts to get public subsidies for new stadiums were rebuffed. Only after the departure of the Colts and sale of the Orioles did public officials accede to Oriole demands for a new public stadium.

This history, along with the financial analysis presented above, is consistent with the following story. Public officials understood that Camden Yards was not an engine of economic revitalization and thus saw no reason to support a move to Camden Yards when the only public benefit was the capture of $3 million in tax and job imports.[81] But in the 1980s the stakes changed: with the Colts gone and the Orioles owned by a Washingtonian, the presence of the Orioles in Baltimore and thus the public consumption benefits were at risk. This tipped the balance in favor of the subsidy. This scenario (and we emphasize that it is but one of many scenarios consistent with the facts) casts Maryland's public officials not as manipulative Romer-Rosenthal agenda setters but as responsible keepers of the public trust.

The Ravens at Camden Yards

The Ravens stadium at Camden Yards is projected to cost approximately $200 million, plus $24 million in luxury boxes to be paid by the Ravens out of the proceeds from personal seat licenses.[82] The Ravens will be responsible for all maintenance but will pay no rent. The "no-rent" clause in the Ravens' contract led to considerable confusion in the Baltimore press. There is a clause in the Orioles' lease with the Maryland

Stadium Authority that entitles them to "parity" with any NFL team.[83] Rent is not the only point at issue regarding the parity clause; it seems likely that the parity clause will oblige the Stadium Authority to make substantial lease concessions to the Orioles.

Since the Orioles pay approximately $6 million in rent, the central rental component of the Ravens' agreement is substantially different from that in the Orioles' lease.[84] But unlike the Orioles, the Ravens will be responsible for maintenance (at a cost of approximately $4 million a year). Thus one major difference is that under their lease the Orioles pay maintenance indirectly (via rent), whereas the Ravens pay it directly.[85] This change was made because of a change in the U.S. tax code in 1986, whereby, as of the time of financing the Ravens' stadium, it is not legal to use tax-exempt bonds to finance a stadium if more than 10 percent of the service on those bonds is secured by rent from the stadium.

As with the Orioles, there will be a 10 percent tax on all stadium tickets. Admission tax revenue is estimated to be $2.6 million.[86] We have no history on what fraction of this tax will be paid by out-of-state residents, nor among those the fraction that will be incremental.[87] Given the presence of the Redskins in the Washington suburbs, it seems highly unlikely that the Ravens will match the Orioles and draw 31 percent of their fans from out of state. Nevertheless, we will provisionally assume that 30 percent of Ravens fans will come from out of state.[88] If 30 percent of the admission tax revenue is attributed to incremental out-of-staters, then the Ravens import $0.8 million in admission tax revenue.

For the other entries in table 8-2, a reasonable upper bound for the Ravens analog to the benefit generated by the Orioles is found by taking 15.6 percent of the Orioles benefit (on the grounds that there will be 10 percent as many Ravens games as Orioles games, but 56 percent more fans per game).[89] On the basis of this simple assumption, table 8-3 shows the Ravens analog to the Orioles net-cost calculation of table 8-2.

Economic projections prepared by various groups assume that part or all of the shortfall (relative to the Orioles) will be made up from non-NFL events staged at the Ravens' stadium.[90] The Maryland Stadium Authority would receive the 10 percent admissions tax for all such events and would receive in addition 50 percent of net (of staging cost) gate receipts for some but not all such events. In one of its hypothetical scenarios, the Department of Fiscal Services estimates that total gate receipts from non-NFL events will be $12.4 million, plus $1.24 million in admission taxes.[91] Depending on staging costs, and assuming the state is

Table 8-3. *Economic Benefit from the Ravens*
Millions of dollars

Benefit	Amount
Benefits of job creation	0.07
Out-of-stadium incremental taxes	0.20
Incremental admission tax	0.80
Sales tax on incremental stadium spending	0.07
Total	1.14

Source: Authors' calculations.

entitled to 50 percent of the gate on all such events, the authority might receive up to $5 million on non-NFL events.

The fundamental problem with these projections is that these non-NFL events (if there is truly a market for them in the first place) could easily be held in other venues around the state. Many events could likely be staged at the baseball park at Camden Yards; thus the economic benefit from such events cannot be used as a justification for building the football stadium. In the five years since Oriole Park at Camden Yards opened, virtually no major non–baseball events have been staged in the stadium, which suggests that somehow the stadium and its primary (base-ball) function is not well suited to concerts and the like. However, Joseph Foss of the Orioles disputes this. He believes that the lack of non–baseball events in Camden Yards is due to a peculiarity (another depar-ture from parity with the Ravens) in the Orioles' lease. Under this lease term, the Orioles receive no revenue from non–baseball events at Cam-den Yards, but they do have veto power over any proposed event. The result is that the Orioles have no incentive to try to market the stadium or to even cooperate with the state. Mr. Foss suggests that with the right incentives the Orioles could easily accommodate concerts and other such events while the Orioles are on the road. As of this writing, the Orioles are negotiating with the state authority for rights to revenue to non–baseball events. Particularly if Oriole Park begins to compete for the concert trade, it seems most unlikely that the football stadium will gen-erate even a substantial fraction of the projected $12 million in concert revenue, and in any case almost all such revenue that is generated will be simply a relocation of such activity from elsewhere in Maryland.

In the case of the Orioles, recall that we estimated a best-case fiscal deficit of approximately $11 million, or $14.70 per Baltimore household. For the Ravens' stadium, it is a deficit of approximately $13 million, or

$17.33 per household per year. The total cost of the stadium (to Maryland-ers) is $14 million in capital cost plus $4 million in maintenance.

The $4 million maintenance cost should count as a part of the cost of the Ravens only to the extent that crowding out of alternative spending does not result in a reduction in maintenance expenditure at other venues. Unfortunately, we have no information on potential savings of maintenance cost elsewhere. Thus the worst-case cost of the Ravens is between $14 million and $18 million per year, or between $18.67 and $24 per household per year.

As with the Orioles, the subsidy is justified if the public consumption benefits exceed the subsidy. And as with the Orioles, we have no adequate method of estimating the magnitude of the public consumption benefit.

Conclusion

Several conclusions can be drawn about the impact of Oriole Park at Camden Yards.[92] First, the new stadium generated sufficient new revenue to more than cover the capital and maintenance cost. Second, the Orioles' fiscal picture improved dramatically as a result of the move; they captured much more than 100 percent of the surplus generated by the move. Third, before considering the external public consumption benefits from the presence of the Orioles, the state and its subdivisions lose approximately $9 million a year on Camden Yards. This is approximately $12 per Baltimore household per year; the public subsidy to the stadium is justified only if the public consumption benefits of the Orioles are at least this large. Fourth, in addition to the deficit borne by the state, the national economy bears approximately another $12 million in costs. We are unable to determine what fraction of this burden is borne by Marylanders, but it seems likely that the majority is borne by non-Marylanders.

With respect to football in Baltimore, one can safely say, first, that, in terms of direct impact, the state and it subdivisions lose approximately $13 million a year on the Ravens stadium, depending on the amount of non-NFL activity generated at the new stadium, and on the fraction of such activity that would not have happened but for the stadium. Second, since the Ravens play many fewer games, the state has fewer opportunities to recoup tax revenue from out-of-state fans than for the Orioles. Induced-employment and out-of-state tax benefits are estimated to be approximately $1 million per year. Third, the costs absorbed by the economy as a whole are comparable to those attributable to the baseball park: approximately $12 million. For both the Orioles and the Ravens, we are unable to estimate the value of the public consumption benefits received by Marylanders. This is unfortunate, because each ballpark is, or is not, worth the subsidy, depending on whether the public consumption benefits are greater than the subsidy.

Notes

1. Jacobs Field in Cleveland is also thought to be an exception.

2. Just as with the four years preceding the move, the five years following the move may be atypical. We discuss the so-called honeymoon effect later in the chapter. *Orioles 1996 Media Guide* (Baltimore Orioles, 1996), p. 368.

3. As shown in figure 8-1, Orioles attendance can be divided into three eras. Until 1979, home attendance was approximately 80 percent of the major league average. After 1979 (the Edward Bennett Williams era of heavy marketing in Washington), team attendance was at about the major league average. In each year since the 1992 move to Camden Yards, attendance was approximately 60 percent above the major league average. For a variety of reasons, it is not clear that the four years preceding the move to Camden Yards is typical (see figure 8-1). It includes 1988, when the Orioles began the season with a twenty-three-game losing streak, but also 1989, 1990, and 1991; in all three of those years attendance exceeded 30,000, demolishing the previous all-time high of 26,918 in 1984. *Baltimore Orioles 1996 Media Guide*, p. 368; John Thorn and others, *Total Baseball: The Official Encyclopedia of Major League Baseball*, 5th ed. (New York: Viking Penguin, 1997).

4. We state this in terms of Baltimore households because we assume Baltimoreans will receive the majority of any benefits, even though the costs are absorbed by all residents of the state of Maryland.

5. See James Edward Miller, "The Dowager of 33rd Street: Memorial Stadium and the Politics of Big-Time Sports in Maryland, 1954–1991," *Maryland Historical Magazine*, vol. 87 (Summer 1992), p. 189. Neither Miller nor his source (the *Baltimore Sun*) states precisely what is measured in this "profit"; most important, we are unable to determine whether the profit was measured gross or net of capital cost.

6. The original stadium had been built with the possibility of adding an upper deck in mind. Ibid., p. 188.

7. Ibid., p. 189; and Michael Gershman, *Diamonds: The Evolution of the Ballpark from Elysian Fields to Camden Yards* (Houghton Mifflin, 1993), p. 173.

8. Miller, "The Dowager of 33rd Street," p. 188. Here we have conflicting reports. Gershman (*Diamonds*, p. 173) reports Dallas Texans, while Miller reports Dallas Colts.

9. Is it coincidence that two of the three teams lured to Baltimore have been nicknamed Browns? Donald Dewey and Nick Acocella, *Ball Clubs: Every Franchise, Past and Present, Officially Recognized by Major League Baseball* (New York: Harper, 1996), pp. xvii, xviii.

10. According to Miller, the most serious threat was from the Pacific Coast League. James Edward Miller, *The Baseball Business: Pursuing Pennants and Profits in Baltimore* (University of North Carolina Press, 1990), pp. 14, 15.

11. Indeed, the Browns attempted to move to Los Angeles in 1941. See Ibid., p. 23.

12. Ibid., p. 16.

13. Before the Browns' move to Baltimore, virtually all baseball stadiums had been owned by the teams rather than municipalities. The Browns owned the baseball stadium in St. Louis and sold it to the Cardinals when they moved to Baltimore. Ibid., p. 32.

14. Ibid., pp. 30, 34–35.

15. Ibid., p. 212

16. Edward Cline, deputy director of the Maryland Stadium Authority, interview with the authors; and Arthur T. Johnson, "Economic and Policy Implications of Housing Sports Franchises: Lessons from Baltimore," *Urban Affairs Quarterly*, vol. 21 (March 1986), pp. 411–33.

17. The Colts won the NFL championship in 1958 and repeated in 1959.

18. Miller, *The Baseball Business*, p. 75.

19. The American League generally lagged well behind the National League in attempts to attract black players. By the time the American League teams began to actively seek black players, the National League had stripped the Negro League of its best talent. Ibid., pp. 65, 96.

20. Ibid., p. 39

21. None of these commercial establishments is adjacent to Memorial Stadium.

22. Miller, *The Baseball Business*, p. 70.

23. Until the Senators left Washington, access to Washington was not a significant issue in any event.

24. This information was received through a personal interview with a former Oriole front office staff member who requested anonymity.

25. The first serious discussion of improvements came in 1957, when the city agreed to replace wooden bleachers with individual seats.

26. From 1903 through 1953 no major league baseball teams moved (see figure 8-1). Beginning in the 1950s, many east coast cities that had two or more franchises saw one move west. The five movers in the 1950s were Boston to Milwaukee, St. Louis to Baltimore, Philadelphia to Kansas City, Brooklyn to Los Angeles, and New York to San Francisco. The three movers in the 1960s were Washington to Minnesota, Milwaukee to Atlanta, and Kansas City to Oakland. The two movers in the 1970s were Seattle to Milwaukee, and Washington to Texas. See Donald Dewey and Nicholas Acocella, *The Ball Clubs' Every Franchise, Past and Present, Officially Recognized by Major League Baseball* (Harper Perennial, 1996), pp. xvii and xviii.

27. Of course, free agency is not sufficient to explain teams' rising payrolls. The "cost" of fielding a competitive baseball team is largely rent; individual franchises "must" pay competitive salaries, but the competitive level of salaries is determined by the sum of direct fan revenues and subsidies paid by cities. Roughly speaking, if other comparable cities are willing to pay $10 million subsidies for sports franchises, then Baltimore must match *this* or lose its franchises. With well-informed cities, and a limited number of franchises, one would expect the subsidy to be bid up to the point where the marginal city achieves no surplus. If there were collusion among the cities rather than among the teams, then in equilibrium all rent would go to the cities rather than the teams and players.

28. Though teams had moved before 1984 (for example, the Colts and the Orioles), the leagues had successfully retained veto power over moves in the past. Until 1984 a city could be sure of retaining its team unless the league approved a move. The Los Angeles court ruling diminished the NFL's prerogative to interfere with franchise moves, but the extension to baseball is far from obvious because of baseball's continuing antitrust exemption.

29. Miller, "The Dowager of 33rd Street," p. 196.

30. The official name of the stadium is a compromise between the Orioles (who wanted Oriole Park) and the then governor of Maryland, William Donald Schaefer, who wanted Camden Yards (the original name of the site from its railroad-terminal days).

31. Miller, *The Baseball Business*, p. 289.

32. Free agency also reduced the ability of clubs to reap the benefits of their farm system investments. Whatever faults the reserve clause had, it did have the virtue of inducing teams to make efficient investments in the human capital of their prospects. (Free agency, on the other hand, gives established players added incentive to invest in themselves.)

33. The Inner Harbor is too shallow and confined for modern ships; Baltimore's port activity is all located to the southeast of the Inner Harbor, away from downtown and where the harbor is wider and deeper.

34. Miller, *The Baseball Business*, pp. 152, 234.

35. Numbers on actual parking were conveyed to us orally by Joseph Foss, vice president of business and operations, of the Baltimore Orioles. As of this writing, the Orioles and Maryland Stadium Authority are negotiating over the resolution of the 5,000-parking-space provision in the Orioles' lease.

36. USA Today, *The Complete Four Sport Stadium Guide* (1996), p. 9.

37. *Orioles 1996 Media Guide*, pp. 362–63.

38. One might argue that 1988 should be disregarded as an anomaly: after going 0 for 23 at the beginning of the season they went on to lose 107 games that year, and they drew only 22,442 per game. But throughout the 1980s they drew in the low- to mid-twenties. In 1983, when they won the World Series, they drew 26,520. Average attendance figures were calculated using information obtained from the *Orioles 1996 Media Guide*, p. 368.

39. A regression of average attendance on winning percentage and a Camden Yards dummy yields the following result:

Attend = 24226 − 11558 · (winning percent) + 26964 · (Camden Yards Dummy)
(−1.00) (8.62)

$R^2 = 0.659$ (*t*-statistics in parentheses).

40. Incremental fans = 45,000 - 29,000 = 16,000; out-of-state fans at Memorial Stadium = 0.1 × 29,000 = 2,900; out-of-state fans at Camden Yards = 45,000 × 0.31 = 13,500. Incremental out-of-state fans = 10,600.

10,600/16000 = 0.7.

See *The Economic Impact of Oriole Park at Camden Yards: Results of a Fan Spending Survey for the 1992 Season* (Baltimore City Department of Planning, December 1992), fig. 3, p. 12.

41. Roger G. Noll, "Attendance and Price Setting," in Roger G. Noll, ed., *Government and the Sports Business* (Brookings, 1974), pp. 115–58.

42. Data for 1996 were supplied by Joseph Foss, vice chairman of business and finance of the Baltimore Orioles.

43. Of course, if one attributes the team's playing-field improvement to the revenue from Camden Yards, then arguably the net (reduced-honeymoon/improved-team) effect may approximate the steady state after all.

44. Joseph Foss and Edward Cline, interviews with the authors.

45. See Federal Reserve Bank of Cleveland, *Economic Trends*, Research Department of the Federal Reserve Bank of Cleveland, May 1996, p. 5.

46. Charles L. Ballard, John B. Shoven, and John Whalley, "The Total Welfare Cost of the United States Tax System: A General Equilibrium Approach," *National Tax Journal*, vol. 38 (June 1985), p. 125.

47. These figures are net of the 20 percent of gate receipts that are remitted to the visiting team.

48. In 1994 gate receipts were $25.6 million and in 1995 $35.4 million during the two strike-shortened seasons. On the other hand, in 1995 Cal Ripken broke Lou Gehrig's consecutive game streak. In addition to the athletic achievement, this was a major media event in Baltimore. See Anthony Baldo and others, "Secrets of the Front Office: What America's Pro Teams Are Worth," *Financial World*, vol. 162 (February 1991), p. 42; Michael K. Ozanian and Stephen Taub, "Big Leagues, Bad Business: It's Time to Restructure Major League Sports, Here's Why. And Here's How," *Financial World*, July 7, 1992, p. 50; Michael K. Ozanian and others, "Foul Ball," *Financial World*, May 25, 1993, p. 28; Michael K. Ozanian and others, "The $11 Billion Pastime: Why Sports Franchise Values Are Soaring Even as Team Profits Fall," *Financial World*, May 10, 1994, p. 52; Michael K. Ozanian and others, "Suite Deals inside the New Stadium Boom," *Financial World*, May 9, 1995, p. 46; and Tushar Atre and others, "Sports—The High-Stakes Game of Team Ownership: Owning a Pro Team Can Be More Lucrative than Owning Stocks and Bonds. But It's Becoming a Lot Easier," *Financial World*, May 20, 1996, p. 56.

49. Stadium revenue includes suites, luxury seating, concessions, parking, and venue advertising. See ibid.

50. Whether the admission tax should be counted as part of the "private" return to Camden Yards depends upon whether we think of it as an ordinary tax or the state's share of the gate. In further calculations in this section, we exclude the admissions tax.

51. Both the "before" and "after" financial figures are somewhat suspect as bases for a steady-state comparison. The "after" figures might be high because of the honeymoon effect. The "before" figures are likely high as well (tending to offset any errors generated by ignoring the honeymoon effect). The last two years at Memorial were extraordinarily successful by historical standards; average attendance in the final two years exceeded the average over the final Memorial decade by 17 percent. Also note that the revenue data were taken from 1990 through 1995; they are not (quite) all dollars of the same value. Offsetting this, we have made no allowance for possible future rises in real ticket and concession prices.

52. Camden Yards is maintained by the Maryland Stadium Authority. At present the Orioles are asking the authority to turn over maintenance to the Orioles. Joseph Foss of the Orioles believes that the team can maintain the stadium for approximately $4 million. Memorial Stadium was maintained by the Baltimore City Department of Parks and Recreation. We have been unable to obtain maintenance cost figures on Memorial Stadium; however, Joseph Foss of the Orioles believes that maintenance cost at Memorial was comparable to that at Camden Yards.

53. Row houses on twenty- by sixty-foot lots sell for approximately $90,000 in the Memorial Stadium neighborhood. If we assume land constitutes 20 percent of house value and that lots cover 70 percent of the land, then land value per acre is $450,000. The Memorial Stadium site, at approximately forty acres, has residual value of $18 million, less the (unknown) cost of demolition of Memorial Stadium. (Estimates of value of row houses were provided by Bill Cassidy, manager of the Fells Point office of Long and Foster Realtors. The estimate of the size of the Memorial Stadium site was provided by Edward Cline, deputy director of the Maryland Stadium Authority.)

54. The Maryland Stadium Authority receives substantial revenue in addition to this rent. Edward Cline, interview with the authors.

55. Calculated using various *Financial World* reports.

56. Calculated using various *Financial World* reports.

57. The period of high operating costs also coincides with the period in which the Orioles' owner then, Eli Jacobs, was facing bankruptcy.

58. Edward Cline and Joseph Foss, interviews with the authors.

59. Calculated by the authors: 10 percent of gate receipts.

60. Of course, if the investment that was crowded out was public rather than private, there is no incremental taxation and therefore no deadweight loss.

61. Actually, it is financed by lottery proceeds, but this has no bearing on the magnitude of the deadweight loss. Even if lotteries are less distortionary than taxes, stadium lotteries crowd out other lotteries that otherwise could have been used to finance state expenditures.

62. Recall that our first focus will be on the "social" return from the perspective of Maryland taxpayers; where appropriate, we note in the text how this diverges from the national social rate of return.

63. In the calculations below, we assume that all expenditure by out-of-staters takes place in the Baltimore metro area. As we will see, the economic benefits of such expenditure are relatively modest; our basic conclusions in the chapter are not affected if some of the imported expenditure takes place in Maryland's hinterland.

64. Joseph Foss, vice chairman for business operations and finance of the Orioles, advises us that as of 1996 at least 35 percent of Camden Yards fans are from out of the state.

65. This comes to approximately $30 per out-of-state fan.

66. Thirty-one percent of 45,000 as opposed to 10 percent of 29,000.

67. This does *not* mean, for example, that average wages should be the same in Baltimore as in Biloxi, even after correcting for cost of living and amenities. The job mix differs substantially across regions, and some workers who earn high incomes in Baltimore would be virtually unemployable in Biloxi (to take a case germane to this discussion, most major league baseball players would earn little outside a Major League Baseball city).

68. Real wages correct for cost of living and amenities.

69. See, for example, Edwin S. Mills and Bruce W. Hamilton, *Urban Economics,* 5th ed. (Harper Collins College, 1994).

70. Labor's share of national income is approximately 73 percent (compensation of employees/national income; U.S. Department of Commerce, *1995 Statistical Abstract,* table 632, p. 457); however, the fraction of this expenditure due to *local* labor is likely to be smaller.

71. A baseball player with a large salary, even if he saves much of his income and spends much of it outside the local economy, is likely to generate at least as much employment with his local spending as a steelworker who never leaves the city.

72. U.S. Department of Commerce, *1995 Statistical Abstract of the United States,* table 632, p. 402.

73. Calculated by the authors: Baltimore 1990 SMSA population (2,382,172) less rural Baltimore SMSA population (305,635) divided by the average Maryland population per household. Population data from U.S. Census of Population, 1990 General Population Characteristics, Metropolitan Areas, table 1. Household size data from U.S. Department of Commerce, *U.S. Statistical Abstract 1995,* p. 60. For completeness, we note that this increase in property values generates an increase in property tax revenues of approximately 2 percent of the value increase, or approximately $0.13 per house per year.

74. The beneficiaries of such a scheme are property owners, and the burden is borne by taxpayers who cover the cost. If the job-import subsidy is financed by local property taxes, there is essentially no redistribution; otherwise there is redistribution from the bearers of the tax burden to the property owners.

75. Thirty-one percent of 45,000 at Camden Yards less 10 percent of 29,000 at Memorial, divided by 45,000.

76. Glenn Blomquist, telephone interview with the authors, July 1996. Blomquist was reporting his own research efforts published in Mark Berger, Glenn Blomquist, and Werner Waldner, "A Revealed Preference Ranking of Quality of Life for Metropolitan Areas," *Social Science Quarterly*, vol. 68 (December 1987), pp. 761–68.

77. If NFL teams continue to move to second-tier cities (see the discussion in chapter 2 in this volume), then in the future the correlation between city size and professional sports activity might be weak enough to facilitate estimation of this effect.

78. Though the burden of the subsidy is borne by citizens throughout the state, it seems reasonable to assume that any public consumption benefits are concentrated in the Baltimore metro area. However, it also seems unlikely that such public consumption benefits stop at the metro area boundary.

79. See U.S Department of Commerce, *Statistical Abstract of the United States 1953*, p. 22; and 1990 Census of Population, General Population Characteristics, Metropolitan Areas, sec. 1 of 3, p. 3.

80. Demolition, for example, is generally not an economically viable option. Demolition of row houses generally costs between $500,000 and $900,000 per acre, and many acres in Baltimore are not worth this much. Mills and Hamilton, *Urban Economics*, p. 145.

81. Had the job-creation and tax-import benefits of Camden Yards been greater than the deficit, then public officials should have immediately embraced the Orioles' earliest request for a new stadium.

82. Maryland Department of Employment and Economic Development, "Estimated Impact of a Football Stadium at Camden Yards," January 1996, p. 7. This $24 million is to be paid over fifteen years; thus the present value is substantially less. Indeed, in the memorandum of agreement between the Ravens and the Maryland Stadium Authority under which the Ravens moved to Baltimore, there is no repayment schedule for this $24 million, nor any interest accrual. Joseph Foss, interview with the authors, August 26, 1996.

83. Before 1979 the city negotiated leases with the Orioles and Colts separately, generally adjusting rent according to ability to pay. The Orioles, being less profitable, paid less rent than the Colts. But in 1979 the Colts got a clause in their lease tying their own rental payments to those of the Orioles. *Baltimore Sun*, August 7, 1979.

84. As of October 1996, the Ravens and the Maryland Stadium Authority had not agreed upon final terms of the lease; rather, there is a memorandum of understanding that leaves substantial room for negotiation.

85. Another difference is that the Ravens' payment is due regardless of the team's financial success. Or at least so the Maryland Stadium Authority believes. Interview with Edward Cline, deputy director of the Maryland Stadium Authority. But inasmuch as the final Ravens' lease is not yet signed, it is not clear whether this term will be a part of it. The Orioles' rent is a proportion of team revenue; thus in the event of poor attendance (or a strike) the team's rent will fall. (Since Orioles' games are virtually all sold out, it is implausible that a revenue-based rent will rise.)

86. This is to be split, with 80 percent, or $2.1 million, going to the Maryland Stadium Authority and 20 percent, or $.5 million, going to the city of Baltimore.

87. To the extent that Ravens' Washington fans would otherwise have attended Redskins games, such tax importing is not attributable to the Ravens, because the Redskins stadium will be in Maryland in any event.

88. This assumption has little bearing on the economic viability of the Ravens' stadium; even assuming that 30 percent of fans are imported, the stadium is even more of an economic drain on Maryland than the baseball stadium.

89. Average baseball attendance is approximately 45,000; the football stadium is projected to hold 70,000. Maryland Department of Employment and Economic Development, "Estimated Impact of a Football Stadium at Camden Yards."

90. One example is a January 1996 projection by the Maryland Department of Fiscal Services (DFS), which critiques earlier studies by the Maryland Department of Business and Economic Development.

91. In their projection, the DFS only assigns incremental attendance (estimated at 15,000) for football games, on the assumption that the games would have occurred anyway, but with lower attendance.

92. All of these conclusions hinge on one crucial intangible: Will attendance hold at its historically phenomenal level? If an expansion team comes to Washington, or if poor playing-field performance reduces fan support, the outlook for the Orioles and the Maryland Stadium Authority might be quite different.

9

SPORTS, POLITICS, AND ECONOMICS

The Cincinnati Story

JOHN P. BLAIR AND DAVID W. SWINDELL

 Ohio has witnessed an explosion of new sport facilities during the 1990s. Inspired by Cleveland's Gateway Complex, several other Ohio cities have joined in the sports boom. Columbus officials are trying to decide how best to build a new facility for their professional Major League Soccer franchise and downtown hockey arena to go along with the new basketball arena at Ohio State University. Akron has completed a new minor league baseball stadium that lured a team away from a five-year-old stadium in nearby Canton. Toledo city officials have been trying to finance a new minor league baseball downtown to lure the Mudhens from a nearby suburb. Dayton continues to look for ways to build a stadium in hopes that the owner of the Cincinnati Reds will allow the city to attract a minor league baseball team. In 1995 Cleveland lost the National Football League Browns to Baltimore, days before area voters approved a tax dedicated to the financing of a new NFL facility.

While each of these deals is significant for its city's tax base, none can match the events that have unfolded in Cincinnati in terms of cost. In 1996, after two years of haggling and a highly charged referendum campaign, Hamilton County/Cincinnati voters approved a sales tax increase to pay a large portion of the $544 million costs for a new football-only stadium for the NFL Bengals and a new baseball-only stadium for the Major League Baseball Reds.[1]

This chapter details how these events came to pass in Cincinnati, how the community addressed the tidal forces of not one but two professional sports franchises demanding new facilities, how local public leaders met the challenge while trying to revitalize the city's downtown, and how a public-private partnership helped resolve some of the city's difficulties. At its core, this is a case study of public finance decisionmaking and the economic impact reports underlying this decisionmaking.

A Case for Welfare

The stadium issue in Cincinnati illustrates a fragmented polity attempting to match local resources with sports franchise needs while faced with the demands of two team owners. After extensive analysis by public and private groups and numerous trial balloons, needs became whatever Marge Schott, principal owner of the Reds, and Mike Brown, principal owner of the Bengals, demanded. In response, local and regional leaders tried several methods of cost sharing in order to match the owners' requirements with those of the larger Cincinnati region. When these attempts failed and the process stalled, the teams began issuing threats. In what was described by the local media as a crisis situation ("the 11th hour," "fourth down," "bottom of the ninth," and so on), city and county officials adopted a plan that called for a complicated series of exchanges for certain service responsibilities along with a sales tax increase and a property tax rollback.

Emerging Needs

What, precisely, were the teams' "needs"? At the time of the crisis, the two teams were playing in Riverfront Stadium, opened in 1970 to replace the Reds' historic ballpark, Crosley Field. In those days, it was considered an advanced design, with 60,000 seats for football and 53,000 for baseball. The facility was instrumental in attracting the NFL Bengals to Cincinnati. However, it does not have many of the amenities currently in vogue in new stadiums and arenas around the nation: in particular, it does not have the club seating and luxury boxes that can substantially increase a facility's revenue. At the same time that the Reds and Bengals' owners were talking about the lack of such amenities, citizens began complaining about the physical appearance of Riverfront. The saucer-like design had become the butt of numerous local jokes.

The teams also were trying to make the case that they had been losing money over the previous few seasons in relation to their respective league averages. External annual estimates provided by *Financial World* magazine indicate that from 1990 through 1993, the Reds did in fact experience a significant drop in their net operating income.[2] This was due in large part to skyrocketing player costs and flat revenues from media and stadium sources (in constant dollars). However, the case for the Bengals was much weaker. According to those same estimates, the Bengals net operating income over that period had been flat, hovering between $6 million and $8 million annually (in constant dollars). Regardless, both owners pleaded for additional revenues through facility enhancements.

Though both teams were locked into leases extending many years into the future, they felt that Riverfront Stadium was outdated. As a result, a redevelopment task force began to consider a new stadium on the northern riverfront in 1993. Almost all observers believed the plan would include only one new stadium. When the initial plan was released in September 1993, it called for a $315 million project consisting of a new stadium along with an update and conversion of Riverfront to a single-purpose stadium for the team that did not get the new facility. The plan did not address the question of which team should occupy the new stadium. As anticipated, a struggle ensued between the Bengals and Reds to determine which team would get the new facility. What was not anticipated was how this struggle would escalate the costs of keeping the teams.

Knowing that the redevelopment plan was soon to be released and what the general recommendations were, the Reds general manager announced that the only way Cincinnati could keep the Reds would be to build a new, baseball-only stadium. Three months later, Mike Brown, the Bengals general manager, announced that his team was losing money and that to stay in Cincinnati it would need a new, football-only facility to replace twenty-four-year-old Riverfront.[3]

Shortly after, the city renegotiated the Bengals' lease for use of Riverfront. Under a new lease, the Bengals agreed to play in Riverfront until at least 1998 and then go to a year-to-year lease if a new stadium was not in the works. The city agreed to pay the Bengals a $2.75 million annual subsidy and to add luxury boxes and a clubhouse to Riverfront.[4] Just as important, the new lease included an escape clause for the Bengals. If Cincinnati was not constructing or about to construct a new football-only stadium by the end of the decade, the lease could be terminated, freeing the Bengals to move.

The new lease enhanced the future mobility of the Bengals, made it more difficult to retire the debt incurred by the city and county to finance Riverfront Stadium, and possibly sent a signal to Schott that the Bengals had the inside track in the quest for the new stadium. In hindsight, it was not surprising that three months after the Bengals renegotiated their lease, Schott grumbled that city officials "don't appreciate us," reiterated her desire for a new baseball park, intimated that America's oldest professional baseball team might leave Cincinnati, and discussed possible locations in northern Kentucky and southeastern Indiana.

The Public Challenge

As public groups sought to clarify and finance the initial stadium plan, they knew both teams had expressed a desire to have their own facility but viewed these statements as bargaining positions. Most observers still believed that renovations to Riverfront Stadium for one team and the construction of a new facility for the other would meet the community's needs. The mayor of Cincinnati and the president of the Hamilton County Commission appointed a twenty-seven-member regional task force of leaders from Ohio, Indiana, and Kentucky to frame the issue: how best to provide a new venue in which the Bengals and/or Reds could play.[5]

In May 1994 Reds' owner Schott suddenly contacted city officials (not the regional task force) expressing interest in buying Riverfront Stadium, along with an attached parking garage that required repair. On the one hand, this move seemed a hopeful sign because it suggested she might be interested in remaining in Riverfront. On the other hand, it diminished the already limited authority of the regional task force.

Schott asked for time to evaluate the structures and develop possible financing options. She hired HOK Sports to do an analysis. City leaders tried to close a deal because the money from the sale of Riverfront could have been used to build a new football stadium while removing the existing stadium from the city's list of debt items.[6] The city hired a local engineering firm to evaluate the costs of rehabilitating the large Riverfront parking garage. The firm's estimate was $40 million.

The city's team of engineers, paid with state grant money, concluded that the renovations to Riverfront Stadium—including added club seating, luxury boxes, and the other revenue-generating amenities that both the Bengals and Reds wanted—would cost approximately $21 million. In order to meet the team owners' requirements, the region's sports facilities were initially expected to cost $61 million for Riverfront and the garage renovations. Additional money would be needed for the new stadium. Still, no one directly addressed the key issue: Who would get the new facility and who would play in the renovated Riverfront?

After the engineers hired by the city released their cost estimates, the consulting firm Schott hired to examine stadium renovations released its results. For football only, the renovation would cost $48 million, and for baseball only, it would cost $44 million, plus the $40 million for the parking garage renovation. The estimates for keeping the teams had just made the first in a series of jumps, from $61 million to around $86 million (the average of the estimated stadium restoration plus garage costs of $40 million), which was nearly a 30 percent increase. The new facility was expected to cost $120 million although in retrospect the estimate was completely blind and greatly underestimated. Thus to satisfy both teams it would take roughly $200 million.

Schott used an HOK Sports press conference to announce that she had decided not buy Riverfront after all but would consider doing so only if the city converted it to a baseball-only facility. In other words, once the Reds were the only possible tenant, she would start negotiations. Some public officials expressed reservations about the sincerity of her intent to buy the facility after renovations.

To defray some of the cost to local taxpayers and to overcome perceived citizen objections to the large public subsidies, the Cincinnati Business Committee (CBC) suggested some private sector support in order to keep the teams. They proposed low-interest loans, luxury suite purchases, and permanent seat licenses (PSLs). The CBC gesture was the first of several public, high-visibility suggestions of private support, none of which became a firm commitment until two years after the initial press conference (which was held six months after the eventual referendum).

The expected cost to local taxpayers was further reduced when the president of the Ohio Senate (Cincinnati's most powerful representative in Columbus) pledged state funding on par with the purported 10 percent paid for Cleveland's Gateway project. The public and private groups that seemed interested in helping resolve the issue now included private organizations, the city of Cincinnati, Hamilton County, the state of Ohio, and numerous smaller governmental units throughout the Tri-State area.

Regional Ties Loosen

Once the HOK Sports study was released, those who might be expected to pay for the stadiums began to raise pointed questions. For instance, who had the right to sell the name of the new facility or of Riverfront? City representatives argued they did because they leased it and were responsible for operating it. The Hamilton County Commissioners argued they did because they owned it.

In the meantime, Schott had decided she was unhappy with the renegotiated Bengals lease. She wanted "parity" with the Bengals (which she felt entitled to on the basis of her lease agreement). In the renegotiation of the Bengals' lease, that team was given an extra $2.75 million by way of an annual subsidy until the end of the decade, when the new stadium was to be finished.[7] Schott wanted the same terms as the Bengals were getting: an immediate profit enhancement in addition to a new facility in the long run. Schott then refused to ratify physical changes to Riverfront and asked for even more than the city was paying Brown to remain in Cincinnati. If Cincinnati tried to meet those demands and also pay the direct subsidies to the Bengals, replied the city manager, the stadium fund would be exhausted by 1996; the city simply could not afford to placate both Brown and Schott with direct subsidies. At this juncture, city representatives turned to Hamilton County Commissioners for help. But the commissioners refused, and the regional ties loosened even further.

Despite the division her demand for a short-term subsidy had caused, Schott continued to press for her long-run goals. In November 1994 she said she now wanted a new, baseball-only stadium downriver from the current stadium. To satisfy her, the city would have to persuade Brown to keep the Bengals in Riverfront Stadium, something he had already said he did not want. Furthermore, officials feared that the location Schott wanted would not allow them to carry out related economic development projects designed to revive the downtown. But local officials were also aware that the Reds were more popular than the Bengals. They play more home games, generate more spending from outside, were the first professional baseball team in the country, and were better than the Bengals on the field.

As momentum grew for a new, old-style ballpark for the Reds, Brown went back to the regional task force to make his case for a new football-only stadium. Without a new stadium and not counting the direct subsidy already in place, he said, the Bengals would be $5.5 million under the average NFL revenues by the year 2000. He made his presentation on the same day that Cleveland Browns owner Art Modell announced that his team needed $130 million worth of renovations to Cleveland's Municipal Stadium.

Threats Become Explicit and Credible

A year after Brown signed the renegotiated lease with the city of Cincinnati, he announced that the Bengals would not play in Cincinnati after the 1999 season unless they were promised a new football stadium. He would not accept a renovated Riverfront, arguing that the HOK Sports numbers did not add up in a way that would keep the Bengals competitive both on the field and financially. He estimated a football stadium would cost $146 million, over and above the rehabilitation or replacement of the parking garage. (Not surprisingly, this estimate later proved too low.) He suggested doubling the county's hotel-motel tax to 6 percent (to export the tax incidence) or levying a regional tax on alcohol and tobacco reaching into Kentucky and Indiana.

What had become a multisided tug-of-war continued into the winter of 1994–95. City leaders who have faced the possibility of losing their home team have said it is like having a gun held to one's head. In this case, perhaps it would be more apt to say that Cincinnati city, county, and regional leaders were caught in a cross-fire. Schott and Brown made no effort to coordinate their demands. They never tried to accommodate each other or the community. Meanwhile, the regional task force was paralyzed, unable or unwilling to suggest which team should receive the new facility. It postponed the date for releasing recommendations until March 1995.

The Cincinnati City Council instructed the city manager to give Schott a $2 million annual subsidy, hoping she would consider the balance with the Bengals restored and that she would start good-faith negotiations. However, this move may have actually weakened the city's bargaining position since it received nothing from the Reds in exchange. Some time later, the Reds threatened to break their lease because they were not satisfied with the progress on the new ballpark plans and felt the subsidy to the Bengals affected the validity of the Reds' lease. When the National League president announced that he would approve a move of the Reds within the Tri-state area, the possibility of losing the team became real. As the threats mounted, the governor decided to step in. Governor George Voinovich immediately berated all parties and tried to persuade everyone involved to reduce the rhetoric. He suggested that regional taxpayers, businesses, and team owners combine their funds to renovate Riverfront or build a new facility before the state would contribute to the project. Voinovich's statement was designed to apply pressure but remain neutral; it was also a portent of future state funding.

The spirit of regionalism withered further in January 1995, when Cincinnati's mayor, Roxanne Qualls, proposed an "interstate compact" to finance the stadium. Some area judges opposed a new tax of any kind that would support private businesses. After the November 1994 congressional elections, citizens began balking at the idea of a new regional level of government built on a new tax. Many residents outside Hamilton County, particularly Kentucky residents, resented the regional plan, asking why their taxes should support downtown Cincinnati.

Seeing that regionalism was faltering, Governor Voinovich created another task force, the Governor's Sports Facility Task Force, to study how the state could help raise money for sports facilities across the state. Again, questions of parity arose, but this time it was between cities, not teams. Since Ohio had contributed toward sport facilities in Cleveland, it was politically difficult for a Republican governor to ignore Hamilton County, a Republican stronghold. Furthermore, the state's actions illustrated the political importance to the entire state of a professional sports presence and the precedents that had been set for sports subsidies.

Several ideas for raising revenues were suggested in political circles and in the press, including a "sin" tax on tobacco and alcohol, a hotel-motel tax, a ticket tax, a regional general sales tax, a lottery game, and a "pop" tax (on the packaging of soft drinks). None of the trial balloons proved successful as various groups fought to shift the incidence of the funding mechanism to others. As the financial options dwindled, so did the prospects of keeping both teams.

In March 1995 Brown was again in the spotlight, putting a new sense of urgency into the search for resources. He proclaimed that the city had broken the 1993 renegotiated lease agreement because a $167,000 payment against the $2.75 million annual city subsidy was three days late. For Brown, it was late enough to consider the lease broken. The team, he said, was now legally free to leave Cincinnati at the end of the next season if he chose. Cincinnati officials disagreed that the lease was broken, but Brown's threat bore some weight in the light of what was happening in Baltimore.

The Bengals and Baltimore

Brown had acquired a suitor: the community leaders in NFL-hungry Baltimore. Furthermore, the NFL, in a recent meeting at which they denied the Rams permission to move to St. Louis from Los Angeles, also discussed the possibility of moving the Bengals to either St. Louis or, if the Rams did move, to Los Angeles. In the midst of growing rumors about the Bengals moving to Baltimore, the consensus of opinion was that the regional task force would recommend a renovated Riverfront for the Bengals. What momentum there was for a new stadium had been aimed at the better-loved Reds, even though they were still locked into a lease agreement to the year 2010. The media coverage stimulated the city council back into action. For the first time, and with a growing sense of urgency, attention was turned to finding a way to make a new football-only stadium happen.

After meeting with Maryland officials in mid-April, Mike Brown issued an ominous ultimatum. Baltimore officials who were charged with bringing NFL football back to Baltimore and were wooing Brown said that the money committed to a new football stadium would have to be recommitted if no team had been secured by June 1. Accordingly, Brown set June 1 as the deadline for the Cincinnati region to close a deal to keep the Bengals. Otherwise, he would take the Baltimore deal: new stadium, direct subsidies, and all.

For the first time, the Cincinnati Business Committee, the city council, and county commissioners began seriously trying to figure out how to finance *two* new facilities and a new parking garage. The regional task force had been meeting for fifteen months without result. Now officials were confronted with a six-week deadline to find a way to finance a project that many more believed would cost close to $500 million.

A group of local executives received headlines when they pledged millions of dollars for a new football stadium. However, no money was actually collected or legally committed. To complicate matters, public support for subsidies was weak. One public opinion poll, taken in March 1995, indicated that citizens wanted a new stadium but did not want to pay for it. Sixty percent of the citizens sampled supported a stadium, but only 27 percent thought that public dollars should be used to build it. A subsequent poll of Cincinnati residents found only 37 percent in favor of the city building new facilities and only 19 percent favored a tax increase to do it. Almost 50 percent of stadium supporters wanted another multipurpose—not football- or baseball-only—facility to replace Riverfront.[8] Many in the county, including those at the *Cincinnati Enquirer* newspaper, seemed to think the Bengals were all but gone.

Ten days before Brown's Baltimore deadline, HOK Sports reestimated the costs of the facilities they had proposed the previous September and concluded it would not be as expensive as originally thought. A new facility for the Bengals could be built from Riverfront's skeletal structure for only $110 million to $160 million, and a new retro-style ballpark would cost between $130 million and $175 million. Again, these estimates would also prove to be far too low.

In spite of the problems, Brown felt there was enough potential support for his position to ignore the Baltimore deadline. But as soon as the deadline passed, opponents renewed their attacks on the various plans. The local teachers' union said sales tax money should be used to support schools before stadiums. The local branches of the American Federation of Labor and Congress of Industrial Organizations did not want pension funds used for such a speculative investment. As a result of the instant cooldown, Mike Brown returned to Baltimore to see if negotiations could continue. In fact, the deadline was not as firm as some were led to believe. Baltimore officials extended talks until June 30, 1994, so the threat of leaving remained viable. Brown had until June 30 to commit.

In Columbus, the Governor's Regional Sport Facilities Task Force unveiled its financing plan. It ignored the multistate region and focused on Hamilton and the three surrounding counties in Ohio for the resources. Kentucky and Indiana were excluded because of their reluctance to contribute resources. The plan called for a new sales tax and a new tax on tobacco and alcohol. The plan's chances of implementation, given its miniregional approach, rested in large measure on the support of the governor and the legislature. But support from the legislature was not forthcoming for two reasons. First, many legislators objected to the idea of supporting a private firm on principle. One influential Republican state senator (Charles Horn) stated emphatically that sports stadiums did not generate economic development.[9] Second, residents in the counties surrounding Hamilton County were reluctant to contribute to a project. As

Table 9-1. *Proposed New Revenue Expenditures from 1 Cent Increase in Hamilton County Sales Tax*

Millions of dollars

New expenditure	Amount
Property tax rollback	40.0
Stadium costs	35.0
300-bed county jail	15.0
Retirement of other long-term debt	6.5
Reduction in real estate transfer tax	2.0
Subsidy for county communications center operations	1.5
Total	100.0

Source: Regional Stadium Task Force, "Stadium Financing," presentation by Public Financial Management, Inc., June 22, 1995.

the Baltimore deadline drew closer, the search for resources was once again paralyzed.

The 1 Cent Solution

On June 22, Hamilton's county commissioner, Republican Bob Bedinghaus, presented a plan to finance two new stadiums along with the long-awaited Regional Stadium Task Force report. The plan called for a twenty-year, 1 cent increase in the county sales tax, raising it to 6.5 percent. According to his calculations, almost $100 million could be collected annually, of which $35 million would be needed to pay the annual financing of two new stadiums (principal and interest). Thirty-five million dollars would amortize approximately $520 million over twenty years. The suggested use for the rest of the money set the Cincinnati deal apart from others around the country and may make it a model for future subsidy efforts.

The original 1 cent increase in the sales tax would have generated $65 million more than what was required for the stadiums. This, Bedinghaus suggested, would make it possible to roll back the property tax an average 17 percent. The property tax rollback proved to be a particularly popular feature. Bedinghaus further planned to use the extra funds to build a needed 300-bed jail for the county, enhance several services, and retire some county debt. Table 9-1 shows the details.

Another of the three Hamilton County commissioners threw his support behind the new plan. As part of the plan, the commission then released the details to the city council along with a list of "nonnegotiable" items the county wanted in return for taking the lead in the offer. These

Table 9-2. *Proposed Stadium-Related Costs*

Millions of dollars

Projected cost	Amount
Retro-style baseball stadium	160.0
Open-air football stadium	170.0
Stadium engineering and architecture	33.0
Repair of old parking garage	54.0
Construction of 1,500 new parking spaces	15.0
Parking engineering and architecture	6.9
Luxury boxes and scoreboards	37.0
Demolition of existing Riverfront Stadium	5.0
Local infrastructure	10.0
Infrastructure engineering	1.0
Land acquisition	25.0
Subsidy to Bengals for two seasons of away games	3.0
Current Riverfront Stadium debt	25.0
Total	544.9

Source: Regional Stadium Task Force, "Stadium Financing," presentation by Public Financial Management, Inc., June 22, 1995.

items included the city's stadium fund, the Bengals' training facility, Riverfront Stadium, all earnings taxes associated with jobs at the stadium, all earnings from ticket surcharges, and operational control of the Metropolitan Sewer District (MSD). Because the plan called for a substantial contribution from the city, it won the immediate support of suburban and business leaders. However, several city councilors objected to the ultimatum, both to the manner of its presentation and the revenue the city would lose. The city manager's initial estimate was that Cincinnati would lose $100 million over twenty years. City commissioners expressed concern about the service cuts that would be necessary in the face of such revenue losses. County commissioners responded that city officials were overreacting, considering how "little" the county was asking in return for assuming the lead in the drive to find a solution that would satisfy both teams. Public bickering lasted several days before county and city administrators started working on a compromise.

The hastily completed stadium task force report detailed the stadium-related expenses. These elements are summarized in table 9-2. The $544.9 million bottom line became the official amount for the project. However, even this number is somewhat ephemeral. For instance, there were no architectural or engineering plans for the facilities so accurate cost estimates were not possible.[10] Cost estimates for the new stadiums themselves were based on recent, similar stadium projects.

The project not only lacked adequate plans, but it overlooked two important costs. First, interest costs were not considered. Depending upon interest rates and construction time, the project costs could increase or decrease significantly. Second, the infrastructure estimate included a footnote mentioning that either Mehring Way or the Fort Washington Way Platform, or perhaps both, might have to be relocated. These additional items could increase the project's infrastructure costs by $60 million to $120 million, a cost that also would be borne by the public.

As the financial plan took shape, team owners kept up the threat. Brown said he was being encouraged by the Maryland Stadium Authority to enter into exclusive negotiations with it by the end of that week. Schott drove to neighboring Warren County to meet with local officials and examine real estate for possible alternatives if Cincinnati failed to meet her ill-defined terms.

On the Tuesday before the Thursday deadline, tensions reached their highest level. County Commissioner John Dowlin bucked rank with his fellow Republicans and said he would vote against the Bedinghaus plan because it raised taxes. Local lawyer Tim Mara indicated that he would lead a grass roots campaign to repeal the tax increase if it passed. The state Senate president, Stanley Aronoff, and Governor Voinovich both distanced themselves from the fray, indicating that the state would not intervene in a local matter.

Fearing the parties might not reach an agreement by Baltimore's deadline, City Manager John Shirey instructed the city solicitor to prepare a team of local lawyers to challenge Brown's contention that his current lease was void because a subsidy payment was three days late. Brown responded that he wanted to change his lease to a year-to-year arrangement in the event that the county imposed a sales tax and it was overturned in a referendum. All the while, city and county administrators negotiated over cost-sharing details. The negotiations covered many issues that would ordinarily be irrelevant to sport projects (such as control over the sewage district) as the county attempted to shift costs to the city and capture resources. On Wednesday, after particularly intense talks, a deal began to take shape. The county agreed not to tap so deeply into the city's revenue sources, and the city promised to address other issues of concern to the county. Brown even relented on his demand for a year-to-year lease if voters rejected the new taxes, further easing the tensions.

Thursday morning, the day of the deadline, a new problem arose. The city faxed its version of the deal signed the night before to the county.

County officials were incensed by the way the city handled unresolved details. County commissioners accused the city of rewriting the agreement. During the early afternoon's shuttle diplomacy, the county and city worked toward an agreement. Mayor Qualls finally reconvened the council that evening. Citizens spoke against the proposal and the councilors made their last speeches, venting their frustration with the entire process; the extortion by Brown, Schott, and the Hamilton County commissioners; and the terms of the deal. Finally, as the midnight deadline approached, Mayor Qualls called the vote. The agreement with the county passed by a vote of 5 to 4, the mayor breaking with the Democrats to join with the Charterite and Republicans in support. The deadline was met, the crisis averted, for the time being. The following morning, Brown showed reporters the note he had prepared to send the council had the vote gone the other way. It read: "Thanks for your support. Goodbye."

After the Storm

The next hurdle for the stadiums project was the actual vote to approve the county tax increase. Given the nature of Ohio law, Hamilton County commissioners would have to approve two, ½-cent increases. Since two of the three commissioners already supported the financing plan, this step was considered a formality. Confidence that the Hamilton County Commission would pass the tax was the key to Brown's rejection of the Baltimore offer. Nevertheless, the two public meetings before the commission's vote were raucous and dominated by antitax speakers. Citizens were particularly concerned that they lacked the opportunity to vote on the levee.

A local antitax group led by Tim Mara, a member of Citizens for Choice in Taxation, promised a vigorous repeal attempt if the commission imposed the tax. Objections to the tax were expressed by pro-education groups disappointed that some of the tax revenues were not earmarked for schools. Even Commissioner Guy Guckenberger, a plan supporter, expressed concern over the decision to deny voters a direct voice. But it was well understood that Brown opposed a referendum. The Bengals' owner believed a tax increase would not be approved if left to the voters. His opinion was supported by poll results and the tone of public opinion. On July 26, Commissioners Bedinghaus and Guckenberger voted yes and Dowlin voted no, exactly as expected. The issue passed and was initially scheduled to take effect on October 1.

The Referendum

The political leaders had reached a solution, but in doing so, had stifled citizen participation. Poll results and the tone of public opinion indicated that citizens were unhappy about the county's decision. They decided to force a referendum. The pro-stadium faction was well organized with clearly defined money interests. The antitax faction was poorly organized, poorly funded, but at the outset appeared to have the votes to win. Yet, through a professional and well-financed campaign that included an economic impact study, the pro-stadium faction was able to change voters' minds.

The Repeal Movement

The tax-repeal group mobilized quickly. By law, they had until the end of August (a little more than one month) to obtain the required 27,000 signatures on each of two separate petitions if the public was to have a vote on the tax. The afternoon that county commissioners approved the tax, lawyer Tim Mara ordered 2,000 petitions printed to start the campaign. Members of the repeal movement were optimistic, but no tax-repeal referendum had ever succeed in the county's history.

The response to the petition drive was substantial. More than 700 volunteers helped collect signatures. After only one week, 17,000 of the approximately 54,000 signatures needed were already in hand.[11] Halfway through the drive, the Citizens for Choice in Taxation had 25,000 signatures. By the end of the third week of the drive, the antitax group had more than 58,000 signatures. By the last day of the drive, Mara turned in a total of 160,000 signatures between the two petitions. It was to be official: the people would get to vote on the tax. The referendum was set for March 19, 1996, along with the presidential primary balloting.

Vote Mobilization

Now it was Cincinnati's pro-stadium groups that mobilized. They began studying similar campaigns and the commissioners contracted out an economic impact analysis. Stuart Dornette, a member of the Bengals' law firm, announced the formation of a "grass roots" organization, Citizens for a Major League Future, to combat the antitax group. They arranged for the governor to be the honorary chair. While calling the pro-stadium group "grass roots" may have been cynical, it was very useful in distancing the pro-stadium groups from the monied interests, namely, team owners and the Cincinnati Business Committee, which had so far led the push for the stadiums.

Dornette hired a professional campaign advertising agency, a campaign director, and a pollster. The uphill nature of the pro-stadium group's battle was indicated by a comment by the chief executive officer of the advertising agency. During the job interview, he said that the referendum was impossible to win; it was already lost.[12]

In early November, however, an outside event dramatically altered the way voters looked at the issue. Art Modell, owner of the Cleveland Browns, announced that he was taking his team to Baltimore. He accepted the same basic package from the Maryland Stadium Authority that the Bengals had rejected. Clevelanders were devastated and incensed. For Cincinnati residents, it was easy to see that the door had been opened for the Bengals to move up Interstate 71 to the new stadium Clevelanders had already decided to build.[13] A survey of Hamilton County residents conducted the weekend after the Cleveland announcement confirmed the shift in public opinion.

Early polls indicated that voters liked the property tax relief. They did not care whether the tax increase was 1 cent or ½ cent. However, the new jail was splitting those in support of the stadium. Even Mayor Qualls still wavered on whether to increase taxes to build a jail. Her Democratic support and support from women was critical to widen voter approval for the overall package, and these groups were cool to the idea. Mara's group fought against taxes to support the private business interests of sports teams. Local labor leaders opposed the project until there were stronger assurances that the jobs created would be union jobs. Other local Democrats were calling for a "sunset" provision on the tax to ensure that it would not be collected forever. In response, the pro-stadium campaign experts appealed to Bedinghaus to drop the jail and other public services and focus on the strong pieces: stadiums and property tax relief. After the meeting, Governor Voinovich persuaded Bedinghaus to drop the new jail, emergency service improvements, some of the property tax relief, and half of the tax increase, making the proposal more popular. Thus the referendum was reduced to only a ½-cent increase in the sales tax.

Crunch Time

By January the pro-stadium forces had taken the momentum and began a flurry of activity. The new half-cent sales tax proposal was unveiled. It would raise approximately $50 million a year. While property taxes were still to be rolled back, they would not be rolled back as much. Interestingly, although the tax rollback and other items were cut, the amount dedicated to the stadium remained the same: $35 million.

The pro-stadium campaign team created television advertisements, mobilized volunteers, and erected signs. Fund-raisers were scheduled to give more legitimacy to the idea that it really was a grass roots effort, not one being spearheaded by the business community. Even the governor made one of several appearances in Cincinnati to support the efforts. In the face of this activity, tracking polls indicated that opposition continued to erode. The predominantly African-American Baptist Ministers Conference dropped its opposition, as did the local branch of the National Association for the Advancement of Colored People. In return, set-asides for minority workers were agreed to as part of the construction contracts.

While the local Democratic party was still officially against the plan, most visible leaders were silent, and the opposition of high-profile opponents was lackluster. The grass roots pro-stadium faction held rallies inside major luxury hotels with guest lists that included high-profile politicians, athletes, and local personalities. The poorly funded antitax groups protested outside in the snow. The athletes for the Bengals and Reds were instructed how to respond to questions about the tax. They were told to emphasize how much they liked being in Cincinnati and that they would not want to move. Almost every major media outlet either strongly supported the tax increase or remained silent. Of particular importance was the strong support of WLW, the high-wattage talk/sports format radio station, and the *Cincinnati Enquirer*. Both outlets had financial interests in keeping the teams in the city.

Economic Impacts

Also in January, the University of Cincinnati, Center for Economic Education (CEE), released an economic impact report prepared for the Hamilton county administrator.[14] The fifty-nine-page report (including about thirty pages of technical notes) examined the costs and benefits of the stadium proposal. The report was organized around numerous "talk-

Table 9-3. *Net Effects of a 1/2 Percent Increase in the Hamilton County Sales Tax*

Dollars

Effect on county residents	Amount
Increased revenues	49,352,114
Increased burden	26,157,222
Property tax relief	14,805,634
Residual burden	11,351,634
Net burden per household	33

Source: University of Cincinnati, Center for Economic Education, "The Effects of the Construction, Operation, and Financing of New Sports Stadium on Cincinnati Economic Growth," January 2, 1996, pp. iii, iv.

ing points" that could be used by stadium proponents. Of particular interest were the conclusions regarding the shifting of the sales tax, the impact of construction costs (treated as a benefit), and the overall annual impacts of the stadiums.

Unfortunately, the report was not organized in a way that allowed clear comparisons of the benefits and costs. On the one hand, the political jurisdiction used for estimating the tax cost was Hamilton County. The relatively small geographic size of Hamilton County allowed the proponents to argue that the costs of the sales tax increase could in large part be shifted to noncounty residents and was therefore small from the perspective of Hamilton County residents. On the other hand, the entire Cincinnati Consolidated Metropolitan Statistical Area (CMSA)—a thirteen-county area—was used in calculating benefits.[15] Therefore, the local spending, direct economic benefits, and the multiplier were much larger than they would have been had Hamilton County remained the geographic unit of analysis. Furthermore, no effort was made to discount future benefits and costs. Hamilton County voters had no basis for estimating their economic benefits. Nevertheless, the CEE report established a prima facie plausible case that the stadiums would generate economic gains for the region and possibly Hamilton County.

SHIFTING COSTS. The CEE analysts reported that the cost of the sales tax to Hamilton County residents would be small because much of the sales tax burden would be shifted to nonresidents. In support of the shifting argument, the CEE analysts used sales data, population estimates for surrounding counties, and license plate surveys conducted at Hamilton County shopping areas. The extent of the shifting can be seen by the analysis summarized by table 9-3.

Table 9-3 shows that $49.35 million would be collected annually. However, the report's authors estimated that only $26.16 million of the revenue would come from Hamilton County residents, and of that amount $14.81 million was to be returned to Hamilton County residents in the form of a property tax rebate. Thus the net burden of the stadiums would be only $33 per household, by their methodology.

A critique of the CEE report released by Citizens for Choice in Taxation questioned the shifting assumption on several technical grounds.[16] There was no discussion of potential job loss from individuals shopping out of the county or of the deadweight costs of tax avoidance, factors that would increase the tax burden. More important, the rebuttal report charged that by combining the method of finance and the cost of the project, the true cost of the stadiums (that is, the opportunity cost) was hidden. For instance, if the stadiums were not built and the sales tax revenues used solely for property tax relief, the total burden to households would change from a burden of $33 per household (see table 9-3) to a net benefit of $63 per household, a $96 turnaround. In other words, the actual annual burden of the stadiums was $96 per household ($33 + $63). In terms of opportunity costs, the $96 represents the per household opportunity forgone. By failing to isolate the cost of the stadiums and ignoring the opportunity costs, the true project costs were obscured.

In defense, the CEE analysts might argue that it was proper to combine the method of finance and the stadiums because they are inseparable. There could be no stadiums without the sales tax. But more important, there could be no sales tax/property tax relief without the stadiums. Perhaps politicians would have never proposed the sales tax/property tax relief plan without the stadiums issue to generate support even if it would have generated major benefits for Hamilton County residents.

The proponents of the stadiums appear to have either been uncomfortable with the shifting argument or did not understand it. Days before the Citizens for Choice in Taxation rebuttal report was released, the sales tax increase was reduced from 1 cent to ½ cent. Part of the property tax relief and other community projects were dropped, while the funds going to the stadiums remained the same. Consequently, the proportion of revenues for property tax rebate declined, the proportion for the stadiums doubled, and the burden to the average Hamilton County resident actually *increased*. In effect, the change suggested that a proposal with a larger burden per Hamilton County household (according to the CEE

Table 9-4. *Impacts of Stadium Construction*

Millions of dollars

Impact	Stadiums	Parking	Infrastructure	Total
Direct spending	407.90	75.90	36.00	519.80
Local spending	367.11	68.31	32.40	467.82
Indirect impact	525.48	91.90	45.47	662.39
Total economic impact	892.59	160.20	77.87	1,130.66
Household earnings	296.33	52.11	24.78	373.23
Number of jobs	14,648	2,582	1,231	18,461

Source: University of Cincinnati, Center for Economic Education, "The Effects of the Construction, Operation, and Financing of New Sports Stadium on Cincinnati Economic Growth." January 2, 1996, p. 14.

study) had a greater likelihood of success: an assumption that implicitly denies the rational, self-interested voting model.

The CEE study also examined the impact of the combined sales tax increase/property tax rollback by income class. The authors concluded that if income were defined as current earnings, the proposal was very regressive, placing a relatively heavy burden on the poor. Among renters, for instance, the lowest fifth of the income scale would experience a tax increase of 0.82 percent compared with 0.18 percent for upper-income renters. A similar but less regressive pattern applied to homeowners. The use of lifetime income reduced but did not eliminate the regressivity.[17]

IMPACT OF NEW STADIUM CONSTRUCTION. Public discussions of the stadiums emphasized the economic impacts more than the issues of shifting. The title of the CEE's section on stadium construction emphasized "economic growth." The fact that the impact was temporary was mentioned in the text, but then was passed over. Table 9-4 shows the estimated impact of the construction projects on the Cincinnati CMSA. Both the geographic area that would receive the spending and the multiplier effects were determined using the thirteen-county CMSA. Consequently, local spending and the multiplier were much greater than if only Hamilton County was considered. Unfortunately, the use of the CMSA as the unit of analysis ensured that the jobs and income derived from the project were never examined for the political jurisdiction whose citizens had to pay the tax.

The estimates of direct local spending by construction contractors were based on "best guesses." Since the configurations and needs of the stadiums were unknown, there were no engineering plans. At the time of the report, there were not even conceptual renderings. But since project spending was expected to reach $520 million, the authors of the report probably estimated how $520 million would be spent on an archetype or a previously constructed stadium. Neither the costs nor the sectors supplying the inputs were known exactly.

Derived spending was based on the RIMS II multiplier for the CMSA. The RIMS II methodology allows researchers to consider different impacts from alternative sectors. For instance, the corresponding effects of a dollar spent on landscaping will be different from a dollar spent on direct construction. A major problem with the CEE technique is that it requires the assumption that there are no supply-side constraints to growth. Theoretically, it is a disaggregated export-base model. Thus increases in employment in one sector will not cause employment to decrease in another in this model. In other words, the model assumes that the contractors and construction workers hired would have been unemployed if not for the stadium project or, alternatively, the model assumes a perfectly elastic supply of resources within the Cincinnati region. This assumption is difficult to support at a time when the unemployment rate for the region was less than 5 percent.[18]

The CEE study estimated that 90 percent of the construction work would be done by area residents. No justification for this critical assumption was given in the report. In fact, if both projects were to come on line at about the same time or if other local construction projects were built, a much higher proportion of the construction work would probably go to outside firms.

Perhaps the greatest problem with the study's measure of stadium impact was that construction spending was treated as though it was being financed by funds coming into the area. In fact, almost all of the funds will come from within the area in the form of increased taxes (which will lead to reduced spending) or from the Cincinnati share of state capital project funds. Thus stadium spending will simply crowd out private spending. Even the state's anticipated contribution will likely simply displace state aid for other projects.

ANNUAL IMPACT OF NEW STADIUMS. The CEE report assumed that if the referendum did not pass both teams would immediately leave the area. Therefore the report's authors calculated the benefit of the two stadiums as the sum of (a) the current impact of Riverfront Stadium, (b) the increased spending from two new stadiums even if there were no new events, and (c) the economic losses from Cincinnati area residents going elsewhere if the teams were to leave. We examine each of these assumptions in turn, along with the CEE's "bottom line."

What was the impact of the existing Riverfront Stadium? The annual operating expenditures were derived as the sum of operations spending, visiting fan spending, and spending from other outside sources. No effort was made to distinguish that portion of the operating expenses that were funded through local spending as opposed to nonlocal spending. To the extent that operating expenses represented a pass-through of dollars that would have been spent for some other local enterprise (for example, a movie), the economic impact should have been reduced. When the RIMS II multiplier was applied to local spending, the total economic impact came to $244.94 million a year. The total impact, in turn, translated into $76.21 million in household earnings and 5,757 jobs. There was no discussion regarding the quality of the jobs created, but the annual earnings per job were estimated to be about $13,238, according to the CEE figures. Although there was no discussion of how local expenditures were distinguished from import spending (dollars flowing out of the area), it appears that player salaries were counted as local spending in spite of the fact that, as noted in chapter 1, most professional players do not tend to spend locally.

Visitor spending for the 1995 season was estimated on the basis of a survey of 651 persons attending Reds' and Bengals' games. According to survey findings, about 50 percent of attendees and about 35 percent of fans using season tickets came from outside the "Greater Cincinnati" area; about 80 percent of the out-of-town fans stated that the primary reason for being in "Greater Cincinnati" was to see the game; average spending before and after games was $13.00 for baseball fans and $16.34 for Bengals attendees; about 75 percent of fan spending was spent directly in "Greater Cincinnati"; and about 76 percent of out-of-town attendees stayed overnight.[19]

In general, the CEE survey concluded that visitor spending accounted for a total economic impact of $66 million annually. Reds fans spent $28 million per season; Bengals fans spent $4 million. The difference is largely due to the greater number of baseball games played, offsetting the larger per game spending attributable to the Bengals.

Media spending from other cities is also attributable to professional sports events and generates export earnings for the community. Media

Table 9-5. *Estimated Impact from Current Riverfront Stadium*

Millions of dollars

Impact	Operations	Visitors	Total
Local spending	98.00	45.24	143.24
Indirect impact	57.01	44.69	101.70
Total economic impact	155.01	89.94	244.94
Household earnings	48.71	27.50	76.21
Number of jobs	3,533	2,224	5,757

Source: University of Cincinnati, Center for Economic Education, "The Effects of the Construction, Operation, and Financing of New Sports Stadium on Cincinnati Economic Growth," January 2, 1996, p. 16.

spending was estimated with the assistance of area television stations and data from broadcasting research reports. The CEE authors concluded that media brought $2.82 million into the area annually. Their total local spending model adjusted direct spending to provide a total media economic impact of $4.84 million, earnings of $1.35 million, and seventy jobs. No deduction was made to account for possible monetary outflows when the Cincinnati media travels outside the area to cover any games and related events.

Local spending generated by other Riverfront events such as concerts was also estimated, but based on a much looser set of assumptions. The resulting estimate was also included in the impact projection. These monetary inflows probably would have occurred in any case because there are numerous alternative venues in the area. Table 9-5 shows the estimated economic impact of Riverfront Stadium for the various sources.

What increased spending would occur as a result of the new stadiums? After estimating the current impact of Riverfront Stadium, the consultants estimated the increased spending that could be attributed to hosting nearly the same events in the proposed new stadiums rather than in Riverfront. Understandably, the methodology regarding how to determine the increased spending in the region was not rigorous. The questions required speculation and there is no known methodology that could provide a precise answer. The CEE authors depended heavily on a report prepared by the Baltimore Department of Planning concerning the impact of Oriole Park at Camden Yards, which opened in 1992.[20] The Baltimore report concluded that, because of the new ballpark, local attendance rose by 500,000, and out-of-town visitors to the park more than doubled.[21] About 35 percent of all Baltimore fans combined their trip to the ballpark with other downtown activities, and this activity generated more than $14 million. The downtown findings were important to emphasize because many stadium proponents argue that the stadiums will generate important externalities for the Cincinnati central business district. More significantly, the Baltimore report indicated that fan spending increased 144 percent after the Orioles moved to the new ballpark.

On the basis of the Baltimore study, league averages, and fragmentary evidence from the newly opened Jacobs Field in Cleveland, the CEE report arrived at a series of assumptions that led the authors to a final estimate of the expected increase in economic activity to be generated by the new stadiums without new events. These assumptions forecast the following increases: spending on stadium operations, 50 percent; operating expenditures of the Reds and Bengals, 12 percent; expenditures for stadium maintenance and operations, 50 percent; concession expenditures, 60 percent;[22] fan spending, 15 percent; and attendance, 15 percent for the Reds and 20 percent for the Bengals.

The heavy reliance on the Baltimore report suggests a possible cumulative bias in sports impact reports. One inaccurate report can become input into other impact studies. The Baltimore report and other reports used by the CEE authors may or may not have been accurate (we do not know), but many are written for clients with definite positions they want supported. They are not refereed, and there is at least the possibility of bias. Rarely do the proponents or the opponents of various impact studies take (or have) the time to consider the accuracy and evaluate the methodology of previous reports. Evaluating the methodology of previous reports is also difficult because it often requires information not made explicit in the reports. Both sides tend to pick and choose information from previous sports studies that is useful at the moment.

The increase in attendance projected by the Baltimore study was assumed to be permanent, not a novelty effect of people wanting to go to an event primarily to see a new facility. Other evidence has suggested that the new-stadium effect weakens over time, as argued by the Citizens for Choice in Taxation.[23]

What if Cincinnati fans spend money out of town? Another loss, according to the CEE report, is that some Cincinnati residents would travel elsewhere to see games if both teams left the area. Perhaps they would travel to Indianapolis (about a two-and-a-half-hour drive one way) to watch professional football. The loss to Cincinnati would be greater if the Reds or Bengals located in an area nearby but outside the Cincinnati area, such as Columbus, Ohio, or Louisville, Kentucky.

The CEE analysts estimated that 0.24 percent of Cincinnati CMSA residents would travel outside the area to attend a baseball game and 0.34 percent would travel to attend a football game. The estimates were based on behaviors of visitors to Cincinnati professional sports events as a proportion of their city of origin. Consequently the estimates were highly speculative. It was not known whether either team would leave or where they might relocate. Furthermore, Cincinnati has many other professional and college sports events that do not exist in the smaller towns and cities where many visitors to the Cincinnati games reside. Consequently, Cincinnati residents might be less likely to travel to see a game than someone living in a city with fewer options. Nevertheless, the region's loss due to this factor was estimated at 762 jobs and $9.34 million in household income.

What was the CEE bottom line? The CEE study suggested a total of 7,645 jobs would be created or saved from the stadium investment. This figure is far too high, for it fails to take into account the fact that sports spending crowds out local private spending and also assumes that the teams would relocate immediately. The CEE estimate translates into a cost of about $68,000 per job on the basis of a $520 million sports project. In contrast to this high cost per job, the cost per job created by state economic development programs is about $6,250 per job.[24]

AN ALTERNATIVE PERSPECTIVE. It is now time to reestimate the impacts of Riverfront by retracing as closely as possible the steps followed in the CEE report. We use the methodologies suggested in chapter 1 by Roger Noll and Andrew Zimbalist and avoid double-counting and other problematic techniques. Unfortunately, some information necessary for this alternative approach is not available in the CEE report. In these instances, plausible estimation techniques can be used to fill the gaps.

The Noll and Zimbalist approach is much more straightforward than the winding CEE approach. Noll and Zimbalist suggest that impact studies should focus on monetary inflows into the area, the income created by the inflows, and the additional consumption made possible due to the increased income (the multiplier).

Construction Impact. Almost all of the money to build the stadiums will come from within the Cincinnati CMSA. Even state money will, for the most part, be deducted from the area's share of state capital aid. In addition, the construction jobs and income will be temporary, and con-

Table 9-6. *Recalculated Visitor Spending, 1995*

Visitor statistic	Reds	Bengals
1. Attendance per game	33,000	55,000
2. Out-of-area visitors (%)	53	46
3. Number visitors/game [(1) × (2)]	17,490	25,300
4. Number home games	81	10
5. Number fan visits/year	1,416,690	253,000
6. Spending before and after game, per person	13.00	16.34
7. Gross annual monetary inflow (millions)	18.42	4.13
8. Fans in area for game (percent)	.80	.80
9. Monetary inflow due to game [(7) × (8)] (millions)	14.73	3.31
10. Visitor/fan spending in Cincinnati area (percent)	.80	.72
11. Net visitor monetary inflow (millions)	11.79	2.38
Total visiting/fan spending:	14,168,057	

Source: University of Cincinnati, Center for Economic Education, "The Effects of the Consruction, Operation, and Financing of New Sports Stadium on Cincinnati Economic Growth," January 2, 1996, pp. 18, 43.

struction employment is already high. Accordingly, the impact of construction will be near zero.

The Impact of Existing Riverfront. Money flowing into the area as a result of the existing sports infrastructure was divided into spending by visitor/fan, team operations, visiting teams, media, and additional events at Riverfront. The CEE study estimated a combined impact of $76.21 million in annual household earnings and 5,757 jobs.[25]

—Visitor/fan spending was derived on the basis of average attendance, the percentage of out-of-area visitors per game, number of games, average spending per game, and the percentage of the game attendees in town for other purposes. The data for all of these factors were taken from the CEE report. Table 9-6 shows the details of the calculation in terms of gross monetary inflows (not income). No multiplier has yet been applied.

—Spending on the operation of Riverfront and the teams also contributed to jobs and income. We make important modifications to the CEE study here. First, only that portion of operations spending attributable to out-of-area sources is included in the impact. Operations spending that originated from local sources is considered displacement rather than a net monetary inflow. Second, the CEE study counts player and coach salaries as local spending, yet the salaries do not tend to create income for Cincinnati area residents. In the alternative estimation, only 50 percent of player salaries is counted as local spending because of the deferred nature of salaries, the out-of-area residents of the majority of players and families, and the high savings rate attributable to the need to save after short careers. Consequently, most salary expenditures do not help the local economy. The 50 percent deduction from player salaries for out-of-area spending is probably too low. Similar adjustments should be made to the salary of coaches and other staff, as well as out-of-area operations (pre-season training), but the data required for accurate adjustments are not available (see table 9-7).

—Media spending constituted another source of monetary inflow. In contrast to the CEE study, we make an adjustment for out-of-town spending by Cincinnati sports/news teams. We deduct 33 percent of media spending from the CEE estimates of these inflows to account for Cincinnati coverage of out-of-area Reds and Bengals events. The calculations are detailed in table 9-8.

—Visiting team spending was also counted in the CEE study. In our alternative estimation, it is considered zero since the home team plays about as many games away as at home. Ideally, the expenditures should have been deducted from operations, but since the exact amount of spending was not known, this approach accomplishes the same result.

—Other events were estimated to contribute $4.80 million in monetary inflows due to concerts and similar events held at Riverfront. However, sites for such events in other public stadiums and university halls are ample in the area. It seems unlikely that an event would not be held in Cincinnati for the lack of a facility. Accordingly, no net monetary inflow was credited to the presence of Riverfront in our alternative approach.

Total monetary inflows attributable to the current Riverfront Stadium are summarized in table 9-9. These inflows are not the same as income since a significant level of spending flows outside the area immediately, to purchase inventories and other items that do not create local income. The CEE report indicated that on average each dollar of monetary inflows created $0.31 in income.[26] Accordingly, monetary inflows based on our alternative methodology can be estimated to generate income of $17.96 million ($57.95 million × 0.31).

The multiplier will act on the initial income increase as money is spent and re-spent in the area. The average multiplier for operations, visitors, and media within the region was 1.7.[27] Therefore, we estimate the total economic impact of monetary inflows resulting from the current Riverfront to be $30.54 million ($17.96 million × 1.7). Setting the average ratio of income to jobs at $13,238,[28] we attribute an estimated 2,307 jobs to Riverfront under the alternative perspective. The CEE report esti-

Table 9-7. Recalculated Operations Spending

Millions of dollars

Operations spending	Reds	Bengals
1. Total[a]	64.90	52.90
2. 50% of player salaries[a]	23.20	17.95
3. Local spending [(1) - (2)]	41.70	34.95
4. Stadium spending by local fans (displaced from region)[b]	24.98	9.79
5. Net monetary inflow due to team [(3) - (4)]	16.72	25.16
Total net local spending:		41.89

	(1) In-stadium spending[c]	(2) Fan/ games[d]	(3) Total in-stadium spending	(4) Number of games	(5) Total spending (3 × 4)	(6) Percentage local[e]	(7) Local spending (5 × 6)
Reds	17.12	0.03	571,052	81	46.26	.54	24.98
Bengals	38.31	0.05	2,082,148	10	20.82	.47	9.79

a. "Suite Deals," *Financial World*, May 9, 1995, p. 47.
b. Gate receipts from *Financial World*; local fans from University of Cincinnati, Center for Economic Education, "The Effects of the Construction, Operation, and Financing of New Sports Stadium on Cincinnati Economic Growth," January 2, 1996, p. 43.
c. Ibid., p. 42.
d. Ibid., p. 18.
e. Ibid., p. 43.

Table 9-8. *Media Spending*

Media spending	Reds	Bengals
1. Per person per game	185.76	185.76
2. Times number of attendees per game	17	87
3. Total per game [(1) × (2)]	3,158	16,161
4. 3d party hires per game	25,800	31,992
5. (3) + (4)	28,958	48,153
6. Times number of games	81	10
7. Annual monetary inflow [(5) × (6)]	2,345,598	481,530
Total	2,827,128	
Deduction for Cincinnati media out-of-area spending @ 33%	932,948	
Net monetary inflow	1,894,180	

Source: Author's calculations and University of Cincinnati, Center for Economic Education, "The Effects of the Construction, Operation, and Financing of New Sports Stadium on Cincinnati Economic Growth," January 2, 1996, p. 41.

mated that Riverfront would produce $76.21 million in household earnings and 5,757 jobs.[29]

At the same time, the CEE study implicitly assumed that if the stadiums were not constructed both the Reds and Bengals would leave the area almost immediately. Alternative possibilities were never discussed in the report. Yet there are several reasons to believe that even if the referendum failed, the Reds would have remained in the area. First, they were committed to a lease that did not expire until 2010.[30] Second, even when they made overtures to find another site, the Reds looked within the Cincinnati area. Finally, many considered it highly unlikely that Major League Baseball would allow the Reds to leave the area. Therefore, an equally probable loss might be about one-third of the previously estimated loss because the Bengals impact is about one-third of the total sports impact. If the Reds remained in the area, the total loss if the

Table 9-9. *Comparison of Annual Monetary Inflows*

Millions of dollars

Monetary inflow	Alternative	CEE estimate
Operations	41.87	98.00
Fan/visitors	14.17	33.00
Media	1.89	2.83
Visiting team	0	4.62
Other	0	4.80
Total	57.95	143.24

Source: Author's calculations and University of Cincinnati, Center for Economic Education, "The Effects of the Construction, Operation, and Financing of New Sports Stadium on Cincinnati Economic Growth," January 2, 1996, pp. 37, 39, 41, 44.

Table 9-10. *Impact on Cincinnati of Two New Stadiums under Alternative Methodology*

Impact	Income	Jobs
Current Riverfront impact	30,538,762	2,307
× 20 percent impact	.20	.20
Total increase	6,107,752	461

Source: Author's calculations.

referendum failed would be $10.18 million in income and 769 in jobs. At the very least, the estimated losses to the area should have been discounted to reflect that they would not occur immediately.

Economic Impact from New Stadiums. The CEE estimated a 20 percent increase in spending due to the new stadiums even without new events.[31] The estimate was not based on rigorous analysis and none exists for exact estimates. Nevertheless, if the percentage increase suggested by the CEE report was applied to the Riverfront impact under our alternative approach, even assuming the immediate loss of the Reds, increases from the new stadiums reach only $6.11 million and 461 jobs, substantially less than the CEE estimates. The results are presented in table 9-10.

Induced Outside Spending. Spending out of the Cincinnati area would occur if the Reds and Bengals left the area and local residents traveled to games outside the area. The CEE report estimated this lost impact as $9.34 million in income and 762 in jobs. If the Reds did not leave, the lost impact would be reduced by two-thirds, to $3.22 million in income and 254 in jobs.

Comparison. Using the alternative approach total, the passage of the referendum is estimated to have an impact of 3,530 jobs (2,307 for Riverfront, 461 for forgone increased spending, and 762 for induced outside spending) *if* both the Reds and Bengals left the area immediately. This amounts to 3,530 jobs, and given the stadium costs of $520 million, the cost per job would be more than $147,000. Assuming the Reds would remain in the area if the issue failed, the jobs created or saved would drop to about one-third of 3,530 or 1,177. In this case, the cost per job would be more than $440,000. In contrast, the CEE study estimated 7,645 jobs, a cost of about $68,000 per job for jobs that will pay substantially less on average.

IMPACT OF THE IMPACT STUDY. The CEE study received significant publicity, although only the general conclusions were discussed in the press.

In letters to the editor and various local talk shows, the total economic impact numbers generated by the CEE study received more attention than the response of the Citizens for Choice In Taxation, which tended to be conceptual and methodological and did not contain original numbers or survey data. Because it included double-counting and money pass-through in the "total impact," the CEE report has little meaning in terms of welfare compared with job creation or income changes; but "impact" was the largest and therefore most impressive number.

The press covered the highlights of both reports but made no attempt to discuss the methodology or even to frame the issue in a rational manner so that costs and benefits could be compared. Because of the way the press reported the studies, citizens were not given the details they needed to reach an informed conclusion regarding the economic merits of the public investment in those sports stadiums. Each side was allotted short sound bites: the pro-stadium faction could cite some numbers, and the opposition could point to flaws.

Did the CEE impact study and the Citizens for Choice in Taxation response have a significant impact on decisionmaking? No one knows for sure, and that will probably keep the impact consulting industry going. The role of economists in wrongful death and injury lawsuits may serve as a metaphor for understanding the influence of impact reports. In a situation where a jury is contemplating a settlement for a wrongfully injured person, it will probably have to listen to conflicting testimony from experts regarding lost wages and future medical costs. Conflicting experts might be difficult for jurors to understand. What the jury would also see, however, is a plaintiff who may be crippled, in pain, or facing a shorter life expectancy. Empathy for the plaintiff, the jurors' views about what constitutes a fair settlement, their own view of how their vote will reflect on them, and other intangibles would probably weigh more heavily than an economist's discounted earnings estimate. Similarly, the remaining weeks of the Cincinnati campaign suggested that the key issues were what the referendum outcome would mean for the community, whether the subsidy was fair, and whether citizens wanted to live in a "major league city." For many people, narrow self-interest was obfuscated by the politics of meaning.

March to the Finish

On February 1 television aired the first advertisement, entitled "What Makes a Major League City?" It was obvious from the start that the public relations campaign was to be fought primarily on emotional grounds, and secondarily on economic grounds. Although the ad did not make much difference in the polls, it confirmed that men were particularly interested in the economic impacts related to the teams.[32] Unfortunately, from a public policy perspective, no one was clarifying or seriously discussing how the economic growth potential related to the investments.

The tax opponents were being vastly outspent during the critical month of February and lacked the resources needed to counter the pro-stadium media effort. The pro-stadium advocates released another media spot with Mayor Qualls spreading the word that "It's not about sports. It's about Cincinnati." That spot pushed support firmly over the halfway point in the polls by attracting more women into the pro-stadium camp.

Everything was going smoothly for the pro-stadium forces until shortly before the election, when Marge Schott was quoted as asking why Mike Brown really thought the Bengals needed a new stadium. The comment had an impact on the polls a few days later: they again fell below the 50 percent approval level.

Schott further hurt the cause when, on March 8, she angrily announced that the city was trying to collect more than $3 million in rent from her when it owed her an even larger sum under an agreement she said she reached in a previous settlement with the city (supposedly the direct subsidy for the Reds to keep them on par with the subsidy to the Bengals). Schott stated that another $4 million would be due on April 15, 1996, and she would withhold the rent payment until after she received her subsidy. The statements made her seem greedy in the light of the money Hamilton County residents were being asked to commit.

As the referendum approached, two events shored support for the stadiums. First HOK Sports released sketches of the stadiums. Although the artist's renderings were conceptual guesses, not architectural plans, they gave the clear impression to voters that the sports project was a concrete idea. Second, Brown announced that the Bengals would contribute $25 million to $35 million to the project cost over twenty years. Brown's announcement was not a legal commitment, but it served to increase popular support. The pro-stadium campaign quickly built a TV spot around the gesture. Not long after, the polls again crawled safely above the 50 percent mark.

On March 19, armed with surprisingly little information, voters cast their votes. They did not know what the stadiums would look like, since there were no real plans. They did not know how much the stadiums would cost without those plans. Few voters had any idea about the economic development impact or monetary costs and benefits. Those voters who followed the issue realized that neither team had committed itself to staying in the new facilities and that neither team nor the business community had actually committed any money to the project. However, and most important, voters believed that without passing a tax increase to commit themselves to build stadiums for the Bengals and the Reds, they would lose their home teams and become a less respected American city.

The turnout was heavy by primary standards and the stadiums proposal passed easily with 61.4 percent in favor. The ½ cent increase in the sales tax was passed; 70 percent of it was earmarked for paying stadium costs and the remaining 30 percent was intended to offset a property tax rollback. The tax took effect June 1, 1996, with the stipulation that if neither team had signed a lease by June 1, 1997, then the tax would automatically be rescinded.

Postscript: Uncomfortable Details and the Long Morning After

After the vote, the rhetoric subsided substantially and negotiations moved behind closed doors. Schott made clear her intentions to have the county build the Reds' new stadium first. When asked how much she was going to contribute to the costs, she said she would pay something but as late as the following November had yet to elaborate on a figure. The Bengals were far more aggressive in the months following the vote. The team contributed $300,000 to the $1 million "grass roots" campaign that won the referendum. Brown was involved in hard negotiations with county officials to get the stadium for his team on line.

Other problems surfaced. The state had finally decided how it was going to pay its share of the project. Since the state government had supported stadium projects elsewhere, including some of the cost overruns of Cleveland's Gateway Complex, the capital improvement funds going to institutions of higher education was to be scaled back. In addition, the money that the Cincinnati sports projects received was counted against the city's capital improvements allotment from the state. Consequently, Cincinnati's other capital projects would go unfunded. Cincinnati officials were angered by this because before the referendum, state officials had promised this would not happen.

The public sector problems did not end there. The city police department and the county sheriff's office began a dispute of their own over who would be responsible for policing the new facilities. County commissioners announced in July that the new property taxes for the next year would be 3.8 percent lower as a result of the rollback funded through the sales tax, significantly less that the 4.29 percent cut predicted by the commission before the election.

The franchises were doing quite well financially, though the Reds had been complaining of yearly operating losses of $10 million. According to the 1997 report of franchise values compiled by *Financial World* magazine, the value of the Reds increased 13 percent over the previous two years, up to $95 million. This increase was due in large part to the promise of new stadium revenues. Their value will increase dramatically when the new stadium lease is completed. The value of the Bengals increased 37 percent, to $188 million (6.8 percent and 29.5 percent growth, respectively, when adjusted for inflation).[33]

By the end of July, following the vote referendum, there was yet another problem. Public and team officials could not agree on where to put the new stadiums. Yet again, the Reds and Bengals sparred, since they both wanted the same parcel. County Commissioner Bedinghaus had come out with a plan earlier in May suggesting a football stadium in a different neighborhood several blocks north of the river, on the northeast side of downtown. Brown said no, made comments about slow negotiations, and gently reminded the county officials that he could still move the team. Even with the tax in place, he was threatening to leave. The threat worked, and attention turned to putting the new baseball stadium in the other neighborhood instead, leaving the Bengals on the riverfront property. The Reds organization disagreed with the logic and this issue continued unresolved for several more months.[34]

In August it became apparent that there was some confusion about where the community was going to find a $29 million piece of the project puzzle. County officials were under the impression that this money was to come from the state Department of Transportation *in addition* to the state's 15 percent contribution. Officials in the department did not share this view. By July 1997 this had yet to be resolved. However, the expectation had changed to 15 percent of the construction costs and 60 percent of the road changes and improvements.

By the end of August there was finally some movement on the stadium negotiations, though fitful. The county had almost closed a deal with Cinergy Corporation (a recently created entity from the merger of Cincinnati Gas and Electric with PSI Energy of Indiana) to sell the naming rights of the existing Riverfront Stadium. Before the press conference announcing the deal, however, the Bengals effectively vetoed the plan, saying that they would not print the new name on tickets or use it in public announcements and advertisements until they had reached an agreement with the county on the new football stadium. Thus the naming deal was put on hold.

In early September the county and Bengals had reached an understanding on most of the outstanding issues clearing the way for the Cinergy deal. On September 9, 1996, Riverfront Stadium officially became Cinergy Field. In return for these naming rights, Cinergy Corporation agreed to pay the county $6 million for the right until 2001 or until a new stadium was constructed (plus $25,000 per post-season game of the Reds and $50,000 per post-season game of the Bengals). The deal did not apply to any new stadiums. The county used the money to pay down the outstanding debt on the existing facility.

The next day, the county and the Bengals held a joint press conference announcing that they had reached an agreement on a new football-only stadium that would keep the Bengals in Cincinnati until 2026. The deal outlined the destination of various revenue streams and each party's responsibilities but avoided the issue of location, which the Reds were still holding out on. Even so, the deal did clear the way for the county to begin searching for an architectural firm to begin the actual design process (assuming the location would be resolved at some point). The delays in getting the negotiations to this point and deciding on a location delayed the expected opening date of any new stadium from 1999 to 2000. Thus the Bengals' deal states that they will occupy the new facility on August 1, 2000. The details of the new agreement include the following provisions: $20 million to $24 million in permanent seat licenses to go to the county for construction costs (considered team money contribution);[35] the first $5 million from the sale of naming rights will be given to the county (considered team money contribution); Bengals will pay $11.7 million in rent for the first nine years, then no rent through the end of the lease; proceeds from surcharge of 25 cents per ticket, worth $4 million over the life of the lease, will go to the county; Bengals promise not to play elsewhere without the county's permission and cannot apply to NFL for transfer; ticket, parking, advertising, and concession revenues go to the team; the county is responsible for the costs of maintaining the facility (estimated to be between $2.5 and $7 million annually); the county must sell $20 million in PSLs by April 30, 1997, and the Bengals must sell 50,000 season tickets and 80 percent of the luxury boxes and club seats by the same date (if either condition is not met, the team can back out of the deal); the Bengals have ten-year exclusive right to bring in a professional soccer team, while the county will seek other events for the facility; Bengals can veto site selection of the facility.

As with most lease agreements, this one contained particular details of revenues and responsibilities. The amount of money counted as team contributions ranged from $40.7 million to $44.7 million toward the construction costs of a 70,000-seat facility with 7,500 club seats, 100 luxury suites, and replay screens over each end zone. This was considerably more than the $25 million to $35 million that Mike Brown pledged in the days preceding the referendum vote. In view of the sources of those funds, however, calling them team contributions seems problematic. For one thing, the team claimed that a portion of the money raised from selling the naming rights of a publicly owned facility would be part of the team's contribution, the remainder belonging to the team. The county was responsible for selling the PSLs, but the revenue was considered team revenue, to be turned back over to the county as another piece of the team's contribution. Furthermore, selling PSLs in a city that already had a team has not met with any success before. The team's weak performance on the field during the early part of the 1996–97 season suggested that this source of revenue was not a given and led the owners to find a new head coach for the team in an effort to bolster sales. When the deal was announced, fans were upset at the use of the PSLs, and in October the Bengals decided that the cost of a PSL would have a discounted price based on the length of time a purchaser had held season tickets. This was later changed to a flat 10 percent discount for current season ticket holders.

The process changed somewhat at this point. The negotiations with the Bengals were relatively open, with frequent public updates, compared with the negotiations with the Reds. Talks with the Reds were assumed to be on hold while the Bengals' Memorandum of Understanding (MOU) was put into action as a prelude to a full lease. The only news from the Reds was the occasional attempt to veto site locations. It was not until records became available in July 1997 that the public realized that negotiations with the Reds had been going on while most of the attention was on the Bengals.

After much wrangling, the county commission voted on a site for the new Bengals stadium in early February 1997. The site was located several blocks west of the prized site that both teams were coveting but included a $10 million three-field practice facility next door on the west side. During the site negotiations, the sales campaign got under way in December. By early February, the county had already reached the necessary $20 million in seat license sales, holding up its end of the MOU and beating the April 30 deadline by almost three months. The Bengals did not have as much success meeting the deadline with the luxury suites and club seats sales. However, team officials announced that the deadline was more a way of testing the degree of support for the team and that the Bengals would continue to negotiate under the terms of the MOU.

By May negotiations had become tense because the county had not secured a formal lease agreement with either of the teams. The referendum on the tax passed fourteen months earlier required at least one signed lease or the tax would automatically be repealed. Thus negotiations gained speed quickly, and, after announcing that the team had reached its sales goals of 80 percent of its luxury suites and club seats, the county and Bengals held a press conference to proclaim a new lease arrangement that would keep the Bengals in town at least to 2026. In accordance with a secret agreement made months earlier, the new stadium is to be named for Brown's father, Paul Brown.

Calling it an "average" deal (because the team could not ask the fans or the community for more than that), the Bengals' new lease looks similar to the MOU signed the previous September, with only minor changes. For instance, the original expectation was that the county would sell $20 million to $24 million in seat licenses. It sold $26 million, which it gets to keep as part of the team's contribution to the construction costs. The county keeps all seat license proceeds until August 1, 2000, at which time the team collects that revenue stream. Also, the team did not sell the naming rights and thus forgoes up to $16.7 million in additional revenues, an unexpected decision given the dire financial condition professed by the team when making its original demands for a new stadium.

The problem with the new football stadium is the price. When the Bengals first released the details in early May, it was priced at $288 million, not including the practice facility, land acquisition, design fees, or the costs of moving utility lines. It did include the construction, parking, and plaza costs. The county quickly began negotiating down to its new target price of $240 million. By the time the lease was signed, the price had only dropped to $270 million, which was $100 million higher than the original $170 million advertised at the time of the referendum. In addition, the land needed for the site was appraised at $28 million, and with a fair market value markup, it could reach $34 million. In the original plan, acquisition costs for the entire two-stadium project were expected to be no more than $25 million.

The Reds were relatively quiet during these months, while the Bengals held the headlines and the high ground on the site location decision. However, several meetings taking place behind the scenes were not made public until July 1997. While the Reds continued to demand the favored site and resolutely refused any other, there was a proposal by the team asking for a 45,000-seat stadium costing at least $235 million and including the outline of a lease deal. County officials said several aspects were impossible and made a counterproposal in May for a $220 million facility.

The Reds were not happy with the counterproposal, and rumors again circulated that the team was looking at properties across the river in northern Kentucky. In light of the new Bengals' lease, however, several issues became clearer for the baseball negotiations. First, the Reds relented on the site issues somewhat, but remained adamant about remaining on the riverfront. Again, they cited "long-term concerns" with a nonriverfront site such as Broadway Commons but offered no elaborations. Wedge supporters and Broadway Commons supporters engaged in demonstrations and countered each other with economic impact analyses. But the Reds ignored them and kept to their long-held position.

In July the Reds responded to the county's May proposal by stating again that the new ballpark might not be enough to help them remain competitive and that they had to have a better deal than the Bengals simply because of the nature of baseball in a small market city. In a subsequent counterproposal to the county (which has become the basis for a draft MOU with the team and a basis for a future lease agreement), the Reds still want a 45,000-seat stadium with 50 luxury suites, 3,000 club seats, and an occupancy date of no later than the 2002 season. The stadium is expected to cost $235 million, and the team would need a renegotiated contract until the new stadium opened. The new interim lease would forgive the outstanding $6.5 million in past rent, establish rent until 2000 at $750,000 per year, and drop the rent to $1 a year from 2000 to 2002.

The team indicated that it would pay $30 million in up-front costs for the new stadium (some of which would be generated by county sales of seat licenses) and an additional $2.5 million in annual rent for the first ten years of occupancy. Rent would then drop to $1 a year for the remaining twenty years of the lease. This would yield approximately $60 million of the expected $80 million in team contribution. Furthermore, the team would collect all revenue from baseball and non–baseball events at the ballpark. An HOK consultant report indicated that parking, demolition, land, infrastructure, and "soft costs" for the new ballpark would raise the overall costs another $54 million at the Broadway Commons site, or $85 million at the Wedge site, increasing the overall ballpark cost to between $289 million and $320 million; slightly higher than the $160 million projection at the time of the referendum.

As of the middle of July 1997, sixteen months after the referendum, the county has yet to secure an MOU (much less a lease) with the Reds on a new ballpark. It has not yet agreed on a site for the park either, so true land costs are not known, and a more accurate estimate of the costs is not available. Furthermore, although the Bengals have committed to a long-term lease in a new stadium, its new $270 million price tag is not final until the engineering plans are finished to determine the "guaranteed maximum price." In addition, the price of the football stadium property alone will exceed the expected costs advertised during the referendum campaign by as much as $9 million (not counting the unknown cost of any ballpark property needed). The Bengals are paying more in team contributions than they said before the referendum, but these contributions come from sources that one could easily argue the county should have a claim to anyway. Both teams will be paying rent for the first ten years of their respective lease, but they both have revenues from the new facilities that far exceed their proportion of the burden of building the facilities. All said, it looks as though the total cost of the project will exceed $750 million; it will be more than $200 million higher than the $545 million estimate at the time of the referendum.

To further complicate matters, city and county officials have not stopped bickering. The city has threatened to withhold land for the football stadium unless certain terms are changed in the Bengals' lease, to which county officials reply that the city is just playing election-year politics. The city raised the admissions tax on for-profit entertainment tickets (in order to fulfill its commitment to the city's public schools), and Mike Brown immediately tried to kill it by saying he would not sign any lease if the increase was there. He eventually backed down and the city did not raise the tax as much as it had intended. Brown and Schott continue to butt heads over the ballpark site as well. Other than these minor details, Cincinnati and Hamilton County are poised to stumble into the twenty-first century as a major league city.

Conclusion

This chapter has shown what a small market city like Cincinnati has to go through to be a "major league city" in today's environment of "franchise free agency." The chronology is particularly important in that it illustrates the failure of regional cooperation among public officials at the interstate, intercounty, and intracounty levels. Attention should also be drawn to the flaws in the economic impact report used to support stadium advocates' claims that the Cincinnati project will be a panacea, with its promise of new jobs and a major boom in the local economy. More realistic assumptions that explicitly take into account the monetary inflows and transfers within the local economy suggest otherwise. Indeed, the results they suggest are in stark contrast to those of the optimistic report sponsored by the county commissioners.

Given the modest number of new jobs that will emerge from this massive investment in sports, we conclude that the deal is clearly an inefficient means of creating jobs. As the public relations campaign surrounding the referendum illustrates, however, this investment was not about economic development per se. It was about image. In a county desperately afraid of being perceived as another Louisville, Lexington, Dayton, or Columbus, voters have bought a lot of image . . . at a pretty high price.

Notes

1. Linda Vaccariello, "The Selling of the Stadium Tax," *Cincinnati Magazine*, vol. 29 (June 1996), p. 68.

2. Anthony Baldo and others, "Secrets of the Front Office: What America's Pro Teams Are Worth," *Financial World*, vol. 14 (July 9, 1991), p. 42; Michael Ozanian and Stephen

Taub, "Big Leagues, Bad Business: It's Time to Restructure Major League Sports, Here's Why. And Here's How," *Financial World*, vol. 14 (July 7, 1992), p. 50; Michael Ozanian and others, "Foul Ball," *Financial World*, vol. 11 (May 25, 1993), p. 28; Michael Ozanian, "The $11 Billion Pastime: Why Sports Franchise Values Are Soaring Even as Team Profits Fall," *Financial World*, vol. 10 (May 10, 1994), p. 52.

3. Never were the costs and revenues defined, so the precise meaning of the term "losing money" was never clear. This and the other historical background in this chapter is drawn from various articles in the *Cincinnati Enquirer*, 1993–94.

4. The improvements to Riverfront had to be approved by Reds owner Marge Schott. She later rebuffed City Manager Shirey and withheld her agreement in an effort to win a larger short-term subsidy for the Reds.

5. The work of the Regional Stadium Task Force was underwritten by a grant from the state of Ohio's capital improvements budget in excess of $1 million.

6. At this time, the county still owed more than $25 million on Riverfront. The city's lease payments were the main source of revenue that the county used to pay the debt. Richard Green, "Schott Seeks Riverfront Link: Firm Developing Plans to Cover Riverfront Freeway," *Cincinnati Enquirer*, February 25, 1995, p. B1.

7. The subsidy was justified on the grounds that it covered the lost revenues for the Bengals since Riverfront did not have the luxury suites and other revenue amenities. The renovations were to provide these new revenues, and after that the direct subsidy would end.

8. Vaccariello, "The Selling of the Stadium Tax," pp. 68–74; Richard Green, "City Poll Shows Most Opposed to New Stadium," *Cincinnati Enquirer*, April 27, 1995, p. A4.

9. "Your Taxes Help Put Team Owners on EZ Street," *USA Today*, December 28, 1995, editorial.

10. Cleveland's Gateway Complex ran more than 30 percent over the cost estimated (and promised) without the aid of actual plans.

11. Since the effort was aimed at repealing two ½ cent increases, the antitax group needed to obtain approximately 27,000 signatures on *each* petition for a total of 54,000. Expecting that 40 percent of the signatures would be invalidated, the group targeted twice that number.

12. Vaccariello, "The Selling of the Stadium Tax."

13. Stadiums have high fixed and low marginal costs. Consequently, in negotiations city officials are tempted to give teams the use of such facilities at low or negative costs, which translate into large subsidies in the United States. Today, there is excess stadium capacity as communities have built expecting to attract events. Alternatively, one could make the argument that the cartel nature of the major leagues undersupplies teams. Either way, subsidies result.

14. University of Cincinnati, Center for Economic Education (CEE), "The Effects of the Construction, Operation, and Financing of New Sports Stadiums on Cincinnati Economic Growth," January 2, 1996.

15. The Cincinnati CMSA includes Hamilton, Brown, Butler, Warren, and Clermont counties in Ohio. It reaches into Kentucky's Boone, Campbell, Kenton, Grant, Gallatin, and Pendleton counties. It also includes two Indiana counties: Dearborn and Ohio.

16. John P. Blair, prepared for Citizens for Choice in Taxation, *A Report on the Impacts of Stadia Construction and Renovation Projects on Hamilton County, Ohio*, Cincinnati, Ohio, January 16, 1996.

17. The reason that the use of lifetime incomes reduces regressivity is that the variations in an individual's income from year to year are greater than income variations over a lifetime. Most people have low earning periods when they are young and tend to earn more as they age, peaking in middle age. Lifetime income effectively averages annual earnings.

18. Ohio Bureau of Employment Services, *Labor Market Review, Ohio Labor Market Information*, March 1997.

19. Although the questionnaire asked whether out-of-town attendees stayed in a hotel or motel and how much they spent, the totals were not included in the report.

20. *The Economic Impact of Oriole Park at Camden Yards*, Baltimore City Department of Planning, December 1992. It seems likely that the Baltimore Department of Planning would wish to portray the city-financed facility as a success.

21. For an alternative view, see the discussion in chapter 8.

22. The high concession expenditure seems inconsistent with increased attendance. However, it may be due to assumed enhanced dining amenities.

23. Anthony Baldo, "Edifice Complex," *Financial World*, November 26, 1991, p. 7.

24. Andrew Zimbalist, "The Economics of Stadiums, Teams, and Cities," written testimony, Hearings before the New York State Senate Legislature, New York City, April 25, 1996.

25. CEE, *The Effects*, p. 45.

26. Ibid.

27. Ibid.

28. Ibid.

29. Ibid., p. 16.

30. Ibid., p. 17.

31. If they broke the lease, the substantial buyout and damages Cincinnati would have claimed should have been included as an offset in the CEE study.

32. Vaccariello, "The Selling of the Stadium Tax."

33. The leaky bucket analogy suggests that it often costs the public more money to subsidize an activity than the value received by the party receiving the subsidy. Thus the subsidy leaks from the bucket as it is being carried to recipient. If the increase in the value of the franchises represents the gain to the owners from the subsidy only, then we can conclude that the commitment of a $520 million subsidy from taxpayers resulted in a combined benefit of $36.7 million in the first season following the vote (adjusted for inflation). A leaky bucket, indeed. The owners received only about 7 percent of the subsidy. If a portion of the increase in value of the franchises was due to things other than the subsidy, the percentage of the taxpayer cost going to the team owners would be even less.

34. As of this writing, there still has been no decision on the location of the new baseball facility which has hampered the architectural and engineering plans considerably.

35. Some refer to these as permanent or personal seat licenses. In the sales campaign, the Bengals organization called them Charter Ownership Agreements, or COAs.

10

BEARING DOWN
IN CHICAGO

Location, Location, Location

ROBERT A. BAADE AND
ALLEN R. SANDERSON

Make no little plans; they have no magic to stir men's blood.
—Daniel Burnham

 Chicago may still do justice to Sandburg's description of it as a city of the Big Shoulders, though he might have been dismayed to see local sporting triumphs and tragedies featured regularly on the front page of its daily newspapers and as the lead story on the ten o'clock evening news. Despite all the attention given to sports, until the decade of the 1990s Chicago had few championship banners to hoist and had not heeded the exhortation of another of its famous citizens to make plans that could stir the blood and the soul. But with the opening of "New" Comiskey Park in April 1991, five National Basketball Association titles in the past seven years for the Bulls, and complicated struggles to resolve the Bears' stadium laments, all that has changed. Having bypassed the national construction wave of the 1960s and 1970s in professional sports, Chicago is now having its turn.

This chapter is about the economics and politics of the ongoing debate over a den for the Bears. Unlike other case studies in this volume, the story of the Chicago Bears does not yet have a conclusion. No formal votes were taken in Springfield (in the state legislature or a statewide bond initiative) or Chicago (in the City Council or a referendum). The governor and mayor have not worked out their differences. The Bears have not left town, or the area; and the plan to build a new stadium is still in its formative stages. Thus what we have to say about the recent proposals and their financial aspects, while not completely devoid of empirical content, is, like the situation itself, somewhat fluid and very much "a work in progress." Our discussion begins with a review of the history of the sports franchises and facilities in Chicago. Throughout, we pay close attention to two factors that have greatly influenced the Bears' case: the other commercial and cultural attractions competing for the mayor's attention and the state's money (airports, convention facilities, casinos, and education); and the intertwined politics and personalities in Chicago and Illinois, including their visions for the city and state.

A Brief Tour of Chicago Sports Facilities

Until the 1990s, Chicago boasted some of the oldest stadiums in professional sports in this country. And despite inevitable changes and innovations, as well as significant demographic and economic shifts, most of the city's franchises and facilities have not wandered far from their neighborhood roots. Even changes in ownership have not taken the teams to suburban or more automobile-friendly sites. This does not mean that stadium economics and politics in Chicago is easy to fathom. As the program vendors inside Wrigley or Comiskey like to say, it is hard to tell the players—or the plays—without a scorecard.

Comiskey Park, on the city's South Side (figure 10-1), opened in 1910 and closed in 1990. The first All-Star game was played there in 1933. Shoeless Joe Jackson roamed the outfield, and owner Bill Veeck, with his avant-garde entrepreneurship, entertained some fans and disgusted others. The National Football League's Chicago Cardinals played in Comiskey Park until they left for St. Louis in 1960 (and, later, for Phoenix). With ninety skyboxes and 100 percent public financing, New Comiskey Park opened across the street from the old park in 1991, the first new baseball-only facility since Royals Stadium (now Kauffman Stadium) opened in 1972. It was also the first new sports facility in Chicago since the construction of Chicago Stadium in 1929.

A source of considerable controversy even before it opened—owing mainly to ugly political fights, a credible threat to become the Florida White Sox, and the commitment of $150 million in state bonds to build

Figure 10-1. *Chicago's Loop and Surrounding Neighborhoods*

it—the new ballpark has been savaged in the local press as a "mallpark" with a foreboding upper deck. Surrounded by the Robert Taylor Homes (a two-mile-long public housing development), an expressway, and railroad tracks on the city's South Side, Comiskey's location (probably owner Jerry Reinsdorf's third choice behind suburban Addison and St. Petersburg, Florida) offered few prospects for economic development. Because a local ordinance restricts street vendors, and the White Sox keep all souvenir shops, food emporiums, and a post-game bar within the confines, commercial activity in the neighborhood has been restricted even further.[1]

Privately owned Wrigley Field, originally known as Weeghman Park but renamed for the Cubs' owner, opened on the North Side in 1914. (The ballpark was originally the home of the Federal League's Chicago Whales.) Apart from a manual scoreboard (1937), ivy on the outfield walls (1938), lights (1988), and a few skyboxes (1989), not much has changed inside the park in eight years, other than to say good-bye to the Bears when they moved to Soldier Field in 1970. Outside the park, the Lakeview, Wrigleyville, and surrounding Northside neighborhoods have emerged as vibrant commercial centers and highly desirable places to live. This growth has accompanied Chicago's strong economic development in the past two decades, rather than being a catalyst for it. Despite fielding mediocre teams, the Cubs continue to draw well from these immediate areas and beyond, in part because of the beauty of the park itself, as well as exposure on WGN's national cable channel.

On the West Side, the Chicago Stadium—the Madhouse on Madison—welcomed the Blackhawks when it opened and the expansion Bulls in 1966. For the start of the 1994–95 season, both franchises moved across the street to the United Center, an arena that received some public financial assistance—$30 million for infrastructure and neighborhood amenities—but otherwise was built (at a cost of $175 million) and is operated privately by its two principal tenants, William Wirtz and Jerry Reinsdorf, owners of the Blackhawks and Bulls, respectively. The United Center has a few thousand more seats than the old arena but, more important, it has 216 luxury suites (whereas the Chicago Stadium had only one makeshift cantilevered booth).

Through some financial concessions and good political instincts, the Bulls and Blackhawks were able to fend off neighbors' objections to the inevitable dislocations caused by a larger facility and more asphalt for parking. The arena is located in what has been essentially a crime-ridden, economically depressed area of the city. However, it is too soon to tell if the arena and recent complementary public decisions and events—removal of some public housing in the area (the now-famous Henry Horner Homes), the 1996 Democratic National Convention at the United Center, subventions for businesses to remodel and a city beautification program along Madison Street—have affected or will affect longer-term economic development, and whether they would pass normal benefit-cost tests. In the very short run, bringing game-day concession activity (that is, food and drink, souvenir merchandise) inside the arena, increasing the amount of parking owned and operated by the teams, and enforcing an antivendor ordinance have reduced economic activity in the area surrounding the arena to a trickle.

The city's fourth major stadium is Soldier Field, its main tenant since 1971 being the Bears. The stadium sits on the lakefront south of the Loop and near three of Chicago's main cultural attractions: the Field Museum of Natural History, Adler Planetarium, and the Shedd Aquarium (figure 10-2). It is also close to the city's three-building convention center complex, known collectively as McCormick Place, and a small commuter landing strip, Meigs Field, which Mayor Richard M. Daley recently attempted to close. The relatively small area from the northern tip of the "Magnificent Mile" shopping and hotel centers along Michigan Avenue to McCormick Place to the south, and the Dan Ryan Expressway to the west and Lake Michigan to the east, contains most of Chicago's well-known architectural landmarks, world-class museums, lakefront parks, and convention and trade-show amenities.

The presence of all the facilities just described is an important factor to consider in assessing the impact of professional sports on Chicago's economy. The idea that "if you build it, they will come"—and in large numbers bringing obscene sums of money and other commercial activity with them—does not apply to Chicago. In this case, the location of an individual football stadium, as well as the type of facility (open-air versus dome, natural versus artificial playing surface, and football-only versus major convention facility), has to be seen in the context of a vision of economic development for the entire city, and in the context of the geographic area depicted in figure 10-2. Equally significant are the political climate and the political chess moves that lurk behind the newspaper headlines and the explicit proposals. Tip O'Neill's contention that all politics is local may well apply here; if not, it's still "up close and [very] personal."

Figure 10-2. *Chicago's Museum Campus*

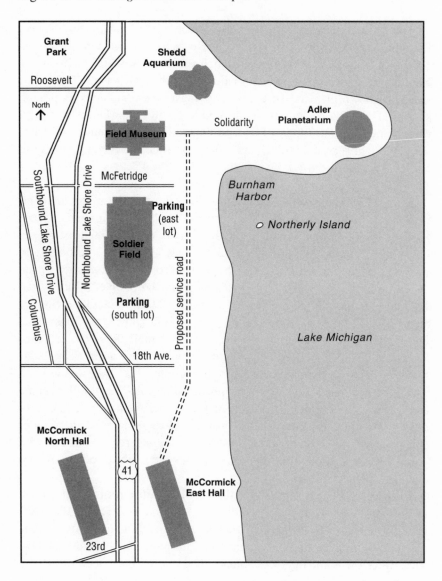

The Bears and Soldier Field

The Chicago Bears originally were formed as the Decatur Staleys. As the name implies, the team resided in Decatur, a city in central Illinois 180 miles from Chicago. A major employer there was the A. E. Staley Manufacturing Company, which made corn syrup and was the defendant in a well-known 1945 antitrust case involving a base-point delivery pricing system. The team became the Chicago Staleys in 1921 when they moved their home games to Wrigley Field. In 1922 the Staleys became the Bears. Wrigley Field served as the Bears' home for almost fifty years, with the last contest there played against the Green Bay Packers on December 13, 1970.[2]

Soldier Field, an open-air stadium built as a memorial to the men and women who served in World War I, opened in 1924 as Municipal Grant Park Stadium; it was renamed a year later. It went up in three stages between 1922 and 1939, and the total cost was $13 million. Soldier Field was not designed to cater to a single sport but to serve as a multipurpose "showcase for events and a playground for all the people."[3] More than 100,000 spectators filled the new stadium in 1927 to watch Gene Tunney, aided by the famous "long count," get off the canvas to defeat Jack Dempsey for the heavyweight boxing title. An equally large crowd heard President Franklin D. Roosevelt deliver a wartime address in 1944. Evanglist Billy Graham addressed a full house in 1962. The site has been used for track meets, concerts, the annual College All-Star football game (until it was discontinued in the 1970s), and the opening ceremonies of the 1994 World Cup. But since 1971—when George Halas, team founder ("Papa Bear" to insiders and followers), signed a three-year lease, with a provision for successive one-year options—the principal tenant has been the Chicago Bears.

Even as the Bears prepared for their six-mile move from Wrigley Field to Soldier Field, Halas was looking at other alternatives in the area, including a return to Wrigley. In the mid-1970s he thought about building a new stadium in Arlington Heights. Periodically, the Chicago Park District, which owns and operates Soldier Field, has proposed adding a dome to the stadium, or building an entirely new stadium on the same spot or at another location in the city. Such proposals surfaced in the late 1960s, even before the Bears arrived there, and again in 1977, 1982, and 1985. In 1980 Halas signed a twenty-year lease for the Bears to play in Soldier Field. In November 1983, following the death of George Halas, his grandson Michael McCaskey became president of the Bears.[4] In 1984 McCaskey began complaining about the Bears' financial situation and the fact all Chicago-area stadiums and arenas were more than fifty years old.

In 1985 the Bears capped off a 15-1 regular season with dominating performances in the playoffs and Super Bowl XX (January 1986). Fortified by the team's success, McCaskey threatened to break the Bears' Soldier Field lease and move to Roselle, an option he did not pursue even though he did enter into a contract to buy 500 acres of land there. Thereupon, Mayor Harold Washington proposed a joint Bears–White Sox facility, a domed stadium to be built not far from McCormick Place and Soldier Field, but McCaskey rejected it. The White Sox, too, had been searching (mainly in the western suburbs) for a new location and a new stadium, to replace Comiskey Park, built in 1910 and the oldest stadium in major league baseball.

Still hoping to be gone from Soldier Field before the end of the 1999 season, when the lease expires, the Bears in 1987 investigated moving to Arlington Heights (beyond O'Hare airport in the northwest suburbs); then they proposed building an open-air, city-subsidized, multipurpose facility near the Chicago Stadium, at the time home to the Bulls and Blackhawks on the city's West Side. This latter proposal, which would have required $90 million in public funds, was received favorably by Chicago's mayors in 1987 (Washington) and 1988 (Eugene Sawyer, following Washington's death), but not by the state legislature (nor by Wirtz and Reinsdorf, much to McCaskey's dismay). In 1988 the legislature, with the strong support of Republican Governor Jim Thompson, provided $150 million in bond financing for the construction of a baseball-only stadium, Comiskey Park, to keep the White Sox from bolting to St. Petersburg, Florida.

In 1990 McCaskey, long an advocate of an open-air, natural-turf facility for his team, agreed to consider, as well as to contribute modestly to, a domed stadium that would be built near McCormick Place. This plan died in the Illinois General Assembly in 1991, in part because of the general feeling that the state had been burned by all of the turmoil and commitments surrounding a publicly financed ballpark for the White Sox. In that same year, Richard M. Daley was elected mayor of Chicago, and Jim Edgar succeeded Thompson as governor.

In 1992 the Park District, hoping to keep the team in the city, offered the Bears more luxury boxes and a better split of Soldier Field revenues. Over the next few years, McCaskey developed a proposal for an open-air stadium. His plan, unveiled in April 1995, called for the state to provide $185 million in bond financing toward the $285 million facility. McCaskey then began to "shop" the plan around suburban sites: Hoffman Estates (where Sears and Ameritech had migrated and opened corporate headquarters), Naperville, Warrenville, West Chicago, Waukegan, Aurora, and other locations around O'Hare. Addison, whose voters rejected a proposal to help relocate the White Sox in the late 1980s, was not considered a viable alternative by McCaskey.

The Bears even went as far as to secure options on parcels of land in Hoffman Estates and Aurora (see figure 10-3).[5] None of these local political entities warmed up to the notion of having their taxpayers provide substantial financial support, and several officials explicitly rejected the Bears' suggestion in this regard. At the same time, the Daley administration proposed three Chicago sites: one old and two new.

As the Bears headed for training camp (in Platteville, Wisconsin) in August 1995, McCaskey announced that a new stadium deal had to be wrapped up within the next few months or he would be forced to consider out-of-state locations for his team. He set December 31, 1995, as the deadline for the city and state to come up with an acceptable alternative. In October Mayor Daley proposed a substantial renovation of Soldier Field, with an initial public price tag of $61 million, which escalated to $171 million within a couple of months. The Bears rejected the mayor's proposal, and any other plan that involved renovating Soldier Field.

About the same time, a prominent development firm, Stein & Co., proposed a "privately financed" domed stadium at or near McCormick Place (quickly dubbed "McDome"). The firm was already managing the McCormick Place extension project and had overseen the construction of the United Center. The 74,000-seat stadium plus land acquisition, parking, and other amenities would cost $350 million. The private financing consisted of luxury box revenues, club seats, personal seat licenses, naming rights, and other venue income, with less taxpayer money than McCaskey's suburban plan.

A third alternative came almost from nowhere in November: Northwest Indiana/Chicagoland Entertainment Inc. ("NICE"), a group with ties to public utilities and other commercial interests, began a serious attempt to lure the Bears to Gary, Indiana, as part of Planet Park, a larger recreational complex being proposed for the area. They offered McCaskey a $312 million open-air stadium, to be financed by local taxes; in February 1996, however, all seven members of the Lake County (In-

Figure 10-3. *A Guide to the Geography of Chicago Sports Facilities*

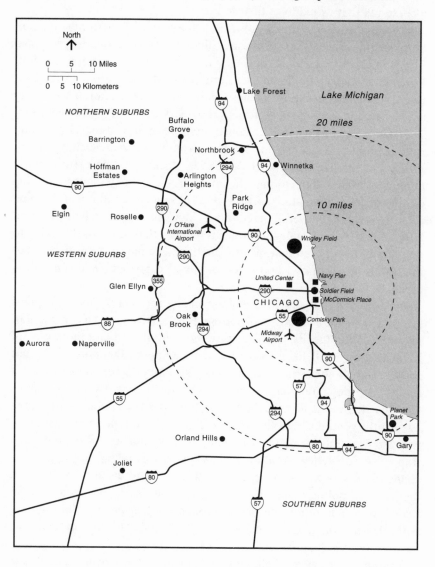

diana) Council voted to reject the 0.5 percentage point increase in the income tax that would have financed it.

Anticipating the eventual political, economic, and environmental collapse of the Planet Park proposal, Illinois Governor Jim Edgar asked McCormick Place officials to work out the details for a domed stadium. Long an advocate of a domed stadium, primarily because he expected it to attract more convention business to the state, Edgar offered McCaskey a $465 million domed-stadium plan near McCormick Place in February 1996. Edgar asked the Bears to contribute $175 million of the $465 million total from in-stadium revenue streams (from luxury suites, club seating, PSLs, and the like). Although McCaskey deemed it "an extraordinary amount to ask the team to pay," he later agreed to think about something on that order of magnitude. At this and subsequent iterations, it became clear that by "that order of magnitude," McCaskey meant a figure around $100 million. Mayor Daley had once remarked that it was like "having to pull teeth" to get even that much from him. The mayor publicly rejected the governor's proposal and stuck by his own Soldier Field renovation plan.

On September 15, 1996, Daley unveiled a retractable dome proposal for Soldier Field, a 73,000 seat stadium for the Bears, and a complementary convention facility. Though seemingly out of the blue, the timing of his plan was in all likelihood related to another contentious (but not sports-related) local-state issue: Daley's plan to seize Meigs Field, a small, lakeside commuter airport, on October 1, 1996 (when the state's fifty-year lease was to expire), and to convert it to a public nature area against the governor's explicit wishes. This tit-for-tat, one-upmanship, or win-win proposal seemed to be giving the governor something the latter wanted—a domed convention facility—while signaling an implicit exchange Daley prized—conversion of an airstrip to a public park. Both men denied publicly that there was any relationship between the two issues. In this iteration the price tag inched up again, to $400 million, with $175 million again penciled in as the Bears' contribution, from the usual stadium-related revenues.

Within two months of the announcement of the mayor's retractable dome plan, revised cost figures, including those for the infrastructure needed to make it accessible to McCormick Place, put the price at $100 million above Daley's publicly stated figure. That nine-figure addendum and convention groups' lukewarm reception to the concept eliminated any lingering enthusiasm for it. But the mayor and McCaskey immediately offered competing alternatives: Daley bid $240 million to modernize Soldier field plus $105 million for an assembly hall west of McCormick Place; McCaskey countered with a new open-air football-only stadium and a high-tech, 20,000-seat meeting hall, though he produced no cost estimates. After the initial announcement, neither plan was ever mentioned again in the press.

Months passed with scant interest in where the Bears would next call home. Then, on March 14, 1997, a front-page *Chicago Sun-Times* headline proclaimed: "McDome Deal Near." Although subsequently denied, or at least downplayed by all camps, the paper reported that Mayor Daley, Governor Edgar, and Bears' owner McCaskey had worked out a plan for a $465 million domed stadium near McCormick Place. The financial aspects were very similar to Edgar's proposal of the year before: $185 million from the Metropolitan Pier and Exposition ("McPier") Authority tourism-related tax revenues, another $55 million in McPier Authority funds for a parking facility and administrative costs, $25 million each from the city and state for land and infrastructure, and $175 million "contributed" by the Bears from the sale of PSLs, luxury boxes, and club seats in the new stadium.

Adding to the seemingly endless iterations and alternatives, in May 1997 Blackhawks' owner William Wirtz and Bulls' owner Jerry Reinsdorf contributed one more. These partners in the privately financed United Center proposed a privately financed $300 million, open-air, football-only home for the Bears on the lakefront. The altruistic aspects include reducing the public subvention from $290 million under a McDome-like plan to direct expenditures of $45 million for land and infrastructure; the self-interest aspects entail fending off competition from a lakefront dome that could siphon off concert, ice show, circus, and other sporting-event revenues from the United Center. Under this plan, the Bears' contribution would be reduced to $100 million (though perhaps only because the principal financial backers would control more of the venue revenues), and McCaskey would get the natural turf, open-air stadium he always favored, albeit at the price of having to be the principal tenant in a facility controlled by two Chicago sports moguls who have been less than amicable toward him over the years.[6] Daley is interested in this plan, in comparison with the McDome alternative, for two main reasons: it would reduce the tax revenues the city would have to provide, and it would offer a way of one-upping Edgar. In Chicago, *plus ça change*!

Financial Underpinnings and Incidence

Two factors have figured prominently in the public debates over what to do for (or to) the Bears: the commitment of $150 million in state bonds to build a new stadium for the White Sox in 1988; and the construction of the $175 million United Center in 1993–94 with private funds (except for the public support for the surrounding infrastructure) from the two principal tenants, Blackhawks' owner William Wirtz and Bulls' owner Jerry Reinsdorf. The Sports Facilities Authority, which operates Comiskey Park, owes $14.65 million each year to bondholders. In addition, it spends another $6 million a year on park administration and maintenance. Revenues come from a 2 percent Chicago hotel tax and rent from the White Sox (which is a stair-step function of attendance).

As noted earlier, even before the first kickoff in Soldier Field against the Steelers on September 19, 1971, the new tenants were already less than thrilled. Subsequently, some modest lease modifications shifted more revenues to the team, but the Bears regard their lease as the worst in the entire NFL.

Never conceived as a venue to watch football, the 100,000-seat bowl was long on seats and short on amenities. Remodeling reduced seating capacity to its current 67,000, but almost two-thirds of the seats are in the end zones. By current NFL standards, there are too few seats, luxury boxes, customer-friendly features (that is, too few rest rooms, food and beverage options, souvenir shops, and museum-like attractions), and player and press facilities. Other than upgrading lighting and seat quality, replacing the artificial playing surface with grass in 1988, and wedging in a few luxury suites, Soldier Field has not changed noticeably over the years. Seven remodeling plans, all with public funds, were implemented between 1971 and 1995. In spite of the alleged stadium deficiencies, an uninviting climate ("Bear weather" to the faithful), and a-win-loss record that has hovered around .500 for the last several years, every home contest has sold out and the waiting list for season tickets is sizable.

With January 1, 2000, fast approaching in Chicago and franchise moves and new construction in other cities, all parties have been thinking seriously about the future of the Bears. Here we summarize the basic features of the proposals that have been put forward in the past two years.

The Owner's Offer

On April 12, 1995, McCaskey unveiled a $285 million plan for a 74,000-seat open-air stadium. Of this amount, $100 million was to come from the Bears and $185 million from the state. The announced figure did not include the cost of land acquisition or infrastructure. Bears' surveys indicate that 60 percent of their season ticket holders live in the suburbs, primarily to the north and west of the city. Consequently, McCaskey indicated a preference for one of three suburban sites: one near O'Hare airport, one in DuPage County, one in Hoffman Estates.

To buttress his case for public support, McCaskey hired Ernst & Young to provide an analysis of the Bears' impact on the Chicago area's economy. It calculated a bottom-line annual impact of $125 million, and $322 million during the construction period.[7] In addition, Bears' operations were expected to generate 872 jobs: 195 full-time, 415 "sustained by related economic activity," and 262 through "trickle down."[8]

Diversions and Sparring

At the same time that McCaskey was roaming the suburbs for parcels of land and political support, the Daley administration countered with three in-town sites. If that was not enough, politically connected developer Richard "Ritchie" Stein complicated everyone's plans and preferences by floating a proposal for an in-town domed stadium near Mc-Cormick Place that allegedly would require relatively little public assistance: "Planners are confident that, using modern stadium financing techniques—including up-front sales of luxury skyboxes and club seats, stadium sponsorships, and permanent seat licenses (PSLs)—to cover construction costs and debt service, the facility could be built with little or no taxpayer money."[9]

Stein's plan called for a 74,000-seat facility, including 200 luxury suites and 10,000 club seats. The price tag was $275 million plus an additional $75 million for land acquisition, parking, and other contingencies. Although officially a dome, the facility was referred to in the plan as having a "portable" grass field. Stein's emphasis on "private" funding immediately put the McCaskey proposal for a publicly financed suburban facility on the defensive. It also put the mayor, who continued to advocate both an open-air facility and the Soldier Field location, on the defensive. Daley accused Stein of "lowballing" his estimate by at least $100 million to drum up political support, a charge with some substance because in 1990 Stein had put forth a first McDome proposal budgeted at $467 million plus $100 million more for land acquisition and parking. The mayor later described the latest project as "astronomically more expensive" than his Soldier Field plan and one that would not work economically.

McCaskey expressly maintained that he was not threatening to move out of the Chicago area, but as the pressure mounted and the deadlines grew closer, that stance changed. In August he stated:

> Four and a half months is all we have left. . . . If it's not looking like it's going to happen in Illinois, or if we get a very attractive offer, then we'll consider something else. . . . We've appealed to the Legislature and the governor and the mayor and said, "Look at the economic contribution and the psychological contribution the Bears make." . . . But as time slips away, you have to consider other alternatives.[10]

That same month, the Bears added another community to their list of non-Chicago options, reserving an option on 207 acres of land in Aurora, a former mill town and now home to riverboat gambling, some high-tech ventures, and the movie *Wayne's World*. The city was willing to consider property-tax abatements as a way of luring the Bears, seeing the franchise as a complementary catalyst for industrial development. "You can't put a price tag on the prestige and recognition that would come with having a major football team," said the director of Aurora's Economic and Development Commission.[11]

Like Addison voters when asked to fund a new White Sox ballpark in the 1980s, most of the suburban areas that the Bears were courting were very willing to put a price tag on prestige. Gayle Franzen, chairman of the DuPage County Board, said it was unlikely that county voters would support a tax increase to generate at least some of the $18 to $20 million annual debt service for the next thirty years: "I don't think there is much support in DuPage County for a local tax support of any kind for a professional team."[12]

Mayor Daley Responds

In October 1995, as the Bears' threats to play elsewhere became uglier and more serious, the mayor suggested Alaska as a location for McCaskey to consider. Daley also unveiled a $156 million reconstruction plan for

Soldier Field. Lowering the field thirteen feet would raise seating capacity to 71,000; the number of skyboxes would be increased from the current 116 to 180; rest room and concession space would more than triple; and other fan amenities such as a high-tech scoreboard and the Bears' Hall of Fame and museum would be added. Earlier, more modest upgrades proposed by the mayor had carried a public price tag of $60 million; in the months that followed Daley's August 1995 announcement, the figure rose from $156 million to $171 million. In addition, the governor agreed to commit $28 million in state funds for necessary public works improvements around Soldier Field to complement the interior renovations.

The mayor's financial plan included selling 15,000 personal seat licenses (PSLs) and assessing annual fees, refinancing $55 million in Park District debt, and issuing $100 million in construction and industrial revenue bonds. McCaskey, with Governor Edgar, gave the plan good marks and indicated a willingness to contribute toward construction expenses. The mayor hinted that the Bears' current lease could be modified to allow them to share in parking and concession revenues. However, no one stated an explicit dollar amount that the Bears would chip in, nor were stadium revenues such as luxury box leases and PSLs credited toward their contribution. Initial estimates suggested that McCaskey could reap $20 million annually from the plan. "This is it," the mayor said. "This is the position we've taken on behalf of Chicago to keep the Chicago Bears here. There's no other way. There's no one walking around with a lot of money in their pockets; let's be realistic. This is our only way to keep the Bears here." [13]

Subsequently, the city made other minor modifications in response to the Bears' review of the plans, including a reconfiguration of some of the luxury seating. It did balk at a $74 million "add-on" that would have rotated the field 90 degrees to get more sideline and fewer end zone seats, which the HOK Sports Facilities Group had proposed to the Bears as early as 1990. But the honeymoon was short: less than two months after calling the mayor's Soldier Field renovation a "bold step," McCaskey denounced Daley's effort as inadequate. While nothing had changed in terms of an attractive financial offer from one of Chicago's "collar-county" suburbs or Springfield, and distant options such as Cleveland or Los Angeles were still considered unrealistic, McCaskey had one new alternative very close to home: Gary, Indiana.

Interstate Commerce

With glossy printed materials and a video presentation, Northwest Indiana business leaders opened their official bidding for the Bears on November 14, 1995. Their plan, Planet Park, consisted of a year-round family resort, a park for recreation vehicles, golf course, restaurants, hotels and shops, and Bears Stadium at Planet Park, a $312 million futuristic open-air facility with 75,000 seats, including 9,000 club seats and 138 skyboxes (the stadium itself would cost $206 million, the other fan-related amenities $106 million). Billed as a public-private partnership, 40 percent of the funding would come from twenty- to thirty-year bonds secured by a 0.5 percentage increase in the income tax for citizens of Lake County, a highly taxed and economically depressed area. Advertising noted that for a household with an annual income of $20,000, the tax would amount to $7.80 a month, and $20 a month for a family with a $50,000 income. The private component was to come from the usual stadium sources.

Planet Park, which carried a total price tag of almost $500 million, stressed employment opportunities and economic development for the area, including 14,000 construction jobs and 2,800 permanent jobs by the time everything was completed. Although sponsored by "NICE," Northwest Indiana/Chicagoland Entertainment, Inc., and supported strongly by the Northwestern Indiana Regional Planning Commission, one of the major political forces was Gary Neale, president and chief executive officer of NIPSCO (Northern Indiana Public Service Company), a public utility that paid $400,000 to work up the Planet Park proposal for the Bears. Neale was also "the Daley ally who helped put together the Chicago-Gary Airport Authority in April [1995] . . . That bit of bureaucratic cunning linked the aviation interests of the two cities on paper, in a move to prevent the Republican-dominated Illinois General Assembly from seizing control of Chicago's airport operations, its patronage and lucrative contracts."[14]

The Bears appeared interested in their latest suitor. Edgar's office offered minimal comment, and Daley immediately ridiculed the Gary plan. One of the first concerns to surface, however, was environmental: the proposed 1,100-acre site contained toxic wastes and was adjacent to a major wetlands area that includes a rare dune and swale system. The second challenge came from a grass roots community group, "This S.T.I.N.C.S." (This Stadium Tax Is Nothing but Corporate Subsidy), which mounted an effective petition and public relations campaign against NICE and Planet Park. In early February 1996, the group prevailed: the Lake County Council voted 7 to 0 against the income tax increase, citing resident opposition and some uncertainties over the financial aspects of the project as the major reasons behind their decision.

Governor Edgar Weighs In

Even before the vote was taken in Indiana, 1996 began with Daley spoiling for a political fight. He agreed to drop his own opposition to a domed stadium near McCormick Place if the governor and GOP legislatures would agree to have "their own" stadium taxed to pay for it (that is, some financing would have to come from the whole six-county metropolitan area, and maybe downstate as well, and not just Chicago), an unattractive proposition in an election year. "If they want to build it," he added, "if Edgar wants to build a dome, it should be done with state money and a regional tax. . . . If they want it, let them build it. Let them pay for it too." [15] Daley was feeling corresponding pressure from trade unions in the area, which very much wanted the construction work a new stadium would provide, and they expected their Democratic mayor to come through for them.

It did not take the governor long to grab the bait or the football, but on his own terms. In early February he produced a formal plan for a $465 million domed stadium, to be built at McCormick Place. It would have 72,000 seats (including 10,000 club seats) and 179 skyboxes, and the now usual array of expected fan amenities. The Metropolitan Pier and Exposition (McPier) Authority would provide $185 million from continuing tourism-related taxes levied in Chicago and Cook County. Edgar asked the city to provide $25 million for land and utility improvements, and he asked the Bears to come up with $175 million from luxury box revenues, club seat charges, PSLs, and other stadium-related revenues. The residual amount would come from the state and other McPier funds.

Daley balked at the plan, the $25 million he was asked to provide, and the continued use of Chicago-area hotel and restaurant taxes. Edgar countered that "a relatively small percentage of Chicagoans pay taxes for McCormick Place" and that "the lion's share is paid for by people outside the city [and the state]." [16] McCaskey praised the plan but deemed his $175 million expected contribution "an extraordinary amount to ask the team to pay" and "a far heavier burden than you'll see in most any other multipurpose facility of this type." He named $100 million as a more reasonable figure.[17] Edgar conceded that the financing plan had room for negotiation.

Mayor Daley's "Soldier Dome"

After a lull of several months, on September 13, 1996, the mayor held a show-and-tell press conference to announce his latest proposal for the Bears: a translucent retractable dome for Soldier Field. Unlike the more sophisticated mechanisms used at Skydome (and planned for other new baseball parks in Phoenix and possibly Houston, Seattle, and Milwaukee), Daley's dome was of a low-tech nature, a roof that could roll back and forth on tracks. This "new" Soldier Field would have 73,000 seats (6,000 more than at present), 176 skyboxes, and the usual array of new fan amenities: restaurants and food courts, gift shops and museums, and more sideline seats. The estimated cost was $395 million, of which $358 million would be for the stadium itself and $37 million for exterior improvements.

Daley's plan represented a bundle of compromises. The Bears would have a natural-grass playing surface and the possibility of open-air games, weather permitting. The governor would have a convention facility. The mayor would "own" the concept and could take credit for initiating a solution that was roughly $100 million less expensive than the governor's McDome plan. The three-year construction plan would not disrupt regular season play, unlike the mayor's earlier plan to rotate the field 90 degrees. By late 1996, the mayor's proposal was one of two still on the table, the other being some variation of McDome.

The $395 million commitment also represented compromises. The Bears would be asked to "contribute" $175 million from the usual in-stadium revenue streams but could earn $30 million annually. The Park District would issue $60 million in revenue bonds and continue to operate Soldier Field. The Metropolitan Pier and Exposition Authority would contribute $160 million in bond financing (paid from tourist-related tax revenues), funds otherwise earmarked for McCormick Place. The mayor would be renouncing his earlier and often-stated criterion that counties around Chicago and the state as a whole should share equally in the cost of any new or renovated facility for the Bears.

Although the Park District's portion of the money would not require legislative approval, the McPier funds would require approval from Springfield. A publicly funded, open-air stadium, such as the model McCaskey had proposed in early 1995, also would require legislative approval. A simple new dome stadium at McCormick Place would not require a General Assembly vote, because the McPier Authority could issue bonds. Furthermore, as titular head of the Chicago Park District, which owns Soldier Field, Daley would control all bond financing and construction work for any renovation project. However, if the McPier Board is a partner instead of the Park District, then Daley would have to share control with Edgar.

As noted earlier, a flurry of activity in late 1996 all but eliminated Daley's retroactive dome from consideration. In addition, the half-hearted counterproposals by the mayor and McCaskey were short on specifics and vision. The only viable options on the table, or in the proverbial smoke-filled back rooms, are a modest recasting of Edgar's February 1996 McDome and the May 1997 surprise proposal by Reinsdorf and Wirtz for a privately financed stadium. (There is one additional option that at this writing looms larger and larger: with legislative elections in 1998 and the Bears' lease expiring at the end of 1999, the Bears may well be forced to extend their Soldier Field lease into the twenty-first century.)

Except for the May 1997 counterstrike by Wirtz and Reinsdorf, the various proposals, summarized in table 10-1, have three features. First, the price tag for a new Bears' stadium is increasing. In his first plan, Mayor Daley started with a modest $60 million renovation, but in his last plan, "Soldier Dome," as revised, the stadium expense had escalated to $492 million. Of course, there has been a concomitant dollar increase in the public contribution to the Bears' stadium project.

Second, the revenue from the operation of the stadium that would accrue to the Bears is increasing. Although estimates on the revenues appropriated by the Bears from the current operation of Soldier Field differ, no estimate exceeds $15 million. In Daley's Soldier Dome proposal, the Bears' "take" from stadium operations has been placed at $30 to $35 million. This amount would put the Bears second to the Dallas Cowboys (whose receipts totaled approximately $40 million in 1996) in the race for venue revenues, and, if 1994 statistics are any indication, comfortably ahead of the third-place team, the Miami Dolphins, with

Table 10-1. Summary Data for Current Facility and Seven Stadium Plans for the Chicago Bears

Plan and date	Facility type and size	Cost (millions of dollars)	Financing (millions of dollars)		PSLs Yes/No	Luxury seating	Bears revenue (millions of dollars)
			Public	Private			
Soldier Field (current)	Open-air, 67,000	n.a.	n.a.	n.a.	No	116 loges	6[a]
McCaskey, 4/12/95	Open-air, 74,000	285	185	100	?		n.a.
Stein, 10/95	Dome, 74,000	350		350	Yes	10,000 club, 200 loges	30–35
Daley I, 10/95	Open-air, 71,000	171	155	16	Yes	180 loges	20–28
Planet Park, 11/15/95	Open-air, 75,000	312[b]	312[b]		?	9,000 club, 138 loges	n.a.
Edgar, 2/8/96 and 3/14/97	Dome (McDome), 72,000	515	340	175[c]	Yes	10,000 club, 179 loges	30–35
Daley II, 9/15/96	Retractable dome, 73,000	395 to 500	220	175[c]	Yes	176 loges	30
Reinsdorf-Wirtz, 5/14/97	Open-air, 70,000+	300	45	255	Yes	n.a.	n.a.

Source: See text.
n.a. Not available.
a. As of 1994, as reported in Bob Verdi, "Browns' Move, Bears Watching and Worrying," Chicago Tribune, November 1, 1995, sec. 4, pp. 1, 5. Other esimates range from $7 million to $14 million.
b. Advertised as a public-private partnership, but the private contribution was to come from stadium revenues.
c. Private contribution was to come from stadium revenues.

$15.4 million in venue receipts in 1994. Since $30 million was proposed by Mayor Daley, it is reasonable to expect the Bears to earn more than that from the operation of their new stadium when the negotiations are completed.

Third, the Bears' financial contribution to the stadium project has increased in dollar terms with each iteration. The proposals indicate that the Bears' support will consist of stadium revenues earmarked for financing the stadium rather than constituting discretionary income for the Bears. This convention is not unique to the Bears but rather represents one development in the public-private partnerships that have been forged to finance stadium construction. Revenues derived from the luxury suite leases, personal seat licenses, and stadium advertising contracts are counted toward the team's, not the city's (or state's) share of stadium construction costs. Thus a football franchise may be credited with $175 million in contributed revenue toward a $300 million facility when, in fact, logic would suggest that all $300 million should be thought of as public support. This accounting convention is particularly misleading if the team is guaranteed a certain dollar amount from the operation of the stadium.

Fourth, all of these plans reserve $100 million to $200 million of McPier tax revenues derived from the 1991 second McCormick Place building to finance a new Bears stadium. Thus all sides claim that no new tax will have to be imposed. This contention ignores various alternative uses of the McPier funds. In economic terms, the opportunity of these funds is certainly not zero.

Financial Impact

In the negotiations between a team and a city, or another governmental entity funding the stadium project, attention usually focuses on the perceived need to improve the team's bottom line, while the public sector's return on its investment is neglected if not ignored. The extent to which a sports team contributes to a city's economy is small in absolute and relative terms. Table 10-2 shows the fraction of service income (SIC 70) constituted by the amusement and recreation industry (SIC 79) and commercial sports (SIC 794) for the city of Chicago in 1992 (the most recent period for which data are available). Commercial sports accounted for less than 1 percent of services income, and this is for a city with five professional sports teams. Even if all entertainment income was gener-

Table 10-2. *Economic Contribution of Stadiums and Professional Sports to the Economy of Chicago, 1992*

Standard Industrial Classification (SIC)	Receipts	Annual payroll	Paid employees
70–89 (services rendered)	20,325,014	8,015,936	279,373
79 except 792, 793,7984 (amusement and recreation services)	397,614	188,307	6,072
794 (commercial sports)	153,666	128,470	1,223
79 as a percentage of 70–89	1.96	2.35	2.17
794 as a percentage of 70–89	0.76	1.60	0.04

Source: U.S. Department of Commerce, Bureau of the Census, *1992 Census of Service Industries, Geographic Area Studies, Illinois* (Washington, D.C.: GPO, December 1994), pp. 45, 48.

ated in conjunction with the use of Chicago's stadiums and arenas, less than 2 percent of services income could be attributed to Chicago's sports facilities. Furthermore, service receipts accounted for approximately 31.22 percent of the payroll in Cook County in 1992.[18] Should this statistic hold for the city of Chicago, commercial sports (794) and amusement and recreation (79) account for approximately 0.24 and 0.61 percent, respectively, of Chicago's personal income.

Furthermore, while service receipts per capita for Chicago with a population of 2.768 million equaled $7,342.85, amusement and recreation and commercial sports receipts per capita were about $143.64 and $55.52, respectively.[19] Professional sports account for approximately 39 percent of commercial sports receipts overall, and only a relatively small fraction of these per capita figures originate through the activities of a single professional sports franchise for which a stadium is constructed.[20] From the combined statistics, it appears that the professional sports industry in total accounts for roughly $22 on average for each citizen of Chicago.

These statistics on the absolute and relative role of professional sports in a metropolitan economy exaggerate the impact of sports. As discussed in chapter 2, the time and money spent spectating at a professional sports event mean less time or money available for other leisure activities. If the fans who attend live professional sports events primarily in the metropolis's environs, then sport realigns spending without increasing it overall. In the absence of an increase in spending in the aggregate, incomes do not increase, jobs are not created, and tax revenues remain the same. Since the labor market for players and owners is national and not local, it may well be that sports diverts spending from locally owned and operated leisure enterprises to those that are national in character.

It is plausible, therefore, that professional sports has a negative effect on local economic activity.

Politics and Personalities

The flurry of Chicago's stadium-related proposals appeared (and disappeared) in a complex historical, political, and economic context. The two features of primary concern here are, first, the personal and professional profile of the various participants and their constituencies and, second, other Chicago-specific public policy actions and agendas.

Politics as Usual and Unusual

Mayor Richard ("Rich" or "Ritchie") M. Daley, son of the late Richard J. Daley, who served as Chicago's mayor for more than thirty years, grew up on the South Side of Chicago. The family home in the blue-collar neighborhood of Bridgeport was within walking distance of Comiskey Park, where father and son cheered for the White Sox and the Cardinals. Family loyalties and feelings run deep. When Mike McCaskey threatened to bolt for a suburb or Gary, the current Daley threatened to bring a second NFL team into the city. The first call he made was to William Bidwell, owner of the Cardinals (who, as luck would have it, was also a long-time friend of the McCaskey family). Daley also carries a grudge against McCaskey for firing Mike Ditka as the Bears' coach in 1992.

Angered by the 1994–95 baseball strike, and expressing his anger against both wealthy owners and high-salaried players, Daley did not return to his box at Comiskey Park until well into the 1996 season. As mayor, he turned much of his personal attention and city coffers toward the "greening" of the city, being generally supportive of business (some political wags refer to him as Chicago's Republican mayor) and engaging in many family-oriented public improvement programs, including park renovations, bicycle paths, ice-skating rinks, signage, neighborhood festivals, and other recreational activities for the average citizen. On the other hand, Daley has proposed two or three "mega-scale" public policy initiatives for the Chicago area, not all of which have been successful, and some of which have stepped on the political and economic toes of his political rivals. Daley was reelected to office in 1995 with overwhelming bipartisan support. He also exercises almost total control over the fifty-member City Council; the recent vote in favor of his proposed budget for fiscal year 1997 was 49 to 1.

Popular Illinois governor Jim Edgar, first elected in 1991 and reelected by margins similar to Daley's in 1995, is a downstate Republican, the same political affiliation as his predecessor (Jim Thompson). In Daley's opinion, Edgar is less attuned to and less supportive of Chicago politics and priorities than was Thompson. Edgar's support is strong in the five "collar counties" around Chicago, and he has personal ties to folks whose interests run counter to those of the mayor.[21]

On average, the Daley-Edgar relationship has been bumpy and contentious. They worked closely together on funding for and control of Chicago public schools. Edgar also was very supportive of the mayor's plans and needs for the 1996 Democratic National Convention in Chicago, for which Daley has been publicly and privately grateful. On other matters, these two public figures have clashed openly and repeatedly in the last five years. Daley wanted state support for a trolley system to help revitalize commercial activity in the city center; Edgar opposed it, and won. Illinois has ten licensed riverboats for gambling, which operate on the Mississippi River (the westernmost part of the state) and the Fox River (Joliet and Aurora areas). Two floating casinos operate in Northwest Indiana (known as Buffington Harbor, rather than the less attractive but perhaps more accurate name, Gary). Edgar has opposed land-based casinos in Illinois, some think to protect horse racing in the state, a sport in which he has personal interests and close friends, such as Richard Duchossois, who owns the Arlington International Racetrack. Daley proposed a 100-acre gambling hall and theme park for downtown Chicago. Edgar refused to support it.

A third major battle between Edgar and Daley was over control of O'Hare and Midway airports and plans for a third airport in the Chicago area. The governor had expressed a preference for a third airport in Peotone, far south of Chicago in Will County. At the same time, Edgar used the Republican majority in the General Assembly to push through legislation to seize control of O'Hare airport operations, which would have meant patronage-like jobs and power over all contracts let for the airport. Daley fought Edgar on both fronts, including brokering the Lake Calumet-Gary Airport Authority (Lake Calumet, south of the city, borders both Illinois and Indiana). Because the airport would have crossed state lines, Edgar and the Republican legislature could not control or stop it. Although the debate over a third major airport for Chicago has subsided, Daley and Edgar are fighting a pitched battle, with the early rounds in and out of court going to Daley over Meigs Field (a small commuter landing strip near McCormick Place), Soldier Field, and three museums.

Other players and personalities have been involved in the struggle over Soldier Field and the alternatives. First on the list are the architectural firms: the Bears' principal firm is Hellmuth, Obatam and Kassabaum (HOK Sports Facilities Group), which did the architectural design for the new Comiskey Park (as well as Oriole Park at Camden Yards and Jacobs Field in baseball and the new football stadiums in St. Louis and Jacksonville); the city is represented by Skidmore, Owings and Merrill, which has put together the Soldier Field renovation and retractable dome proposals. Second, Richard "Richie" Stein, the politically connected developer in charge of McCormick Place, was a Daley ally until he announced his support for a domed stadium instead of the mayor's proposed renovation plan for Soldier Field. Daley responded by denying Stein interest in a lucrative contract at O'Hare airport. Third, Reinsdorf and Wirtz are wary of McCaskey since his 1987 attempt to cut into their West Side territory. Concerned that a domed facility near McCormick Place would cut significantly into concerts, ice shows, circuses, and other sports events at the United Center, they opposed all McDome-like construction and then made their 1997 foray into McCaskey's lakefront territory. Fourth, Gary Neale, chairman of NIPSCO (Northern Indiana Public Service Co.) and one of the driving forces behind the NICE Planet Park proposal to lure the Bears to Gary, was the Daley ally who helped put together the Chicago-Gary Airport Authority in 1995. Fifth, Jim Reilly, Edgar's former chief of staff, is the head of the Metropolitan Pier and Exposition Authority, which operates Navy Pier and McCormick Place. He prefers a domed stadium near McCormick Place to add to its marketability.

A complementary twist in the pro-dome saga started in early 1996 with the contention that the Bears' limited use of McDome would only be the tail. The dog would be conventions, sporting events, and other attractions for which the city does not now compete, allegedly because it lacks adequate indoor meeting space. Supporters claim that these events would pump almost $400 million annually into the state's economy, most of which would originate from outside the area and thus be "new money." With three separate buildings, McCormick Place alone has 2.2

million square feet of exhibition space and small meetings rooms, but no large hall.

Dome opponents, including the mayor, note that the metropolitan area has 4.3 million square feet of exhibition space—more than twice as much as any other entire city in the country (New Orleans is the only other U.S. city with more than 1 million square feet); and it already attracts approximately 40,000 conventions, trade shows, and corporate meetings each year. The United Center was able to accommodate the Democratic National Convention in 1996, which argues that further construction to attract additional conventions may be a substitute for current facilities. Local media investigations have come to that same conclusion, and recent national reviews confirm a convention space glut across the country. Nevertheless, when Daley unveiled his retractable-roof plan for Soldier Field in September, he felt compelled to argue that the facility could accommodate and help attract more conventions and other sporting events to Chicago, though no other domed facility in the country has to contend with and preserve a grass field in the process.

Chicago's two newspapers, the conservative *Chicago Tribune* and the more moderate *Chicago Sun-Times*, have consistently and repeatedly taken pro-McDome stances on their editorial pages. With eleven editorials in six months from August 16, 1995, through February 11, 1996, and at the rate of about one a month since then, the *Tribune* has made its position quite clear:[22]

> Consider the merits of a domed stadium immediately west of McCormick Place—a dome that could double as the Bears' den and as a multi-use facility capable of hosting mega-events ranging from the Super Bowl to national religious conventions.[23]
>
> The city and the Bears would be wasting each other's money upgrading a facility [Soldier Field] that, when complete, still will be located in a bad place and still won't be a good place to watch a football game.[24]

Chicago: Urbs in Horto ("City in the Garden")

As noted earlier, Chicago and its mayor have been involved in several public policy plans and disputes in the 1990s concerning schools, airports, gambling, a national political convention, and the completion of the third building for McCormick Place. Several others, as well, impinge directly on plans for any home for the Bears, and some of them involve commitments of public funds that are both complementary to and a substitute for a new or renovated football stadium.

Renovated with $200 million in state funds and some private and corporate support, Navy Pier opened in 1995. Fashioned after Faneuil Hall in Boston, Pike Place Market in Seattle, and the Inner Harbor area in Baltimore, the Pier offers strollers everything from restaurants and souvenir shops to a concert stage, cultural exhibition area, and a 148-foot Ferris wheel. The Metropolitan Pier and Exposition Authority, which owns and operates Navy Pier, projects an $8.6 million deficit from fiscal year 1997 through 2000, then a profit to be reinvested in the pier starting in 2001. Worries about cost overruns have been dampened by attendance numbers, which are almost 50 percent above original estimates. Surveys indicate that about two-thirds of visitors are local, with a slight majority from the surrounding suburbs.

On November 9, 1996, the first phase of a two-year, $90 million urban planning project was completed as automobile traffic flowed across the new lanes of Lake Shore Drive. The purpose of relocating all the lanes of this important artery to the west of Soldier Field, unlike recent highway projects in Chicago, was not to improve the lives of motorists. Instead, when the second phase—landscaping the area into a grass-and-tree mall—is completed in 1997, pedestrians and cyclists will enjoy immediate and uninterrupted access to the lakefront and the three museums. Street signs already point visitors to the "Museum Campus" (see figure 10-2).

To the extent that there is a third phase, or "hidden agenda," to the Lake Shore Drive project to return the lakefront to "the people," to nature, and to Daniel Burnham's 1909 Plan of Chicago, it was revealed officially in early July 1996 (though rumored for months) when the Chicago District announced that the city would not renew the state's fifty-year lease on Meigs Field when it expired on September 30, 1996. Instead the District planned to convert the small commuter airstrip to a nature preserve, Northerly Island Park, with playgrounds, beach, botanic garden, wetlands, and a nature center. The price tag, $27.2 million, was to be paid from a federal grant, Park District funds, and a bond issue. Some revenues would accrue from parking, concessions, and other use fees. Friends of Meigs Field, opposed to the conversion, estimated that the airport adds $57 million to the region's economy; city officials put the figure at less than $5 million.

From July through September 1996, and into the late fall and early winter, local supporters of Meigs Field and the governor continued their struggle with Mayor Daley and the Park District in court. The governor threatened to reclaim the land for the state and retain it as an airport. He made good on that threat as the GOP-controlled General Assembly (which would return to Democratic hands on January 8, 1997) and the state Senate voted in early December for a transfer of the land to the state, a bill Edgar signed on December 16, 1996.

In the course of raw political maneuvering and rather unseemly political exchanges in the media between the mayor and governor, the Miegs-for-McDome swap resurfaced. The *Chicago Sun-Times* led with a large front-page headline on December 18, 1996: "Daley: Edgar Broke Deal." The alleged pre-signing agreement worked out by the two camps would have given Daley his $27.2 million nature park and Edgar his $465 million domed stadium. On the day of Christmas Eve, Edgar proposed a compromise: Meigs would be reopened and operated for seven years, after which Daley would be free to convert the area to any other use in 2003. After months of angry, personal attacks, and an estimated $2.7 million in legal fees, the two sides agreed on January 7, 1997, that Meigs would serve as an airport for five more years; the land and facility would then revert to the city.

Daley has committed substantial public funds to other projects in the central city and neighborhoods. After failing to obtain state assistance for his trolley initiative, he spearheaded a $24.5 million plan (featuring new sidewalks, landscaping, lightning) to return State Street to automobile traffic and thus revitalize the Loop for shopping. Another $15 million has been earmarked for a dozen outdoor neighborhood ice-skating rinks distributed throughout the city. Neighborhood fountains will come next. A 1996 landscape and beautification plan, certainly not unrelated to the 1996 Democratic National Convention, has cost another $28.9 million for trees, flowers, planters, and signage. Initial estimates, pieced together from several fiscal entities, suggest that a total of $180 million in local, state, and federal funds may have been spent on the convention.[25] This includes the capital projects noted above, plus $81 million from the Chicago Housing Authority to renovate the Horner Homes near the United Center, and $28 million simply to run the convention. In addition, millions of dollars in private support were raised for it. Revamping and shoring up the Chicago Transit Authority and improving public education are Daley's top priority for his next visit to Springfield.

Conclusions

Before the start of the 1996 season, Bears' coach Dave Wannstedt made an ill-advised and ill-timed comment: "All of the pieces [necessary for the Bears to go to the Super Bowl that season] were in place." As the Bears completed another lackluster season on the field, the press never let him forget it. Off the field, all of the financial and political pieces are not in place either. The final disposition of Meigs Field, how the city and state will eventually respond on the gambling front, and whether there will be a third airport in the area are still up in the air.

However, some things seem likely. First, the Bears will no doubt remain inside Chicago city limits. Second, the team will have a new home within ten years, though it may well open the 2000 season in Soldier Field. Third, both the total and public component of the price for that stadium will be larger than any figure noted in table 10-1. In addition, and in his own way, Richard M. Daley will still be trying to make Daniel Burnham's memory proud of the city and what it has become.

Notes

1. For a detailed review of pre-construction history and controversies, see Charles Euchner, *Playing the Field* (Johns Hopkins University Press, 1993). On employment effects of stadiums and information on attendance for the first six years, see chapter 3 in this volume.

2. Because Wrigley Field was also the home field for the Chicago Cubs, each fall the Bears usually played their first three or four games on the road, waiting for the baseball season to end. Given the Cubs' infrequent appearance in post-season play, the Bears' wait was shorter than for other football teams that shared a facility with a baseball team.

3. Chicago Park District Commissioners, *Soldier Field*, n.d.

4. Seven members of the McCaskey family are currently on the Bears' corporate payroll.

5. Chicago is located in Cook County; there are five surrounding "collar" counties: Lake, Kane, Kendall, DuPage, and Will. All of the other sites McCaskey and the Bears have considered are in one of these five areas. Politically, the city is overwhelmingly Democratic, while the neighboring counties are Republican strongholds.

6. John Kass and Jacquelyn Heard, "Wirtz, Reinsdorf Have Plan for a Bears Stadium," *Chicago Tribune*, May 14, 1997, sec. 2, p. 1.

7. Don Pierson, "McCaskey: New Stadium a Necessity, Not a Luxury," *Chicago Tribune*, April 13, 1995, sec. 4, p. 1.

8. Jim Kirk, "The Bears Mean Bucks," *Chicago Sun-Times*, October 22, 1995, p. 1.

9. Jeff Borden, "Stein Makes Bears Pass," *Crain's Chicago Business*, vol. 18 (April 1995), p. 1.

10. Mike Mulligan and Fran Spielman, "McCaskey: Build It or We May Go," *Chicago Sun-Times*, August 11, 1995, p. 14.

11. Peter Baniak, "Bears Select Aurora Site in Draft for New Stadium," *Chicago Tribune*, August 10, sec. 2, p. 8.

12. Rick Pearson, "DuPage Leader Shuns Footing Bill for Bears," *Chicago Tribune*, April 19, 1995, sec. 2, p. 2.

13. John Kass and Julie Deardorff, "Stadium Plan to Enter the Negotiating Arena," *Chicago Tribune*, October 19, 1995, sec. 1, p. 1.

14. John Kass and Nancy Ryan, "Daley, Gary Tossing Bombs in Stadium Battle," *Chicago Tribune*, November 18, 1995, sec. 1, p. 1.

15. John Kass and Rick Pearson, "Daley Dares GOP on McDome," *Chicago Tribune*, January 4, 1996, sec. 1, p. 1.

16. Sue Ellen Christian and John Kass, "Edgar's Dome Plan Filled with Many Ifs," *Chicago Tribune*, February 9, 1996, sec. 1, p. 1.

17. Michael Gills and Fran Spielman, "Edgar Fields McDome Details," *Chicago Sun-Times*, February 9, 1996, p. 1.

18. U.S. Department of Commerce, *County Business Patterns*, 1994.

19. The population figure is from Department of Commerce, *Statistical Abstract of the United States, 1994*.

20. U.S. Department of Commerce, *Country Business Patterns, 1994*.

21. With regard to politics in the Illinois General Assembly in Springfield: Democrats, who have generally held the majority until the 1994 elections, regained control—by a 60 to 58 margin—of the House of Representatives. The Republicans have a small majority in the fifty-nine-member state Senate. The Republicans controlled both Houses and the governorship from 1994 to 1996, the only time that has happened in the past twenty-five years. Neither party has been anxious to have financing for a Bears' stadium come up for a vote in the legislature.

22. "McDome Still Makes Sense" (May 1, 1995); "Baltimore Bluff Is unBearable" (August 16, 1995); "Flames Football? Try McDome" (September 17, 1995); "Another 20 years at Soldier Field?" (September 21, 1995); "Old Soldier Fields Never Die" (October 22, 1995); "How (Not) to Send the Bears Packing" (November 8, 1995); "Time for Leadership—and McDome" (December 17, 1995); "Starting to See the Light on McDome" (December 27, 1995); "Whenever You're Ready, Gentlemen" (January 3, 1996); "Daley's Key to the McDome" (January 14, 1996); "Edgar's Turn to Advance McDome" (February 5, 1996); "Daley Owes Answers on McDome" (February 11, 1996); "Time Now for McDome Homework" (July 13, 1996); "Soldier Dome Advances in Ball" (September 17, 1996).

23. "McDome Still Makes Sense," *Chicago Tribune*, May 1, 1995, sec. 1, p. 14.

24. "Another 20 Years at Soldier Field?" *Chicago Tribune*, September 21, 1995, sec. 1, p. 30.

25. Greg Hinz, "The $180-million Party," *Crain's Chicago Business*, vol. 19, no. 34 (August 1996), p. 1.

11

CLEVELAND'S GATEWAY TO THE FUTURE

ZIONA AUSTRIAN AND MARK S. ROSENTRAUB

 A decade or so ago there was no shortage of sarcastic jokes about Cleveland and its downtown area. A declining Rust Belt city, Cleveland was a ponderous relic with a decaying and dying core. The image of Cleveland as a shrinking and dirty city with a deteriorating center was poignantly framed by the fires on the Cuyahoga River. Named for one of the Native American tribes that lived in the area, the Cuyahoga winds its way through parts of the downtown area and actually caught fire in 1969, with locally generated pollutants a contributing cause. The burning of the river provided additional material for late-night comics who, with humor, debased the city as a place to live. Cleveland in the 1970s and early 1980s had become somewhere to be from, not a desirable destination or an attraction. After dark, downtown Cleveland was a foreboding and lonely place.

Today, quite a different reality and image exist. In the wake of a three-day civic birthday party to commemorate Moses Cleveland's landing at Founder's Point on the banks of the Cuyahoga River two hundred years ago, downtown Cleveland is now a focal point for recreation, civic celebrations, entertainment, and professional sports. In 1996 attendance at events at Gund Arena, home to the Cleveland Cavaliers, and Jacobs Field, home to the Cleveland Indians, exceeded four million.[1] Playhouse

Square, an expanding theater district close to the sports facilities, also attracts suburbanites back to the city for entertainment. West of the sports complexes, and adjacent to the Cuyahoga River, is the "flats," site of numerous restaurants and clubs; several redeveloped apartments and condominium complexes now exist nearby. Located on the shores of Lake Erie, in an area now identified as the "North Coast Harbor," are a series of museums, which stand next to the site of the old Municipal Stadium, the former home of the Browns and Indians. Recently the Municipal Stadium was razed, and plans are now being developed for a new facility for a new Cleveland Browns team, expected to begin play before the end of the century. When one stands near either of Cleveland's new sports facilities on a game day, it is virtually impossible to be unaffected by both the excitement that now exists in the downtown area and the large number of people attending events. Both Jacobs Field and the Gund Arena are entertainment destinations and provide an image of vitality, a stark juxtaposition to earlier views of life in downtown Cleveland.

These changes are in vivid contrast to the past images of downtown Cleveland. With fewer than five thousand residents, the downtown area had a "ghost town" look after the business day. With no real residential base, downtown's survival depended on its centrality as a place to work. Here, too, there was little growth for several years. From 1970 to 1980 the total number of private sector jobs in the entire county increased by just two-tenths of 1 percent; this rate of job growth was considerably smaller than the growth rates in other areas, including Indianapolis, Cincinnati, Louisville, Columbus, and Pittsburgh. With a very low population base and stagnant job levels, Cleveland's leadership was understandably attracted to several initiatives to revitalize downtown.

Redevelopment in Downtown Cleveland

The rebuilding of downtown Cleveland has involved several initiatives. One, as briefly mentioned, is a museum district on the shores of Lake Erie and on the most northern extent of downtown Cleveland. This area is home to the newly opened Rock 'n' Roll Hall of Fame and Museum and the Great Lakes Science Center (with a large screen theater). It also has a maritime museum in a Great Lakes shipping vessel. The three museums are immediately east of Cleveland (Municipal) Stadium, the future site of the new facility for Cleveland's promised NFL team.

Immediately south of the museum district, and across an interstate highway, lies a large corporate headquarters and the Galleria Mall. The mall is part of the real estate holdings in which the owners of the Cleveland Indians have a share. A second mall, Tower City Center, a third redevelopment initiative, was part of the refurbishing of Public Square. Terminal Tower, a leading corporate office building in downtown Cleveland for decades, now sits atop and adjacent to the new mall and at the junction of Cleveland's mass transit system. This retail and shopping complex is connected to the Gund Arena and Jacobs Field by a pedestrian walkway. The footpath connects the mall and train station with the sports complexes and provides suburbanites convenient access to several of the new amenities in downtown Cleveland. The "flats," located west of Public Square and north of the sports facilities, is an extensively redeveloped restaurant and entertainment area and was one of the earliest efforts to help revitalize downtown Cleveland by changing recreational patterns within the region. The adjacent warehouse district also includes restaurants and several apartment and condominium projects.

Sports Facilities and Redevelopment

While each of these initiatives, and many others (new office buildings, Playhouse Square, renovation and addition of the municipal library), have been critical to the effort to define downtown Cleveland's image and underscore its role as a recreational, cultural, and shopping center for the region, the "crown jewel," or catalyst, in this set of activities consists of the two large facilities built for the Cleveland Indians and Cleveland Cavaliers. The sporting venues generate considerable regional and national publicity for downtown Cleveland. The recent success of the Indians, combined with the architectural splendor of Jacobs Field, has enhanced the popularity of the stadium as a destination for recreation.

At least three goals inspired the building of both sports facilities. Cleveland wanted, first, to retain the Indians, who were threatening to move; second, to bring the Cavaliers back to the downtown area. The Indians had threatened to leave the city, and Major League Baseball had repeatedly declared its support for either a new stadium for the team or a move to another city if a new facility was not forthcoming. The Cavaliers had left an inner-city location for suburban Richfield in 1974. Their ownership made it clear that the return to a downtown location depended wholly on the building of a new facility. Third, Cleveland's leadership hoped (or believed) that the presence of the teams and the new facilities on the southern boundary of the downtown area would lead to more growth for this part of the city's center. This attraction to downtown sports facilities as a tool for reinvigorating a section of its downtown area certainly mirrors the development policies implemented by numerous cities.

Previous chapters have clearly demonstrated that sports facilities and teams offer a region little in the way of economic growth. What happens when the focus of redevelopment is only a small area, as in the case of Cleveland's downtown area, now the site of two new facilities for their big league teams? Can a scheme to attract millions of visitors to a section of a downtown area stimulate development and reinvigorate a small portion of a central business district? That is to say, do sports teams and the facilities they use have an impact on economic development at a micro level? It is to this issue that we turn our attention through an analysis of changing employment levels and opportunities in the area adjacent to Cleveland's Jacobs Field and Gund Arena. The discussion opens with a brief review of the project itself.

Cleveland's Gateway

Cleveland's giant leap into the financing of professional sports facilities was its Central Market Gateway Project (popularly known as the Gateway Project). Michael White, elected mayor in 1989, joined several other elected officials and the Indians' owners in supporting the building of two facilities, one for the Indians and another—an indoor arena—to lure the Cavaliers back from the suburbs. Thus the initial impetus behind the Gateway Project was not the redevelopment of a section of downtown. Rather, as noted, the explicit goal was to save the Indians for Cleveland. An earlier effort to build a domed stadium for the team had been rejected by voters. The Indians' owners were growing impatient as they wanted to leave aging Cleveland Stadium, where they were tenants of Art Modell and his Cleveland Browns. As the only Major League Baseball team that was not the prime tenant of the facility used for home games, the Indians wanted a new stadium in Cleveland. If that was not forthcoming, the owners were prepared to move the team to a city that would provide a state-of-the-art facility. There was no doubt that Major League Baseball would support the move of the Indians to another city. Commissioner

Fay Vincent made that absolutely clear in testimony before the Cleveland City Council. In his remarks before the public vote on the Gateway Project, Vincent declared that the Indians had met three of the four criteria for an approved move: the team was losing money, the team had poor attendance, and if a new stadium was not built, evidence of a lack of community support would exist.[2]

Although the initial Gateway concept was limited to a facility for the Indians, when Mayor White assumed office, the building of an arena for a basketball team and other events was quickly added to the project. A baseball facility, it was argued, would limit the year-round impacts of the Gateway Project since there would be no activities in the area during the winter months. This "economic" justification for the "need" for two facilities was merely a rationalization to obscure a direct political initiative or agenda. Mayor White, it seemed to some of the community's leaders, wanted to add his own policy twist or signature to what would become the "the centerpiece" of Cleveland's redevelopment efforts. The proposed stadium for the Indians was actually a legacy of a previous (Republican) administration. Adding another facility to the project not only redefined the entire concept, but it established the White administration's perspective for creating a twelve-month entertainment complex in downtown Cleveland. Instead of simply building a facility to ensure that the Indians would remain in Cleveland, the Gateway Project was to be a tool for economic development through the creation of an entertainment center with events every month of the year. There were, however, some crucial and unplanned outcomes from the rather hasty addition of a multipurpose arena to the Gateway redevelopment effort.

First, the new facility drastically changed the overall funding requirements of the project. The public's resources for its investment in the Gateway Project were to come from a sales tax on alcohol and tobacco products, but this levy would not generate sufficient funds to support both facilities. Second, the addition of the arena to the proposed development without any guarantees from the owners of the Cavaliers that they would return to Cleveland also meant the owners of the basketball team would be in the highly desirable position of being able to negotiate a lucrative lease. If the facility and the proposed lease did not meet their specifications and demands, they would simply stay in the suburbs. This would not only jeopardize the entire Gateway Project but raise the possibility that the Indians would be playing baseball in another city.

Table 11-1. *The Original Financial Plan for the Gateway Project: A Proposed Baseball Stadium and Arena for Basketball*
Millions of 1990 dollars

Source of costs and revenues	Amount
Anticipated costs	
Stadium construction	128.5
Arena construction	75.0
Land acquisition	22.0
Land for future development	36.0–51.0
Financing and working capital	67.5
Total	343.5
Anticipated revenues	
Total private investment	174.0
Luxury seats	99.0
Cleveland Tomorrow	18.0–20.0
Property loans[a]	38.5
Interest earnings	16.5
"Sin tax" commitment[b]	169.5
Total	343.5

Source: Gateway to the Future Committee.
a. Property loans were to be repaid by income earned by the Gateway Corporation.
b. The "sin tax" revenues would be used to pay for the bonds sold to generate $169.5 million.

Mindful of the public's reluctance to use property taxes for sports facilities (the failed domed stadium proposal had pledged property taxes) and recognizing the need to include Mayor White's proposal for a "year-round" entertainment complex, on March 21, 1990, the Cuyahoga County commissioners

> approved a public/private partnership to develop the Central Market Gateway Project, an economic development zone that includes a new publicly owned stadium and arena. The 50/50 partnership includes a $174 million commitment of private sector funds for the Gateway Project. To finance the public portion of the $344 million development, the Commissioners today placed an initiative on the May 8 ballot seeking voter approval of a small excise tax on the purchase of alcoholic beverages and cigarettes.[3]

The $174 million in private funds was to come from several sources (see table 11-1). The press announcement issued by the Cuyahoga County commissioners indicated that the majority of the private funds, 56.9 percent, or $99 million, would come from the teams or the sale of luxury boxes (loges) or club seats. Cleveland Tomorrow, a nonprofit organization supported by the city's leading businesses, was prepared to commit $20 million, and $38.5 million in property loans was expected from banks. The loans were to be repaid by Gateway from anticipated income that the nonprofit corporation would earn from facility leases and other activities. The commissioners estimated that Gateway's earnings from interest would be $16.5 million. The commissioners also declared that the facility for the Indians would cost $128 million to build and that a facility for the Cavaliers would cost $75 million. A total of $22 million was budgeted to secure the land for the sports facilities and another $36 to $51 million was set aside to acquire other lands for continued development. A budget line of $67.5 million for financing and working capital was also included in the public announcement, and the material circulated by the committee was designed to secure the public's approval of a "sin tax" referendum, a tax on alcoholic beverages and cigarette and tobacco products.

When interviewed years later, leaders involved with the development of the proposed plan said they did not really expect the "sin tax" to generate sufficient funds to support the public sector's share of the costs for both the baseball stadium and the basketball arena. Yet, knowing that the Indians would leave if their new stadium was not built and that the political coalition needed to secure passage of the tax plan would erode if the arena was not part of the package, the leaders put a proposed plan before the voters in Cuyahoga County: it called for the building of two facilities at a cost of $174 million. The public's share was to be supported only with the sales tax on alcohol and tobacco products. As would soon become clear, not only was the revenue estimate too low, but the cost estimates for both facilities were entirely unrealistic.

Voters approved the financing plan by only a slight majority. The measure actually failed within the city of Cleveland, 56 percent to 44 percent. In the suburban areas, 55 percent of the voters supported the tax plan. The larger turnout in the suburbs gave the plan 51.9 percent of the total votes cast.[4] The facilities that were finally built were the state-of-the-art venues that their owners demanded. A summary of what was finally built, the proposed and actual costs of each facility, and the percentage of the construction cost that represented an "overrun" are presented in table 11-2.

The stadium for the Indians did not cost $128 million. The final cost, as tabulated by Gateway, was between $176 million and $180 million. The figures differ, depending on which of three possible sources are used: the Gateway Corporation itself, the Cuyahoga County Auditor's Office, or several media sources. Part of the reason for this discrepancy was that

Table 11-2. *Characteristics of Gund Arena and Jacobs Field*

	Facility	
Characteristic	Gund Arena	Jacobs Field
Start date	1991	1991
Opening date	1994	1994
Seating capacity	20,562	42,865
Club seats	2,000	2,064
Suites	92	122
Estimated cost (millions of dollars)	75	128
Final estimated cost (millions of dollars)	148–157	176–180
Overrun (percent)	97.3–109.3	37.5–40.6
Team investment (millions of dollars)	41.6–60.5	63.5

Sources: Mark S. Rosentraub, *Major League Losers: The Real Costs of Professional Sports and Who's Paying for It* (New York: Basic Books, 1997); Friedman and Much, *Inside the Ownership of Professional Sports Teams*, 1997.

some costs were classified as either construction or operating costs. To minimize the size of the overrun, some costs were treated as operational charges. At the lower figure of $176 million cited by the Gateway Corporation, construction costs were 37.5 percent higher than the costs forecast during the campaign for the sin tax and when the county commissioners announced their support for the project. If the actual cost was $180 million, as reported by the media and the County Auditor's Office, Jacobs Field cost 40.6 percent more than what was anticipated.

Although it was originally believed that the proposed arena for the Cavaliers would cost $75 million, the actual cost was substantially higher. In May of 1994 the estimated cost was $130 million. This was an update on a previous estimate of $118 million, which itself was $43 million more than the original proposal. In reporting that the cost had increased to $130 million, Thomas V. Chema, executive director of the Gateway Economic Redevelopment Corporation, noted that the final cost would be " 'somewhat north of' $130 million."[5] On December 15, 1994, the *Cleveland Plain Dealer* reported the total cost of the arena would be $148 million.[6] Earlier in 1994 the Cuyahoga County auditor had estimated the arena would cost $124.25 million, but additional cost overruns were found. With a $148 million price tag, the cost overrun was 97.3 percent of the original figure presented to voters by the Cuyahoga commissioners. In October 1996, as the Gateway Corporation and the team's owners were still debating who was responsible for certain changes in construction, some people estimated that the facility cost $157 million, or 109.3 percent more than the original cost presented to the voters in 1990.[7] The total cost of the Gateway project, including infrastructure, was approximately $467 million.

Why did the facilities cost so much? To begin with, when the original proposal was presented to the county commissioners, no plans existed for either facility. The county's leadership essentially approved a financing plan for a concept that lacked any specific details. Cost estimates were drawn from other cities, but since no plans existed for either facility, no one could be sure what was to be built and how much it would cost. Then, after the voters had approved the concept and financing plan, Gateway's leadership began working with the teams and their owners to find out what they wanted to see included in the new facilities. Since the voters and commissioners had already given their approval for the project, the teams did not feel compelled to show any restraint in their demands. Indeed, if they were not satisfied, they could simply withdraw or threaten to withdraw, and the political and economic costs would fall on the mayor and the leadership of the Gateway Redevelopment Corporation. The Indians' owners already had permission from Major League Baseball to move if the city did not give the team the support it needed. The owners of the Cavaliers had their own facility in a suburban area and could have simply stayed where they were if their demands were not met. Thus the teams were in a much stronger bargaining position than the Gateway Corporation. This meant that the facilities built would likely exceed the projected costs. With the political leadership clearly committed to building the facilities, even if Gateway's director and board had tried to reduce the scale of the projects, the teams would likely have had their demands met.

What did the teams want that raised Gateway's cost? First, luxurious food facilities were built in both cases. Premier restaurants were added, and the one in Jacobs Fields had enormous glass windows installed to permit diners to view activities on the field from several levels. Some tables in this restaurant sit in alcoves overlooking the playing field. Second, both ownership groups were also given offices in the facilities. Third, the scoreboard and sound system in Gund Arena were upgraded to ensure that the facility had state-of-the-art equipment. Another series of construction cost overruns, not unusual for projects of this size, arose because the users were able to request changes without adversely affecting their own budgets.

Ironically, elected officials have felt little political repercussions from the cost overruns. Michael White was reelected mayor. Governor Voinovich, who initiated the idea of a new facility for the Indians when he was mayor of Cleveland and who remained an ardent supporter of the project, has also remained politically popular. Gateway's administrator and the individual who supervised the building of both facilities, Tom Chema, did not fare as well, however. When the overruns became an economic liability for the Gateway Redevelopment Corporation and the county, Gateway's board looked for answers, and there was substantial criticism of the construction oversight. As the controversy over costs escalated into the summer of 1995, Chema resigned.

The project's problems did not end there. As already noted, Gateway's leadership was well aware that the taxes approved and the teams' financial investments would never pay for both a baseball stadium and a multi-event arena. The initial shortfall would have to be paid for by the county through a bond issue guaranteed by property taxes. But in 1996 the overruns continued as the Cavaliers and Gateway disagreed over which costs were operational and which were capital. Under the terms of the lease, the team's management company is responsible for operating costs, including maintenance, but capital costs are the responsibility of the Gateway Redevelopment Corporation. The Cavaliers have the unilateral right to declare costs capital expenses (Gateway can refer the matter to arbitration if they object) and subtract those payments from any rent due to Gateway. Sufficient capital costs were cited in the first fiscal year to eliminate all rental payments for the team. It is likely in the second year of operation that a portion, if not all of the rent to be paid, will also be offset by "capital costs."

Both teams were given favorable leases for the use of their new facilities; as has become typical of arrangements in which the public makes a rather large investment, the team retains most if not all of the revenues. In both cases here, this was done by assigning ticket and luxury seating revenues to the teams themselves and all other revenues to the facility management company. (In the lease with the Cavaliers, Gateway does receive a portion of luxury seat revenues as part of the rental payment). For both Jacobs Field and Gund Arena, the team's owners also own the facility management companies. For these favorable terms the teams have very different commitments or lease requirements. The Indians agreed to pay $20 million as an initial fee and then assumed fiscal responsibility for a small part of the construction cost of the stadium. The present value of that obligation is $31 million. The Indians also pay a small fee based on attendance. If three million fans attend games, the per ticket rental income is $1.175 million through 2004. If fewer fans attend games, the rental charge is lower. If the Indians average three million people in paid attendance, the present value of their contribution to Jacobs Field will be $63.5 million. The fee paid by the Jacobs family for naming rights is not included in this total because that investment was not made by the team.[8]

The Cavaliers actually paid less for their lease for Gund Arena. The Cavaliers' payment, as noted, is based on a share of the sale of luxury seating less any agreed to costs the team incurs for capital construction. In the first year of occupancy, Gateway and the team agreed that there would be no rental payment required as a result of capital costs incurred by the team. The team is also demanding that a large portion, if not all, of the rent payment for the second year of their lease be eliminated.[9] Should this pattern continue for a few years, the team's total investment in the facility might decline to about the $40 million level.[10] If the final price for Jacobs Field is $180 million, the Indians paid 35.2 percent. If the final cost of Gund Arena is $157 million, the team's share could be as little as 25.5 percent. Both of these percentages could shrink if attendance levels decline.

The Effects of Gateway on Its Immediate Area

With a substantial portion of the financial burden for the facilities assumed by the public sector, it is fair to ask, "What did Cleveland and Cuyahoga County receive for their investment?" In terms of the initial goal, saving the Indians for Cleveland, the team has a new twenty-year lease for the use of Jacobs Field. The second goal, to bring the Cavaliers back to the downtown area from the suburbs, was also achieved. But what of the third goal? Did the Gateway Project ignite or stimulate economic development in the immediate area? Can sports facilities contribute to micro-level economic development in a small part of a downtown area if the facilities are well-integrated into the fabric of the area? Cleveland may well be the perfect setting in which to analyze this question. The building of new homes for the Indians and Cavaliers has established a new nexus point for the region's recreation. With more than four million people attending events at these two facilities, if any set of facilities could have realigned some dimension of economic activity, it should be apparent in downtown Cleveland.

The most appropriate manner in which to analyze changes in economic activity would be to use a pooled time-series, cross-sectional data set covering all downtown neighborhoods for several years before construction of the facilities, for the years during construction, and for several years after. Any changes in employment or development in the area adjacent to the facilities over these periods could be compared with development in other parts of downtown and in other parts of the region in the same time periods. A data set does exist that permits an analysis at this level for the small geographic areas. The newly created Ohio Economic Development Information database, compiled from ES202 data, can be used to estimate industry employment and payroll changes at these different geographic levels. The ES202 data are taken from quarterly unemployment compensation reports compiled by each state under federal mandate. Nearly all employers with paid employees are required to file unemployment reports to their respective states. It is estimated that 99 percent of paid employees and 90 percent of all employees are included in this database. The ES202 database was created by the Ohio Bureau of Employment Services for tax collection purposes. Employers are required to provide quarterly summaries that include their name, address, zip code, county, industrial classification, employment levels, and payroll.

Several problems need to be addressed when using this data set, however. In particular, extensive procedures must be followed to avoid errors and overestimations. Each address in the database must be verified, because some firms do not furnish this information. Each time the ownership structure of any business changes, the Bureau of Employment Services creates a new entry to reflect the firm's new legal status. Unfortunately, the system frequently does not adjust to indicate the continuation of only one business entity when ownership structures are altered. As a result, the reports from each employer must be checked to ensure that changes in ownership are not counted as the closing of one firm and the creation of a new business. Employees of companies with multiple locations that reported a headquarters site had to be divided along the lines of the specific geographic area in which their jobs were located. This is also a time-consuming effort. The resources required to perform this "cleaning" for the entire region, or even the entire downtown area, could not be secured for this initial inquiry. Instead, telephone directories and industrial or corporate listings were used to refine the data for the three zip code areas that constitute the immediate Gateway area (see figure 11-1). The Haines Criss-Cross Directory was used to identify additional businesses in the Gateway area that are not reported in the ES202

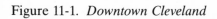

Figure 11-1. *Downtown Cleveland*

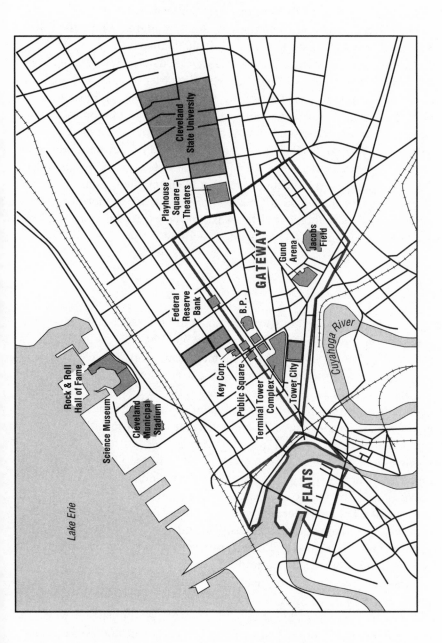

data in the correct zip codes. In this manner it was possible to ensure that all employees (full and part-time) were included in the database and that any improper records were properly eliminated.[11]

Data were geocoded to identify companies by address within the Gateway area boundaries and to locate individual companies on maps using a Geographic Information System (GIS). The data reviewed were from the first quarter of 1989 through the second quarter of 1995. The analysis compares economic activities during the pre-Gateway years of 1989 to 1992 (half-year intervals to half-year intervals) and outcomes during Gateway's construction and first year of operation, the post-Gateway period, or 1992 to 1995. Throughout 1995 and 1996 several additional businesses opened that were not part of the database for this analysis. Several housing developments have also been initiated. Some of these developments were added to the analysis to provide a more complete "first look" at development in the wake of the excitement generated by the opening of both Jacobs Field and the Gund Arena.

Job Creation

The opening of a large sports complex in an area of downtown that was suffering from blight and abandoned buildings has the potential to attract new businesses. Such development can occur in two broad patterns. First, a portion of the recreational activity associated with the facilities in the region can be channeled into the downtown area. This occurs through the opening of new restaurants and other businesses that complement the sporting and other events at the new facilities. Recreational activity concentrated in one area might also attract a major restaurant chain that does not have any facilities in the general region. In either case, although regional growth may be minimal, the movement of recreational activity into the Gateway area represents export activity for the city of Cleveland. Second, some businesses may be drawn into the Gateway area that could just as easily locate in the suburbs. The special services and office work that frequently define downtown economies are replicated in suburban locations.

Another concern of this analysis was to compare the growth of new employment opportunities in Gateway with the job growth in Cuyahoga County and the Cleveland metropolitan area. A comparison with job creation before the project was undertaken is also included since expan-

Table 11-3. *Job Creation in Gateway and the Cleveland Metropolitan Areas, 1989–95*

Location	Total employment[a]			Percent change	
	1989	*1992*	*1995*	*1989–92*	*1992–95*
Cleveland PMSA	1,022,139	1,007,339	1,068,010	−1.4	6.0
Cuyahoga County	764,059	739,491	770,155	−3.2	4.1
Gateway area	44,387	46,166	47,417	4.0	2.7

Source: Gateway Database, developed from the Ohio Bureau of Employment Services' Covered Employment and Payroll Data (ES202 Data).
a. Totals represent averages of the first two quarters in each year.

sion in the downtown area could well account for some of the job growth in the study area. In this manner, it is possible to estimate how much of the job creation in the Gateway area is due to the development of sports facilities or structural changes in local companies and industries.

The Gateway area, which includes sections of downtown Cleveland, was experiencing some growth and recovery before the construction of the new facilities. Total employment in Gateway actually increased by 1,779, or 4.0 percent, during the initial or preconstruction period (1989 to 1992). During the same period, both Cuyahoga County and the Cleveland metropolitan area recorded job losses of 3.2 percent and 1.4 percent, respectively (table 11-3). Despite the 4 percent increase in Gateway's total employment, however, the total number of jobs added was quite small. The trend of higher growth levels in the Gateway area compared with the county and region was reversed in the years after the facilities were built. From 1992 to 1995, although employment levels in the Gateway area continued to increase, growth was more robust elsewhere.

In contrast to the growth in employment before construction, the number of businesses in Gateway between the first half of 1989 and the first half of 1992 declined by 39 (2.9 percent). As a result, the average number of employees per business rose from 32.5 to 35. In the 1992–95 period, the number of businesses continued to decline (by 1.8 percent), while employment increased. Business size in the area, then, continued to grow and the average firm had 36.4 employees.

Type of Jobs Created

It is reasonable to expect different employment trends in the Gateway area, Cuyahoga County, and Metropolitan Cleveland. The economies of each are substantially different: the Gateway area is a downtown econ-

Table 11-4. *The Job Structure of Three Economies, 1995*[a]

Percent

Industry	Gateway area	Cuyahoga County	Cleveland PMSA
Construction	0.2	3.2	3.6
Manufacturing	7.4	18.2	21.3
TCPU[b]	7.5	5.9	5.3
Wholesale trade	4.6	7.2	6.3
Durable goods	1.0	5.0	4.4
Retail trade	6.1	16.6	17.4
Eating and drinking places	3.4	5.9	6.1
FIRE[c]	36.4	7.3	6.3
Services	36.6	36.5	34.5
Business	7.4	6.6	5.7
Health	0.5	11.3	10.4
Legal	7.7	1.1	0.9
Educational	1.7	6.8	7.3
Engineering and management	8.2	2.8	2.4
Government	1.4	4.6	4.3

Source: Gateway Database, developed from the Ohio Bureau of Employment Services' Covered Employment and Payroll Data (ES202 Data).

a. Detailed industries (two-digit) are presented in the table if they account for at least 5 percent in any of the areas.

b. Transportation, communication, and public utilities.

c. Finance, insurance, and real estate.

omy with a high concentration of finance and service industries, while the surrounding region includes a concentration of manufacturing firms. Table 11-4 shows the industrial makeup of the Gateway area, Cuyahoga County, and the Cleveland region. Given its proximity to the downtown area, Gateway has few manufacturing firms, whereas almost one-fifth of the county's jobs are in manufacturing. (Although BP America's only facility in downtown Cleveland is its administrative headquarters, the Standard Industrial Classification reflects the corporation's status as a manufacturing concern.) Also, employment in finance, insurance, and real estate (FIRE) accounts for 36.4 percent of the jobs in the Gateway area, whereas this same sector accounts for only 7.3 percent of all jobs in Cuyahoga County.

The employment trends presented in table 11-3 mask opposing trends in different industries as the character of the Gateway area changes. Table 11-5 records the changes in job levels within the study area by type of industry. Some of these changes can be attributed to structural changes, but others might be related to the development of the sports facilities. Measured both by the number of jobs and busi-

Table 11-5. *Employment Trends by Major Industry in the Gateway Area, 1989–95*

Wages in 1995 dollars

Industry	Employment[a]			Percent Change	
	1989	1992	1995	1989–92	1992–95
Total employment	44,387	46,166	47,417	4.0	2.7
Construction	67	104	74	55.6	−29.0
Manufacturing	5,438	5,002	3,474	−8.0	−30.5
TCPU[b]	4,097	3,776	3,517	−7.8	−6.9
Wholesale trade	1,870	1,967	2,143	5.2	8.9
Retail trade	3,241	3,341	2,887	3.1	−13.6
FIRE[c]	13,749	15,648	17,138	13.8	9.5
Services	15,514	15,723	17,227	1.4	9.6
Public administration (government)	406	596	636	46.8	6.7
Number of establishments	1,364	1,325	1,301	−2.9	−1.8
Average wages (all employees)	$37,048	$36,760	$38,856	−0.8	5.7
Average wages (excluding players)	$37,048	$36,760	$38,057	−0.8	3.5
Average wages (50 percent players)	$37,048	$36,760	$38,434	−0.8	4.6

Source: Gateway Database, developed from the Ohio Bureau of Employment Services' Covered Employment and Payroll Data (ES202 Data).
a. Averages of first and second quarters in each year. Total employment is larger than the sum of major industries because some companies do not report their industry classification.
b. Transportation, communication, and public utilities.
c. Finance, insurance, and real estate.

nesses, firms in the service and FIRE sectors, were, as would be expected, the largest industrial sectors in the Gateway area in both the pre- and post-Gateway periods. Each of these sectors of the economy had more than 17,000 employees by 1995.[12] Most of the service job growth in the Gateway area occurred during the post-Gateway period, increasing by almost 10 percent between 1992 and 1995. Between 1989 and 1992, service jobs grew by 1.4 percent. Jobs in the FIRE industries rose in both periods as a result of increased activity among bank headquarters in the downtown area. The largest service industries in the Gateway area were engineering and management services (SIC 87), legal services (SIC 81), and business services (SIC 73). Of these industries, engineering and management services and business services enjoyed some job gains during the post-Gateway period, reversing a similar-size decline during the earlier three years.

Retail employment increased in the pre-Gateway period but declined between 1992 and 1995. Most of these losses could be attributed to changes in one or two firms as a result of national restructuring trends. The two department stores located in Downtown Cleveland were purchased by national chains. One company decided to close its downtown outlet, while the other reduced the size of its store. Ironically, these changes took place despite the development of the two sports facilities and other business openings that had the potential to create additional demand for retail shopping through the presence of more employees and visitors to the Gateway area.

Another unrelated employment loss in the Gateway area occurred in manufacturing industries; the number of jobs in this sector of the economy declined by 30.6 percent from 1992 to 1995. The majority of these job losses are related to the restructuring and the downsizing of BP America, a large British petroleum company with headquarters in Cleveland. In the 1992 to 1995 period many of BP's administrative jobs were either eliminated or reassigned to England.

The large majority of construction and trade workers who built the sports facilities are not included in this database. These workers were employed by companies located outside the Gateway area; only a few small construction companies are located in Gateway. In addition, for an analysis of this nature, construction related to the facilities cannot be counted as these workers would likely have been employed had other projects been built with the tax dollars collected.

Wage Levels

Three separate calculations were made to measure changes in average wage levels per employee. First, all employees, including the players for both the Cavaliers and the Indians, were included in the calculation. The players and the jobs they represent were increments to the employment base of the Gateway area since neither team played in this section of downtown Cleveland before the facilities were built. Second, since an issue of this analysis was the related development or the employment gains made as a result of the presence of the teams, average wage increases excluding the players were also tabulated. A third calculation including only 50 percent of the players' salaries was made to reflect the observation that at least half of the income of many players is never spent in the local economy.

If the players' salaries are included, workers in the Gateway area earned $458 million (quarterly average): this represented a real increase of 7.9 percent from 1992; average per employee wages increased 5.7 percent. With the players excluded, average wages increased 3.5 percent, which somewhat exceeded the average payroll increases in Cuyahoga County and the Cleveland PMSA (2.7 percent and 2.6 percent, respectively). In the years before the facilities were built, average wages per employee in the Gateway area declined by 0.8 percent.

Sports-Related Industries

Many of the documented changes that occurred in businesses in the vicinity of Gateway—including the recovery of certain downtown industries and the restructuring of certain retail vendors—were the result of factors other than the sports facilities. Of the several industries or businesses that did experience sports-related growth, it seemed to be a direct result of the presence of the Gateway complex. These businesses serve the fans and visitors to the complex and include general merchandise stores (SIC 53), apparel and accessory stores (SIC 56), eating and drinking places (SIC 58), hotels and motels (SIC 70), and amusement and recreation (SIC 79) firms.

Employment in Gateway's sports-related industries as a group increased by 22.6 percent in the post-Gateway period, from 1992 to 1995, following a 10.2 percent increase from 1989 to 1992. As can be seen in table 11-6, most of the job growth occurred in the amusement and recreation industry (SIC 79), especially in sports clubs (SIC 7941). This is a direct result of the relocation of the Indians and Cavaliers into the Gateway area. The other two sports-related industries that posted some employment growth during the post-Gateway period were eating and drinking establishments and hotels and motels. The increase in the number of workers in eating and drinking businesses was the same in the pre- and post-Gateway periods, even though in relative terms, job growth was less in the post-Gateway period. Employment in the hotel and motel industry grew less in the years after the facilities were built than in the pre-Gateway period.

Average wages in the area's sports-related industries rose in the post-Gateway period following a decline in the 1989 to 1992 period. If the players' salaries are included, the increase from 1992 to 1995 was 68.3 percent. If the players' salaries are removed altogether, the increase was 17.2 percent. Average wages in the sports-related businesses were lower than the average wages for all industries in the Gateway area. This was to be expected as many of those employed in restaurant and retail jobs are primarily part-time and low-wage workers.

Table 11-7 compares employment changes in the Gateway area's sports-related industries with changes in the county and the metropolitan area. The two industries that lost employment in the Gateway area during the 1992–95 period also lost jobs in the larger regions. More than one-half of the growth in the amusement and recreation jobs in the metropolitan area occurred in the Gateway area as a result of the move of the Cavaliers from Richfield. Employment opportunities in hotels and motels in the 1992–95 period declined in Cuyahoga County, but rose in the Gateway area.

*Dynamic Changes in Employment: Openings, Closings,
and Relocations*

In both the pre- and post-Gateway periods, the number of business openings was larger than the number of closings, and the number of job gains attributable to openings was larger than job losses due to closings.[13] Between the first quarter of 1989 and the fourth quarter of 1991, 177 new establishments opened in the Gateway area, creating almost 1,950 jobs. During the post-Gateway period, 183 establishments opened, creating 2,251 jobs (table 11-8). In contrast, 123 establishments closed between

Table 11-6. *Employment Trends in Sport-Related Industries in the Gateway Area, 1989–95*

Wages in 1995 dollars

	Employment[a]			Percent change	
Related industry	*1989*	*1992*	*1995*	*1989–92*	*1992–95*
Related employment	3,730	4,110	5,039	10.2	22.6
General merchandise	1,145	919	439	−19.7	−52.2
Apparel and accessories	322	381	351	18.3	−7.9
Eating and drinking	1,153	1,384	1,621	20.1	17.1
Hotels and motels	779	1,019	1,087	30.8	6.7
Amusement and recreation	331	407	1,541	23.0	278.6
Number of establishments	141	154	155	9.2	0.7
Average wages (all employees)	$17,444	$15,042	$25,316	−13.8	68.3
Average wages (excluding players)	$17,444	$15,042	$17,630	−13.8	17.2
Average wages (50 percent players)	$17,444	$15,042	$21,377	−13.8	42.1

Source: Gateway Database, developed from the Ohio Bureau of Employment Services' Covered Employment and Payroll Data (ES202 Data).

a. Average of first and second quarters in each year.

Table 11-7. *Employment Growth Changes in Sports-Related Industries by Area/Region, 1992–95*

	Gateway area		Cuyahoga County		Cleveland PMSA	
Related industry	*Change*	*(%)*	*Change*	*(%)*	*Change*	*(%)*
Related employment	929	22.6	3,314	4.3	7,337	6.8
General merchandise	−480	−52.2	−2433	−16.7	−907	−4.4
Apparel and accessories	−29	−7.7	−505	−6.0	−444	−4.4
Eating and drinking	236	17.1	4,598	11.3	6,562	11.2
Hotels and motels	68	6.7	−232	−4.4	−2	−0.0
Amusement and recreation	1,134	279	1,886	23.9	2,128	18.2

Source: Gateway Database, developed from the Ohio Bureau of Employment Services' Covered Employment and Payroll Data (ES202 Data).

1989 and 1992, with nearly 1,600 jobs lost; and a total of 133 businesses closed between 1992 and 1995, with 1,972 jobs lost (table 11-9). On balance, through the process of business openings and closings, the Gateway area gained 54 and 50 establishments in the pre- and post-Gateway periods, respectively. The industries that contributed most to business starts in the pre-Gateway period were services and retail trade, while services, retail, and financial industries accounted for most business openings in the post-Gateway period.

As can be seen in table 11-8, the number of business openings and jobs created in the post-Gateway area as a result of these openings was larger than the number during the pre-Gateway area. The location of the

Table 11-8. *Business Openings in the Gateway Area by Major Industry, 1989–92 and 1992–95*

	Before Gateway, 1989–92		After Gateway, 1992–95	
Industry	*Number of establishments*	*Employment gains*	*Number of establishments*	*Employment gains*
Total	177	1,947	183	2,251
Construction	1	3	1	6
Manufacturing	5	33	2	9
TCPU[a]	3	35	2	31
Wholesale trade	5	37	8	58
Retail trade	50	746	41	307
FIRE[b]	19	95	41	916
Services	94	999	88	925

Source: Gateway Database, developed from the Ohio Bureau of Employment Services' Covered Employment and Payroll Data (ES202 Data).
a. Transportation, communication, and public utilities.
b. Finance, insurance, and real estate.

Table 11-9. *Business Closings in the Gateway Area by Major Industry,*
1989–92 and 1992–95

	Before Gateway, 1989–92		After Gateway, 1992–95	
Business	Number of establishments	Employment loss	Number of establishments	Employment loss
Total	123	1,578	133	1,972
Construction	0	0	2	55
Manufacturing (only nondurable)	7	320	5	24
TCPU[a]	3	37	8	52
Wholesale trade	5	19	4	44
Retail trade	19	168	47	722
FIRE[b]	21	241	19	870
Services	68	791	48	204

Source: Gateway Database, developed from the Ohio Bureau of Employment Services' Covered Employment and Payroll Data (ES202 Data).
a. Transportation, communication, and public utilities.
b. Finance, insurance, and real estate.

businesses that opened can be seen in figure 11-2, which shows all openings identified in our database between the first quarters of 1992 and 1995. However, because the database covers only one year after the opening of the sport facilities, and new developments continue to occur, figure 11-2 also includes new restaurants that opened in 1995 (after the second quarter) and in 1996, as well as two new hotels, along with four multifamily housing projects that are bringing the first middle-income residents into this part of downtown Cleveland in decades.

The number of business closings in the post-Gateway period, most of which occurred in the service and retail industries, was slightly higher than in earlier periods (table 11-9). Interestingly, more retail stores closed during the post-Gateway period. It may be that some older stores were displaced by restaurants. In addition, some older restaurants are being replaced by newer and larger facilities. To summarize, during the post-Gateway period more establishments opened than closed and the number of jobs gained through openings was greater than the number of jobs lost due to closings. It is obvious that most of the dynamic changes in the Gateway area are typical of changes in a downtown economy, which relies heavily on service-producing industries.

Regional employment is also affected by the relocation of companies into and out of the region.[14] As shown in table 11-10, more establishments moved out of the Gateway area than moved into it both before and after the construction periods. During the pre-Gateway period, the moves in and out caused employment to drop by almost 1,190. During the post-

Figure 11-2. *Business Openings in the Gateway Area*

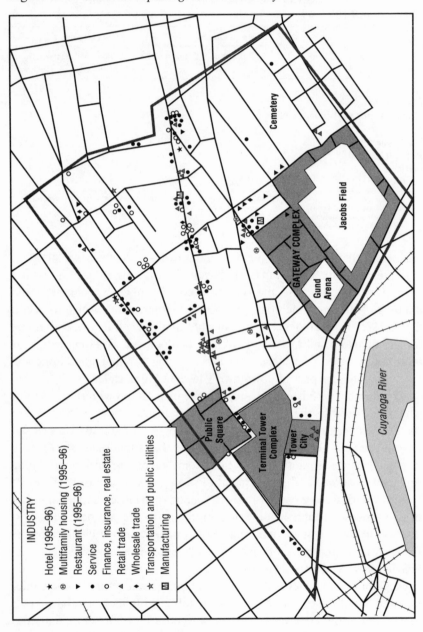

INDUSTRY

★ Hotel (1995–96)
⊕ Multifamily housing (1995–96)
▶ Restaurant (1995–96)
● Service
○ Finance, insurance, real estate
◀ Retail trade
◆ Wholesale trade
☆ Transportation and public utilities
Ⅲ Manufacturing

Cemetery

Jacobs Field

GATEWAY COMPLEX

Gund Arena

Cuyahoga River

Public Square

Terminal Tower Complex

Tower City

Table 11-10. *Total Relocations into and out of the Gateway Area,*
1989–92 and 1992–95

	Within area		Into area		Out of area	
Period	Businesses	Jobs	Businesses	Jobs	Businesses	Jobs
1989–92	102	4,067	34	428	95	1,618
1992–95	49	1,643	15	1,572	49	1,318

Source: Gateway Database, developed from the Ohio Bureau of Employment Services' Covered Employment and Payroll Data (ES202 Data).

Gateway period, however, even though more companies moved out than in, the number of jobs added as a result of companies coming in (1,572) was larger than the job losses associated with companies going out (1,318).

Conclusions

Cleveland built the Gateway Complex to serve three main purposes: maintain the city as the home for the Indians, bring the Cavaliers back to the downtown area from suburban Richfield, and increase job levels and wages in the area adjacent to the facilities and in the downtown area. With the building of the facilities and the negotiation of leases with the teams, the city attained its first two objectives. As for the economic impact of the development, the preliminary assessment in this chapter suggests that Cleveland has been successful in redirecting or reshuffling patterns of recreational spending within the region. Although changes of this nature do not imply economic growth at the regional level, they do represent real enhancements and job growth for the economy of downtown Cleveland.

Excluding the players' salaries, real wages per employee in the Gateway area increased, and that increment exceeded the growth rate for the county and the metropolitan area. There has been an increase in sports-related jobs as a result of the opening of new restaurants and hotels and the presence of the teams. Furthermore, from 1992 to 1995 there was a net increase in the number of businesses established.

Some less positive changes should also be pointed out. On the employment front, 1,779 jobs were added in the Gateway area in the years immediately preceding the building of the two facilities, but only 1,251 jobs were added in the three years after construction was initiated. Thus a pattern of slow job growth continued despite the presence of the two sports facilities. Moreover, the rate of job growth since construction began is actually less than the rate in Cuyahoga County and the Cleveland metropolitan area.

Two important caveats are also in order here. First, the foregoing analysis covers only a short term, since each facility had been in operation for just one year; but it should also be remembered that the 1994 baseball season ended early because of a strike. This labor dispute between the baseball players and owners was not settled until days before the beginning of the 1995 season. As a result, there was some doubt about whether the players would be part of the 1995 season. (The owners had proposed using replacement players). Some business investment may have been postponed as a result of the labor dispute and the observed impacts reduced accordingly. In addition, it takes a long time to redevelop and reuse older urban areas, which means that some of the new and planned developments may not be captured in the years studied. Future developments have the potential to add to the job base in the Gateway area.

Second, the years studied must also be considered the "honeymoon" period for both facilities. Although the strike by baseball players may have reduced attendance, the attractiveness of the facilities made visits to the ballpark and arena a recreational "happening" in Cleveland. The design of the facilities and their integration into downtown Cleveland have made both the ballpark and the arena an important recreation destination. A longer-term analysis will be needed to determine if short-term trends or changes in regional recreational activities have become permanent. Since the opening of Jacobs Field, the Indians in successive years have won the American League pennant and their division title. While the Cavaliers have been somewhat less successful, they, too, qualified for the playoffs. In most cities, attendance at sporting events is conditional on the performance of the team. In losing seasons, then, teams tend to attract fewer fans, and some sports-related businesses may fail. One factor that certainly does affect future attendance levels and economic spillover is the facility's design. Ballparks and arenas that are integrated into a downtown area tend to attract more fans and create spillover effects. Jacobs Field and Gund Arena were designed with that purpose in mind. However, it is too early to tell if Jacobs Field and Gund Arena will be more like Baltimore's Camden Yards (a continuing recreation destination) or Chicago's Comiskey Park (a ballpark that is some-

Table 11-11. *Other Large Economic Development Projects in Downtown Cleveland, 1991–95*

Project	Year of completion	Cost (millions of dollars)
Great Lakes Science Center	1996	55
Rock and Roll Hall of Fame and Museum	1995	92
Wyndham Hotel	1995	27
Convocation Center, Cleveland State University	1991	47
Society Bank/KeyCorp Tower Center	1991	400
Bank One Center	1991	95
Reserve Square Hotel renovation	1991	20

Source: Greater Cleveland Growth Association, Research Department.

what isolated from other neighborhood activities with lower attendance levels after the end of the "honeymoon period").

The full impact of the Gateway Project cannot be assessed without taking into account other related developments as well. Since the completion of the public/private partnership for the building of both facilities in 1990, several other large-scale projects have been initiated in downtown Cleveland. Many political leaders interviewed as part of this project cited the synergistic relationship between the Gateway Complex and the projects listed in table 11-11. Although no one would suggest that there was either a causal or catalytic relationship, the Gateway complex was among the first large-scale public/private partnerships in downtown Cleveland and represented a clear commitment of both the public and private sectors to the revitalization of downtown Cleveland. In view of the substantial conflict in the late 1970s and early 1980s between Cleveland's public and private sectors, this successful partnership has made more development possible.[15]

Interviews with local developers have identified several other projects in the Gateway area that are believed to be a result of the building of the two sports facilities. First, the planning phases of the Gateway Project included investments to the area's streets, sidewalks, curbs, vaults under the sidewalks, lighting, landscape, and signage. Second, during 1996 an estimated thirteen additional restaurants were opened, occupying 100,000 square feet in the Gateway area. Most of these establishments, especially those nearest the facilities, are a direct result of the presence of Jacobs Field and Gund Arena. It is hoped that a few of them will attract additional people to the area. These places are unique and offer entertainment services that are not available in the suburbs (large or special restaurants, a comedy club, and breweries).

Third, because of the new vitality of the Gateway area, many buildings are being considered and studied for possible conversion into multifloor housing units. The first apartment development project was recently opened and 22 of the 36 apartments have already been rented.[16] The first condominium project has also been initiated. Four other redevelopment proposals are under consideration with a possible 250 additional apartments. Three factors bode well for a housing development in the Gateway area. The improvements brought in by the Gateway Project made the area ready for development. Also, the area is now perceived to be safe, after many years of stagnation and increased blight, and this change will increase the demand for housing and redevelopment. The demand for downtown housing is already on the rise, as is evident from the redevelopment and the conversion of upper-floor empty space into housing units in Cleveland's warehouse district. Furthermore, financing is now available for the conversion of older buildings into apartments.

All of these outcomes, however, must be measured against the public sector's fiscal commitments to attracting the teams to downtown Cleveland and enhancing economic development in the Gateway area. The public sector's investment in the Gateway Complex will be approximately $289 million.[17] Inasmuch as the teams' payments to the Gateway Corporation depend on attendance levels and the sale of luxury seating for the Cavaliers, the public sector's fiscal responsibilities for Gateway may escalate.

This financial investment should be weighed against the goals achieved. Both the Indians and the Cavaliers have long-term leases to stay in Cleveland, more than $700 million has been spent on other major developments in downtown Cleveland since 1991, and approximately 1,750 jobs have been created in the Gateway area in the post-Gateway period, which includes the construction period and the first year of operation. If the public sector's investment of approximately $289 million is weighed against the 1,251 jobs created, the cost per job is $231,000. Some may argue that additional jobs in the future could reduce the cost per job and that economic development is a long-term process. Yet, available research on the factors affecting attendance suggests that the initial impact of a new stadium occurs within three years.[18] If attendance at games is a significant factor in influencing job creation in the surrounding area, then one would expect most new jobs related to the new stadium to be created within three years. However, if one expects economic development to occur over a longer time period, then the number of jobs in subsequent years could be higher. It now remains for Cuyahoga County's residents to decide whether the public's investment in the Gateway complex has been worth the benefits received.

Notes

1. Alan Friedman and Paul J. Much, *Inside the Ownership of Professional Sports Teams: The Complete Directory of the Ownership and Financial Structure of Pro Sports* (Chicago: Team Marketing Report, Inc., 1997).

2. Bob Becker and Lou Mio, "Baseball Chief Opposes City Losing Indians, but Says Move Is Possible," *Cleveland Plain Dealer,* May 3, 1990, pp. 1, 10.

3. Press release by Cuyahoga County, Ohio, "Cuyahoga County Commissioners Approve Financial Package for the Economic Development of the Central Market Gateway Project," March 21, 1990.

4. "Gateway Project Takes First Big Step: Voters Narrowly Approve Sin Tax," *Cleveland Plain Dealer,* May 9, 1990, p. A1.

5. Catherine L. Kissling, "Gateway Arena Costs Soaring," *Cleveland Plain Dealer,* May 26, 1994, pp. 1, 11.

6. Stephen Koff, "Gateway Financial Disclosure Sought," *Cleveland Plain Dealer,* December 15, 1994, p. 1b.

7. Roldo Bartimole, "If You Build It, Baseball Holds a City Hostage," *The Progressive,* June 1994, pp. 28–31.

8. Mark S. Rosentraub, *Major League Losers: The Real Cost of Sports and Who's Paying for It* (New York: Harper Collins, 1997), pp. 273–75.

9. Bartimole, "If You Build It,", p. 28–29.

10. Rosentraub, *Major League Losers,* p. 275.

11. Only companies with confirmed location and correct address were included in the Gateway database. Companies with local addresses reported in the ES202 data that were not confirmed were excluded from the analysis. Also, only companies with at least one paid employee are included; companies reporting zero employment were excluded.

12. The service sector is defined here as SICs 70–89. It does not include wholesale and retail trade, transportation and public utilities, and finance and real estate industries.

13. An opening is defined as an establishment that opened between 1989 and 1991 for the pre-Gateway period and between 1992 and 1995 for the post-Gateway period. Employment associated with these openings was calculated on the basis of employment in 1991 and 1995, respectively.

14. Relocation of an establishment is defined here as a confirmed change of address. Address changes were either provided in the ES202 data, and thus were checked and confirmed, or were identified through the data verification process described in the methodology section. Establishments that moved from outside Ohio into Gateway, or moved from Gateway to other states, might have been identified as openings or closings, respectively.

15. Todd Swanstrom, *The Crisis of Growth Politics: Cleveland, Kucinich, and the Challenge of Urban Populism* (Temple University Press, 1985).

16. Stan Bullard, "Developers Cooing That Occupancy Is Better than Expected," *Crain's Cleveland Business,* October 21, 1996, p. 3.

17. Bartimole, "If You Build It," p. 31; Rosentraub, *Major League Losers,* p. 278.

18. William N. Kinnard Jr., Mary Beth Geckler, and Jake W. DeLottie, "Team Performance, Attendance and Risk for Major League Baseball Stadiums: 1970–1994," *Real Estate Issues,* vol. 22 (April 1997), pp. 8–15.

12

Stickball in San Francisco

Stephen J. Agostini, John M. Quigley, and Eugene Smolensky

This is a simple game: you throw the ball,
you hit the ball, you catch the ball. You got it?

—*Bull Durham*

 On July 11, 1961, one year after opening, San Francisco's Candlestick Park was the site of baseball's thirtieth All-Star Game. The new stadium, built to lure the former New York Giants to the West Coast, became the stage for a most unusual comedy. As the *New York Times* described it, "For eight innings, in the stillness of an unusually hot and almost windless afternoon, brilliant National League pitching, starting with Warren Spahn, had held the vaunted American League to just one hit while the senior loop piled up a 3-1 lead."[1] But in the ninth inning, the already infamous Candlestick Point winds picked up. While "local fans, knowing full well what was coming, were heading for the exits before being blown into the bay," the National League made three errors, including a comical muff of a pop foul by catcher Smoky Burgess. Finally, with runners on first and second, right-hander Stu Miller was brought in to replace Sandy Koufax. As he wound up for his first pitch, a sudden gust blew Miller off the pitcher's

This chapter received research support from the Koret Foundation. Quigley's research is supported by the Fisher Center for Real Estate and Urban Economics, University of California, Berkeley. We acknowledge the able assistance provided by Sandra Sullivan in archival research and data analysis. The discussion benefited from the comments of Randall Hamilton, Dennis Howard, Roger Noll, and Andrew Zimbalist.

rubber, and the runners advanced on a rare balk. Another gust helped Rocky Colavito's grounder get past Ken Boyer. The American League scored two runs, pushing the game into extra innings. Eventually, however, the National Leaguers pulled it out in the tenth.

The wind did not change the game's outcome, but this did not spare Candlestick from the players' utter and vocal disdain. In the clubhouse afterward, Colavito declared, "If I was traded to the Giants and had to play here all the time, I'd quit baseball."[2] Yogi Berra grumbled, "You can have this park," while Arthur Daley of the *Times* pontificated, "Candlestick Park is like nothing else in the world. Whatever it is, though, it is definitely not a major league ballpark."[3]

But Willie Mays summed up the local perspective. "What can you do about it? You do the best you can in a park in which you got to play, and you just hope you don't look too foolish too often."[4] Mays's forbearance turned out to be a grim necessity. Giants players and fans have lived with the consequences of hasty decisions about the site and design of their stadium for three decades, despite endless and repetitive battles about fixing or replacing Candlestick.

This is the story of the ballpark that replaced Coogan's bluff. It covers the financial analyses underlying proposals for building a new ballpark to replace the embarrassment of Candlestick. It also covers the political economy surrounding public choices in San Francisco about the design, location, and public involvement in a new ballpark. Our conclusion is clear and somewhat surprising, at least to us. The procedures adopted to make complicated decisions about the baseball stadium in San Francisco are, we conclude, probably as good as one could expect. The mechanism used—a single-issue ballot initiative—is exactly the one favored by those who subscribe to the model of public choice.

As professional policy analysts, we would, of course, prefer to see the consumer surplus of each of the affected individuals added up, rather than their votes. But the procedures adopted in San Francisco dominate most of those found outside of economic textbooks. The ballot initiative provides ample opportunity for political elites and interest groups to affect the outcome, but their analyses and exhortations are inputs in a local plebiscite. The plebiscite represents a choice about public investment, but also about public consumption. Clearly, a reckoning of the investment costs and benefits is important, but the issue does not turn on a cost-benefit analysis alone.

Our review of the financial analysis underlying the stadium proposals suggests that much of it is flawed and self-serving. However, these analytical documents are only inputs to voters' decisions. Certainly, the electoral process is improved if the analyses presented are more credible. It is not clear, however, that the information available for baseball stadiums is systematically worse than the information relied on in other areas of public choice.

History

The debacle of the All-Star Game arose only a year after Candlestick Park had been opened. The stadium itself, and the financial deal behind it, was the crucial factor in inducing owner Horace Stoneham to move the Giants from New York for the 1958 season. Bayview Point, the specific site of Candlestick Park, was available immediately. This permitted San Francisco's mayor George Christopher to promise that the Giants could begin playing in a new ballpark soon after their arrival. On August 19, 1957, the New York Giants Board of Directors voted 8 to 1 to move to San Francisco. Within a matter of weeks, the Brooklyn Dodgers also decided to flee New York. Baseball was forever changed.

For several years, Stoneham and Dodgers' owner Walter O'Malley had made no secret of their dissatisfaction with the Polo Grounds and Ebbets Field, respectively. Despite a quite public scramble for alternative sites in the local area, there had been little enthusiasm in New York for providing government subsidies to the Giants or Dodgers. A majority of New York City's Board of Estimate (New York's equivalent to San Francisco's Board of Supervisors, for these purposes) was opposed to granting funds to construct a new stadium for either team.[5] Mayor Robert Wagner expressed similar views: "If we began to subsidize baseball teams, all sorts of business enterprises would demand the same things. Our feeling is that professional ball clubs class as private enterprise. They have to carry their own weight. We will not be blackjacked."[6]

Ironically, Wagner mused years later that New York City in 1957 was simply not ready to do what history and technological change had made necessary: put public funds into keeping a ball club in the city. "Had it all happened five years later, the outcome would probably have been different. The idea of municipalities building stadiums or helping in the building of stadiums was not really politically possible in New York City in 1957."[7]

A public subsidy for a baseball franchise was unthinkable in New York, but out in California it was quite doable. The deal offered by the city and county of San Francisco was an attractive one. The government agreed to use the proceeds from a $5 million bond issue already approved to build a 40,000- to 45,000-seat stadium at Bayview Point, with a 12,000-car parking lot. Contractor Charles Harney, who conveniently owned most of the land around Bayview Point (and could therefore promise rapid construction), was commissioned to build the park. He agreed to provide all additional financing to meet the total expected cost of $10 to $12 million. The city agreed to repay Harney with interest from stadium revenues, after which the park would be owned by the city.[8]

In addition to the friendly business climate proffered by city officials in San Francisco, the chimera of pay-TV appeared to make the West Coast far more attractive for professional baseball than New York City. Pay-TV seemed likely to become a reality very quickly in California, while its future in New York was far less certain. The financial appeal of pay-TV was significant. In 1956 the Giants received $603,000 for commercial radio and TV rights to their games. Under the proposed pay-TV system, Stoneham anticipated net receipts of $2.2 million a season by airing home games.[9]

While other publicly financed baseball stadiums at the time commanded a rent of at least 7 percent of net receipts, the Giants negotiated the surprising figure of 5 percent. The agreement did specify a minimum rent payment of $125,000 each year, but it also allowed the Giants to pocket all revenue from the stadium concessions.[10] The agreement specified the standard split of advertising revenues: the city would keep receipts from advertising under the stands, while the team would receive income from advertising on the stadium fences.[11]

The city expected to recoup its investment primarily through parking fees, with gross parking revenues anticipated to be $368,000.[12] After Harney's investment was repaid, the controller predicted complacently that the city could add the half million dollars in stadium receipts to its general fund each year.[13] A grand jury investigation of a possible "secret deal" between Mayor Christopher and developer Harney found no conflict of interest, but the grand jury report characterized the agreement on the Candlestick location and related economic terms as "a bad deal."[14]

A wind study commissioned by Mayor Christopher shortly after the 1961 All-Star Game recommended a dome for the stadium. By 1967 there were discussions of either expanding Candlestick or razing it. In 1968 the influential San Francisco Planning and Urban Research Association (SPUR) recommended a downtown ballpark, citing the high cost of operating Candlestick.

In 1969, when the city expanded Candlestick to facilitate play by football's 49ers, the situation got even worse for baseball. The front row in left field was pushed further back, away from the field, and the artificial turf made play more dangerous.[15]

The wind study commissioned in 1961 was only the first reanalysis of housing for the Giants. Two decades later, in the spring of 1981, the Giants released a 254-page report declaring Candlestick "unfit for baseball" and offering two options: build a new domed stadium, at an estimated cost of $100 million; or put a dome on Candlestick, at an estimated cost of $60 million.[16] The report set off years of debate, site studies, economic analyses, stadium proposals, and bond initiatives, which have continued to the present day. The alternatives discussed in the wake of the 1981 study are those that have been reexamined throughout the intervening decade and a half: make improvements to Candlestick, build a downtown stadium, build a stadium at China Basin, or do nothing at all.

The Giants' 1981 report led Mayor Dianne Feinstein to impanel a task force that identified four sources of funding for a new stadium: the sale or lease of private luxury boxes, tax benefits for stadium developers, corporate sponsorships and advertising revenue from the scoreboard and the media, and sale of the Candlestick property. The city still owed $20 million in bond payments for the improvements to Candlestick made for the benefit of the 49ers. The task force hoped that proceeds from the sale of the land would exceed this amount,[17] but other observers were less optimistic.[18] The mayor's task force also proposed that $3.5 million in hotel occupancy tax revenues be earmarked each year for Candlestick Park.

In October 1982, after studying ten sites, the task force proposed a new stadium at China Basin. The advantages of the site included the fact that the land was owned by two public agencies: the state of California and the San Francisco Port Commission. The task force hoped that both agencies could be persuaded to give up the land at very reasonable prices. In addition, the task force anticipated that the stadium could share parking facilities with the planned Mission Bay development project, which was expected to combine commercial and retail facilities with affordable housing.

However, some pointed out that the low-cost donation of China Basin land was not really a bargain. The task force valued the land at $58 to $65 a square foot, for a total cost of $32.8 to $36.8 million. If used for a new city-owned stadium, this land would produce no property taxes and could not be used for other attractive purposes. According to the city budget analyst, such alternatives might include 700 single-family homes, valued at $100,000 each, which would yield $651,000 per year in property taxes.[19]

Meanwhile, former mayor George Christopher went on record in support of doming Candlestick. He criticized the $100 million estimate put forth in the Giants' report for building a new stadium, noting that with the cost of land at China Basin, the project would require a minimum of $165 million. Since city regulations on debt financing would further increase the cost of financing the project, he declared that the Giants' report was written by "people who haven't studied San Francisco government" and recommended building a $60 million dome using the city's $187 million budget surplus.[20] In December, the San Francisco Board of Supervisors approved $300,000 for a feasibility study for a new stadium. Its members conditioned their approval on assurances that the study would focus not just on Mayor Feinstein's favored China Basin site, but on other possible locations, as well as on continued use of Candlestick.[21]

For the next five years, feasibility was studied and restudied. In 1987 Giant owner Robert Lurie persuaded Mayor Feinstein to put a proposal for a new stadium on the ballot. Feinstein warned Lurie that the proposal was not likely to succeed, but he persisted. Thus San Francisco voters had their first opportunity to express their preferences about a new stadium for the Giants. According to the Registrar of Voters, "Proposition W would make it the official policy of the people of San Francisco to build a baseball park at 7th and Townsend Streets on land provided at no cost to the city. There would be no increases in taxes, and all debt [would be] repaid with non-tax money."[22] According to proponents, the new ballpark would be financed by $45 million in bonds guaranteed by the private sector; $35 million would come from the sale of luxury boxes and the name of the new park, from corporate sponsorships associated with it, from proceeds of the sale of Candlestick Park, and from "surplus" hotel transient occupancy tax receipts.[23]

Opponents took issue with the claim that the ballpark could be constructed at no cost to the city. Although the industrial or revenue bonds proposed would be sold to private investors, the bonds would be guaranteed by the city, and the city could not allow a default without damaging its own bond rating and increasing the cost of financing future projects. Furthermore, the land was to be "donated" by the Santa Fe Corporation, developer of the adjacent Mission Bay development. Skeptics suggested that there was no such thing as a free acre and that Santa Fe undoubtedly expected subsidies for its project in return for this donation. Opponents also emphasized that while Proposition W ruled out tax *increases* to finance the stadium, there was nothing to prevent *current* tax funds from being diverted to stadium construction. In fact, the city planned to use some of the proceeds from the current tax on hotel occupancy.[24]

Mayor Feinstein, a majority of the Board of Supervisors, numerous law enforcement officials, labor groups, SPUR, and the San Francisco Chamber of Commerce all supported Proposition W. The ballot initiative was opposed by three supervisors, by a vocal urban environmental group (San Francisco Tomorrow), and by a variety of neighborhood groups. Most important, the proposition was opposed by mayoral candidate Art Agnos, who felt that the financial package left the city with an unacceptable budgetary risk. Agnos ran against a strong ballpark supporter who had a large early lead in the polls. Agnos was elected, and his success was reflected in the fate of Proposition W, which the voters rejected by a 53 to 47 margin. This defeat stood in sharp contrast to the voters' concurrent approval of $99 million for parks, streets, health centers, and police stations.[25]

Giants owner Bob Lurie initially seemed to take the vote personally, as if San Francisco voters were rejecting the team itself rather than a particular stadium financial arrangement. He announced that the Giants would leave San Francisco no later than 1994, when their Candlestick lease expired. In fact, Lurie announced that he wished to move his team to a South Bay location. Civic leaders in the South Bay communities responded positively to this message.

Over the next year and a half, various communities on the peninsula, including Santa Clara, East Palo Alto, San Jose, and Half Moon Bay, lobbied Lurie. However, key staff members to Mayor Agnos aggressively pursued efforts to keep the Giants in San Francisco. In October 1988, they solicited bids for a 42,000-seat downtown baseball stadium along with a 20,000-seat entertainment and sports arena. Meanwhile, Santa Clara was conducting a feasibility study, and Lurie commissioned a marketing study to see whether Santa Clara could support a ballpark.

On July 27, 1989, the mayor and Bob Lurie announced their plan for a 45,000-seat stadium at China Basin. The economics of the new deal, along with the participation of the Spectacor Management Group (experienced veterans at constructing and managing new sporting facilities) convinced Lurie that the ballpark should be put before San Francisco voters one more time. Mayor Agnos was willing to support a stadium with a more clearly defined financing package if it meant keeping the Giants from moving to the South Bay. In Lurie's view, however, this was the last shot for San Francisco. During negotiations with the mayor, he demanded, and received, a provision that would release the Giants from their Candlestick lease starting in 1990 if the proposal were defeated by the voters. This lease amendment was approved by the Board of Supervisors in early October.

Although there was no legal requirement that this ballpark agreement had to be approved by the voters, the mayor decided to put the proposal on the November ballot in light of the voters' rejection of the 1987 initiative. Thus, in Proposition P, voters were asked to approve the financial package contained in Memoranda of Understanding between San Francisco and the Giants and between San Francisco and the Spectacor Management Group.[26]

Debate over Proposition P was intense. Stadium proponents described the city's financial commitment to building the stadium as a mere $20 million, plus $10 million in loans. This money would be paid to the developer, Spectacor, in $3 million increments over ten years, starting in 1995, out of the city's hotel tax. Carol Wilkins, deputy mayor for finance, projected a return of $80 million over forty years on the $20 million investment. She also estimated that the investment in the ballpark would generate $230 million in additional sales, property, and payroll taxes.[27]

Opponents pointed to additional costs to the city beyond the $30 million commitment. For example, the city accepted liability for up to $10 million in cost overruns. The city would purchase and prepare the land. While the city would retain title to the parcel, it would give up the right to assess property taxes on it. In order to purchase the land, the city intended to sell a municipal bus lot, valued at about $18 million. In addition, under the Memoranda of Understanding, the city would be required to relocate port facilities and tenants, at an estimated cost of between $2 million and $7 million. The most unpredictable portion of the cost involved toxic cleanup of the China Basin property. While the city projected these costs at $2 million, subsequent testing could reveal a price tag of anywhere from $2 to $20 million.

The city was responsible for constructing a 1,500-car parking garage; it was unclear how this structure would be financed, especially when 1,200 of the spaces would be given free to luxury box owners and Giants affiliates. Critics argued that, to ensure proper access to the ballpark, the city would have to finance significant transit improvements to the municipal systems.

The city agreed it would not assess an admissions tax for the duration of the lease. In addition, the city would agree to give the Spectacor Management Group the exclusive right to develop a multipurpose arena adjacent to the ballpark. In return, the city would receive 20 percent of any stadium net cash flows for forty years. The city would retain title to the land. Giants officials confirmed that their rent—to be paid to Spectacor—would increase from about $700,000 at Candlestick (which represented the five percent of revenues specified in the Giants' original lease) to $7 million at China Basin.

Spectacor would pay the remainder of the $115 million in construction costs. These would be financed in part through $50 million in tax-exempt bonds, authority for which had been obtained by Mayor Feinstein as a special provision of the Tax Reform Act of 1986 (and which otherwise would expire at the end of 1990). The remaining $46 million required to build the park would be financed by Spectacor through taxable bonds. Spectacor planned to repay these bonds through revenues from luxury boxes, concessions, and rent. Spectacor also had the right to sell the park's name and to set ticket prices. At Candlestick, prices were set by a San Francisco city agency.

The battle over the initiative looked very close indeed. Proposition P was supported by most of the city's political establishment, by SPUR, by the League of Conservation Voters, by the San Francisco Chamber of Commerce, by both political parties, and by some affordable housing groups. In addition, elites in the gay community generally supported the ballpark, despite organized baseball's perceived hostility.

Nevertheless, in mid-September, polls showed the ballpark trailing slightly. But public opinion polls lost most of their relevance on October 17, 1989. On that date, just before the beginning of the third game of the San Francisco–Oakland World Series, a major earthquake hit San Francisco. Many observers believed that this, more than anything else, doomed the ballpark proposal. Candlestick was damaged, but it did withstand the earthquake, while other infrastructure and buildings crumbled. Suddenly building a new ballpark seemed far less important than housing the homeless and rebuilding the city.

The leaders of the mayor's "Yes on P" campaign were immediately diverted to Red Cross stations and relief offices. The mayor concentrated on raising money for disaster relief. Mayor Agnos did send out previously printed materials on the ballpark with a revised message: the ballpark was needed now, more than ever, for economic development and also to send a message of vitality to the rest of the country. In a cover letter, Agnos made a personal appeal: "I need to draw private investment into the city. I need to stimulate the economy. And construction of the new ballpark will help me do that. And this election will send a signal to the rest of the world that we believe in our future. The new construction methods used for the downtown high-rises, built on landfill, showed that we can build safely by anchoring foundations deep in the earth. The same will be true with the ballpark at China Basin."[28]

A few days before the vote, the campaign took a bizarre twist. It was revealed that a contractor in the employ of a prominent Sacramento financier, Gregg Lukenbill, had contributed $12,500 to a little-known ballpark opposition group known as "Yes on V/No on P." Mayor Agnos angrily charged that Lukenbill meant to "loot San Francisco of its baseball team in order to complete a financing package that is necessary for him to get the (Los Angeles) Raiders in Sacramento."[29] While some observers raised their eyebrows, noting that Lukenbill was a business partner of Angelo Tsakopoulos, a close friend and political supporter of Mayor Agnos, the media picked up on the charges that outsiders were trying to steal the Giants. The mayor urged San Francisco voters to defeat the efforts of these "outsiders" by supporting Proposition P.

Agnos's appeal was not enough. Proposition P lost by fewer than 2,000 votes.

During the next seven years, the Giants looked south to Santa Clara County, to San Jose, to Tampa, and finally back to San Francisco, seeking a home. South Bay voters twice showed their reluctance to pay higher utility taxes to finance a stadium, and Tampa lost out when Major League Baseball owners rescinded a sale of the team to interests in Tampa, forcing fed-up owner Bob Lurie to accept $15 million less in selling the team to a group of San Francisco investors cobbled together by Mayor

Frank Jordan. The new owners set out to develop a new kind of stadium proposal.

On December 21, 1995, the Giants once again announced their intention to build a 42,000-seat ballpark at the China Basin site. A ballot initiative was drafted, providing an exemption from zoning regulations. This initiative did not ask voters to approve a detailed financial understanding, but rather a policy statement: the ballpark would be privately financed. The private financing aspect drew the support of many who had opposed previous stadium initiatives. The campaign for the stadium was chaired by the conservative state senator Quentin Kopp, the liberal supervisor Roberta Achtenberg, and the well-known black clergyman Reverend Cecil Williams. The campaign would be chaired by Mayor-elect Willie Brown's campaign manager Jack Davis, who along with Kopp had actively worked against the 1987 and 1989 proposals.[30]

The ballpark was expected to cost $255 million. Of this, $140 million would be raised through a private bond issue, and $90 million would come from the sale of the stadium name, personal seat licenses for 15,000 seats, advertising and concession rights, and luxury boxes. Direct public money would be limited to tax-increment financing from the Redevelopment Agency. Of the $3.5 million in property taxes projected to be generated by the stadium, 60 percent would be invested by the city to improve public spaces around the ballpark. The other 40 percent would be invested in education and low-income housing. While this $6 million in tax increment financing from the Redevelopment Agency was clearly public funding, the Giants argued that the tax revenues were inextricably linked to the new stadium.

Many of the financial details between the Giants and the city remained to be worked out. The Port of San Francisco would purchase the portion of the property owned by the California Department of Transportation, and negotiate lease terms with the Giants. Once again, opponents pointed to indirect costs: purchase and preparation of the land, toxic cleanup, relocation of tenants, and increased security and transit improvements.

Many observers were skeptical that the Giants could undertake the private financing successfully. Personal seat licenses had never been used for baseball before, and the originator of the concept, Max Muhleman, expressed doubt that the Giants could raise significant funds in this way. Others noted that sports franchises had not had much success in issuing private bonds.[31] If the $140 million were successfully raised, debt service would require the team to attract 2.6 million fans per year, an increase of approximately 1 million over recent years.[32]

Nevertheless, the support from the entire political establishment, leaders of business, labor, education, the gay community, and many planning and environmental groups (together with assurances that a stadium would *not* be built unless privately financed) combined finally to provide the Giants with a victory. On May 26, 1996, Proposition B passed in every district but one. Two-thirds of the voters were recorded in favor of the zoning changes and the statement of principle.

The history of the past forty years can be summarized as a long convoluted struggle to fix a mistake. Study after study, plan after plan, and repeated efforts by the city's power structure and its political elite could not get a new stadium approved until a credible case could be made that the Giants would *not* receive a substantial direct subsidy.

The Lesson of History

One logical inference from this narrative is that it is acceptable to the voters for the city to provide infrastructure support and assistance with land assembly, but not to provide a direct subsidy to a private firm. A cash subsidy is just one benefit a city can provide to a sports franchise, and other support may be of equal importance. In San Francisco, it is simply inconceivable that the Giants or their fans could have a new ballpark without the city managing the process.

Imagine a private firm setting out to build a ballpark in China Basin on its own. Starting in the upper left-hand corner, figure 12-1 shows the steps the firm would have to take simply to acquire a site. Initially, a tract of land, large by any measure, would have to be assembled. Once a site had been chosen, elected government officials would be required to act. The colossal height of a major stadium requires a zoning variance by the Zoning Board, by the Board of Supervisors, or by an initiative. Because stadiums are controversial, local politicians prefer an initiative. So site assembly, at least in San Francisco, is going to involve an initiative whether a subsidy is involved or not. Approval of the city's political elite is not sufficient condition for approval of an initiative, as noted earlier, but it is probably necessary.

If the ballot measure were approved, as figure 12-1 indicates, a host of further approvals would be required from the city to meet environ-

Figure 12-1. *Steps Toward Private Construction of China Basin Ballpark*

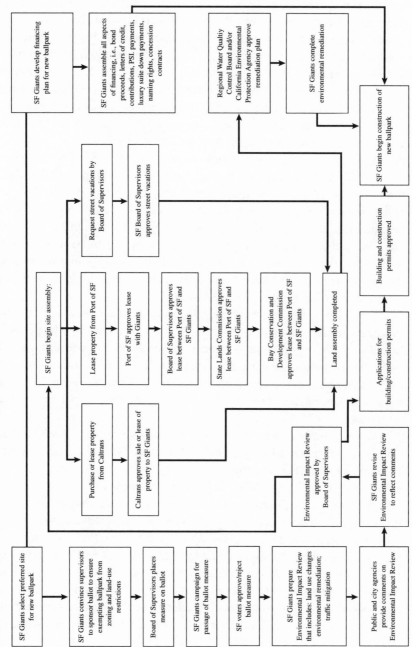

mental remediation and traffic mitigation requirements, culminating once again with a vote of the Board of Supervisors. If that hurdle were passed, consider what would have to happen next if this very large site was to be acquired from the city. Many agencies would have to sign off, and once again the Board of Supervisors would have to give its assent. Getting environmental, safety, and traffic approvals as well as acquiring city land would be easier if an organ of government, say the Port of San Francisco, were the applying agency. Government agencies have credibility before other public agencies—and probably before the press and the public, too—that private firms do not have. It is hard to imagine a private firm working through the twenty-eight steps in figure 12-1 without the prior agreement of the mayor and a majority of the Board of Supervisors, even if no cash subsidy to the firm were contemplated. The 47 to 66 percent of the voters who want major league baseball in the city need the commitment of the city government if they are to be able to get a commodity that they must consume collectively. Such a commitment from the city is necessary to help manage the process of complying with law, tradition, and local political expectations.

In addition to site selection and preparation, financing is another area in which the city must play a key role, whether a stadium is to be privately or publicly developed. This is a consequence of the huge federal subsidy available for finance using tax-exempt bonds. "A $225 million stadium built today and financed 100 percent with tax-exempt bonds might receive a lifetime federal tax subsidy as high as $75 million, 34 percent of construction costs."[33]

So, if a sizable minority (recall that the smallest vote a stadium received in the three initiatives in San Francisco was 47 percent) want a baseball stadium, how are they to get it? San Francisco's history suggests a two-step procedure that economists should applaud:

—Supporters of the stadium first demonstrate that they are willing to pay for it privately or are willing to finance some portion publicly.

—Then they convince the median voter that it would be desirable for the city to arrange to assemble the land and make it ready for construction, arrange access to the federal subsidy, and provide a local subsidy. Many economists would be happier if the local subsidy were zero. Almost all economists would be happier if the federal subsidy were zero. But the local subsidy, at least, is a matter of local tastes for a local consumption good.

Quantifying the Costs and Benefits of a China Basin Ballpark

As already mentioned, San Franciscans have had three opportunities to register their opinions on the replacement of Candlestick Park: Proposition W (which lost, 47 to 53 percent, in 1987); Proposition P (which lost, 49 to 51 percent, in 1989); and Proposition B (which passed, 66 to 34 percent, in 1996). Of these, Proposition P underwent the most intense scrutiny. It was the subject of three fiscal analyses: one produced by then Mayor Agnos's Office; an independent review of that report produced by the San Francisco Board of Supervisors' budget analyst, Harvey Rose; and a third, authored by an economics professor for San Franciscans for Planning Priorities (SFPP). In contrast, Proposition B received somewhat less financial scrutiny, perhaps because public funds were less of an issue.[34] Proposition W received even less in the way of systematic analysis.

Proposition P generated significant analytical attention, and that attention arguably clarified the debate over the financial benefits of a new ballpark. The mayor's office, as well as the campaign apparatus in support of Proposition P, argued that the investment "would generate net benefits of $31.5 million" and that "even in the worst case, if the intangible benefits often associated with major league sports are considered, along with the quantifiable benefits estimated . . . , it would appear that this investment is worth undertaking."[35]

The budget analyst disagreed with this contention, arguing that "the estimated net cost/benefit of the downtown ballpark proposal is significantly less than the mayor's report has projected."[36] The analysis prepared for SFPP also took issue with the mayor's report, arguing that there would be no net benefits associated with this investment.[37] In the end, the three analyses rendered inconclusive the public debate over the extent of financial benefits to a new ballpark. In the aftermath of the Loma Prieta earthquake in October 1989, this debate became largely irrelevant.

While the voters considering Proposition B in 1996 were not subjected to contradictory analyses, the financial review conducted by the budget analyst was, by its own admission, "unable to make a definitive calculation of the total costs and benefits to the City."[38] In spite of this, the San Francisco Giants, in a letter to the budget analyst, hailed the report: "We agree with your overall findings that *the benefits of the new ballpark far exceed any potential costs* associated with the new China Basin Ballpark."[39] Mayor Willie Brown concurred with the Giants' assessment: "In fact, [the budget analyst] shows that the city stands to gain more than $1.5 million annually in additional tax revenues from the presence of the Giants in a new downtown ballpark," an assessment the budget analyst took pains to refute.[40] Curiously, the Giants went on to report (in the very next sentence of their letter) that they "also agree that *no definitive cost estimate can be made at this time* given the current information available."[41] A voter considering these seemingly contradictory assessments of the same report could be forgiven for being somewhat confused. Did the benefits of Proposition B indeed "far exceed" the potential costs, as the Giants believed? Or was the existing information insufficient to reach a definitive conclusion, as the budget analyst originally stated? Confused or not about the financial implications of a new ballpark, San Franciscans approved Proposition B by a huge margin in March 1996. The Giants were clearly pleased by the outcome. As "the man who crafted the financial plan for the Giants' China Basin ballpark [stated], the election victory means 'the hardest part is over. The rest is a cakewalk.' "[42]

For many of the proponents of Proposition P, the choice was simple: the financial returns associated with the proposed ballpark, combined with the prospect of retaining the Giants in San Francisco, provided ample reasons for investing city resources—directly—in a new ballpark. For Proposition B's proponents the choice was equally simple: the absence of a direct public subsidy, and the prospect of retaining the Giants, were compelling reasons for voting to exempt the ballpark project from zoning and land-use restrictions. To their respective advocates, these were two distinctly different approaches—public subsidy versus no public subsidy—to resolving the same problem: retaining major league baseball in San Francisco. And if the votes on the two measures were any indication, voters were very clear about which approach they preferred: a new ballpark without public subsidy.

The financial analysis reported in the appendix to this chapter evaluates the claims made by proponents for the two most recent China Basin ballot initiatives—Propositions B and P—by quantifying some of the public costs, benefits, and transfers associated with each proposal. This is a somewhat speculative endeavor, since San Francisco has yet to construct a replacement for Candlestick Park. Consequently, hard data about construction costs are simply unavailable for San Francisco. While our

Table 12-1. *Estimates of Net Fiscal Impact of Propositions B and P*
Millions of 1996 dollars

	Year	Net fiscal impact	
		Upper bound	*Lower bound*
Proposition B	1996	− 12.1	2.0
Proposition P	1989	− 18.4	0.9

Source: See tables 12A–4 through 12A–7. Negative numbers represent net fiscal costs.

estimates do not use ex-post financial statements, a wealth of information is available to construct plausible inferences about impacts. Note that the evaluation reported in the appendix is based on the data available to voters at the time the decisions were made.

No comprehensive benefit-cost analysis (as described in chapter 2) was ever conducted for any of the San Francisco stadium proposals. Rather, as the appendix to this chapter explains, there were several fiscal impact studies. The political debate about Proposition P, in particular, featured dueling studies and attacks on parts or all of each. Here we summarize what the informed, involved voter could have deduced from the debate swirling around these fiscal impact studies, for the elite, informed voters may play the pivotal role in determining whether a complicated initiative passes.[43]

The central finding for Propositions P and B is that the key difference between the two was the decline in downside risk to the taxpayer, particularly the decline in the upper-bound estimates of the public subsidy (see table 12-1 and appendix tables 12A-1 through 12A-7). The major reason for this decline was the elimination of promises of cash by the city. Proposition P offered Spectacor cash in three forms: a contribution for operations and maintenance, a loan, and reimbursement of the costs imposed by other jurisdictions. In eliminating these costs ($16 million) in the transition from Propositions P to B, the city gave up a share in the ballpark's cash flow and payroll taxes ($10.5 million). Moreover, the city substantially reduced its net downside risk.

To make these comparisons, informed voters had to work their way from the flawed data in studies as they first appeared (summarized in appendix tables 12A-1 and 12A-2) to extract the information presented in appendix tables 12A-3 through 12A-7. They then had to appraise the remaining uncertainties that are captured in the differences between the upper- and lower-bound estimates. Also important, the voter had to shift the focus of the accounting system for benefits and costs from the perspective of the city's general fund to the perspective of citizens as federal as well as local taxpayers. Of course, the voter had to understand the concept of net present value and interest rate sensitivity. The relevant opinion leaders were certainly capable of making these calculations, in a very rough and ready way, of course. The gross errors and the more subtly misleading implications that come from evaluating the benefits and costs of a stadium from the perspective of the general fund of the city are clear in the detailed discussion of the appendix tables.

One illustration of the consequences of accounting for benefits and costs from a city's financial perspective involved reckoning the costs of the site. Initially, the city put the value of the land at 9 percent of the original acquisition cost of the land (which the city already owned). This was because city officials expected the remainder to be borne by the federal government. Of course, city residents lose when the federal government loses. Moreover, in this case, the cost used would have been less than the opportunity cost of the land *to the city*. Even valuing the land at acquisition cost would have underestimated the true economic cost (that is, the current opportunity cost) of the stadium. Undervaluing the site in calculating the costs of the stadium foreclosed any other use of the land that would have had greater economic benefits for the city.

As these important details illustrate, calculating costs and benefits from the perspective of the city's operating budget makes no economic sense. Indeed, there is something terribly peculiar about categorizing any increase in taxes collected by the city as a benefit! Yet it is from this very perspective that the economic debate about stadiums has been pursued in San Francisco and, most likely, everywhere else.

The Use of Analysis

It has often been noted that studies analyzing the impact of sports stadiums on the local economy are flawed and self-serving. As reported in the appendix, the analyses of the 1989 proposal are replete with errors and are based on specialized (or peculiar) assumptions. They are, to some extent, political documents meant to influence the political process.

It is crucial to recognize, however, that in San Francisco these analytical studies were inputs in local plebiscites. They were hardly intended to rank public investment projects according to principles of cost-benefit analysis so that experts could determine the most socially beneficial in-

Table 12-2. *Voting on 1989 Stadium Initiative in San Francisco*

t-ratios in parentheses

Independent variable	Model					
	I	*II*	*III*	*IV*	*V*	*VI*
Median income (thousands)	0.011 (3.16)			−0.000 (0.84)		
College graduate (fraction)		0.239 (9.86)				0.227 (4.60)
Executive (fraction)			0.721 (8.92)			0.489 (4.02)
Male (fraction)	−0.072 (1.01)	−0.071 (1.35)	−0.084 (1.54)	−0.192 (3.04)	−0.076 (1.36)	−0.112 (2.04)
Hispanic (fraction)	−0.137 (2.74)	0.060 (1.33)	0.047 (1.01)	−0.080 (1.84)	0.055 (1.10)	0.019 (0.41)
Asian (fraction)	0.029 (1.28)	0.121 (5.96)	0.113 (5.39)	0.120 (5.25)	0.123 (5.77)	0.131 (6.02)
White (fraction)				0.167 (7.24)	0.010 (0.28)	0.071 (2.53)
Constant	0.511 (11.23)	0.429 (13.20)	0.443 (13.23)	0.499 (12.87)	0.430 (13.13)	0.440 (13.36)
R^2	0.194	0.497	0.455	0.421	.497	0.480

Source: Authors' calculations.
Dependent variable: percentage of voters supporting initiative by census tract. Precinct voting data for 1989 were
aggregated to the level of census tracts and merged with the U.S. Census STF3 data for San Francisco for 1990,
yielding 140 observations on aggregate voting by census tract.

vestment projects to undertake. On the contrary, these studies were used
by citizens in making judgments in a single-issue ballot. The issue to be
decided was partly about public investment, but only partly. It was also
about public consumption. The issue was much the same as decisions
about the appropriate level of support for the San Francisco opera and
symphony, or about the decision to enhance the public park adjoining
the municipal art gallery at Yerba Buena.

A careful reckoning of costs and benefits is clearly important to these
public choice decisions, but these issues do not turn solely on benefit-
cost ratios that fail to take into account the willingness-to-pay of those
most intensely interested in keeping or attracting a team. The decisionmaking process differs between, say, opera and baseball in San Francisco
in that the latter is based on citizen ballot. Proposition P failed. Why did
it fail? Which segments of the population were willing to provide substantial up-front money to build a municipal ballpark in China Basin?

Table 12-2 provides some evidence. It reports a series of regression
results based on the 1989 ballot initiative. Voting returns by precinct
were aggregated to the level of census tracts and matched to 1990 tract

data. The regressions report the fraction of the vote favoring the initiative as a function of the demographic composition of the tracts. The six regressions differ in the measures used to represent more sophisticated voters (median income, or the fraction of adults who are college graduates, or the fraction employed in executive or managerial positions).

As table 12-2 indicates, the 1989 baseball stadium was a superior good: an extra thousand dollars in income increased the propensity to vote in favor of the stadium by about one percentage point. College graduates were substantially more likely to favor the stadium proposal, as were those in executive and managerial occupations. There is some evidence that those living in census tracts with larger male populations (including San Francisco's homosexual community) were more likely to oppose the initiative. Asians were generally in favor of the initiative as were white voters. There is weak evidence of systematic differences between Hispanic and other voters. Other evidence, not reported, suggests that there was little difference in voting behavior in the 1989 initiative by age group, homeownership, or other demographic considerations.[44] Overall, the statistical models explain somewhat less than half of the variance in voting behavior.

Table 12-3 presents the same regressions applied to the 1996 voter initiative. The pattern of the estimated coefficients is strikingly similar. Higher-income, better-educated San Franciscans were more likely to favor the initiative, as were those in professional and executive jobs. Those living in census tracts with higher fractions of males were less likely to favor the ballpark proposal. Asian voters were more likely to favor the initiative, while Hispanics were, perhaps, more likely to oppose it.

The similarity of voting patterns in the two plebiscites suggests that voter preferences for a new ballpark to keep the Giants in San Francisco are stable, but that the price of achieving this varied in the two elections. Table 12-4 tests this hypothesis more formally. It reports coefficient estimates when the voting data for the two elections are combined. The same models are estimated, adding a dummy variable for the 1996 election.

Here, the larger sample improves the precision of the coefficient estimates and the explanatory power of the statistical models. The dummy variable for the 1996 election indicates that, when the public subsidy to the franchise was eliminated (or at least reduced substantially), voter approval increased by roughly fifteen percentage points.

The F tests indicate that the coefficients on the demographic variables are, indeed, identical for the two elections.

Table 12-3. *Voting on the 1996 Stadium Initiative in San Francisco*[a]
t-ratio in parentheses

Independent variable	Model					
	I	II	III	IV	V	VI
Median income (thousands)	0.001 (1.92)			0.001 (1.15)		
College graduate (fraction)		0.087 (3.18)			0.184 (3.34)	
Executive (fraction)			0.316 (3.62)			0.461 (3.47)
Male (fraction)	−0.128 (1.95)	−0.144 (2.40)	−0.143 (2.43)	−0.142 (2.09)	−0.105 (1.68)	−0.126 (2.10)
Hispanic (fraction)	−0.249 (5.43)	−0.183 (3.57)	−0.172 (3.39)	−0.242 (5.18)	−0.139 (2.51)	−0.154 (2.70)
Asian (fraction)	0.016 (0.77)	0.044 (1.91)	0.049 (2.17)	0.027 (1.11)	0.029 (1.22)	0.038 (1.57)
White (fraction)				0.021 (0.83)	−0.082 (2.02)	−0.044 (1.45)
Constant	0.716 (17.20)	0.704 (19.15)	0.698 (19.32)	0.715 (17.13)	0.698 (19.12)	0.700 (19.45)
R^2	0.300	0.331	0.345	0.304	0.351	0.355

Source: Authors' calculations.
a. Dependent variable: percentage of voters supporting initiative. Precinct voting data for 1996 were aggregated to the level of census tracts and merged with U.S. Census STF3 data for San Francisco, yielding 140 observations on aggregate voting by census tract.

One further aspect of these results is consistent with the combined investment-and-consumption nature of the public choice. More sophisticated voters—better-educated, higher-income voters with higher-status jobs—were consistently more strongly *in favor* of these initiatives than other voters. If the ballpark choice were simply an investment in local economic development, we would expect these voters to be more easily able to discern the fact that a new ballpark was a dubious proposition in purely fiscal terms. That these very voters were more likely to approve the propositions reinforces the consumption aspects of the choice. A new ballpark to keep the Giants in San Francisco is a normal economic good, and higher-income households are more likely to support it. If the price is lower, as it was in 1996, citizens are more likely to approve the package.

Conclusion

In most cities, major changes to the infrastructure are commonly proposed and discussed. Citizens almost always have some ways, formal

Table 12-4. *Voting on San Francisco Stadium Initiatives of 1989 and 1996*[a]

t-ratios in parentheses

Independent variable	Model					
	I	II	III	IV	V	VI
Median income (thousands)	0.009 (3.63)			0.000 (0.25)		
College graduate (fraction)		0.163 (8.65)			0.205 (5.38)	
Executive (fraction)			0.519 (8.56)			0.475 (5.11)
Male (fraction)	−0.100 (2.07)	−0.108 (2.62	−0.114 (2.77)	−0.167 (3.49)	−0.090 (2.01)	−0.119 (2.83)
Hispanic (fraction)	−0.193 (5.70)	−0.061 (1.74)	−0.062 (1.76)	−0.161 (4.89)	−0.042 (1.09)	−0.067 (1.86)
Asian (fraction)	0.022 (1.47)	0.082 (5.24)	0.082 (5.24)	0.074 (4.25)	0.076 (4.61)	0.085 (5.06)
White (fraction)				0.094 (5.37)	0.036 (1.28)	0.013 (0.62)
1996 election (dummy)	0.151 (29.42)	0.151 (32.43)	0.151 (32.35)	0.151 (30.88)	0.151 (32.47)	0.151 (32.32)
Constant	0.538 (17.41)	0.491 (19.37)	0.495 (19.64)	0.532 (18.03)	0.488 (19.21)	0.495 (19.56)
R^2	0.766	0.816	0.815	0.798	0.817	0.815
F-ratio[b]	0.311	1.291	0.979	1.380	1.469	1.424

Source: Authors' calculations.

a. Dependent variable: percentage of voters supporting initiatives Regressions are based on 140 observations on aggregate census tract votes for 1989 and 140 observations on aggregate voting patterns in 1996.

b. The critical value of F (6,267) exceeds 2.10 at the .05 level.

and informal, to influence these decisions. Rarely, however, is the process as open as it was in the recent history of baseball stadiums in San Francisco. Even in San Francisco, major expenditures for the opera and symphony, and large changes in the allocation of retail space, are made without the systematic involvement of all citizens.

It is also rarely the case that analysis plays as prominent a role in decisionmaking. As we have shown, the analyses presented were deeply flawed. Sometimes assumptions were unrealistic. Perhaps in some cases, the analyses were simply dishonest. But, criticisms and countercriticisms of all the studies were given considerable coverage by the media. Most important, perhaps, those who were supporters and those who were opposed were well known. Political analyses of other initiative elections in California suggest that "uninformed" voters often emulate the behavior of "informed" voters when the right cues are available. The cues of particular relevance are the identities of public figures who support and oppose the initiative.[45] The key to the final passage of a stadium initiative may well have been that well-known political figures shifted from opposing to supporting the stadium. If these politicians made the switch on the basis of the elimination of any direct subsidy to the Giants, as they claimed, the process appears to have worked well.

The defects of analysis and public choice that remain should be compared against specific real world alternatives. Is the analytical support for the B-1 Bomber superior? Are the projected consequences of a 15 percent tax reduction, by any of the disputants, more credible?

Appendix

This appendix presents the critical financial elements of Propositions P and B, the prior financial analyses provided to the public during the debates over each, and our own estimates (lower and upper bounds) of the "net fiscal impacts" of the two proposals.

Proposition P (1989): The Financial Analysis

On July 27, 1989, San Francisco mayor Art Agnos, San Francisco Giants owner Bob Lurie, and Spectacor Management Group (SMG) vice president Don Webb announced that they had signed Memoranda of Agreement to build a new downtown ballpark for the Giants for $95.8 million (1989 dollars), a facility the Giants would call home for the next forty years. The new ballpark, to be located in an area known as China Basin, was to be constructed and operated by a public-private partnership between SMG and the city. This public-private partnership (a precursor to similar arrangements that would soon become common), was designed to limit the city's financial exposure for constructing Candlestick Park's replacement.

SMG's responsibilities in this arrangement were significant: it was to assemble the financing necessary for construction through pre-sales of luxury suites and premium seating, handle the sale of naming and scoreboard rights, manage construction of the facility to ensure availability for opening day, and operate the facility with the Giants as tenants over the next forty years.[46] In exchange, SMG would keep 80 percent of the "net cash flow" from operation of the ballpark, along with the exclusive right to develop a sports and entertainment arena in the city, a potentially lucrative option for SMG.[47]

The city's responsibilities in the partnership were equally significant: San Francisco was to issue $50 million in tax-exempt bonds for the new ballpark under city authority (retained in the transition rules to the Federal Tax Reform Act of 1986);[48] acquire and assemble the land for the ballpark; prepare the site for construction; contribute up to $10 million, if necessary, for construction cost overruns (above the original $96.8 million estimate);[49] and disburse $3 million a year for the first ten years of the ballpark's operations, $2 million as an investment in the ballpark, and $1 million as a market rate loan to the ballpark's operators.

For the city, these expenditures would not only ensure that the Giants remained in San Francisco, but they would also secure for the city the remaining 20 percent of the net cash flow of the ballpark's operations over SMG's forty-year lease (in exchange for the $2 million investment); and they would provide title to the entire facility to the city at the end of SMG's initial lease, as "repayment" for the $10 million loan.

The city's financial contributions were not trivial. Land assembly, expected to be completed in 1991, would require pulling together Port of San Francisco property at Pier 46B and property owned by the state of California's Department of Transportation (Caltrans), "which was originally intended to be part of the uncompleted Interstate 280 freeway."[50] The Port's property would require payment for the opportunity costs that would be incurred by the Port, estimated by the mayor's office at between $4.2 million (1989 dollars) and $7.1 million. This would be financed from the proceeds of the sale of municipal bus yards. The Caltrans property would require the city to pay $1.3 million, an amount reflecting the actual cost for site acquisition by Caltrans. Since the property was originally acquired with a 91 percent match from the federal government, a waiver of the requirement to reimburse the federal government for the property would mean that Caltrans could be paid only 9 percent of the total value of the property ($12.94 million). At the time, the mayor's office was confident that the federal government would waive its reimbursement requirement for properties purchased for the federal highway system. The waiver would therefore have saved Caltrans, and the ballpark project, an $11.78 million payment that would otherwise have been required by the federal government.[51]

Site preparation, scheduled for 1992, would require: relocation of the Port's central maintenance facility, which was contemplated as part of a city Redevelopment Agency project; partial or complete demolition of the deck on Pier 46B, estimated between $1.8 million and $7 million; environmental remediation of the site, estimated at $2 million; and $1 million for infrastructure improvements, exclusive of transit improvements, which had already been contemplated for the area by the Municipal Railway. A contingency of $2 million, principally for environmental remediation, was also budgeted.

The city also agreed to waive property or possessory interest taxes on the new facility. This meant that the city would make payments in lieu of taxes to other governmental jurisdictions on behalf of the ballpark and SMG over the life of the lease.

As calculated by the mayor's office, the nominal costs totaled $62.9 million (1989 dollars) or about $26.5 million in net present value (NPV). Yet the mayor's office argued that there were sizable financial benefits associated with retaining the team, although it qualified its estimate of these benefits in an entirely overlooked passage regarding "substitution effects."[52] Direct tax revenues generated by the Giants and indirect tax revenues generated by the ballpark, along with the city's 20 percent share of the ballpark's cash flow, provided net benefits that were greater than the costs that might be incurred, even in the "worst-case" scenario envisioned in the report.

The city's share of the ballpark's cash flow was estimated at $6.1 million in present value terms.[53] Direct city revenues, estimated to be $34.7 million in the expected case, were revenues from taxes directly imposed on the Giants or the operation of the ballpark. These taxes were limited to payroll taxes paid on the players' salaries and other personnel of the Giants, payroll taxes on concessionaire personnel, and sales taxes on concessions.[54] Indirect city revenues, estimated at $17.2 million (NPV 1989 dollars), assumed that the Giants' payroll and the expenditures on the ballpark and its operations generated a multiplier impact, calculated at 1.44, which created wealth throughout San Francisco's economy and additional revenues for the city's treasury.

Within days of the release of the mayor's office analysis, the budget analyst employed by the Board of Supervisors released a detailed critique, substantially revising the estimates of the potential costs and benefits of the ballpark proposal. The budget analyst pointed out that the mayor's office had neglected to include the opportunity costs incurred by the Port of San Francisco for surrendering its land for the project, was overly optimistic regarding the Caltrans waiver, and had neglected the potential costs for providing security within the new ballpark (a cost accepted by the city in the Memorandum of Agreement with SMG). The budget analyst also questioned the value of the benefits calculated by the mayor's office, arguing (correctly) that the salaries of nonplayers had been inflated at the rate projected for players. According to the budget analyst, if Proposition P were approved, the city risked incurring a "negative benefit of $21.3 million"[55] in the worst case, ensuring that "the City would lose money over the long term."[56] The costs and benefits described in the mayor's analysis are summarized in table 12A-1. The Board of Supervisors and budget analyst's revisions to these estimates are summarized in table 12A-2.

The SFPP analysis was a third assessment of the new ballpark's potential costs and benefits, coming on the heels of the budget analyst's revision. It also called into question many of the assumptions underlying the report from the mayor's office. It focused on two issues in particular. First, it called the failure to account for the Port's opportunity costs "an egregious oversight," since "the stock of city assets has been reduced to build the new stadium."[57] Second, the report challenged "the entire notion of using a standard measure of spin-off benefits to estimate the impact of a ballpark on city finances. The money that Giants fans will spend at the new stadium may be largely money they would have spent in the city, . . . and simply shifting that spending from one type of business to another or from one ballpark site to another won't lead to any net economic benefits."[58]

The three separate analyses contributed to a heated, if inconclusive, debate about the proposed ballpark. The debate, the stadium proposal itself, the earthquake, and a variety of other factors affected the vote. The proposal lost by 49 to 50 percent. If 1,055 additional voters had been convinced of the virtues of the China Basin ballpark, the initiative would have passed.

Proposition B (1996): Financial Analysis

On December 21, 1995, Peter Magowan, the president and general managing partner of the San Francisco Giants, announced plans for a $255 million, 42,000-seat ballpark, the "first privately financed major league ballpark to open in three decades" at a familiar downtown location: the same China Basin site proposed in 1989.[59] The new stadium plan called for $50 million in naming rights from Pacific Bell, to be paid

Table 12A-1. *Costs and Benefits of Proposition P as Portrayed by Mayor's Office, 1989*

All figures are in hundreds of thousands of 1989 dollars

	Nominal costs		
	Worst case	*Expected case*	*Best case*
Costs			
China Basin land assembly	(1,300)	(1,300)	(1,300)
China Basin site preparation	(6,800)	(6,800)	(6,800)
City share of construction costs	(10,000)	(10,000)	0
City contribution for ballpark operation and maintenance	(20,000)	(20,000)	(20,000)
City loan to ballpark operations	(10,000)	(10,000)	(10,000)
City payments to other jurisdictions	(14,745)	(14,745)	(12,094)
Total estimated costs	(62,845)	(62,845)	(50,194)
Revenues			
City share of ballpark cash flow	71,004	75,203	75,203
Retained tax revenue	159,253	495,375	1,782,160
Spectacor payroll taxes	75,920	252,393	925,324
Total estimated revenues	306,177	822,971	2,782,687
Net impact	243,332	760,126	2,732,493

	Net present values		
	Worst case	*Expected case*	*Best case*
Costs			
China Basin land assembly	(973)	(973)	(973)
China Basin site preparation	(4,737)	(4,737)	(4,737)
City share of construction costs	(6,028)	(6,028)	0
City contribution for ballpark operation and maintenance	(8,275)	(8,275)	(8,275)
City loan to ballpark operations	(4,137)	(4,137)	(4,137)
City payments to other jurisdictions	(2,348)	(2,348)	(1,926)
Total estimated costs	(26,498)	(26,498)	(20,048)
Revenues			
City share of ballpark cash flow	5,619	6,130	6,130
Retained tax revenue	14,723	34,665	102,340
Spectacor payroll taxes	6,730	17,198	52,581
Total estimated reveneus	27,072	57,993	161,051
Net impact	574	31,495	141,003

Soruce: Carol Wilkins and Stephen J. Agostini, *Building a New Home for the San Francisco Giants: A Cost-Benefit Analysis of the Proposed China Basin Ballpark*, San Francisco, Office of the Mayor, October 2, 1989, tables 2, 3, and 4.

Table 12A-2. *Costs and Benefits of Proposition P as Portrayed by Board of Supervisors—Budget Analyst, 1989*
Hundreds of thousands of 1989 dollars

	Nominal costs		
	Worst case	Expected case	Best case
Costs			
Port of SF opportunity costs	(7,000)	(7,000)	(4,200)
China Basin land assembly	(11,500)	(1,300)	(1,300)
China Basin site preparation	(11,900)	(6,900)	6,800
City share of construction costs	(10,000)	(10,000)	(2,500)
City contribution for ballpark operation and maintenance	(20,000)	(20,000)	(20,000)
City loan to ballpark operations	(10,000)	(10,000)	(10,000)
City payments to other jurisdictions	(18,700)	(16,880)	(14,745)
SFPD costs for security	(12,080)	(12,080)	(12,080)
Total estimated costs	(101,180)	(84,160)	(71,625)
Revenues			
City share of ballpark cash flow	71,004	75,203	75,203
Retained tax revenue	124,462	345,417	1,192,807
Spectacor payroll taxes	75,920	252,393	925,324
Total estimated revenues	271,386	673,013	2,193,334
Net impact	170,206	588,853	2,121,709

	Net present values		
	Worst case	Expected case	Best case
Costs			
Port of SF opportunity costs	(5,240)	(5,240)	(3,145)
China Basin land assembly	(8,600)	(973)	(973)
China Basin site preparation	(8,290)	(4,737)	(4,737)
City share of construction costs	(6,028)	(6,028)	(1,500)
City contribution for ballpark operation and maintenance	(8,275)	(8,275)	(8,275)
City loan to ballpark operations	(4,137)	(4,137)	(4,137)
City payments to other jurisdictions	(2,980)	(2,688)	(2,348)
SFPD costs for security	(2,270)	(2,270)	(2,270)
Total estimated costs	(45,820)	(34,348)	(27,385)
Revenues			
City share of ballpark cash flow	5,619	6,130	6,130
Retained tax revenue	12,157	25,267	69,807
Spectacor payroll taxes	6,730	17,198	52,581
Total estimated reveneus	24,506	48,595	128,518
Net impact	(21,314)	14,247	101,133

Source: Letter. Board of Supervisors—Budget Analyst, to Supervisors Hongisto. Hsieh, and Nelder, October 6, 1989, pp. 31–33.
ɣ, pp. ɔɪ–ɔɔ.

over 24 years;[60] between $35 million and $45 million from the sale of premium seat licenses;[61] $145 million in private financing "through a consortium of banks and other investors;"[62] and $10 million to $15 million in tax increment financing from the San Francisco Redevelopment Agency.[63]

Many were pleased with this latest proposal, particularly in view of Magowan's insistence on financing the facility privately: "If the Giants are successful here, the days of [sports franchise] owners putting a gun to the heads of a city and saying 'Build a stadium or I'll move,' are over," Magowan said.[64] State Senator Quentin Kopp, a vociferous opponent of Proposition P, supported the plan principally because it did not require public financing: "It looks feasible, and it looks desirable and in the public interest . . . I have not supported previous plans because those plans utilized taxpayers' money for the cost. The forthcoming plan does not."[65]

Outside observers, however, questioned the feasibility of privately financing the new ballpark. Jerry Reinsdorf, owner of the Chicago White Sox and Chicago Bulls, argued: "The best they will be able to do is cover their debt service. So what's the point of building it?"[66] John H. McHale Jr., president of the Detroit Tigers, observed: "Obviously, they want to stay in San Francisco very badly. . . . People don't commit economic suicide on purpose. It is possible, but it is a thin deal financially."[67]

To buttress their claims that the privately financed ballpark would be a boon to San Francisco, on February 26, 1996, the Giants released an economic impact report, prepared by Economics Research Associates (ERA), that stated the ballpark would have "a first year impact of $124.8 million" on the city and create 6,455 jobs.[68] This report, an update of an earlier report prepared by ERA for the Giants,[69] considered as the counterfactual, "the Giants have left the West Coast entirely, and no new major league fianchise has moved into San Francisco to replace them."[70] The report then sought to quantify direct economic impacts by projecting attendance at the new ballpark, examining surveys of patrons' purchasing habits within and outside recently constructed ballparks around the country, examining surveys of spending by fans from outside of San Francisco, and estimating the percentage of the Giants' operating expenses spent within San Francisco. Indirect economic impacts were then estimated using the Regional Input-Output Modeling System (RIMS II) developed by the U.S. Department of Commerce, which provided a multiplier between 1.83 and 1.90.

Less than a week later, the Board of Supervisors' budget analyst issued his report on the prospective public costs and benefits of the Giants' proposed ballpark:

> Our review has found that potential costs to the city and County of San Francisco include the areas of Municipal Railway (Muni) transit services, traffic control and security performed by the Police Department and the Department of Parking and Traffic, the Port, and various capital projects. However, sufficient information has not been provided to the Budget Analyst to clearly specify the amount of all such costs to the City. Until such time as the environmental review process has been completed and a long term ground lease between the Giants and the Port has been negotiated and approved, the Budget Analyst is unable to make a definitive calculation of the total costs and benefits to the City.[71]

The budget analyst stated that the costs for land assembly and site preparation "are ultimately to be paid by the Giants . . . under the long-term lease to be negotiated between the Port and the Giants."[72] These costs would include: $11 million (if not more) to purchase the Caltrans site at China Basin, as much as $7 million to relocate the Port's maintenance facility, between $2 million and $7 million for demolition of the "deck" and structures on Pier 46B, and between $5 million and $20 million for the remediation of toxics on the site.

According to the budget analyst, the city would incur costs for additional Municipal Railway service that would be needed to service the new ballpark, estimated at $300,000 annually; the loss of lease revenue at Candlestick Park, estimated at between $1 million and $1.2 million annually; some indeterminate cost for security and traffic control around the ballpark; debt-service costs of $920,700 a year for twenty years to finance $10 million in tax increment revenue bonds that would be issued by the San Francisco Redevelopment Agency; an annual set-aside of $184,200 for housing, mandated by state law, to be paid by the San Francisco Redevelopment Agency; and some as yet undetermined amount for transit-related capital improvements to meet increased demand for transit services that result from increased attendance at the new ballpark (average attendance increases for the period 1986–95 are shown in table 12A-3).

The budget analyst argued that the possessory interest taxes that would be generated by the construction of the new ballpark, estimated at $3.5 million, would be more than sufficient to pay the SFRA's costs associated with issuing debt and paying the housing set-aside. In fact, he argued that

Table 12A-3. *Average Annual Attendance for New Baseball Facilities,*
1986–95

	Before new ballpark		After new ballpark		
Facility	Time period	Average attendance	Time period	Average attendance	Percent increase
Baltimore	6 yrs. (1986–91)	27,369	4 yrs. (1992–95)	44,327	62.0
Chicago	6 yrs. (1985–90)	17,861	5 yrs. (1991–95)	31,039	73.8
Cleveland	6 yrs. (1988–93)	21,532	2 yrs. (1994–95)	36,649	70.2
Texas	6 yrs. (1988–93)	26,212	2 yrs. (1994–95)	34,999	33.5

Source: Authors' calculations based on John Thorn and Peter Palmer with Michael Gershman, eds., *Total Baseball*, 4th ed. (Viking, 1995), p. 109.

the remaining possessory interest taxes would generate an annual net increase in direct city revenues of approximately $1.4 million.[73]

The budget analyst also stated that "retention of the Giants in San Francisco will maintain certain direct revenues now being received by the City and County from the Giants."[74] These direct revenues, estimated at $2.7 million for the first year of the new ballpark and $2.5 million annually thereafter, included payroll taxes, sales taxes, parking taxes, and admission taxes for the school sports program. In addition, the budget analyst restated the economic impacts identified by ERA in its February report for the Giants.

The budget analyst's report was accompanied by a letter from the Giants' vice president and chief financial officer, John Yee, praising certain aspects of the report while objecting to others. Yee applauded what he believed to be the overall finding of the report, that "the benefits of the ballpark far exceed any potential costs,"[75] an interpretation that the budget analyst disputed: "We did not make such a finding."[76] Yet, Yee also took pains to make the following points: "*There is no use of General Fund money* to support any portion of the ballpark project";[77] "*no definitive cost estimate can be made at this time given the current information available*;"[78] "the proposed ballpark creates substantial value in a site . . . which is of, at best, questionable worth now;"[79] and, with respect to the estimate of possessory interest taxes, "the actual amount will depend upon the final assessment to be determined once the project is completed."[80]

On March 26, 1996, the Giants and their numerous political supporters put the disagreements with the budget analyst and others behind them. San Franciscans approved Proposition B by 66 percent to 34 percent, and in the process provided the Giants with a margin "sufficient for the

Table 12A-4. *Lower-Bound Net Fiscal Impact on San Francisco City and County for Proposition P, 1989 China Basin Ballpark Proposal*
Hundreds of thousands of 1996 dollars

	Nominal value	Net present value
Costs		
Port of SF opportunity costs	(5,147)	(3,854)
China Basin land assembly	(1,428)	(1,069)
China Basin site preparation	(11,128)	(7,751)
City share of construction costs	(12,255)	(7,387)
City contribution for ballpark operation and maintenance	(24,510)	(10,141)
City loan to ballpark operations	(12,255)	(5,070)
City payments to other jurisdictions	(12,506)	(1,387)
SFRA annual housing set-aside	0	0
SF MUNI staffing	(22,620)	(3,292)
SFPD costs for security	(9,240)	(1,345)
Total estimated costs	(111,088)	(41,295)
Revenues		
City share of ballpark cash flow	108,350	10,377
Retained tax revenue	237,708	31,569
Spectacor payroll taxes	1,713	249
Total estimated revenues	347,772	42,195
Net fiscal impact	236,683	900

Source: Authors' calculations.

Giants to claim a mandate for the nation's first privately financed major-league baseball stadium in 32 years."[81]

The Fiscal Impacts of Propositions P and B

For reasons just discussed, the analyses provided by the mayor's office and the budget analyst regarding Propositions P and B were insufficient for measuring the fiscal impacts of the two proposals on the city. The following tables represent our attempt to measure the lower- and upper-bound net fiscal impacts of the two propositions. Wherever possible, and relevant, we have sought to use the most recent information and assumptions to construct these measures.

NET FISCAL IMPACTS FOR PROPOSITION P. Table 12A-4 provides our lower-bound estimate of the net fiscal impact of Proposition P had it been approved in 1989. All estimates have been converted into 1996 dollars using the GDP implicit price deflator. The city discount rate is assumed to be 7.5 percent (nominal). The time frame for the investment is from 1989 to 2034, the fortieth year of the proposed ballpark, and corresponds with the assumed useful life of the stadium.

Assumptions regarding costs listed in table 12A-4 are as follows: the Port of San Francisco would incur opportunity cost corresponding to the low estimate ($4.2 million) calculated in 1989. With the passage of Proposition H in 1990, which restricted development on Port property, it is unlikely that the Port would have realized its higher income projection for the property, which assumed lucrative development adjacent to Pier 46B. China Basin land assembly assumes that the federal government would have granted Caltrans a waiver of the reimbursement requirement. The city's cost for the property would have been nine percent of the value of the property. China Basin site preparation assumes $2 million for demolition costs, $1 million for infrastructure improvements, and $2 million for relocation costs (these 1989 estimates have been adjusted to reflect 1996 dollars) and a recent estimate, $5 million (1996 dollars), for environmental remediation. The city's share of construction costs assume that final construction costs would have reached $116.5 million, which was the experience for new ballparks that opened between 1991 and 1994. For example, final construction costs for Camden Yards exceeded $140 million according to published reports. The city contribution for ballpark operation and maintenance and its loan to ballpark operations assume the city proceeded with its $3 million "investment" in the ballpark. City payments to other jurisdictions assumes an "income-based" approach to the assessment value of the ballpark and uses 1995 San Francisco property tax rates.[82] There are no San Francisco Redevelopment Agency costs for housing set-asides, since tax-increment financing was not contemplated for the project. San Francisco Municipal Railway costs are included.[83] San Francisco Police Department costs for security inside the ballpark assume an additional annual cost of $100,000, beginning in 1995, which is inflated annually by 3 percent.

Assumptions regarding revenues listed in table 12A-4 are as follows. The city's share of ballpark revenues represents 20 percent of the ballpark's "cash flow" and utilizes the same assumptions included in the mayor's 1989 analysis with one exception: average attendance in the new ballpark is assumed to be 40,300 per game in 1995 and 34,400 per game in 1996 and beyond, on the basis of actual experience for new stadiums in Baltimore, Chicago (American League), Cleveland, and Texas (see table 12A-3).[84] Retained tax revenue follows the original assumptions of

Table 12A-5. *Upper-Bound Net Fiscal Impact on San Francisco City and County for Proposition P, 1989 China Basin Ballpark Proposal*
Hundreds of thousands of 1996 dollars

	Nominal value	Net present value
Costs		
Port of SF opportunity costs	(5,147)	(3,854)
China Basin land assembly	(15,862)	(11,877)
China Basin site preparation	(23,382)	(16,287)
City share of construction costs	(12,255)	(7,387)
City contribution for ballpark operation and maintenance	(24,510)	(10,141)
City loan to ballpark operations	(12,255)	(5,070)
City payments to other jurisdictions	(12,506)	(1,387)
SFRA annual housing set-aside	0	0
SF MUNI staffing	(22,620)	(3,292)
SFPD costs for security	(9,240)	(1,345)
Total estimated costs	(113,777)	(60,639)
Revenues		
City share of ballpark cash flow	108,350	10,377
Retained tax revenue	237,708	31,569
Spectacor payroll taxes	1,713	249
Total estimated revenues	347,771	42,195
Net fiscal impact	209,994	(18,444)

Source: Authors' calculations.

the mayor's 1989 analysis with three exceptions: Giants' player salaries are assumed to grow by 10 percent a year, which is lower than the average annual increase of 13 percent experienced between 1988 and 1996; parking tax revenue, which was omitted from the 1989 analysis, is included here and is based on 3.1 patrons per car, paying $8.00 per car for parking, 25 percent of which is collected as taxes; the admission tax, which was imposed after 1989, is also included and assumes 5,270 tickets per game will be sold at an average ticket price above $25.01, $0.50 of which is collected as taxes; all other tickets sold include $0.25 in an admission tax. Spectacor payroll taxes follows the original assumption of the 1989 analysis.

Table 12A-5 provides our upper-bound estimate of the net fiscal impact of Proposition P had it been approved in 1989. The same assumptions used in table 12A-4 are employed with three exceptions: land assembly costs assume that the federal government would not have waived its reimbursement requirement for Caltrans and that the city would have paid for the full value of the parcel; site preparation assumes $7 million

Table 12A-6. *Lower-Bound Net Fiscal Impact on San Francisco City and County for Proposition B, 1996 China Basin Ballpark Proposal*
Hundreds of thousands of 1996 dollars

	Nominal value	Net present value
Costs		
Port of SF opportunity costs	(5,147)	(4,143)
China Basin land assembly	(15,862)	(12,768)
China Basin site preparation	(11,128)	(8,332)
City share of construction costs	(27,622)	(8,143)
City contribution for ballpark operation and maintenance	0	0
City loan to ballpark operations	0	0
City payment to other jurisdictions	0	0
SFRA annual housing set-aside	(5,524)	(1,629)
SF MUNI staffing	(22,620)	(3,804)
SFPD costs for security	0	0
Total estimated costs	(87,903)	38,819)
Revenues		
City share of ballpark cash flow	0	0
Retained tax revenue	288,178	40,803
Spectacor payroll taxes	0	0
Total estimated revenues	288,178	40,803
Net fiscal impact	200,276	1,984

Source: Authors' calculations.

for demolition costs and $7 million for relocation costs, along with $1 million for infrastructure and $5 million for environmental remediation; and the San Francisco Municipal Railway incurs additional costs for providing additional service to the ballpark.

NET FISCAL IMPACTS OF PROPOSITION B. Table 12A-6 provides our lower-bound estimate of the net fiscal impact of Proposition B. The city discount rate is again assumed to be 7.5 percent (nominal). The time frame for the investment is from 1996 to 2039, the fortieth year of the proposed ballpark, and corresponds with the assumed useful life of the stadium. Land assembly assumes Caltrans will not waive reimbursement and that the Port of San Francisco will pay the entire cost of the property to Caltrans ($12.94 million, 1989 estimate, converted to 1996 dollars). Site preparation includes $2 million for demolition costs, $1 million for infrastructure improvements, and $2 million for relocation costs. As in table 12A-3, these 1989 estimates have been adjusted to reflect 1996 dollars. Site preparation also includes a recent estimate, $5 million for environ-

Table 12A-7. *Upper-Bound Net Fiscal Impact on San Francisco City and County for Proposition B, 1996 China Basin Ballpark Proposal*
Hundreds of thousands of 1996 dollars

	Nominal value	Net present value
Costs		
Port of SF opportunity costs	(5,147)	(4,143)
China Basin land assembly	(15,861)	(12,768)
China Basin site preparation	(23,382)	(17,509)
City share of construction costs	(41,433)	(12,214)
City contribution for ballpark operation and maintenance	0	0
City loan to ballpark operations	0	0
City payment to other jurisdictions	0	0
SFRA annual housing set-aside	(8,287)	(2,443)
SF MUNI staffing	(22,620)	(3,804)
SFPD costs for security	0	0
Total estimated costs	(116,731)	(52,881)
Revenues		
City share of ballpark cash flow	0	0
Retained tax revenue	288,178	40,801
Spectacor payroll taxes	0	0
Total estimated revenues	288,178	40,803
Net fiscal impact	171,447	(12,078)

Source: Authors' calculations.

mental remediation. We have assumed that the Port of San Francisco will pay all of these costs. SFRA funding of ballpark construction assumes debt service on $10 million for thirty years at 8.4 percent. SFRA annual housing set-aside assumes 20 percent of annual debt-service cost for thirty years. San Francisco Municipal Railway staffing costs assume $300,000 in new annual costs, inflated by 3 percent a year. Retained tax revenue follows the same assumptions listed in tables 12A-3 and 12A-4.

Table 12A-7 provides our "upper-bound" estimate of the net fiscal impact of Proposition B. The same assumptions employed in table 12A-5 are operative for table 12A-6, with three exceptions: site preparation assumes $7 million for demolition costs and $7 million for relocation costs, along with $1 million for infrastructure and $5 million for environmental remediation; San Francisco Redevelopment Agency funding of ballpark construction assumes debt service on $15 million of tax-increment bonds; and the San Francisco Redevelopment Agency's annual housing set-aside of 20 percent increases accordingly.

The costs listed in tables 12A-6 and 12A-7 are based on two important assumptions. The first concerns the Giants' ability to compensate the Port of San Francisco for any costs it would incur for land assembly and site preparation, including opportunity costs. We estimate that these costs were likely to be between $32 million and $44 million. This would represent a significant additional cost to the Giants for the ballpark project (an increase of between 12.5 percent and 17.2 percent of the project's $255 million price tag). Given the increasing possibility that additional San Francisco Redevelopment Agency funding will be needed for the project (no doubt the result of shortfalls in private financing), we doubt that the Giants will have the financial wherewithal to pay the Port for the costs of land assembly and site preparation. The options for addressing this issue are limited: either the Port will have to absorb these costs, or the city will have to dedicate other resources to assemble the land and prepare the site in order make this "financially thin" proposal reality. Or the ballpark will not be built.

The second assumption concerns possessory interest taxes to be paid by the Giants on the new facility. The budget analyst estimated that new possessory interest taxes of approximately $3.5 million annually would be available to the city's treasury once the new facility was completed. These taxes would then be available to pay the costs associated with debt service on the tax-increment financing, the annual housing set-aside, and, presumably, other costs that might be incurred for additional Municipal Railway service.

We are very skeptical that the Giants will pay any possessory income taxes, for two reasons. The Giants will no doubt expect their property assessment to be based on an income approach, since an income approach would ensure that the Giants, who reportedly lost $10.3 million in 1994[85] and $1.9 million in 1995,[86] would have lower tax liabilities. Second, the private financing underpinning this "financially thin" deal will require that the Giants pledge every available revenue stream to repay this private debt. This will leave very little revenue for paying a new, and very sizable, tax they currently avoid; an additional tax will only make completion of the ballpark project difficult. This will again place the city on the horns of a dilemma: Will it pursue the imposition of a sizable possessory interest tax to pay for the costs that it will incur, and risk stalling (if not dooming) the ballpark project, or will the city simply absorb the costs that the possessory interest taxes were projected to pay?

For the purposes of this analysis, we have assumed that the city will absorb the costs of land assembly and site preparation, as well as the costs for servicing debt for the tax-increment financing, the costs of the housing set-aside, and the costs of additional Municipal Railway services.

Conclusions

For the most part, the budget analyses accompanying the various proposals to build a ballpark in San Francisco were done from the perspective of the city government's treasury. Taxes collected, for example, were invariably defined as "benefits" (as opposed to transfers). There have been no true benefit-cost analyses of stadiums in San Francisco.

As calculated here, the net fiscal impacts vary from slightly positive to significantly negative. To believe the net fiscal impact will be neutral, the most positive estimate has to be four times as likely to be realized as the most pessimistic estimate.

When San Franciscans overwhelmingly approved Proposition B—the first initiative on a ballpark in San Francisco to pass in recent memory— the impacts on city finances were apparently an important factor in the affirmative vote. That is to say, the fact that the ballpark project did not carry a significant city subsidy, as underscored by Proposition B's proponents, swayed many voters to support the initiative. This outcome has caused many to conclude that a replacement for Candlestick will finally be built.

Yet, given the magnitude of the task and the potential difficulties the Giants are likely to face in assembling the financing for the new stadium, it seems a reasonable likelihood that the city's financial contribution to the new ballpark will grow, if only to ensure site assembly and preparation. If such financial support is not forthcoming from the city, it will place the completion of the new China Basin ballpark at risk. At that juncture, San Franciscans may have to contemplate yet again the extent of their financial commitment to retaining the San Francisco Giants.

Notes

1. John Drebinger, "Hit By Clemente Ends 5-4 Contest," *New York Times,* July 12, 1961, p. 22.

2. Phil Berman, "Colavito: Play Here? I'd Quit First," *San Francisco Chronicle,* July 12, 1961, p. 37.

3. Arthur Daley, "Life in a Wind Tunnel," *New York Times*, July 12, 1961, p. 22.

4. Milton Gross, "It Proved Two Things," *San Francisco Chronicle*, July 13, 1961, p. 38.

5. Philip Benjamin, "Closed TV Linked to Baseball Shift," *New York Times*, June 1, 1957, p. 15.

6. Bruce Lee, "Stadium Set for Two Years," *San Francisco Chronicle*, June 1, 1957, p. 2H.

7. Harvey Frommer, *New York City Baseball: The Last Golden Age, 1947–1957* (New York: Atheneum, 1985) p. 15.

8. "Giants Here in '58: Mayor Tells Terms," *San Francisco Chronicle*, August 20, 1957, pp. 1–2.

9. "Stoneham: Giants headed for SF," *San Francisco Chronicle*, July 18, 1957, p. 1H.

10. Darrell Wilson, "City's Loot to Come from Parking Lot in Bay View," *San Francisco Chronicle*, August 20, 1957, p. 1H.

11. "This Is What Brought Giants Here," *San Francisco Chronicle*, August 20, 1957, p. 3H.

12. Darrell Wilson, "City's Loot to Come from Parking Lot at Bay View," *San Francisco Chronicle*, August 20, 1957, p. 1H.

13. The city controller added up the parking fees, the minimum rent, and the estimated $25,000 in advertising revenues. He estimated annual receipts to the city of $518,000, which would pay off Harney within twenty-one years. The $5 million bond issue would cost San Francisco taxpayers $420,000 annually in additional sales taxes for the next fifteen years.

14. "Grand Jury Majority Report Calls Stadium Proposal a 'Bad Deal,'" *San Francisco Chronicle*, December 30, 1958, p. 1.

15. Glenn Dickey, "Why Candlestick Isn't Working: A Lesson in Obsolescence," *San Francisco Chronicle*, December 20, 1982, p. 6.

16. *The Future of Candlestick Park* was compiled for the San Francisco Giants by Laventhol and Horwath, and released on May 19, 1981.

17. Allan Temko, "SF Officials Optimistic about a New Stadium," *San Francisco Chronicle*, August 11, 1982, p. 6.

18. Richard Leger, "The Staggering Costs of a New SF Stadium," *San Francisco Chronicle*, December 21, 1982, pp. 1, 6.

19. Ibid., p. 6.

20. Harry Jupiter, "Ex-Mayor Wants a Dome," *San Francisco Chronicle*, September 30, 1982, p. 3.

21. Evelyn Hsu, "$300,000 OK'd for Sports Stadium Feasibility Study," *San Francisco Chronicle*, December 2, 1982, p. 4.

22. Office of the Registrar of Voters, City and County of San Francisco. *San Francisco Voter Information Pamphlet*, Municipal Election, November 3, 1987.

23. The arguments of proponents were spelled out in ibid.

24. Ibid., p. 26.

25. Gary Enos, "San Franciscans to Vote Again on Sports Stadium," *City and State*, October 23, 1989, p. 3.

26. Ibid.

27. Letter, Carol Wilkins to San Francisco citizens, September, 1989.

28. Letter, Art Agnos to San Francisco citizens, October, 1989.

29. Jim Balderston, "Prop. P, R.I.P.," *San Francisco Bay Guardian*, November 15, 1989, p. 15.

30. Phillip Matier and Andrew Ross, "Ballpark Win a Fine-Tuned Political Effort," *San Francisco Chronicle*, March 27, 1996, p. A11.

31. Edward Epstein, "Giants Need a Lot More than Voter OK for Ballpark," *San Francisco Chronicle*, February 12, 1996, p. A13.

32. Dan McGraw, "Playing the Stadium Game," *U.S. News and World Report*, June 3, 1996, pp. 50–51.

33. Dennis Zimmerman, *Tax-Exempt Bonds and the Economics of Professional Sports Stadiums*, Congressional Research Service, Library of Congress, May 29, 1996, Summary.

34. Budget Analyst, Board of Supervisors, City and County of San Francisco, *Review of the Projected Costs and Economic Benefits Associated with the San Francisco Giants' Proposed Ballpark at China Basin*, March 1996.

35. Carol Wilkins and Stephen J. Agostini, *Building a New Home for the San Francisco Giants: A Cost-Benefit Analysis of the Proposed China Basin Ballpark*, San Francisco, Office of the Mayor, October 2, 1989, p. 13.

36. Letter, Board of Supervisors—Budget Analyst to Supervisors Hongisto, Hsieh, and Nelder, October 6, 1989, p. 4.

37. Jim Balderston, "Say It Ain't So, Art," *San Francisco Bay Guardian*, October 18, 1989 pp. 15–17.

38. Budget Analyst, Board of Supervisors, City and County of San Francisco, *Review of the Projected Costs and Economic Benefits*, p. 2.

39. Letter, John F. Yee, Vice President and Chief Financial Officer, San Francisco Giants, to Ken Bruce, Budget Analyst's Office, February 29, 1996, attachment to ibid.

40. Edward Epstein, "Giants Tout Tax Benefits of China Basin Ballpark, But Analyst Says Overall Effect Unclear," *San Francisco Chronicle*, March 5, 1996, p. A1.

41. Letter, John F. Yee, Vice President and Chief Financial Officer, San Francisco Giants, to Ken Bruce, Budget Analyst's Office, February 29, 1996.

42. Eric Brazil, "After Giants' Big Hit, 'It's a Cakewalk'," *San Francisco Examiner*, March 28, 1996, p. A8.

43. Arthur Lupia, "Shortcuts versus Encyclopedias: Information and Voting Behavior in California Insurance Reform Elections," *American Political Science Review*, vol. 88 (March 1994), pp. 63–76.

44. Our complete analysis included separate estimates of voter turnout and estimates using the fraction of adults (rather than voters) supporting the initiative. In addition, we investigated more elaborate specifications using logit and logarithmic models. The simple models reported in the text adequately capture the results of the more elaborate statistical models.

45. Lupia, "Shortcuts versus Encyclopedias."

46. These terms were originally laid out by SMG in its original proposal, *Downtown Baseball Stadium and Sports/Entertainment Arena, A Proposal to the City and County of San Francisco* by Spectacor Management Group, January 11, 1989. SMG's responsibilities did not materially change during the negotiations.

47. At the time, SMG was part of a group that, among other business interests, owned and operated the Spectrum in Philadelphia, home to the National Basketball Association's 76ers and the National Hockey League's Flyers, who were also owned by SMG's parent company. Many observers, including members of the mayor's staff, believed that SMG offered their ballpark proposal as a means to ensure control of an arena project in San Francisco, especially given the possibility that the NBA's Golden State Warriors would relocate to San Francisco.

48. The transition rules regarding tax-exempt financing for stadiums are discussed by Zimmerman in *Tax-Exempt Bonds and the Economics of Professional Sports Stadiums*, p. 5.

49. This critical cost element was, in essence, conceded to SMG early in the negotiations by city representatives.

50. Chester Hartman, *The Transformation of San Francisco* (Totowa, N.J.: Rowan and Allanheld, 1984), p. 210.

51. Waivers such as the one pursued by San Francisco are not unique. For example, the city of Milwaukee unsuccessfully pursued a downtown location for a new ballpark for the Milwaukee Brewers in 1995 and 1996. This site would have also required a federal waiver of a reimbursement by the state of Wisconsin's Department of Transportation to the Federal Highway Administration for the decommission and teardown of a highway spur in downtown Milwaukee.

52. Wilkins and Agostini, *Building a New Home for the San Francisco Giants*, fn. 8, p. 7.

53. This estimate (figures in 1989 dollars) assumed average game-day attendance of 24,000 for seventy-nine dates for each of the forty years; an average ticket price of $11; average per capita concession income of $9.50; average per capita novelty item income of $1; seven non–baseball events per year with attendance of 17,900; average rentals for the 120 luxury suites of $40,000, increased every ten years by a factor equal to 5 percent a year for the preceding nine years; naming rights of $40 million; scoreboard revenues of $2 million in the first year, increased annually by 5 percent; and revenues from electronic marquees equal to $500,000 in the first year, increased annually by 5 percent.

54. The estimates assumed that player salaries would increase by 14 percent a year over the succeeding forty years.

55. Letter, Board of Supervisors—Budget Analyst to Supervisors Hongisto, Hsieh, and Nelder, October 6, 1989, p. 4.

56. Ibid., p. 30.

57. Balderston, "Say It Ain't So, Art," p. 16.

58. Ibid., p. 17.

59. Katherine Seligman and Eric Brazil, "Giants Take Wraps Off Design for New Ballpark," *San Francisco Examiner,* December 21, 1995, p. A1.

60. Edward Epstein, "Name's a Big Deal for Giants, Pac Bell," *San Francisco Chronicle,* April 4, 1996, p. A13.

61. Edward Epstein, "Giants Brass Poised to Move Quickly, Seat Licenses Go on Sale This Summer," *San Francisco Chronicle,* March 27, 1996, p. A1.

62. McGraw, "Playing the Stadium Game," p. 50.

63. Glenn Dickey, "New Giants Ballpark Right on Track," *San Francisco Chronicle,* August 14, 1996, p. B3; Seligman and Brazil, "Giants Take Wraps Off Design For New Ballpark," p. A1.

64. Seligman and Brazil, "Giants Take Wraps Off Design For New Ballpark," p. A1.

65. Rachel Gordon and Eric Brazil, "Giants Want New Ballpark on Ballot," *San Francisco Examiner,* December 19, 1995, p. A18.

66. Edward Epstein, "Experts Debate Wisdom of Giants' Ballpark Plan," *San Francisco Chronicle,* February 2, 1996, p. A17

67. Ibid.

68. Eric Brazil, "Giants Say SF Will Score Big with Ballpark," *San Francisco Examiner,* February 27, 1996, p. A4.

69. Economic Research Associates, *Economic and Fiscal Impacts of the Giants Franchise on San Francisco,* January 13, 1994.

70. Ibid., p. II-3.

71. "Review of the Projected Costs and Economic Benefits . . . Board of Supervisors—Budget Analyst," March 1996, pp. 1–2.

72. Ibid., p. 2.

73. Ibid., pp. 10–11.

74. Ibid., p. 16.

75. Letter, John F. Yee to Ken Bruce, February 29, 1996, p. 1.

76. Eric Brazil, "Ballpark Debated at City Hearing," *San Francisco Examiner,* March 7, 1996, p. A4.

77. Letter, John F. Yee to Ken Bruce, February 29, 1996, p. 3.

78. Ibid., p. 3.

79. Ibid., p. 3.

80. Ibid., p. 4.

81. Eric Brazil, "Two-Decade Effort to Build New SF Stadium Finally Wins Voter Approval on Fifth Try," *San Francisco Examiner,* March 27, 1996, p. A12.

82. Municipal assessors typically utilize an "income approach" to value property when the property in question is publicly owned or otherwise exempt, yet some form of profit-making activity takes place on that property. The income approach has been utilized here, since the property in question is owned by at least one governmental unit (the state of California, leased to the Port of San Francisco) and a lease is contemplated to a for-profit concern, the Giants. As for the methodology of calculating the income approach see Alfred A. Ring, *The Valuation of Real Estate,* 2d ed. (Prentice-Hall, 1970).

83. No San Francisco Municipal Railway operating or capital costs were included in the original 1989 proposal because capital improvements in the ballpark area were to be funded principally (if not entirely) by the federal government and it was unclear what impact the ballpark would have on service. An argument could made that Muni patrons whose lives were disrupted by longer travel times caused by ballpark-induced Muni congestion would simply "absorb" these costs and be worse off. While this would not have entered the analysis from the perspective of the city treasury, an accurate cost-benefit analysis would have captured this cost to Muni patrons. More recent discussions have acknowledged the need to add additional buses to the fleet if the China Basin stadium is built.

84. According to Mitchell Zeits, senior managing consultant, Public Financial Management, Inc., the assumptions regarding per capita ticket prices and concession and novelties revenues included in the 1989 Mayor's Office analysis remain reasonable today, even after adjusting for 1996 dollars. Assumptions regarding luxury suite revenues (an average of $49,000 per suite, 1996 dollars) are lower than prices recently advertised by the Giants: $65,000 to $95,000 per suite, depending on location.

85. Michael K. Ozanian and others, "Suite Deals," *Financial World,* May 9, 1995, p. 46.

86. Tushar Atre and others, "Sports, the High Stakes Game of Team Ownership," *Financial World,* May 20, 1996, p. 56.

13

SPRING TRAINING

JOHN F. ZIPP

 The timeliness of this volume stems from the increased wanderlust and new stadium mania on the part of professional franchises and the heightened willingness of public officials to accommodate these desires. Although almost all the national attention paid to this mania has focused on the permanent locations and new facilities for major league teams, a similar and perhaps even greater amount of competition has been occurring for baseball's spring training sites. Between 1984 and 1996, seventeen of the twenty-eight major league teams changed spring training locations, with new homes bringing new or improved facilities.[1] Six and possibly seven more clubs will be in new quarters in 1998.[2] The quest of major cities for a professional franchise and the associated designation of being a "major league" city are mirrored in the competition for a similar status among smaller cities and counties seeking to host a spring training team.

The work on this chapter was supported in part by the Department of Sociology, University of Wisconsin-Milwaukee. I would like to thank the Florida Sports Foundation, the Florida Department of Revenue, the *Sporting News*, and the National Baseball Hall of Fame for providing some of the data used here; Chris Anderson, Dan Yoder, and Helen Yoder for research assistance; and John Crompton for his very helpful comments. None of the above bear any responsibility for the interpretations or conclusions.

The purpose of this chapter is to provide another assessment of the impact of professional sports by evaluating the economic effect of spring training on the Florida counties that host major league teams. Twenty of the twenty-eight Major League Baseball teams train in thirteen Florida counties, and the "Grapefruit League" has long been considered a major economic asset to the state.[3] To help appraise these claims, I have taken advantage of the disruptions in spring training caused by the 1994–95 baseball strike. As is well known, the strike caused the cancellation of the 1994 World Series and delayed the opening of the 1995 season. Because the strike was continuing unabated in February, Major League Baseball teams opened their 1995 spring training camps with "replacement" players, using them instead of their normal rosters to play the regularly scheduled spring training games in March. Two teams (Toronto and Baltimore) did not field replacement teams, and overall attendance was down 62 percent (942,518 fewer fans than in 1994).[4] In view of this development, the role of tourism in the Florida economy, and the small size of many of these counties (especially compared with large cities that are home to major league teams), the effects of hosting a franchise might be expected to be greater than in the larger metropolitan areas. Thus, unless there was a marked decline in economic indicators during the 1995 spring training season, it is extremely difficult to contend that professional franchises have a major economic impact on their host communities.

Spring Training in Florida

For more than a century, baseball teams have traveled to warmer climes to escape winter's harshness and to help prepare for the next season. Initially training in Arkansas, Louisiana, Texas, California, and a handful of southeastern states, spring training now is confined to Arizona and Florida. Since only eight clubs play in Arizona, in the minds of many, spring training is virtually synonymous with Florida.

The first team to use Florida specifically for spring training was the Washington Statesmen in 1888.[5] In contrast to the red carpets that communities now roll out for the teams, the locals were decidedly less hospitable on this initial visit. Since baseball players were held to be unsavory characters at the time, the Statesmen and their fifteen players, including reserve catcher Connie Mack, were repeatedly turned away from hotels. They were able to secure lodging only when they promised not to mingle with the other guests, not to eat in the hotel's dining room, or even to mention that they played baseball.[6]

Throughout the first two decades of this century, teams held spring training at various sites throughout the South (especially Florida, Georgia, North Carolina, Arkansas, and Louisiana) and West (mainly Texas and California).[7] Although various teams trained in Florida at different points (for example, as manager, Connie Mack brought his Philadelphia Athletics back to Jacksonville for one season in 1903), it was not until 1914 that more than two teams were in Florida at the same time. Even though the Grapefruit League was formed then, Florida did not establish a major spring training presence until the 1920s, with much of the credit for this due to the efforts of Al Lang.[8]

A Pittsburgh businessman, Lang moved to St. Petersburg in 1911 for health reasons and embarked on a mission to get major league teams to train there. After being spurned by his hometown Pirates, Lang persuaded the St. Louis Browns to move to St. Petersburg in 1914. In 1920 Lang raised money to build a new ballpark—Waterfront Park—and by 1925 three teams were training in town: the Browns, the Boston Braves, and the New York Yankees. Lang's efforts to attract teams were not limited to St. Petersburg. He also helped to find a home for the Washington Senators in Tampa, assisted the move of the Dodgers to Clearwater in 1923, and persuaded Sarasota to extend an invitation to the New York Giants. The end result of these efforts was that by the end of the decade, ten of the sixteen major league teams held spring training in the Sunshine State.[9]

Despite this commitment to Florida, teams changed spring training sites frequently during the 1920s and 1930s as they shopped around for the best locations. One indication of this mobility is that the three teams with the longest stays at one location in Florida—the Cardinals (in St. Petersburg from 1946 to 1997), the Tigers (in Lakeland since 1946), and the Phillies (in Clearwater since 1947)—each played at eight different sites between 1920 and 1940.[10]

Teams continued to move a bit in the postwar years, but with a few exceptions most settled in for longer stays until the mid-1980s. Part of this new wanderlust was facilitated by the state of Florida, which in 1985 allowed counties to devote revenues from their tourist development tax to baseball. This gave counties a new source of funds to finance stadiums.[11] Between 1985 and 1996, eleven of Florida's twenty teams changed locations (see table 13-1), with at least five more clubs pulling up stakes

Table 13-1. *Spring Training Relocations of Major League Baseball,*
1984–96

Year	Team	Moved from	Moved to
1984	Athletics	Scottsdale	Phoenix
	Giants	Phoenix	Scottsdale
1985	Astros	Cocoa Beach	Kissimmee
1986	Brewers	Sun City	Chandler
1987	Rangers	Pompano Beach	Port Charlotte
1988	Mets	St. Petersburg	Port St. Lucie
	Reds	Tampa	Plant City
	Royals	Ft. Myers	Baseball City
1989	Orioles	Miami	Miami/Sarasota
1991	Twins	Orlando	Ft. Myers
	Orioles	Miami/Sarasota	Sarasota
1993	Angels	Mesa/Palm Springs	Mesa/Tempe
	Indians	Tucson	Winter Haven
	Mariners	Tempe	Peoria
	Orioles	Sarasota	Sarasota/St. Petersburg
	Red Sox	Winter Haven	Ft. Myers
1994	Marlins	Cocoa	Melbourne
	Padres	Yuma	Peoria
1996	Orioles	St. Petersburg	Ft. Lauderdale
	Yankees	Ft. Lauderdale	Tampa

Source: Myles E. Friedman, "Spring Training," in John Thorn and Pete Palmer, eds., with Michael Gerschman, *Total Baseball,* 4th ed. (New York: Viking Press, 1995).

in 1998.[12] This latest round of activity was kicked off in 1985 by the Astros, who were lured to Kissimmee from Cocoa Beach. Two years later a new facility enticed the Rangers to move from Pompano Beach to Port Charlotte. In 1988 the Mets, Royals, and Reds moved. The Orioles started to leave Miami in 1989 for Sarasota, split time between Sarasota and St. Petersburg for three years, and moved to the Yankees' former facilities in Ft. Lauderdale in 1996.[13] To recover from the loss of the Royals, Ft. Myers landed the Twins in 1991. Two years later, the Red Sox left Winter Haven for Ft. Myers, while Winter Haven became home to the Indians.[14] The Marlins stayed one year in Cocoa before putting down stakes in Melbourne in 1994, while the long-rumored move of the Yankees to Tampa finally occurred in 1996. And in 1998 the White Sox will leave Sarasota for Tucson, and at least four other teams—the Blue Jays, Braves, Cardinals, and Expos—will be in different locations.[15]

Nine of the eleven teams—all but the Indians and Orioles—that changed locations between 1985 and 1996 were enticed to do so with offers of new facilities.[16] A decade ago new stadiums for the Astros and

Rangers each cost approximately $5.5 million. Lee County provided $15 million to lure the Twins to Ft. Myers in 1991, while two years later the city of Ft. Myers spent $25 million on the City of Palms Park to attract the Red Sox. Hillsborough County spent $17 million for the new Yankees' facility, and although the team is responsible for maintenance, the Yankees get to keep all revenue from it. Perhaps most telling, the Marlins sent out a ten-page proposal to numerous cities throughout Florida *before* any prospective suitor contacted them. The proposal detailed what the club would need (for example, an $8.5 million to $15 million dollar facility, excluding the cost of land), right down to the type of grass on the field. The Marlins' approach appears to have paid off: a one cent increase to the tourist development tax financed the construction of Space Coast Stadium in Melbourne, with the land donated by a local developer. The twenty-year lease required the team to operate the facility and to build their minor league complex next door, but the club receives all the revenue from tickets, parking, concessions, and advertising at the ball park.[17] Finally, in what may be a wave of the future, at the end of the 1997 season, the Atlanta Braves opened their new spring training home as the baseball part of Disney's $110 million, thirty-sport Wide World of Sports complex in Orlando.[18]

Perhaps not surprisingly, in view of what has occurred for large cities interested in professional franchises (see chapter 2), an assortment of studies claim that hosting spring training has a sizable economic impact. In 1960, over and above the spending by the teams and their players, the twelve teams that then trained in Florida were reported to have brought half a million dollars into the local economy.[19] More recently, in anticipation of possible disruptions in 1995's spring training, the U.S. Conference of Mayors surveyed each of the cities hosting spring training to assess the impact of a cancellation of the spring games. Complete responses were obtained for twelve Florida teams: each lost game of spring training was estimated to cost the state $640,000.[20] In addition, both business and public leaders see hosting spring training as a way to spur additional residential development. For instance, the Viera Company, a land development corporation, donated a sixty-five-acre parcel, valued at $1 million, for the Marlins' Space Coast Stadium in the hope that the team would help attract residents for its planned community.[21]

Perhaps the most cited evidence, however, of the economic impact of spring training is a 1991 study done by Van Horn Associates for the Florida Department of Commerce.[22] Van Horn Associates surveyed 12 of the 18 teams then playing in Florida, 12 of the 16 stadium managers, and 10 of the 16 concessionaire operators, in addition to interviewing 872 fans at home games of all 18 teams. On the basis of these data, they estimated that non-Floridians spent $91.5 million dollars outside the stadiums in 1991. Using a standard economic impact model with a very high multiplier of 3.1, they estimated that these nonresidents attending spring training generated $285 million in new business activity in the Sunshine State.

As noted in chapter 2, public and team officials have a vested interest in showing relatively low costs and high benefits, and all too often their figures are victimized by faulty methods.[23] Even though it is difficult to place much faith in studies touting the impact of spring training, the absence of other sorts of analyses have created a situation in which their conclusions have gone largely unchallenged.

In this chapter, I attempt to provide an alternative view of the impact of spring training on Florida. Instead of confronting these impact studies head on, I take a more indirect approach, drawing on my previous work.[24] Recently, I used the canceled games from the 1994 baseball strike as a natural experiment of sorts for analyzing the impact of professional sports. Comparing all U.S. cities with teams and four cities without clubs, I found that the relationship between a city's economic performance before and during the strike was virtually the same for cities that hosted major league clubs as it was for those without them, for small and large market towns, and for cities that lost more home games and fans as a result of the strike.

Here I extend this earlier analysis and examine the impact that the strike had on the Florida counties that are home to the spring training camps of major league teams. Once again, the strike has created a natural experiment for understanding the economic impact of professional sports. Spring training is purported to be an economic asset to a community (and to the state as a whole) primarily because it attracts non-Floridians who come in March to see spring training games. For instance, the Florida Department of Commerce's 1991 study found that 80.8 percent of the $113.2 million in direct spending due to spring training—$91.5 million—came from spending by nonresident fans.[25] These tourists spend money on food, lodging, transportation, souvenirs, and so on, all of which pumps up the Florida economy. Thus the key to the economic impact of spring training is the number of nonresident fans and how much money they spend locally. Since replacement games attracted

Table 13-2. *Home Attendance at Florida Spring Training Games,
1993–95*

County	Teams	1993	1994	1995
Brevard	Marlins	105,183	93,831	36,842
Broward	Yankees	122,379	89,957	35,951
Charlotte	Rangers	61,565	67,416	17,198
Hillsborough	Reds	72,895	71,191	18,524[a]
Indian River	Dodgers	55,031	55,031	31,758
Lee		200,130	191,923	109,500
	Red Sox	103,077	108,869	58,992
	Twins	97,053	83,054	50,508
Manatee	Pirates	68,975	67,404	19,613
Osceola	Astros	59,217	57,400	16,429
Palm Beach		152,862	163,302	52,358
	Braves	90,004	95,546	31,074[a]
	Expos	62,858	67,756	21,284
Pinellas		314,321	280,476	61,408
	Blue Jays	80,178	73,115	—
	Cardinals	70,974	64,971	29,574
	Phillies	98,811	83,221	31,834
	Orioles	64,358	59,169	—
Polk		235,602	214,300	105,813
	Indians	80,000	55,215	46,944
	Tigers	87,832	88,810	25,024[a]
	Royals	67,770	70,275	33,845
St. Lucie	Mets	79,405	58,900	27,816
Sarasota	White Sox	115,366	95,850	31,253
Total		1,642,931	1,506,981	564,463

Source: Florida Sports Foundation.
a. Obtained from the respective teams.

63 percent fewer fans during the 1995 spring training season, compared
with the 1994 season, and presumably fewer non-Floridians, counties
hosting teams should have been particularly hard hit (see table 13-2).
Unless there was a marked decline in economic indicators during the
1995 spring training season, it will be difficult to contend that spring
training in particular, and professional franchises more generally, have a
major economic impact on their host communities.

Data and Methods

In 1995 twenty teams trained in thirteen Florida counties, clustered
along I-4 between Tampa and Orlando, along the west coast between
Fort Myers and Dunedin, or near I-95 between Melbourne and Ft. Lau-

Figure 13-1. *Baseball Spring Training Sites in Florida, 1995*

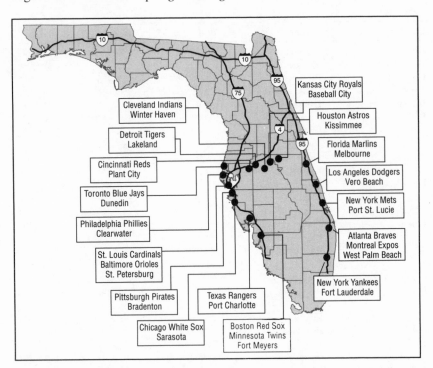

derdale (see figure 13-1). Eight counties were host to a single club, and Pinellas County to four.[26]

Spring training is said to boost the Florida economy in a number of ways. First, the teams, stadiums, and concessionaire operators pay wages and salaries to local employees and also spend money on food, lodging, supplies, equipment, transportation, repairs, and maintenance. Second, fans from outside the state visit to see spring training games, and they spend money both inside (for example, tickets, concessions, parking) and outside the ballpark (for example, hotels, restaurants, gas, entertainment, souvenirs, transportation). Finally, the media descend on Florida to cover the camps and the actual spring training games.

These *direct* expenditures that stem from spending by the teams, players, and fans on goods and services in the local economy also result in a set of *secondary* economic impacts. Because local businesses and workers earn income from this direct spending, and they in turn spend some of this locally, a series of *induced* expenditures ripples through the area's economy. *Indirect* expenditures are usually calculated by invoking a multiplier that represents the degree to which successive rounds of direct spending are captured in the local market. It was this sort of analysis that estimated non-Floridians attending spring training generated $285 million in business activity (in 1991).[27]

For the purposes of this analysis, the economic impact of spring training can be measured by analyzing taxable sales, reported monthly, at the county level to the Florida Department of Revenue. Taxable sales should capture the bulk of the spending by tourists visiting for spring training. The only major category of retail spending exempted from sales taxes by Florida is food bought in grocery stores; thus these data should represent a reasonably good indicator of overall business activity in each of the state's counties.[28] This should capture the initial spending done by those nonresidents attending spring training, and some of the indirect and induced spending as well.[29]

The objective here is to see if Florida counties hosting spring training teams were hurt economically by the players' strike. Given the relatively small size of some of these counties, I used an average of the county's economic performance in the prior two years as a baseline with which to compare the county's 1995 results.[30] Using two instead of only one prior year as a point of comparison should help adjust for any irregularities that might have occurred in one of the years.

Overall, these data and my use of them have their strengths and weaknesses, and it is important to mention both. On the positive side, there are three reasons why these data may be able to yield solid insights on the impact that replacement games had on the Florida economy. First, most of the economic effect of spring training comes from fans' spending. As noted earlier, 80.8 percent of the direct spending associated with spring training comes from spending by nonresident fans.[31] It appears reasonable to assume that virtually all of this direct spending—for example, in the renting of rooms and in the purchase of tickets, souvenirs, food in restaurants, and the like—takes place around the time of spring training and typically in locations in some proximity to the home of the ballpark. For instance, a study done in Lee County found that 57.7 percent of spring training attendees were visitors staying in Lee County.[32] Although I do not know how representative this is for all counties hosting teams, public and business officials involved in attracting teams to their communities clearly act as if this is the case.

Second, since most of the other expenditures should be relatively the same in strike and nonstrike years, the largest difference between the two years is in attendance at the games.[33] More specifically, the clear logic of those who claim a major economic impact from spring training is that most of the decline is from out of state fans. I can illustrate this by drawing on the discussion in chapter 2.

The analysis there suggests that fans attending spring training games can be divided into three types: local residents; those who are visiting Florida for other reasons; and those non-Floridians who are there primarily to attend spring training. Only the third group can be counted toward the economic impact of spring training. Thus, if spring training is supposed to have a substantial economic impact, it must be because nonresidents flock to Florida to attend spring training games. It stands to reason, then, that those who defend the economic impact of spring training must take the position that most of the decline in attendance was from this third group of fans. If the attendance loss was primarily among locals and those who were in Florida anyway, this would imply that the number of tourists coming to replacement games was similar to the number attending regular spring training, a fact that undercuts the drawing power of spring training.

Third, it is important to note that, in one sense, I may be estimating the upper bound of the impact of spring training. This is because I am analyzing only one type of revenue that is generated from these games, and I am not considering any of the expenses incurred by the local municipalities or opportunity costs of these investments (see chapter 2 for a discussion of these). For instance, it is indeed possible for me to find that hosting a team boosts tourism and thus taxable sales but does not generate enough revenue to cover whatever the interest and amortization and publicly defrayed operating expense might be on the loan required to land the team in the first place.[34]

These measures also have some shortcomings. First, given the uncertainty surrounding the baseball strike, it is possible that those non-Floridians who attend spring training had already made their plans to visit in 1995 and did not change them in the face of replacement games. Similarly, it is possible that these tourists originally came to Florida at this time of year to attend spring training and enjoyed themselves so much that they got in the habit of coming, with or without spring training. Thus these "snowbirds" still came but did not attend, or went to fewer games. This could account both for lower attendance and not significantly lower taxable sales.

I cannot completely rule out these possibilities; however, if either were true, it would indicate that the other joys of visiting Florida in March outweigh the interest in spring training. In other words, people—even those fans devoted enough to travel to see spring training (at least at one time)—are willing to come to Florida at this time of year without attending spring training games. This surely undercuts a central argument of those who tout the economic benefits of spring training on the counties hosting teams.

Second, it is possible that my reliance on observing changes at the county level does not capture fully the impact of spring training. It could be the case that significant numbers of those attending spring training may very well obtain accommodations in counties other than those hosting the team these tourists came to see. For example, the Lee County study found that one-quarter of those attending spring training were "day trippers" originating outside of the county.[35] In the results section, I report some analyses designed to address this point.

Results

In attempting to determine if lower attendance at 1995 spring training games (most of which is assumed to be the result of fewer non-Florida fans) had a noticeable negative impact on the economies of Florida counties hosting major league teams, I ask two primary questions: Was there a significant decline in taxable sales in 1995 as compared with an average of the same month in 1993 and 1994? and Did any such declines follow a pattern consistent with the baseball strike (was it more pronounced, for example, in counties hosting teams, or in counties whose teams "lost" more home fans)?

The first step in this process is to see if taxable sales were less than expected. Table 13-3 presents the changes in taxable sales between comparable months across 1993–95. These data are listed separately for counties hosting and counties not hosting spring training clubs.

The most relevant data are for March, as these represent the changes in taxable sales between the average of March 1993 and 1994 ("normal" spring training years) and March 1995 (the spring training with "replacement" players). As can be seen there, taxable sales were 4.7 percent higher (an increase of $318 million) in counties with teams in 1995 but

Table 13-3. *Percent and Real Dollar Changes in Taxable Sales in Florida Counties, 1993/94–95*[a]

Millions of dollars

Counties	November	December	January	February	March	April
With teams[b]	6.5	6.1	5.5	5.5	4.7	2.4
	370.2	440.4	323.2	330.7	318.1	152.3
Without teams[c]	8.0	8.9	6.4	7.3	8.2	3.3
	274.8	379.4	220.5	257.3	331.5	127.5

Source: Author's calculations based on data obtained directly from Florida Department of Revenue.
a. The 1993 and 1994 figures are adjusted for inflation.
b. N = 13.
c. Dade and Orange counties are excluded (N = 52).

increased even more—8.2 percent (+ $331.5 million)—in counties without teams.[36] At first glance, then, this would seem to indicate that counties hosting teams were hurt economically by the strike. Before accepting this conclusion, one should take note of two points. First, although the relative gap in March was the largest, counties without teams outperformed counties with teams in every month between November and April. And, second, the relative increase in taxable sales in counties home to spring training declined uniformly from November to April. Perhaps this indicates that March's results reflect not lower tourism associated with replacement spring training, but some longer-term economic trend. Thus, without attempting to minimize the March shortfalls, it may be premature to attribute them prima facie to the lower attendance associated with the baseball strike.

I next conducted a series of multiple regressions to determine if the economic changes in March represent a statistically significant deviation from previous trends, especially for those counties thought to be especially vulnerable to the strike (for example, those that hosted teams, or lost more fans). In my primary equations the dependent variable is the dollar change in taxable sales between March 1993/94 and March 1995. Although March is the major tourist month for spring training, because the camps open in February and because some tourists may stay into April, I also replicated these models for changes in February and in April.

Two key questions are addressed by the regression models: Did any changes in February's, March's, or April's taxable sales deviate from what would have been expected given the recent pattern of changes in these economic indicators? and Did any economic declines follow a pattern consistent with what might have been expected by the lower attendance at replacement games (that is, was it greater in counties that hosted teams or in ones that "lost" more home fans)?

To answer these questions I needed several different types of measures. First and most basically, I needed a way to judge whether the changes between 1993/94 and 1995 (in February, March, and April, respectively) were greater or less than what might be expected given the county's performance across other months. For instance, a particular county's March 1995 taxable sales may have been $10 million less than its 1993/94 figures, but before this decline is attributed to the baseball strike it needs to be placed in a context of overall changes in taxable sales in that county. In order to capture the latter, I used two variables. To begin with, I included the absolute value of average taxable sales in the same month of the previous two years: what I have defined above as my baseline measure of taxable sales. In addition, I used the monthly economic changes for November, December, and January as indicators of the expected change in economic activity in each county. These prior economic performance measures, then, represent the economic trend confronting the county at the beginning of the replacement spring training in 1995.

The second sort of required variables are ones that specifically focus on the effect of the baseball strike on the economies of Florida's different counties. I have several measures here. To begin with, since the most fundamental expectation is that counties hosting teams would be at greater risk due to the strike, I have a dichotomous variable (0 = no, 1 = yes) measuring whether the *county hosts a team*. Furthermore, it might be expected that counties whose teams lost more home fans during the replacement games would have been harder hit economically. Thus I have measured the change (in the thousands) in home attendance between the 1993/94 average and 1995 (*attendance change*).

Finally, the most relevant question for this analysis is whether the relationship between how a county performed in the prior years and how it performed in 1995 is different for counties hosting teams, or for counties whose teams lost more home fans. This asks if there are statistical interactions among March's (or another month's) dollar change in taxable sales, the baseline level of taxable sales in March, and the various measures of vulnerability to the baseball strike. For the replacement games to be seen as having a sizable impact, there should be a significant discontinuity in the economic performance of counties hosting teams and of counties whose teams lost more fans.

Table 13-4. *Dollar Change in Taxable Sales, 1993/94–95*[a]

Millions of dollars

Taxable sales	Dollar change		
February 1993/94–95			
County hosts team[b]	20.490[c]	6.637[c]	7.751[c]
Taxable sales, February 1993/94		0.034[c]	−0.037[c]
Percentage change in November[d]		1.003[c]	1.210
Percentage change in December[d]		6.630	5.962
Percentage change in January[d]		2.825	2.531
County hosts team × February sales			−0.004
Constant	4.948	2.134	1.938
R^2	0.387[c]	0.698[c]	0.699[c]
March 1993/94–95			
County hosts team[b]	18.094[c]	−4.734	−0.731
Taxable sales, March 1993/94		0.051[c]	0.068[c]
Percentage change in November[d]		3.631	4.976
Percentage change in December[d]		7.282	4.678
Percentage change in January[d]		7.784	5.994
County hosts team × March sales			−0.022[c]
Constant	6.375	1.498	0.264
R^2	0.215[c]	0.803[c]	0.820[c]
April 1993/94–95			
County hosts team[b]	9.264[c]	0.704	0.888
Taxable sales, April 1993/94		0.021[c]	0.022[c]
Percentage change in November[d]		4.019	4.080
Percentage change in December[d]		4.979	4.858
Percentage change in January[d]		2.995	2.913
County hosts team × April sales			−0.001
Constant	2.452	0.199	0.143
R^2	0.190[c]	0.494[c]	0.494[c]

Source: Author's calculations based on data obtained directly from Florida Department of Revenue.
a. Unstandardized regression coefficients. $N = 65$ (Dade and Orange counties excluded from all analyses).
b. County hosts team is a dichotomous variable, 0 = no, 1 = yes.
c. $p < .05$.
d. Refers to percentage change in taxable sales between (month) 1994/95 compared with average taxable sales in that month in the previous two years.

Table 13-4 shows the first set of regressions that addresses these questions. Here I have regressed the dollar change in taxable sales between 1993/94 and 1995 for February, March, and April on a number of independent variables. First is a dichotomous variable distinguishing whether a county was host to any major league team (0 = no, 1 = yes). My second independent variable taps the average dollar of taxable sales in the same month in the prior two years. Third, I have included three variables measuring the percentage changes in taxable sales in November, December, and January, respectively. Finally, in the last equation for each dependent variable, I include a cross-product term measuring whether there is a statistical interaction among that month's dollar change in taxable sales, the baseline level of taxable sales, and whether the county hosted a spring training team.

A number of significant points can be drawn from this analysis. First, as indicated in the first column of results, counties with teams had a larger increase in taxable sales than did counties without teams in all three months. For instance, on average, taxable sales increased by $20.5 million more in February, $18.1 million more in March, and $9.3 million more in April in counties hosting spring training than in counties without clubs.

Part of this stems from the larger economies of counties hosting teams; on average, taxable sales are four to five times as great in the thirteen counties with teams as in the fifty-two counties without them.[37] Thus, before drawing any conclusions, it is important to adjust both for these differences and for the changes in taxable sales in the months leading up to 1995 spring training. These latter results, listed in the second column of table 13-4, are revealing. After adjusting for a county's economic base and prior economic performance, spring training counties outperformed other counties only in February (and even here, the $20.5 million advantage decreased to $6.6 million). The apparent March and April increases in spring training counties were primarily a reflection of the larger economic size of these counties.[38]

Third, I checked to see if there were any significant statistical interactions between hosting a team, baseline levels of taxable sales, and dollar change in taxable sales in February, March, and April. The objective here is to determine if the way in which the change in a county's taxable sales in 1995 is related to its previous level of taxable sales is different for counties that do and do not host teams. The underlying logic is that, given the greater attendance at spring training games in March 1993/94 compared with March 1995, it is possible that there is a difference in the way in which taxable sales in prior years relate to 1995 taxable sales in counties with and without major league teams. Counties with teams would be expected not to receive the same increase in economic activity in 1995 that they received in earlier years, while counties without teams should be relatively unaffected. If this occurred, there should be a noticeable divergence between these two groups of counties in the way in which prior economic trends are able to predict current taxable sales.

The results for the test of these interactions are presented in the third column of table 13-4. Although all three coefficients are negative, only the coefficient for March is significant. The sign of this coefficient means that taxable sales increased more slowly in March 1995 compared with March of the prior two years in spring training counties than in counties without teams. At first glance, this would seem to indicate that replacement games had a negative impact on the Florida counties hosting teams.

It is worth considering some additional results before accepting this interpretation. I estimated the same interaction models portrayed in column 3 of table 13-4 for the months of November, December, and January.[39] Obviously, since spring training did not begin until mid-February, there should be no differences in the ways in which 1994/95 taxable sales relate to prior years' sales between these two types of counties. Yet, the interaction terms were statistically significant in both December (− .042) and January (− .047).[40] Thus in two of the three months before replacement spring training could possibly have any effect, counties hosting teams had less steep increases in taxable sales compared with counties without teams. Since this clearly is not a result of the baseball strike, the March fall-off in spring training counties may be part of a larger trend not accounted for by my measures here. Thus it is probably best to conclude that counties with teams fared no worse in early 1995 than counties without teams.

Before continuing, it is possible that my findings on spring training's negligible impact are an artifact of my method. As noted earlier, my measures have assumed that the only counties to benefit from spring training are those that host the teams. Clearly, tourists can spend significant amounts of money in other counties, and by not allowing for this, I may have underestimated the statewide impact of spring training. Again, this explanation cannot be entirely eliminated, although I have tried to bring some data to bear on it. Following this logic, the most obvious beneficiaries are the counties that border those counties hosting spring training. For instance, in the Lee County study cited earlier, almost 75 percent of those coming that day to see a spring training game stayed the previous night in one of two adjacent counties.[41] Admittedly, there is no clear definition of what constitutes a valid border county, but it seemed reasonable to see the sixteen counties south of Citrus, Sumter, Lake, and Volusia that do not host spring training as neighboring counties.[42] I included a term distinguishing these neighboring counties from those in the rest of the state in my basic regression models. In no case were the coefficients associated with this term statistically significant. Thus it appears that any losses in taxable sales have not been obscured by my focusing only on counties with hosting teams.

In a similar vein, it is possible that my results may be confounded by the degree to which a county depends on tourism versus having a more diverse economic base.[43] To assess this, I measured employment in hotels, motels, camps, rooming houses, and other lodging places as a percentage of a county's labor force and included this as a term in my regression models.[44] In no case was this significant, nor did its presence substantially change any other result.

In all the above results, I indexed a county's vulnerability to the strike by measuring whether a county hosts a team.[45] Although the logic in these comparisons appears adequate, further refinement could be of benefit to the analysis. For instance, it seems reasonable that the counties most affected by the strike should be the ones that "lost" the most out-of-town fans in 1995. In other words, if non-Floridians attending spring training games directly spent $91.5 million in 1991 (this would be $102.5 million in 1995 dollars), then those counties that witnessed the steepest declines in out-of-state fans between 1993/94 and 1995 also should have witnessed the largest declines in taxable sales.

Unfortunately, since there are no data for every team that list the number of in-state and out-of-state fans for spring training in 1993, 1994, and 1995, I had to estimate it. To do so I computed a general attendance change variable that subtracted the 1993/94 average home attendance from the 1995 figures (expressed in thousands). Although this clearly provides an accurate index of the changes across these years, it does not capture the change in the number of non-Floridians attending games. This may not be as serious a problem as it first seems, since it is likely that the steepest drop in 1995 attendance occurred among out-of-state fans.[46] In addition, this measure would be biased only if the relative declines in the percentage of non-Floridian fans in 1995 was significantly different across teams. Since there is little reason to believe that the latter occurred, my measure should provide a reasonable estimate of the loss of out-of-state fans during the March 1995 replacement games.

Because there are only thirteen counties with major league teams, it is perhaps best to see this analysis of the impact of home attendance on taxable sales as more exploratory than definitive. However, the expectations surrounding these relationship are clear: counties that lost fewer fans in 1995 should have larger increases in taxable sales. Thus there

Table 13-5. *Dollar Change in Taxable Sales in Counties Hosting Spring Training Teams, 1993/94–95*[a]

Millions of dollars

Taxable sales		Dollar change	
February 1993/94–95			
Attendance change (thousands)	−0.167	−0.106	−0.064
Taxable sales in February, 1993/94		0.031[b]	0.026
Percentage change, November–January		39.431	40.924
Attendance change × February sales			−0.000
Constant	12.438	−4.949	−3.000
R^2	0.248	0.703[b]	0.705[b]
March 1993/94–95			
Attendance change (thousands)	−0.081	0.038	0.139
Taxable sales in March, 1993/94		0.052[b]	0.043
Percentage change, November–January		83.097	86.573
Attendance change × March sales			−0.000
Constant	18.176	−16.040	11.377
R^2	0.031	0.846[b]	0.851[b]
April 1993/94–95			
Attendance change (thousands)	−0.101	−0.073	−0.107
Taxable sales in April, 1993/94		0.020[b]	0.023
Percentage change, November–January		48,112	46,891
Attendance change × April sales			0.000
Constant	3.879	−12.926	−14.532
R^2	0.162	0.553[b]	0.555[b]

Source: Author's calculations based on data obtained directly from Florida Department of Revenue.
a. Unstandardized regression coefficients. $N = 13$.
b. $p < .05$.

should be a positive relationship between attendance change and the change in taxable sales.

As table 13-5 indicates, once again I have estimated models for February, March, and April, and once again my dependent variable is the dollar change in taxable sales in that month in 1995 as compared with the 1993/94 baseline. My independent variables include the baseline level of taxable sales, the change in attendance from 1993/94 to 1995, and the total percentage change in taxable sales between November and January.[47]

There are three interesting results. First and perhaps unexpectedly, not only was the change in attendance unrelated to changes in taxable sales in all three months (see column 1), but also smaller losses in attendance tend to be associated with declines in taxable sales (the signs of all three coefficients are negative). This is counterintuitive and may again reflect differences in economic size across the counties.

The results in column 2 of table 13-5 adjust for these sorts of differences, in that here the effects of lower attendance are net of a baseline level of taxable sales and prior economic trends. Despite these adjustments, attendance change remains unrelated to changes in taxable sales, although the sign of the coefficient for March changed from negative ($-.081$ in column 1) to positive ($.038$ in column 2). This latter is a slight, though statistically insignificant, indication that smaller losses in home attendance in March were associated with greater gains in taxable sales. One way to see this effect is to evaluate the expected losses in taxable sales for a county with an average loss in home attendance (approximately 78,000 fans; see table 13-2). Doing these calculations indicates that the average county would have had $3 million less in additional taxable sales in March 1995 than expected on the basis of its taxable sales in 1993 and 1994. Although this figure is not statistically significant, it does represent approximately 12 percent of the average gain in taxable sales in these counties in 1995, and should not be dismissed out of hand.

Notwithstanding this point, one way to put this in context is to see if attendance change was related to changes in taxable sales in these counties in the November, December, and January, months preceding spring training. Interestingly enough, net of prior levels of taxable sales, smaller losses in 1995 spring training attendance were associated with greater gains in taxable sales in December 1994.[48] Applying the same logic in assessing this effect as above, the average county would have had taxable sales $15 million lower than expected in December (42 percent of the average gain in taxable sales). Since 1995 attendance losses cannot explain taxable sales in December 1994, it is likely that both the December and March results may stem from some other unmeasured economic indicator.

The last column of table 13-5 reports whether there were any statistical interactions among the 1995 change in taxable sales, the baseline level of sales, and the change in the number of home fans. None of the coefficients is significant, and only the April one is in the expected direction. Thus it is fairly safe to conclude that losses in home attendance had no clear negative impact on taxable sales in counties hosting spring training.

Discussion

The most general conclusion that can be drawn from the foregoing analysis is that, whatever losses in tourism occurred with replacement spring training in 1995, these did not have a noticeable negative impact on one indicator of economic performance—taxable sales—in the Florida counties that host spring training. In contrast, how these counties did in the spring of 1995 is largely a function of how they did previously. This seems to indicate that, even in the relatively small economies of these Florida counties, professional sports can produce rather limited economic benefits.

Before turning to the implications of these results, it is important to note some qualifications. First, although hosting spring training may not be a powerful independent tourist attraction for a particular county, this does not mean that spring training is not a key attraction to the state of Florida as a whole.[49] Each individual spring training camp might be best seen as part of a "cumulative attraction" to the state. As the tourism literature suggests, tourist attractions will draw better if they are some-how linked to one another (en route, in close proximity, and the like) than if they are widely scattered, and it is important to consider their cumulative impact, not just their independent appeals.[50] Thus, although no individual county may see significant effects of hosting spring training, collectively the state of Florida may benefit from the increased tourism that spring training as a whole brings.[51]

Second, it is possible that spring training attracts lots of tourists, but that they do not spend very much money that is taxable in Florida. For instance, those coming to see the games may stay with friends or relatives, stay in inexpensive campgrounds (taxable, but not generating much revenue), and instead of eating in restaurants, buy their food in grocery stores (not taxable). This state of affairs could generate tourism and spark some business but not show up in substantial taxable sales for the state.[52] Although I cannot eliminate this possibility, should it constitute a large part of the spring training tourism saga, it would mean that the fiscal revenue benefits to Florida and its counties of hosting spring training would be constrained markedly by the types of tourists the games attract.

These qualifications noted, my results have several implications. First, the lack of impact on taxable sales and on tourist development tax revenues may indicate that spring training is not the major tourist draw that many claim. In my search for sources of data on the impact of spring training I had the occasion to speak with various tourism researchers and officials in Florida. After outlining my project and reasons for wanting this information, one tourist researcher noted that not only did her organization not see any declines in March 1995, but also that she never expected to see any such shortfalls. Her focus group research over the years has clearly indicated that, although some tourists visit expressly to see spring training, most snowbirds come to Florida mainly for the weather. Her view is supported by other studies of the impact of spring training on Florida. A report done for Lee County—a county with two spring training sites—found that spring training attendees represented just 5.1 percent of March 1994 tourists.[53] Similarly, a survey of local tourists in Broward County found sports to be relatively low in their priorities.[54] In this survey, only 7 to 17 percent of revenues from lodging during spring training in most cities came from baseball fans.[55] To pick an example, it may be unwise to use the Michigan plates on cars in Lakeland as evidence of the drawing power of the Tigers.

Second, in line with other research on the economic impact of professional sports, it is possible that the main effect on these Florida counties is noneconomic or symbolic. Focusing on a county's economic performance in March as an indicator of the impact of spring training ignores the clear tendency among clubs now to include a minor league complex as part of their spring training home. For instance, when the Astros left Cocoa Beach for Kissimmee in 1985, their Florida State affiliate, the Daytona Beach Astros, also moved to Osceola County. Similar changes have accompanied other moves, such that by 1996 twelve of the fourteen Florida State League Class A clubs played in the same county in which their affiliated major league team trained.[56] Thus it is important to realize that landing a spring training team helps a municipality become home to a minor league club. And, even though these teams probably do not attract much in the way of tourists, they do establish another tie between what is usually a relatively small city or county and the major leagues.

As noted earlier, most of the literature on this topic has analyzed the impact of professional sports on large metropolitan areas. Because of their size and diversity, it may be unreasonable to expect sports teams to have a noticeable effect in these communities. For instance, Rosentraub has reported that the maximum share of local jobs associated with professional sports in any U.S. county with at least 300,000 residents is 0.4 percent. Similarly, the average franchise has a budget that is approximately 20 percent of the average urban university. In many respects it may be no surprise that professional sports teams cannot drive their local economies.[57]

In a similar fashion, spring training's relatively short span and the lower attendance associated with it clearly limits its economic impact. However, the communities hosting spring training in Florida are generally quite small, especially in comparison to those that are home to major league franchises. For instance, almost half the counties had fewer than 400,000 residents in 1990; three of these—Charlotte, Indian River, and Osceola—had approximately 100,000 residents each. Not seeing an impact in such small municipalities represents one more significant piece of evidence which undermines the claim that professional sports have a substantial impact on their host communities.

Notes

1. Myles E. Friedman, "Spring Training," in John Thorn and Pete Palmer, eds., with Michael Gerschman, *Total Baseball: The Official Encyclopedia of Major League Baseball*, 4th ed. (New York: Viking Press, 1995), pp. 573–76.

2. David Sweet, "New Baseball Complexes Are a Rite of Spring," *Wall Street Journal*, Interactive Edition, March 21, 1997, p. 1.

3. Kevin M. McCarthy, *Baseball in Florida* (Sarasota, Fla.: Pineapple Press, 1996), pp. 163–65. This will change slightly in 1998, as the White Sox will move from Sarasota, Florida, to Tucson, Arizona. Sweet, "New Baseball Complexes," p. 3.

4. Most of the attendance figures for spring training were provided by The Florida Sports Foundation, with the 1995 figures for the Braves, Tigers, and Reds coming from the teams themselves.

5. They also were known as the Capitals, Senators, and Nationals.

6. Mike Shatzkin and Jim Charlton, *The Baseball Fan's Guide to Spring Training: 1989 Season* (Reading, Mass.: Addison-Wesley, 1989), p. 11; William Zinsser, *Spring Training* (Harper and Row, 1989), p. 18.

7. The first permanent spring training facility was not established until 1908, by the New York Giants in Marlin Springs, Texas. Shatzkin and Charlton, *The Baseball Fan's Guide to Spring Training*, p. 12.

8. McCarthy, *Baseball in Florida*, pp. 143–47; Zinsser, *Spring Training*, pp. 18–19.

9. Friedman, "Spring Training," pp. 575–76; McCarthy, *Baseball in Florida*, pp. 143–54; Shatzkin and Charlton, *The Baseball Fan's Guide to Spring Training*, p. 13; Zinsser, *Spring Training*, p. 19.

10. Friedman, "Spring Training," pp. 575–76.

11. Robyne Turner, "Fort Lauderdale, Florida!" in Arthur T. Johnson, ed., *Minor League Baseball and Local Economic Development* (University of Illinois Press, 1993), p. 158.

12. Sweet, "New Baseball Complexes," p. 1.

13. The Orioles are somewhat of an exception in choosing spring training sites, as they are the only Florida-based team not to have a permanent location at this writing. According

to Orioles vice president Joe Foss, the team moved back to Florida's east coast because this is where its fan base from Maryland and vicinity is more likely to have relocated or to visit. Joe Foss, personal communication, October 21, 1996.

14. Homestead, a small community thirty miles south of Miami, spent $22 million in 1991 to build a modern facility for the Indians, only to see it severely damaged in 1992 by Hurricane Andrew. Even though the town spent $8 million to repair it, neither the Indians nor any other team has been willing to locate there, either out of fear of another hurricane or because of the distance between Homestead and most of the other spring training sites. McCarthy, *Baseball in Florida*, p. 165.

15. Sweet, "New Baseball Complexes," p. 1.

16. The Indians play in Chain O'Lakes Stadium, originally built for the Red Sox thirty years ago, while the Orioles currently play in Fort Lauderdale Stadium, recently vacated by the Yankees.

17. McCarthy, *Baseball in Florida*, pp. 164–65; Larry Rohter, "The Games, Practice; The Money, Real," *New York Times*, March 14, 1995, p. F6.

18. Sweet, "New Baseball Complexes," p. 1.

19. McCarthy, *Baseball in Florida*, p. 163.

20. The U.S. Conference of Mayors, *The Economic Impact of the Baseball Strike on Spring Training Cities* (Washington, D.C., December 1994).

21. McCarthy, *Baseball in Florida*, p. 165.

22. Van Horn Associates, *Economic and Fiscal Impacts Associated with Major League Baseball Spring Training Operations in the State of Florida* (Tallahassee: Florida Department of Commerce, 1991), pp. 19, 27.

23. See John L. Crompton, "Economic Impact Analysis of Sports Facilities and Events: Eleven Sources of Misapplication," *Journal of Sports Management*, vol. 9 (1995), pp. 14–35.

24. John F. Zipp, "The Economic Impact of the Baseball Strike of 1994," *Urban Affairs Review*, vol. 32 (1996), pp. 157–85.

25. In contrast, wages and salaries paid by the teams accounted for only $3.2 million. Van Horn Associates, *Economic and Fiscal Impacts*, p. 22.

26. During this time, the Orioles played their games in Pinellas County (St. Petersburg), but trained in Sarasota County.

27. As noted in chapter 2, sales multipliers are not especially appropriate, since they do not capture what is most important: how much extra income the local community receives from the spending by visitors to the sports event. Thus this $285 million figure undoubtedly overstates the impact of spring training, as these dollars do not necessarily remain in the state.

28. Florida also reports total sales information by county, and I initially planned to include this in my analysis instead. Although this would have the benefit of including the sale of food in grocery stores, I chose to use taxable sales for two additional reasons. First, total sales include numerous transactions (for example, wholesale sales) that are unrelated to the tourist traffic associated with spring training. Second and relatedly, there was much greater instability in the counties' total sales than in their taxable sales. More than likely, this reflects wholesale transactions and thus supports my reliance on taxable sales.

29. Clearly some of this secondary spending takes place well after spring training is finished, but this fact does not invalidate the analyses here. Since I am mainly interested in comparisons between comparable months in different years, the real threat is if the proportion of secondary spending that was done during versus after spring training was significantly less in 1995 than in earlier years. Although I have no data on this, there seems to be no compelling reason to think that this sort of problem has occurred. Thus taxable

sales across the two years should represent a reasonable method for capturing the economic impact of spring training.

30. The prior two years' figures are adjusted for inflation.

31. Van Horn Associates, *Economic and Fiscal Impacts*, p. 22.

32. Research Data Services, Inc., "Spring Training in Lee County," prepared for the Lee Country (Florida) Board of County Commissioners and Lee Island Coast Visitor and Convention Bureau, June 15, 1994, p. 7.

33. The largest other categories of direct expenditures are by the teams (11.9 percent) and the stadiums (5.3 percent). Teams (except for Baltimore and Toronto) fielded players and played games, stadiums were maintained, and the media covered it all. Van Horn, *Economic and Fiscal Impacts*, p. 22.

34. This is not just fanciful reasoning on my part. Prior to relocating in Tampa, the Yankees approached Osceola County with a $50 million proposal to move there. Since most of the costs would have been borne by the local government, the county decided not to pursue it. The county manager, Bill Goazlou, concluded that "in 30 days you don't get enough out of spring training to pay the interest on a $50 million project." Rohter, "The Games, Practice," p. F6.

35. Research Data Services, Inc., "Spring Training in Lee County," p. 7.

36. Because they are outliers and they drastically skew the overall results, I have omitted both Dade and Orange counties from all my analyses. During this period, taxable sales in Dade County dropped precipitously. For instance, between November 1994 and April 1995, the fifty-two counties without teams (not including Dade and Orange) gained almost $1.6 billion in taxable sales (over the prior two-year average); during this same period, Dade County lost almost $530 million in taxable sales. Relatedly, Orange County, home to the Disney Complex, is an outlier on the other end: during these months, taxable sales in Orange County increased by almost $480 million.

37. Recall that this comparison excludes both Dade and Orange counties.

38. However, it is important to note that although the regression coefficient for whether the county hosted spring training was not statistically significant, it was negative in sign, perhaps suggesting that counties with teams fared worse in March than expected.

39. For all three months I used whether the county hosted a team, the baseline level of taxable sales, and the cross-product of them as independent variables. For January, I also included the percentage change in taxable sales in November and December; for December, I included the percentage change in taxable sales for November.

40. To conserve space, I have not reported the complete results, but they are available upon request.

41. Research Data Services, Inc., "Spring Training in Lee County," p. 4.

42. This includes all counties that actually border on a host county and others in their immediate proximity, again except for Dade and Orange.

43. Professor Art Johnson, University of Maryland, Baltimore County, suggested this possibility.

44. U.S. Department of Commerce, *County Business Patterns 1993: Florida* (Washington, D.C.: GPO, 1993).

45. I replicated all these results by using the number of teams that a county hosted instead of the dichotomous variable assessing just whether or not a county was home to a team. Although there are some minor differences between the two sets of results, no conclusions would be different using either measure.

46. Although this is not a precise comparison, it is worth noting that in 1991 non-Floridians accounted for 61.4 percent of fans, and 1995 attendance was down by almost the same percentage (62 percent from 1994).

47. With only thirteen cases, it made more sense to include one summary measure rather than variables for each individual month, as I did previously.

48. Once again, to save space I have not reported these results, but they are available upon request.

49. This point was brought to my attention by John Crompton of Texas A&M University.

50. Chi-Chuan Lue, John L. Crompton, and Daniel R. Fesenmaier, "Conceptualization of Multi-Destination Pleasure Trips," *Annals of Tourism Research*, vol. 20 (1993), p. 297.

51. If this is true, the best situation for a county might be not to host spring training and thus incur possible revenue shortfalls, opportunity costs, and so on, but to be adjacent to counties that are home to teams. In addition, this situation suggests that the costs of spring training be borne by entities larger than a city or county (for example, metropolitan areas, the state).

52. This point was also raised by John Crompton.

53. Research Data Services, Inc., "Spring Training in Lee County," p. 8.

54. Turner, "Fort Lauderdale, Florida!" p. 155.

55. Ibid.

56. Author's computations.

57. Mark S. Rosentraub, "Does the Emperor Have New Clothes? A Reply to Robert J. Baade," *Journal of Urban Affairs*, vol. 18, no. 1 (1996), pp. 23, 25.

14

MINOR LEAGUE TEAMS AND COMMUNITIES

ROBERT A. BAADE AND
ALLEN R. SANDERSON

 Since the mid-1970s substantial economic change has taken place at every level of professional sports. The impact has been felt not only by owners, players, and fans, but also by the communities that host professional teams. Many of the communities discussed in this volume thus far are major metropolitan areas, but smaller cities and towns have experienced the economic upheaval as well. This is particularly true of communities that host minor league baseball.

The 1990 Professional Baseball Agreement (PBA) speaks volumes, between the lines, about shifting financial fortunes in major and minor league baseball and about Major League Baseball's response to the changing economic circumstances. Nowhere is this economic dynamic more apparent than in Attachment 58 to the 1990 PBA, Minor League Facility Standards and Compliance Inspection Procedures. Figure 14-1 shows the facility standards, review procedures, and the table of contents for Attachment 58.[1] Almost twenty pages of the PBA are devoted to the stadium mandate.

This chapter examines changes in the economics of major and minor league baseball, their contribution to the development of Attachment 58 (hereafter referred to as A58), and the extent to which this agreement has imposed a financial burden on minor league baseball communities. Several related issues are also discussed: What motivated MLB to author A58 and the minor leagues to agree to it? To what extent have minor league communities financed A58? Why did these host towns and cities accede to baseball's demands for ballpark replacement or renovation? And if minor league communities have financed a large part of MLB's stadium directive, has the investment nevertheless been worthwhile for them?

Though different in some respects from federal government unfunded mandates, the MLB stadium directive rivals such mandates in its impact, as measured by the financial commitment and compliance rate among minor league communities. Like many government mandates, the MLB stadium directive "encourages" cooperation by penalizing a community for noncompliance: failure to comply terminates the minor league club. The effectiveness of this threat depends on MLB's ability to control the minor leagues and the extent to which minor league owners recognize that the stadium directive bolsters their own financial interests. The 1990 PBA, the result of protracted and contentious negotiations between MLB and the minor leagues, indicates that MLB retains control. The enthusiastic acceptance of A58 by minor league owners suggests that they expected new and renovated stadiums to enhance their bottom lines.

Although professional baseball leagues and teams exhibit some fiscal and political autonomy at all levels, baseball's structure is clearly hierarchical, with MLB heading the organization chart. Ultimate authority arguably rests with the owners of the thirty major league franchises, including the two new teams in Florida (Devil Rays) and Arizona (Diamondbacks) that will begin play in 1998.[2]

MLB uses the 1990 agreement to force minor league communities to improve its financial performance in the following fashion. First, MLB decrees that minor league clubs must renovate old or construct new stadiums. In particular, A58 identifies a comprehensive list of stadium specifications with which minor league teams must comply. Clubs that fail to abide by the MLB edict risk losing their major league affiliation and, most important, their player development contracts, the financial lifeblood of the minor leagues. Second, in response to this threat, minor league clubs pressure their host communities to provide the requisite funding, often by threatening to cease operations or abandon these cities. In a 1990 survey of minor league baseball, twenty-four of sixty-six communities sampled indicated that team demands for financial assistance

Figure 14-1. *Attachment 58: Minor League Facility Standards and Compliance Inspection Procedures*

Standards

Unless expressed as recommendations, these facility standards are minimum requirements for all new Minor League facilities. Notwithstanding its facility's designation as a "new facility," a Minor League Club which can demonstrate that its new facility construction planning and approval process was at such a stage as of November 17, 1990 that requiring compliance with a minimum new facilities standard (other than those outlined in Sections 11, 12 and 13) will cause it to suffer a material hardship, may apply to the President of the Minor League Association for a variance from such standard. The standards outlined in Sections 11, 12 and 13 are applicable to *both* new and existing facilities.

New Facilities

Any facility which is scheduled for a construction starting date of January 1, 1991 or later shall be considered a "new facility." All plans for new facilities, including construction time schedules, must be submitted to field inspection personnel designated by the Commissioner's office and the President of the Minor League Association, for review and approval by the field inspection personnel prior to the start of construction. Such review must be completed within 30 days after submission or the plans shall be deemed approved. If such plans meet the standards they shall be approved.

Existing Facilities

Any facility other than a "new facility" as defined above shall be considered an "existing facility." All existing facilities must meet the standards outlined in Sections 11, 12 and 13 (playing field and other team facilities) by no later than April 1, 1995. All plans for additions, alterations or renovations of such facilities, including new turf installations, must be submitted to field inspection personnel designated by the Commissioner's office and to the President of the Minor League Association, for review and approval by the field inspection personnel (including construction time schedules) prior to the start of construction. Such review must be completed within 30 days after submission or the plans shall be deemed approved. If such plans meet the standards they shall be approved.

TABLE OF CONTENTS

were accompanied by threats to relocate.[3] Our own research indicates that teams have carried out these threats and in some cases have moved to other areas that are less-capital-poor or more willing to comply: sixty-six minor league baseball relocations occurred between 1985 and 1995. Third, as minor league teams obtain new stadiums, their financial performance improves. This improvement enables major league clubs to reduce the subsidies that they provide for the minor leagues.

We believe that for owners and players at both the major and minor league level the impact of A58 has been positive. For the communities that fund this decree, or a good portion of it, the 1990 agreement represents an economic burden since the economic benefits of operating a minor league club are insufficient to offset the cost of renovating an old stadium or constructing a new one. This is precisely what other chapters in this book have said about cities that host major league sports. The difference between major and minor league communities as it relates to new stadium construction is a matter of degree, not kind. In most instances, justification for the stadium subventions has to be based on qualitative or psychic benefits to the community; however, these benefits are more ambiguous for minor league baseball than for a city that hosts an MLB club.

The consensus among minor league team officials appears to be that either through accident or design, A58 has precipitously improved the financial condition of many minor league teams. But what about the general criticism of unfunded mandates? Are they not promulgated to serve the narrowly defined financial and political interests of the authority imposing them, at the expense of those in a politically vulnerable position? To answer that question, one must identify who in society has shouldered the financial burden imposed by the stadium mandate, and why.

MLB's Motivation for Imposing Attachment 58

According to MLB owners, the financial returns to most of their teams have declined since the mid-1970s (a period that corresponds roughly to the coming of player unionization and free agency). There is, however, considerable evidence to the contrary: a good deal of research indicates that owning a professional sports franchise continues to be profitable.[4] Irrespective of the past or current bottom financial line, profitability can be improved, or losses can be mitigated, by increasing revenues or by reducing costs. Possible revenue enhancements include sharing revenue from sales of minor league logo merchandise and venue receipts. On the cost side of the ledger, major league owners spend sizable amounts on developing players and operating a farm system. Thus MLB is motivated to have its minor league affiliates assume greater fiscal responsibility and autonomy. The 1990 PBA codified MLB's intent to reduce its financial support to teams.

This objective has been bolstered by renewed fan interest in minor league baseball in recent years and a corresponding improvement in the financial performance of many of its teams. Historically, minor league baseball attendance set records in the late 1940s, reaching a peak of more than 40 million in 1949.[5] Attendance plummeted to 15.5 million in 1957 as television brought major league baseball into the living rooms of minor league towns.[6] But in the late 1970s interest in minor league baseball revived, and between 1979 and 1989 attendance increased 51 percent, from 15.3 million to 23.1 million.[7] During the late 1980s and early 1990s, minor league baseball attendance continued to climb, and in 1995 almost 31 million tickets were sold for games played in 156 cities in the United States and Canada.[8] Developments in the major leagues, particularly the strike-shortened 1994 season and the delayed start of the 1995 season, explain, at least in part, the improvement in minor league attendance.

To provide some perspective on minor league attendance, we calculated summary statistics on total attendance in 1995 as a fraction of community population—that is, the rate of attendance—for a sample of minor league teams from leagues at the AAA, AA, and A levels in comparison with MLB teams (see table 14-1). The results–attendance rates are considerably higher in minor league communities than in major league cities—are not surprising in that baseball may have fewer competitors for citizens' recreational dollars in small communities than in major metropolitan areas. The actual differences may even be larger since major league teams are more likely than minor league teams to draw some fans from beyond the immediate area, especially during the summer.

Another way of gauging fan interest in minor league baseball in comparison with major league baseball, as well as potential "demand-side" pressure for a larger facility, is to compute stadium utilization rates, that is, actual attendance as a percentage of stadium capacity. For the sample of communities that host minor league baseball in table 14-1, attendance

Table 14-1. *Rate of Attendance for Selected and All Minor League Teams, 1995[a]*

League[a]	Rate (attendance/population x 100)
MLB	38.8
AAA[c]	116.2
AA[d]	201.4
A[e]	136.5
Minor League sample (all)	153.7

Sources: Minor league attendance: National Association of Professional Baseball Leagues, Inc., "1995 Minor League Regular Attendance Survey: 1984 to Present," n.d., processed. MLB attendance rates: Shannon Dortch, "The Future of Baseball," *American Demographics and Consumer Trends*, April 1996, p. 26.

a. Population statistics for minor league communities are for 1990 and have been derived from U.S. Department of Commerce, Economics and Statistics Administration, *County and City Databook 1994* (Washington, D.C.: GPO, August 1994).

b. The league acronyms represent, from top to bottom, major league baseball overall, the highest level of minor league play (AAA), the next highest level (AA), and the lowest level (A) of minor league play.

c. Communities in the AAA sample are Buffalo, Indianapolis, Louisville, New Orleans, Charlotte, Columbus, Richmond, Rochester, Albuquerque, Colorado Springs, Las Vegas, and Tacoma. Rate of attendance for these cities ranged from 50 (Indianapolis) to 274.5 (Buffalo).

d. Communities in the AA sample are Binghamton, Harrisburg, Trenton, Birmingham, Knoxville, Memphis, El Paso, Shreveport, and Tulsa. Rate of attendance ranged from 36.3 (Memphis) to 511.9 (Trenton).

e. Communities in the A sample are Modesto, San Jose, Stockton, Augusta, Savannah, and Asheville. Rate of attendance ranged from 18.0 (San Jose) to 383.4 (Augusta).

averaged 48.6 percent of stadium capacity, which approximates the utilization rate for the major leagues as a whole. This statistic also shows little variation across the levels of minor league play: AAA, AA, and A capacity utilization rates averaged 48.8, 48.6, and 47.8 percent, respectively, for these sample communities.

Apart from longer-term or steady-state averages, new stadiums and new teams, irrespective of the level of play, also generate a "novelty effect." Whether a stadium, a mall, or a restaurant, newness attracts the curious and usually is a short-term phenomenon. There is evidence to suggest that a minor league team experiences a substantial attendance spurt when this effect is most pronounced, that is, during the year in which a team moves into a new community or occupies a new stadium. Table 14-2 shows the increase in attendance the year after a team moved or a stadium was built during the 1985–95 period for all AAA, AA, and A minor league teams by level of play.

MLB is motivated to stipulate new or improved stadiums at the minor league level for at least three reasons: financial returns to the major leagues have increased in the wake of their own new stadiums; minor league attendance patterns are rising (table 14-2); and the financial prospects of minor leagues on the whole are positive, particularly with respect to franchise appreciation. The major leagues have found that substantial stadium revenues can be derived from upgrading seating—segmenting

Table 14-2. *Average Increase in Attendance the Year Following Move of a Minor League Franchise or Construction of a New Stadium, 1985–95*
Percent

League	Change after a team moves[a]	Change after a new stadium is built[b]
AAA	193.7	107.3
AA	91.1	119.8
A	158.6	71.2
Overall	147.5	98.6

Source: National Association of Professional Baseball Leagues, Inc., "1995 Minor League Regular Season Attendance Survey: 1984 to Present," n.d., processed.

a. The number of franchise shifts during the period 1985 through 1995 (a move from 1984 to a new location in 1985 was counted) for all AAA, AA, and A teams was 66. AAA, AA, and A league relocations numbered 6, 14, and 46, respectively. Attendance declined in 18 percent of the moves (12 of the 66 changes), but many of the negative changes can be explained by a very popular team moving up a league, and the league filling the void with a team that did not draw as well in another community. For example, when MLB's Denver Rockies began play in 1993, the AAA franchise moved to New Orleans, where they did not draw well in comparison with Denver's AAA team. The standard deviations for the attendance changes were large: 160.1 percent (AAA), 99.9 percent (AA), and 163.4 percent (A).

b. Although 67 new ballparks were constructed for NAPBL teams during the period 1985–95, 15 of them were built in cities that already had a stadium in which minor league baseball was played. Of these 15 stadiums, 6, 4, and 5 were constructed in AAA, AA, A League communities, respectively. In no instance did attendance decline after the construction of a new stadium. Attendance increases in these communities ranged from 19 percent (Yakima, Washington; A League) to 260 percent (Shreveport, Louisiana; AA League).

the market for spectating—and providing other amenities. Hence MLB sought to improve the financial performance of minor league stadiums by upgrading and standardizing ballpark seating according to minor league classification (A58, Section 1.2). Although MLB has not specified minimums for luxury loges or club seats, "minor league stadiums are fast becoming miniatures of modern major league facilities, complete with skyboxes, restaurants, picnic areas, effective lighting for the playing field and modern amenities for the players and umpires."[9]

The new generation of stadiums can be particularly lucrative if revenues do not have to be shared with the public agencies financing their construction. Here, too, the minor leagues are mimicking the practice of the majors. Minor league clubs do not share stadium revenues with their host communities, either:

Beyond stadium rental fees, local governments tend not to share directly in the revenues produced by the teams. Fewer than half (47.1 percent) of the 34 communities whose teams generate parking revenue share in the parking receipts and only 4 of these local governments retain all of them. With only two exceptions, all the sample communities which disclosed financial data reported that their teams generate revenue from advertising within the ball park. However, only 19.5 percent of these communities share in stadium advertising receipts. Finally, 65.5 percent of the teams generate radio/television revenue, but only four of the reporting communities share in this revenue.[10]

Nothing has encouraged MLB to restructure its financial relationship with the minor leagues more than the improving financial performances and prospects of their minor league affiliates. In negotiating the 1990 PBA, MLB undoubtedly focused on identifying the optimum level of subsidization of minor league clubs. The uppermost question for MLB was how to maintain control of the minor leagues while cutting its costs in supporting them? A number of economic changes had occurred to give these questions greater urgency:

> To major league owners, a transaction such as this proved their growing suspicion that they were subsidizing the literal fortunes of their minor league counterparts. Again, South Bend was hardly alone. The market for minor league ball clubs—and a market was what the buying and selling of franchises had become by now—was yielding one Xerox-in-1952 bonanza after another: Harrisburg, Pennsylvania, bought in 1980 (in Nashua, New Hampshire) for $85,000, sold for $3 million; Peoria, Illinois, bought in 1983 (in Danville, Illinois) for $125,000, sold for $1.2 million; Durham, North Carolina . . . bought in 1979 for $2,400, sold for $4 million.[11]

Similar trends have reportedly occurred in Albany, Oklahoma City, and Louisville.[12] It did not help the minor league financial cause for an occasional owner to flaunt the primary reason for his financial success:

> Take the case of Joseph Buzas, 68, who has owned and operated 64 different minor league teams during his career. In 1978 Buzas paid the awesome sum of $1 to acquire the bankrupt Reading Phillies. Last year Buzas resold the franchise for an astounding $1 million. Says he, "the majors are subsidizing us tremendously. You have to be real stupid if you can't make money in this environment."[13]

In this environment, it would have been surprising if MLB had not taken steps to reduce its farm-system subsidy. The major leagues have been castigated for their greedy behavior, and their aggressive tactics in their 1990 negotiations with the National Association of Professional Baseball Leagues (NAPBL) did not play well throughout the United States and Canada, despite the evidence just cited. Perhaps MLB felt it useful, at least in the arena of public opinion, to strengthen the financial performance of the minor leagues further before reducing in more obvious and extensive ways its financial support for them. Whatever the reason, the 1990 PBA was structured in a way that allowed for greater

MLB participation in the financial success of the minor leagues in exchange for the continuation of the player development contracts.[14]

Attachment A to the 1990 PBA contains measures that allow MLB to reduce expenditures on the minor leagues and yet participate in their financial success. Some of the more important cuts pertained to the "special considerations" fee, player and staff travel (new limitations were imposed for minor league clubs), and the $35 transaction fee (the fee MLB paid the NAPBL every time it made a minor league roster change). The formula for an MLB sharing of minor league revenues appears in the 1996 version of the 1990 PBA (page 13). In brief, NAPBL will pay MLB a flat fee ($2 million in 1994) that is based on a maximum contribution of 5 percent of revenues for each minor league club.[15] MLB's cost cutting alone reduced the Waterloo Diamonds' (Class A) revenue by $20,000 to $25,000.[16] Although the percentage of revenues shared declines as revenues increase, this framework still provides MLB an unambiguous incentive to amplify the financial success of its affiliates. We contend that Attachment A to Article IX (the revenue-sharing schedule) and A58 were designed in part to enhance the MLB's bottom line.

Depending on the length of the new stadium novelty effect, the increased attendance and revenues that correlate with a new ballpark may well provide a short-term rationale for MLB either to reduce its financial support to its affiliates or to increase its revenue-sharing percentage, beginning with the expiration of the 1990 PBA in 1997. MLB reportedly is already considering taking a bold step to reduce its minor league expenses further by limiting the number of minor league affiliates any one MLB team can have. Currently, the average MLB team has six to seven affiliates, and the total player development costs incurred by MLB teams average $7 million to $9 million. The proposal reportedly under discussion will limit the number of farm teams to four per MLB franchise.[17] This would reduce expenses approximately $1 to $3 million per big league team.

The proposition reflects another reality of player development: intercollegiate baseball is providing an increasingly attractive alternative for training baseball players, one with significant cost-saving advantages from MLB's perspective (similar to advantages enjoyed by the NBA and NFL). The reduction in the number of affiliates suggests not only that MLB is interested in cutting costs but that it is also relying more on colleges and universities to weed out the 90 percent of minor league players who fail in their quest to reach the majors. In noting, perhaps, the slim chance of success in big league baseball, MLB aspirants are hedging their bets by attending colleges and universities in greater numbers.[18]

If MLB is regarded as the head of a trade association or franchising corporation, it has an interest, just as McDonald's does across its thousands of outlets, in ensuring that its major league members and minor league affiliates reflect well on the umbrella operation in terms of both personnel and property. No doubt A58 and other operating regulations in part serve this function for MLB. However, when MLB has considerable cartel control over entry and also uses its power to extract substantial subventions from the communities in which major and minor league teams reside, providing quality control and ensuring a uniform product are more than likely not the primary purpose of the PBA.

In addition, signing bonuses and other sizable dollar commitments that parent clubs have in some of their minor league prospects could also account for MLB's insistence on better minor league facilities to protect their investments in human capital. However, this narrow interest could be satisfied through requirements in Section 12 of A58. which pertain to field conditions and lighting (see figure 14-1). It is hard to see how the specifications in the other areas apply.

In sum, Attachment 58 to the 1990 PBA was authored in large measure because it serves MLB's bottom line over the life of the 1990 PBA and beyond. Renewed interest in and increased attendance at minor league baseball games has improved the financial health of MLB's farm system, and this reality has not escaped MLB owners. In fact, it has allowed MLB to justify its reduced financial support of the minors to the government— although antitrust immunity remains an issue—and the general public.

Does it require a suspension of belief to accept the premise that MLB has linked renewed interest in minor league baseball, the financial vigor of the minors, new stadiums, and its bottom line? We think not. Indeed, it would be surprising if, in future negotiations with the NAPBL, MLB did not seek further financial concessions based on improving financial prospects for the minors in response to the ballpark improvements mandated by A58.

Minor League Response to Attachment 58

At first, minor league owners responded tepidly to the 1990 PBA and Attachment 58. Since then, owners have seen attendance (and presumably revenues) increase at the new ballparks, and their initial grudging acceptance of Attachment 58 has turned into effusive praise. According to Rick Smith, the general manager of the Class A California League Bakersfield Dodgers,

> Now that we're being required to upgrade our facilities, it makes professional baseball that much more appealing. The minor league owners should have been able to figure this out on their own and didn't. The problem was that minor leagues sat on their duffs for 20 years, and they needed a kick in the pants to get going on these ballparks. I think it's one of the best things that ever happened to the minor leagues.[19]

Despite the lack of input from the minor leagues, General Manager Tim Marting of the Modesto A's, also in the California League, was positive about the MLB action: "In terms of the concept of facility standards, there's no question it's for the betterment of the game."[20]

Franchise appreciation of the magnitude exhibited by the minor leagues could not have occurred in the absence of a robust demand for franchises. It should be emphasized that the increased demand for minor league clubs has been motivated primarily by the promise of franchise appreciation, not by past high annual rates of return through the operation of the team. (Teams that appreciate in value even though they operate in the red is explained by anticipated positive future earnings.)[21] The minor leagues, one observer has pointed out, "are major business nowadays."

> Although very few franchises offer substantial annual profits, almost all of them experienced a geometric rise in their market value. . . .
>   . . . But even if a team is losing money on an annual basis, its franchise value continues to appreciate.[22]

If a particular community does not offer sufficient support to generate at least a competitive return on the investment in the baseball club, investors can move the team to a locale that provides heightened interest, greater public sector support, and a greater return. Profitable relocation requires a demand for franchises that exceeds the available supply. Minor league owners, like their major league counterparts, understand that if their host city does not support them adequately through attendance levels or stadium subsidies, other cities might. The incidence of franchise relocation in minor league baseball offers compelling evidence that there exists no shortage of suitor cities (see the notes to table 14-2).

League cartels contribute positively to individual franchise valuations by limiting the supply of teams. At the major league level, substantial political pressure is often necessary to induce expansion. In all likelihood, NAPBL exercises less control over the supply of teams than do other professional sports cartels. Demand for minor league baseball can be met through independent leagues, for example. However, the established minor leagues, particularly at the highest level, have the advantage of name identification, a league tradition, and ballparks that now meet minimum standards. Independent league teams must find teams to compete with and a stadium in which to play. The new generation of expensive and more luxurious minor league stadiums represents a barrier to entry, since new, independent teams may have trouble finding comparable facilities. Nonetheless, barriers to entry in minor league baseball are less formidable than those in the major leagues, and it follows that excess demand is less likely to persist in the minor leagues than in the majors.

Prospects for profits, substantial appreciation in the value of teams, and complexities and risks inherent in managing a larger enterprise have produced a new breed of owners. They are driven by something more than a passion for minor league baseball, and they are also more willing to uproot a team:

> Unlike the locals who used to run minor league clubs on a virtually not-for-profit basis, or fans "who got involved out of love of baseball but found they could also turn a profit," today's owners are in many cases "outsiders who, however fond of the sport, [consider] their acquisitions in business terms only. . . . [T]hey changed the economic structure of the minors. They imposed a subtle pressure on other clubs to conform to their standards, at least at first; eventually, a not-so-subtle pressure; and now, through the new PBA, a mandate."[23]

This change in ownership occurred over a ten-year period, beginning in 1980 and culminating in the 1990 PBA. This trend is continuing, and, not surprisingly, the franchise moves have accelerated. Between 1987 and 1996 there have been sixty-eight franchise relocations, and thirty-five of them (51 percent) have occurred since 1993.[24] As mentioned earlier, the financial gains have been facilitated in part by moving clubs from one community to another. When the baseball novelty wears off or the community becomes more parsimonious, the club moves to greener pastures. These nomadic tendencies are particularly evident at the lower minor league level. In a survey of eight-eight communities with minor league stadium leases, 72.4 percent had leases of five years or less. Those hosting AAA and AA teams appeared to negotiate longer-term leases (55.5 percent have leases of five years or more) than communities with A and Rookie league teams (only 17.5 percent of this group had longer leases). Furthermore, 75.3 percent of the communities reported that their teams had made demands on them within the three years preceding the survey (1986–88).[25]

More business-oriented ownership has also brought minor leagues business acumen, particularly in the area of marketing.[26] One of their new strategies is to relocate minor league teams to "edge cities," which are self-contained developments in close proximity to old central cities. These "galactic cities" are to be distinguished from the expanding rings of suburbs.

The increasing incidence of edge cities hosting Class A minor league baseball is one important manifestation of A58. The trends that correlate with the mandate fall into three categories: an existing market renovates an old stadium or builds a new one; a new market, larger than the old markets characteristic of a league, builds a new facility; or the edge city, a new type of market altogether and larger than the other new markets, builds a new facility.

Edge city hosts bring minor league clubs closer to markets that enhance their prospects for increasing stadium revenues through the sale or lease of luxury seating and corporate sponsorship in the form of stadium signage and advertising. The character of the new minor leagues can be seen in Rancho Cucamonga, a recent addition to the California League. It replaced San Bernardino, a city that had failed to fund a new ballpark. When the franchise's first manager showed up for a press conference, he received a briefing on what to expect:

> Fourteen skyboxes, an elevator to the front offices, a receptionist to lead visitors through the carpeted suites. [The manager] looked out at the grape arbors across the road, and he imagined the subdivisions that were sure to emerge there by the turn of the century. Rancho Cucamonga lay forty miles east of Los Angeles, had been one of the nation's top-twenty-five fastest growing communities of the 1980s, and promised to become the Kane County of the California League. "I've died and gone to heaven," [he] said.[27]

The Class A Midwest League has evolved in much the same way as many minor leagues. Before 1981 the league consisted of eight stable teams, three in Wisconsin and five in Iowa. All eight teams were locally owned and operated. At present, the Midwest League is composed of fourteen teams, two in Wisconsin, four in eastern Iowa, three in Illinois, two in Indiana, and three in Michigan. Of the fourteen teams, only five are locally owned and operated. In contemplating a new president for the league, the owners favored replacing George Spelius, the current president and a florist from Beloit, Wisconsin, with a marketing specialist headquartered in Chicago.

Perhaps the best example of the audiences that the minor leagues are now seeking comes from Kane County, Illinois, which runs a franchise in the Midwest League and is home to service industries, corporate headquarters, and research laboratories. The audience the Kane County franchise "coveted" consisted of

> first, a core of more than 150 corporate sponsors to buy blocks of box seats and provide the franchise with a substantial and stable attendance base, from American Express to Zenith, with stops along the alphabet for national names such as Amoco Oil Company, Armour-Swift Eckrich, McDonald's Corp. and Stroh Brewery, . . . the employees of all these businesses and the thousands of others lining the access roads and crowding the cul-de-sacs in a fifteen- or twenty-mile radius; and finally, and especially, their children—and all of them, from CEOs to six-year-olds, with bountiful disposable incomes.[28]

Edge city relocation of many minor league franchises has compelled both major and minor league groups to establish strict territorial boundaries for all (these boundaries are identified in the 1996 version of the 1990 PBA):

> For more than 60 years, Major League Baseball teams controlled their cities plus a surrounding five-mile zone; no other club, major or minor, could move in without the approval of the team controlling the territory. Under the new guidelines . . . the majors have claimed larger, county-based territories as well as a 15-mile buffer beyond the new territories. The minors also were allowed to create new territories based on counties.[29]

The fact that such boundaries had to be defined at all indicates that minor league teams have been moving uncomfortably close to major league markets.

The revenue-sharing scheme codified in the 1990 PBA, under which the major league share declines as revenues increase, encourages minor league clubs to expand revenues as much as possible. Of course, this incentive would be present without revenue sharing, but it is safe to assume that MLB would have demanded some form of revenue sharing or additional cost cutting in their 1990 negotiations with the National Association. Clearly a regressive arrangement offers a greater incentive to expand revenue than does a proportional or a progressive scheme.

The astute entrepreneur who has come to dominate minor league ownership is well aware that attendance and revenues go up when new ballparks open. Given the recent sales prices of minor league franchises, it is highly probable that club purchases are highly leveraged, and that stadiums must now produce considerably more revenue than stadiums of the past. These new owners have come to embrace the MLB stadium mandate because it has supported high franchise prices overall by improving the financial performance of the clubs.[30] The "David" role NAPBL played in negotiations with the MLB "Goliath" before the 1990 accord has enabled teams to portray themselves as the victims of the mandate, since its costs have been passed on to them.

The fact that excess demand exists for minor league franchises—no direct fault can be ascribed to an individual team in this regard—has served in turn to induce the public sector to underwrite the risk inherent in investing in sports infrastructure. If MLB succeeds in limiting the number of minor league affiliates, the surviving teams will likely appreciate further. Indeed, when all is said and done, the strongest supporters of A58 are likely to be the strongest minor league franchises.

Ironically, the financial success of the minor leagues in the past two decades has put minor league communities at financial risk. How? The financial success of the minor leagues, particularly as it relates to franchise appreciation, induced MLB to reconsider its financial relationship with them. The 1990 PBA codifies the particulars of MLB's reassessment. Because the new PBA allows MLB to share in the financial success of its affiliates, a clear incentive for MLB's A58 exists. In the longer term, the improved financial health that minor league clubs might derive from A58 could justify additional reductions in MLB "farm" subsidies. Under the MLB stadium initiative, the brunt of all the resulting changes falls squarely on minor league host communities.

Financial Implications of Attachment 58 for Communities

The details of stadium costs and the financial burden of MLB's stadium mandate presented in this section are drawn from several sources,

Table 14-3a. *Number of NAPBL Ballparks Constructed or Renovated by Minor League Classification, 1985–2000*

Period	AAA	AA	A	All
1985–90				
New	3	2	7	12
Renovated	0	3	2	5
1991–95				
New	6	7	26	39
Renovated	9	9	43	61
1996–2000				
New	6	2	4	12
Renovated	1	2	7	10

the most important of which is our September 1996 survey of all minor league clubs—AAA, AA, regular A and short-season A leagues—identified in note 8. (A copy of the telephone survey instrument we employed is included in the appendix to this chapter. Of the 156 minor league teams, 143, or more than 92 percent, responded to the survey. Only 1 team refused to answer our questions; the remaining 12 were simply unavailable because their seasons had ended and their administrative offices were closed.)

Substantial stadium construction activity in the minor leagues certainly predated the 1990 PBA. The surge in minor league attendance and improved financial prospects in the 1980s clearly encouraged new ballpark construction and renovations. Increases in attendance alone, however, cannot explain the frenetic pace at which minor league facilities were constructed in the 1990s. Indeed, the increased seating capacity provided through new stadiums—A58 defines a minimum number of seats and their distribution by "luxury" level for new ballparks at each minor league level and seating capacity clearly affects attendance—may account for at least some of the attendance increases. Arguably, the primary impetus for stadium construction activity can be traced to A58, Facility Standards and Compliance Inspection Procedures, specified in the 1996 version of the Professional Baseball Agreement.

Table 14-3a records information by league classification on the number of minor league ballparks and stadiums constructed and renovated for the periods 1985 to 1990, 1991 to 1995, and under construction or projected to be built in 1996 through the year 2000. Table 14-3b shows the average cost incurred in constructing new or renovating ballparks for the

Table 14-3b. *Average Construction or Renovation Costs for NAPBL Ballparks Built or Renovated during 1985–2000, by Minor League Classification*

Millions of current dollars

Period	AAA	AA	A	All
1985–90				
New	32.7	3.5	2.6	7.3
Renovated	0.0	2.0	2.2	2.1
1991–95				
New	18.9	7.8	6.8	8.8
Renovated	2.8	1.2	0.8	1.1
1996–2000				
New	26.5	20.0	11.0	20.0
Renovated	12.0	3.3	1.3	2.8

periods 1985 to 1990 and 1991 to 1995, and for average costs for stadiums slated for construction after 1996 to 2000; table 14-3c provides total construction and renovation costs in current dollars for these same periods.

Of the 143 teams that constituted our sample, 51 built new stadiums between 1985 and 1995. Approximately 76 percent of the new minor league stadiums constructed between 1985 and 1995 were built after 1991 (according to published NAPBL mimeographed reports, only 63 percent were built during this time period).[31] For those stadiums built or reno-

Table 14-3c. *Construction or Renovation Costs for NAPBL Ballparks Built or Renovated during 1985–2000 by Minor League Classification*

Millions of current dollars

Period	AAA	AA	A	All
1985–90				
New	98.0	7.0	18.5	123.5
Renovated	0.0	6.0	4.3	10.3
1991–95				
New	113.4	54.4	175.6	343.4
Renovated	25.0	10.9	33.0	68.9
1996–2000				
New	159.0	40.0	44.0	243.0
Renovated	12.0	6.5	9.4	27.9

Sources: Telephone survey of all minor league teams conducted at Lake Forest College, September 12–29, 1996. Of the 156 teams that constitute the population of all NAPBL AAA, AA, and A teams, 138 responses were secured. National Association of Professional Baseball Leagues, "NAPBL Ballparks Constructed since 1985," n.d., processed.

vated after the 1990 PBA, more than 66 percent of the respondents cited Attachment 58 as the driving force for the ballpark construction project.

To the extent that increased fan incomes could have created the demand for new or improved facilities, in the same way that consumers are motivated to "trade up" automobile models, clothing lines, or other income-elastic commodities, one would expect to see more construction as a natural course of events. However, the "spike" in building so evident in the middle period at all three levels of play in table 14-3a points strongly to an exogenous cause. A58 is, in our opinion, that factor.

Furthermore, in more than 67 percent of the survey cases, the new or renovated ballpark was financed primarily through public means.[32] Also, stadium construction costs incurred during the 1991–95 period exceeded the current-dollar stadium costs incurred during the previous five-year period by almost $280 million (see note 32). After adjusting for inflation, the real cost of stadium construction during the 1991–95 period exceeded that of the 1985–1990 period by 141 percent, according to the results of our survey only.[33] (See appendix table 14A-1 for complete survey results by minor league classification.)

Taken together, the evidence recorded in tables 14-3a through 14-3c indicates that more stadiums were built at a higher cost in the years following the imposition of Attachment 58 than was true for the five-year period preceding the 1990 PBA. Inasmuch as the majority of survey respondents indicated that the MLB stadium mandate had been decisive in compelling ballpark construction, it is safe to conclude that Attachment 58 has imposed a substantial demand on the capital resources of minor league communities. Indeed, the survey results indicated that 29 minor league communities (21 percent of the respondents) incurred stadium costs that exceeded $100 per capita, and of those 29 teams, 20 financed the stadium mostly or completely with public funds.

Why Did Minor League Communities Accede to MLB Demands?

In recent times communities that host baseball teams often have found themselves forced to choose between retaining the franchise or assuming the cost of a new ballpark. A58 lent greater urgency and authority to minor league ballpark construction. If teams did not comply with the stadium mandate by April 1, 1995, or were not exempted from compliance, the minor league club lost its MLB affiliation. This threat, of course, induced a great deal of stadium construction, but it does not explain all the construction activity noted earlier. Furthermore, it does not explain how the supporters of the use of public funds to build ballparks have rationalized such subventions or otherwise convinced themselves and a skeptical public of their merits.

The rationale most often used recognizes the stadium as a public investment that yields benefits in excess of the costs incurred. Benefits are often broadly defined to include those that qualify as psychic or nonmonetary in nature and are generally related to the enhanced quality of life professional sports provide for participating communities. From the point of view of the community, it may well be that minor league baseball is less about baseball than family entertainment, helping to define a city's livability.[34] From this perspective, the stadium issue is best described as a public choice question in which economics plays a role but may not be decisive in the public funding decision. There is, however, the ubiquitous use of an economic rationale, and evaluating its merits helps focus the public debate.

As noted earlier, minor league clubs are not particularly profitable in terms of their annual operations. Only through long-run capital appreciation are the returns attractive. If teams invested in new stadiums without public support, the already thin profit margins would erode further, if not disappear altogether. In the minor leagues, barriers to team movement are weak; in fact, the statistics cited previously indicate that teams move with impunity. Thus the threat to abandon a community in the minor leagues has to be taken seriously. The inequality of the bargaining positions between a community and team is exacerbated by the excess demand for the finite number of franchises, but other factors relating more to structural changes in the U.S. economy help explain why communities accede to team demands for new or refurbished facilities.[35]

In this regard it is important to interpret decisions to finance stadiums not as an isolated practice, but rather as part of a larger strategy that has its roots in trade theory and the "new federalism" of the 1980s and into the present decade. By new federalism we mean increased state and local fiscal autonomy, with the federal government sharing less federal tax revenue with state and local governments, and state governments sharing less of their revenues with local governments. Less money from higher levels of government, coupled with other growing demands on city financial resources, forced local governments to become more creative and enterprising in dealing with their financial crises that cut into both their revenues and costs. To be more precise, direct local government spending in nominal terms increased by 90 percent over the Reagan years (from $259 million in 1980 to $491 million in 1988), while the fraction of total state and local government revenue provided by the federal government decreased from 18.4 percent in 1980 to 13.3 percent in 1988.[36] Thus local government can now be characterized as more entrepreneurial than before, but also as more prone to taking risks.

Such risk-taking sometimes produces unfortunate outcomes (Orange County, California, being one recent example). But local and state governments are more likely to exercise risk in business ventures than in financial "wheeling and dealing." These levels of government have invested heavily in entertainment-related activities. The proliferation of theme parks, convention centers, and festivals complement more traditional commercial and industrial investments. All are manifestations of local government entrepreneurial urges that attempt to garner more local residents' discretionary income as well as to lure new dollars from beyond the local area.[37] From a balance-of-payments perspective, community officials hope that the investment in sports infrastructure will induce an increase in net receipts or dollar inflows to their communities from the world outside. We are entering, it seems, "the entrepreneurial phase of municipal government. . . . You are seeing a linkage between airport, highway, convention center, stadia financing. They are being integrated into a single economics package that's designed to draw people into that entity—a destination city."[38]

The city as a destination, a cultural destination, substitutes the money spent by "foreign interests" drawn to its entertainment attractions previously provided by larger governmental entities. That is the hope of local government officials, and professional sports stadiums are an important spoke in a strategy born out of economic imperative or opportunity. This is the model city of the twenty-first century. Nevertheless, vying for a professional sports franchise, including construction of a stadium to attract or retain a team, differs substantially from negotiating with, say, a department store or an assembly plant. In the former case, the cartel has the power to restrict or relocate the supply of teams, whereas Nordstrom cannot prevent Saks from selling shirts or perfume in any location it chooses. The territorial prerogatives that professional sports teams exercise "unlevels" the playing field immediately and implies that communities are dependent on the goodwill of teams to receive fair compensation for their sports entertainment investment.

Another reason for continued public support for sports facilities is that misinformation abounds. Estimates by local business interests of job creation and new tax revenues, including multiplier effects, are always optimistic, as are economic impact studies commissioned by a franchise or locality. In fact, it may not be possible to find even one example of an impact study or chamber of commerce claim that does not support building a new facility or luring a franchise to town. These create dreams and irresistible temptations for elected officials and unrealistic expectations for citizens and taxpayers. Estimated costs, on the other hand, are often either not fully disclosed or prove wide of the mark when final bills come due.

Evaluating the Stadium Rationale

Public resistance to stadium subsidies has galvanized as taxpayers have grown wary of promises of significant economic returns from stadium subsidies. The inability of stadiums to deliver on their economic promises is attributable in part to the fact that many stadiums are replacement facilities. Once the construction phase of the project is over, the new facility cannot contribute significantly more to community output and employment than the old facility did unless the new structure is far more successful in attracting fans from beyond the community's borders. In the case of replacement facilities, it is more accurate to promise that they will maintain current employment. To suggest or imply that a replacement facility creates new jobs, without inducing an increase in spending overall, has no theoretical foundation and almost certainly exaggerates its economic impact.

Despite growing scholarly evidence that professional sports teams do not contribute significantly to a community's economy, supporters of stadium subventions in both the major and minor leagues persist in using the promise of substantial stadium-induced economic activity as a rationale for them.[39] The United States is replete with examples of communities that have built stadiums on the basis of this promise. Is it a Faustian bargain for cities?

In most cases, minor league communities feel compelled to build ball-parks either to retain or to attract a baseball team. The games and other events held in the stadium do induce spending, but do the activities hosted by the sports facility increase spending in the aggregate in the community? At the major league level, the evidence overwhelmingly indicates that professional sports and stadiums do not generate sufficient additional spending to induce a statistically significant change in either income or jobs.[40]

Blending a professional sports team into the local economic mix trig-gers a variety of changes in financial inflows and outflows to that economy, as explained in chapter 2. Dollars flow into the economy through the sharing of broadcast revenues and the "export" of professional sports entertainment. Dollars flow out of the economy when the professional sports expenditures are converted into salaries for athletes and owners and are repatriated to the primary residences of absentee players and owners. What happens to a community's balance of payments depends on the extent to which spending on professional sports originates beyond the economy's borders (exports) or substitutes for spending that would have resulted in dollar outflows (import substitution).

Given the complexities involved in precisely measuring sports-induced changes in the balance of payments, prospective analysis (building a model and projecting dollar flows) is likely to be inadequate. At the very least, the projections should be filtered through the past experience of stadiums and teams in expanding local economies. The retrospective analysis that has been done indicates that professional sports teams and stadiums are not significant contributors to local or regional economies. This is true in part because the professional sports industry is small in absolute dollar terms. It has been said that "minor league baseball . . . has an economic impact equivalent to a large pet shop (the 122 largest pet shops in the U.S. grossed an average of $1.4 million in 1987)."[41]

A more fundamental reason why professional sports are not likely to induce any statistically significant change in economic activity is that they are largely local in nature. Spectator sports are part of the amusement and recreation industry. Individuals and families have limited leisure budgets defined in terms of both time and money. Fundamental budget constraints mean that more time and money spent spectating at profes-sional sports events leaves less of both for other entertainment activities. To the extent that the fan base is contained within the community hosting the team, baseball realigns leisure spending rather than increasing spending in the aggregate. To represent the contribution of sports to the local economy by summing all spending that takes place in conjunction with it is to fundamentally exaggerate the impact a sport has on the local economy. Unfortunately, this fundamental error is endemic to studies supporting subventions for minor league baseball.

To estimate the impact of minor league baseball, one approach would be to compare the community's economic landscape before and after the introduction of baseball or the completion of a new (or renovated) facility. Although this has been accomplished for major league baseball, the data are insufficient at the minor league level to perform comparable analysis. For small communities data that would enable meaningful analysis are not available in general at the two-digit Standard Industrial Classification (SIC) level, let alone the three-digit level in the amusement and recreation industry. Another approach would be to examine tax revenue by source for minor league communities to determine if sales tax revenues, for example, correlate with investments in baseball infrastructure. Such data, always scarce for smaller communities, have become even less available in the 1990s as a result of government budget cutbacks.

As a consequence, a different strategy must be employed to evaluate the economic impact of minor league baseball. Our strategy combines the extensive retrospective work that has been performed for major league sports (see note 40) with characteristics of minor league sports. We conclude that the statistically insignificant economic impact imparted by major league sports is, if anything, more likely to occur at the minor league level. It should also be recognized that since private minor league interests seek public funding for their infrastructure, the burden of proof is on them to demonstrate that baseball does have a statistically significant impact, or at least an impact sufficient to justify the use of public funds.

To have an impact, minor league baseball must draw fans from outside the community. Others have concluded that this effect does not occur:

> A major league team is capable of attracting millions of fans to a stadium in one season, whereas even a successful minor league team rarely draws more than a few hundred thousand fans. A major league team attracts many fans from beyond its local jurisdiction, especially for postseason play, but this is not the case with a minor league team. A major league team brings national recognition to a city, but it is arguable that the average minor league team brings even regional recognition to its host community.[42]

Our survey respondents admitted freely that they had very little solid information on where their fans came from.

There are other reasons to conclude that the major and minor leagues differ not only in scale but in the kind of spending and economic impact that they generate. The minors do not share in national broadcast revenues, they have greater absentee ownership, and they have many more leagues and thus owners can hold many franchises simultaneously. This implies that much of the profit from minor league games is likely to leave the local economy. The salaries of players and coaches are paid by the major league affiliate, and so the part of the salaries that is spent locally is a net gain to the community; however, few players and coaches live in the local area, which means that few of these payments are likely to be spent locally. To the extent that minor league baseball replaces locally owned and operated leisure businesses, baseball could actually have a deleterious effect on the local economy. In the minors the star players that attract more than a local following are a short-term phenomenon. The purpose of the minors is to develop or rehabilitate out of them.

For these reasons and others noted earlier, the realistic economic experience of minor league communities is likely to fall short of the rosy scenarios so often portrayed in impact studies and presentations made to (and by) local public officials. The current situations in four locations are sufficiently representative of the minor leagues to alert the public to the problems associated with stadium economics across professional sports leagues: Trenton, New Jersey (East); Charlotte, North Carolina (South); LaCrosse, Wisconsin (Midwest); and Lake Elsinore, California (West).

Trenton is a community with a decaying downtown that decided to invest $12 million (the cost eventually rose to $18 million) in a stadium in the hopes of encouraging people to visit downtown and spend money at the minor league baseball games and ancillaries.[43] Waterfront Stadium officially opened on May 9, 1994. The initial returns on the investment have not been promising. (There is some evidence that the Trenton economy has improved in the past two years. However, there is no indication that the stadium played a role in this change.) One small example of the lack of economic spillover for businesses in the ballpark's environs comes from Lamberton Street, a block away from the stadium:

> On the corner is a sandwich shop that changed its name to Ball Park Deli, and promises to remain open on game days until 7 p.m., when the first pitch is thrown. The shop was closed an hour before one recent game, and neighborhood residents said the manager gave up trying to lure baseball fans sometime around midseason, and reverted to his earlier closing time.[44]

In Charlotte, as entertainment options expand in this rapidly growing community, the reality of substitutions within the amusement and recreation industry are abundantly clear:

Lagging attendance for Charlotte's three summer minor league sports franchises is bad enough that one of the clubs—the Charlotte Express—may not return next season.

"There's one thing sports franchises need to understand—they're no longer under the unique purview of sports fans," says John Connaughton, University of North Carolina at Charlotte sports economist. "These teams need to market to the casual fan; they've already got hard-core fans. And they need to understand their market, who their competition is."[45]

The Charlotte case demonstrates the proposition that sports spectating is but one leisure option, and that minor league sports are particularly vulnerable to changes in the entertainment industry. In selling the idea of subsidies for minor league sports to a community, these realities are often ignored.

LaCrosse, Wisconsin, provides a complementary case study. Some leaders in this community of 50,000 proposed building a stadium to attract a Class A Midwest League franchise. Supporters of a public subsidy estimated the team would add $4.3 million to the city's economy annually. Three economists from the University of Wisconsin-LaCrosse performed their own analysis and estimated spending injections of $478,083 for LaCrosse and 30.5 new jobs for the entire region.[46] With the stadium construction costs estimated at $3.595 million, each job would cost more than $100,000 to create. For communities large and small, this represents a very expensive job creation program.

From an investor's point of view, return on equity (ROE) is essential in evaluating the merits of any potential investment. The impartial estimated dollar return (total revenue estimated from the operation of the team) on the LaCrosse stadium investment was $478,083, which represents 13.3 percent of the $3.595 million stadium investment. If the government appropriated all $478,083, the return on equity for taxpayers' investment of $3.595 million would be less than the 13.5 percent on average in the leisure industry.[47] Of course, the government's share (increased tax revenues) of $478,083 is likely to be less than 10 percent of the total, and the ROE for taxpayers no more than 1 percent.

In all likelihood, the promised impact on the community measured in dollar terms exaggerated the actual impact approximately ninefold. The

degree to which the economic impact is embellished by subvention supporters at the minor league level roughly parallels major league overstate-
ments. We have found job creation estimates in major league cities mag-
nified by a factor of at least ten.[48]

In the case of Lake Elsinore, the city council opted to support the
construction of a stadium for a Class A team. A recent review of the
actual impact and budgetary problems experienced there illustrates the
differences between ex-post and pre-commitment expectations and
prospects:

> What seemed like a good idea in 1994 when the project was fast-tracked
> for the Class A team has become the mistake on the edge of the lake.
>
> Originally targeted as an $8.5 million Redevelopment Agency Project,
> the 6,066 seat red-brick jewel of a stadium eventually cost more than $24
> million, taxing the city's general fund to the max. . . .
>
> The city, which recently took over operation of the facility from a private
> company, can't afford the $1 million a year it takes to turn on the lights,
> cut the grass and maintain the grounds. . . .
>
> Here in Lake Elsinore, 70 miles north of San Diego, that kind of full
> faith and credit has been tapped. Social programs have been scrapped.
> Plans to utilize the stadium for events other than minor-league baseball
> have proved fruitless.[49]

Despite the lack of discernible economic impact from the stadiums in
Trenton, Lake Elsinor, and a host of other minor league baseball communities, an investment in a stadium may help a community achieve
some of its development objectives, but it must be planned "using a
development logic that complements other community development planning objectives. These outcomes, however, rarely will be measurable
directly in terms of economic growth. More often, they will enhance
other aspects of a community's development efforts."[50] The comprehensive planning required does not usually occur at the major league level,
let alone among minor league communities. Most stadium projects are
approved under legislative duress at the midnight hour. Hence "the economic impact of a minor league team is not sufficient to justify the
relatively large public expenditure necessary for a minor league stadium."[51]

In evaluating any investment, risk as well as return needs to be considered. While many major league stadium leases are for thirty years,
most minor league stadium leases are for five years or less. In one study
of eighty-four minor league communities, 72.4 percent of the leases were

for five years or less.[52] Since the communities almost always own the stadium but not the team, the community is investing in an asset that depreciates in value while facing the additional risk of losing the team in five years or less. On the basis of risk and return, investing in minor league stadiums does not appear financially prudent.

If there is little merit to the economic argument to subsidize stadiums at the minor league level, the decision to invest must be rationalized on other grounds. Subvention supporters are quick to assert that minor league baseball yields psychological benefits through identification with a professional baseball team. There is risk in emotional commitment, particularly given the rate at which minor league communities are abandoned, and fairness dictates admitting that the psychic dimension cuts both ways: if hosting a team improves the collective community psyche, losing a team must induce a deterioration in a locale's sense of self. This symmetry in feelings was demonstrated in a recent editorial in the *Waterloo Courier* eulogizing the loss of the local minor league baseball team. It referred to the departure as a "real, or perceived, blow to the image of Waterloo, to say nothing of the lost entertainment and financial benefits."[53]

The question that remains is whether the $960 per capita stadium expense incurred by the people of Lake Elsinore or the $40 per capita expense assumed by citizens of Buffalo (see appendix table 14A-1) is less than, or equal to, the external benefits that citizens (consumers) derive from minor league baseball. As pointed out in chapter 2, it is not implausible that consumer surplus exists at the major league level, but it would seem much less plausible at the minor league level. (Continuing voter approval of referenda for funding sports facilities, along with the notion of socially induced consumption, could be manifestations of this implicit benefit; the theory of public choice, however, offers an alternative explanation.) After all, minor league baseball is, in terms of the quality of play, second or third best, and our culture does not ascribe much significance to finishing second, whether it be in the sports world or elsewhere.

Summary and Conclusions

Communities that host minor league baseball have been pressured to substantially renovate or build new stadiums. This insistence on better playing facilities was articulated in Attachment 58 to the Professional Baseball Agreement of 1990. To comprehend how Major League Baseball could mandate stadium construction on such a massive scale requires more than an understanding of the formal organizational apparatus characterizing professional baseball. Financial developments in both the minor and major leagues have provided ample justifications for the mandate, at least in the minds of major league owners. These financial developments include the increased profitability of minor league teams but most importantly the substantial appreciation in the value of minor league franchises.

Financial developments on their own are not sufficient to explain the massive new stadium construction. The manner in which the market for professional baseball is structured is critical to securing the public funding for stadium construction. As long as league cartels are able to constrain the supply of teams, the excess demand for franchises can be parlayed into public funds for the construction of facilities that the private sector would be unable or unwilling to provide.

Stadium construction for minor league teams should not be viewed as an isolated or unique development. The same forces that compel major league cities to build these facilities move minor league communities. In short, new stadiums translate into greater revenues that enhance the value of franchises. New stadiums represent an important element in maximizing the returns from investments in professional sports.

The opportunity for substantial capital gains has encouraged a new breed of aggressive owner in the minor leagues. Tactics that have proved successful in enhancing profits in the major leagues have been adopted by minor league teams. What distinguishes the financial pressures for stadium construction in the minors is that it partly reflects imperatives emanating from the major leagues. Minor league communities, through formal arrangement, are vulnerable to MLB pressure, and MLB has displayed a marked proclivity to exploit this financial opportunity. The end result is that major league financial ambitions are realized at the expense of citizens in communities large and small in the United States.

One could legitimately ask why, if MLB has substantial control over the number of minor league franchises around the country as well as contractual rights to their chief input (that is, minor league players), the "parent cartel" does not or cannot extract virtually all of the monopoly rents from both minor league communities and, especially, minor league owners, such that the latter could only enjoy normal rates of return on their investments, rather than permitting them to earn above-average returns (principally in the form of franchise appreciation). This possible inconsistency is due in large part to imperfect information, heterogeneity (in the quality of play and the community demographics in the minor leagues in comparison with the majors), and risk. Major league owners undoubtedly expropriate some of these rents, but they are dependent on the continued loyalty and support of investors in minor league teams and the communities in which these franchises are located. In addition, the minor leagues are politically important to MLB in defending its antitrust exemption. Furthermore, MLB has more to fear from entry, including disaffiliation (that is, disaffected owners forming independent leagues) at the minor league level, than it does at the major league level, which dilutes its power over minor league owners. (It is worth noting that public sentiment, as articulated in newspapers across the country, also clearly favored the minor leagues in their dispute with MLB over the substance of the 1990 PBA.) Driving owners and communities to the margin, which could result in instability in the industry, may not be to MLB's ultimate advantage.

A full analysis of the extent to which MLB expropriates minor league returns is beyond the scope of this discussion. It can be said, however, that the basic justification for stadium subventions is the same at the minor and major league levels. Subsidy advocates argue the facility expense is properly viewed as an investment. The stream of revenues that stadiums generate, say boosters, negates the argument that these facilities force painful civic trade-offs; rather, sports facilities make possible investments in schools, streets, and other public goods in the minds of their supporters. Scholarly evidence would dispute the claim that professional sports contribute much to local economies at the major or minor league levels. In the final analysis, the beneficiaries of stadium subsidies throughout baseball are owners and players. In addition, MLB has used its executive privilege and power to appropriate a share of the financial benefit accruing from subsidies extended to minor league clubs by their host cities. This exploitation by professional sports interests will continue until the structure of professional sports at all levels is altered.

Appendix: *Minor League Survey Questionnaire*

Team: _____ Affiliation: _____ Level: _____

City/State: _____ Phone number: _____

Name & Title of Respondent: _____

1. Has the team moved in the last six years?
    ☐ Yes; if yes, when: _____ ☐ No

2. Has the stadium/ballpark been renamed recently?
    ☐ Yes; if yes, new name: _____
        and date of change: _____
    ☐ No

3. Has a new stadium/ballpark been built or the old stadium been renovated in the last six years?
    ☐ Yes, new construction; if yes, cost of the construction: _____
    ☐ Yes, renovation; if yes, cost of the renovation: _____
    ☐ No

4. Did the 1990 Professional Baseball Agreement concerning stadium regulations determine your decision to build or renovate?
    ☐ Yes
    ☐ No; if no, why did you renovate? _____

5. How was the stadium construction or renovation financed?
    ☐ All private funds   ☐ Mostly public / some private
    ☐ Mostly private / some public ☐ All public
    ☐ About half private and half public

6. Was your team exempted from making the stadium improvements stipulated by the 1990 Professional Baseball Agreement?
    ☐ Yes; if yes, why? _____
    ☐ No

7. Of those fans who attend your games, what percentage of them do you think travel more than an hour to get to the game? _____ % (verbatim)

Interviewer: _____ Date of call: _____ Time of call: _____

No answer: _____ Disconnected number: _____ Refusal: ☐ soft ☐ hard ☐ hostile

Instructions for call back: _____

Interviewer notes:

Table 14A-1. Survey Data[a]

Team name[b]	Year of construction or renovation	Stadium cost (millions of dollars)[c]	Stadium capacity	Affected by PBA[d]	Public private[e]	Stadium cost per capita per year ($)
American Association (AAA)						
Buffalo Bisons	1988	56.00	21,050	n.a.	5	170.67
Indianapolis Indians	1996	18.00	12,100	No	1	24.61
Iowa Cubs	1992	14.00	10,800	Yes	3	72.54
Louisville Redbirds	1981	4.50	33,500	No	n.a.	16.72
Nashville Sounds	1993–96	1.00	17,000	Yes	1	0.51
New Orleans Zephyrs	U.C.	23.00	n.a.	Yes	5	46.98
Oklahoma City 89ers	U.C.	28.00	n.a.	No	4	61.67
Omaha Royals	1992–96	17.00	23,000	Yes	5	10.13
International League (AAA)						
Charlotte Knights	1990	17.00	10,000	No	1	3,448.28
Columbus Clippers	1932	n.a.	15,000	No	n.a.	n.a.
Norfolk Tides	1993	20.00	12,059	Yes	5	76.56
Ottawa Lynx	1993	12.41	10,332	Yes	5	n.a.
Pawtucket Red Sox	*Proposed*	12.00	7,002	Yes	4	165.19
Richmond Braves	1990–96	1.84	12,146	Yes	5	1.29
Rochester Red Wings	U.C.	33.00	n.a.	Yes	3	142.46
Scranton/Wilkes-Barre Red Barons	1989	25.00	10,832	No	5	114.13
Syracuse Chiefs	U.C.	28.00	n.a.	Yes	4	170.88
Toledo Mud Hens	1991–96	2.00	10,025	Yes	1	1.00
Pacific Coast League (AAA)						
Albuquerque Dukes	*1992, 1994*	*0.30*	10,510	Yes	5	0.39
Calgary Cannons	*1995*	*2.10*	8,000	Yes	4	n.a.
Colorado Springs Sky Sox	*1992, 1993, 1996*	*0.45*	9,000	No	2	0.53

Table 14A-1. (continued)

Team name[b]	Year of construction or renovation	Stadium cost (millions of dollars)[c]	Stadium capacity	Affected by PBA[d]	Public private[e]	Stadium cost per capita per year ($)
Edmonton Trappers	1995	10.00	10,000	Yes	3	n.a.
Las Vagas Stars	1995	0.03	9,334	No	5	0.12
Phoenix Firebirds	1992	35.00	11,200	No	5	269.09
Salt Lake Buzz	1994	22.00	15,500	Yes	5	137.56
Tacoma Rainers	1992–93	0.30	9,600	Yes	1	0.85
Tucson Toros	Proposed	29.00	na.a	No	5	71.54
Vancouver Canadians	1951	n.a.	6,500	n.a.	n.a.	n.a.
Eastern League (AA)						
Binghamton Mets	1992	4.50	6,042	Yes	2	84.89
Bowie Baysox	1994	11.00	10,000	No	4	292.64
Canton/Akron Indians	U.C.	30.00	n.a.	Yes	4	356.46
Hardware City Rock Cats	1996	10.00	6,125	Yes	5	132.47
Harrisburg Senators	1991, 1993	3.00	6,300	Yes	4	57.28
New Haven Ravens	1994	n.a.	6,200	n.a.	n.a.	n.a.
Norwich Navigators	1995	8.33	6,000	Yes	5	32.66
Portland Sea Dogs	1994	3.50	6,500	Yes	4	54.38
Reading Phillies	1991–96	2.00	8,500	Yes	n.a.	25.52
Trenton Thunder	1994	17.10	6,300	Yes	5	192.84
Southern League (AA)						
Birmingham Barons	1993	0.01	10,800	Yes	5	0.04
Carolina Mudcats	Proposed	6.00	6,000	Yes	5	1,890.95
Chattanooga Lookouts	1989	2.00	7,500	No	5	13.12
Greenville Braves	1984	n.a.	7,027	No	n.a.	n.a.
Huntsville Stars	1995	0.10	10,200	Yes	2	0.63

Team	Year		Attendance			
Jacksonville Suns	*1996*	*0.80*	8,200	No	5	1.26
Knoxville Smokies	*1993*	*0.15*	6,412	Yes	5	0.91
Memphis Chicks	*1991*	*3.10*	10,000	Yes	5	5.08
Orlando Cubs	*1990*	*2.00*	5,104	Yes	3	12.14
Texas League AA)						
Arkansas Travelers	*1996*	*0.51*	6,083	No	1	2.91
El Paso Diablos	*1990*	*7.00*	10,000	Yes	5	13.58
Jackson Generals	*1990*	*4.00*	5,200	Yes	5	20.34
Midland Angels	*1990–96*	*1.50*	5,000	Yes	5	16.77
San Antonio Missions	*1994*	*10.00*	8,300	Yes	5	10.68
Shreveport Captains	*1985*	n.a.	6,200	No	n.a.	n.a.
Tulsa Drillers	*1992–96*	*0.05*	10,809	Yes	2	0.14
Wichita Wranglers	*1995*	*1.00*	6,058	Yes	5	3.29
California League (A)						
Bakersfield Blaze	*1993*	*0.70*	4,300	Yes	1	4.00
High Desert Mavericks	*1991*	*6.00*	3,808	Yes	5	704.47
Lake Elsinor Storm	*1994*	n.a.	7,866	n.a.	n.a.	n.a.
Lancaster Jethawks	*1995*	*14.50*	7,000	Yes	5	149.04
Modesto A's	*1996*	*3.00*	2,500	Yes	4	18.21
Rancho Cucamonga Quakes	*1993*	*20.00*	6,665	Yes	5	197.22
San Bernardino Spirit	*1996*	*1.00*	5,000	Yes	5	6.09
San Jose Giants	*1994*	*1.50*	4,200	Yes	3	1.92
Stockton Ports	*1994*	*0.25*	3,500	Yes	3	1.19
Visalia Oaks	*1946*	n.a.	1,800	No	n.a.	
Carolina League (A)						
Durham Bulls	*1995*	*16.10*	9,033	Yes	2	117.85
Frederick Keys	*1989*	*5.30*	5,400	No	4	132.01
Kinston Indians	*1993*	*1.00*	4,100	Yes	5	39.53
Lynchburg Hillcats	*1939*	n.a.	4,000	No	n.a.	n.a.
Prince William Cannons	*1992, 1994*	*0.50*	6,000	yes	5	18.94

Table 14A-1. (*continued*)

Team name[b]	Year of construction or renovation	Stadium cost (millions of dollars)[c]	Stadium capacity	Affected by PBA[d]	Public private[e]	Stadium cost per capita per year ($)
Salem Avalanche	1995	11.00	6,000	No	5	$463.04
Wilmington Blue Rocks	1993	4.00	5,911	No	5	55.92
Winston-Salem Warthogs	1993, 1994	1.80	6,280	Yes	3	12.54
Florida State League (A)						
Brevard County Manatees	1994	15.00	8,100	Yes	3	37.60
Charlotte Rangers	1996	0.03	6,000	n.a.	5	0.23
Clearwater Phillies	1990, 1993, 1996	1.55	6,902	Yes	1	15.69
Daytona Cubs	1930	n.a.	4,200	n.a.	n.a.	n.a.
Dunedin Blue Jays	1990	2.20	6,201	No	5	64.68
Fort Myers Miracle	1992	26.00	7,500	No	5	575.14
Kissimmee Cobras	1989–90	1.20	5,200	No	5	9.98
Lakeland Tigers	1994	0.64	7,100	No	3	9.07
Sarasota Red Sox	1989	n.a.	7,500	No	4	n.a.
St. Lucie Mets	1988	11.00	7,347	No	n.a.	196.90
St. Petersburg Cardinals	1995	1.00	7,004	Yes	5	4.19
Tampa Yankees	1996	27.00	10,387	No	4	96.42
Vero Beach Dodgers	1995	0.35	6,500	No	1	20.17
West Palm Beach Expos	1992–96	0.25	4,404	No	5	3.70
Midwest League (A)						
Battle Creek Golden Kazoos	1989	n.a.	6,200	n.a.	5	n.a.
Beloit Snappers	1994	1.00	3,501	Yes	3	28.11
Burlington Bees	1996, 1997	0.05	3,500	No	5	1.84
Cedar Rapids Kernals	1991–94	0.25	6,000	Yes	4	2.30
Clinton Lumber Kings	1990–96	0.30	3,000	Yes	4	10.27

Team	Year					
Fort Wayne Wizards	1993	5.60	7,100	Yes	4	32.36
Kane County Cougars	1991	6.00	5,900	Yes	5	18.90
Peoria Chiefs	1992	2.20	6,200	No	4	19.38
Quad City River Bandits	1931	n.a.	5,200	No	n.a.	n.a.
Rockford Cubbies	1992	0.05	4,300	Yes	5	0.36
South Bend Silver Hawks	1992–96	0.40	5,000	No	2	3.79
Sultans of Springfield	n.a.	n.a.	5,000	n.a.	n.a.	n.a.
West Michigan Whitecaps	1994	8.00	10,000	Yes	1	1,225.11
Wisconsin Timber Rattlers	1995	5.25	5,500	Yes	1	79.91

South Atlantic League (A)

Team	Year					
Albany Polecats	1993	n.a.	4,200	n.a.	n.a.	n.a.
Asheville Tourists	1992	3.50	3,400	No	4	56.81
Augusta Greenjackets	1995	3.20	5,000	Yes	5	71.69
Capital City Bombers	1991	1.50	6,000	No	3	15.30
Charleston (W.Va.) Alley Cats	1996	0.05	6,800	Yes	5	0.87
Charleston (S.C.) River Dogs	U.C.	16.00	n.a.	Yes	5	198.97
Columbus Redstixx	1995	5.00	2,000	No	4	27.98
Fayetteville Generals	1987	n.a.	4,200	No	n.a.	n.a.
Greensboro Bats	1993	0.25	7,500	No	1	1.36
Hagerstown Suns	1993,1994	0.60	4,600	Yes	4	16.93
Hickory Crawdads	1993	4.50	4,800	Yes	2	159.00
Macon Braves	1995	1.00	3,785	Yes	4	9.38
Piedmont Phillies	1995	6.00	4,700	No	1	202.05
Savannah Cardinals	1994–95	1.00	8,000	Yes	4	7.27

New York-Penn League (SS-A)

Team	Year					
Auburn Astros	1995	3.50	2,800	Yes	4	111.97
Batavia Clippers	1995	3.40	2,600	Yes	1	208.46
Elmira Pioneers	1939	n.a.	5,000	n.a.	n.a.	n.a.
Erie Sea Wolves	1995	9.00	6,000	Yes	5	82.78
Hudson Valley Renegades	1994	n.a.	4,300	n.a.	n.a.	n.a.

Table 14A-1. (continued)

Team name[b]	Year of construction or renovation	Stadium cost (millions of dollars)[c]	Stadium capacity	Affected by PBA[d]	Public private[e]	Stadium cost per capita per year ($)
Jamestown Jammers	1993	0.50	3,324	Yes	5	14.42
New Jersey Cardinals	1994	7.00	4,341	No	4	53.46
Oneonta Yankees	1939	n.a.	4,200	n.a.	n.a.	n.a.
Pittsfield Mets	1994	0.40	4,200	Yes	5	8.23
St. Catherines Stompers	1995	0.15	3,000	Yes	5	n.a.
Utica Blue Sox	U.C.	0.80	4,000	Yes	5	11.66
Vermont Expos	1995	1.00	4,000	Yes	3	150.40
Watertown Indians	1994	0.75	3,269	Yes	5	25.49
Williamsport Cubs	1994	0.40	4,200	Yes	4	12.53
Northwest League (SS-A)						
Bellingham Giants	1964	n.a.	2,200	n.a.	n.a.	n.a.
Boise Hawks	1989	n.a.	4,500	No	n.a.	n.a.
Eugene Emeralds	1991–96	0.07	6,800	No	1	0.62
Everett Aquasox	U.C.	n.a.	2,285	No	n.a.	n.a.
Portland Rockies	1995–96	0.03	23,105	No	1	0.06
Southern Oregon Athletics	1993–99	5.50	2,900	Yes	1	117.14
Spokane Indians	1992–96	0.50	7,101	Yes	4	2.82
Yakima Bears	1993	1.50	3,000	Yes	4	27.36
Appalachian League						
Bluefield Orioles	1994	n.a.	3,000	n.a.	n.a.	n.a.
Bristol White Sox	1994	0.25	2,500	Yes	4	13.57
Burlington Indians	1995	0.30	3,500	Yes	3	7.60
Danville Braves	1993	5.00	2,700	No	4	94.24
Elizabethton Twins	1995–96	0.20	1,500	Yes	3	16.76

Johnson City Cardinals	*1995–96*	*0.35*	3,800	Yes	5	7.09
Kingsport Mets	1995	n.a.	2,500	n.a.	n.a.	n.a.
Martinsville Phillies	1994	0.30	3,200	Yes	3	18.56
Princeton Reds	*1991–96*	*0.50*	1,537	Yes	1	70.99
River City Rampage	n.a.	n.a.	3,100	n.a.	n.a.	n.a.
Pioneer League						
Billings Mustangs	1948	n.a.	4,400	No	n.a.	n.a.
Butte Copper Kings	*1995*	*0.10*	2,500	Yes	1	n.a.
Great Falls Dodgers	*1980–96*	*0.40*	3,834	Yes	5	n.a.
Helena Brewers	1995	*0.50*	1,800	Yes	3	n.a.
Idaho Falls Braves	*1994–96*	*0.17*	2,800	Yes	3	n.a.
Lethbridge Mounties	1996	n.a.	2,750	Yes	5	n.a.
Medicine Hat Blue Jays	n.a.	n.a.	2,000	Yes	5	n.a.
Ogden Raptors	n.a.	n.a.	2,500	n.a.	n.a.	n.a.

Sources: Bruce Adelson, and others, *The Minor League Baseball Book* (New York: Simon & Schuster, 1995; Michael Benson, *Ballparks of North America* (Jefferson, N.C.: McFarland). 1989: "Telephone Survey of All Minor League Teams," conducted at Lake Forest College. September 12–29, 1996 (of the 155 teams contacted. 145 teams responded): National Association of Professional Baseball Leagues. www.minorleaguebaseball.com. September 29, 1996; U.S. Department of Commerce. Economics and Statistics Administration. *County and City Databook 1994.* (Washington, D.C.: GPO, August 1994.

a. Various NAPBL publications show inconsistencies, most notably with regard to stadium seating capacities. If a team in the survey indicated a cost figure for both renovation and new stadium construction, the cost of the most recent stadium expense was recorded. This convention was necessary to eliminate skewing, which could occur if all teams did not answer or interpret the survey question in exactly the same way. Since there were only six teams for which this problem existed, we decided to count only the most recent stadium expense. (8) Population statistics (necessary for computing stadium costs per capita) were based on the following convention: the name of the host community or county identified in the team title was used whenever possible. When no population statistic for the host community in the team title was available, the city or town in which the stadium was located was then used. If that population statistic was unavailable, the county population statistic for the host community was then used as the population base statistic.

b. Team name changes that have occurred since the *Minor League Baseball Book* was published in 1995 include Auburn Doubledays (Astros), Michigan Battle Cats (Battle Golden Kazoos), Piedmont Boll Weevils (Phillies), San Bernardino Stampede (Spirit), and Savannah Sand Gnats (Cardinals). New teams established in 1996 not included in the *Minor League Baseball Book* are Delmarva Shorebirds, Lancaster JetHawks, Lansing Lugnuts, Lowell Spinners, and Port City Roosters.

c. Renovation costs are indicated in italics. Ottawa's stadium construction cost was converted from Canadian to U.S. dollars at an exchange rate of 1.37 Canadian dollars/U.S. dollars.

d. n.a. = not available.

e. 1 = all private; 2 = mostly private/some public; 3 = half private/public; 4 = mostly public/private; 5 = all public.

Notes

1. National Association of Professional Baseball Leagues, Inc., *Professional Baseball Agreement*, 1996.

2. Although MLB owners arguably have the final voice on a variety of issues, it is worthwhile at this juncture to identify and discuss briefly professional baseball's organizational structure. The National Association of Professional Baseball Leagues (NAPBL) governs the minor leagues. The relationship between MLB and the NAPBL is defined by the Professional Baseball Agreement (PBA). Major league teams supply players to their NAPBL affiliates. The specific financial arrangements between a major league club and its affiliates are established by a player development contract. These contracts are for short periods of time, usually two years, and at expiration the affiliates and their parents are free to negotiate a new PDC or change their affiliation. Bruce Adelson and others, *The Minor League Baseball Book* (Simon and Schuster, 1995).

3. Arthur T. Johnson, "Professional Baseball at the Minor League Level: Considerations for Cities Large and Small," *State and Local Government Review*, Spring 1990, p. 94.

4. See, for example, Gerald W. Scully, *The Market Structure of Sports* (University of Chicago Press, 1995); James Quirk and Rodney D. Fort, *Pay Dirt: The Business of Professional Team Sports* (Princeton University Press, 1992); and Andrew Zimbalist, *Baseball and Billions: A Probing Look inside the Big Business of Our National Pastime* (New York: Basic Books), 1992.

5. William G. Colclough and others, "Estimating the Economic Impact of a Minor League Baseball Stadium," *Managerial and Decision Economics*, vol. 25 (1994), pp. 497–502.

6. Ira Horowitz, "Sports Broadcasting," in Roger G. Noll, ed., *Government and the Sports Business* (Brookings, 1974).

7. Elizabeth Comte, "Minors Turn Major Profit," *Sporting News*, June 18, 1990, p. 48.

8. Independent, instructional, Dominican, and Mexican leagues are not included in the city figure. The 156 cities include the following leagues: American Association (AAA), International League (AAA), Pacific Coast League (AAA), Eastern League (AA), Southern League (AA), Texas League (AA), California League (A), Carolina League (A), Florida State League (A), Midwest League (A), South Atlantic League (A), New York/Pennsylvania League (Short-Season A), Northwest League (Short-Season A), Appalachian League (Rookie Advanced), Pioneer League (Rookie Advanced). The number of communities represented in each league are 8, 10, 10, 10, 9, 9, 10, 8, 14, 14, 14, 14, 8, 10, and 8, respectively. For a list of specific cities, see Adelson and others, *Minor League Baseball Book*, pp. 8–9. It should be noted that the number of minor league clubs operating in 1949 was 464, more than twice the number of minor league clubs in operation at present. Average attendance per club in 1949 was 90,301, while average attendance per minor league team was 140,741 in 1991. Zimbalist, *Baseball and Billions*.

9. Arthur T. Johnson, "Different Aims Put Two Levels at Odds," *USA Today Baseball Weekly*, April 7–13, 1993, p. 129.

10. Johnson, "Professional Baseball at the Minor League Level," p. 94.

11. Richard Panek, *The Waterloo Diamonds* (New York: St. Martin's Press, 1995), p. 173.

12. Jerome Holtzman, "Majors-Minors Rift Based on Bottom Line," *Chicago Tribune*, November 28, 1990, sec. 4, p. 8.

13. Richard Behar, "Take That Peter Uberroth," *Forbes*, February 9, 1987, p. 36.

14. For a discussion of the principal financial elements of the 1990 PBA, see Zimbalist, *Baseball and Billions*, p. 115.

15. Ibid.

16. Panek, *Waterloo Diamonds*, p. 174.

17. Jerome Holtzman, "Majors-Minors Rift Based on Bottom Line," *Chicago Tribune*, November 26, 1995, sec. 3, p. 4.

18. Other alternatives exist to developing baseball players for play in U.S. major leagues. The search for professional athletes has become global, and it makes economic sense for MLB to allow other countries to assume the costs of player development and import the "finished-player" product. In addition, winter leagues allow players to develop throughout the year with little if any MLB financial support. If MLB reduces player development expenses, it has more funds to compete for the finished player product. Casual empiricism would suggest that for professional baseball, the United States is running a player trade deficit. That is, it is importing more playing talent than it is exporting. This deficit is made possible in part through the higher salaries MLB pays on average.

19. Andrew Cohen, "As Next Spring's Renovation Deadline Nears, Minor-League Teams Are Struggling to Meet the Professional Agreement's Facility Standards," *Athletic Business*, November 1994, p. 39.

20. Ibid.

21. For a discussion of franchise valuations and their relationship to current earnings, see Quirk and Fort, *Pay Dirt*, pp. 67–77.

22. Steve Wulf, "Down on the Farm," *Sports Illustrated*, July 23, 1990, pp. 35, 38.

23. Panek, *Waterloo Diamonds*, pp. 175–76.

24. Arthur T. Johnson, "Minor League Franchise Relocations 1987–1996," 1996, photocopy.

25. Johnson, "Different Aims," pp. 26–27.

26. Our attention on the changing character of minor league owners is not meant to suggest that there is something inherently wrong with their motivations, but it is meant to emphasize that the incentives for owning minor league teams revolve more around profit than in the past. This more profit-centered perspective has implications for the communities that host minor league teams. In particular, host communities are seeing an increase in the costs and risks associated with minor league baseball. The evidence to date indicates that small communities are having more difficulty retaining their teams even in cases in which fan support is not an issue. The changing economics of minor league sports as noted by Panek in *Waterloo Diamonds* has facilitated the development of A58, and many small communities cannot afford the new or renovated ballparks mandated. Furthermore, if team ownership is not local, what social strictures exist to discourage movement of the club whenever a better offer comes along? If the community has invested in the team by providing a stadium or other form of financial support, does the public sector have the right to expect a reasonable return on that investment? The professional sports cartel, mainly through its ability to control supply, can wring concessions from a host community, which distinguishes this industry from other private enterprises that operate in the community (such as department stores, banks, and restaurants).

27. Panek, *Waterloo Diamonds*, p. 347.

28. Ibid., p. 300.

29. Stefan Fatsis, "Major Leagues Keep Minors at a Distance," *Wall Street Journal*, November 8, 1995, p. B1.

30. In the minors, unlike the majors, the financial benefits flowing from the public provision of ballparks do not have to be shared with players. As a consequence, there is a

stronger financial incentive for the minor league owners to support stadium subsidies than is true of major league owners.

31. NAPBL records indicate that sixty stadiums were built between 1985 and 1995, and 63 percent of them were built after 1990. The difference in stadium numbers can be accounted for by those teams that did not respond to our survey, and by the convention we employed, which was not to count both renovations and new stadium construction if they occurred during the 1985–95 period. We counted only the most recent stadium expense incurred (see convention notes at the end of table 14A-1) to ensure uniformity in our approach. These differences can be reconciled by splicing information from several different sources; we can provide this information to readers upon request.

In addition, the construct of survey question number 6 has resulted in more complete stadium expense information for the 1991–95 period than for the 1985–90 period. We were, however, able to obtain information from other sources, and those additional data were used to gauge the extent of any bias. We have incorporated this information into the text where necessary.

32. If stadium construction is separated from renovations, 70 percent of the stadiums were financed from mostly public or all public funds. This figure resembles the percentage of new stadium costs financed by the public sector (61 percent) in the 1990s at the major league level for professional baseball, basketball, football, and hockey. See David Swindell, "Public Financing of Sports Stadiums: How Cincinnati Compares," Buckeye Center for Public Policy Solutions, January 30, 1996, p. 8, photocopy.

33. The construction cost index used in this analysis was the E. H. Boeckh and Associates Construction Cost Index (1994 = 100). This index can be found in U.S. Department of Commerce, *Statistical Abstract of the United States* (Washington, D.C.: GPO), various years.

34. According to some, baseball is something a city of a certain stature should have. See Panek, *Waterloo Diamonds*, p. 203. Panek argues that baseball's contribution to a city's welfare can be quantified and is incorporated in livability indices calculated by standard reference guides such as *Places Rated Almanac*. In his study of Waterloo, Iowa, Panek found that the loss of the minor league baseball Class A Diamonds dropped Waterloo's overall livability ranking by 10 percent. Panek, *Waterloo Diamonds*, pp. 203–04.

35. Euchner has explained in great detail why communities agree to team demands, and rather than replicating his arguments here, we will augment them. Charles Euchner, *Playing the Field: Why Sports Teams Move and Cities Fight to Keep Them* (Johns Hopkins University Press, 1993).

36. Paul G. Merski and others, *Facts and Figures on Government Finance* (Johns Hopkins University Press, 1991).

37. We have not attempted to differentiate between entrepreneurial activities that originate from pressure derived from federal government budgetary constraints or, in this case, from MLB, versus those cases in which cities are simply responding to increased demands on the part of their citizens and the national population for more or improved recreational options. Public support for and subsidies to professional sports stadiums are not substantially different from other urban strategies. For example, Cleveland's decision to spend $100 million for the Rock & Roll Hall of Fame and Museum is only a difference in degree, not in kind, from its $400 million plus commitment to build Jacobs Field for the MLB Indians and Gund Arena for the NBA Cavaliers.

38. Peter Heap, "Cities Often Dream Up Stadiums before Thinking of Payment," *Bond Buyer*, June 11, 1996.

39. The lack of economic impact is based on the operation of elementary budget constraints. If local residents spend more on professional sports spectating, it is axiomatic

that they will have less time and money to spend on other recreational pursuits. Unless professional sports trigger a significant inflow of funds from outside the area, the activity will not contribute measurably to the local economy. See, for example, Robert A. Baade and Richard F. Dye, "The Impact of Stadiums and Professional Sports on Metropolitan Area Development," *Growth and Change*, Spring 1990, pp. 1–14; Zimbalist, *Baseball and Billions;* Quirk and Fort, *Pay Dirt;* Benjamin A. Okner, "Subsidies of Stadiums and Arenas," in Roger G. Noll, ed., *Government and the Sports Business* (Brookings, 1974), pp. 325–47; Mark S. Rosentraub and others, "Sport and Downtown Development Strategy: If You Build It, Will Jobs Come?" *Journal of Urban Affairs*, vol. 16, no. 3 (1994), pp. 221–39.

40. See Robert A. Baade, "Professional Sports As Catalysts for Metropolitan Economic Development." *Journal of Urban Affairs*, vol. 18 (April 1996); and chapter 3 in this volume.

41. John J. Siegfried, "Minor League Baseball and Local Economic Development" (review of Arthur T. Johnson's Book), *Southern Economic Journal*, vol. 61 (January 1995), pp. 899–900.

42. Johnson, "Different Aims," p. 7

43. To put the stadium expense in perspective, using the 1990 Trenton population statistic (88,675), an $18 million stadium expense averages out to $203 per resident of Trenton, which is several times as much per capita as the new stadium for the White Sox ($169 million) averaged for residents of Chicago and Illinois taxpayers in general. U.S. Department of Commerce, *Statistical Abstracts of the United States, 1990*; and Andrew W. Lehren, "Minor League Towns Wait to Score Bonanza from their Baseball Teams," *Philadelphia Business Journal*, September 16–33, 1996.

44. Lehren, "Minor League Towns Wait to Score Bonanza," p. 17.

45. Erik Spanberg, "Minor League Teams Losing the Battle for the Sports Buck," *Business Journal*, vol. 10, no. 4 (1995), p. 1.

46. Colclough and others, "Estimating the Economic Impact of a Minor League Baseball Stadium," p. 500.

47. Based on the average return on equity for first quarters of 1994 and 1995, industry composite, as reported by *Business Week*, May 16, 1994; May 15, 1995.

48. See chapter 3 in this volume.

49. Barry M. Bloom, "Hits, Overruns, Errors Batter Stadium," *San Diego Union-Tribune*, September 8, 1996, pp. A1, A21.

50. Johnson, "Different Aims," pp. 245–46.

51. Johnson, *Minor League Baseball and Local Economic Development* (University of Illinois Press), p. 245.

52. The length of the lease is directly related to the caliber of baseball. The longest leases are found in MLB; the shortest leases in general are found in the lowest levels of the minor leagues.

53. Panek, *Waterloo Diamonds*, p. 366.

15

SPORTS, JOBS, AND TAXES

The Real Connection

ROGER G. NOLL AND
ANDREW ZIMBALIST

 The United States is clearly experiencing a sports construction boom. Industry experts estimate that more than $7 billion will be spent on new sports facilities before 2006. Lexiconic legerdemain notwithstanding, much of this money will come from public sources. The average subsidy from a host city to its sports team most likely will exceed $10 million a year.

Although some of this support might rationally flow in recognition of the positive externalities engendered by sports teams, for the most part it is made necessary by the noncompetitive structure of the U.S. team sports industry. Major sports leagues are monopolies. They maximize the profits of their members by keeping the number of franchises below the number of cities that are economically viable locations for a team. As a result, cities are thrust into competition with one another to procure or to retain teams. The form this competition takes is a bidding war, whereby cities bid their willingness to pay to have a team, not the minimum amount that would be necessary to keep a team viable.

The tendency of sports teams to seek more hospitable venues has been exaggerated in recent years by new stadium technology. Replacing the rather ordinary cookie-cutter, concrete slab, multipurpose facility of the 1960s and 1970s is the single-sport, more aesthetically pleasing facility that features numerous new revenue opportunities: luxury suites, club boxes, elaborate concessions, catering, signage, parking, advertising, theme activities, and even bars, restaurants, and apartments with a view of the field. Depending on the sport and the circumstance, a new stadium or arena can add anywhere from $10 to $30 million a year to a team's revenues for the first few years after the stadium is constructed. Consequently, new stadiums can be so alluring to a team that demographically lesser cities with new stadiums (such as Charlotte, Jacksonville, and Nashville) can compete effectively for teams against larger cities with older stadiums.

The new stadium technology, by enhancing revenue opportunities, can increase the number of cities that are economically viable franchise sites, thereby exacerbating the imbalance between the supply and demand for sports franchises. This imbalance, in turn, leads cities imprudently to offer the kitchen sink in their effort to retain existing teams or to attract new ones. Including site acquisition and supporting infrastructure, a new stadium costs at least $200 million, and in several cases much more. To date, the most expensive stadiums have been in the range of $400 million to $500 million, although New York City is contemplating a home for the Yankees that will cost about $1 billion. Furthermore, when a state government becomes involved in financially supporting the effort, it generally requires the approval of parallel pork projects elsewhere in the state to secure the necessary votes in the legislature.

Teams do not have sufficient revenues from their own sources to pay for investments in stadiums of this magnitude. A sports franchise is simply too small and earns too little profit to pay the full cost of even a $200 million facility. But, of course, in recent years almost no team has had to pay the full cost of its playing facility. Local and state governments bear part—and sometimes virtually all—of the stadium costs. Usually the stadium lease is so favorable to the team that the city cannot cover its incremental debt service with rent and other stadium revenues. Indeed, the city must not receive enough direct revenues from the stadium to recover its debt cost or the debt that finances the facility will not qualify for the federal tax exemption on municipal bonds.

While the public ends up paying for a substantial part of most stadiums, highly paid players and wealthy owners divide nearly all of the millions in extra revenue. Since public financing often comes in the form of regressive sales taxes or lottery revenues, the distributional consequences of stadium projects are not salutary for those concerned with inequality. To some degree, this consequence has been mitigated by the growing use of new types of user fees (such as personal seat licenses and naming rights).

Although the drive to build new stadiums permeates all team sports, it has been most pronounced in the National Football League. There are two reasons for this. First, an NFL team derives a lower proportion of its revenues from regular ticket sales than teams in other sports. Football derives about 70 percent of its income from league revenues from television rights and licensing, and most of the rest is from gate receipts that are shared between the home and visiting team.[1] Thus more cities are potentially viable locations for a team in professional football, so more competition emerges when a franchise becomes available. Second, because the NFL practices extensive revenue sharing, NFL teams have a powerful incentive to maximize the components of stadium revenues that are not shared, such as premium seating and fancy concessions.

Economic Impact

Three questions might be asked about the economic impact of a professional sports team or facility: Does it promote the general economic development of a metropolitan area? Can it significantly assist in maintaining the vitality of the central city? Can it stimulate microdevelopment in a small, defined district within a city? The studies in this volume uniformly conclude that metropolitan and central city economic development is not likely to be affected by a sports team or facility.

Whether core centrality or microdevelopment can be supported by a team or facility will depend on a number of factors: the development plan; the area's physical, economic, and demographic characteristics; and the facility's financing and lease arrangements. But even under the best of circumstances, any such effect is modest at best.

These results are in sharp contrast to the claims of the dozens of promotional studies that have been performed by consulting firms under contract with the affected city or team. Predictably, their reports conclude that a sports team produces a substantial, positive impact. Yet their analyses are fraught with methodological difficulties. First, they often confuse new spending with spending that is diverted from other local activities. Second, they attribute all spending by out-of-town visitors to the sports team regardless of the motive for the visit. Third, they overstate the multiplier by ignoring crucial characteristics of sports spending. Fourth, they apply this inflated multiplier to gross spending, rather than local value added. Fifth, they omit the negative effects from the taxation that is used to finance construction and operating deficits of the facility.

When promotional studies go beyond estimates of economic impact and attempt an elementary cost-benefit analysis, they frequently introduce even more faulty assumptions. For example, some assume that a site has zero opportunity cost or that a stadium does not impose additional security, infrastructural, or environmental costs on the city. The ubiquitous claims that a professional sports team will convert the metropolitan area into a "big league city" and attract new businesses to the area is more than offset by the heightened possibility of fiscal distress and the resulting challenge to the city's educational system, tax rates, and services in general.

The magnitude of the errors in these studies can be quite large indeed. Consider the following hypothetical example. Suppose that a typical day at Yankee Stadium has 30,000 in attendance, 3,000 (10 percent) of whom are from out of town. Half of the latter group (1,500) have come to New York explicitly to see the Yankees.[2] Further, suppose that each fan spends $10 on food and concessions at the park, of which 40 percent is local value added. In addition, suppose that the out-of-towners drove to the game, buying $20 of gasoline in New York (of which 25 percent is local income, including taxes). Finally, suppose that 200 visitors spent the night in New York, each spending $100, of which $50 is local content, and that half of these people are in New York to see the Yankees.

Now consider the economic impact of consumption spending at the ballpark. For a promotional study making all of the errors alluded to, the estimate of the impact is straightforward. Take the 30,000 fans and multiply by $10 of spending for an impact of $300,000. Then, attribute the $20 in gas from 3,000 out-of-towners to the game, as well as the $100 from 200 all-night visitors, for another $80,000 impact. The total first-round economic benefit is then $380,000. Next, use a multiplier of 2 to estimate the total economic benefit from each Yankee game to the city, and the answer is $760,000.

A proper assessment would recognize that only 1,500 of the fans from out of town came to New York to see the Yankees. Moreover, because most of the expense of attending the game is for goods and services imported from outside New York, each out-of-town visitor spends enough to add $4 of value added locally. Thus the actual economic benefit of the stadium is $6,000, which is fifty times less than the promotional estimate of the impact. Then, only $5 of the gasoline from 1,500 fans and $50 of the overnight costs from 100 fans are a net benefit, accounting for an additional $12,500, rather than the $80,000 estimated in the promotional study. The last step is to undertake a multiplier analysis. The actual multiplier is more like 1.2, so that the proper estimate should be $18,500 times 1.2, or $22,200, rather than $760,000.[3]

Of course, most promotional studies do not make all of these errors, in which case the overestimate of the benefits is not this large. Yet, even the best of these studies leads one to question the economic sense of facility construction projects. Two promotional studies were undertaken for the new football facility at Camden Yards in Baltimore. One estimated that the new stadium would generate 1,394 full-time equivalent jobs, for a cost per job of $127,000; the other estimated 534 jobs, for a cost per job of $331,000. A study by Deloite and Touche concluded that the Arizona Diamondbacks' stadium (projected to cost $280 million) will create a total of 400 jobs, at a cost of $700,000 per job. Peat Marwick's 1996 study on the proposed new stadium for the Yankees over the West Side Railyards reported that a new baseball-only stadium would create 440 jobs at a cost of $800 million, or $1.82 million per job. In contrast, the cost per job generated by the incentive program of the Maryland state economic development agency is only $6,250.

To the extent that a new stadium is a central element of an urban redevelopment plan and its location and attributes are carefully set out to maximize synergies with local business, and to the extent that the terms of its lease are not negotiated under duress and are relatively fair to the city, the local community may derive some modest economic benefit from a sports team. The problem is that these two conditions rarely apply to monopoly sports leagues. Cities are forced to act hastily under pressure and to bargain without any leverage. Properly reckoned, the value of a sports team to a city should not be measured in dollars of new income but should be appreciated as a potential source of entertainment and civic pride that comes with a substantial net cost.

What Can Be Done

The abuses perpetrated by exorbitant stadium packages, sweetheart leases, and footloose franchises have left many citizens and politicians crying foul. What remedy is available, if any, to curb the monopoly excesses of the sports leagues and to protect the emotional and financial investments of fans and their cities? Fledgling efforts by cities to join together and form a sports-host cartel have foundered. The incentives to cheat on any such cartel are too strong to preserve concerted behavior. In effect, absent effective national legislation, cities are on their own and have only ineffective weapons.

Protections in Stadium Leases

Several cities have included in their facility leases provisions to deter team relocation, but these provisions tend to be quite weak. Most have escape clauses that allow the team to move if attendance falls below a certain level or if the facility is not maintained in state-of-the-art condition.[4] Of course, leases without such provisions formally require clubs to complete the term of the lease, but with or without such provisions teams generally have not viewed their lease terms as binding constraints. Rather, they argue that breach of contract by the city or stadium authority releases them from any contractual obligation. Some leases contain liquidated damages or performance provisions requiring teams to reimburse the city for tens of millions of dollars if they vacate their facility prior to lease expiration.[5] These provisions, though, also come with qualifying covenants.

Still other leases grant the city or an investor group approved by the city the right of first refusal to buy the team before it is sold or relocated.[6] The major problem here is the price. If an owner wants to move a team from city A to city B (or to sell the team to someone who will move it), the team probably is worth more in city B. This might be because city B is building a new facility with strong revenue potential and favorable lease terms or because city B possesses more auspicious demographic, geographic, or economic characteristics. If the team is worth, say, $30 million more in city B than city A, then at what price does one offer the team to a buyer from city A? If it is at the market price (the franchise value in city B), then city A or an investor in city A would be foolish to pay $30 million more for the franchise than it is worth there. If the transaction price is at an arbitration-determined value of the franchise value in city A, then the owner is being deprived of his property rights. The only provisions we know about stipulate a market price criterion and hence provide little protection to the existing host city.

Eminent Domain

Another possible defense for cities attempting to hold on to a franchise is the invocation of eminent domain.[7] This defense was attempted by both Oakland when the Raiders moved to Los Angeles in 1982 and Baltimore when the Colts moved to Indianapolis in 1984. In the former case, the California Court of Appeals ruled that condemnation of a football franchise would violate the commerce clause of the U.S. Constitution. In the latter, the condemnation was upheld by the Maryland Circuit Court, but the Colts then removed the action to the U.S. District Court, which ruled that Baltimore no longer had jurisdiction since the team had moved out of the state by the time the condemnation was declared. Eminent domain, while not constitutionally impossible, is not a promising vehicle for cities to retain their sports teams.

Tax Reform

Although one may legitimately argue that the benefits of a team to a particular metropolitan area exceed the costs, there is no rationale whatsoever for the federal government to subsidize the financial tug-of-war among the cities to host ball clubs. If net welfare increases because a team moves from city A to city B (because city A may be larger or have more avid sports fans), then city A ought to be able to pay for that gain without a subvention from Washington, D.C.

In 1986 Congress appeared to have convinced itself of the irrationality of allowing tax exemption for the interest on municipal bonds for city projects where the benefit was to be privately appropriated (as in the case of a municipally owned stadium that is leased to a privately owned team). The 1986 Tax Reform Act stipulated that the interest exemption would not apply to facilities for which more than 10 percent of the bond debt service was financed from revenues generated at the facility. The apparent intention of this provision was to end the federal subsidies for sports facilities.[8] But the provision was replete with loopholes that, if anything, have increased local subsidization of stadiums.

The 10 percent private financing limit applies only to yearly flows of finance; it does not apply to funds raised up front. Thus if the stadium authority was to receive, say, 20 percent of gross concessions revenues of $25 million per year, then this $5 million would count toward the 10 percent limit. If the concessionaire paid the city $30 million up front for the concession rights over a ten-year period, however, this sum would not apply to the income limit. The same reasoning applies to naming rights, long-term luxury or club box leases, pouring rights, PSLs, and other such items. Furthermore, if the lease were to provide that instead of paying rent (which would count toward the limit) the team paid for facility maintenance expenses, then again there would be no offset against the limit.

Along with still other loopholes, the 1986 tax reform provision has meant that teams have received more favorable leases than before. By preventing rental payments and little or no sharing of stadium-generated revenues, the act prevents cities from directly tying their revenues to the revenues of the team. As a result, the city cannot share in the bonanza that takes place in the especially lucrative early years of the stadium. Meanwhile, the team owner holds the appreciating asset (the franchise), and the city owns the depreciating asset (the stadium).

By adopting these lease provisions, sports facilities constructed during the 1990s have continued to benefit from the municipal tax exemption. Senator Daniel Patrick Moynihan, cognizant of this irony and concerned about the prospect of a tax exemption for a debt of $800 million to $1 billion on a new stadium in New York City, introduced a bill, S. 1880, in June 1996 that would eliminate the tax-exempt financing for professional sports stadiums. In its original drafting, the bill appears to have eliminated the existing loopholes. If such a bill were to become law, the good news is that the irrational federal subsidy would be eliminated, but the bad news is that in the present institutional environment cities might absorb all or most of the additional financing cost.

Antitrust and Regulation

Because the monopolistic structure of sports leagues accounts for most of the subsidy for stadiums, the natural policy response is to invoke the standard methods to control monopoly: antitrust and regulation. The regulatory approach would establish a permanent public body to supervise team location decisions, league expansions, and stadium construction and finance agreements. The antitrust approach would force each sport to divide into two or more competing leagues and bar them from making joint decisions about team location and league expansion.

Antitrust is a potential solution to the subsidy problem because the monopoly structure of leagues creates the scarcity in teams that leads to bidding wars among cities. Of course, for antitrust to be applicable, sports monopolies must be illegally acquired or maintained and must take actions that undermine competition. In all four sports, the existing monopoly leagues were created from mergers of competing leagues. In only one case, the merger of the American Football League and the National Football League, did these combinations obtain an antitrust exemption. Even in the case of football, the exemption was solely to allow merger, not to exempt the combined league from antitrust if it subsequently pursued anticompetitive strategies. Thus in all four sports, any increase in anticompetitive conduct that arose from the formation of a single league falls within the scope of antitrust law.

League decisions about franchise locations raise two antitrust issues. First, collaboration among all owners about entry into the sport and the location of league members eliminates competition among championship units—the leagues, conferences, and divisions within each sport—for members and home cities. The American League in baseball, the Western Conference in the NBA, and the National Conference in the NFL have no valid business reason for exercising control over which teams are admitted to the other league or conference, or where they play. Their reason for participating in this decision is solely the desire to maximize joint profits by eliminating competition among leagues and conferences for stadium agreements, broadcast rights, ticket sales, and prices for franchises. Second, collaboration among owners even within a league about whether a team should relocate, and if so, how much it should pay other teams for the privilege, also raises an antitrust concern. Teams can put a competing team in the same league at a disadvantage by blocking a move that would improve its financial performance (and hence its ability to field a stronger team in competition with other league members) or by taxing away the financial gains from the move. All members of a league have a valid interest in team relocations in that if one team irrationally makes a bad decision about relocation and so becomes much weaker, the rest of the league can suffer as fans lose interest in games involving the weak team. At most this justifies scrutiny of location decisions and the financial arrangements between a team and a host city to ensure that the team will not be made worse off. It does not justify denying relocation if a team can pass this test, or taxing the move should it occur.

The structure of the National Collegiate Athletic Association illustrates that sports can be organized as multiple independent leagues with minimal central supervision. The NCAA sets standards for participation in each of its athletic divisions and in particular requires that members of its "major league"—Division I—satisfy minimum standards about playing facilities, managing intercollegiate sports, and scheduling. The NCAA also organizes post-season championships and bowl games. The leagues determine their own membership and revenue-sharing rules and frequently compete for teams. A recent example is the demise of the Southwest Conference, with its most powerful members joining the Big Eight (now Big Twelve) and the rest joining other conferences. The NCAA has engaged in anticompetitive practices, notably with respect to pooling national broadcasting rights and establishing strict rules about recruiting and paying athletes; however, its policies regarding the structure and membership of leagues have been procompetitive and provide a useful example of an alternative approach that would be practical in professional sports.

Congress has considered applying antitrust and regulation to expansion and location issues on numerous occasions. The first round of congressional "city relocation and fan protection" proposals came in the early 1970s. When the Washington Senators departed for Texas, members of Congress who were baseball fans were not amused, and they commissioned an inquiry into professional sports. The inquiry soon focused on the fact that baseball, alone among professional sports, enjoys an antitrust immunity. The investigating committee concluded that baseball's antitrust immunity ought to be removed, but rather than pass a legislative recommendation, it proposed that another committee be established to make detailed proposals.[9] This recommendation was not acted upon by the full House.

In 1984–85, pursuant to the relocation of the Oakland Raiders and the Baltimore Colts, another inquiry was launched. One of the bills that came out of this investigation contained a provision to create a federal sports arbitration board that would preside over issues of team relocation and sale. The same bill would have exempted the NFL from its provisions if the league expanded by two teams and placed one of them in Baltimore, thus laying bare the parochial impulse behind the bill. None of the 1984–85 proposals came to a vote on either the House or Senate floors.

The actions of major league baseball to thwart the relocation of the San Francisco Giants to St. Petersburg generated another wave of congressional interest. In this case, the issue again was whether to withdraw baseball's cherished antitrust exemption.[10] The debate was driven by regional loyalties rather than political ideology. California's liberal

Democratic senator, Barbara Boxer, hardly known as a close ally of big business, favored retaining baseball's antitrust immunity to save her hometown Giants. Florida's conservative Republican senator, Connie Mack, the grandson of the legendary owner-manager of the great Philadelphia A's during the period when they wrested several America League championships from the famed Yankees of Lou Gehrig and Babe Ruth, argued strongly for lifting the immunity to free the Giants to come to Florida. As before, nothing came of this congressional inquiry.

Similarly, the 1995–96 congressional initiatives were inspired by the departure of the Cleveland Browns to Baltimore. Representative Louis Stokes, who was from Cleveland, and Ohio senator John Glenn introduced a bill that would grant the NFL an antitrust exemption for franchise relocation matters and establish a right of first refusal for the host city. The exemption was intended to give the NFL clearer power to thwart team movement, but it ran the risk ultimately of giving the league greater bargaining leverage over cities. The first refusal provision did not deal with the franchise price issue in a manner that would protect the existing host city.

Representative Martin Hoke, who was from another Cleveland district, proposed a bill that would allow teams to move but would obligate the league to restore a team to the bereft city within three years, through expansion or relocation of another franchise. It also extended a limited antitrust exemption to the NFL for relocation issues. Hoke's bill also did not deal adequately with determining the price to be paid for the recovered franchise.

Like the earlier initiatives, none of these bills reached the floors of Congress. Congressional initiatives have been plagued by geographical chauvinism and myopia, as witnessed by the nearly simultaneous proposals to create an antitrust exemption for football but to eliminate the exemption for baseball. The sponsors invariably are reacting to a team movement problem in their state or district and are opportunistically seizing the occasion to defend their constituents. The remaining members of Congress are reluctant to support any measure, largely because they want to remain in the good graces of sports owners so that their districts and states will be treated kindly by the leagues.

Prospects for a Federal Solution

Legislation related to sports leagues, such as the municipal exemption limitation in the 1986 Tax Reform, has a sorry history. If the past is a guide, legislation is likely to be either blatantly favorable to monopoly leagues or sufficiently vitiated and riddled with loopholes to make effective implementation improbable. Because net global welfare is arguably higher when a team can relocate to a better market, policy should not focus on regulating team movements. Instead, the proper course for public policy is to focus on balancing the supply and demand for sports franchises so that all economically viable cities can have a team. Mandating league expansion through congressional action, especially in the current political context, is probably impossible, given the political power of sports owners, but even if such legislation could be passed, the task of deciding who deserves a team would be an administrative nightmare.

A more attractive approach would be to use antitrust policy to divest existing leagues into several competing business entities. These entities would be allowed to collaborate on playing rules and on interleague and post-season play, but they would not be able to divvy up metropolitan areas, establish common drafts or players' markets, collude on broadcasting policy, and so forth. Under these circumstances, no league would be likely to vacate an economically viable city, and, if it did, a competing league would be likely to jump in. Other consumer-friendly consequences would flow from such an arrangement. For one thing, competition from better-managed teams would force ineffective owners to sell or go into bankruptcy. Taxpayers would benefit from lower local, state, and federal subsidies, which would reduce the revenues, owner profits, and player salaries of the clubs. But competition would compel more efficient management practices, and teams would remain solvent, albeit with reduced cost structures.

Unfortunately, the same forces that have impeded effective legislation also stand in the way of antitrust action that would lead to divestiture. Like Congress, the Antitrust Division of the Department of Justice is susceptible to political pressure not to upset sports, and so a large, influential monopoly remains unregulated and de facto immune from antitrust prosecution by the government. Private parties do frequently launch and win antitrust complaints against sports leagues; however, these plaintiffs, as profit-seeking entities, usually want membership in the cartel, not divestiture. The first priority of the U.S. Football League (USFL), when it sued the NFL, was to claim monetary damages, and the second was to be admitted into the NFL. After its Pyrrhic victory— the NFL was found to have violated the antitrust laws but the USFL was given $1 in damages and denied membership in the NFL—the USFL asked for some sort of divestiture. But this was too little and too late, for the case had already been argued on the wrong grounds to sustain this kind of decision.

Local Political Resistance

The most likely source of reform, though still a long shot, will be grass roots disgruntlement and citizen education. These forces have already taken hold in some cities. Voters, cognizant that sports teams will bring little benefit to the local economy and concerned about the distributional consequences of facility subventions, rejected the idea of public support for stadiums on ballot initiatives in San Francisco, San Jose, and Seattle. However, in no case has this caused a stadium not to be built. Nevertheless, more guarded, limited, and conditional support from constituents will prompt political leaders to be more careful in promoting a team or negotiating a stadium deal.

Ultimately, cities acting on their own will have little leverage because they will be competing with others for a limited number of teams. Cities with greater demographic and corporate bases, of course, will have more leverage than smaller cities with fewer corporations. In any event, initiatives that place a greater share of the public financing burden on facility users (through revenues from luxury or club box leases, PSLs, naming rights, or ticket taxes) are more likely to be supported.

Unfortunately, complete private financing is not a viable option for most stadiums, for two reasons. First, the disposition of the money that is collected from PSLs, naming rights, pouring rights, and other private financing options is a matter to be negotiated by teams, cities, and leagues. The NFL, in recognizing this fact, imposed "franchise relocation fees" on the Oakland Raiders, Cleveland Browns, Houston Oilers, and Los Angeles Rams. These fees amount to nothing more than an attempt by the league to capture some of the (unshared) revenues from these sources, rather than to have them pay for the stadium. Competition among cities for teams is not likely to leave any more money on the table for local government than is absolutely essential to induce them to bid for a team.

Second, the amount of revenue that is available from these sources is not likely to be adequate to avoid large public subsidies. Even in the best circumstances, as in the case of the NFL's Charlotte Panthers, local governments are still stuck with supporting investments, and the federal government still pays an interest subsidy for the local government share. In any event, the Charlotte case is unique in that so much was privately raised. At the other end of the spectrum is the disaster in Oakland, where the demand for PSLs was far too small to cover the stadium costs that local government had agreed to underwrite, and the farce in Seattle, where one of the world's richest men obtained a $300 million subsidy for his football team.

We conclude this analysis on a pessimistic note. It is difficult to see an end to the growing public subsidization of sports facilities. Whereas the superficial explanations for this phenomenon lie in the details of federal, state, and local politics, the ultimate reason can be found by looking in the mirror. Professional sports in the United States are subsidized because they are very popular monopolies. While grass roots movements in local areas may achieve modest successes in slightly altering the terms of stadium subsidies, until the structural monopoly and cultural centrality are modified, large-scale public subsidies to wealthy team owners and athletes will be a feature of the professional sports landscape.

Notes

1. Sixty percent of ticket revenues, after deducting an allowance for rent and taxes, is retained by the home team. As a fraction of gross revenues, the revenue split is roughly 66-34 between the home and visiting teams, respectively.

2. This estimate is not fanciful. In several surveys of visitors attending a local sporting event, half or more were in the city for another reason. John L. Crompton, "Economic Impact Analysis of Sports Facilities and Events: Eleven Sources of Misapplication," *Journal of Sport Management,* vol. 9 (January 1995), pp. 27–29.

3. The multiplier (m) of 1.2 is derived from chapter 3 as follows: $m = 1/(1 - s)$, where $s = c * f$, and $c = $ the fraction of the increment to pre-tax income that is spent on consumption, and $f = $ the fraction of consumption expenditures that generates an increase in local net income. Assuming state and federal taxes are equal to one-third of pre-tax income, savings equal to one-fourth of disposable income, local value added equal to half of local spending, and one-fourth of consumption expenditures are made outside the area, then c is .5, f is .3 and s is .15, and the multiplier becomes 1.18.

4. The leases of the Orlando Magic, Colorado Rockies, Baltimore Orioles, Baltimore Ravens, Seattle Mariners, and Minnesota Twins all have relocation clauses. The Mariners' lease allows relocation if attendance falls below 90 percent of the American League average, and the Twins have a similar right if attendance falls below 80 percent of the league average.

5. The New Orleans Saints, Minnesota Timberwolves, and Tennessee Oilers have this provision in their leases.

6. The Indiana Pacers have such a provision in their lease, which requires that if the team finds a qualified buyer, the stadium authority—the Capital Improvements Board—

must be permitted to buy the team at the agreed price. Of course, the board would exercise this right only if a prospective owner would move the team.

7. For a discussion of this issue, see Martin J. Greenberg and James T. Grey, *The Stadium Game* (Milwaukee: Sports Law Institute, 1996), chap. 8.

8. Congressional intent is, of course, an elusive concept. In this case, New York senator Daniel Patrick Moynihan states: "Congress intended to eliminate the issuance of tax-exempt bonds to finance professional sports facilities as part of the Tax Reform Act of 1986"; *Congressional Record* vol. 142, no. 97, Part 1 (June 27, 1996), p. S7205. Unfortunately, statements ten years after the fact are not a credible part of the legislative history.

9. U.S. House of Representatives, "Inquiry into Professional Sports: Final Report of the Select Committee on Professional Sports," 94 Cong. 2 sess., H. Rept. 94-1786, January 3, 1977.

10. U.S. Senate, *Baseball's Antitrust Immunity: Hearing before the Subcommittee on Antitrust, Monopolies and Business Rights*, December 10, 1992.

CONTRIBUTORS

Stephen J. Agostini, San Francisco Redevelopment Agency
Ziona Austrian, Levin College of Urban Affairs, Cleveland State
  University
Robert A. Baade, Department of Economics, Lake Forest College
John P. Blair, Department of Economics, Wright State University
Rodney Fort, Department of Economics, Washington State University
Bruce W. Hamilton, Department of Economics, Johns Hopkins
  University
Peter Kahn, Department of Economics, Johns Hopkins University
Roger G. Noll, Department of Economics, Stanford University
John M. Quigley, School of Public Policy, University of California,
  Berkeley
James Quirk, Professor of Economics (retired), California Institute of
  Technology
Mark S. Rosentraub, Center for Urban Policy and the Environment,
  School of Public and Environmental Affairs, Indiana University,
  Indianapolis
Allen R. Sanderson, Department of Economics, University of Chicago
Eugene Smolensky, School of Public Policy, University of California,
  Berkeley

David W. Swindell, Center for Urban and Public Affairs, Wright State University
Andrew Zimbalist, Department of Economics, Smith College
Dennis Zimmerman, Congressional Research Service, Library of Congress
John F. Zipp, Department of Sociology, University of Wisconsin, Milwaukee

INDEX